THIS BOOK BELONGS TO:

....,
Factamaniac

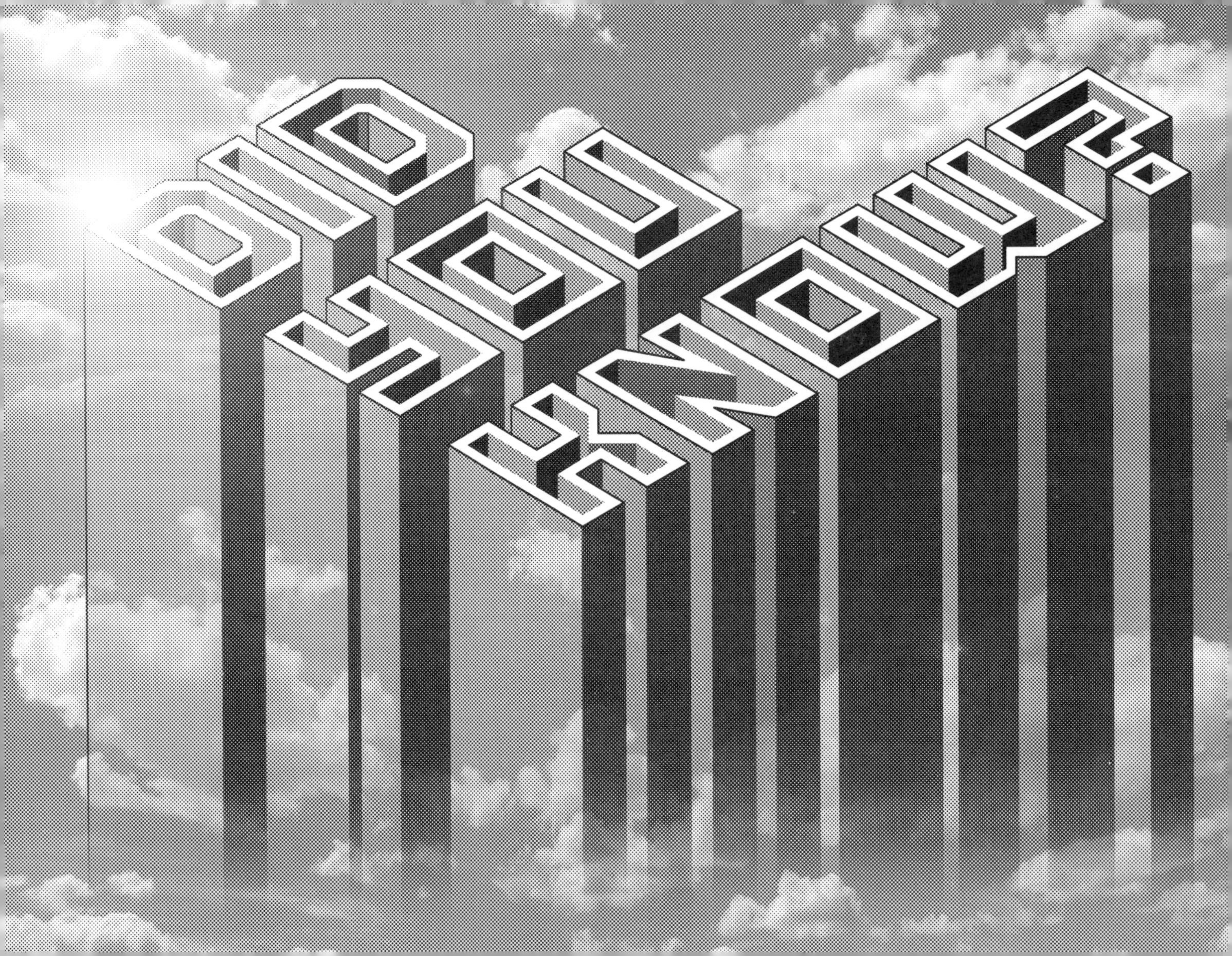
DID YOU KNOW?

THE COLLECTED

Amazing Facts... & Beyond!
with Leon Beyond

~ 2008 - 2012 ~

by

Dan Zettwoch and **Kevin Huizenga**

with Ted May

(and Ron Weaver)

Uncivilized Books

Minneapolis   **St. Louis**   **New York**   **Warsaw**

UNCIVILIZED BOOKS
P.O. BOX 6534
MINNEAPOLIS, MN 55406
USA
uncivilizedbooks.com

First Edition, April 2013

KH28

X IX VIII VII VI V IV III II I

ISBN 978-0-9846814-6-4

DISTRIBUTED TO THE TRADE BY:
Consortium Book Sales & Distribution, LLC.
34 Thirteenth Avenue, NE, Suite 101
Minneapolis, MN 55413-1007
cbsd.com
Orders: (800) 283-3572

Printed in China

These strips originally appeared in the *Riverfront Times* in St. Louis, MO, between **January 31, 2008**, and **October 30, 2012**. That's 1735 days. In 1735 Linnaeus published his *Systema Naturae*. That's 4 years and 9 months, the amount of time you have to wait to apply for U.S. citizenship, and about 247 weeks (rounded down), which is, of course, the number of hours in a day and the days in a week (24/7).

This book is set in the GEORGIA font, which was developed by Matthew Carter in 1996 for use in Microsoft Windows and websites on computer screens. Page numbers on the left are set in ***Helvetica*** and those on the right are set in **Arial**.

Specifications (approximate):
size by volume: 1
weight: 1 lb. 6 oz.
Printed on **Springmill Stone SSX97** (fine-toothed) 8.03 lb. paper, with stochastic whole-dot screens. Inks: a black blend of **Ebon Abyss FF#ddd133** and **SuperBlack 666** primarily, with hints of Focoltone Process Uncoated #02544 (all anti-biotic non-GM vegetable-based). CMYK: cyan, **Azuline 4343;** magenta, **Badious XL-67;** yellow, **Pyse U_U;** black, see above. Conforms to International Book Safety Code, registered, **LB-443-KD-OU812**. Binding glues: Det-LocTM Acrylic Polymer Epoxy (note: may lose strength in some aquatic environments). Do not smoke it. Cardboard case: Cypresine 54 gram, catnip blend, encased in one-week anti-radiation negative ION soak.

More Leon Beyond strips can be found at whatthingsdo.com.

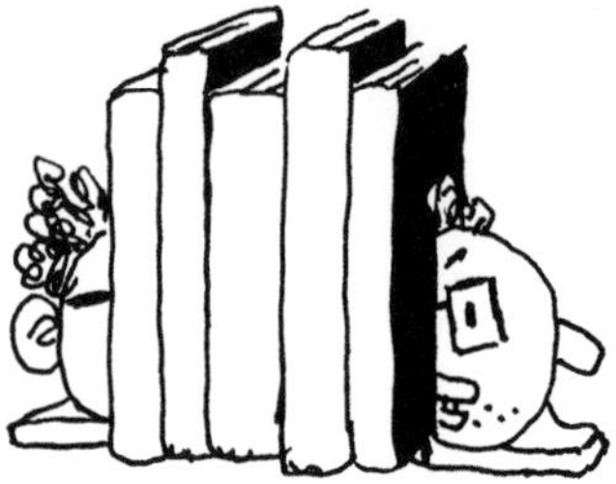

Previous Collections:

The Factoids of Life
Fact Parader
Back That Fact Up
Brain Dump
Factual Healing
...and Trivia for All
Is That a Fact?
Facts On a Plane
Stop Boring Yourself
That's a Spicy Factoid!
Varieties of Verité
Hallowed Be These Facts
Brain Storm!
Blame it on the Brain
Brain Sandwich, 50¢
Facts Machine
No Brain, No Gain
Brainiac Attack
Random Facts of Violence
Cheese Quiz
Facts for Dummies
Word is BEYOND
Fact-Bottomed Girls
Girl You Know It's True

see
usscatastrophe.com/store
for purchasing information

Archiving Information

Authors.
Huizenga, Kevin
Zettwoch, Dan
May, Ted
Weaver, Ron
Beyond, Leon

Title.
Amazing Facts...and Beyond! with Leon Beyond

Subject.
1. Trivia--Comic books, strips, etc.
2. Reference--Comic books, strips, etc.
3. Comic books, strips, graphica--reference.
4. Reference--Trivia
5. Art--General
6. Webcomics--SFW
7. Humor--humorous humor
8. Books with "!" in the title
9. St. Louis

ZZZ6727.H83W5.4 200.13
741.5'973'456'999'ZZZ
CZCZ2013-90s6027-2.1/2

The authors are saying THANKS to:

Tom K, Tom Carlson, Sammy Harkham, the fans and factamaniacs, the STL Drawing Crew, Star Clipper, Les, Kate, Candy, and Sunshine

The authors especially thank the *Riverfront Times* for support.

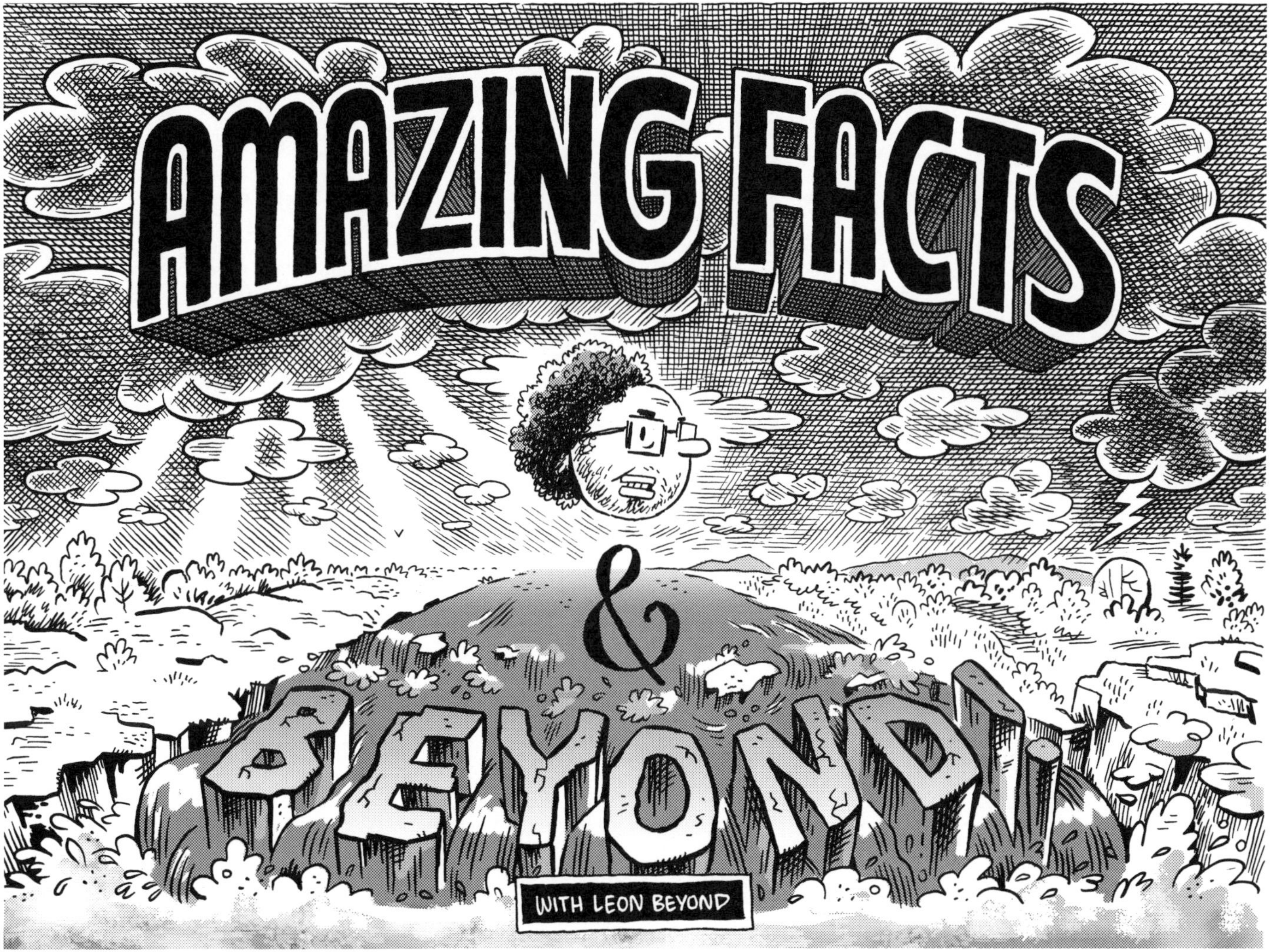
AMAZING FACTS
&
BEYOND!
WITH LEON BEYOND

TABLE... OF BEYONTENTS

DID YOU KNOW?

KEY

by Dan Zettwoch
by Kevin Huizenga
by Ted May
by Ron Weaver

HOLIDAYS AND OCCASIONS

TRAVEL

SAINT LOUIS

FOOD

GAMES

ANIMALS

ADVENTURES OF THE MIND

FASCINATING ESOTERICA

SPORTS

FURTHERMORE, DID YOU ALSO KNOW?

CHAINSAWS

TIPS AND TRICKS

MINDBLOWERS

BEYOND THE BEYOND

3D / SCRATCH 'n' SNIFF SECTION

Did you know? There are important differences between a FOREWORD, a PREFACE, and an INTRODUCTION:

Let's take them alphabetically. Scholars generally date the "introduction" to around the 5th century BCE. Nowadays, an introduction is usually written by someone else besides the author and is not intended to be read. On the other hand, the "foreword" is usually written by the author and contains technical details and things about the book that are unimportant. Is it supposed to be a pun? Well, we find a clue in that there is also something called an "afterword." It should be noted that a foreword is always to be balanced with an afterword of precisely equal length. The "preface" is a later development in book architecture, and is pronounced "preh-ffssse." Written by either the author or someone else, the preface will introduce the topic or something about the book for the reader. Generally, the preface comes before the main text but after the table of contents, though I could name a few books where this is not the case. A preface is always only used in non-fiction books (like this one) because it functions as a "pre-facing" of the facts to follow.

AUTHOR'S PREFACE

There is a vast difference, De Quincey pointed out, between the man who wants to know facts, and the man who wants facts to know. There is also a world of difference between what is termed the known fact and the unknown fact. Now, I won't pretend to know what is amazing and what is not. But an "amazing fact" is something I've always treasured, ever since I was a young boy, traveling this wide, magical world with my beloved mother and father, whose deaths from Roman fever while I was only eight now makes impossible an in-person presentation of this book, which is an ever-present ache and dream, as it represents some small karmic payment for their kind attention and friendship in my youth, before the lonely years of boarding school and later, the grunge years in Seattle.

I have always treasured the Amazing Fact because it is a reminder that the world and life are miraculous and interesting. The Spanish call it "hecho asombroso." The strongest affection and utmost zeal should, I think, promote the study and memorization of glittering trivial factoids. People love to hear something interesting. It helps pass the time. It may gain you a new friend, someone with whom you can share a life of mutual curiosity and discovery. Be careful—I can guarantee you that some will pay you the tribute of protest: show me the proof of this or that, they'll say. I welcome doubters, or any response at all. I like to point out to people that I have indeed made my home in the "Show Me" state.*

My sincere hope is that this book may serve as a bridge between persons with similar interests and outlooks, though too much lending out to friends is not encouraged. A reading group-type setting is ideal, I have found, for bringing together people who will listen to you for some time.

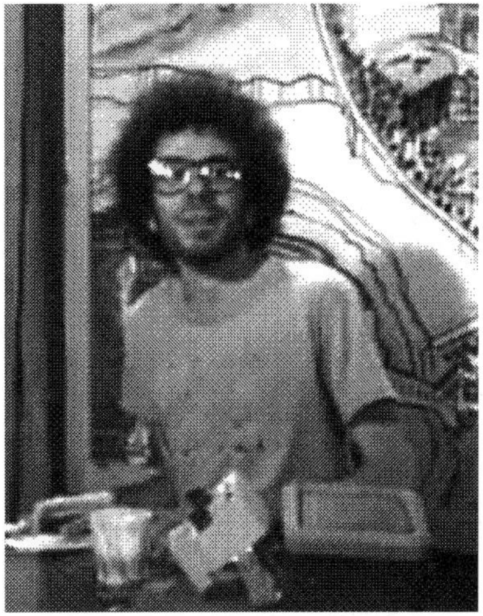

To such as ask no "amazing facts and beyond," but only some light eyebrow-raisers, some mitigation of the daily grind of banalities, this book should also have an appeal. To those looking for a map of the heavens, a polity more enlightened than that which rules the world today, maybe I'll get around to that in a future book.

When I bring each week's "AF&B" to Dan or Kevin, I'm grateful they take them and do their best...to meet the deadline.

Leon

St. Louis, 2012

*Missouri.

Note: If you are one of the purchasers of the Deluxe TEAM BEYOND: DEATH OF THE M'UN D'ANE Edition of this book, AND if you are able to solve the puzzle box you find in the second suitcase, AND it contains one of three Golden Trivia Card Download Keys, congratulations. Just enter your information in the download, and within 6-8 weeks you will receive a packet of seeds and instructions for their care. Remember to use purified water and proper grafting twine, and wait about one (1) week before bringing the ensuing fruit to the Secret Location hidden in the meta-code level of Chapter 5. Please email ahead if you have any special dietary needs. I'll be waiting!

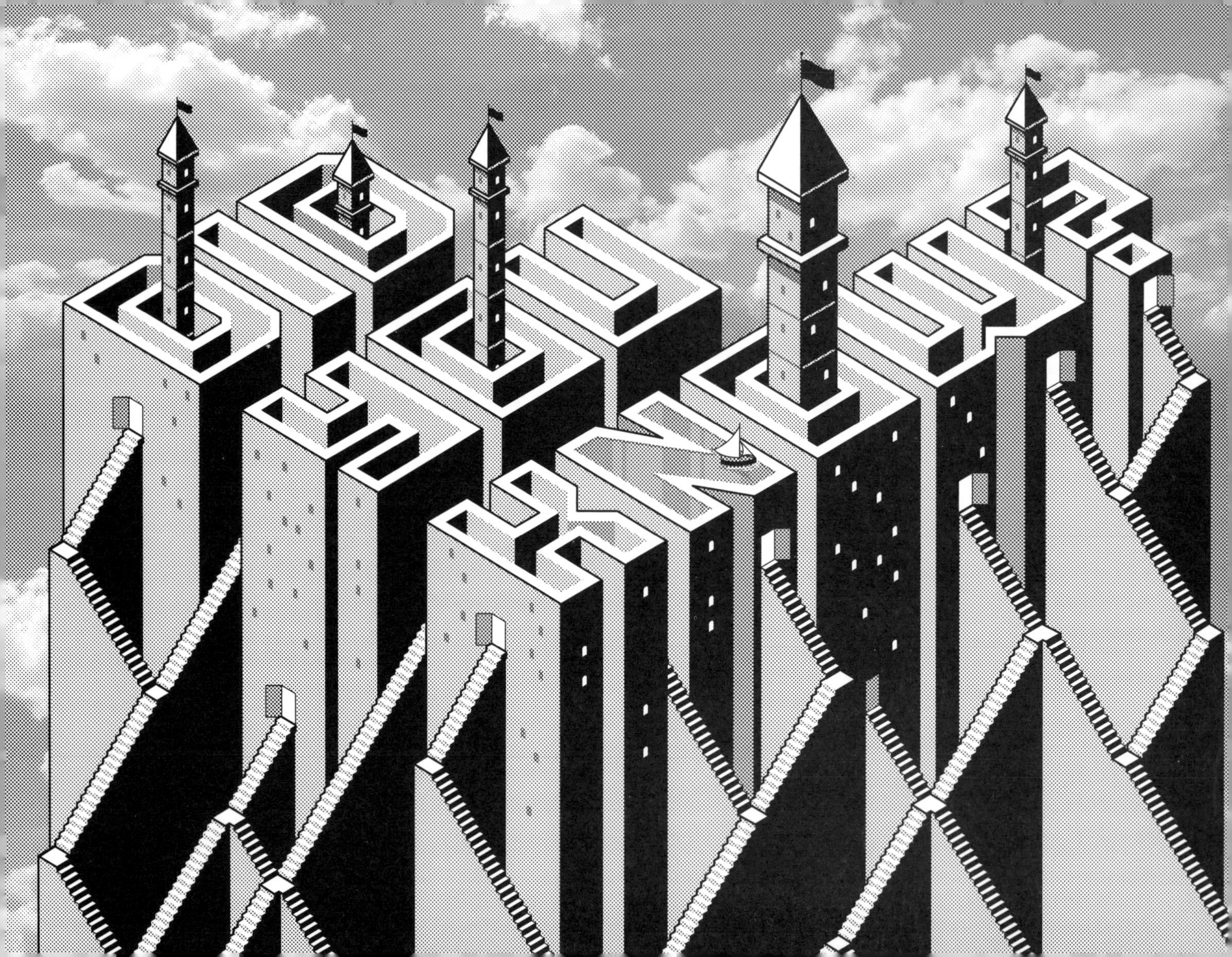

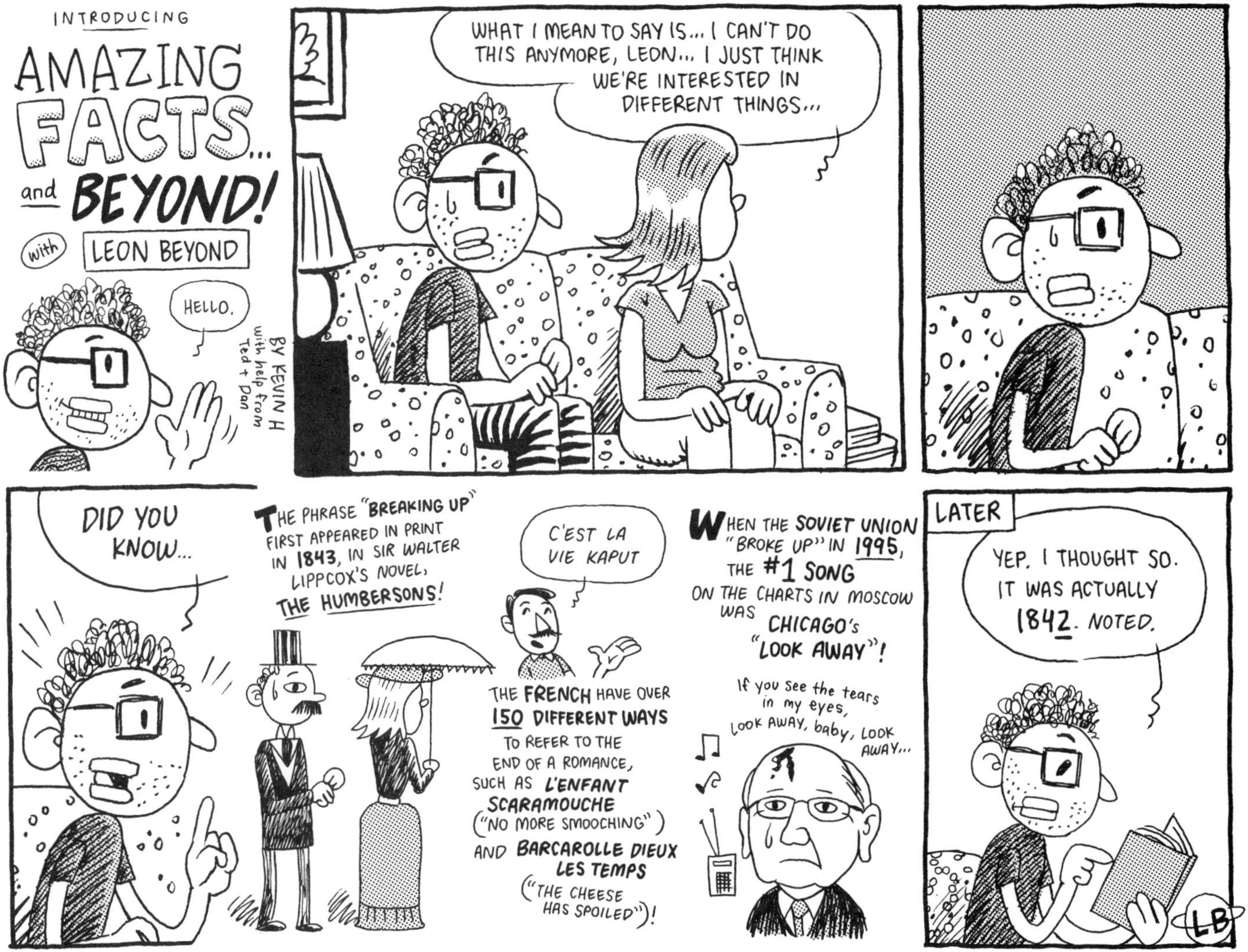
INTRODUCING
AMAZING FACTS... and BEYOND!
with LEON BEYOND
HELLO.
BY KEVIN H with help from Ted + Dan
WHAT I MEAN TO SAY IS... I CAN'T DO THIS ANYMORE, LEON... I JUST THINK WE'RE INTERESTED IN DIFFERENT THINGS...
DID YOU KNOW...
THE PHRASE "BREAKING UP" FIRST APPEARED IN PRINT IN 1843, IN SIR WALTER LIPPCOX'S NOVEL, THE HUMBERSONS!
C'EST LA VIE KAPUT
THE FRENCH HAVE OVER 150 DIFFERENT WAYS TO REFER TO THE END OF A ROMANCE, SUCH AS L'ENFANT SCARAMOUCHE ("NO MORE SMOOCHING") AND BARCAROLLE DIEUX LES TEMPS ("THE CHEESE HAS SPOILED")!
WHEN THE SOVIET UNION "BROKE UP" IN 1995, THE #1 SONG ON THE CHARTS IN MOSCOW WAS CHICAGO'S "LOOK AWAY"!
If you see the tears in my eyes, LOOK AWAY, baby, LOOK AWAY...
LATER
YEP. I THOUGHT SO. IT WAS ACTUALLY 1842. NOTED.
LB

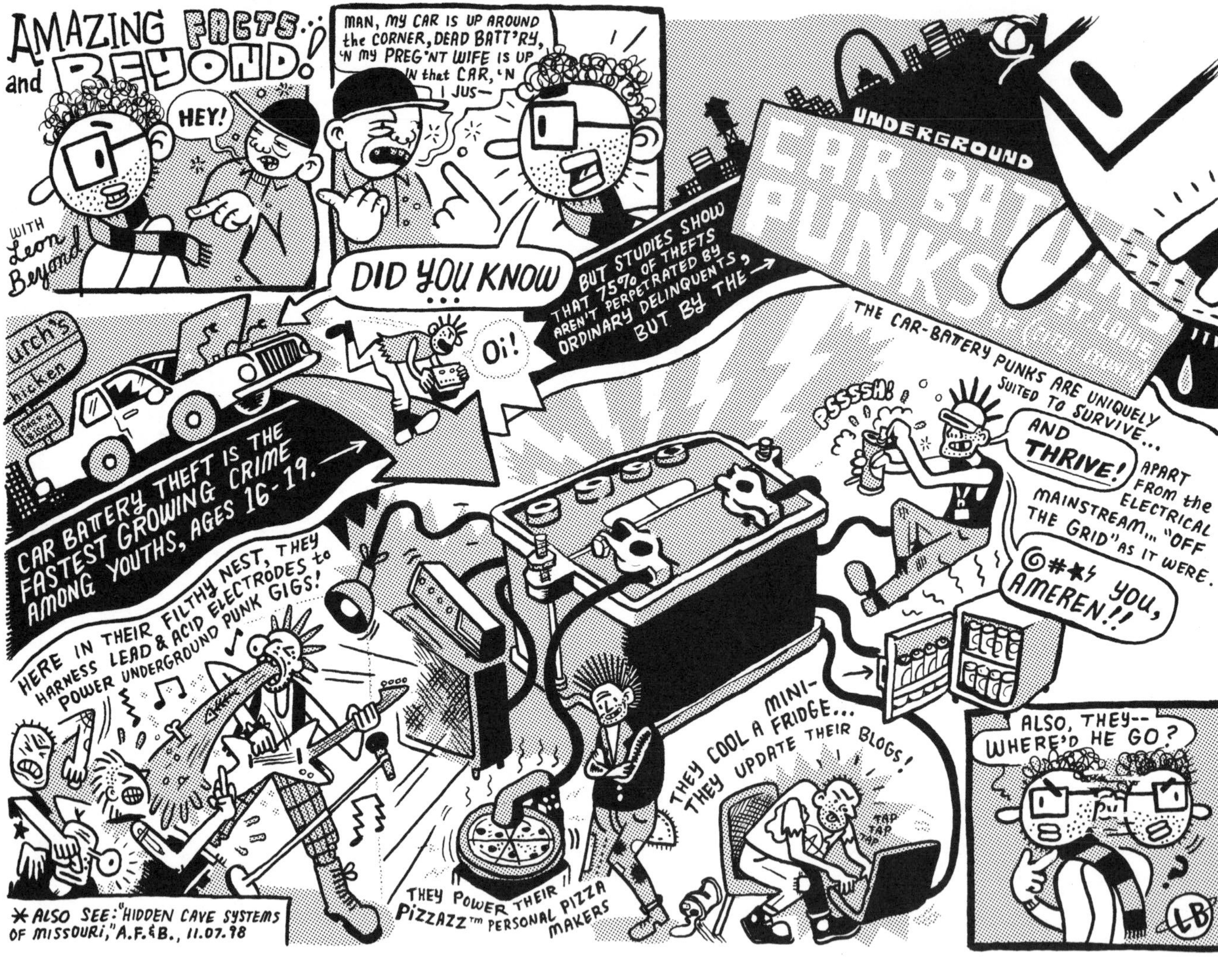
AMAZING FACTS and BEYOND!
WITH Leon Beyond
HEY!
MAN, MY CAR IS UP AROUND the CORNER, DEAD BATT'RY, 'N MY PREG'NT WIFE IS UP IN that CAR, 'N I JUS—
DID YOU KNOW ...
BUT STUDIES SHOW THAT 75% OF THEFTS AREN'T PERPETRATED BY ORDINARY DELINQUENTS, BUT BY THE →
UNDERGROUND
CAR BAT
PUNKS
Oi!
CAR BATTERY THEFT IS THE FASTEST GROWING CRIME AMONG YOUTHS, AGES 16-19. →
THE CAR-BATTERY PUNKS ARE UNIQUELY SUITED TO SURVIVE...
PSSSSH!
AND THRIVE!
APART FROM the ELECTRICAL MAINSTREAM,, "OFF THE GRID" AS IT WERE.
@#*$ YOU, AMEREN!!
HERE IN THEIR FILTHY NEST, THEY HARNESS LEAD & ACID ELECTRODES to POWER UNDERGROUND PUNK GIGS!
THEY POWER THEIR PIZZAZZ™ PERSONAL PIZZA MAKERS
THEY COOL A MINI-FRIDGE... THEY UPDATE THEIR BLOGS!
TAP TAP TAP
ALSO, THEY-- WHERE'D HE GO?
LB
* ALSO SEE: "HIDDEN CAVE SYSTEMS OF MISSOURI," A.F.&B., 11.07.98

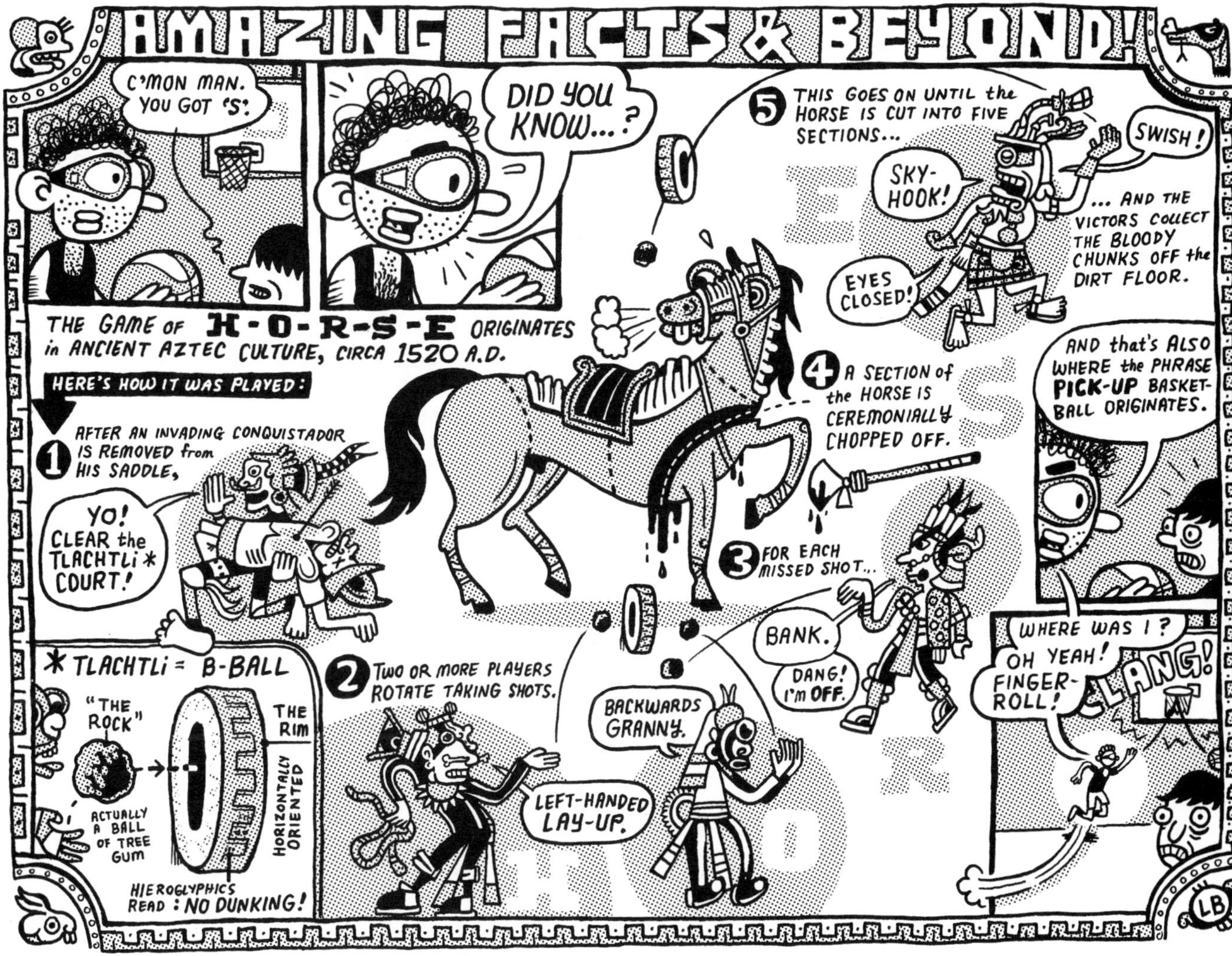
AMAZING FACTS & BEYOND!
C'MON MAN. YOU GOT 'S'.
DID YOU KNOW...?
THE GAME OF H-O-R-S-E ORIGINATES in ANCIENT AZTEC CULTURE, CIRCA 1520 A.D.
HERE'S HOW IT WAS PLAYED:
1 AFTER AN INVADING CONQUISTADOR IS REMOVED from HIS SADDLE,
YO! CLEAR the TLACHTLi * COURT!
* TLACHTLi = B-BALL
"THE ROCK"
ACTUALLY A BALL OF TREE GUM
THE RIM
HORIZONTALLY ORIENTED
HIEROGLYPHICS READ : NO DUNKING!
2 TWO OR MORE PLAYERS ROTATE TAKING SHOTS.
LEFT-HANDED LAY-UP.
BACKWARDS GRANNY.
3 FOR EACH MISSED SHOT...
BANK.
DANG! I'm OFF.
4 A SECTION of the HORSE IS CEREMONIALLY CHOPPED OFF.
5 THIS GOES ON UNTIL the HORSE IS CUT INTO FIVE SECTIONS...
SKY-HOOK!
SWISH!
EYES CLOSED!
... AND THE VICTORS COLLECT THE BLOODY CHUNKS OFF the DIRT FLOOR.
AND that's ALSO WHERE the PHRASE PICK-UP BASKET-BALL ORIGINATES.
WHERE WAS I? OH YEAH! FINGER-ROLL!
CLANG!
LB

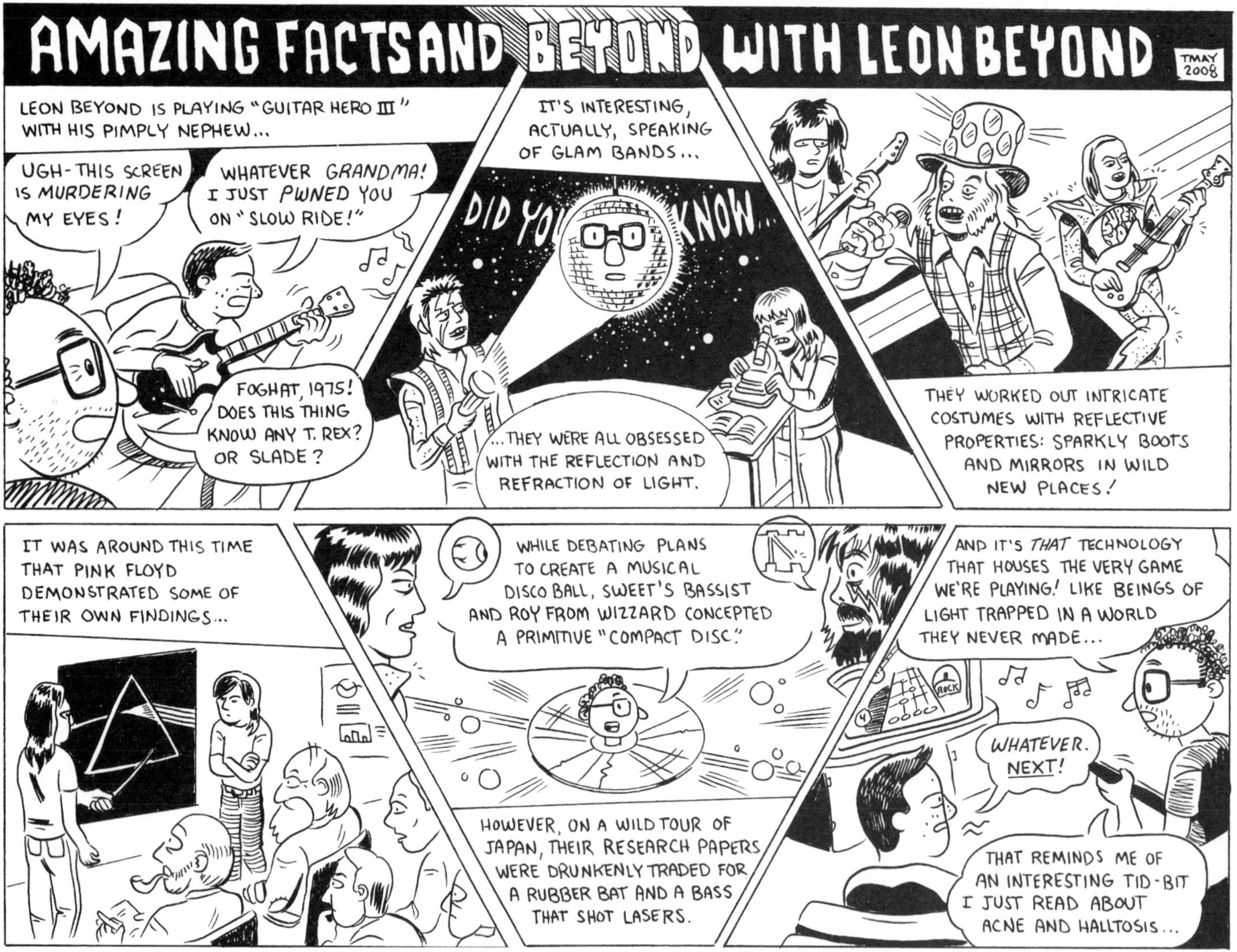
AMAZING FACTS AND BEYOND WITH LEON BEYOND
TMAY 2008
LEON BEYOND IS PLAYING "GUITAR HERO III" WITH HIS PIMPLY NEPHEW...
UGH- THIS SCREEN IS MURDERING MY EYES!
WHATEVER GRANDMA! I JUST PWNED YOU ON "SLOW RIDE!"
FOGHAT, 1975! DOES THIS THING KNOW ANY T. REX? OR SLADE?
IT'S INTERESTING, ACTUALLY, SPEAKING OF GLAM BANDS...
DID YOU KNOW...
...THEY WERE ALL OBSESSED WITH THE REFLECTION AND REFRACTION OF LIGHT.
THEY WORKED OUT INTRICATE COSTUMES WITH REFLECTIVE PROPERTIES: SPARKLY BOOTS AND MIRRORS IN WILD NEW PLACES!
IT WAS AROUND THIS TIME THAT PINK FLOYD DEMONSTRATED SOME OF THEIR OWN FINDINGS...
WHILE DEBATING PLANS TO CREATE A MUSICAL DISCO BALL, SWEET'S BASSIST AND ROY FROM WIZZARD CONCEPTED A PRIMITIVE "COMPACT DISC."
HOWEVER, ON A WILD TOUR OF JAPAN, THEIR RESEARCH PAPERS WERE DRUNKENLY TRADED FOR A RUBBER BAT AND A BASS THAT SHOT LASERS.
AND IT'S THAT TECHNOLOGY THAT HOUSES THE VERY GAME WE'RE PLAYING! LIKE BEINGS OF LIGHT TRAPPED IN A WORLD THEY NEVER MADE...
WHATEVER. NEXT!
THAT REMINDS ME OF AN INTERESTING TID-BIT I JUST READ ABOUT ACNE AND HALLTOSIS...

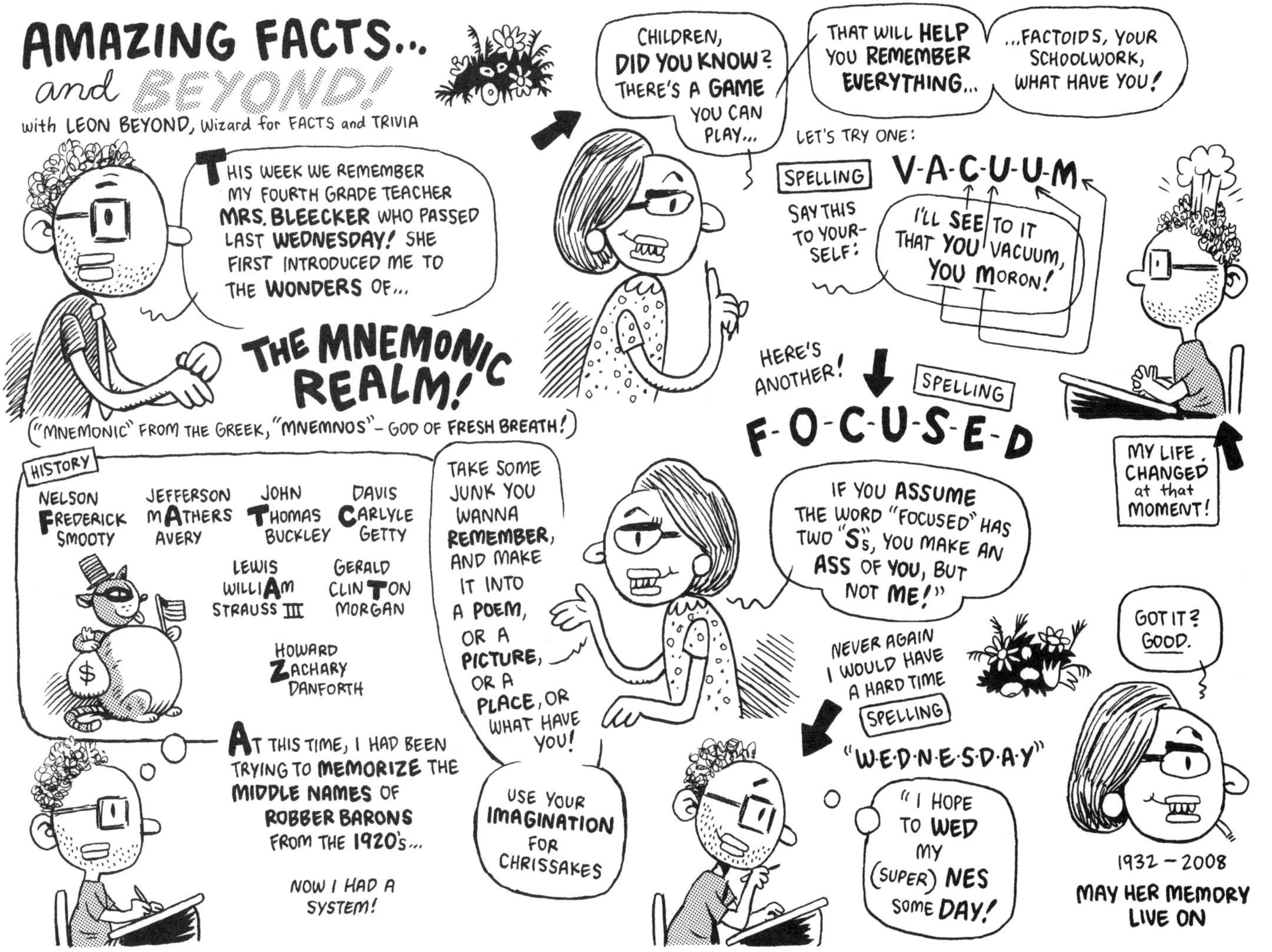
AMAZING FACTS... and BEYOND!
with LEON BEYOND, Wizard for FACTS and TRIVIA
THIS WEEK WE REMEMBER MY FOURTH GRADE TEACHER MRS. BLEECKER WHO PASSED LAST WEDNESDAY! SHE FIRST INTRODUCED ME TO THE WONDERS OF...
THE MNEMONIC REALM!
("MNEMONIC" FROM THE GREEK, "MNEMNOS" – GOD OF FRESH BREATH!)
CHILDREN, DID YOU KNOW? THERE'S A GAME YOU CAN PLAY...
THAT WILL HELP YOU REMEMBER EVERYTHING...
...FACTOIDS, YOUR SCHOOLWORK, WHAT HAVE YOU!
LET'S TRY ONE:
SPELLING
V-A-C-U-U-M
SAY THIS TO YOURSELF:
I'LL SEE TO IT THAT YOU VACUUM, YOU MORON!
HERE'S ANOTHER!
SPELLING
F-O-C-U-S-E-D
IF YOU ASSUME THE WORD "FOCUSED" HAS TWO "S"s, YOU MAKE AN ASS OF YOU, BUT NOT ME!"
MY LIFE CHANGED at that MOMENT!
HISTORY
NELSON FREDERICK SMOOTY
JEFFERSON MATHERS AVERY
JOHN THOMAS BUCKLEY
DAVIS CARLYLE GETTY
LEWIS WILLIAM STRAUSS III
GERALD CLINTON MORGAN
HOWARD ZACHARY DANFORTH
$
AT THIS TIME, I HAD BEEN TRYING TO MEMORIZE THE MIDDLE NAMES OF ROBBER BARONS FROM THE 1920's...
NOW I HAD A SYSTEM!
TAKE SOME JUNK YOU WANNA REMEMBER, AND MAKE IT INTO A POEM, OR A PICTURE, OR A PLACE, OR WHAT HAVE YOU!
USE YOUR IMAGINATION FOR CHRISSAKES
NEVER AGAIN I WOULD HAVE A HARD TIME
SPELLING
"W·E·D·N·E·S·D·A·Y"
"I HOPE TO WED MY (SUPER) NES SOME DAY!"
GOT IT? GOOD.
1932 – 2008
MAY HER MEMORY LIVE ON

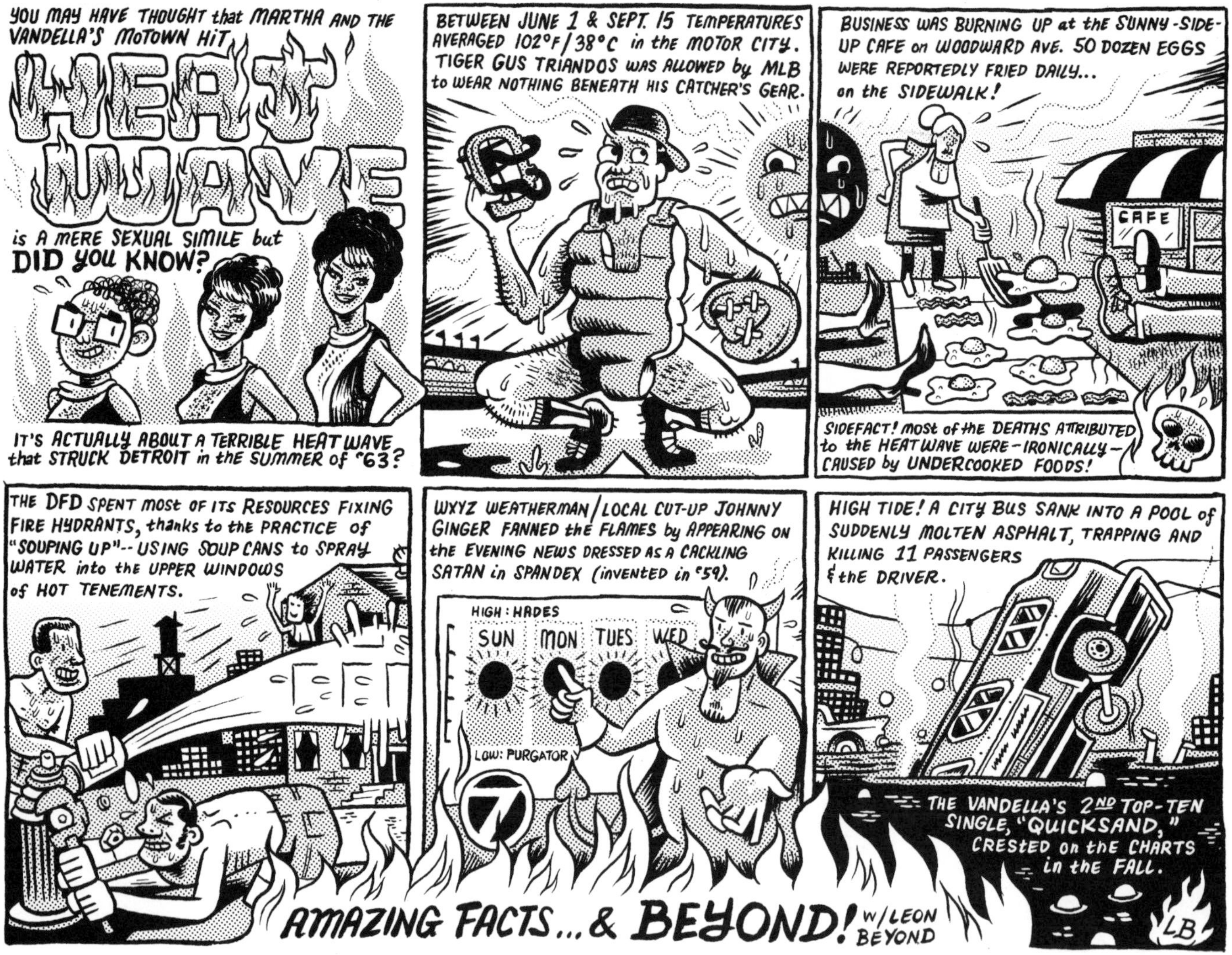
YOU MAY HAVE THOUGHT that MARTHA AND THE VANDELLA'S MOTOWN HIT
HEAT WAVE
is A MERE SEXUAL SIMILE but DID YOU KNOW?
IT'S ACTUALLY ABOUT A TERRIBLE HEAT WAVE that STRUCK DETROIT in the SUMMER of '63?
BETWEEN JUNE 1 & SEPT. 15 TEMPERATURES AVERAGED 102°F / 38°C in the MOTOR CITY. TIGER GUS TRIANDOS WAS ALLOWED by MLB to WEAR NOTHING BENEATH HIS CATCHER'S GEAR.
BUSINESS WAS BURNING UP at the SUNNY-SIDE-UP CAFE on WOODWARD AVE. 50 DOZEN EGGS WERE REPORTEDLY FRIED DAILY... on the SIDEWALK!
CAFE
SIDEFACT! most of the DEATHS ATTRIBUTED to the HEATWAVE WERE—IRONICALLY—CAUSED by UNDERCOOKED FOODS!
THE DFD SPENT MOST OF ITS RESOURCES FIXING FIRE HYDRANTS, thanks to the PRACTICE of "SOUPING UP"-- USING SOUP CANS to SPRAY WATER into the UPPER WINDOWS of HOT TENEMENTS.
WXYZ WEATHERMAN / LOCAL CUT-UP JOHNNY GINGER FANNED the FLAMES by APPEARING ON the EVENING NEWS DRESSED AS A CACKLING SATAN in SPANDEX (invented in '59).
HIGH : HADES
SUN MON TUES WED
LOW: PURGATOR
7
HIGH TIDE! A CITY BUS SANK INTO A POOL of SUDDENLY MOLTEN ASPHALT, TRAPPING AND KILLING 11 PASSENGERS & the DRIVER.
THE VANDELLA'S 2ND TOP-TEN SINGLE, "QUICKSAND," CRESTED on the CHARTS in the FALL.
AMAZING FACTS... & BEYOND! W/ LEON BEYOND
LB

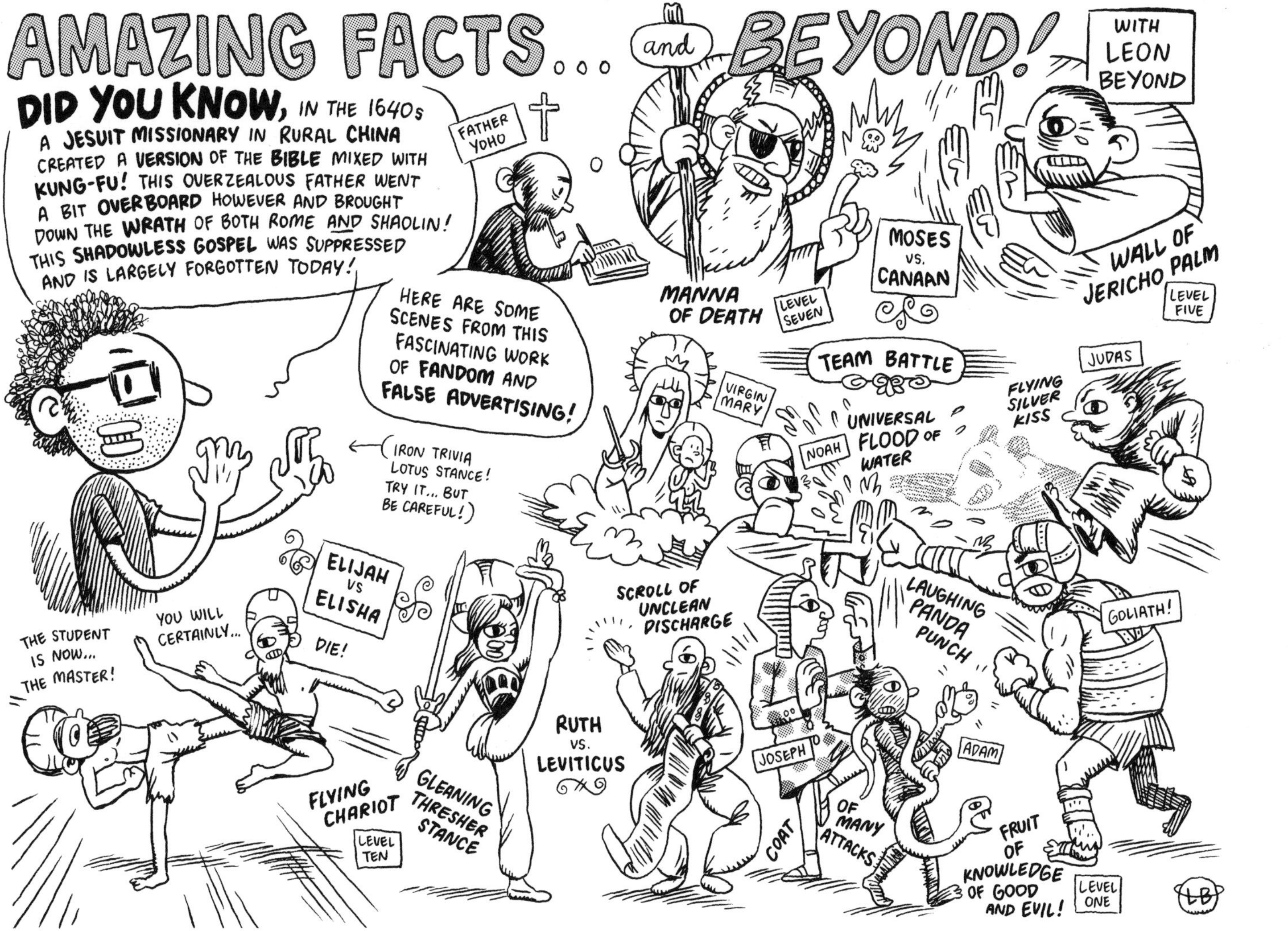
AMAZING FACTS... and BEYOND!
WITH LEON BEYOND
DID YOU KNOW, IN THE 1640s A JESUIT MISSIONARY IN RURAL CHINA CREATED A VERSION OF THE BIBLE MIXED WITH KUNG-FU! THIS OVERZEALOUS FATHER WENT A BIT OVERBOARD HOWEVER AND BROUGHT DOWN THE WRATH OF BOTH ROME AND SHAOLIN! THIS SHADOWLESS GOSPEL WAS SUPPRESSED AND IS LARGELY FORGOTTEN TODAY!
FATHER YOHO
HERE ARE SOME SCENES FROM THIS FASCINATING WORK OF FANDOM AND FALSE ADVERTISING!
(IRON TRIVIA LOTUS STANCE! TRY IT... BUT BE CAREFUL!)
MANNA OF DEATH
LEVEL SEVEN
MOSES VS. CANAAN
WALL OF JERICHO PALM
LEVEL FIVE
TEAM BATTLE
VIRGIN MARY
NOAH
UNIVERSAL FLOOD OF WATER
JUDAS
FLYING SILVER KISS
LAUGHING PANDA PUNCH
GOLIATH!
ELIJAH VS ELISHA
THE STUDENT IS NOW... THE MASTER!
YOU WILL CERTAINLY...
DIE!
FLYING CHARIOT
LEVEL TEN
GLEANING THRESHER STANCE
RUTH VS. LEVITICUS
SCROLL OF UNCLEAN DISCHARGE
JOSEPH
COAT OF MANY ATTACKS
ADAM
FRUIT OF KNOWLEDGE OF GOOD AND EVIL!
LEVEL ONE
LB

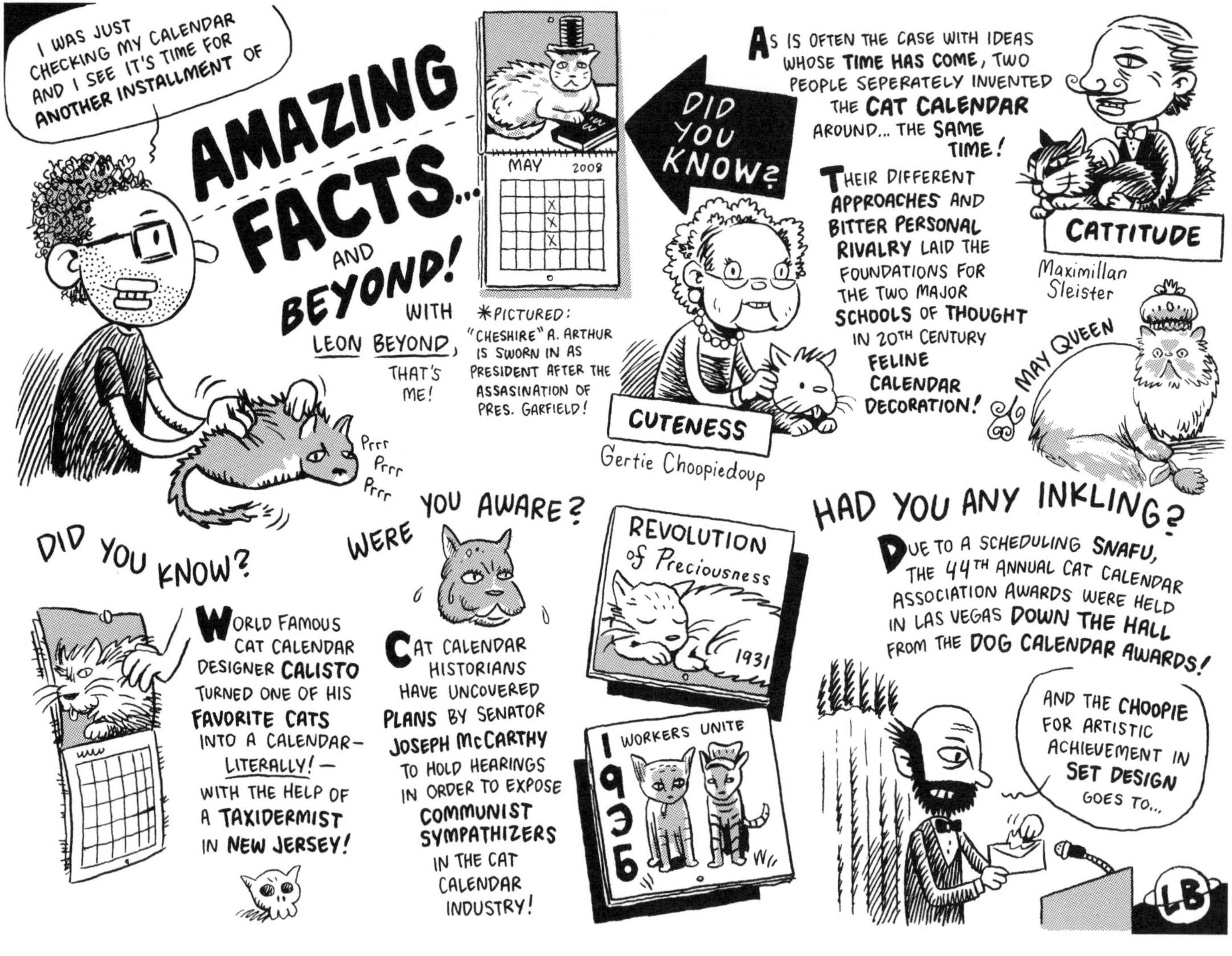
I WAS JUST CHECKING MY CALENDAR AND I SEE IT'S TIME FOR ANOTHER INSTALLMENT OF
AMAZING FACTS... AND BEYOND!
WITH LEON BEYOND, THAT'S ME!
MAY 2008
*PICTURED: "CHESHIRE" A. ARTHUR IS SWORN IN AS PRESIDENT AFTER THE ASSASINATION OF PRES. GARFIELD!
Prrr Prrr Prrr
DID YOU KNOW?
AS IS OFTEN THE CASE WITH IDEAS WHOSE TIME HAS COME, TWO PEOPLE SEPERATELY INVENTED THE CAT CALENDAR AROUND... THE SAME TIME!
THEIR DIFFERENT APPROACHES AND BITTER PERSONAL RIVALRY LAID THE FOUNDATIONS FOR THE TWO MAJOR SCHOOLS OF THOUGHT IN 20TH CENTURY FELINE CALENDAR DECORATION!
CATTITUDE
Maximillan Sleister
CUTENESS
Gertie Choopiedoup
MAY QUEEN
DID YOU KNOW?
WORLD FAMOUS CAT CALENDAR DESIGNER CALISTO TURNED ONE OF HIS FAVORITE CATS INTO A CALENDAR– LITERALLY!– WITH THE HELP OF A TAXIDERMIST IN NEW JERSEY!
WERE YOU AWARE?
CAT CALENDAR HISTORIANS HAVE UNCOVERED PLANS BY SENATOR JOSEPH McCARTHY TO HOLD HEARINGS IN ORDER TO EXPOSE COMMUNIST SYMPATHIZERS IN THE CAT CALENDAR INDUSTRY!
REVOLUTION of Preciousness
1931
WORKERS UNITE
1935
HAD YOU ANY INKLING?
DUE TO A SCHEDULING SNAFU, THE 44TH ANNUAL CAT CALENDAR ASSOCIATION AWARDS WERE HELD IN LAS VEGAS DOWN THE HALL FROM THE DOG CALENDAR AWARDS!
AND THE CHOOPIE FOR ARTISTIC ACHIEVEMENT IN SET DESIGN GOES TO...
LB

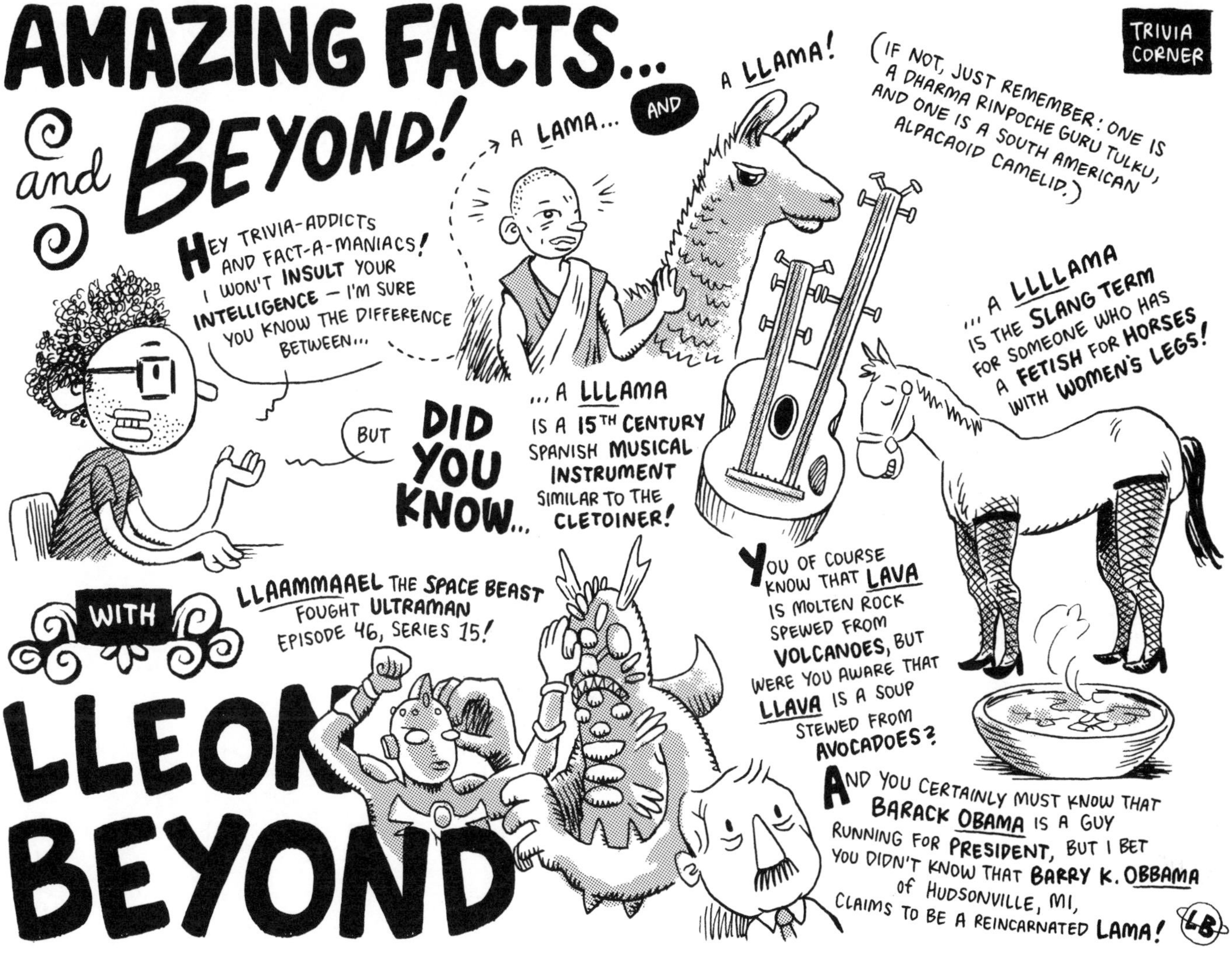
AMAZING FACTS... and BEYOND!
TRIVIA CORNER
HEY TRIVIA-ADDICTS AND FACT-A-MANIACS! I WON'T INSULT YOUR INTELLIGENCE — I'M SURE YOU KNOW THE DIFFERENCE BETWEEN...
A LAMA... AND A LLAMA!
(IF NOT, JUST REMEMBER: ONE IS A DHARMA RINPOCHE GURU TULKU, AND ONE IS A SOUTH AMERICAN ALPACAOID CAMELID.)
BUT DID YOU KNOW...
...A LLLAMA IS A 15TH CENTURY SPANISH MUSICAL INSTRUMENT SIMILAR TO THE CLETOINER!
... A LLLLAMA IS THE SLANG TERM FOR SOMEONE WHO HAS A FETISH FOR HORSES WITH WOMEN'S LEGS!
LLAAMMAAEL THE SPACE BEAST FOUGHT ULTRAMAN EPISODE 46, SERIES 15!
YOU OF COURSE KNOW THAT LAVA IS MOLTEN ROCK SPEWED FROM VOLCANOES, BUT WERE YOU AWARE THAT LLAVA IS A SOUP STEWED FROM AVOCADOES?
AND YOU CERTAINLY MUST KNOW THAT BARACK OBAMA IS A GUY RUNNING FOR PRESIDENT, BUT I BET YOU DIDN'T KNOW THAT BARRY K. OBBAMA OF HUDSONVILLE, MI, CLAIMS TO BE A REINCARNATED LAMA!
WITH LLEON BEYOND
LB

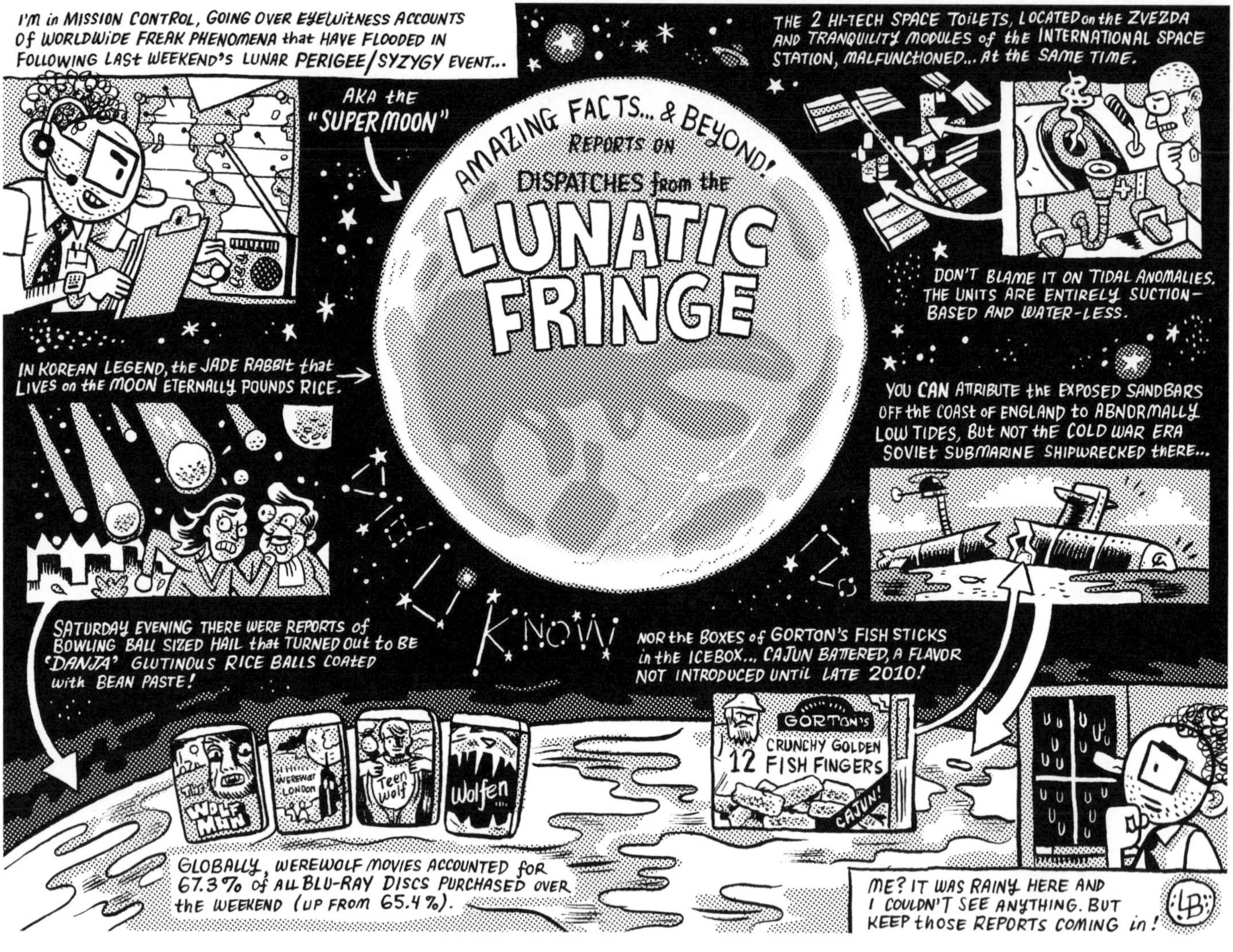
I'M in MISSION CONTROL, GOING OVER EYEWITNESS ACCOUNTS Of WORLDWIDE FREAK PHENOMENA that HAVE FLOODED IN FOLLOWING LAST WEEKEND'S LUNAR PERIGEE/SYZYGY EVENT...
AKA the "SUPERMOON"
AMAZING FACTS... & BEYOND!
REPORTS ON
DISPATCHES from the
LUNATIC FRINGE
THE 2 HI-TECH SPACE TOILETS, LOCATED on the ZVEZDA AND TRANQUILITY MODULES of the INTERNATIONAL SPACE STATION, MALFUNCTIONED... At the SAME TIME.
DON'T BLAME IT ON TIDAL ANOMALIES. THE UNITS ARE ENTIRELY SUCTION-BASED AND WATER-LESS.
IN KOREAN LEGEND, the JADE RABBIT that LIVES on the MOON ETERNALLY POUNDS RICE.
YOU CAN ATTRIBUTE the EXPOSED SANDBARS OFF the COAST of ENGLAND to ABNORMALLY LOW TIDES, But NOT the COLD WAR ERA SOVIET SUBMARINE SHIPWRECKED there...
KNOW
SATURDAY EVENING THERE WERE REPORTS of BOWLING BALL SIZED HAIL that TURNED OUT to BE 'DANJA' GLUTINOUS RICE BALLS COATED with BEAN PASTE!
NOR the BOXES of GORTON'S FISH STICKS in the ICEBOX... CAJUN BATTERED, A FLAVOR NOT INTRODUCED UNTIL LATE 2010!
WOLF MAN
Teen Wolf
Wolfen
GORTON'S
12 CRUNCHY GOLDEN FISH FINGERS
CAJUN!
GLOBALLY, WEREWOLF MOVIES ACCOUNTED for 67.3% of ALL BLU-RAY DISCS PURCHASED OVER the WEEKEND (UP FROM 65.4%).
ME? IT WAS RAINY HERE AND I COULDN'T SEE ANYTHING. BUT KEEP those REPORTS COMING in!
LB

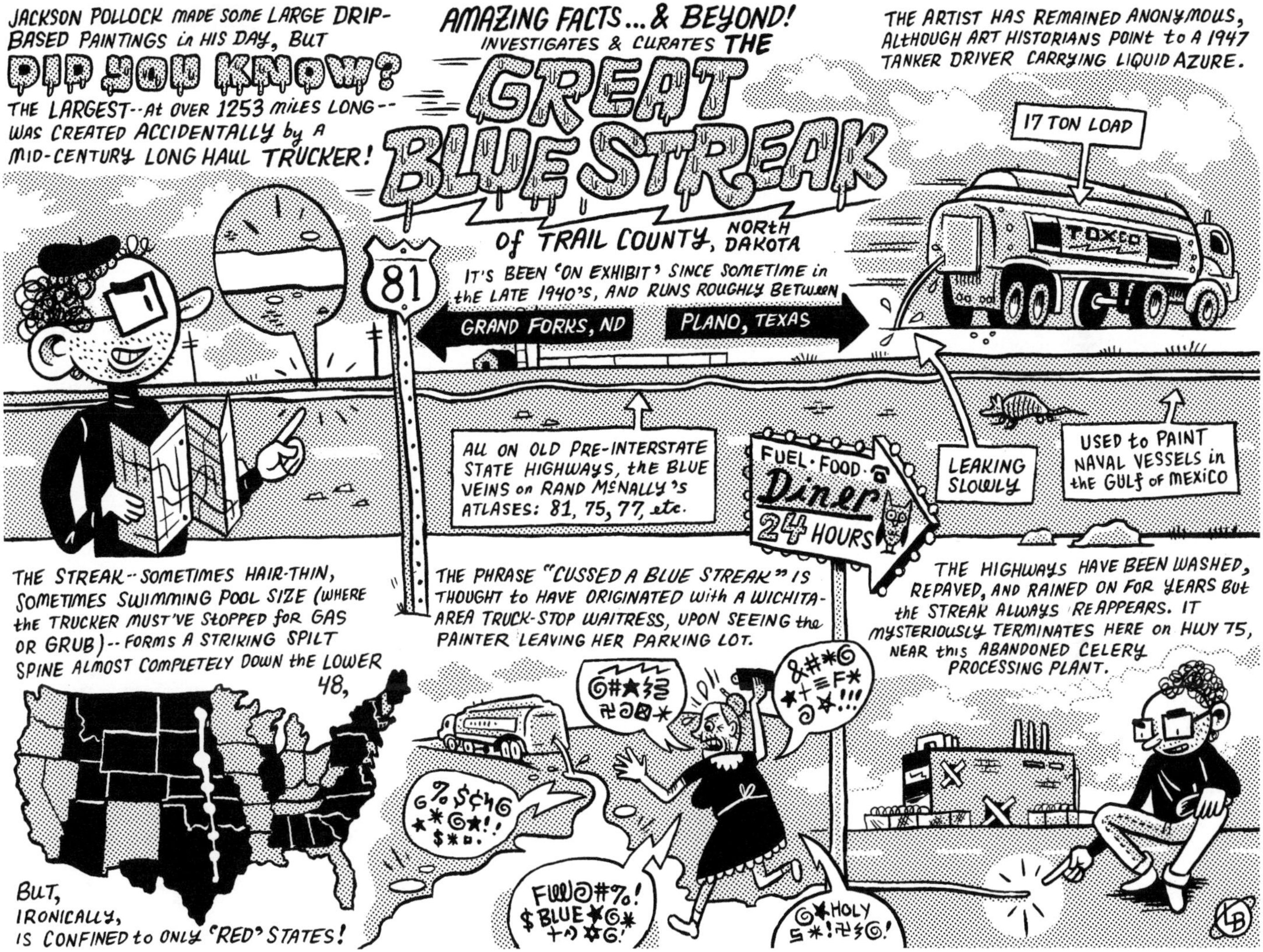
JACKSON POLLOCK MADE SOME LARGE DRIP-BASED PAINTINGS IN HIS DAY, BUT
DID YOU KNOW?
THE LARGEST--AT OVER 1253 MILES LONG--WAS CREATED ACCIDENTALLY BY A MID-CENTURY LONG HAUL TRUCKER!
AMAZING FACTS... & BEYOND! INVESTIGATES & CURATES THE
GREAT BLUE STREAK
OF TRAIL COUNTY, NORTH DAKOTA
THE ARTIST HAS REMAINED ANONYMOUS, ALTHOUGH ART HISTORIANS POINT TO A 1947 TANKER DRIVER CARRYING LIQUID AZURE.
17 TON LOAD
TOXCO
81
IT'S BEEN 'ON EXHIBIT' SINCE SOMETIME IN THE LATE 1940'S, AND RUNS ROUGHLY BETWEEN
GRAND FORKS, ND
PLANO, TEXAS
ALL ON OLD PRE-INTERSTATE STATE HIGHWAYS, THE BLUE VEINS ON RAND McNALLY'S ATLASES: 81, 75, 77, ETC.
FUEL · FOOD
Diner
24 HOURS
LEAKING SLOWLY
USED TO PAINT NAVAL VESSELS IN THE GULF OF MEXICO
THE STREAK--SOMETIMES HAIR-THIN, SOMETIMES SWIMMING POOL SIZE (WHERE THE TRUCKER MUST'VE STOPPED FOR GAS OR GRUB)--FORMS A STRIKING SPILT SPINE ALMOST COMPLETELY DOWN THE LOWER 48,
BUT, IRONICALLY, IS CONFINED TO ONLY 'RED' STATES!
THE PHRASE "CUSSED A BLUE STREAK" IS THOUGHT TO HAVE ORIGINATED WITH A WICHITA-AREA TRUCK-STOP WAITRESS, UPON SEEING THE PAINTER LEAVING HER PARKING LOT.
THE HIGHWAYS HAVE BEEN WASHED, REPAVED, AND RAINED ON FOR YEARS BUT THE STREAK ALWAYS REAPPEARS. IT MYSTERIOUSLY TERMINATES HERE ON HWY 75, NEAR THIS ABANDONED CELERY PROCESSING PLANT.
LB

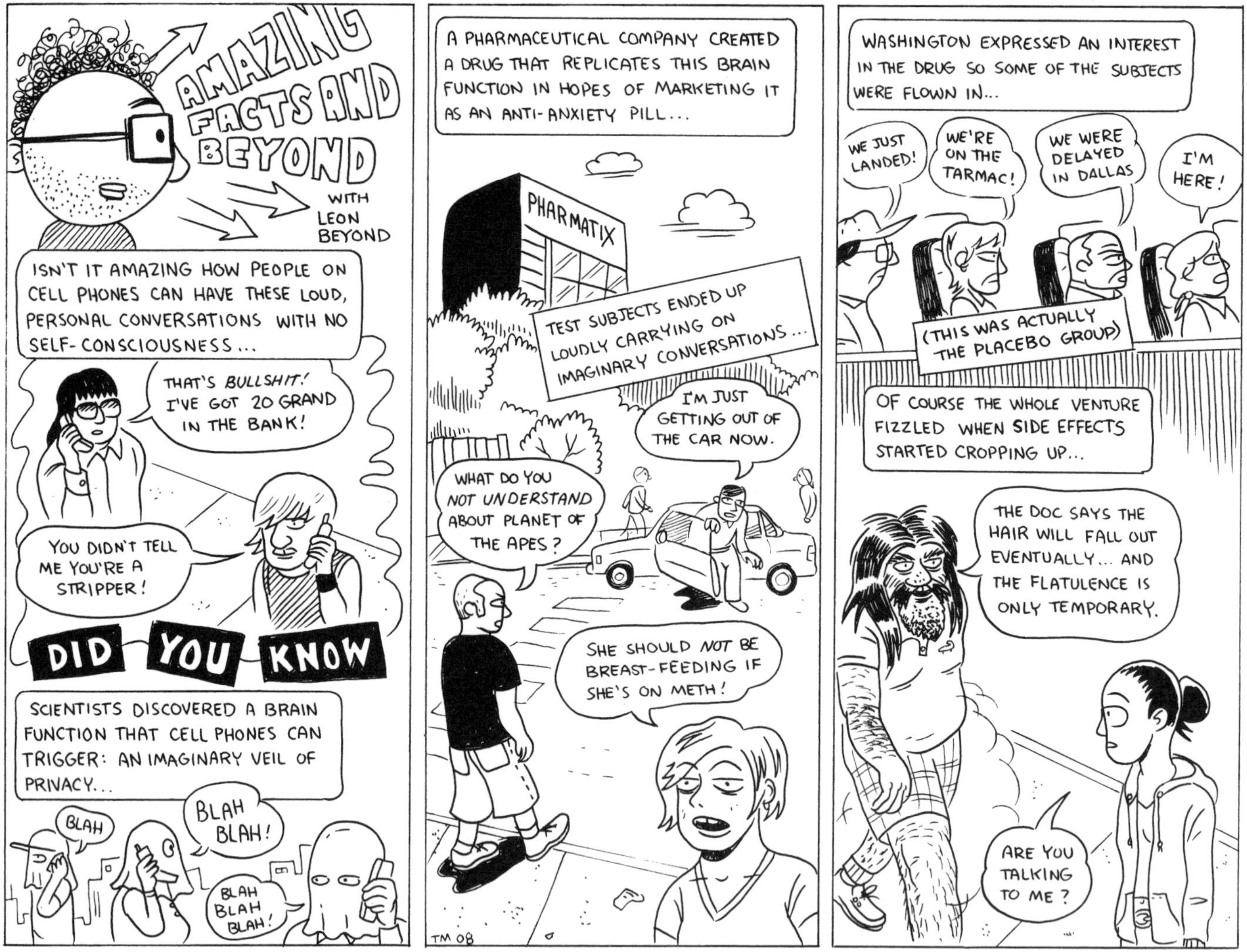
AMAZING FACTS AND BEYOND
WITH LEON BEYOND
ISN'T IT AMAZING HOW PEOPLE ON CELL PHONES CAN HAVE THESE LOUD, PERSONAL CONVERSATIONS WITH NO SELF-CONSCIOUSNESS...
THAT'S BULLSHIT! I'VE GOT 20 GRAND IN THE BANK!
YOU DIDN'T TELL ME YOU'RE A STRIPPER!
DID YOU KNOW
SCIENTISTS DISCOVERED A BRAIN FUNCTION THAT CELL PHONES CAN TRIGGER: AN IMAGINARY VEIL OF PRIVACY...
BLAH
BLAH BLAH!
BLAH BLAH BLAH!
A PHARMACEUTICAL COMPANY CREATED A DRUG THAT REPLICATES THIS BRAIN FUNCTION IN HOPES OF MARKETING IT AS AN ANTI-ANXIETY PILL...
PHARMATIX
TEST SUBJECTS ENDED UP LOUDLY CARRYING ON IMAGINARY CONVERSATIONS...
I'M JUST GETTING OUT OF THE CAR NOW.
WHAT DO YOU NOT UNDERSTAND ABOUT PLANET OF THE APES?
SHE SHOULD NOT BE BREAST-FEEDING IF SHE'S ON METH!
TM 08
WASHINGTON EXPRESSED AN INTEREST IN THE DRUG SO SOME OF THE SUBJECTS WERE FLOWN IN...
WE JUST LANDED!
WE'RE ON THE TARMAC!
WE WERE DELAYED IN DALLAS
I'M HERE!
(THIS WAS ACTUALLY THE PLACEBO GROUP)
OF COURSE THE WHOLE VENTURE FIZZLED WHEN SIDE EFFECTS STARTED CROPPING UP...
THE DOC SAYS THE HAIR WILL FALL OUT EVENTUALLY... AND THE FLATULENCE IS ONLY TEMPORARY.
ARE YOU TALKING TO ME?

AMAZING FACTS & BEYOND

RATS, LEON! THIS NOVEL I'M WRITING IS GOING *NOWHERE*! I THINK IT'S GIVING ME O.C.D.!

YEAH! THAT'S YOUR SEVENTH BEER LABEL NINJA STAR.

DID YOU KNOW THERE'S A GREAT METHOD FOR BUSTING WRITER'S BLOCK? -- STREAKING!

OH, COOL! I'LL DO IT RIGHT NOW!

WAIT- I HAVEN'T TALKED ABOUT IT YET! SO, YEAH, DICKENS, MARK TWAIN, TOLSTOY- ALL MAJOR LEAGUE STREAKERS!

FLAUBERT

STREAK!

MADAME BOVARY

EXISTENTIALISM NEVER REALLY TOOK OFF UNTIL SARTRE... WELL, TOOK OFF!

STREAK!

TALK ABOUT "NOTHINGNESS"!

IT BECAME A LITTLE *TOO* POPULAR. BUT THE TREND MYSTERIOUSLY DIED DOWN. IT MAY HAVE BEEN DUE TO THE ADVENT OF THE POLAROID...

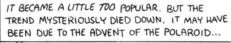

HEMINGWAY

FAULKNER

STREAK!

JACKPOT!

SO... UP FOR ANOTHER...

...UH-OH.

MONTHS LATER...

...AND I SAID, "BOOK JACKET?? I DON'T THINK SO!!"

TODAY THE NAKED AUTHOR READS FROM HIS BEST SELLER

I WAS *THIS* CLOSE TO SUGGESTING "PILATES"...

23

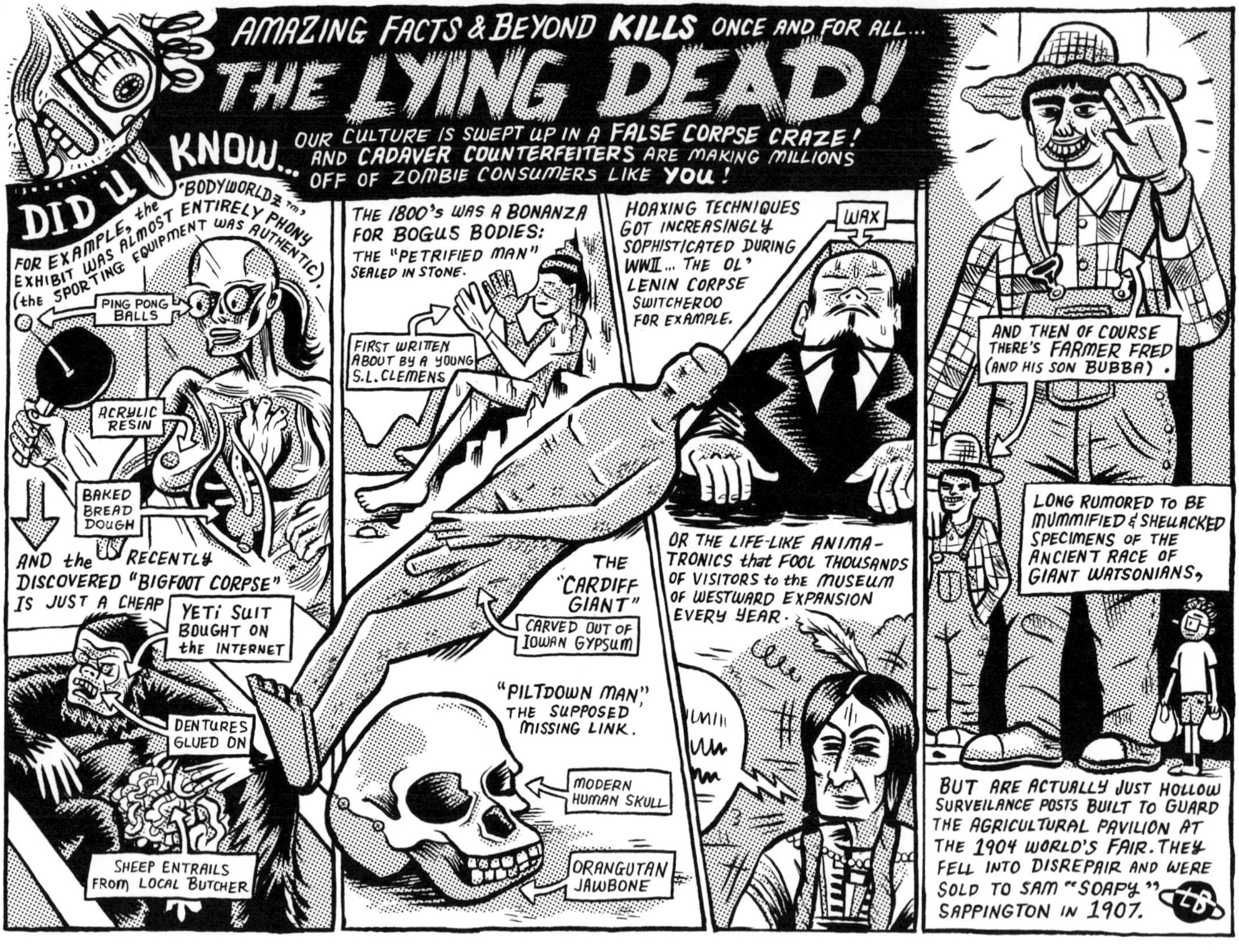

AMAZING FACTS & BEYOND KILLS ONCE AND FOR ALL...
THE LYING DEAD!
DID U KNOW...
OUR CULTURE IS SWEPT UP IN A FALSE CORPSE CRAZE! AND CADAVER COUNTERFEITERS ARE MAKING MILLIONS OFF OF ZOMBIE CONSUMERS LIKE YOU!
FOR EXAMPLE, the "BODYWORLDZ™" EXHIBIT WAS ALMOST ENTIRELY PHONY (the SPORTING EQUIPMENT WAS AUTHENTIC).
PING PONG BALLS
ACRYLIC RESIN
BAKED BREAD DOUGH
AND the RECENTLY DISCOVERED "BIGFOOT CORPSE" IS JUST A CHEAP
YETI SUIT BOUGHT ON the INTERNET
DENTURES GLUED ON
SHEEP ENTRAILS FROM LOCAL BUTCHER
THE 1800's WAS A BONANZA FOR BOGUS BODIES:
THE "PETRIFIED MAN" SEALED IN STONE.
FIRST WRITTEN ABOUT BY A YOUNG S.L. CLEMENS
THE "CARDIFF GIANT"
CARVED OUT OF IOWAN GYPSUM
"PILTDOWN MAN," THE SUPPOSED MISSING LINK.
MODERN HUMAN SKULL
ORANGUTAN JAWBONE
HOAXING TECHNIQUES GOT INCREASINGLY SOPHISTICATED DURING WWII... THE OL' LENIN CORPSE SWITCHEROO FOR EXAMPLE.
WAX
OR THE LIFE-LIKE ANIMATRONICS that FOOL THOUSANDS OF VISITORS to the MUSEUM OF WESTWARD EXPANSION EVERY YEAR.
AND THEN OF COURSE THERE'S FARMER FRED (AND HIS SON BUBBA).
LONG RUMORED TO BE MUMMIFIED & SHELLACKED SPECIMENS OF THE ANCIENT RACE OF GIANT WATSONIANS,
BUT ARE ACTUALLY JUST HOLLOW SURVEILANCE POSTS BUILT TO GUARD THE AGRICULTURAL PAVILION AT THE 1904 WORLD'S FAIR. THEY FELL INTO DISREPAIR AND WERE SOLD TO SAM "SOAPY" SAPPINGTON IN 1907.

THE WORLD'S LARGEST MAN-MADE SWIMMIN' HOLE, ALL 1 1/3 SQ. MILES AND 5.5 TRILLION FRESHWATER GALLONS OF IT, WAS BRIEFLY FOUND OUTSIDE STOCKTON, TEXAS.

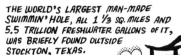

DID YOU KNOW?! IT WAS AN EXACT 1:1000 SCALE REPLICA OF CHINA'S BIGGEST BODY OF WATER! **AMAZING FACTS...& BEYOND!** DIVES INTO the

AQUATIC WILDLIFE NATIVE to THE ORIGINAL POYANG LAKE WERE IMPORTED TO SWIM ALONGSIDE the THOUSANDS THAT VISITED the VAST COMPLEX DAILY from 1969-71.

GREAT POYANG
POOL of Pecos County

IT WAS SO BIG THAT, to PATROL, LIFEGUARDS JERRY-RIGGED SNOWMOBILES for WATER-USE... INVENTING the JET-SKI!

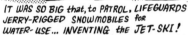

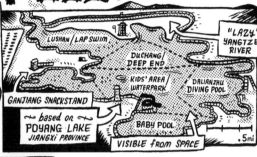

LUSHAN / LAP SWIM

DUCHANG / DEEP END

KIDS' AREA / WATERPARK

DALIANZHU DIVING POOL

"LAZY" YANGTZE RIVER

GANJIANG SNACKSTAND

→ based on POYANG LAKE JIANGXI PROVINCE

BABY POOL

VISIBLE from SPACE

.5mi

SIBERIAN CRANE

JIANGZHU "RIVER PIG"

BAIJI "RIVER DOLPHIN"

THE BATTLE OF POYANG LAKE OF 1343 -- the LARGEST NAVAL BATTLE in HISTORY WHICH SAW THE MIGHTY MING DEFEAT THE HAN -- WAS REENACTED by HUNDREDS of LOCAL TEENAGERS JULY 4TH, 1970.

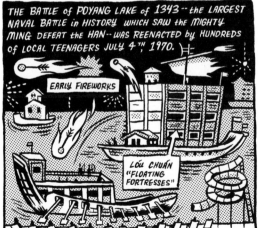

EARLY FIREWORKS

LÓU CHUÁN "FLOATING FORTRESSES"

UNLIKE the ORIGINAL POYANG LAKE -- KNOWN AS the "CHINESE BERMUDA" -- the POOL MYSTERIOUSLY CLAIMED NOT SHIPS 'N' LIVES, BUT GOGGLES, BIKINI BOTTOMS, & STYROFOAM TUBES CALLED "NOODLES."

(THERE WAS NO LOST 'N' FOUND.)

FORCED to CLOSE in EARLY '72 (WATER QUALITY, HEALTH CONCERNS, LAWSUITS), the POOL IS NOW FILLED with GRAVEL & SAND. FEW RELICS of the ORIENTAL CRAZE THAT SWEPT the SOUTHWEST REMAIN.

Welcome to OYANG OOL

NOTICE there IS NO "P"

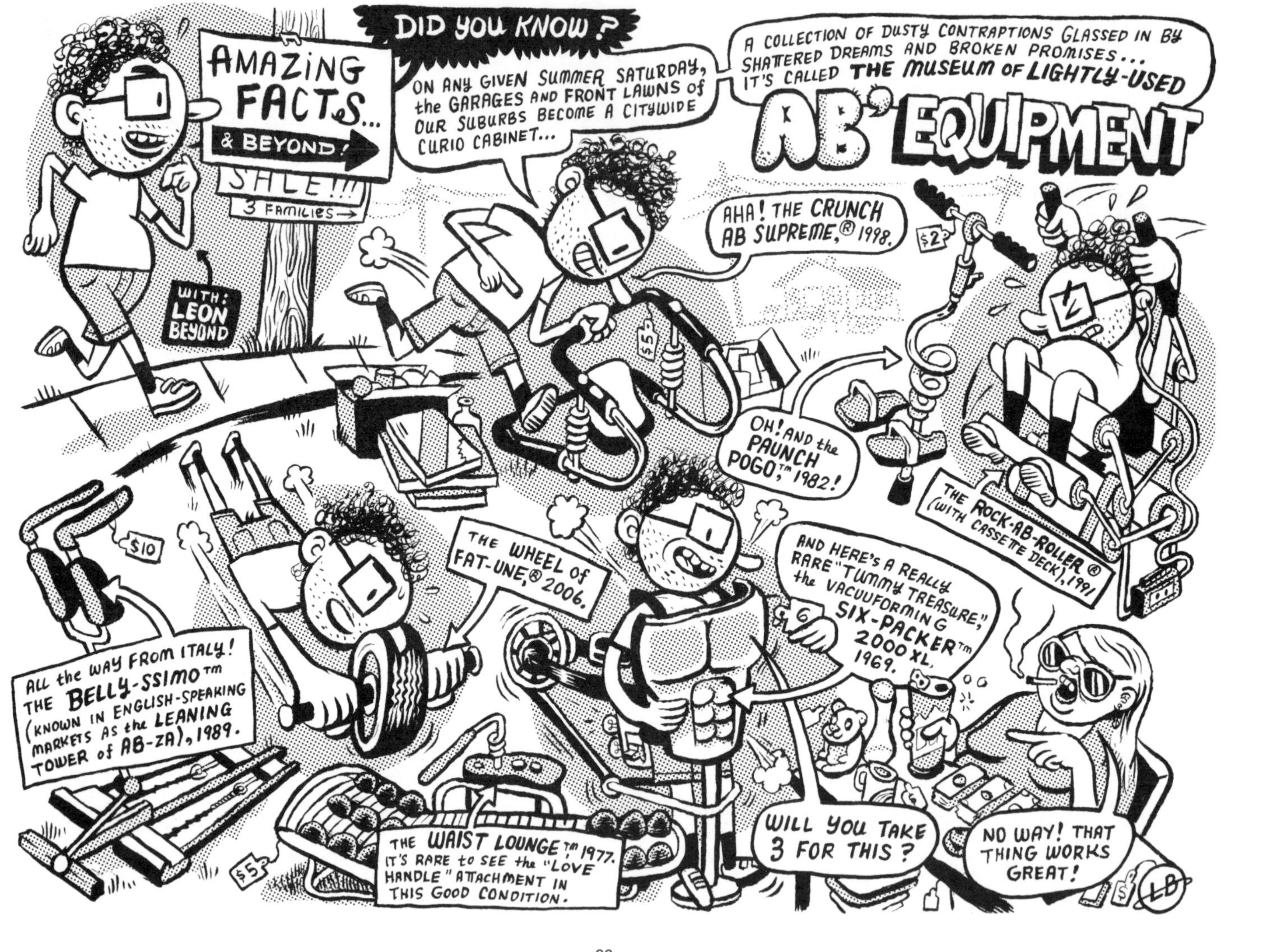
AMAZING FACTS... & BEYOND!
SALE!!!
3 FAMILIES →
WITH: LEON BEYOND
DID YOU KNOW?
ON ANY GIVEN SUMMER SATURDAY, the GARAGES AND FRONT LAWNS of OUR SUBURBS BECOME A CITYWIDE CURIO CABINET...
A COLLECTION OF DUSTY CONTRAPTIONS GLASSED IN BY SHATTERED DREAMS AND BROKEN PROMISES... IT'S CALLED THE MUSEUM of LIGHTLY-USED
AB' EQUIPMENT
AHA! THE CRUNCH AB SUPREME,® 1998.
$5
$2
OH! AND the PAUNCH POGO,™ 1982!
THE ROCK-AB-ROLLER ® (WITH CASSETTE DECK), 1991
$10
THE WHEEL of FAT-UNE,® 2006.
AND HERE'S A REALLY RARE "TUMMY TREASURE," the VACUUFORMING SIX-PACKER™ 2000 XL, 1969.
ALL the WAY FROM ITALY! THE BELLY-SSIMO™ (KNOWN IN ENGLISH-SPEAKING MARKETS AS the LEANING TOWER of AB-ZA), 1989.
$5
THE WAIST LOUNGE,™ 1977. IT'S RARE to SEE the "LOVE HANDLE" ATTACHMENT IN THIS GOOD CONDITION.
WILL YOU TAKE 3 FOR THIS?
NO WAY! THAT THING WORKS GREAT!
LB

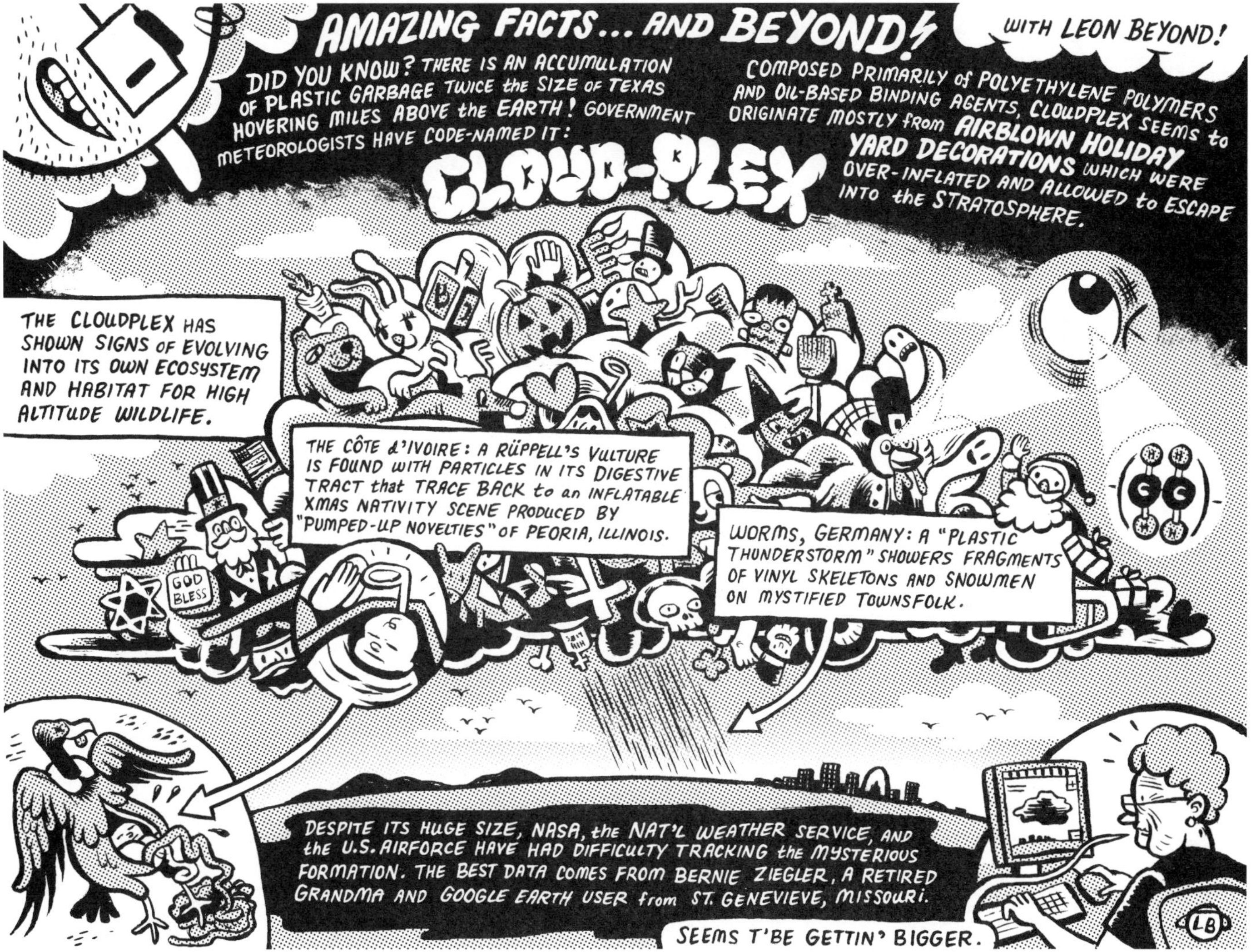
AMAZING FACTS... AND BEYOND!
WITH LEON BEYOND!
DID YOU KNOW? THERE IS AN ACCUMULATION OF PLASTIC GARBAGE TWICE THE SIZE OF TEXAS HOVERING MILES ABOVE THE EARTH! GOVERNMENT METEOROLOGISTS HAVE CODE-NAMED IT:
CLOUD-PLEX
COMPOSED PRIMARILY OF POLYETHYLENE POLYMERS AND OIL-BASED BINDING AGENTS, CLOUDPLEX SEEMS TO ORIGINATE MOSTLY FROM AIRBLOWN HOLIDAY YARD DECORATIONS WHICH WERE OVER-INFLATED AND ALLOWED TO ESCAPE INTO THE STRATOSPHERE.
THE CLOUDPLEX HAS SHOWN SIGNS OF EVOLVING INTO ITS OWN ECOSYSTEM AND HABITAT FOR HIGH ALTITUDE WILDLIFE.
THE CÔTE d'IVOIRE: A RÜPPELL'S VULTURE IS FOUND WITH PARTICLES IN ITS DIGESTIVE TRACT THAT TRACE BACK TO AN INFLATABLE XMAS NATIVITY SCENE PRODUCED BY "PUMPED-UP NOVELTIES" OF PEORIA, ILLINOIS.
GOD BLESS
WORMS, GERMANY: A "PLASTIC THUNDERSTORM" SHOWERS FRAGMENTS OF VINYL SKELETONS AND SNOWMEN ON MYSTIFIED TOWNSFOLK.
DESPITE ITS HUGE SIZE, NASA, THE NAT'L WEATHER SERVICE, AND THE U.S. AIRFORCE HAVE HAD DIFFICULTY TRACKING THE MYSTERIOUS FORMATION. THE BEST DATA COMES FROM BERNIE ZIEGLER, A RETIRED GRANDMA AND GOOGLE EARTH USER FROM ST. GENEVIEVE, MISSOURI.
SEEMS T'BE GETTIN' BIGGER.
LB

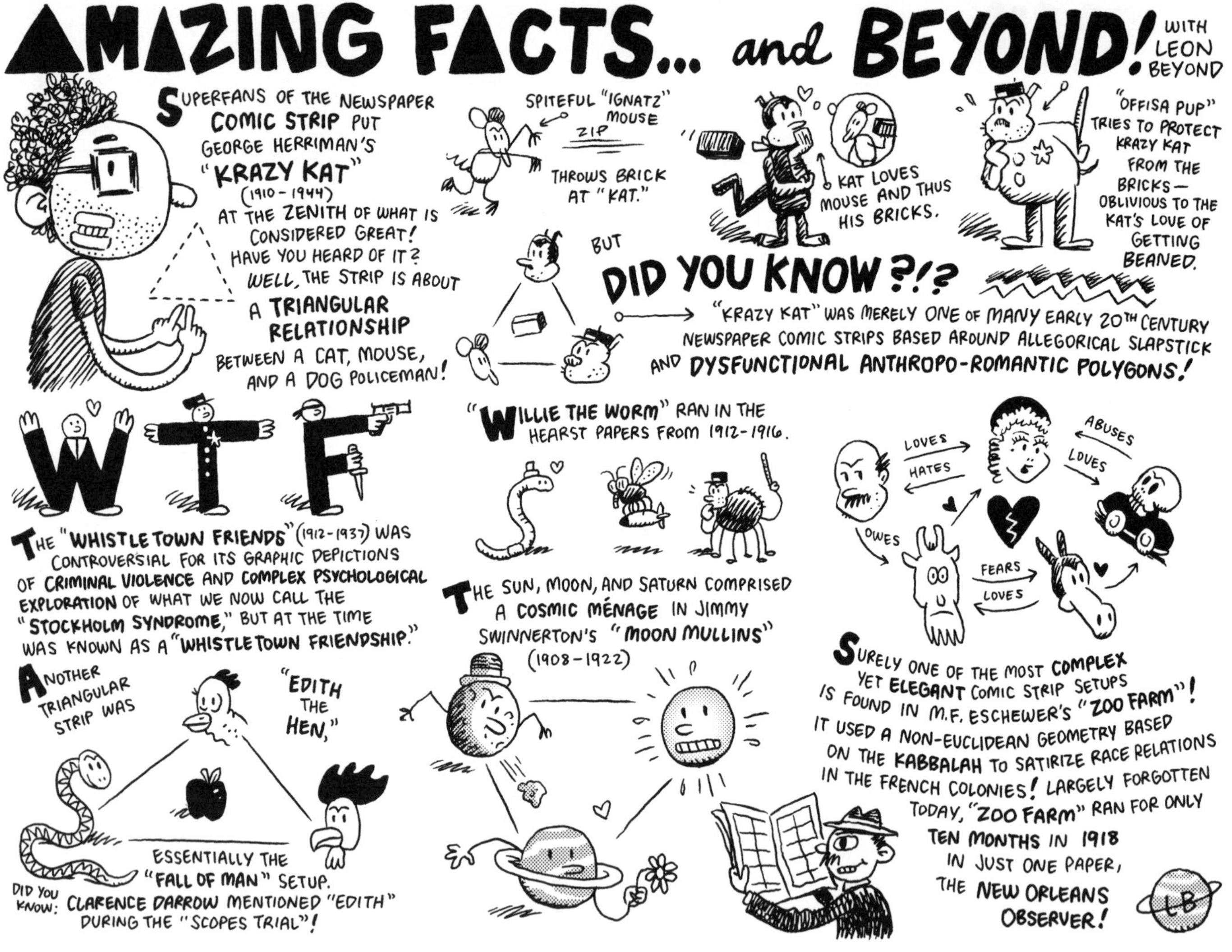
AMAZING FACTS... and BEYOND! WITH LEON BEYOND
SUPERFANS OF THE NEWSPAPER COMIC STRIP PUT GEORGE HERRIMAN'S "KRAZY KAT" (1910–1944) AT THE ZENITH OF WHAT IS CONSIDERED GREAT! HAVE YOU HEARD OF IT? WELL, THE STRIP IS ABOUT A TRIANGULAR RELATIONSHIP BETWEEN A CAT, MOUSE, AND A DOG POLICEMAN!
SPITEFUL "IGNATZ" MOUSE
ZIP
THROWS BRICK AT "KAT."
KAT LOVES MOUSE AND THUS HIS BRICKS.
"OFFISA PUP" TRIES TO PROTECT KRAZY KAT FROM THE BRICKS— OBLIVIOUS TO THE KAT'S LOVE OF GETTING BEANED.
BUT
DID YOU KNOW?!?
"KRAZY KAT" WAS MERELY ONE OF MANY EARLY 20TH CENTURY NEWSPAPER COMIC STRIPS BASED AROUND ALLEGORICAL SLAPSTICK AND DYSFUNCTIONAL ANTHROPO-ROMANTIC POLYGONS!
WTF
THE "WHISTLE TOWN FRIENDS" (1912-1937) WAS CONTROVERSIAL FOR ITS GRAPHIC DEPICTIONS OF CRIMINAL VIOLENCE AND COMPLEX PSYCHOLOGICAL EXPLORATION OF WHAT WE NOW CALL THE "STOCKHOLM SYNDROME," BUT AT THE TIME WAS KNOWN AS A "WHISTLE TOWN FRIENDSHIP."
"WILLIE THE WORM" RAN IN THE HEARST PAPERS FROM 1912-1916.
LOVES
HATES
ABUSES
LOVES
OWES
FEARS
LOVES
ANOTHER TRIANGULAR STRIP WAS "EDITH THE HEN,"
ESSENTIALLY THE "FALL OF MAN" SETUP.
DID YOU KNOW: CLARENCE DARROW MENTIONED "EDITH" DURING THE "SCOPES TRIAL"!
THE SUN, MOON, AND SATURN COMPRISED A COSMIC MÉNAGE IN JIMMY SWINNERTON'S "MOON MULLINS" (1908–1922)
SURELY ONE OF THE MOST COMPLEX YET ELEGANT COMIC STRIP SETUPS IS FOUND IN M.F. ESCHEWER'S "ZOO FARM"! IT USED A NON-EUCLIDEAN GEOMETRY BASED ON THE KABBALAH TO SATIRIZE RACE RELATIONS IN THE FRENCH COLONIES! LARGELY FORGOTTEN TODAY, "ZOO FARM" RAN FOR ONLY TEN MONTHS IN 1918 IN JUST ONE PAPER, THE NEW ORLEANS OBSERVER!
LB

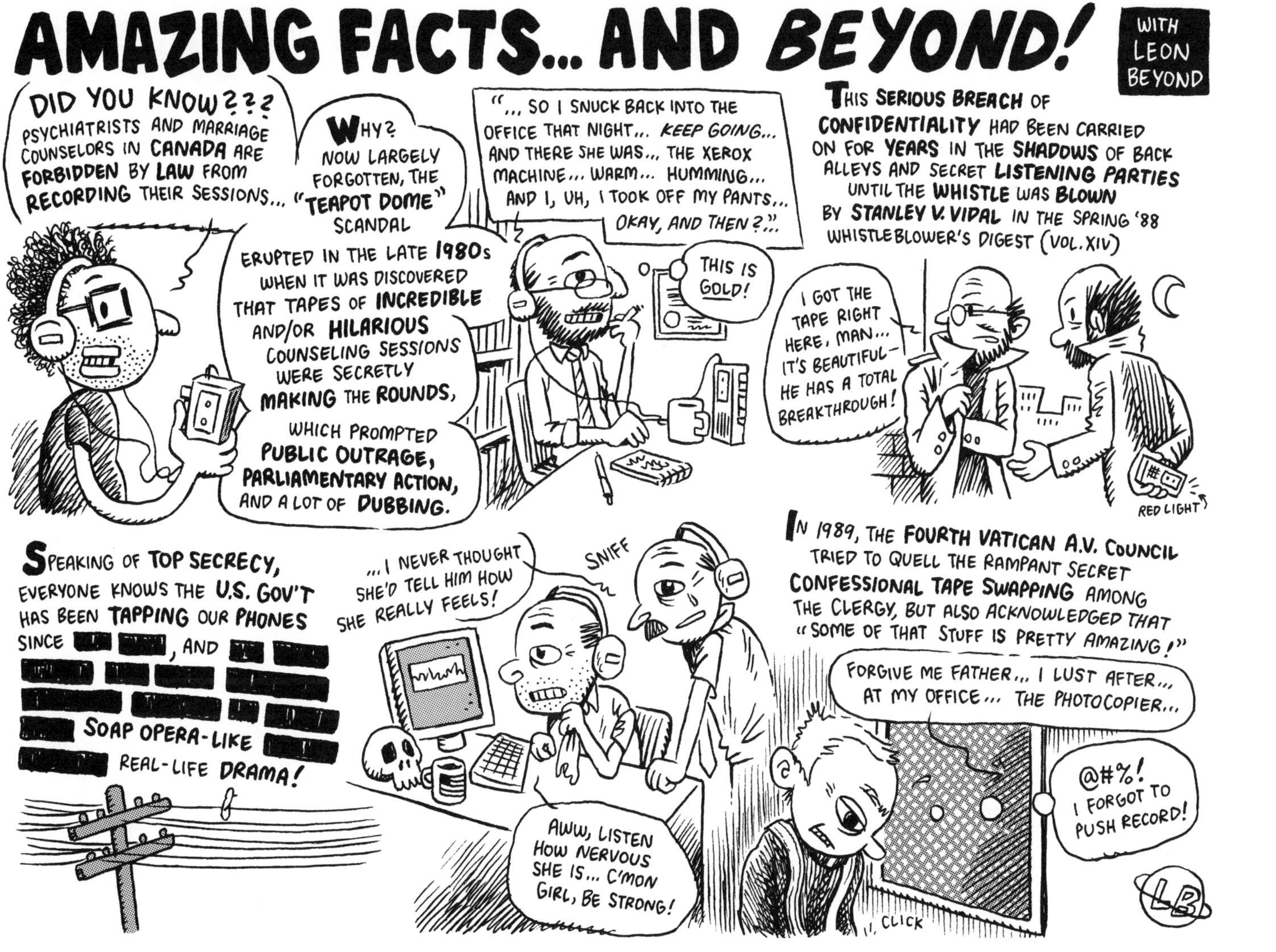
AMAZING FACTS... AND BEYOND!
WITH LEON BEYOND
DID YOU KNOW??? PSYCHIATRISTS AND MARRIAGE COUNSELORS IN CANADA ARE FORBIDDEN BY LAW FROM RECORDING THEIR SESSIONS...
WHY? NOW LARGELY FORGOTTEN, THE "TEAPOT DOME" SCANDAL
ERUPTED IN THE LATE 1980s WHEN IT WAS DISCOVERED THAT TAPES OF INCREDIBLE AND/OR HILARIOUS COUNSELING SESSIONS WERE SECRETLY MAKING THE ROUNDS,
WHICH PROMPTED PUBLIC OUTRAGE, PARLIAMENTARY ACTION, AND A LOT OF DUBBING.
"... SO I SNUCK BACK INTO THE OFFICE THAT NIGHT... KEEP GOING... AND THERE SHE WAS... THE XEROX MACHINE... WARM... HUMMING... AND I, UH, I TOOK OFF MY PANTS... OKAY, AND THEN?..."
THIS IS GOLD!
THIS SERIOUS BREACH OF CONFIDENTIALITY HAD BEEN CARRIED ON FOR YEARS IN THE SHADOWS OF BACK ALLEYS AND SECRET LISTENING PARTIES UNTIL THE WHISTLE WAS BLOWN BY STANLEY V. VIDAL IN THE SPRING '88 WHISTLEBLOWER'S DIGEST (VOL. XIV)
I GOT THE TAPE RIGHT HERE, MAN... IT'S BEAUTIFUL- HE HAS A TOTAL BREAKTHROUGH!
RED LIGHT
SPEAKING OF TOP SECRECY, EVERYONE KNOWS THE U.S. GOV'T HAS BEEN TAPPING OUR PHONES SINCE [redacted], AND [redacted] SOAP OPERA-LIKE [redacted] REAL-LIFE DRAMA!
...I NEVER THOUGHT SHE'D TELL HIM HOW SHE REALLY FEELS!
SNIFF
AWW, LISTEN HOW NERVOUS SHE IS... C'MON GIRL, BE STRONG!
IN 1989, THE FOURTH VATICAN A.V. COUNCIL TRIED TO QUELL THE RAMPANT SECRET CONFESSIONAL TAPE SWAPPING AMONG THE CLERGY, BUT ALSO ACKNOWLEDGED THAT "SOME OF THAT STUFF IS PRETTY AMAZING!"
FORGIVE ME FATHER... I LUST AFTER... AT MY OFFICE... THE PHOTOCOPIER...
@#%! I FORGOT TO PUSH RECORD!
CLICK
LB

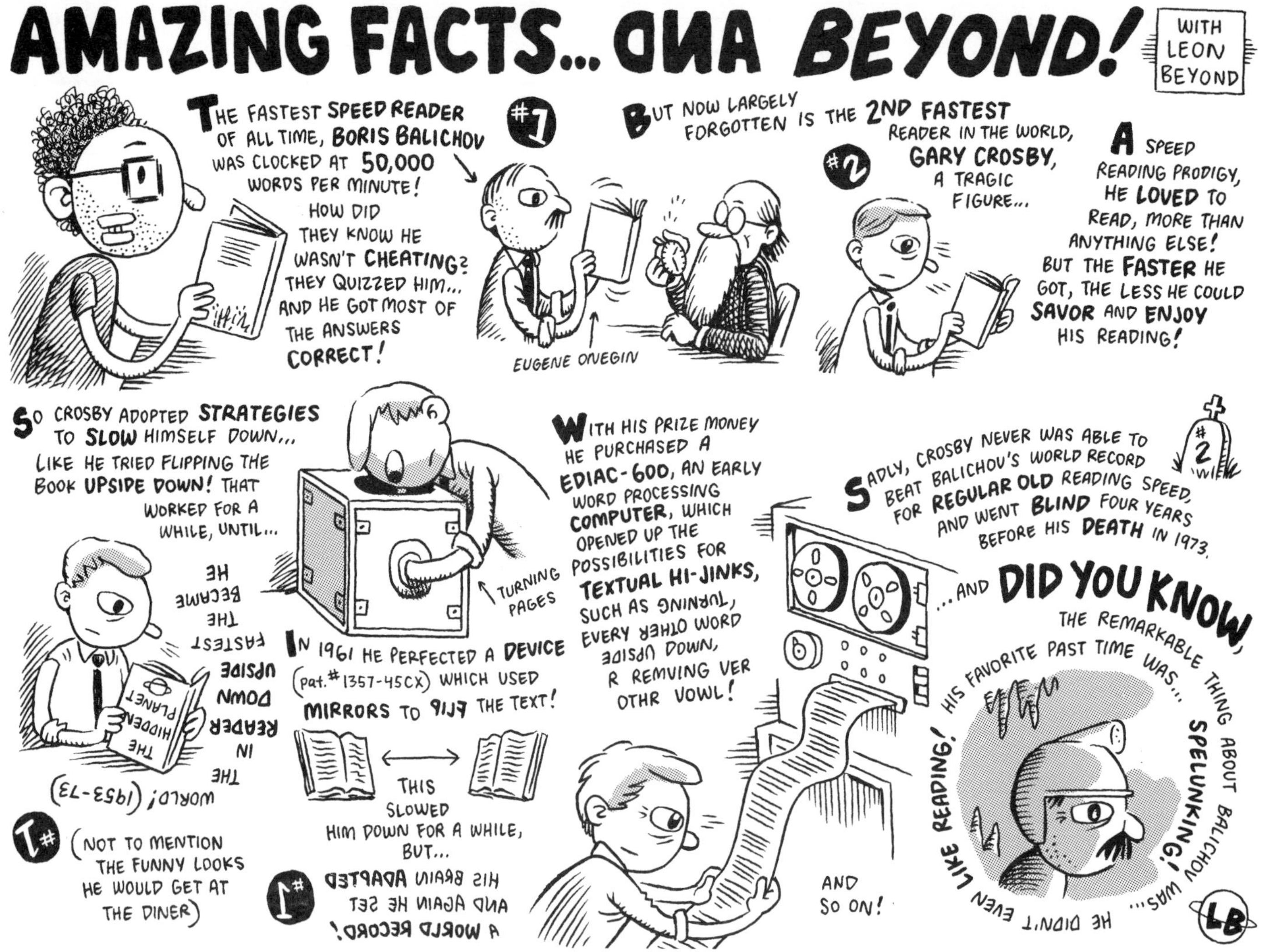

AMAZING FACTS... AND BEYOND!
WITH LEON BEYOND
THE FASTEST SPEED READER OF ALL TIME, BORIS BALICHOV WAS CLOCKED AT 50,000 WORDS PER MINUTE!
HOW DID THEY KNOW HE WASN'T CHEATING? THEY QUIZZED HIM... AND HE GOT MOST OF THE ANSWERS CORRECT!
#1
EUGENE ONEGIN
BUT NOW LARGELY FORGOTTEN IS THE 2ND FASTEST READER IN THE WORLD, GARY CROSBY, A TRAGIC FIGURE...
#2
A SPEED READING PRODIGY, HE LOVED TO READ, MORE THAN ANYTHING ELSE! BUT THE FASTER HE GOT, THE LESS HE COULD SAVOR AND ENJOY HIS READING!
SO CROSBY ADOPTED STRATEGIES TO SLOW HIMSELF DOWN... LIKE HE TRIED FLIPPING THE BOOK UPSIDE DOWN! THAT WORKED FOR A WHILE, UNTIL...
HE BECAME THE FASTEST UPSIDE DOWN READER IN THE WORLD! (1953-73)
THE HIDDEN PLANET
#1 (NOT TO MENTION THE FUNNY LOOKS HE WOULD GET AT THE DINER)
TURNING PAGES
IN 1961 HE PERFECTED A DEVICE (pat. # 1357-45CX) WHICH USED MIRRORS TO FLIP THE TEXT!
THIS SLOWED HIM DOWN FOR A WHILE, BUT...
#1 HIS BRAIN ADAPTED AND AGAIN HE SET A WORLD RECORD!
WITH HIS PRIZE MONEY HE PURCHASED A EDIAC-600, AN EARLY WORD PROCESSING COMPUTER, WHICH OPENED UP THE POSSIBILITIES FOR TEXTUAL HI-JINKS, SUCH AS TURNING EVERY OTHER WORD UPSIDE DOWN, R REMVING VER OTHR VOWL!
AND SO ON!
SADLY, CROSBY NEVER WAS ABLE TO BEAT BALICHOV'S WORLD RECORD FOR REGULAR OLD READING SPEED, AND WENT BLIND FOUR YEARS BEFORE HIS DEATH IN 1973.
#2
...AND DID YOU KNOW, THE REMARKABLE THING ABOUT BALICHOV WAS... HIS FAVORITE PAST TIME WAS... SPELUNKING!
HE DIDN'T EVEN LIKE READING!
LB

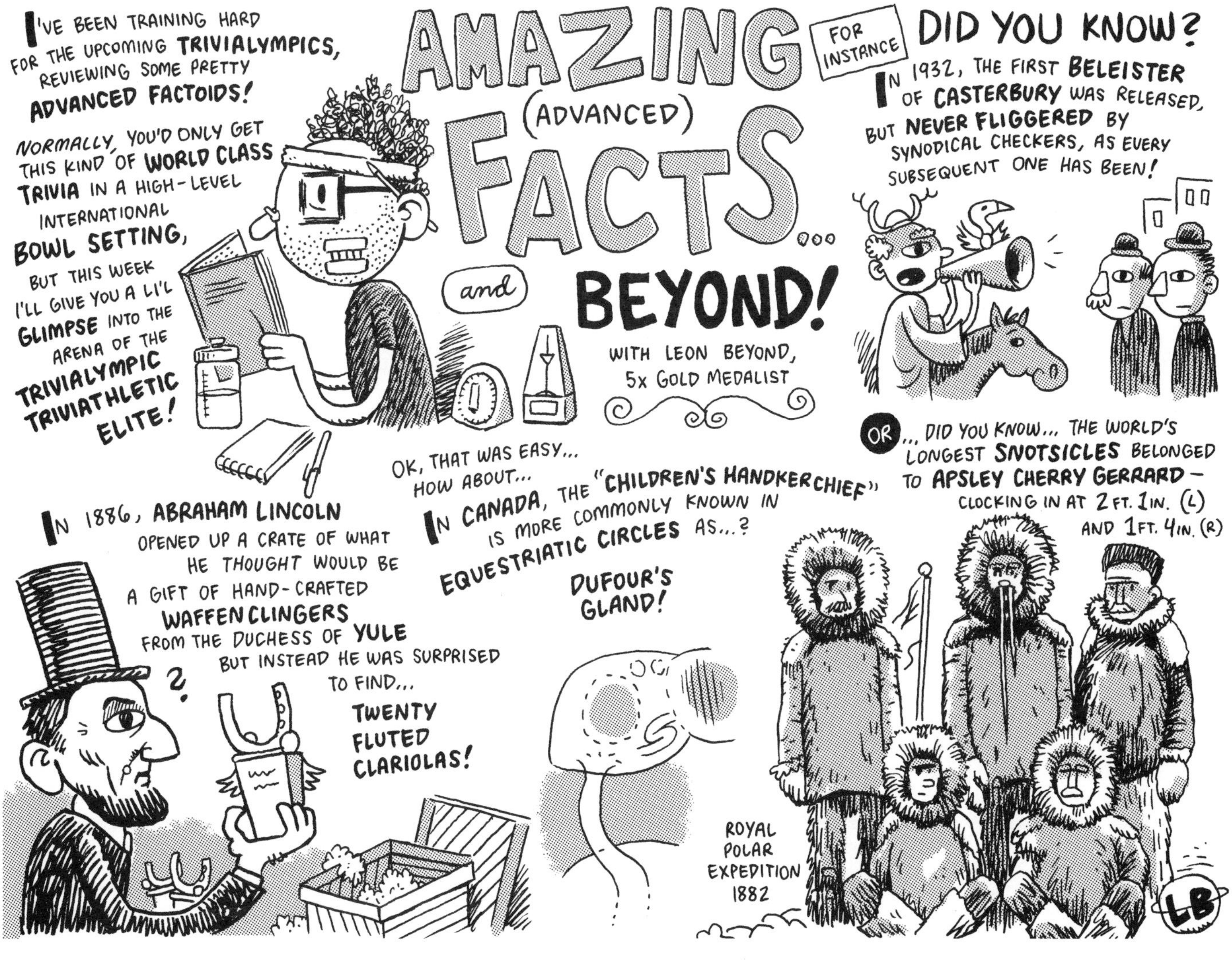
AMAZING (ADVANCED) FACTS... and BEYOND!
WITH LEON BEYOND, 5x GOLD MEDALIST
I'VE BEEN TRAINING HARD FOR THE UPCOMING TRIVIALYMPICS, REVIEWING SOME PRETTY ADVANCED FACTOIDS!
NORMALLY, YOU'D ONLY GET THIS KIND OF WORLD CLASS TRIVIA IN A HIGH-LEVEL INTERNATIONAL BOWL SETTING,
BUT THIS WEEK I'LL GIVE YOU A LI'L GLIMPSE INTO THE ARENA OF THE TRIVIALYMPIC TRIVIATHLETIC ELITE!
FOR INSTANCE
DID YOU KNOW?
IN 1932, THE FIRST BELEISTER OF CASTERBURY WAS RELEASED, BUT NEVER FLIGGERED BY SYNODICAL CHECKERS, AS EVERY SUBSEQUENT ONE HAS BEEN!
OR ...DID YOU KNOW... THE WORLD'S LONGEST SNOTSICLES BELONGED TO APSLEY CHERRY GERRARD – CLOCKING IN AT 2 FT. 1 IN. (L) AND 1 FT. 4 IN. (R)
OK, THAT WAS EASY... HOW ABOUT...
IN CANADA, THE "CHILDREN'S HANDKERCHIEF" IS MORE COMMONLY KNOWN IN EQUESTRIATIC CIRCLES AS...?
DUFOUR'S GLAND!
IN 1886, ABRAHAM LINCOLN OPENED UP A CRATE OF WHAT HE THOUGHT WOULD BE A GIFT OF HAND-CRAFTED WAFFENCLINGERS FROM THE DUCHESS OF YULE
BUT INSTEAD HE WAS SURPRISED TO FIND...
TWENTY FLUTED CLARIOLAS!
?
ROYAL POLAR EXPEDITION 1882
LB

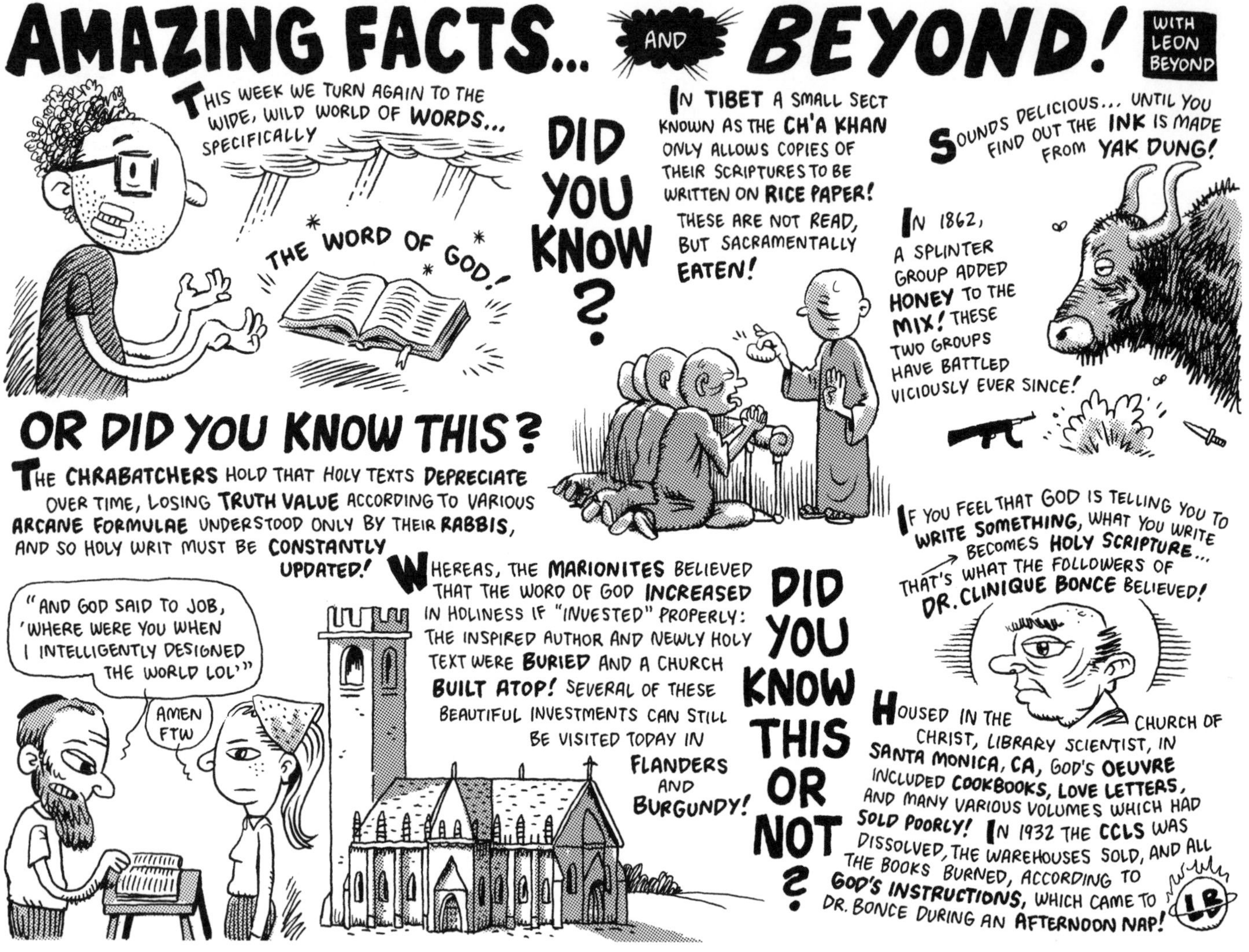
AMAZING FACTS... AND BEYOND!
WITH LEON BEYOND
THIS WEEK WE TURN AGAIN TO THE WIDE, WILD WORLD OF WORDS... SPECIFICALLY
THE WORD OF GOD!
DID YOU KNOW ?
IN TIBET A SMALL SECT KNOWN AS THE CH'A KHAN ONLY ALLOWS COPIES OF THEIR SCRIPTURES TO BE WRITTEN ON RICE PAPER!
THESE ARE NOT READ, BUT SACRAMENTALLY EATEN!
SOUNDS DELICIOUS... UNTIL YOU FIND OUT THE INK IS MADE FROM YAK DUNG!
IN 1862, A SPLINTER GROUP ADDED HONEY TO THE MIX! THESE TWO GROUPS HAVE BATTLED VICIOUSLY EVER SINCE!
OR DID YOU KNOW THIS?
THE CHRABATCHERS HOLD THAT HOLY TEXTS DEPRECIATE OVER TIME, LOSING TRUTH VALUE ACCORDING TO VARIOUS ARCANE FORMULAE UNDERSTOOD ONLY BY THEIR RABBIS, AND SO HOLY WRIT MUST BE CONSTANTLY UPDATED!
"AND GOD SAID TO JOB, 'WHERE WERE YOU WHEN I INTELLIGENTLY DESIGNED THE WORLD LOL'"
AMEN FTW
WHEREAS, THE MARIONITES BELIEVED THAT THE WORD OF GOD INCREASED IN HOLINESS IF "INVESTED" PROPERLY: THE INSPIRED AUTHOR AND NEWLY HOLY TEXT WERE BURIED AND A CHURCH BUILT ATOP! SEVERAL OF THESE BEAUTIFUL INVESTMENTS CAN STILL BE VISITED TODAY IN FLANDERS AND BURGUNDY!
DID YOU KNOW THIS OR NOT ?
IF YOU FEEL THAT GOD IS TELLING YOU TO WRITE SOMETHING, WHAT YOU WRITE BECOMES HOLY SCRIPTURE... THAT'S WHAT THE FOLLOWERS OF DR. CLINIQUE BONCE BELIEVED!
HOUSED IN THE CHURCH OF CHRIST, LIBRARY SCIENTIST, IN SANTA MONICA, CA, GOD'S OEUVRE INCLUDED COOKBOOKS, LOVE LETTERS, AND MANY VARIOUS VOLUMES WHICH HAD SOLD POORLY! IN 1932 THE CCLS WAS DISSOLVED, THE WAREHOUSES SOLD, AND ALL THE BOOKS BURNED, ACCORDING TO GOD'S INSTRUCTIONS, WHICH CAME TO DR. BONCE DURING AN AFTERNOON NAP!
LB

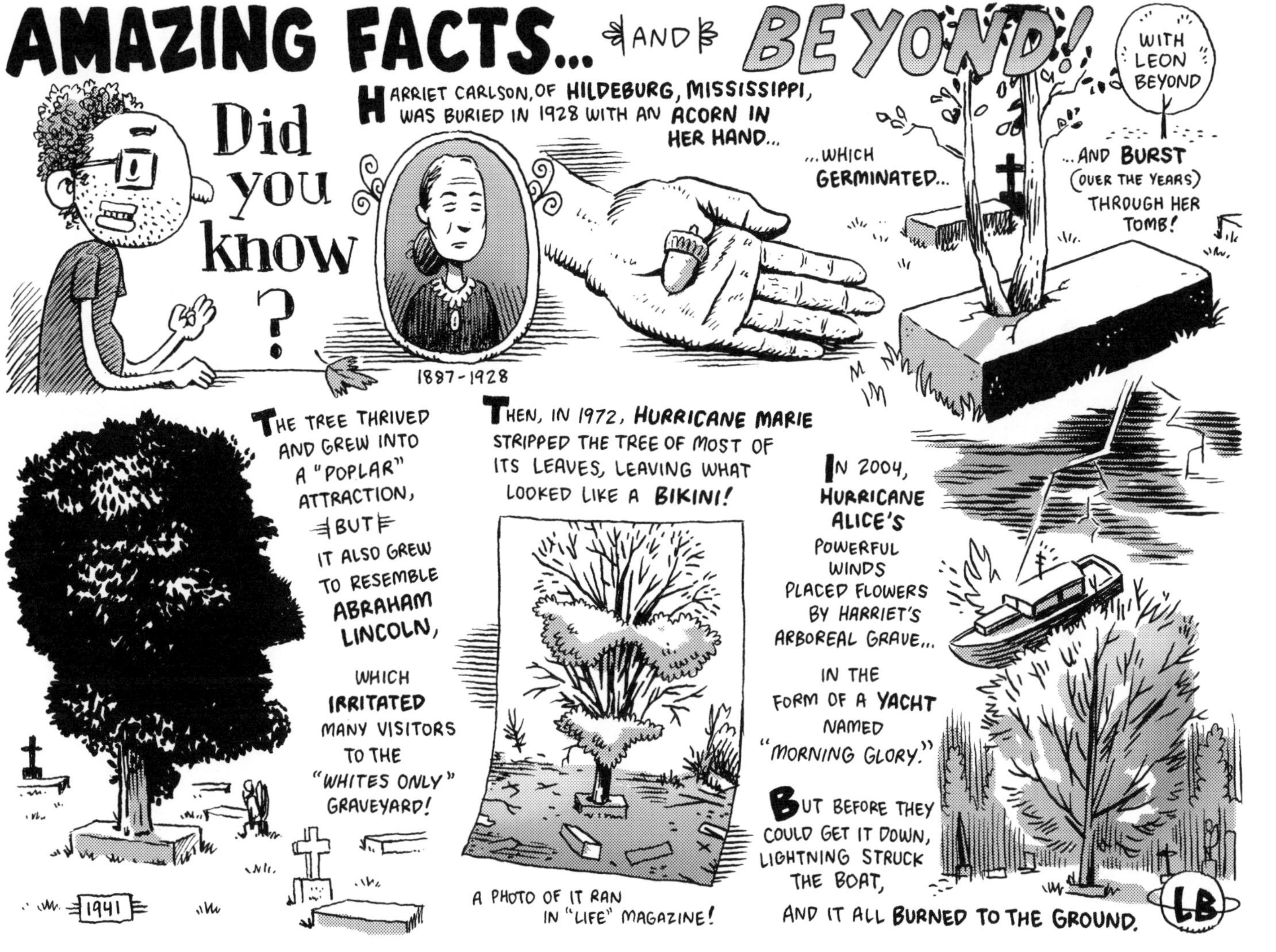
AMAZING FACTS... AND BEYOND!
WITH LEON BEYOND
Did you know?
HARRIET CARLSON, OF HILDEBURG, MISSISSIPPI, WAS BURIED IN 1928 WITH AN ACORN IN HER HAND...
1887-1928
...WHICH GERMINATED...
...AND BURST (OVER THE YEARS) THROUGH HER TOMB!
THE TREE THRIVED AND GREW INTO A "POPLAR" ATTRACTION,
BUT
IT ALSO GREW TO RESEMBLE ABRAHAM LINCOLN,
WHICH IRRITATED MANY VISITORS TO THE "WHITES ONLY" GRAVEYARD!
1941
THEN, IN 1972, HURRICANE MARIE STRIPPED THE TREE OF MOST OF ITS LEAVES, LEAVING WHAT LOOKED LIKE A BIKINI!
A PHOTO OF IT RAN IN "LIFE" MAGAZINE!
IN 2004, HURRICANE ALICE'S POWERFUL WINDS PLACED FLOWERS BY HARRIET'S ARBOREAL GRAVE...
IN THE FORM OF A YACHT NAMED "MORNING GLORY."
BUT BEFORE THEY COULD GET IT DOWN, LIGHTNING STRUCK THE BOAT,
AND IT ALL BURNED TO THE GROUND.
LB

HOLIDAYS
and OCCASIONS

97 YEAR OLD WOMAN of
KYIANG-TONG, MYANMAR
HAS NEVER CELEBRATED
A SINGLE HOLIDAY

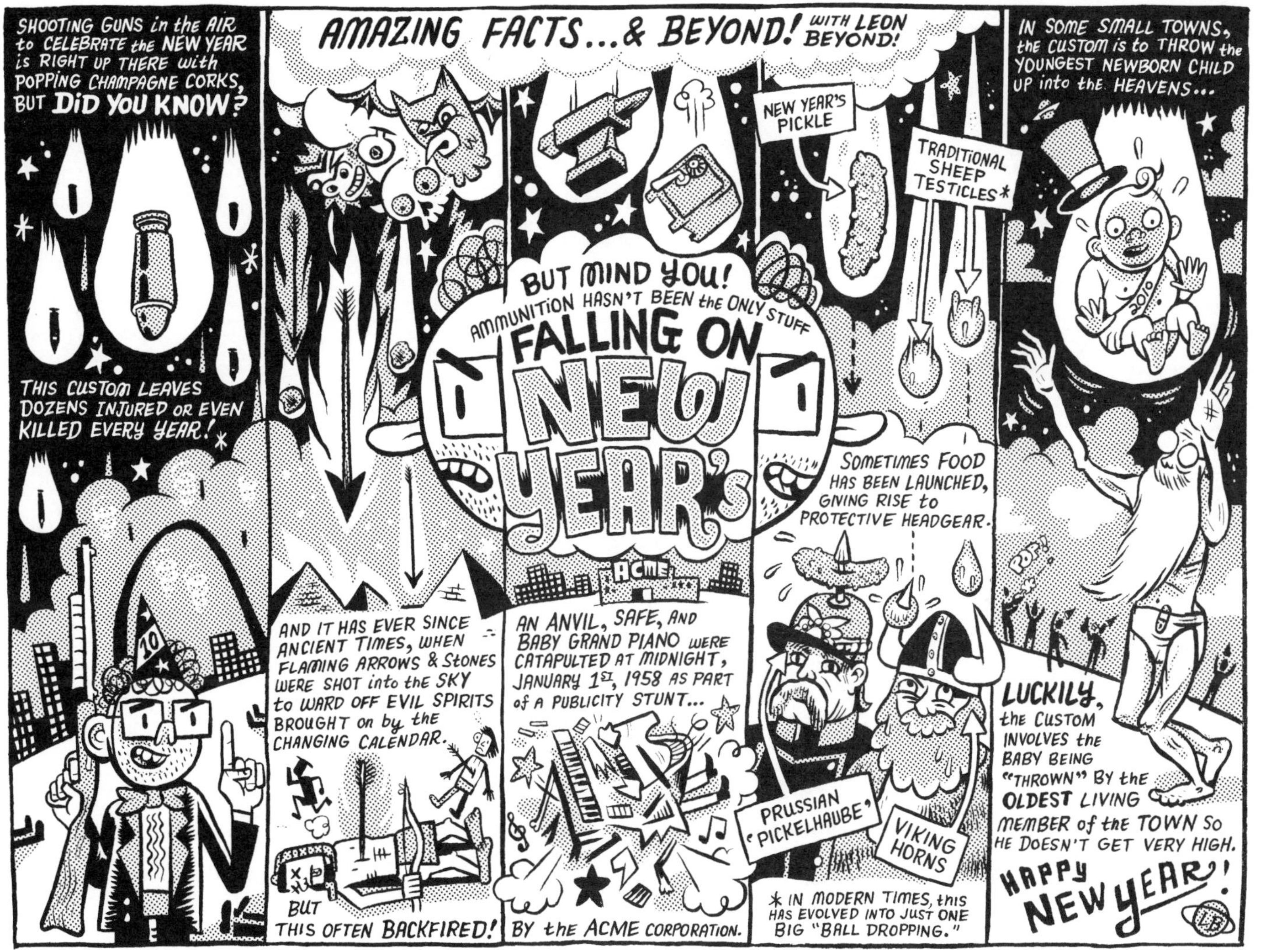
AMAZING FACTS...& BEYOND! WITH LEON BEYOND!
SHOOTING GUNS in the AIR to CELEBRATE the NEW YEAR is RIGHT UP THERE with POPPING CHAMPAGNE CORKS, BUT DID YOU KNOW?
THIS CUSTOM LEAVES DOZENS INJURED OR EVEN KILLED EVERY YEAR!*
BUT MIND YOU! AMMUNITION HASN'T BEEN the ONLY STUFF FALLING ON NEW YEAR'S
AND IT HAS EVER SINCE ANCIENT TIMES, WHEN FLAMING ARROWS & STONES WERE SHOT into the SKY to WARD OFF EVIL SPIRITS BROUGHT on by the CHANGING CALENDAR.
BUT THIS OFTEN BACKFIRED!
ACME
AN ANVIL, SAFE, AND BABY GRAND PIANO WERE CATAPULTED AT MIDNIGHT, JANUARY 1ST, 1958 AS PART of A PUBLICITY STUNT...
BY the ACME CORPORATION.
NEW YEAR'S PICKLE
TRADITIONAL SHEEP TESTICLES*
SOMETIMES FOOD HAS BEEN LAUNCHED, GIVING RISE to PROTECTIVE HEADGEAR.
PRUSSIAN 'PICKELHAUBE'
VIKING HORNS
* IN MODERN TIMES, this HAS EVOLVED INTO JUST ONE BIG "BALL DROPPING."
IN SOME SMALL TOWNS, the CUSTOM is to THROW the YOUNGEST NEWBORN CHILD UP into the HEAVENS...
2010
POP!
LUCKILY, the CUSTOM INVOLVES the BABY BEING "THROWN" BY the OLDEST LIVING MEMBER of the TOWN SO HE DOESN'T GET VERY HIGH.
HAPPY NEW YEAR!
LB

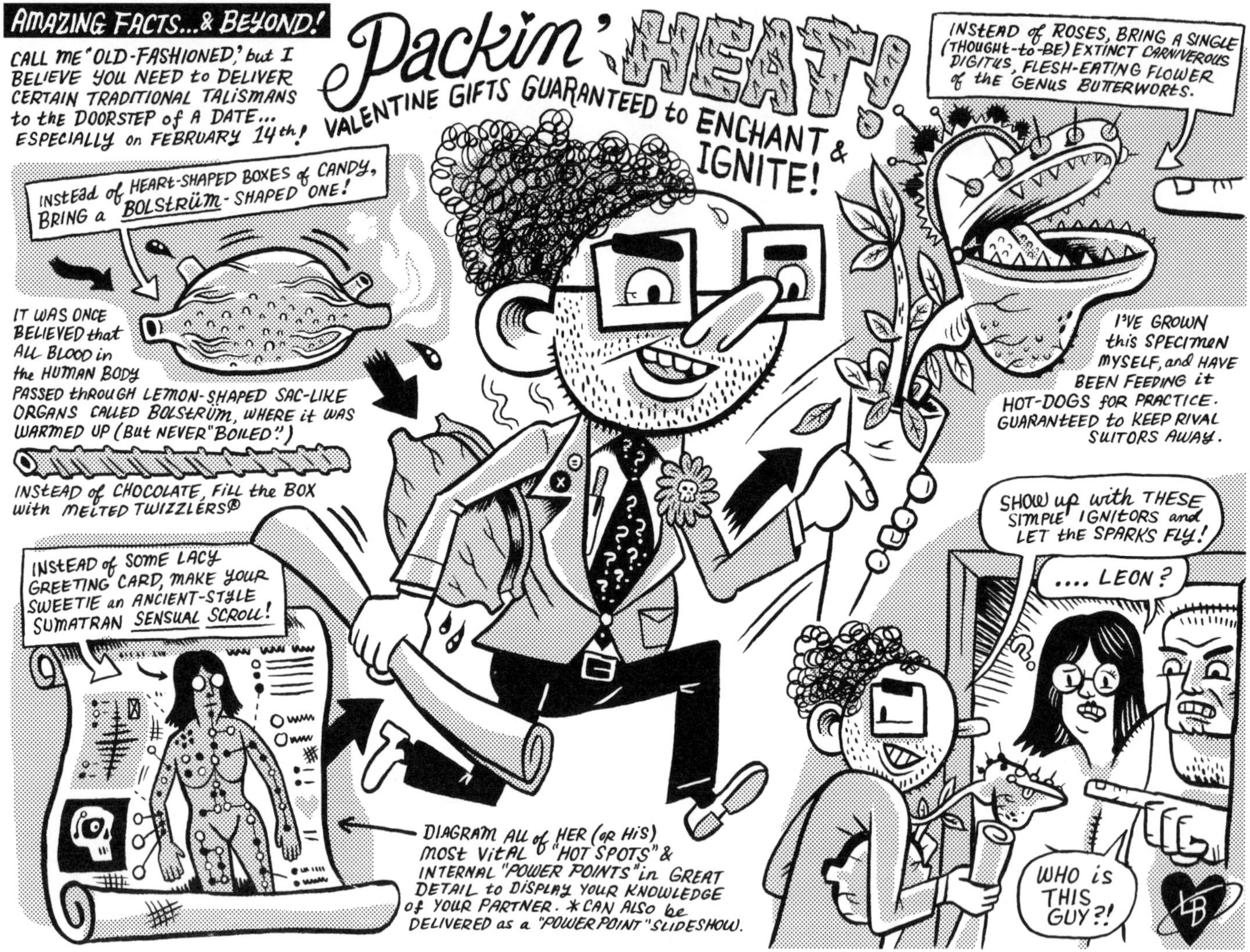
AMAZING FACTS...& BEYOND!
Packin' HEAT!
VALENTINE GIFTS GUARANTEED to ENCHANT & IGNITE!
CALL ME "OLD-FASHIONED," but I BELIEVE YOU NEED to DELIVER CERTAIN TRADITIONAL TALISMANS to the DOORSTEP of A DATE... ESPECIALLY on FEBRUARY 14th!
INSTEAD of HEART-SHAPED BOXES of CANDY, BRING a BOLSTRÜM-SHAPED ONE!
IT WAS ONCE BELIEVED that ALL BLOOD in the HUMAN BODY PASSED through LEMON-SHAPED SAC-LIKE ORGANS CALLED BOLSTRÜM, WHERE it WAS WARMED UP (But NEVER "BOILED.")
INSTEAD of CHOCOLATE, FILL the BOX with MELTED TWIZZLERS®
INSTEAD of ROSES, BRING A SINGLE (THOUGHT-to-BE) EXTINCT CARNIVEROUS DIGITUS, FLESH-EATING FLOWER of the GENUS BUTTERWORTS.
I'VE GROWN this SPECIMEN MYSELF, and HAVE BEEN FEEDING it HOT-DOGS for PRACTICE. GUARANTEED to KEEP RIVAL SUITORS AWAY.
INSTEAD of SOME LACY GREETING CARD, MAKE YOUR SWEETIE an ANCIENT-STYLE SUMATRAN SENSUAL SCROLL!
DIAGRAM ALL of HER (or HIS) MOST VITAL "HOT SPOTS" & INTERNAL "POWER POINTS" in GREAT DETAIL to DISPLAY YOUR KNOWLEDGE of YOUR PARTNER. *CAN ALSO be DELIVERED as a "POWERPOINT" SLIDESHOW.
SHOW up with THESE SIMPLE IGNITORS and LET the SPARKS FLY!
.... LEON?
WHO is THIS GUY?!
LB

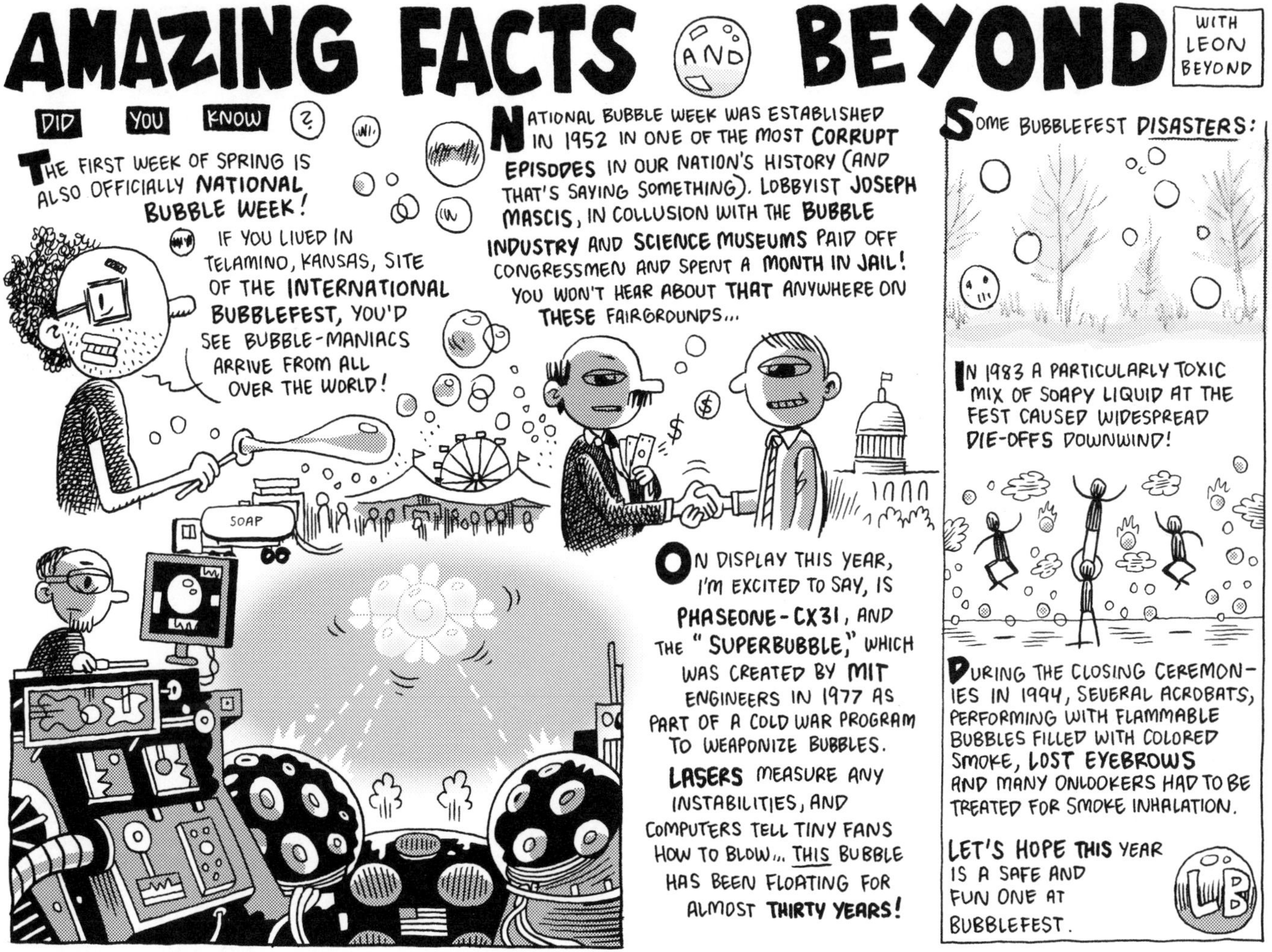
AMAZING FACTS AND BEYOND
WITH LEON BEYOND
DID YOU KNOW ?
THE FIRST WEEK OF SPRING IS ALSO OFFICIALLY NATIONAL BUBBLE WEEK!
IF YOU LIVED IN TELAMINO, KANSAS, SITE OF THE INTERNATIONAL BUBBLEFEST, YOU'D SEE BUBBLE-MANIACS ARRIVE FROM ALL OVER THE WORLD!
SOAP
NATIONAL BUBBLE WEEK WAS ESTABLISHED IN 1952 IN ONE OF THE MOST CORRUPT EPISODES IN OUR NATION'S HISTORY (AND THAT'S SAYING SOMETHING). LOBBYIST JOSEPH MASCIS, IN COLLUSION WITH THE BUBBLE INDUSTRY AND SCIENCE MUSEUMS PAID OFF CONGRESSMEN AND SPENT A MONTH IN JAIL! YOU WON'T HEAR ABOUT THAT ANYWHERE ON THESE FAIRGROUNDS...
ON DISPLAY THIS YEAR, I'M EXCITED TO SAY, IS PHASEONE-CX31, AND THE "SUPERBUBBLE," WHICH WAS CREATED BY MIT ENGINEERS IN 1977 AS PART OF A COLD WAR PROGRAM TO WEAPONIZE BUBBLES. LASERS MEASURE ANY INSTABILITIES, AND COMPUTERS TELL TINY FANS HOW TO BLOW... THIS BUBBLE HAS BEEN FLOATING FOR ALMOST THIRTY YEARS!
SOME BUBBLEFEST DISASTERS:
IN 1983 A PARTICULARLY TOXIC MIX OF SOAPY LIQUID AT THE FEST CAUSED WIDESPREAD DIE-OFFS DOWNWIND!
DURING THE CLOSING CEREMONIES IN 1994, SEVERAL ACROBATS, PERFORMING WITH FLAMMABLE BUBBLES FILLED WITH COLORED SMOKE, LOST EYEBROWS AND MANY ONLOOKERS HAD TO BE TREATED FOR SMOKE INHALATION.
LET'S HOPE THIS YEAR IS A SAFE AND FUN ONE AT BUBBLEFEST.
LB

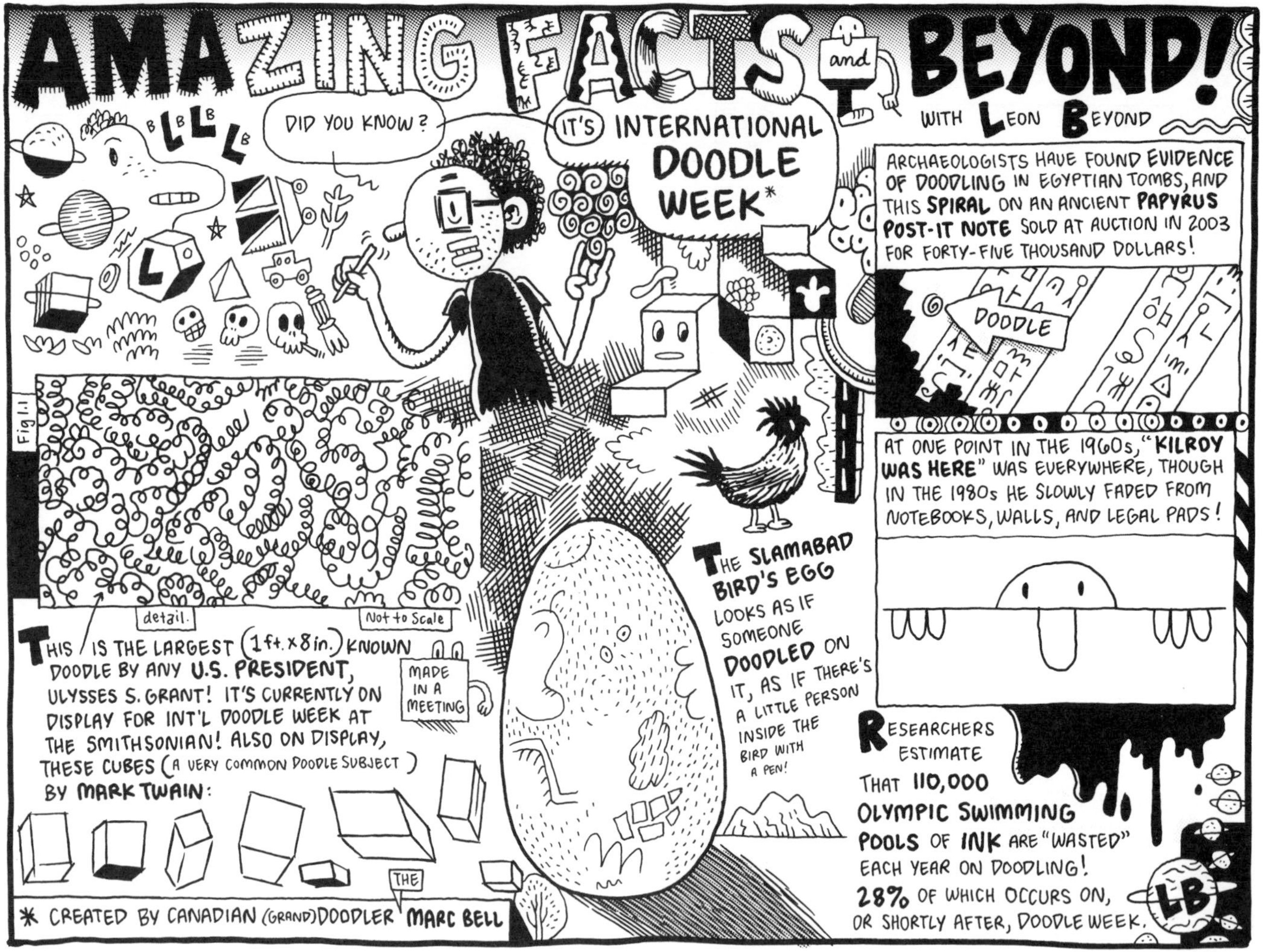
AMAZING FACTS and BEYOND!
WITH LEON BEYOND
DID YOU KNOW?
IT'S INTERNATIONAL DOODLE WEEK*
ARCHAEOLOGISTS HAVE FOUND EVIDENCE OF DOODLING IN EGYPTIAN TOMBS, AND THIS SPIRAL ON AN ANCIENT PAPYRUS POST-IT NOTE SOLD AT AUCTION IN 2003 FOR FORTY-FIVE THOUSAND DOLLARS!
DOODLE
Fig 1.1
detail.
Not to Scale
THIS IS THE LARGEST (1 ft. x 8 in.) KNOWN DOODLE BY ANY U.S. PRESIDENT, ULYSSES S. GRANT! IT'S CURRENTLY ON DISPLAY FOR INT'L DOODLE WEEK AT THE SMITHSONIAN! ALSO ON DISPLAY, THESE CUBES (A VERY COMMON DOODLE SUBJECT) BY MARK TWAIN:
MADE IN A MEETING
AT ONE POINT IN THE 1960s, "KILROY WAS HERE" WAS EVERYWHERE, THOUGH IN THE 1980s HE SLOWLY FADED FROM NOTEBOOKS, WALLS, AND LEGAL PADS!
THE SLAMABAD BIRD'S EGG LOOKS AS IF SOMEONE DOODLED ON IT, AS IF THERE'S A LITTLE PERSON INSIDE THE BIRD WITH A PEN!
RESEARCHERS ESTIMATE THAT 110,000 OLYMPIC SWIMMING POOLS OF INK ARE "WASTED" EACH YEAR ON DOODLING! 28% OF WHICH OCCURS ON, OR SHORTLY AFTER, DOODLE WEEK.
LB
* CREATED BY CANADIAN (GRAND) DOODLER THE MARC BELL

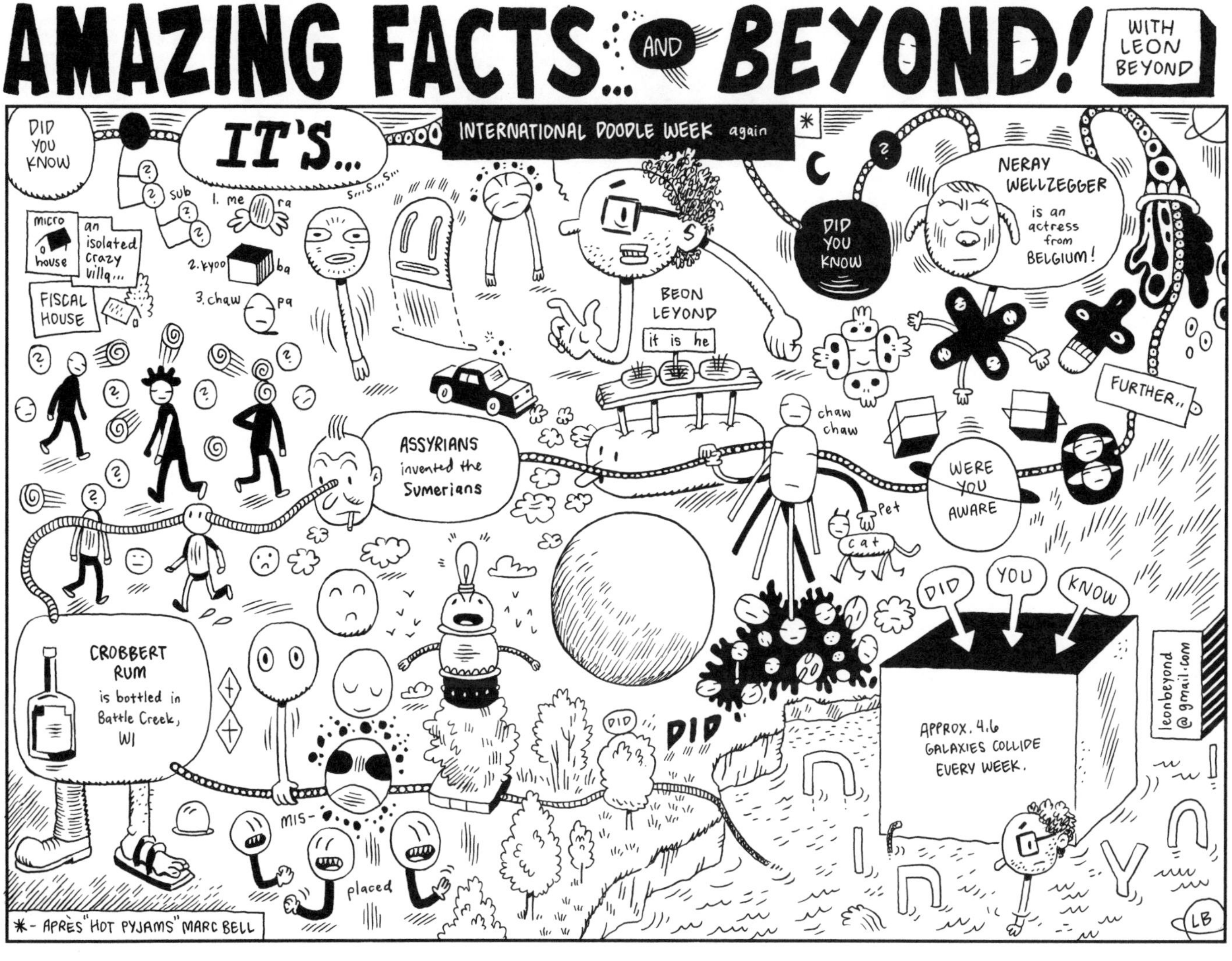
AMAZING FACTS... AND BEYOND!
WITH LEON BEYOND
DID YOU KNOW
IT'S...
INTERNATIONAL DOODLE WEEK again
*
micro a house
an isolated crazy villa...
FISCAL HOUSE
sub
1. me ra
2. kyoo ba
3. chaw pa
NERAY WELLZEGGER is an actress from BELGIUM!
DID YOU KNOW
BEON LEYOND
it is he
FURTHER..
ASSYRIANS invented the Sumerians
chaw chaw
WERE YOU AWARE
Pet cat
DID YOU KNOW
CROBBERT RUM is bottled in Battle Creek, WI
leonbeyond@gmail.com
APPROX. 4.6 GALAXIES COLLIDE EVERY WEEK.
DID
DID
mis- placed
*- APRÈS "HOT PYJAMS" MARC BELL
LB

AMAZING FACTS... AND BEYOND!

WELL, IT'S HERE AGAIN! YOU KNOW WHAT I'M REFERRING TO, RIGHT?

OH.

I'M PLEASED TO **INFORM** YOU, THEN, THAT THIS WEEK IS **INTERNATIONAL BRA WEEK!**

WOMEN ALL OVER THE WORLD ARE EXCITEDLY LINING UP FOR BRA-FITTINGS, BRA-RAFFLES EXHIBITIONS, ETC. ETC.!

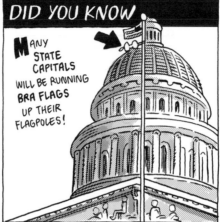

DID YOU KNOW

MANY STATE CAPITALS WILL BE RUNNING BRA FLAGS UP THEIR FLAGPOLES!

KEN BURNS' SHORT DOCUMENTARY "THE BRA IN AMERICA" WILL PLAY TUES-THURS ON PBS! I'LL BE ALL UP ON THERE, FOLKSILY ANECDOTALIZING SOME OLD CHESTNUTS FROM BRA HISTORY:

LEON BEYOND, writer

EXCERPT FROM 'KEN BURNS' THE BRA'

... THE TORNADO HAD APPARENTLY SLIPPED THE BRA RIGHT OFF MRS. NELSON...

MUST'A BEEN TERRIFYING!

..., ALL THE WHILE, HER FEET NEVER LEFT THE GROUND.

THEY FOUND ONE CUP IN GREENVILLE, TENNESSEE, AND THE OTHER 5 MILES AWAY, OVER THE KENTUCKY STATE LINE IN HARLAN, WHERE IT CAN STILL BE VIEWED, SOMEWHAT WORSE FOR WEAR, AT THE HISTORICAL SOCIETY.

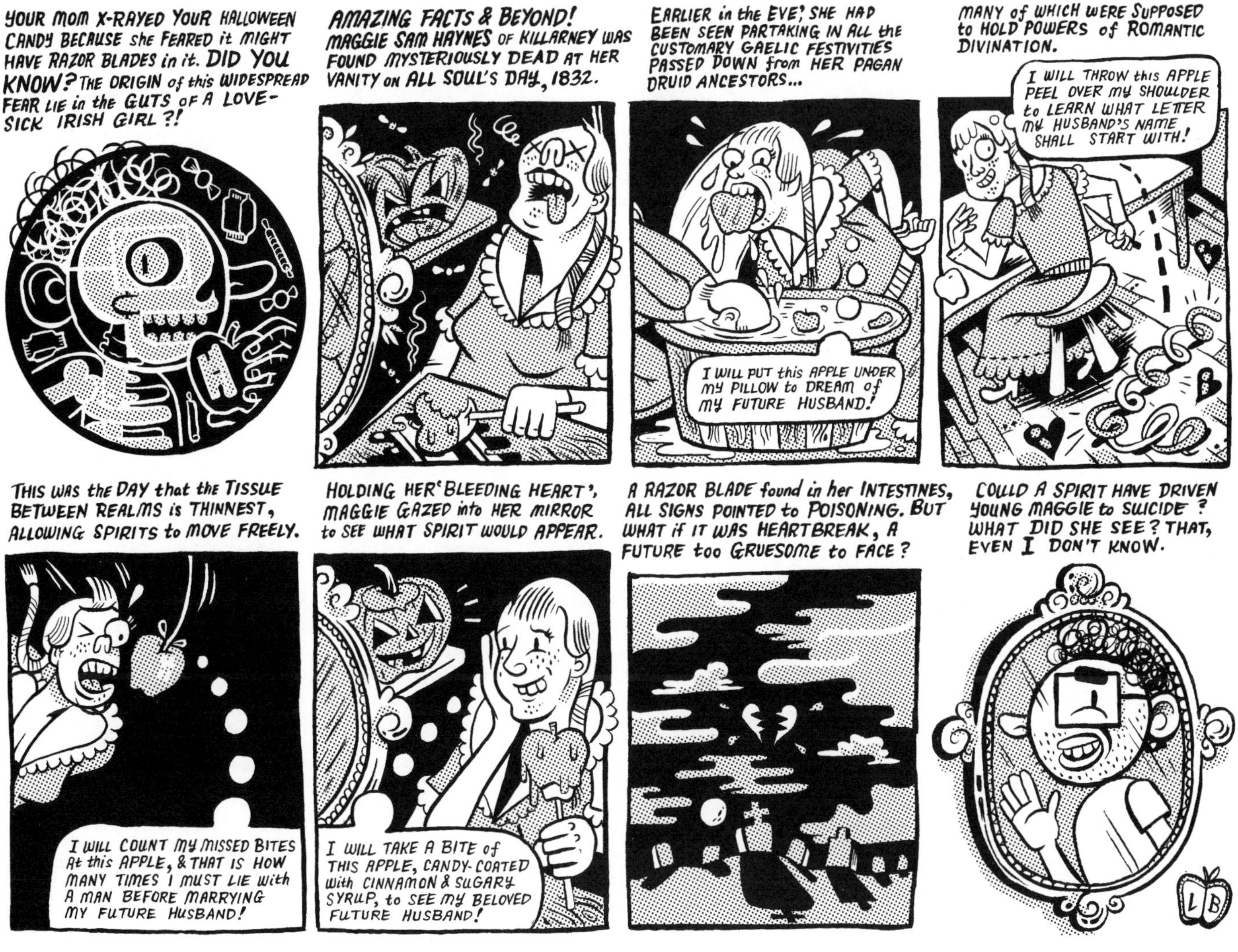
YOUR MOM X-RAYED YOUR HALLOWEEN CANDY BECAUSE she FEARED it MIGHT HAVE RAZOR BLADES in it. DID YOU KNOW? THE ORIGIN of this WIDESPREAD FEAR LIE in the GUTS OF A LOVE-SICK IRISH GIRL?!
AMAZING FACTS & BEYOND! MAGGIE SAM HAYNES OF KILLARNEY WAS FOUND MYSTERIOUSLY DEAD AT HER VANITY ON ALL SOUL'S DAY, 1832.
EARLIER in the EVE, SHE HAD BEEN SEEN PARTAKING IN ALL the CUSTOMARY GAELIC FESTIVITIES PASSED DOWN from HER PAGAN DRUID ANCESTORS...
I WILL PUT this APPLE UNDER MY PILLOW to DREAM of MY FUTURE HUSBAND!
MANY of WHICH WERE SUPPOSED to HOLD POWERS of ROMANTIC DIVINATION.
I WILL THROW this APPLE PEEL OVER MY SHOULDER to LEARN WHAT LETTER MY HUSBAND'S NAME SHALL START WITH!
THIS WAS the DAY that the TISSUE BETWEEN REALMS is THINNEST, ALLOWING SPIRITS to MOVE FREELY.
I WILL COUNT MY MISSED BITES At this APPLE, & THAT IS HOW MANY TIMES I MUST LIE with A MAN BEFORE MARRYING MY FUTURE HUSBAND!
HOLDING HER 'BLEEDING HEART', MAGGIE GAZED into HER MIRROR to SEE WHAT SPIRIT WOULD APPEAR.
I WILL TAKE A BITE of THIS APPLE, CANDY-COATED with CINNAMON & SUGARY SYRUP, to SEE MY BELOVED FUTURE HUSBAND!
A RAZOR BLADE found in her INTESTINES, ALL SIGNS POINTED to POISONING. BUT WHAT if IT WAS HEARTBREAK, A FUTURE too GRUESOME to FACE?
COULD A SPIRIT HAVE DRIVEN YOUNG MAGGIE to SUICIDE? WHAT DID SHE SEE? THAT, EVEN I DON'T KNOW.
L B

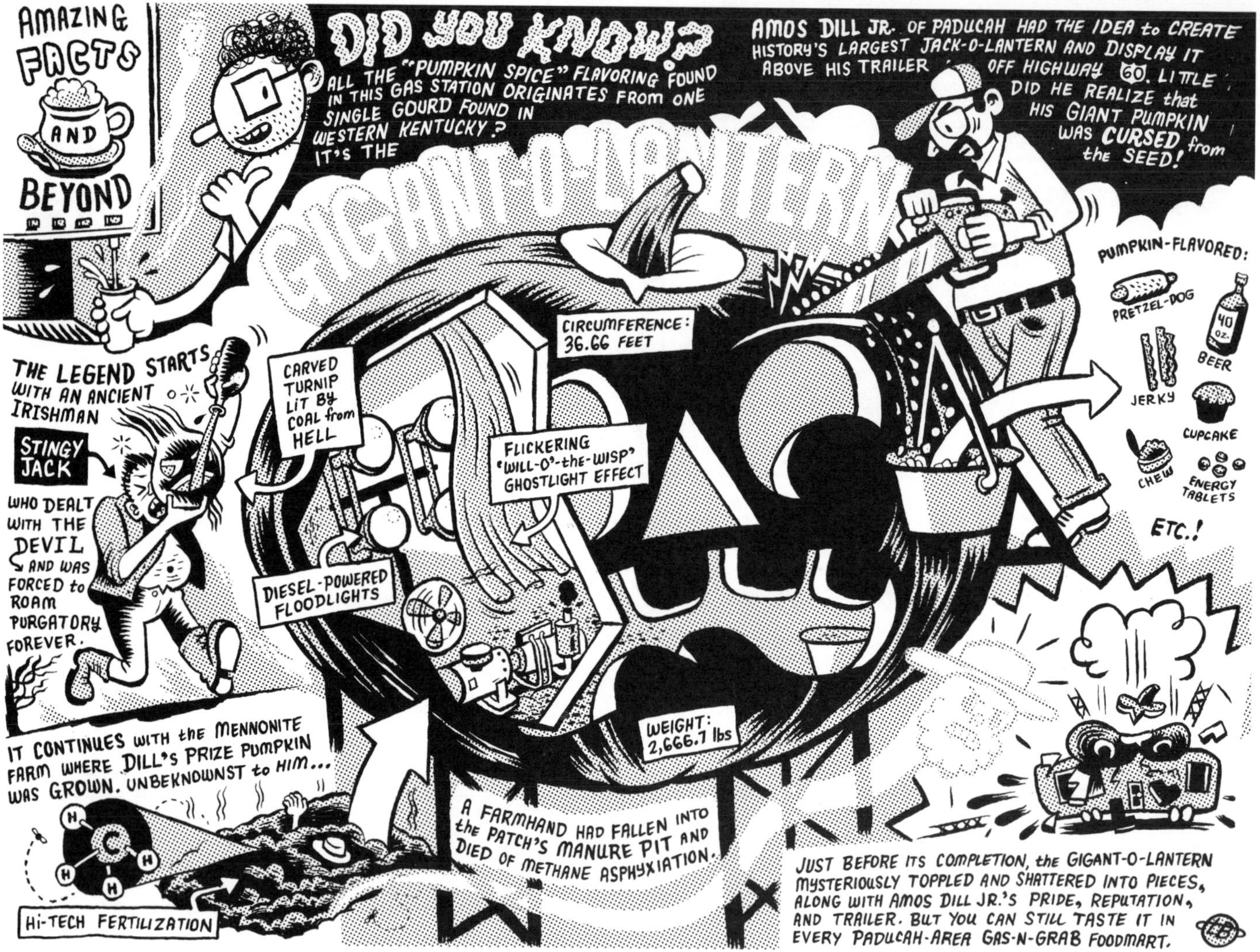
AMAZING FACTS AND BEYOND
DID YOU KNOW?
ALL THE "PUMPKIN SPICE" FLAVORING FOUND IN THIS GAS STATION ORIGINATES FROM ONE SINGLE GOURD FOUND IN WESTERN KENTUCKY? IT'S THE
GIGANT-O-LANTERN
AMOS DILL JR. OF PADUCAH HAD THE IDEA to CREATE HISTORY'S LARGEST JACK-O-LANTERN AND DISPLAY IT ABOVE HIS TRAILER OFF HIGHWAY 60. LITTLE DID HE REALIZE that HIS GIANT PUMPKIN WAS CURSED from the SEED!
THE LEGEND STARTS WITH AN ANCIENT IRISHMAN
STINGY JACK
WHO DEALT WITH THE DEVIL AND WAS FORCED to ROAM PURGATORY FOREVER.
CARVED TURNIP LIT BY COAL from HELL
CIRCUMFERENCE: 36.66 FEET
FLICKERING 'WILL-O'-the-WISP' GHOSTLIGHT EFFECT
DIESEL-POWERED FLOODLIGHTS
PUMPKIN-FLAVORED:
PRETZEL-DOG
BEER
40 OZ.
JERKY
CUPCAKE
CHEW
ENERGY TABLETS
ETC.!
WEIGHT: 2,666.7 lbs
IT CONTINUES WITH the MENNONITE FARM WHERE DILL'S PRIZE PUMPKIN WAS GROWN. UNBEKNOWNST to HIM...
A FARMHAND HAD FALLEN INTO the PATCH'S MANURE PIT AND DIED OF METHANE ASPHYXIATION.
Hi-TECH FERTILIZATION
JUST BEFORE ITS COMPLETION, the GIGANT-O-LANTERN MYSTERIOUSLY TOPPLED AND SHATTERED INTO PIECES, ALONG WITH AMOS DILL JR.'S PRIDE, REPUTATION, AND TRAILER. BUT YOU CAN STILL TASTE IT IN EVERY PADUCAH-AREA GAS-N-GRAB FOODMART.

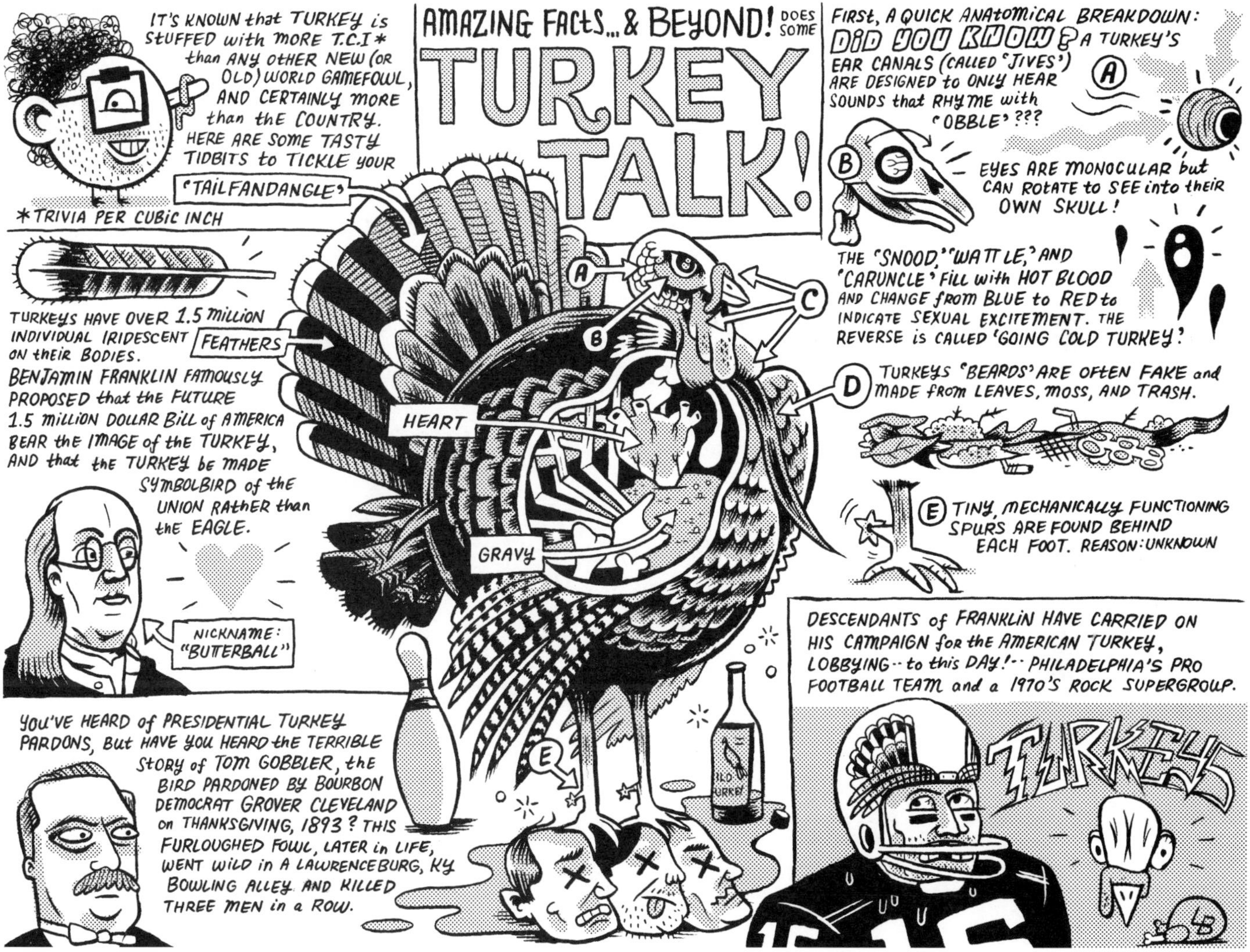
AMAZING FACTS... & BEYOND! DOES SOME
TURKEY TALK!
IT'S KNOWN that TURKEY is STUFFED with MORE T.C.I * than ANY OTHER NEW (OR OLD) WORLD GAMEFOWL, AND CERTAINLY MORE than the COUNTRY. HERE ARE SOME TASTY TIDBITS to TICKLE YOUR
'TAILFANDANGLE'
* TRIVIA PER CUBIC INCH
TURKEYS HAVE OVER 1.5 MILLION INDIVIDUAL IRIDESCENT
FEATHERS
ON THEIR BODIES.
BENJAMIN FRANKLIN FAMOUSLY PROPOSED that the FUTURE 1.5 MILLION DOLLAR BILL of AMERICA BEAR the IMAGE of the TURKEY, AND that the TURKEY be MADE SYMBOLBIRD of the UNION RATHER than the EAGLE.
NICKNAME: "BUTTERBALL"
HEART
GRAVY
A
B
C
D
E
FIRST, A QUICK ANATOMICAL BREAKDOWN:
DID YOU KNOW? A TURKEY'S EAR CANALS (CALLED 'JIVES') ARE DESIGNED to ONLY HEAR SOUNDS that RHYME with 'OBBLE'???
EYES ARE MONOCULAR but CAN ROTATE to SEE into their OWN SKULL!
THE 'SNOOD,' 'WATTLE,' AND 'CARUNCLE' FILL with HOT BLOOD AND CHANGE from BLUE to RED to INDICATE SEXUAL EXCITEMENT. THE REVERSE is CALLED 'GOING COLD TURKEY.'
TURKEYS 'BEARDS' ARE OFTEN FAKE and MADE FROM LEAVES, MOSS, AND TRASH.
TINY, MECHANICALLY FUNCTIONING SPURS ARE FOUND BEHIND EACH FOOT. REASON: UNKNOWN
DESCENDANTS of FRANKLIN HAVE CARRIED ON HIS CAMPAIGN for the AMERICAN TURKEY, LOBBYING -- to this DAY! -- PHILADELPHIA'S PRO FOOTBALL TEAM and a 1970'S ROCK SUPERGROUP.
TURKEYS
YOU'VE HEARD of PRESIDENTIAL TURKEY PARDONS, BUT HAVE YOU HEARD the TERRIBLE STORY of TOM GOBBLER, the BIRD PARDONED BY BOURBON DEMOCRAT GROVER CLEVELAND on THANKSGIVING, 1893? THIS FURLOUGHED FOWL, LATER in LIFE, WENT WILD in A LAWRENCEBURG, KY BOWLING ALLEY AND KILLED THREE MEN in a ROW.
OLD TURKEY
LB

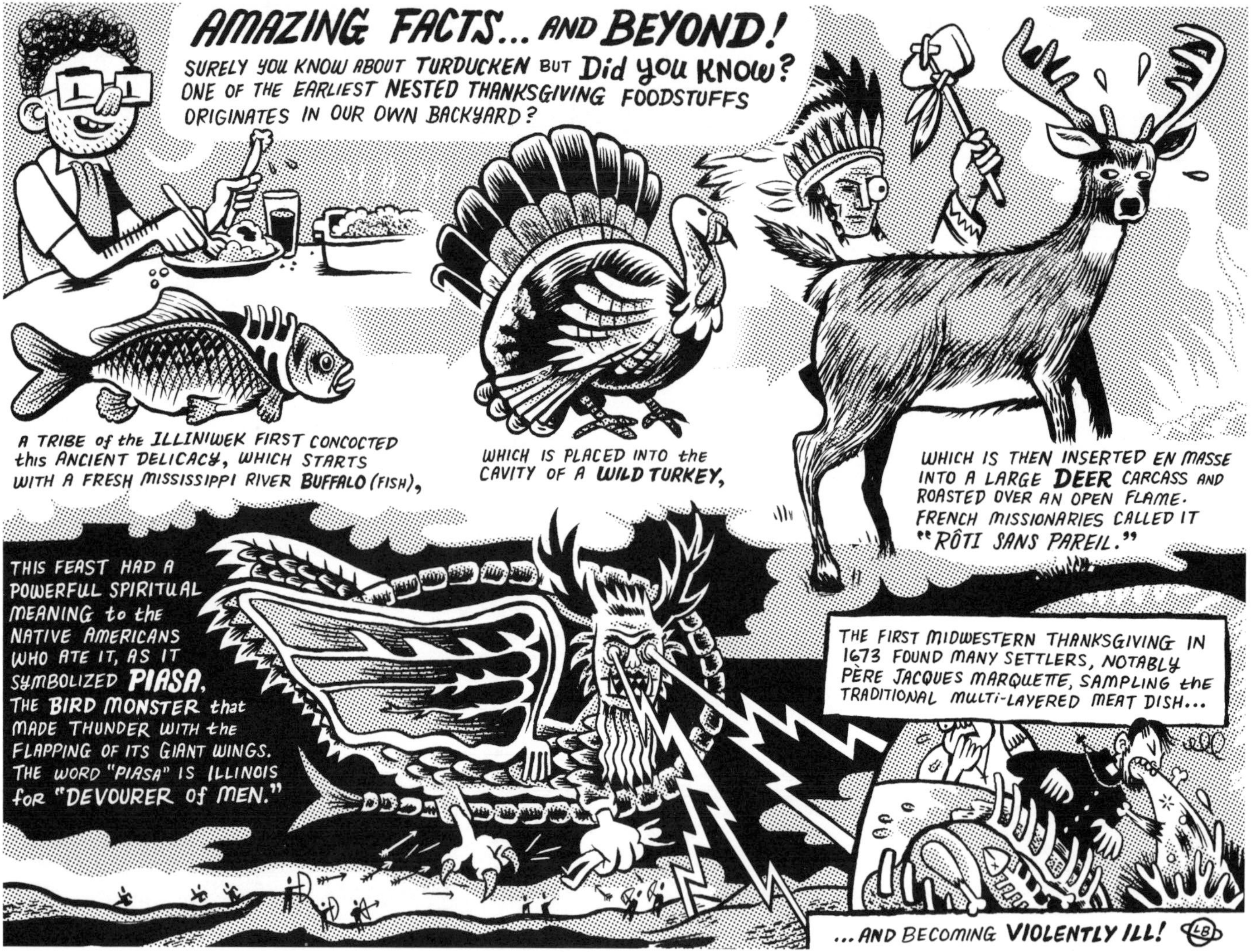
AMAZING FACTS... AND BEYOND!
SURELY YOU KNOW ABOUT TURDUCKEN BUT Did you KNOW? ONE OF THE EARLIEST NESTED THANKSGIVING FOODSTUFFS ORIGINATES IN OUR OWN BACKYARD?
A TRIBE of the ILLINIWEK FIRST CONCOCTED this ANCIENT DELICACY, WHICH STARTS WITH A FRESH MISSISSIPPI RIVER BUFFALO (FISH),
WHICH IS PLACED INTO the CAVITY OF A WILD TURKEY,
WHICH IS THEN INSERTED EN MASSE INTO A LARGE DEER CARCASS AND ROASTED OVER AN OPEN FLAME. FRENCH MISSIONARIES CALLED IT "RÔTI SANS PAREIL."
THIS FEAST HAD A POWERFUL SPIRITUAL MEANING to the NATIVE AMERICANS WHO ATE IT, AS IT SYMBOLIZED PIASA, THE BIRD MONSTER that MADE THUNDER WITH the FLAPPING OF ITS GIANT WINGS. THE WORD "PIASA" IS ILLINOIS for "DEVOURER of MEN."
THE FIRST MIDWESTERN THANKSGIVING IN 1673 FOUND MANY SETTLERS, NOTABLY PÈRE JACQUES MARQUETTE, SAMPLING the TRADITIONAL MULTI-LAYERED MEAT DISH...
...AND BECOMING VIOLENTLY ILL!
LB

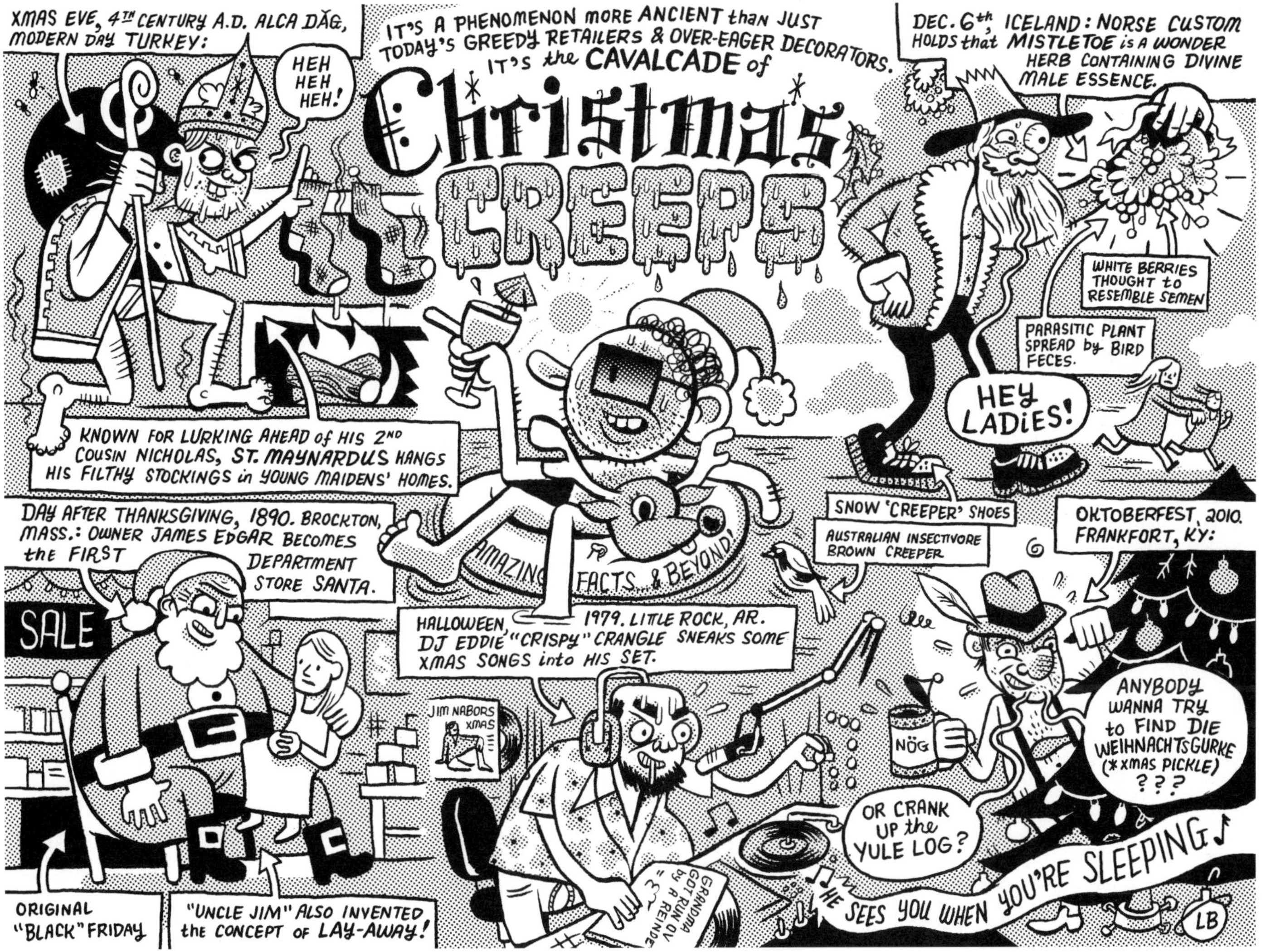
IT'S A PHENOMENON MORE ANCIENT than JUST TODAY'S GREEDY RETAILERS & OVER-EAGER DECORATORS. IT'S the CAVALCADE of
Christmas CREEPS
XMAS EVE, 4TH CENTURY A.D. ALCA DĂG, MODERN DAY TURKEY:
HEH HEH HEH!
KNOWN FOR LURKING AHEAD of HIS 2ND COUSIN NICHOLAS, ST. MAYNARDUS HANGS HIS FILTHY STOCKINGS in YOUNG MAIDENS' HOMES.
DEC. 6th, ICELAND: NORSE CUSTOM HOLDS that MISTLETOE is A WONDER HERB CONTAINING DIVINE MALE ESSENCE.
WHITE BERRIES THOUGHT to RESEMBLE SEMEN
PARASITIC PLANT SPREAD by BIRD FECES.
HEY LADIES!
SNOW 'CREEPER' SHOES
AUSTRALIAN INSECTIVORE BROWN CREEPER
AMAZING FACTS...& BEYOND!
DAY AFTER THANKSGIVING, 1890. BROCKTON, MASS.: OWNER JAMES EDGAR BECOMES the FIRST DEPARTMENT STORE SANTA.
SALE
ORIGINAL "BLACK" FRIDAY
"UNCLE JIM" ALSO INVENTED the CONCEPT of LAY-AWAY!
HALLOWEEN, 1979. LITTLE ROCK, AR. DJ EDDIE "CRISPY" CRANGLE SNEAKS SOME XMAS SONGS into HIS SET.
JIM NABORS XMAS
GRANDMA GOT RUN OV by A REINDE
OKTOBERFEST, 2010. FRANKFORT, KY:
NÖG
ANYBODY WANNA TRY to FIND DIE WEIHNACHTSGURKE (* XMAS PICKLE) ???
OR CRANK UP the YULE LOG?
HE SEES YOU WHEN YOU'RE SLEEPING
LB

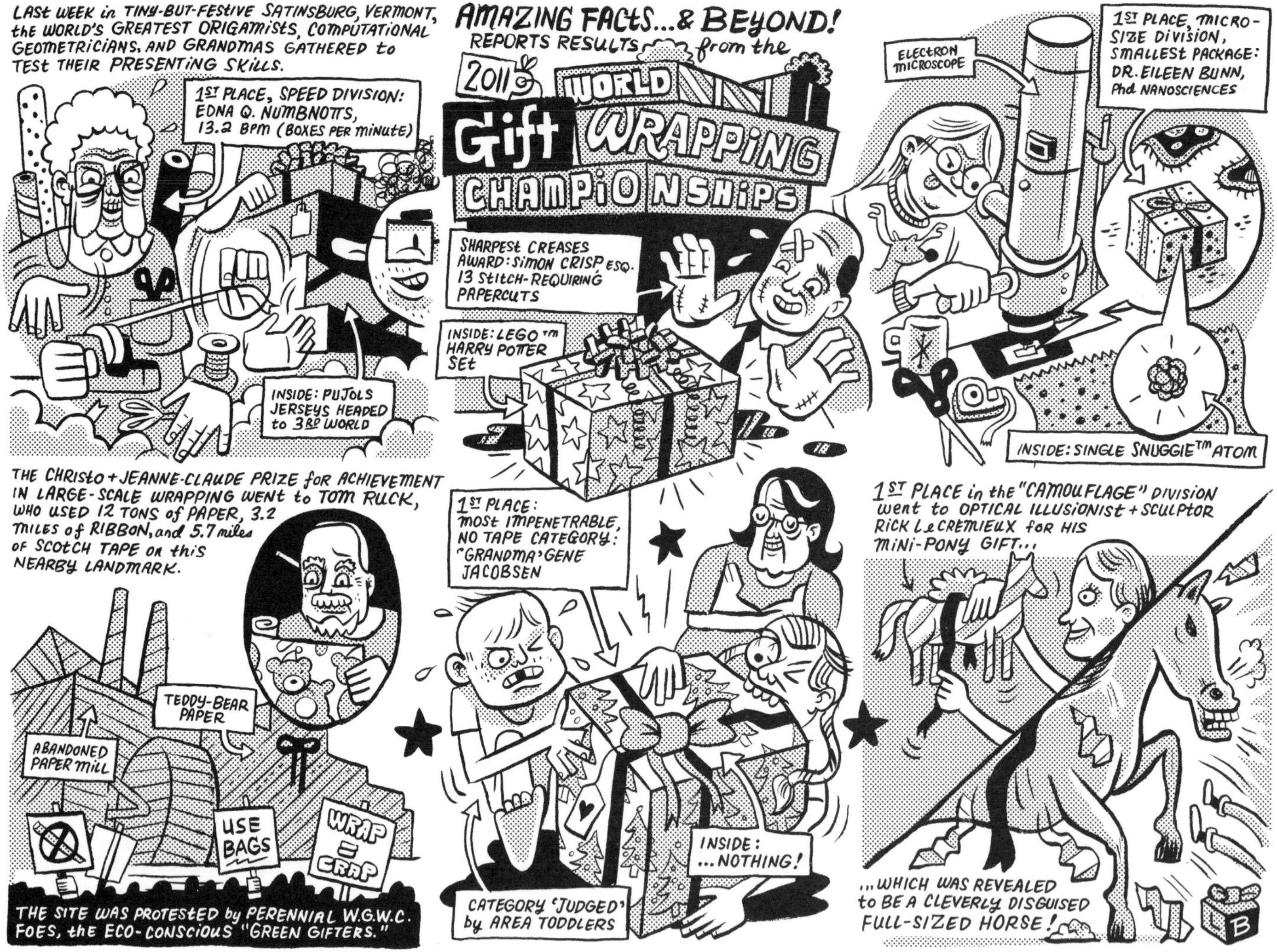
LAST WEEK in TINY-BUT-FESTIVE SATINSBURG, VERMONT, the WORLD'S GREATEST ORIGAMISTS, COMPUTATIONAL GEOMETRICIANS, AND GRANDMAS GATHERED to TEST THEIR PRESENTING SKILLS.
AMAZING FACTS...& BEYOND! REPORTS RESULTS from the 2011 WORLD GIFT WRAPPING CHAMPIONSHIPS
1ST PLACE, SPEED DIVISION: EDNA Q. NUMBNOTTS, 13.2 BPM (BOXES PER MINUTE)
INSIDE: PUJOLS JERSEYS HEADED to 3RD WORLD
SHARPEST CREASES AWARD: SIMON CRISP ESQ. 13 STITCH-REQUIRING PAPERCUTS
INSIDE: LEGO TM HARRY POTTER SET
ELECTRON MICROSCOPE
1ST PLACE, MICRO-SIZE DIVISION, SMALLEST PACKAGE: DR. EILEEN BUNN, PhD NANOSCIENCES
INSIDE: SINGLE SNUGGIE TM ATOM
THE CHRISTO + JEANNE-CLAUDE PRIZE for ACHIEVEMENT IN LARGE-SCALE WRAPPING WENT to TOM RUCK, WHO USED 12 TONS of PAPER, 3.2 MILES of RIBBON, and 5.7 miles of SCOTCH TAPE on this NEARBY LANDMARK.
TEDDY-BEAR PAPER
ABANDONED PAPER MILL
USE BAGS
WRAP = CRAP
THE SITE WAS PROTESTED by PERENNIAL W.G.W.C. FOES, the ECO-CONSCIOUS "GREEN GIFTERS."
1ST PLACE: MOST IMPENETRABLE, NO TAPE CATEGORY: "GRANDMA" GENE JACOBSEN
INSIDE: ...NOTHING!
CATEGORY 'JUDGED' by AREA TODDLERS
1ST PLACE in the "CAMOUFLAGE" DIVISION went to OPTICAL ILLUSIONIST + SCULPTOR RICK LeCREMIEUX FOR HIS MINI-PONY GIFT...
...WHICH WAS REVEALED to BE A CLEVERLY DISGUISED FULL-SIZED HORSE!
B

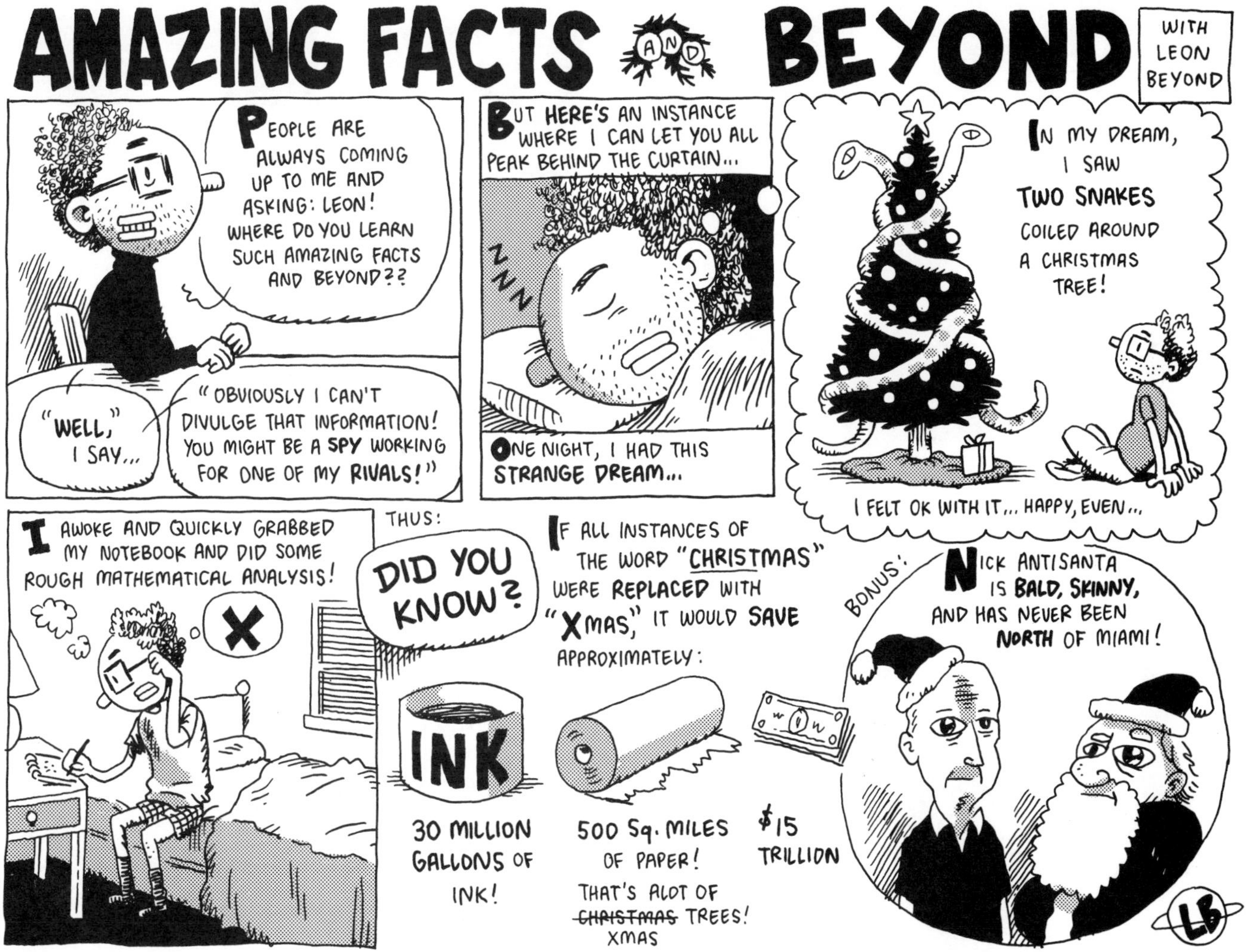
AMAZING FACTS AND BEYOND
WITH LEON BEYOND
PEOPLE ARE ALWAYS COMING UP TO ME AND ASKING: LEON! WHERE DO YOU LEARN SUCH AMAZING FACTS AND BEYOND??
"WELL," I SAY...
"OBVIOUSLY I CAN'T DIVULGE THAT INFORMATION! YOU MIGHT BE A SPY WORKING FOR ONE OF MY RIVALS!"
BUT HERE'S AN INSTANCE WHERE I CAN LET YOU ALL PEAK BEHIND THE CURTAIN...
ZZZ
ONE NIGHT, I HAD THIS STRANGE DREAM...
IN MY DREAM, I SAW TWO SNAKES COILED AROUND A CHRISTMAS TREE!
I FELT OK WITH IT... HAPPY, EVEN...
I AWOKE AND QUICKLY GRABBED MY NOTEBOOK AND DID SOME ROUGH MATHEMATICAL ANALYSIS!
X
THUS:
DID YOU KNOW?
IF ALL INSTANCES OF THE WORD "CHRISTMAS" WERE REPLACED WITH "XMAS," IT WOULD SAVE APPROXIMATELY:
INK
30 MILLION GALLONS OF INK!
500 Sq. MILES OF PAPER!
THAT'S ALOT OF ~~CHRISTMAS~~ XMAS TREES!
$15 TRILLION
BONUS:
NICK ANTISANTA IS BALD, SKINNY, AND HAS NEVER BEEN NORTH OF MIAMI!
LB

AMAZING FACTS... AND BEYOND!

GIFT GUIDE 2010

Here are some 'Tis-the-Season product procurement proposals for the brainiacs and fact-a-maniacs on your list:

BUT FIRST, I SHOULD MENTION THIS, BECAUSE IT HAPPENS EVERY YEAR — PLEASE, TO MY FANS, DO **NOT** SEND ME ANY GIFTS! I'M ALL SET —

MY TRIVIA CHAMPIONSHIP WINNINGS AND SPONSORSHIPS, AS WELL AS THE SALES OF MY BOOKS — SUCH AS "THE FACTOIDS OF LIFE," "FACT PARADER" (AND NEW THIS YEAR:) "BACK THAT FACT UP" (AVAILABLE AT USSCATASTROPHE.COM) HAVE MADE ME VERY COMFORTABLE!

I HAVE EVERYTHING — OR ACCESS TO EVERYTHING — I COULD EVER WANT OR NEED!

MANY OF YOU TRY TO 'BLOW MY MIND' WITH PUZZLERS OR RARE, MYSTERIOUS ITEMS —

I LOVE THAT STUFF, BUT TRUST ME, I HAVE PROBABLY SEEN OR SOLVED IT BEFORE!

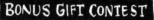

I APPRECIATE THE **FAN-ART** AND CHARMING **HANDMADE TRIBUTES**, I REALLY DO, BUT I'M RUNNING OUT OF **ROOM!**

IF YOU **MUST,** PLEASE KNOW, ALL ITEMS WILL BE DONATED FOR AUCTION TO THE **WORLD CHILDREN TRIVIA FUND!**

SAVE ME SOME PAPERWORK AND DONATE DIRECTLY TO THE WCTF — (SEE MY BLOG FOR INFO)

OK SO, FOR THE **TRIVIA LOVER** ON YOUR LIST — NATURALLY YOU'RE THINKING,

"LEON WILL PROBABLY RECOMMEND ONE OF HIS BOOKS, SINCE THEY **ARE** THE PERFECT GIFTS FOR LOVERS OF TRIVIA!"

IT'S TRUE — THEY ARE! TOO PERFECT! CHANCES ARE, THEY ALREADY HAVE MY BOOKS!

INSTEAD: RUBIK'S CUBE TRIVIA DAYPLANNER.

BONUS GIFT CONTEST

The most-wrapped gift was wrapped by Marjorie Requiette as a "GAG GIFT" FOR THE LUMBER PRODUCTS ASSOCIATION CHRISTMAS PARTY IN 1972! AFTER PICKING THE WINNING NUMBER FROM A SANTA-HAT, GEORGE McBRAHMS UNWRAPPED ALL <u>422</u> LAYERS —

? WHAT WAS INSIDE ?

FIRST CORRECT ANSWER TO: leonbeyond@gmail.com WINS A "BACK THAT FACT UP" BOOK!

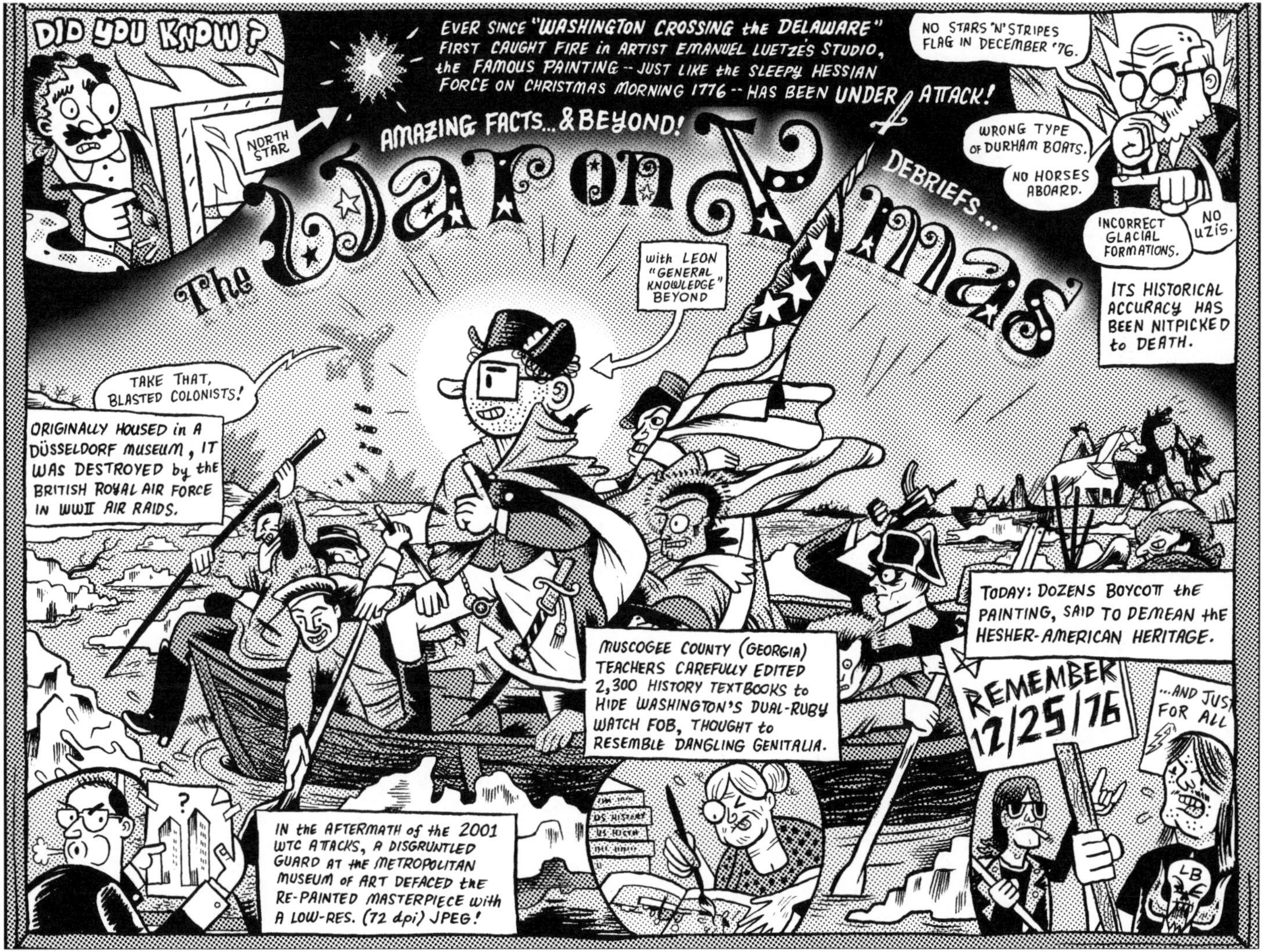
DID YOU KNOW?
EVER SINCE "WASHINGTON CROSSING the DELAWARE" FIRST CAUGHT FIRE in ARTIST EMANUEL LUETZE'S STUDIO, the FAMOUS PAINTING -- JUST LIKE the SLEEPY HESSIAN FORCE ON CHRISTMAS MORNING 1776 -- HAS BEEN UNDER ATTACK!
NORTH STAR
AMAZING FACTS... & BEYOND!
The War on Xmas
DEBRIEFS...
NO STARS 'N' STRIPES FLAG IN DECEMBER '76.
WRONG TYPE OF DURHAM BOATS.
NO HORSES ABOARD.
INCORRECT GLACIAL FORMATIONS.
NO UZIS.
ITS HISTORICAL ACCURACY HAS BEEN NITPICKED to DEATH.
with LEON "GENERAL KNOWLEDGE" BEYOND
TAKE THAT, BLASTED COLONISTS!
ORIGINALLY HOUSED in A DÜSSELDORF MUSEUM, IT WAS DESTROYED by the BRITISH ROYAL AIR FORCE IN WWII AIR RAIDS.
TODAY: DOZENS BOYCOTT the PAINTING, SAID TO DEMEAN the HESHER-AMERICAN HERITAGE.
MUSCOGEE COUNTY (GEORGIA) TEACHERS CAREFULLY EDITED 2,300 HISTORY TEXTBOOKS to HIDE WASHINGTON'S DUAL-RUBY WATCH FOB, THOUGHT to RESEMBLE DANGLING GENITALIA.
REMEMBER 12/25/76
...AND JUST FOR ALL
IN the AFTERMATH of the 2001 WTC ATTACKS, A DISGRUNTLED GUARD AT the METROPOLITAN MUSEUM of ART DEFACED the RE-PAINTED MASTERPIECE with A LOW-RES. (72 dpi) JPEG!
?
LB

YOU MAY THINK EDISON INVENTED the LIGHT BULB, BUT **DID YOU KNOW?** NYC MECHANIC HEINRICH GÖBEL INSTALLED an IDENTICAL RED VERSION ABOVE his SHOPPE 25 YEARS EARLIER!

JEWELRY, HOROLOGY — OPTICAL PORNOGRAPHY

Open

AMAZING FACTS... & BEYOND!
SEEING RED!

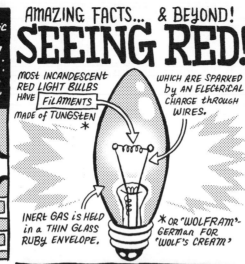

MOST INCANDESCENT RED LIGHT BULBS HAVE FILAMENTS MADE of TUNGSTEN *

WHICH ARE SPARKED by AN ELECTRICAL CHARGE through WIRES.

INERT GAS is HELD in a THIN GLASS RUBY ENVELOPE.

* OR "WOLFRAM"- GERMAN FOR "WOLF'S CREAM"

BEFORE OUTDOOR "ICICLE" STYLE XMAS LIGHTS BECAME DE RIGUEUR, SATANIST FAMILIES HUNG SIMILAR STYLES in RED to REPRESENT OLD-FASHIONED RIVULETS of BLOOD.

K-CHUNK!

IT'S NOT JUST for CARTOONS, FOLKS! RECENT INFRARED BRAINSCANS HAVE SHOWN that WHEN CERTAIN PEOPLE HAVE GOOD IDEAS **, the SCARLETTERAL LOBE BURSTS with PINK LIGHT.

** FOR OTHERS IT'S PORNOGRAPHIC IDEAS

THE NORTHERN STOPLIGHT LOOSEJAW (MALACOSTA NIGER) is the ONLY DEEP-SEA DRAGONFISH to EMIT RED LIGHT.

FLUORESCENT SACS of PIGMENT CALLED PHOTOPHORES

THE ONLY KNOWN MAMMAL to POSSIBLY EX-HIBIT SIMILAR BIOLUMINESCENCE was the PREHISTORIC STAG-MOOSE (CERVALCES SCOTTI). FOSSILS INDICATE a DISGUSTING SAC of REFLECTIVE GLANDS HANGING from its SNOUT.

YOU WOULD EVEN SAY it GLOWS.

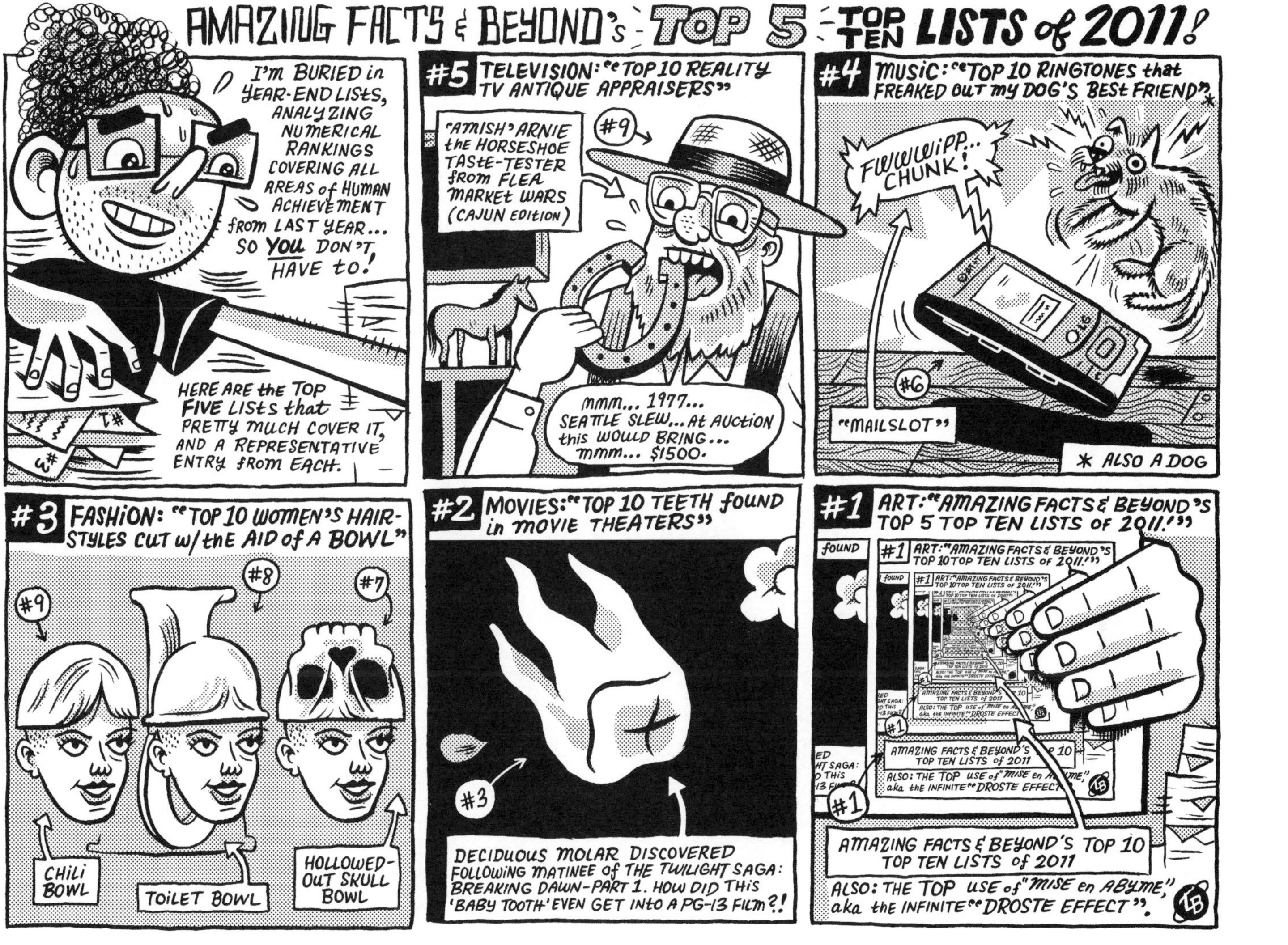
AMAZING FACTS & BEYOND'S TOP 5 TOP TEN LISTS of 2011!
I'm BURIED in YEAR-END LISTS, ANALYZING NUMERICAL RANKINGS COVERING ALL AREAS of HUMAN ACHIEVEMENT from LAST YEAR... SO YOU DON'T HAVE to!
HERE ARE the TOP FIVE LISTS that PRETTY MUCH COVER IT, AND A REPRESENTATIVE ENTRY from EACH.
#5 TELEVISION: "TOP 10 REALITY TV ANTIQUE APPRAISERS"
'AMISH' ARNIE the HORSESHOE TASTE-TESTER from FLEA MARKET WARS (CAJUN EDITION)
#9
mmm... 1977... SEATTLE SLEW... At AUCTION this WOULD BRING... mmm... $1500.
#4 MUSIC: "TOP 10 RINGTONES that FREAKED OUT my DOG'S BEST FRIEND"*
FWWWIPP... CHUNK!
#6
"MAILSLOT"
* ALSO A DOG
#3 FASHION: "TOP 10 WOMEN'S HAIR-STYLES CUT w/ the AID of A BOWL"
#9
#8
#7
CHILI BOWL
TOILET BOWL
HOLLOWED-OUT SKULL BOWL
#2 MOVIES: "TOP 10 TEETH found in MOVIE THEATERS"
#3
DECIDUOUS MOLAR DISCOVERED FOLLOWING MATINEE of THE TWILIGHT SAGA: BREAKING DAWN-PART 1. HOW DID THIS 'BABY TOOTH' EVEN GET INTO A PG-13 FILM?!
#1 ART: "AMAZING FACTS & BEYOND'S TOP 5 TOP TEN LISTS of 2011!"
#1
AMAZING FACTS & BEYOND'S TOP 10 TOP TEN LISTS of 2011
ALSO: THE TOP USE of "MISE en ABYME," aka the INFINITE "DROSTE EFFECT".

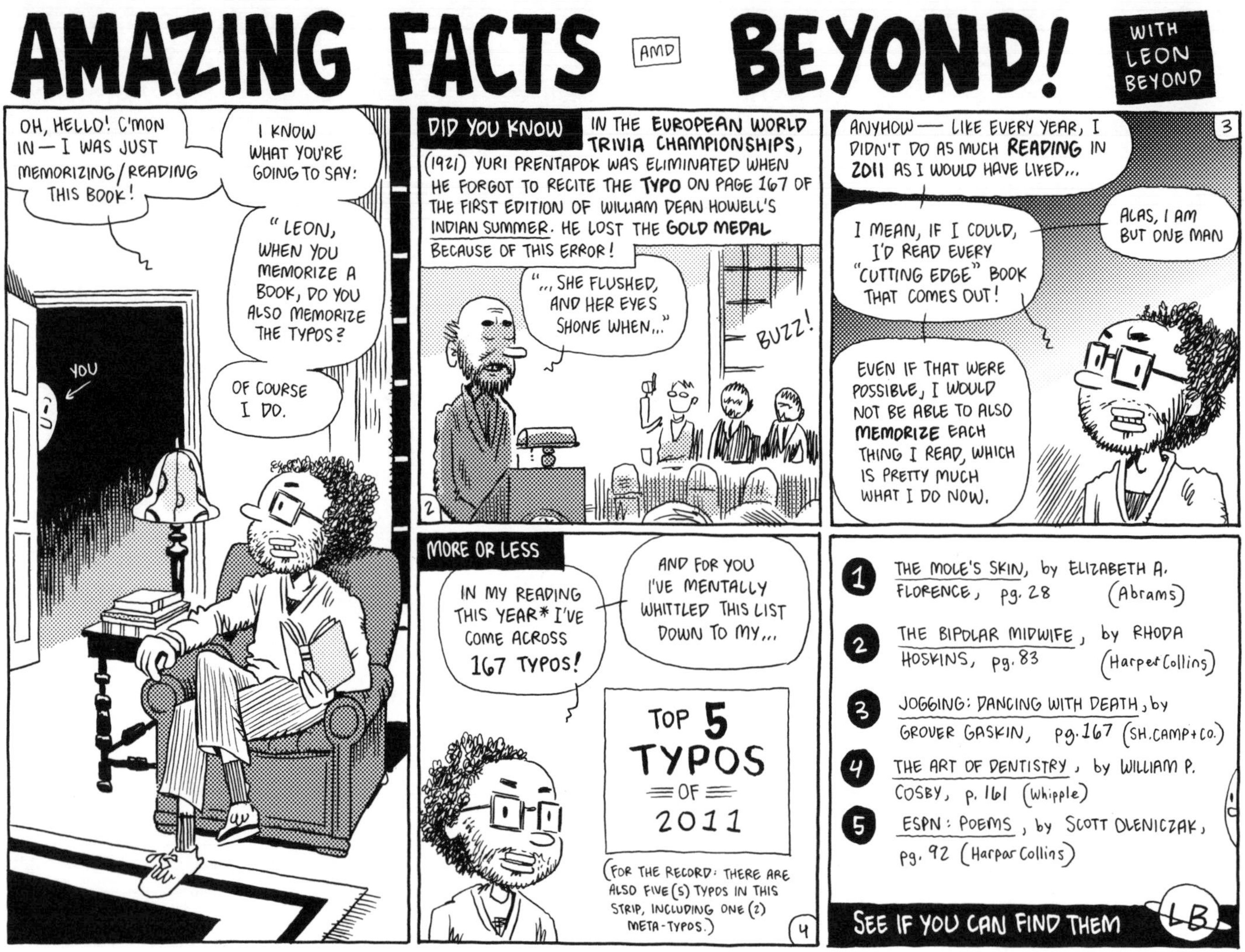
AMAZING FACTS AMD BEYOND! WITH LEON BEYOND
OH, HELLO! C'MON IN — I WAS JUST MEMORIZING/READING THIS BOOK!
I KNOW WHAT YOU'RE GOING TO SAY:
"LEON, WHEN YOU MEMORIZE A BOOK, DO YOU ALSO MEMORIZE THE TYPOS?
OF COURSE I DO.
YOU
DID YOU KNOW
IN THE EUROPEAN WORLD TRIVIA CHAMPIONSHIPS, (1921) YURI PRENTAPOK WAS ELIMINATED WHEN HE FORGOT TO RECITE THE TYPO ON PAGE 167 OF THE FIRST EDITION OF WILLIAM DEAN HOWELL'S INDIAN SUMMER. HE LOST THE GOLD MEDAL BECAUSE OF THIS ERROR!
"... SHE FLUSHED, AND HER EYES SHONE WHEN..."
BUZZ!
2
ANYHOW — LIKE EVERY YEAR, I DIDN'T DO AS MUCH READING IN 2011 AS I WOULD HAVE LIKED...
3
I MEAN, IF I COULD, I'D READ EVERY "CUTTING EDGE" BOOK THAT COMES OUT!
ALAS, I AM BUT ONE MAN
EVEN IF THAT WERE POSSIBLE, I WOULD NOT BE ABLE TO ALSO MEMORIZE EACH THING I READ, WHICH IS PRETTY MUCH WHAT I DO NOW.
MORE OR LESS
IN MY READING THIS YEAR* I'VE COME ACROSS 167 TYPOS!
AND FOR YOU I'VE MENTALLY WHITTLED THIS LIST DOWN TO MY...
TOP 5 TYPOS OF 2011
(FOR THE RECORD: THERE ARE ALSO FIVE (5) TYPOS IN THIS STRIP, INCLUDING ONE (2) META-TYPOS.)
4
1 THE MOLE'S SKIN, by ELIZABETH A. FLORENCE, pg. 28 (Abrams)
2 THE BIPOLAR MIDWIFE, by RHODA HOSKINS, pg. 83 (HarperCollins)
3 JOGGING: DANCING WITH DEATH, by GROVER GASKIN, pg. 167 (SH. CAMP + CO.)
4 THE ART OF DENTISTRY, by WILLIAM P. COSBY, p. 161 (Whipple)
5 ESPN: POEMS, by SCOTT OLENICZAK, pg. 92 (Harpar Collins)
SEE IF YOU CAN FIND THEM
LB

AMAZING FACTS... AND BEYOND!

WITH LEON BEYOND

ASTRONOMY BUFFS ARE CELEBRATING 2012: YEAR OF THE NEBULA!

HERE'S A PRIMER ON NEBULAR CURRENT EVENTS SO YOU WON'T EMBARRASS YOURSELF AT PARTIES!

KNOW YOUR HOT NEBULAS 2012

SHIT NEBULA

THIS EMISSION CLOUD IS FORTY LIGHT YEARS ACROSS AND IS SHOWN BRIEFLY IN THE VIDEO "SHIT ASTRONOMERS SAY." NGC 1835 F71

OTHER INTERNET MEME NEBULAS

PANCAKE AND EGGS

ROLLING STONES NEBULA

NSFW NEBULA

BIRD NEBULA

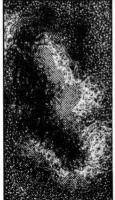

SOUTHERN CRAB

ALASKAN SALMON

HUGO NEBULA

BONUS FACT

SINCE THE LATE 1970'S SOMEONE HAS BEEN MAILING PHOTOS OF HIS BUTT TO RANDOM STRANGERS ALL OVER THE WORLD! A TEAM OF DETECTIVES HAS BEEN UNABLE TO LOCATE THE IDENTITY OF THIS MAN.

I HAVE BEEN ASKED TO JOIN THE TEAM, BUT I AM NOT INTERESTED.

TRAVEL

FAMOUS HANGING GARDENS
of COOPER PARK, BABYLON,
NEW JERSEY

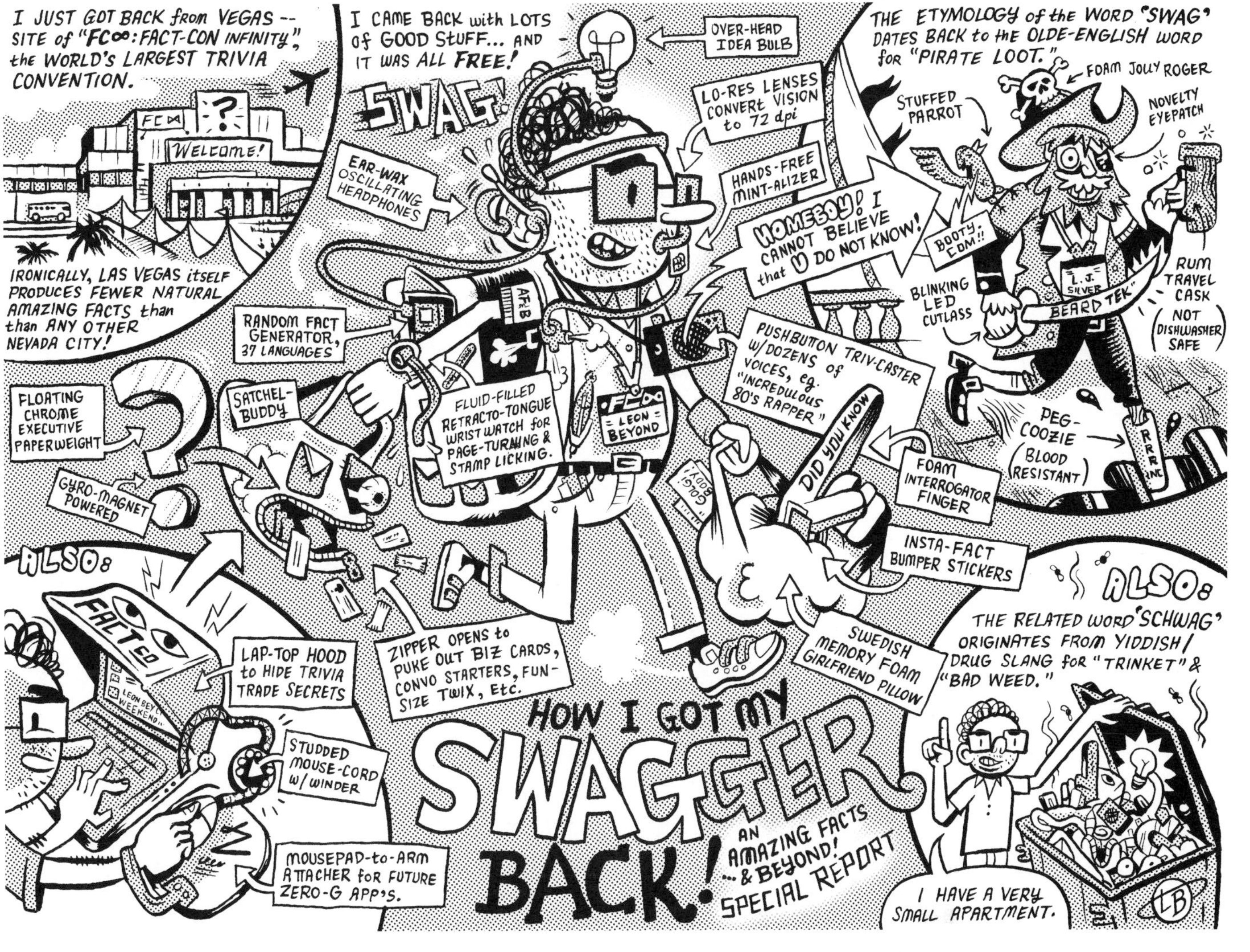

I JUST GOT BACK from VEGAS -- SITE of "FC∞: FACT-CON INFINITY", the WORLD'S LARGEST TRIVIA CONVENTION.
FC∞
WELCOME!
IRONICALLY, LAS VEGAS itself PRODUCES FEWER NATURAL AMAZING FACTS than than ANY OTHER NEVADA CITY!
I CAME BACK with LOTS of GOOD STUFF... AND IT WAS ALL FREE!
SWAG!
OVER-HEAD IDEA BULB
LO-RES LENSES CONVERT VISION to 72 dpi
EAR-WAX OSCILLATING HEADPHONES
HANDS-FREE MINT-ALIZER
HOMEBOY! I CANNOT BELIEVE that U DO NOT KNOW!
RANDOM FACT GENERATOR, 37 LANGUAGES
SATCHEL-BUDDY
FLUID-FILLED RETRACTO-TONGUE WRISTWATCH for PAGE-TURNING & STAMP LICKING.
FC∞ LEON BEYOND
PUSHBUTTON TRIV-CASTER w/DOZENS of VOICES, eg. "INCREDULOUS 80'S RAPPER"
DID YOU KNOW
FLOATING CHROME EXECUTIVE PAPERWEIGHT
GYRO-MAGNET POWERED
FOAM INTERROGATOR FINGER
INSTA-FACT BUMPER STICKERS
SWEDISH MEMORY FOAM GIRLFRIEND PILLOW
ZIPPER OPENS to PUKE OUT BIZ CARDS, CONVO STARTERS, FUN-SIZE TWIX, Etc.
THE ETYMOLOGY of the WORD "SWAG" DATES BACK to the OLDE-ENGLISH WORD for "PIRATE LOOT."
FOAM JOLLY ROGER
STUFFED PARROT
NOVELTY EYEPATCH
BOOTY.COM!!
L.J. SILVER
BEARD TEK
BLINKING LED CUTLASS
RUM TRAVEL CASK (NOT DISHWASHER SAFE)
PEG-COOZIE (BLOOD RESISTANT)
R R R INC
ALSO:
FACT CO
LAP-TOP HOOD to HIDE TRIVIA TRADE SECRETS
STUDDED MOUSE-CORD w/WINDER
MOUSEPAD-to-ARM ATTACHER for FUTURE ZERO-G APP'S.
HOW I GOT MY SWAGGER BACK!
AN AMAZING FACTS ...& BEYOND! SPECIAL REPORT
ALSO:
THE RELATED WORD "SCHWAG" ORIGINATES FROM YIDDISH/DRUG SLANG for "TRINKET" & "BAD WEED."
I HAVE A VERY SMALL APARTMENT.
LB

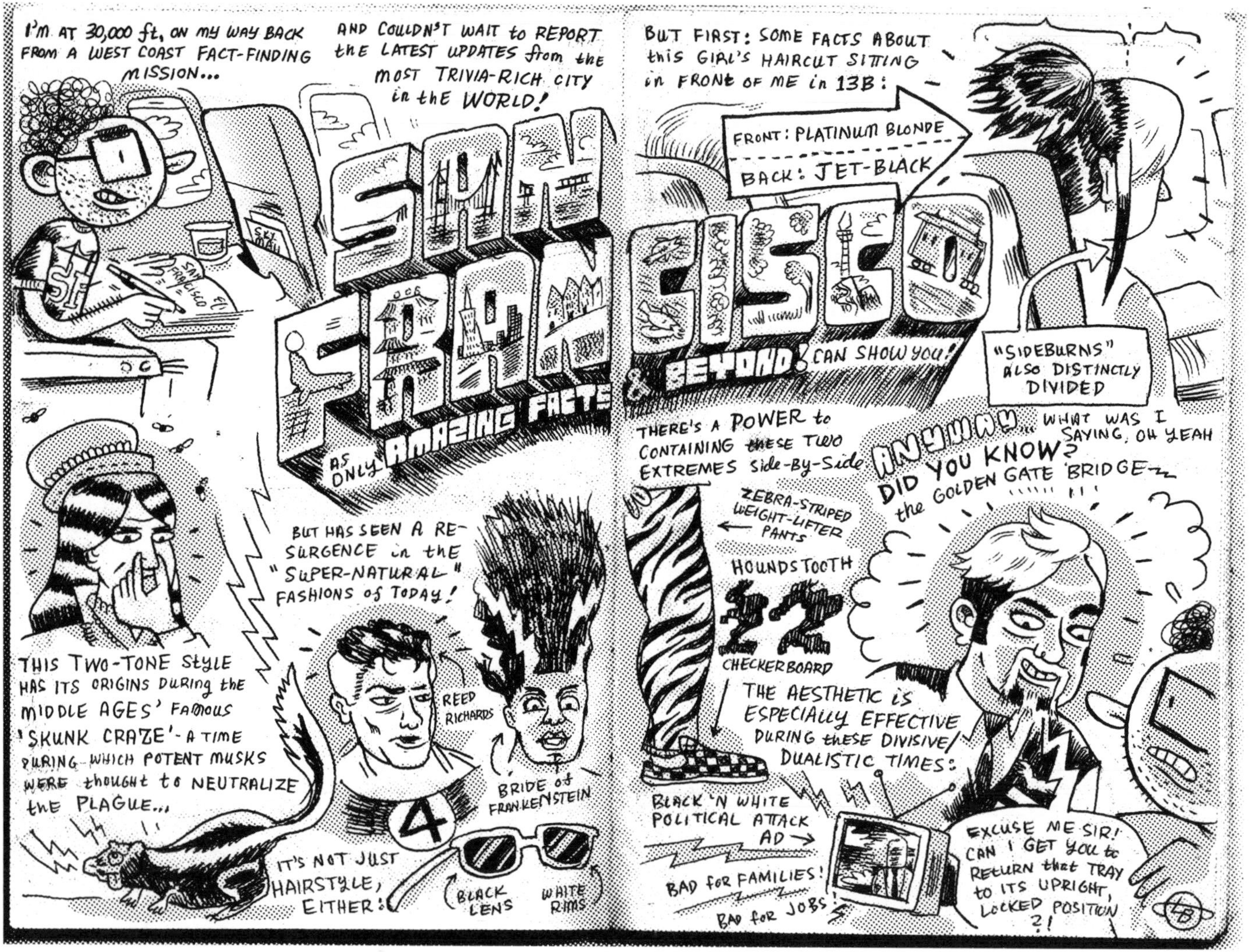
I'M AT 30,000 ft, ON MY WAY BACK FROM A WEST COAST FACT-FINDING MISSION...
AND COULDN'T WAIT to REPORT the LATEST UPDATES from the MOST TRIVIA-RICH CITY in the WORLD!
SAN FRANCISCO & BEYOND!
AS ONLY AMAZING FACTS CAN SHOW YOU!
BUT FIRST: SOME FACTS ABOUT this GIRL'S HAIRCUT SITTING in FRONT OF ME in 13B:
FRONT: PLATINUM BLONDE
BACK: JET-BLACK
"SIDEBURNS" ALSO DISTINCTLY DIVIDED
THIS TWO-TONE STYLE HAS ITS ORIGINS DURING the MIDDLE AGES' FAMOUS 'SKUNK CRAZE' - A TIME DURING WHICH POTENT MUSKS WERE thought to NEUTRALIZE the PLAGUE...
BUT HAS SEEN A RE-SURGENCE in the "SUPER-NATURAL" FASHIONS of TODAY!
REED RICHARDS
BRIDE of FRANKENSTEIN
4
IT'S NOT JUST HAIRSTYLE, EITHER:
BLACK LENS
WHITE RIMS
THERE'S A POWER to CONTAINING these TWO EXTREMES side-by-side
ZEBRA-STRIPED WEIGHT-LIFTER PANTS
HOUNDSTOOTH
CHECKERBOARD
THE AESTHETIC is ESPECIALLY EFFECTIVE DURING these DIVISIVE/DUALISTIC TIMES:
BLACK 'N WHITE POLITICAL ATTACK AD
BAD for FAMILIES!
BAD for JOBS!
ANYWAY... WHAT WAS I SAYING. OH YEAH
DID YOU KNOW? the GOLDEN GATE BRIDGE—
EXCUSE ME SIR! CAN I GET YOU to RETURN that TRAY to ITS UPRIGHT, LOCKED POSITION?!

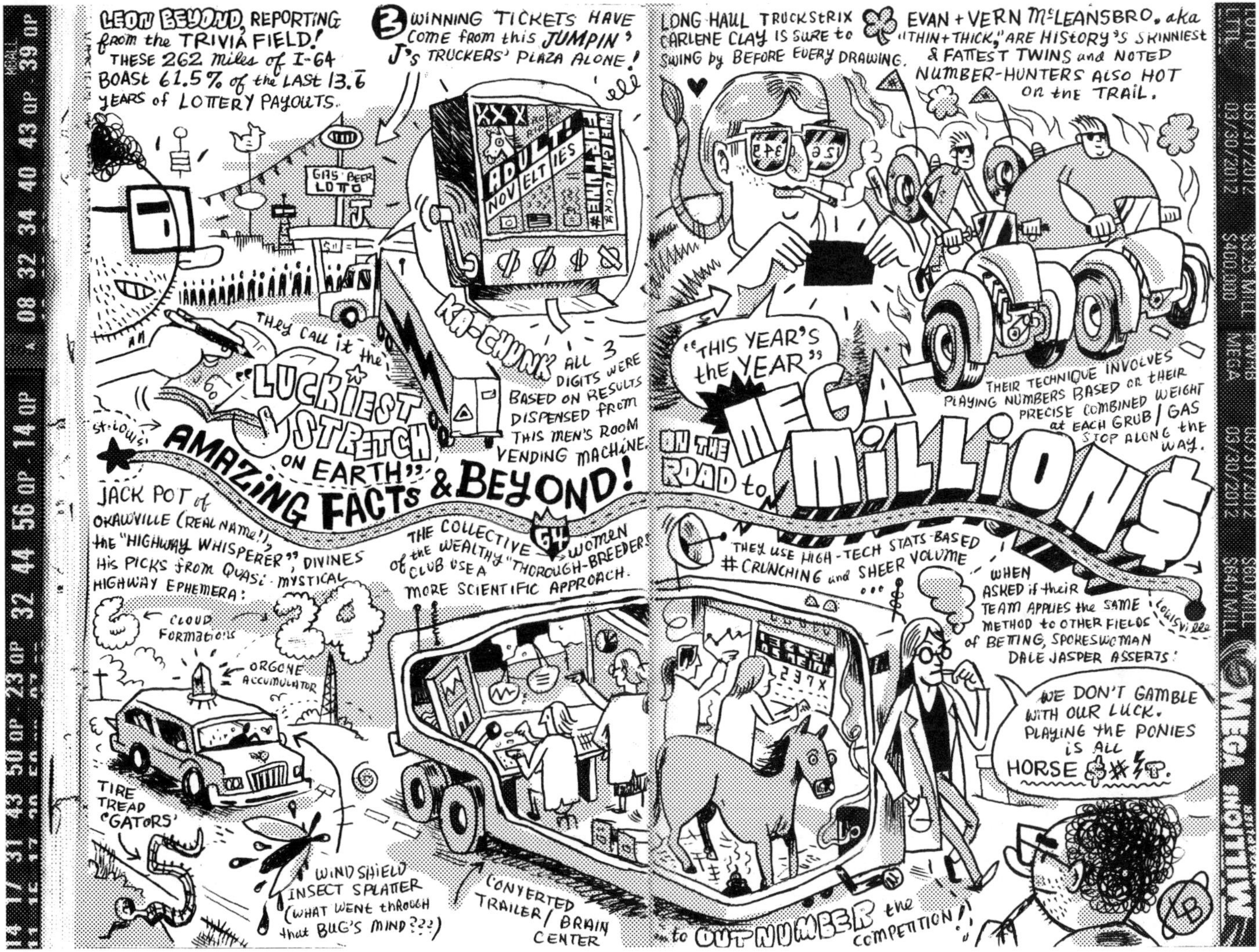
LEON BEYOND, REPORTING from the TRIVIA FIELD! THESE 262 miles of I-64 BOAST 61.5% of the LAST 13.6 YEARS of LOTTERY PAYOUTS.
3 WINNING TICKETS HAVE COME from this JUMPIN' J's TRUCKERS' PLAZA ALONE!
GAS BEER LOTTO
XXX
ADULT NOVELTIES
WEIGHT FORTUNE
KA-CHUNK
ALL 3 DIGITS WERE BASED ON RESULTS DISPENSED FROM THIS MEN'S ROOM VENDING MACHINE.
THEY CALL IT THE "LUCKIEST STRETCH ON EARTH"
ST. LOUIS
AMAZING FACTS & BEYOND!
JACK POT of OKAWVILLE (REAL NAME!), the "HIGHWAY WHISPERER", DIVINES HIS PICKS FROM QUASI-MYSTICAL HIGHWAY EPHEMERA:
CLOUD FORMATIONS
ORGONE ACCUMULATOR
TIRE TREAD 'GATORS'
WINDSHIELD INSECT SPLATTER (WHAT WENT THROUGH THAT BUG'S MIND???)
64
THE COLLECTIVE of the WEALTHY "THOROUGH-BREEDERS" WOMEN CLUB USE A MORE SCIENTIFIC APPROACH.
CONVERTED TRAILER/BRAIN CENTER
LONG HAUL TRUCKSTRIX CARLENE CLAY IS SURE to SWING BY BEFORE EVERY DRAWING.
EVAN + VERN McLEANSBRO, aka "THIN + THICK," ARE HISTORY'S SKINNIEST & FATTEST TWINS and NOTED NUMBER-HUNTERS ALSO HOT ON THE TRAIL.
"THIS YEAR'S THE YEAR"
ON THE ROAD to MEGA-MILLION$
THEIR TECHNIQUE INVOLVES PLAYING NUMBERS BASED ON THEIR PRECISE COMBINED WEIGHT AT EACH GRUB/GAS STOP ALONG THE WAY.
THEY USE HIGH-TECH STATS-BASED # CRUNCHING and SHEER VOLUME ... to OUTNUMBER the COMPETITION!
WHEN ASKED if their TEAM APPLIES the SAME METHOD to OTHER FIELDS of BETTING, SPOKESWOMAN DALE JASPER ASSERTS:
LOUISVILLE
WE DON'T GAMBLE WITH OUR LUCK. PLAYING THE PONIES IS ALL HORSE $#!T.
LB
MEGA MILLIONS

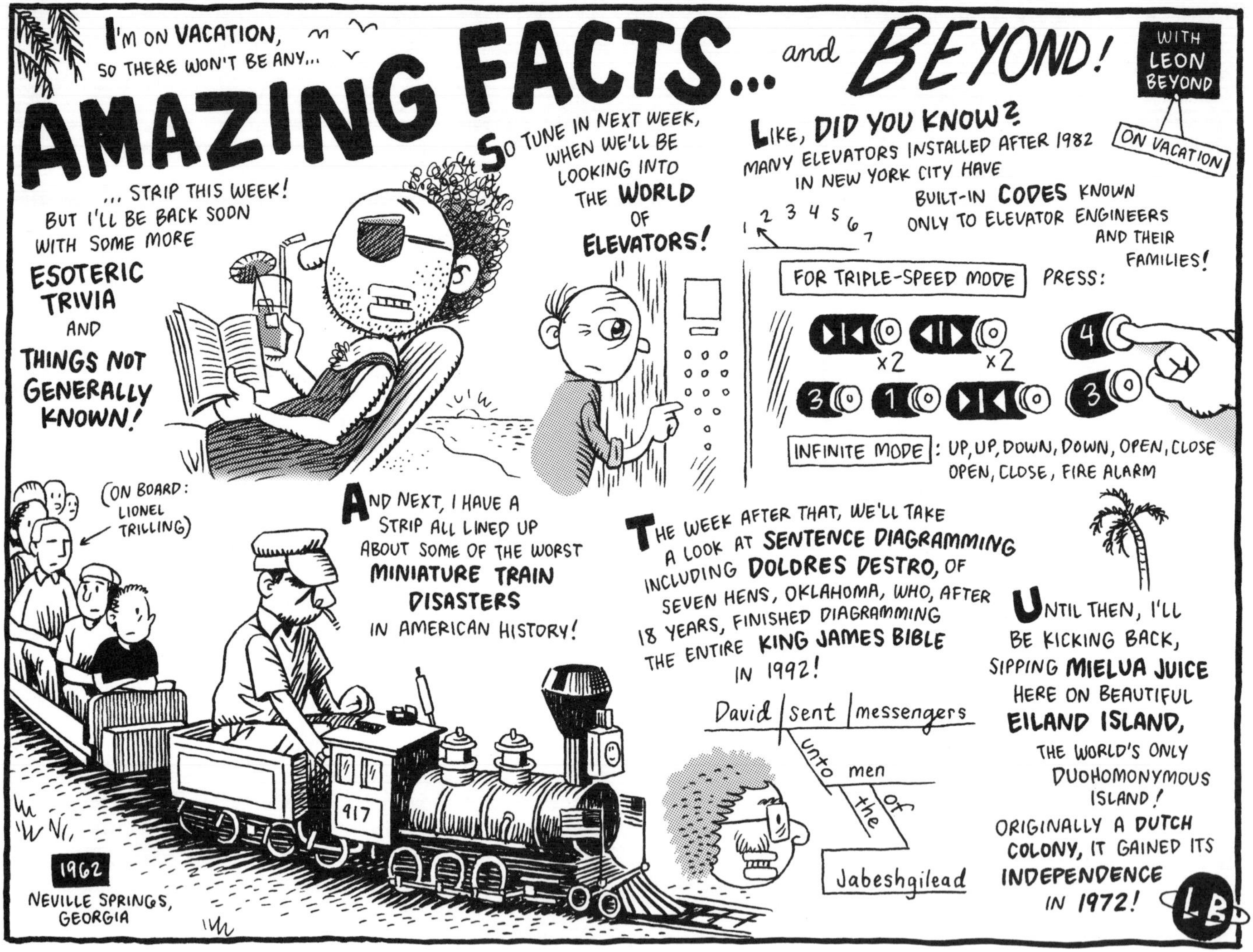
I'M ON VACATION, SO THERE WON'T BE ANY...
AMAZING FACTS... and BEYOND!
WITH LEON BEYOND
ON VACATION
... STRIP THIS WEEK! BUT I'LL BE BACK SOON WITH SOME MORE ESOTERIC TRIVIA AND THINGS NOT GENERALLY KNOWN!
SO TUNE IN NEXT WEEK, WHEN WE'LL BE LOOKING INTO THE WORLD OF ELEVATORS!
LIKE, DID YOU KNOW? MANY ELEVATORS INSTALLED AFTER 1982 IN NEW YORK CITY HAVE BUILT-IN CODES KNOWN ONLY TO ELEVATOR ENGINEERS AND THEIR FAMILIES!
1 2 3 4 5 6 7
FOR TRIPLE-SPEED MODE
PRESS:
x2
x2
4
3
1
3
INFINITE MODE: UP, UP, DOWN, DOWN, OPEN, CLOSE OPEN, CLOSE, FIRE ALARM
(ON BOARD: LIONEL TRILLING)
AND NEXT, I HAVE A STRIP ALL LINED UP ABOUT SOME OF THE WORST MINIATURE TRAIN DISASTERS IN AMERICAN HISTORY!
417
1962
NEVILLE SPRINGS, GEORGIA
THE WEEK AFTER THAT, WE'LL TAKE A LOOK AT SENTENCE DIAGRAMMING INCLUDING DOLDRES DESTRO, OF SEVEN HENS, OKLAHOMA, WHO, AFTER 18 YEARS, FINISHED DIAGRAMMING THE ENTIRE KING JAMES BIBLE IN 1992!
David | sent | messengers
unto
men
of
the
Jabeshgilead
UNTIL THEN, I'LL BE KICKING BACK, SIPPING MIELUA JUICE HERE ON BEAUTIFUL EILAND ISLAND, THE WORLD'S ONLY DUOHOMONYMOUS ISLAND! ORIGINALLY A DUTCH COLONY, IT GAINED ITS INDEPENDENCE IN 1972!
LB

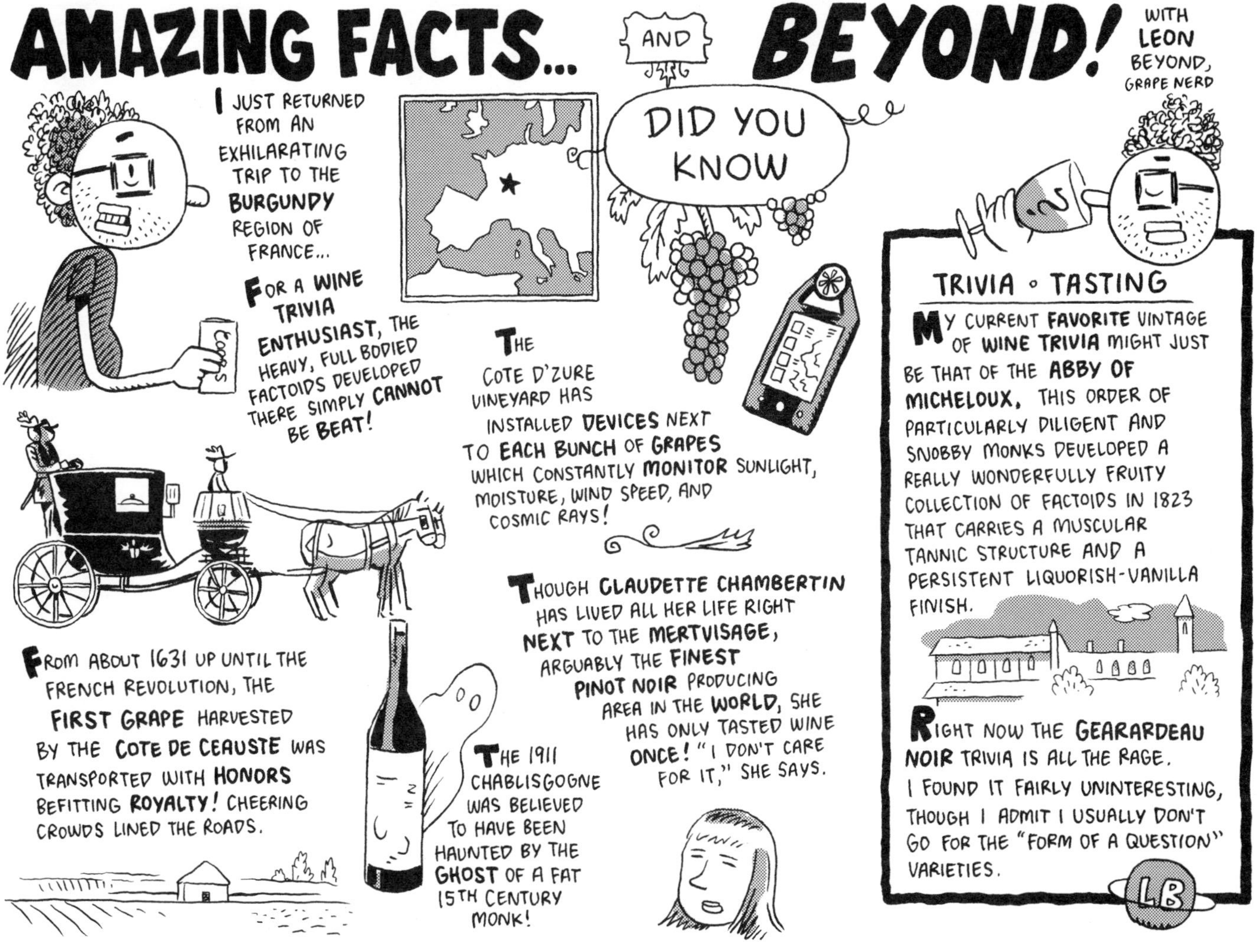
AMAZING FACTS... AND BEYOND!
WITH LEON BEYOND, GRAPE NERD
I JUST RETURNED FROM AN EXHILARATING TRIP TO THE BURGUNDY REGION OF FRANCE...
FOR A WINE TRIVIA ENTHUSIAST, THE HEAVY, FULL BODIED FACTOIDS DEVELOPED THERE SIMPLY CANNOT BE BEAT!
DID YOU KNOW
THE COTE D'ZURE VINEYARD HAS INSTALLED DEVICES NEXT TO EACH BUNCH OF GRAPES WHICH CONSTANTLY MONITOR SUNLIGHT, MOISTURE, WIND SPEED, AND COSMIC RAYS!
FROM ABOUT 1631 UP UNTIL THE FRENCH REVOLUTION, THE FIRST GRAPE HARVESTED BY THE COTE DE CEAUSTE WAS TRANSPORTED WITH HONORS BEFITTING ROYALTY! CHEERING CROWDS LINED THE ROADS.
THE 1911 CHABLISGOGNE WAS BELIEVED TO HAVE BEEN HAUNTED BY THE GHOST OF A FAT 15TH CENTURY MONK!
THOUGH CLAUDETTE CHAMBERTIN HAS LIVED ALL HER LIFE RIGHT NEXT TO THE MERTVISAGE, ARGUABLY THE FINEST PINOT NOIR PRODUCING AREA IN THE WORLD, SHE HAS ONLY TASTED WINE ONCE! "I DON'T CARE FOR IT," SHE SAYS.
TRIVIA ◦ TASTING
MY CURRENT FAVORITE VINTAGE OF WINE TRIVIA MIGHT JUST BE THAT OF THE ABBY OF MICHELOUX. THIS ORDER OF PARTICULARLY DILIGENT AND SNOBBY MONKS DEVELOPED A REALLY WONDERFULLY FRUITY COLLECTION OF FACTOIDS IN 1823 THAT CARRIES A MUSCULAR TANNIC STRUCTURE AND A PERSISTENT LIQUORISH-VANILLA FINISH.
RIGHT NOW THE GEARARDEAU NOIR TRIVIA IS ALL THE RAGE. I FOUND IT FAIRLY UNINTERESTING, THOUGH I ADMIT I USUALLY DON'T GO FOR THE "FORM OF A QUESTION" VARIETIES.
LB

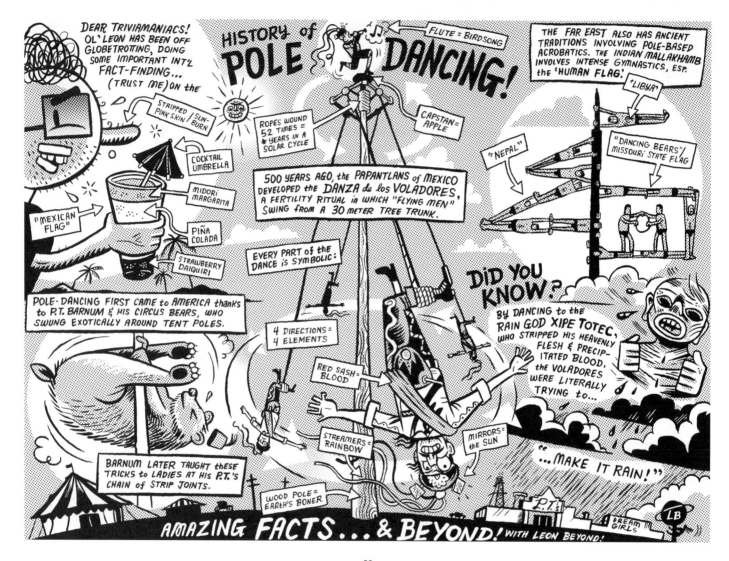

DEAR TRIVIAMANIACS! OL' LEON HAS BEEN OFF GLOBETROTTING, DOING SOME IMPORTANT INT'L FACT-FINDING... (TRUST ME) ON the

HISTORY of POLE DANCING!

FLUTE = BIRDSONG

THE FAR EAST ALSO HAS ANCIENT TRADITIONS INVOLVING POLE-BASED ACROBATICS. THE INDIAN MALLAKHAMB INVOLVES INTENSE GYMNASTICS, ESP. the 'HUMAN FLAG.'

STRIPPED/SUN-BURN PINK SKIN

COCKTAIL UMBRELLA

MIDORI MARGARITA

PIÑA COLADA

STRAWBERRY DAIQUIRI

"MEXICAN FLAG"

ROPES WOUND 52 TIMES = # YEARS IN A SOLAR CYCLE

CAPSTAN = APPLE

"LIBYA"

"NEPAL"

"DANCING BEARS", MISSOURI STATE FLAG

500 YEARS AGO, the PAPANTLANS de MEXICO DEVELOPED the DANZA de los VOLADORES, A FERTILITY RITUAL IN WHICH "FLYING MEN" SWING FROM A 30 METER TREE TRUNK.

EVERY PART of the DANCE IS SYMBOLIC:

POLE-DANCING FIRST CAME to AMERICA thanks to P.T. BARNUM & HIS CIRCUS BEARS, WHO SWUNG EXOTICALLY AROUND TENT POLES.

DID YOU KNOW?

BY DANCING to the RAIN GOD XIPE TOTEC, WHO STRIPPED HIS HEAVENLY FLESH & PRECIPITATED BLOOD, the VOLADORES WERE LITERALLY TRYING to...

4 DIRECTIONS = 4 ELEMENTS

RED SASH = BLOOD

STREAMERS = RAINBOW

MIRRORS = the SUN

"... MAKE IT RAIN!"

BARNUM LATER TAUGHT these TRICKS to LADIES at HIS P.T.'S CHAIN of STRIP JOINTS.

WOOD POLE = EARTH'S BONER

P.T.'s

DREAM GIRLS

LB

AMAZING FACTS... & BEYOND! WITH LEON BEYOND!

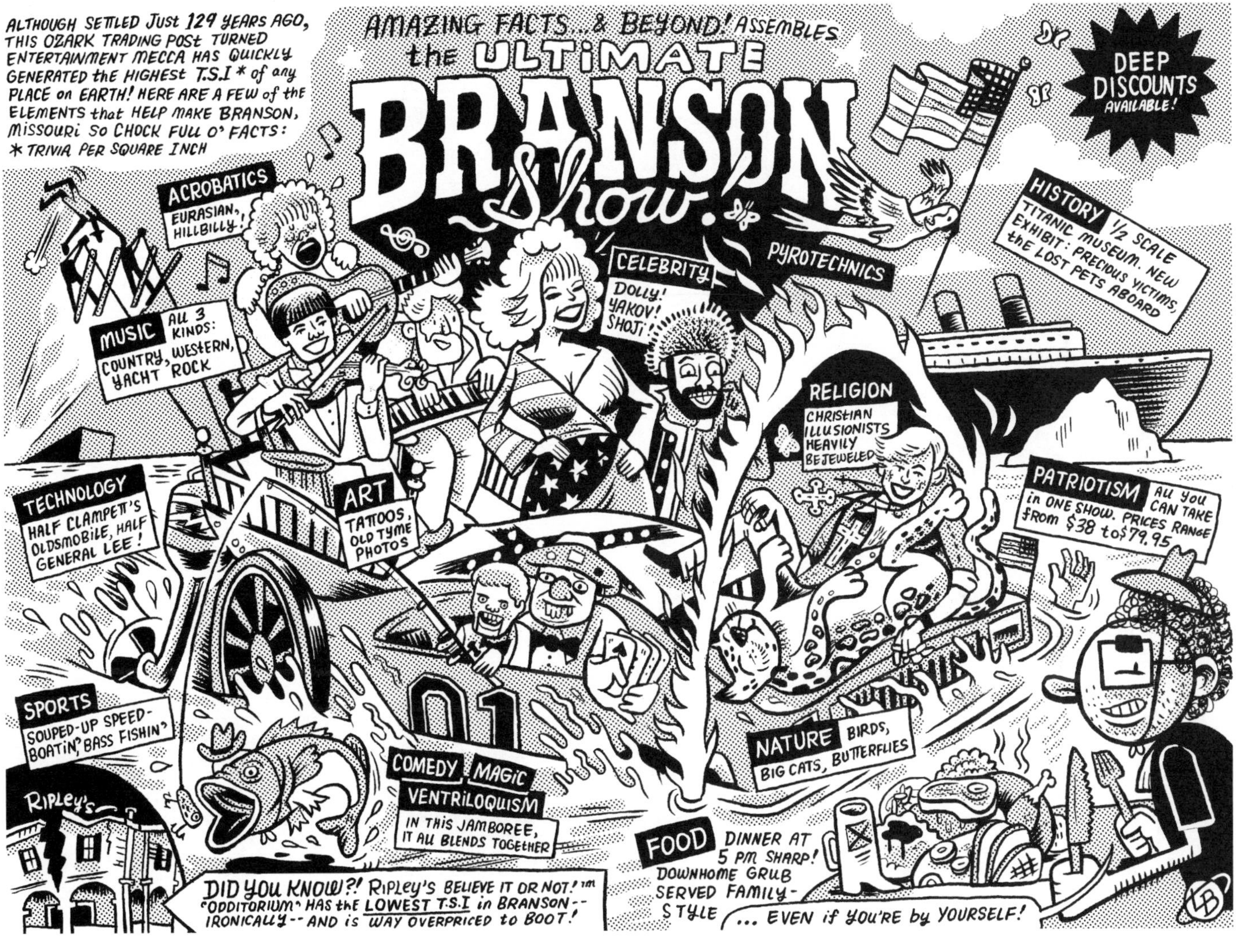

ALTHOUGH SETTLED JUST 129 YEARS AGO, THIS OZARK TRADING POST TURNED ENTERTAINMENT MECCA HAS QUICKLY GENERATED THE HIGHEST T.S.I * OF ANY PLACE ON EARTH! HERE ARE A FEW OF THE ELEMENTS THAT HELP MAKE BRANSON, MISSOURI SO CHOCK FULL O' FACTS:
* TRIVIA PER SQUARE INCH
AMAZING FACTS...& BEYOND! ASSEMBLES
THE ULTIMATE
BRANSON
SHOW!
DEEP DISCOUNTS AVAILABLE!
ACROBATICS
EURASIAN, HILLBILLY!
MUSIC
ALL 3 KINDS: COUNTRY, WESTERN, YACHT ROCK
CELEBRITY
DOLLY! YAKOV! SHOJI!
PYROTECHNICS
HISTORY
1/2 SCALE TITANIC MUSEUM. NEW EXHIBIT: PRECIOUS VICTIMS, THE LOST PETS ABOARD
RELIGION
CHRISTIAN ILLUSIONISTS HEAVILY BEJEWELED
TECHNOLOGY
HALF CLAMPETT'S OLDSMOBILE, HALF GENERAL LEE!
ART
TATTOOS, OLD TYME PHOTOS
PATRIOTISM
ALL YOU CAN TAKE IN ONE SHOW. PRICES RANGE FROM $38 TO $79.95
01
SPORTS
SOUPED-UP SPEED-BOATIN', BASS FISHIN'
NATURE
BIRDS, BIG CATS, BUTTERFLIES
COMEDY
MAGIC
VENTRILOQUISM
IN THIS JAMBOREE, IT ALL BLENDS TOGETHER
RIPLEY'S
FOOD
DINNER AT 5 PM SHARP! DOWNHOME GRUB SERVED FAMILY-STYLE
... EVEN IF YOU'RE BY YOURSELF!
DID YOU KNOW?! RIPLEY'S BELIEVE IT OR NOT!™ "ODDITORIUM" HAS THE LOWEST T.S.I IN BRANSON -- IRONICALLY -- AND IS WAY OVERPRICED TO BOOT!
LB

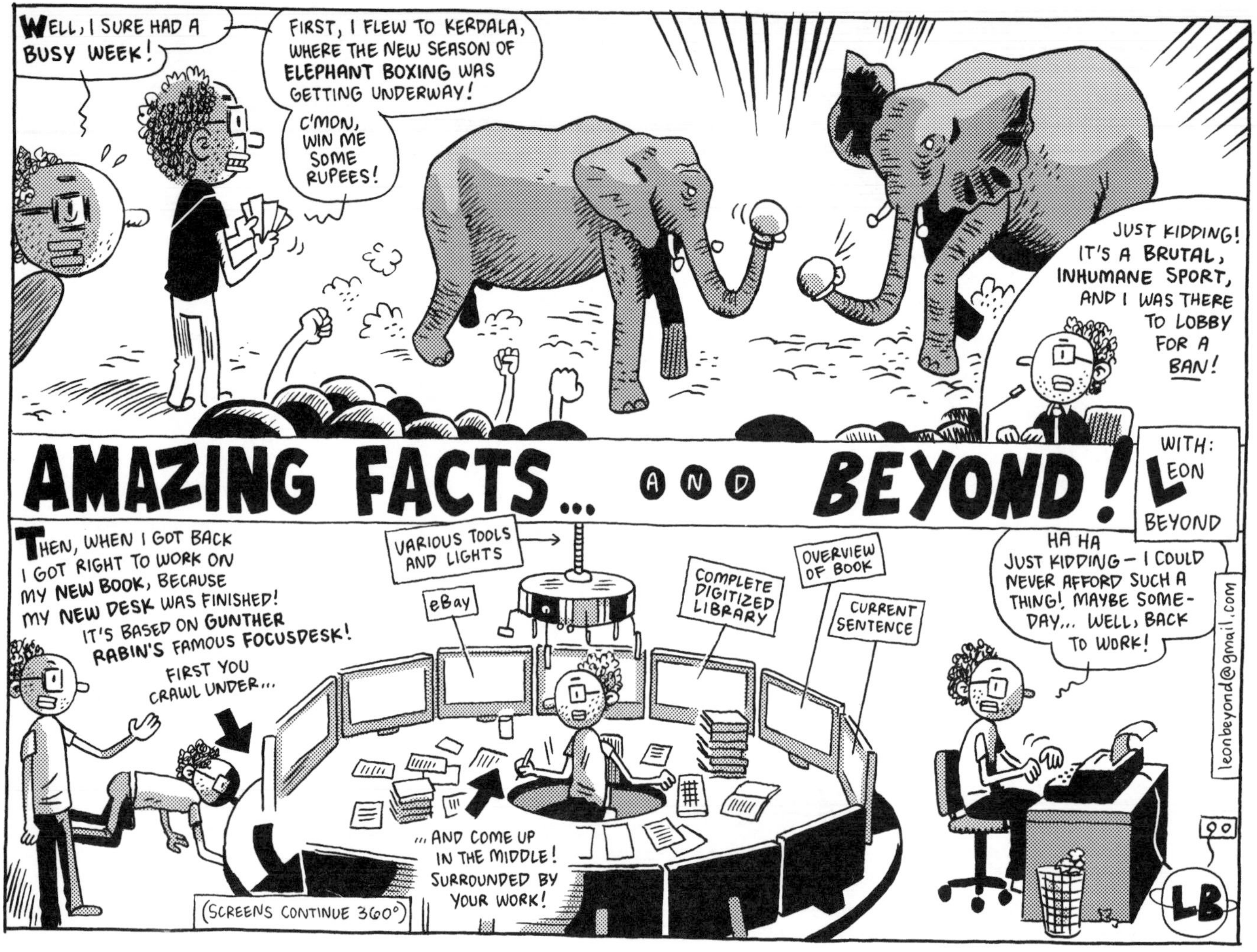
WELL, I SURE HAD A BUSY WEEK!
FIRST, I FLEW TO KERDALA, WHERE THE NEW SEASON OF ELEPHANT BOXING WAS GETTING UNDERWAY!
C'MON, WIN ME SOME RUPEES!
JUST KIDDING! IT'S A BRUTAL, INHUMANE SPORT, AND I WAS THERE TO LOBBY FOR A BAN!
AMAZING FACTS... AND BEYOND!
WITH: LEON BEYOND
THEN, WHEN I GOT BACK I GOT RIGHT TO WORK ON MY NEW BOOK, BECAUSE MY NEW DESK WAS FINISHED! IT'S BASED ON GUNTHER RABIN'S FAMOUS FOCUSDESK!
VARIOUS TOOLS AND LIGHTS
eBay
COMPLETE DIGITIZED LIBRARY
OVERVIEW OF BOOK
CURRENT SENTENCE
FIRST YOU CRAWL UNDER...
...AND COME UP IN THE MIDDLE! SURROUNDED BY YOUR WORK!
(SCREENS CONTINUE 360°)
HA HA JUST KIDDING — I COULD NEVER AFFORD SUCH A THING! MAYBE SOME-DAY... WELL, BACK TO WORK!
leonbeyond@gmail.com
LB

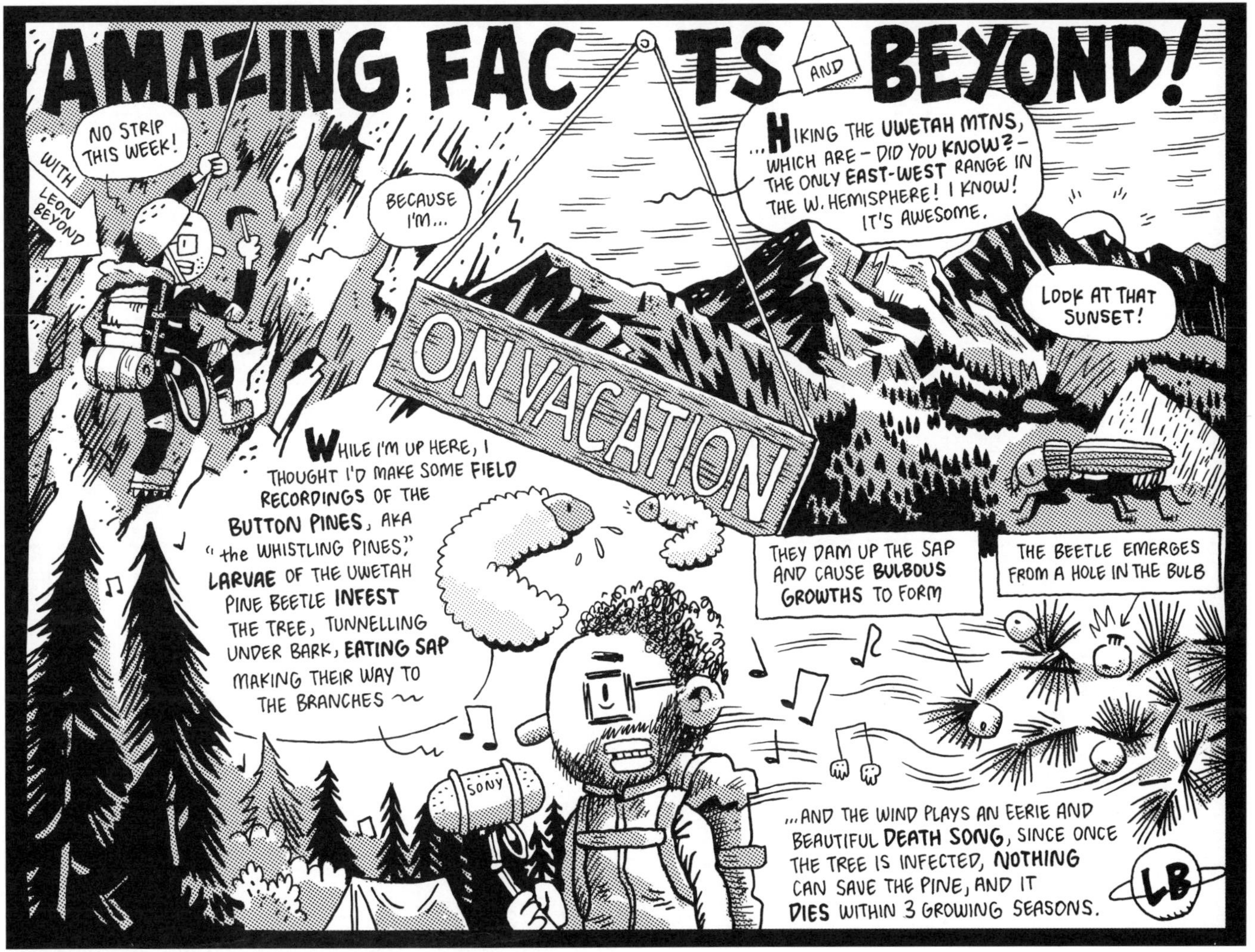
AMAZING FACTS AND BEYOND!
WITH LEON BEYOND
NO STRIP THIS WEEK!
BECAUSE I'M...
ON VACATION
...HIKING THE UWETAH MTNS, WHICH ARE - DID YOU KNOW? - THE ONLY EAST-WEST RANGE IN THE W. HEMISPHERE! I KNOW! IT'S AWESOME.
LOOK AT THAT SUNSET!
WHILE I'M UP HERE, I THOUGHT I'D MAKE SOME FIELD RECORDINGS OF THE BUTTON PINES, AKA "the WHISTLING PINES." LARVAE OF THE UWETAH PINE BEETLE INFEST THE TREE, TUNNELLING UNDER BARK, EATING SAP MAKING THEIR WAY TO THE BRANCHES ~
THEY DAM UP THE SAP AND CAUSE BULBOUS GROWTHS TO FORM
THE BEETLE EMERGES FROM A HOLE IN THE BULB
...AND THE WIND PLAYS AN EERIE AND BEAUTIFUL DEATH SONG, SINCE ONCE THE TREE IS INFECTED, NOTHING CAN SAVE THE PINE, AND IT DIES WITHIN 3 GROWING SEASONS.
SONY
LB

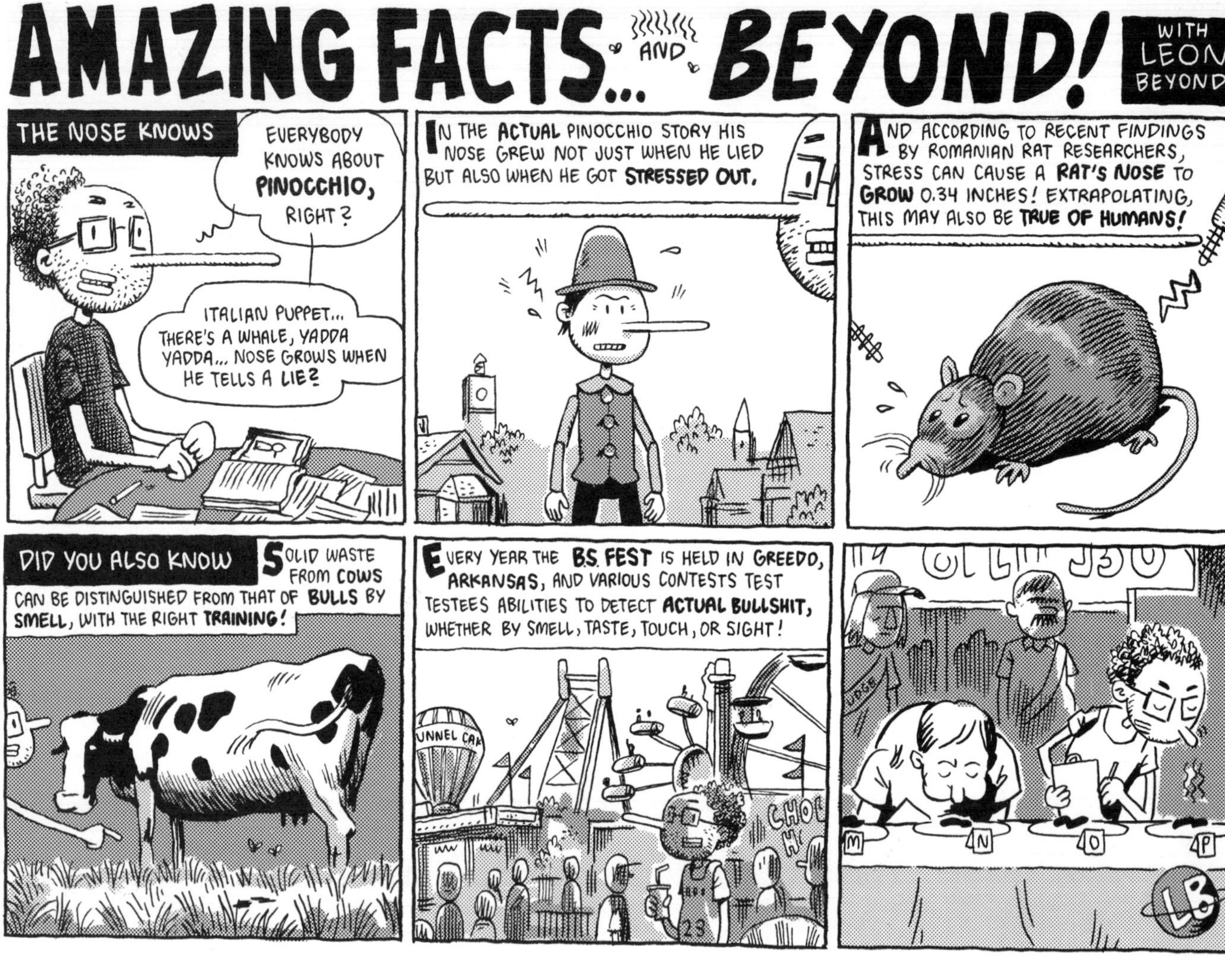
AMAZING FACTS... AND BEYOND!
WITH LEON BEYOND
THE NOSE KNOWS
EVERYBODY KNOWS ABOUT PINOCCHIO, RIGHT?
ITALIAN PUPPET... THERE'S A WHALE, YADDA YADDA... NOSE GROWS WHEN HE TELLS A LIE?
IN THE ACTUAL PINOCCHIO STORY HIS NOSE GREW NOT JUST WHEN HE LIED BUT ALSO WHEN HE GOT STRESSED OUT.
AND ACCORDING TO RECENT FINDINGS BY ROMANIAN RAT RESEARCHERS, STRESS CAN CAUSE A RAT'S NOSE TO GROW 0.34 INCHES! EXTRAPOLATING, THIS MAY ALSO BE TRUE OF HUMANS!
DID YOU ALSO KNOW
SOLID WASTE FROM COWS CAN BE DISTINGUISHED FROM THAT OF BULLS BY SMELL, WITH THE RIGHT TRAINING!
EVERY YEAR THE B.S. FEST IS HELD IN GREEDO, ARKANSAS, AND VARIOUS CONTESTS TEST TESTEES ABILITIES TO DETECT ACTUAL BULLSHIT, WHETHER BY SMELL, TASTE, TOUCH, OR SIGHT!
M
N
O
P

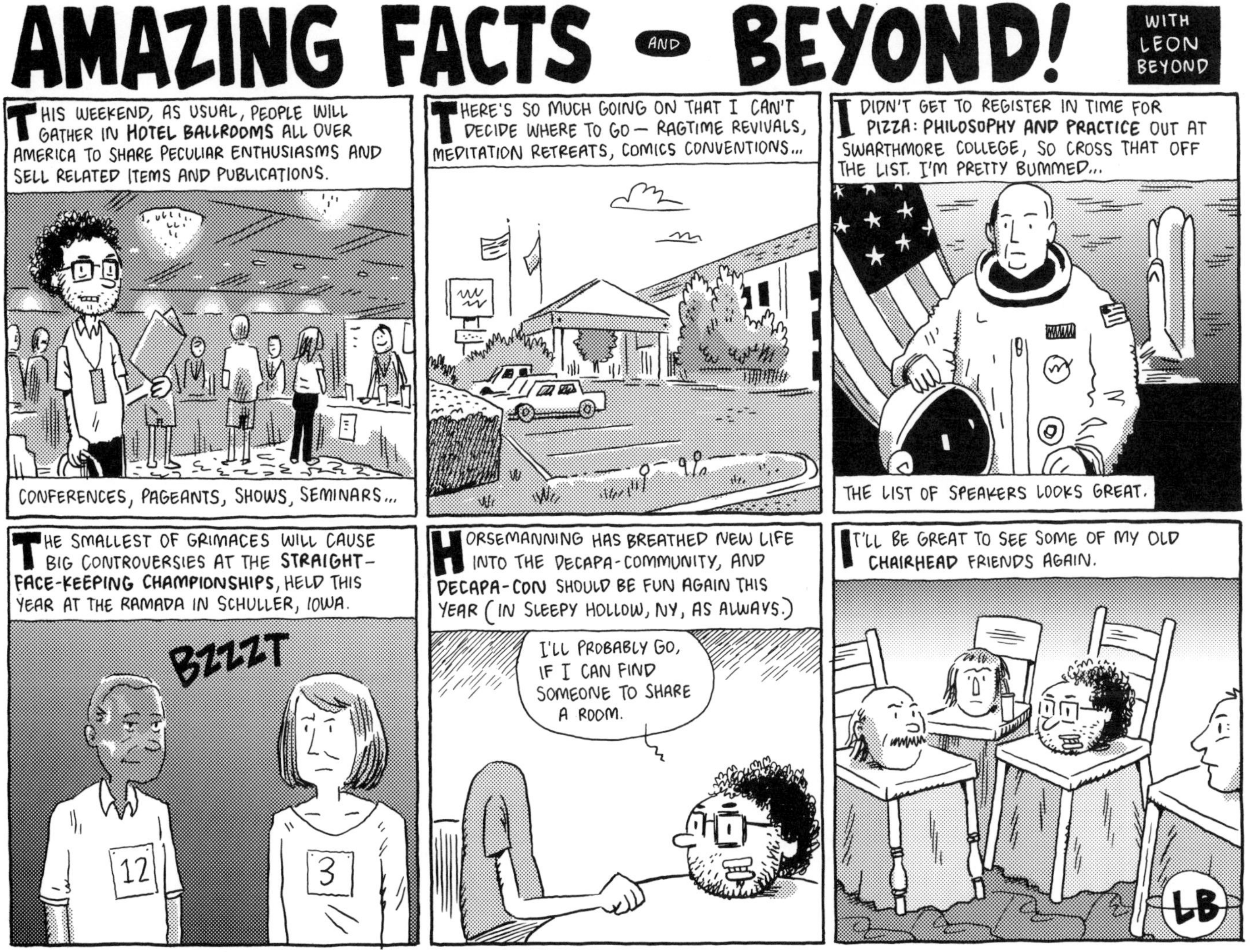
AMAZING FACTS AND BEYOND!
WITH LEON BEYOND
THIS WEEKEND, AS USUAL, PEOPLE WILL GATHER IN HOTEL BALLROOMS ALL OVER AMERICA TO SHARE PECULIAR ENTHUSIASMS AND SELL RELATED ITEMS AND PUBLICATIONS.
CONFERENCES, PAGEANTS, SHOWS, SEMINARS...
THERE'S SO MUCH GOING ON THAT I CAN'T DECIDE WHERE TO GO — RAGTIME REVIVALS, MEDITATION RETREATS, COMICS CONVENTIONS...
I DIDN'T GET TO REGISTER IN TIME FOR PIZZA: PHILOSOPHY AND PRACTICE OUT AT SWARTHMORE COLLEGE, SO CROSS THAT OFF THE LIST. I'M PRETTY BUMMED...
THE LIST OF SPEAKERS LOOKS GREAT.
THE SMALLEST OF GRIMACES WILL CAUSE BIG CONTROVERSIES AT THE STRAIGHT-FACE-KEEPING CHAMPIONSHIPS, HELD THIS YEAR AT THE RAMADA IN SCHULLER, IOWA.
BZZZT
12
3
HORSEMANNING HAS BREATHED NEW LIFE INTO THE DECAPA-COMMUNITY, AND DECAPA-CON SHOULD BE FUN AGAIN THIS YEAR (IN SLEEPY HOLLOW, NY, AS ALWAYS.)
I'LL PROBABLY GO, IF I CAN FIND SOMEONE TO SHARE A ROOM.
IT'LL BE GREAT TO SEE SOME OF MY OLD CHAIRHEAD FRIENDS AGAIN.
LB

ST. LOUIS

STATUE OF KING LOUIS IX
OF FRANCE, NAMESAKE
OF ST. LOUIS, MISSOURI

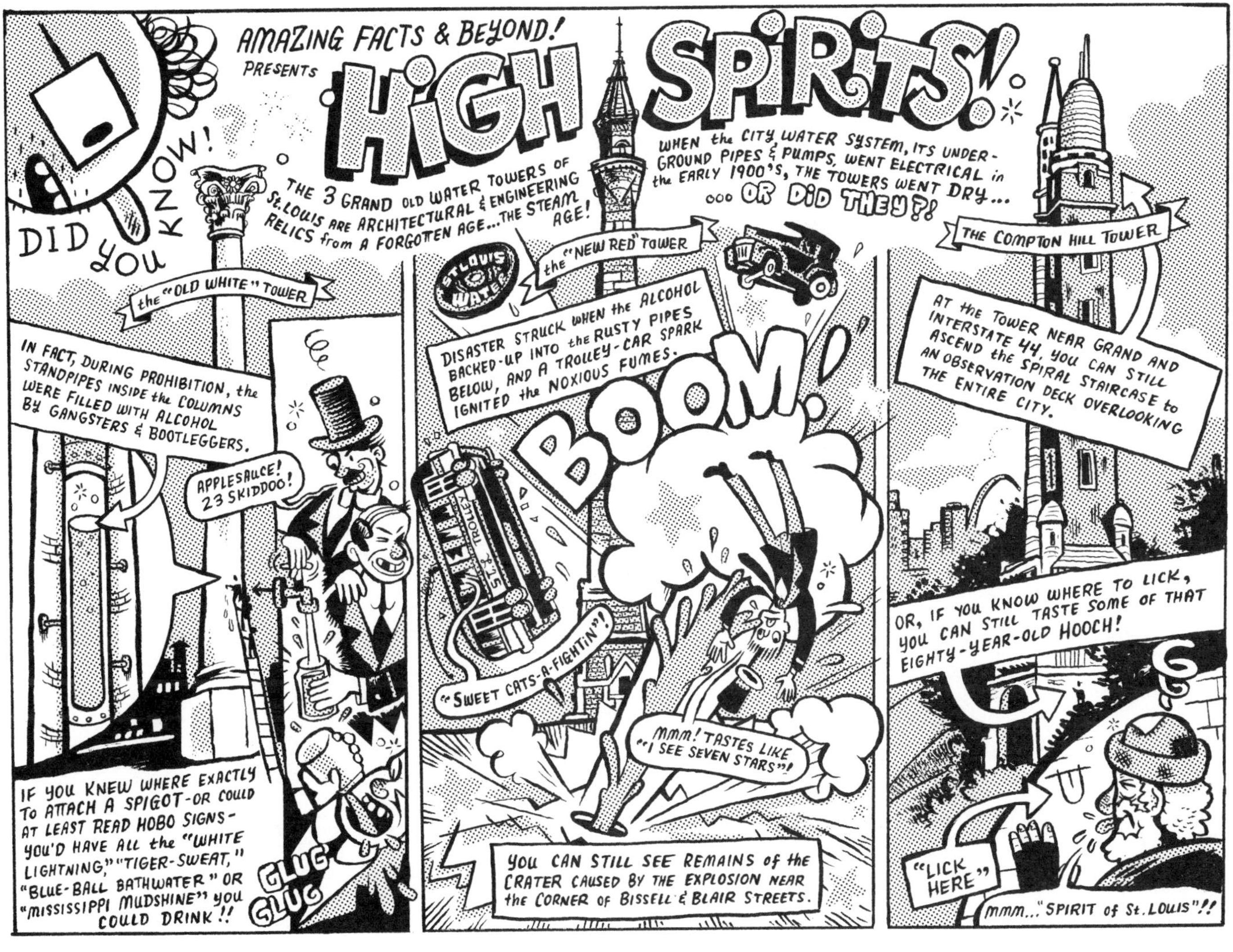
AMAZING FACTS & BEYOND!
PRESENTS
HIGH SPIRITS!
DID YOU KNOW!
THE 3 GRAND OLD WATER TOWERS OF ST. LOUIS ARE ARCHITECTURAL & ENGINEERING RELICS FROM A FORGOTTEN AGE... THE STEAM AGE!
WHEN THE CITY WATER SYSTEM, ITS UNDERGROUND PIPES & PUMPS, WENT ELECTRICAL IN THE EARLY 1900'S, THE TOWERS WENT DRY...
... OR DID THEY?!
THE "OLD WHITE" TOWER
THE "NEW RED" TOWER
THE COMPTON HILL TOWER
ST. LOUIS WATER
IN FACT, DURING PROHIBITION, THE STANDPIPES INSIDE THE COLUMNS WERE FILLED WITH ALCOHOL BY GANGSTERS & BOOTLEGGERS.
APPLESAUCE! 23 SKIDDOO!
IF YOU KNEW WHERE EXACTLY TO ATTACH A SPIGOT - OR COULD AT LEAST READ HOBO SIGNS - YOU'D HAVE ALL THE "WHITE LIGHTNING," "TIGER-SWEAT," "BLUE-BALL BATHWATER" OR "MISSISSIPPI MUDSHINE" YOU COULD DRINK!!
GLUG GLUG
DISASTER STRUCK WHEN THE ALCOHOL BACKED-UP INTO THE RUSTY PIPES BELOW, AND A TROLLEY-CAR SPARK IGNITED THE NOXIOUS FUMES.
BOOM!
ST. L. TROLLEY
"SWEET CATS-A-FIGHTIN'!"
MMM! TASTES LIKE "I SEE SEVEN STARS"!
YOU CAN STILL SEE REMAINS OF THE CRATER CAUSED BY THE EXPLOSION NEAR THE CORNER OF BISSELL & BLAIR STREETS.
AT THE TOWER NEAR GRAND AND INTERSTATE 44, YOU CAN STILL ASCEND THE SPIRAL STAIRCASE TO AN OBSERVATION DECK OVERLOOKING THE ENTIRE CITY.
OR, IF YOU KNOW WHERE TO LICK, YOU CAN STILL TASTE SOME OF THAT EIGHTY-YEAR-OLD HOOCH!
"LICK HERE"
MMM..."SPIRIT OF ST. LOUIS"!!

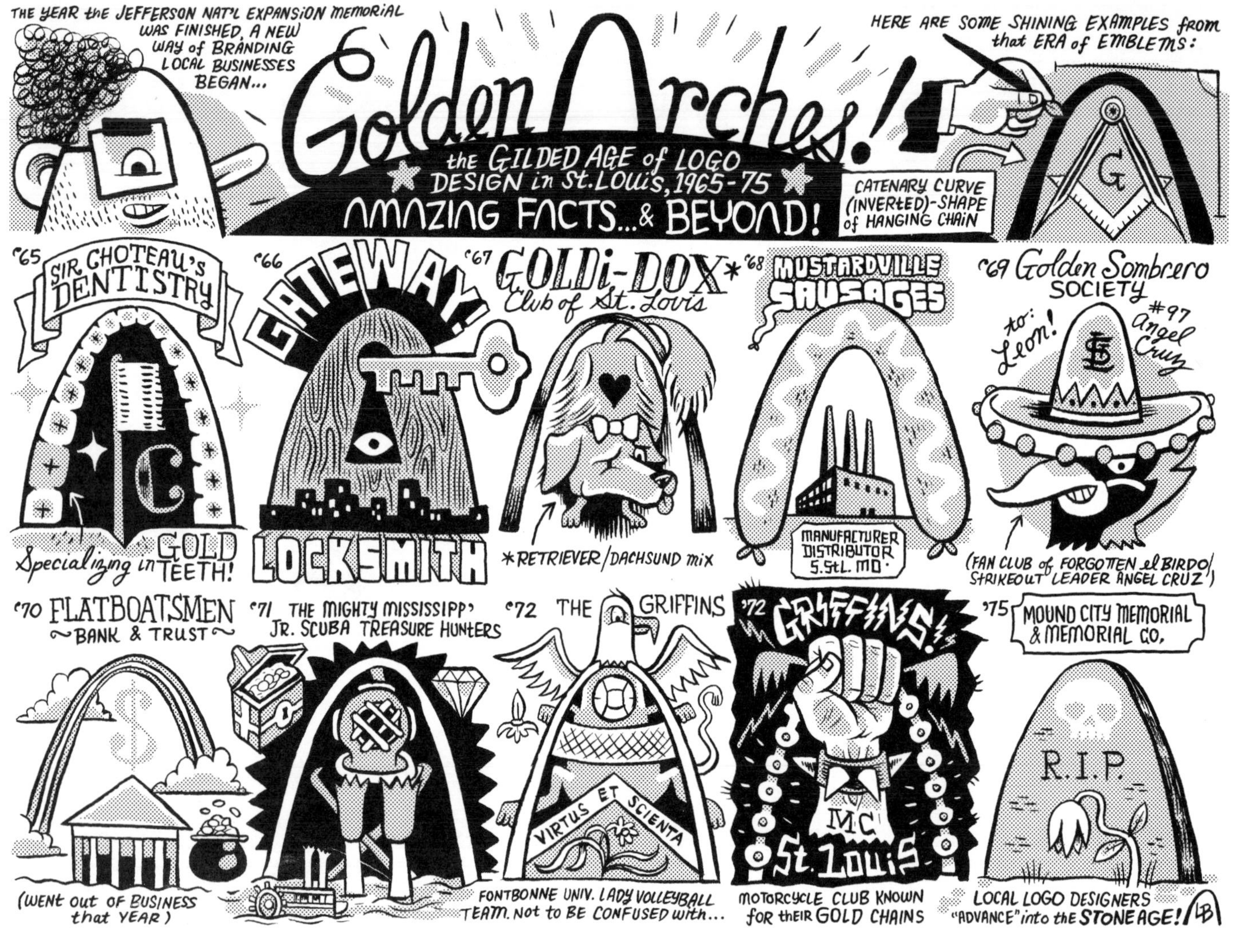

THE YEAR the JEFFERSON NAT'L EXPANSION MEMORIAL WAS FINISHED, A NEW WAY of BRANDING LOCAL BUSINESSES BEGAN...
Golden Arches!
the GILDED AGE of LOGO DESIGN in St. Louis, 1965-75
AMAZING FACTS...& BEYOND!
HERE ARE SOME SHINING EXAMPLES from that ERA of EMBLEMS:
CATENARY CURVE (INVERTED)-SHAPE of HANGING CHAIN
G
'65 SIR CHOTEAU's DENTISTRY
C
Specializing in GOLD TEETH!
'66 GATEWAY! LOCKSMITH
'67 GOLDi-DOX* Club of St. Louis
*RETRIEVER/DACHSUND mix
'68 MUSTARDVILLE SAUSAGES
MANUFACTURER DISTRIBUTOR S.Stl. MO.
'69 Golden Sombrero SOCIETY
to: Leon!
#97 Angel Cruz
(FAN CLUB of FORGOTTEN el BIRDO/ STRIKEOUT LEADER ANGEL CRUZ)
'70 FLATBOATSMEN ~BANK & TRUST~
$
(WENT out of BUSINESS that YEAR)
'71 THE MIGHTY MISSISSIPP' JR. SCUBA TREASURE HUNTERS
'72 THE GRIFFINS
VIRTUS ET SCIENTA
FONTBONNE UNIV. LADY VOLLEYBALL TEAM. Not to BE CONFUSED with...
'72 GRIFFINS!
MC
St. Louis
MOTORCYCLE CLUB KNOWN FOR their GOLD CHAINS
'75 MOUND CITY MEMORIAL & MEMORIAL CO.
R.I.P.
LOCAL LOGO DESIGNERS "ADVANCE" into the STONE AGE!
LB

AMAZING FACTS... AND BEYOND!

WITH LEON BEYOND

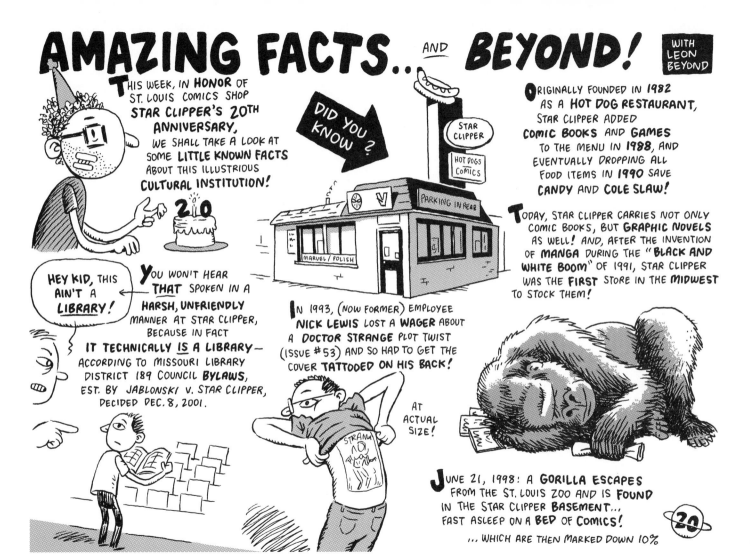

THIS WEEK, IN **HONOR** OF ST. LOUIS COMICS SHOP **STAR CLIPPER'S 20TH ANNIVERSARY**, WE SHALL TAKE A LOOK AT SOME **LITTLE KNOWN FACTS** ABOUT THIS ILLUSTRIOUS **CULTURAL INSTITUTION!**

DID YOU KNOW?

STAR CLIPPER

HOT DOGS COMICS

PARKING IN REAR

MARVEL / POLISH

ORIGINALLY FOUNDED IN **1982** AS A **HOT DOG RESTAURANT**, STAR CLIPPER ADDED **COMIC BOOKS** AND **GAMES** TO THE MENU IN **1988**, AND EVENTUALLY DROPPING ALL FOOD ITEMS IN **1990** SAVE **CANDY** AND **COLE SLAW!**

TODAY, STAR CLIPPER CARRIES NOT ONLY COMIC BOOKS, BUT **GRAPHIC NOVELS** AS WELL! AND, AFTER THE INVENTION OF **MANGA** DURING THE "**BLACK AND WHITE BOOM**" OF 1991, STAR CLIPPER WAS THE **FIRST** STORE IN THE **MIDWEST** TO STOCK THEM!

HEY KID, THIS AIN'T A **LIBRARY!**

YOU WON'T HEAR **THAT** SPOKEN IN A **HARSH, UNFRIENDLY** MANNER AT STAR CLIPPER, BECAUSE IN FACT **IT TECHNICALLY IS A LIBRARY**— ACCORDING TO MISSOURI LIBRARY DISTRICT 189 COUNCIL **BYLAWS**, EST. BY JABLONSKI V. STAR CLIPPER, DECIDED DEC. 8, 2001.

IN 1993, (NOW FORMER) EMPLOYEE **NICK LEWIS** LOST A **WAGER** ABOUT A **DOCTOR STRANGE** PLOT TWIST (ISSUE #53) AND SO HAD TO GET THE COVER **TATTOOED ON HIS BACK!**

AT ACTUAL SIZE!

STRANGE

JUNE 21, 1998: A **GORILLA** ESCAPES FROM THE ST. LOUIS ZOO AND IS **FOUND** IN THE STAR CLIPPER BASEMENT... FAST ASLEEP ON A **BED** OF COMICS! ... WHICH ARE THEN MARKED DOWN 10%

20

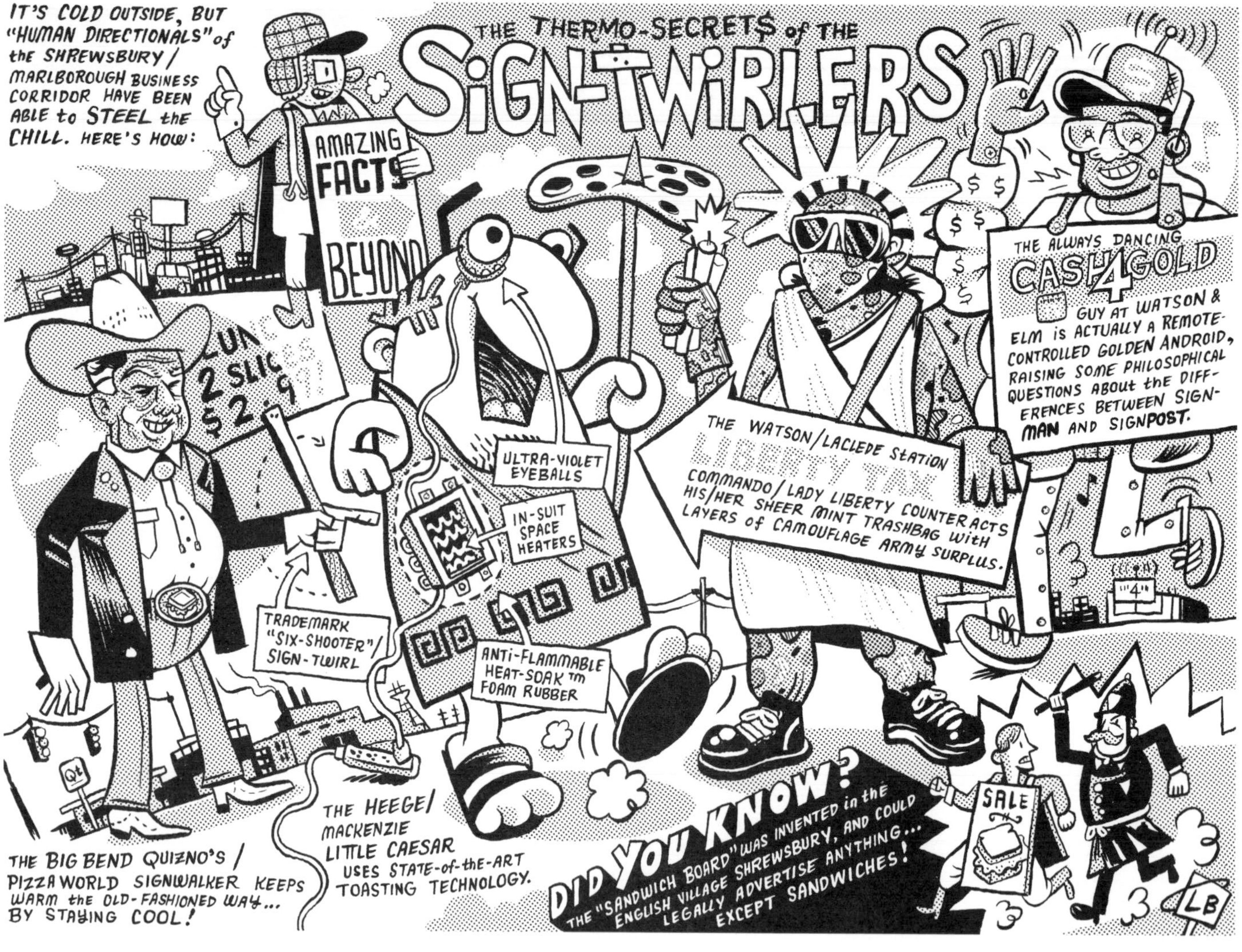
IT'S COLD OUTSIDE, BUT "HUMAN DIRECTIONALS" of the SHREWSBURY/ MARLBOROUGH BUSINESS CORRIDOR HAVE BEEN ABLE to STEEL the CHILL. HERE'S HOW:
THE THERMO-SECRET$ of THE SIGN-TWIRLERS
AMAZING FACTS & BEYOND
THE ALWAYS DANCING CASH 4 GOLD GUY AT WATSON & ELM is ACTUALLY A REMOTE-CONTROLLED GOLDEN ANDROID, RAISING SOME PHILOSOPHICAL QUESTIONS ABOUT the DIFFERENCES BETWEEN SIGN-MAN AND SIGNPOST.
ULTRA-VIOLET EYEBALLS
IN-SUIT SPACE HEATERS
THE WATSON/LACLEDE STATION COMMANDO/LADY LIBERTY COUNTERACTS HIS/HER SHEER MINT TRASHBAG WITH LAYERS of CAMOUFLAGE ARMY SURPLUS.
TRADEMARK "SIX-SHOOTER"/ SIGN-TWIRL
ANTI-FLAMMABLE HEAT-SOAK™ FOAM RUBBER
THE BIG BEND QUIZNO'S / PIZZA WORLD SIGNWALKER KEEPS WARM the OLD-FASHIONED WAY... BY STAYING COOL!
THE HEEGE/ MACKENZIE LITTLE CAESAR USES STATE-of-the-ART TOASTING TECHNOLOGY.
DID YOU KNOW? THE "SANDWICH BOARD" WAS INVENTED in the ENGLISH VILLAGE SHREWSBURY, AND COULD LEGALLY ADVERTISE ANYTHING... EXCEPT SANDWICHES!
SALE
LB

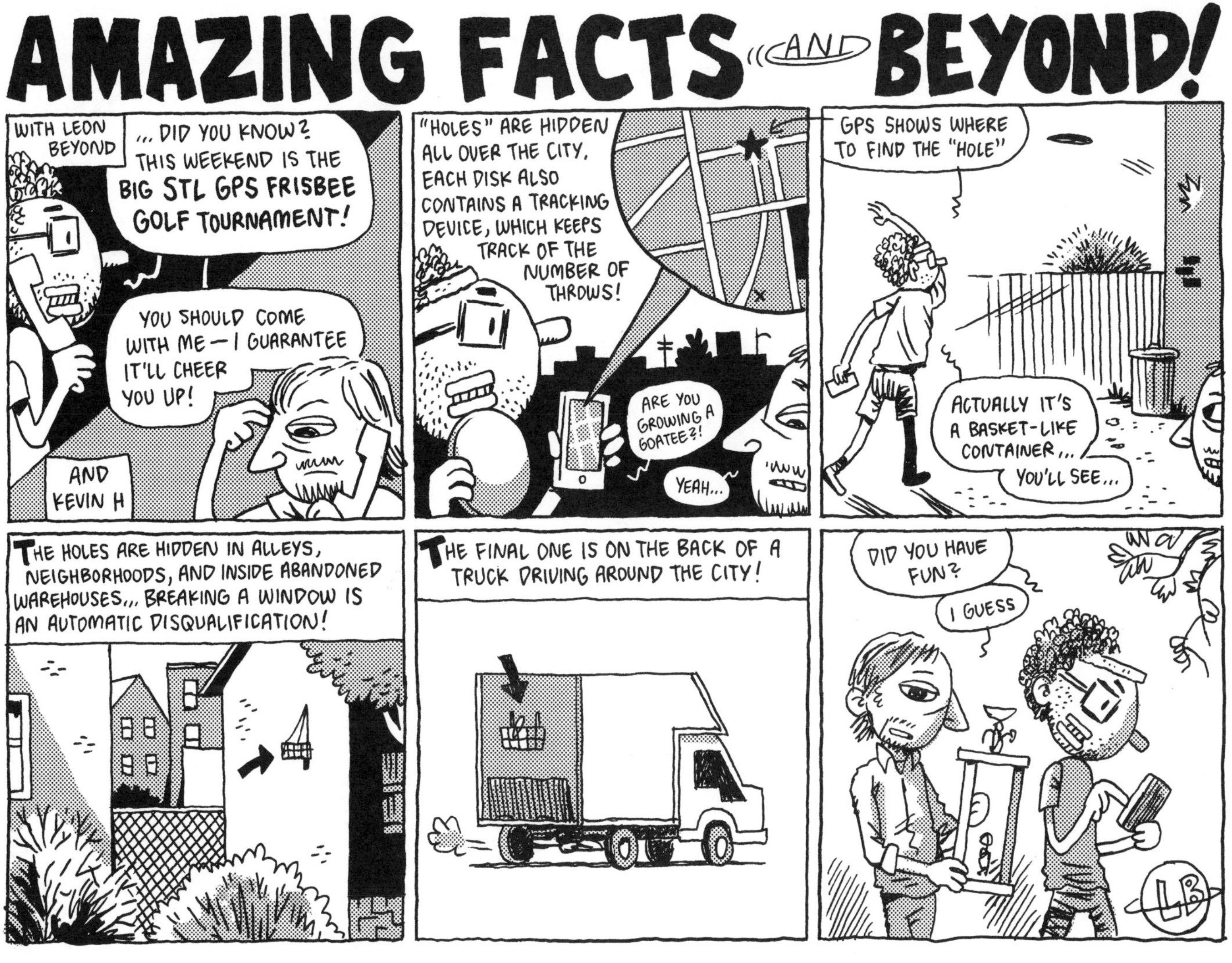
AMAZING FACTS AND BEYOND!
WITH LEON BEYOND
... DID YOU KNOW? THIS WEEKEND IS THE BIG STL GPS FRISBEE GOLF TOURNAMENT!
YOU SHOULD COME WITH ME — I GUARANTEE IT'LL CHEER YOU UP!
AND KEVIN H
"HOLES" ARE HIDDEN ALL OVER THE CITY, EACH DISK ALSO CONTAINS A TRACKING DEVICE, WHICH KEEPS TRACK OF THE NUMBER OF THROWS!
ARE YOU GROWING A GOATEE?!
YEAH...
GPS SHOWS WHERE TO FIND THE "HOLE"
ACTUALLY IT'S A BASKET-LIKE CONTAINER...
YOU'LL SEE...
THE HOLES ARE HIDDEN IN ALLEYS, NEIGHBORHOODS, AND INSIDE ABANDONED WAREHOUSES... BREAKING A WINDOW IS AN AUTOMATIC DISQUALIFICATION!
THE FINAL ONE IS ON THE BACK OF A TRUCK DRIVING AROUND THE CITY!
DID YOU HAVE FUN?
I GUESS
LB

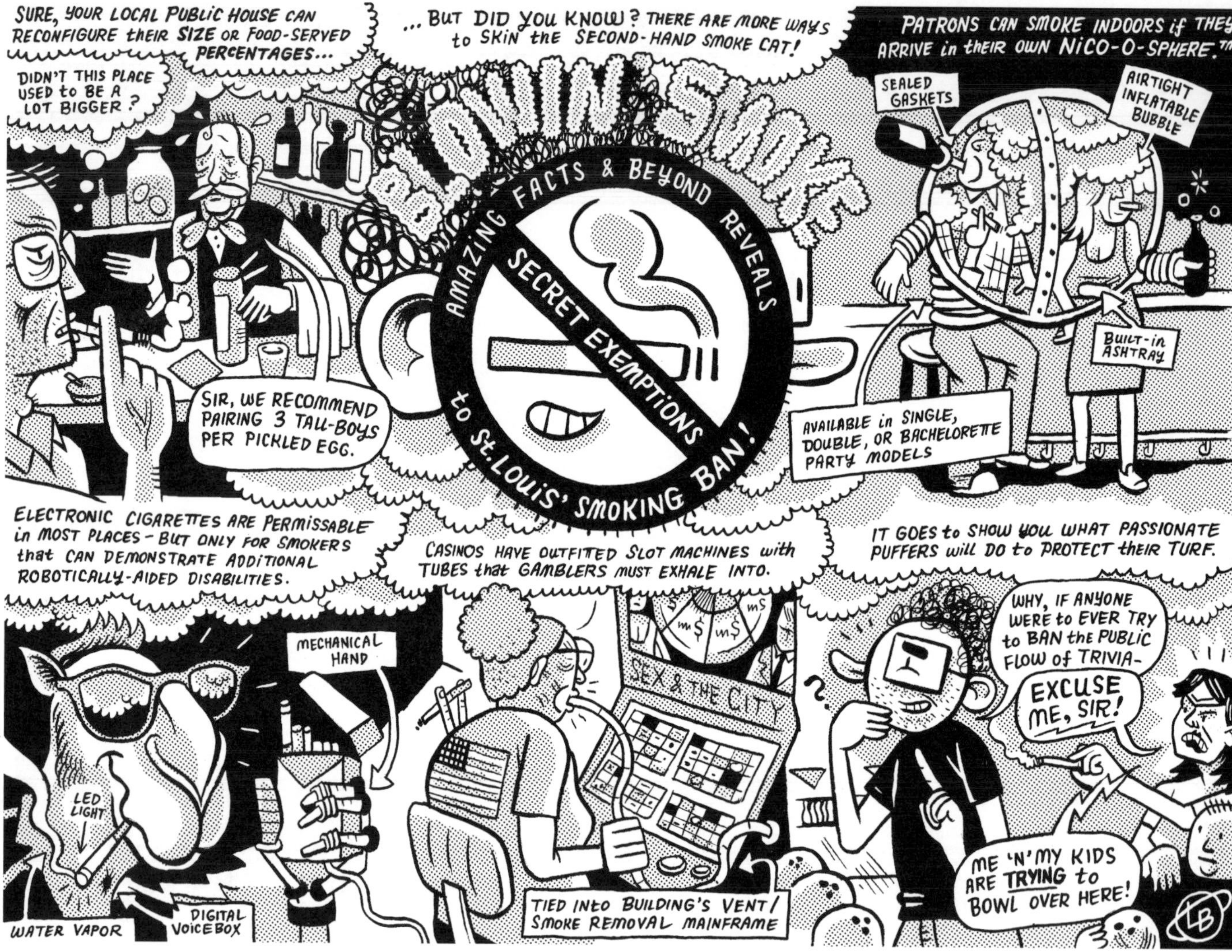

SURE, YOUR LOCAL PUBLIC HOUSE CAN RECONFIGURE their SIZE OR FOOD-SERVED PERCENTAGES...
...BUT DID YOU KNOW? THERE ARE MORE WAYS to SKIN the SECOND-HAND SMOKE CAT!
BLOWIN' SMOKE
AMAZING FACTS & BEYOND REVEALS
SECRET EXEMPTIONS
to St. Louis' SMOKING BAN!
DIDN'T THIS PLACE USED to BE A LOT BIGGER?
SIR, WE RECOMMEND PAIRING 3 TALL-BOYS PER PICKLED EGG.
PATRONS CAN SMOKE INDOORS if THEY ARRIVE in their OWN NICO-O-SPHERE.™
SEALED GASKETS
AIRTIGHT INFLATABLE BUBBLE
BUILT-in ASHTRAY
AVAILABLE in SINGLE, DOUBLE, OR BACHELORETTE PARTY MODELS
ELECTRONIC CIGARETTES ARE PERMISSABLE in MOST PLACES - BUT ONLY FOR SMOKERS that CAN DEMONSTRATE ADDITIONAL ROBOTICALLY-AIDED DISABILITIES.
MECHANICAL HAND
LED LIGHT
WATER VAPOR
DIGITAL VOICEBOX
CASINOS HAVE OUTFITTED SLOT MACHINES with TUBES that GAMBLERS MUST EXHALE INTO.
SEX & THE CITY
TIED INTO BUILDING'S VENT/ SMOKE REMOVAL MAINFRAME
IT GOES to SHOW YOU WHAT PASSIONATE PUFFERS will DO to PROTECT their TURF.
WHY, IF ANYONE WERE to EVER TRY to BAN the PUBLIC FLOW of TRIVIA-
EXCUSE ME, SIR!
ME 'N' MY KIDS ARE TRYING to BOWL OVER HERE!
LB

FOOD

FRUIT ROLL-UP CRANE FLAMBÉ

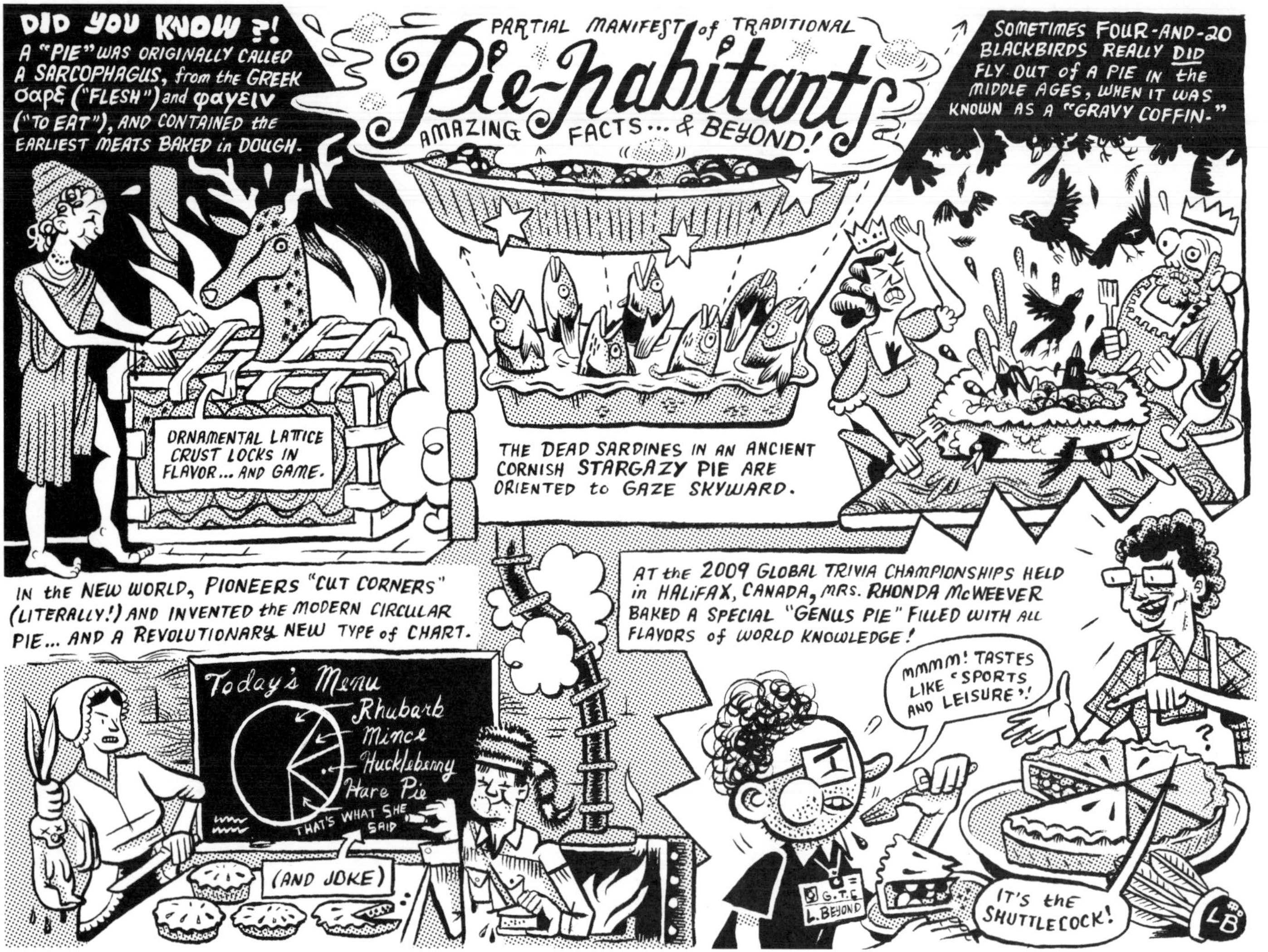
PARTIAL MANIFEST of TRADITIONAL
Pie-habitants
AMAZING FACTS... & BEYOND!
DID YOU KNOW ?!
A "PIE" WAS ORIGINALLY CALLED A SARCOPHAGUS, from the GREEK σαρξ ("FLESH") and φαγειν ("TO EAT"), AND CONTAINED the EARLIEST MEATS BAKED in DOUGH.
ORNAMENTAL LATTICE CRUST LOCKS IN FLAVOR... AND GAME.
THE DEAD SARDINES IN AN ANCIENT CORNISH STARGAZY PIE ARE ORIENTED to GAZE SKYWARD.
SOMETIMES FOUR-AND-20 BLACKBIRDS REALLY DID FLY OUT of A PIE IN the MIDDLE AGES, WHEN IT WAS KNOWN AS A "GRAVY COFFIN."
IN the NEW WORLD, PIONEERS "CUT CORNERS" (LITERALLY!) AND INVENTED the MODERN CIRCULAR PIE... AND A REVOLUTIONARY NEW TYPE of CHART.
Today's Menu
Rhubarb
Mince
Huckleberry
Hare Pie
THAT'S WHAT SHE SAID
(AND JOKE)
AT the 2009 GLOBAL TRIVIA CHAMPIONSHIPS HELD in HALIFAX, CANADA, MRS. RHONDA McWEEVER BAKED A SPECIAL "GENUS PIE" FILLED WITH ALL FLAVORS of WORLD KNOWLEDGE!
MMMM! TASTES LIKE 'SPORTS AND LEISURE'!
G.T.C.
L. BEYOND
IT'S the SHUTTLECOCK!
LB

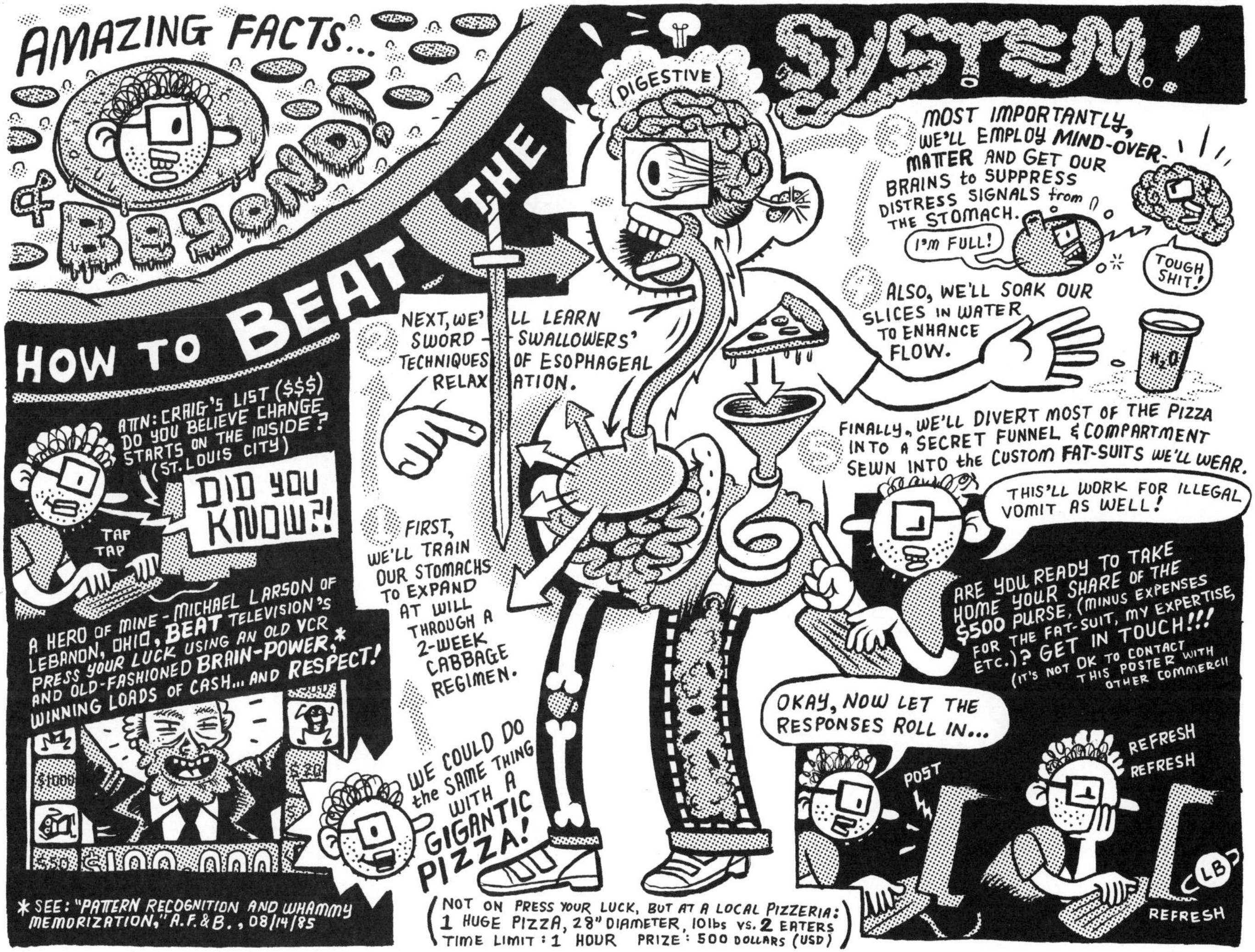
AMAZING FACTS...
& BEYOND!
HOW TO BEAT THE (DIGESTIVE) SYSTEM!
ATTN: CRAIG'S LIST ($$$) DO YOU BELIEVE CHANGE STARTS ON THE INSIDE? (ST. LOUIS CITY)
TAP TAP
DID YOU KNOW?!
A HERO OF MINE - MICHAEL LARSON OF LEBANON, OHIO, BEAT TELEVISION'S PRESS YOUR LUCK USING AN OLD VCR AND OLD-FASHIONED BRAIN-POWER,* WINNING LOADS OF CASH... AND RESPECT!
$100,000
WE COULD DO the SAME THING WITH A GIGANTIC PIZZA!
* SEE: "PATTERN RECOGNITION AND WHAMMY MEMORIZATION," A.F.&B., 08/14/85
FIRST, WE'LL TRAIN OUR STOMACHS TO EXPAND AT WILL THROUGH A 2-WEEK CABBAGE REGIMEN.
NEXT, WE'LL LEARN SWORD-SWALLOWERS' TECHNIQUES OF ESOPHAGEAL RELAXATION.
MOST IMPORTANTLY, WE'LL EMPLOY MIND-OVER-MATTER AND GET OUR BRAINS to SUPPRESS DISTRESS SIGNALS from THE STOMACH.
I'M FULL!
TOUGH SHIT!
ALSO, WE'LL SOAK OUR SLICES IN WATER TO ENHANCE FLOW.
H₂O
FINALLY, WE'LL DIVERT MOST OF THE PIZZA INTO A SECRET FUNNEL & COMPARTMENT SEWN INTO the CUSTOM FAT-SUITS WE'LL WEAR.
THIS'LL WORK FOR ILLEGAL VOMIT AS WELL!
ARE YOU READY TO TAKE HOME YOUR SHARE OF THE $500 PURSE, (MINUS EXPENSES FOR THE FAT-SUIT, MY EXPERTISE, ETC.)? GET IN TOUCH!!!
(IT'S NOT OK TO CONTACT THIS POSTER WITH OTHER COMMERCI
OKAY, NOW LET THE RESPONSES ROLL IN...
POST
REFRESH
REFRESH
REFRESH
(NOT ON PRESS YOUR LUCK, BUT AT A LOCAL PIZZERIA: 1 HUGE PIZZA, 28" DIAMETER, 10lbs vs. 2 EATERS TIME LIMIT: 1 HOUR PRIZE: 500 DOLLARS (USD))
LB

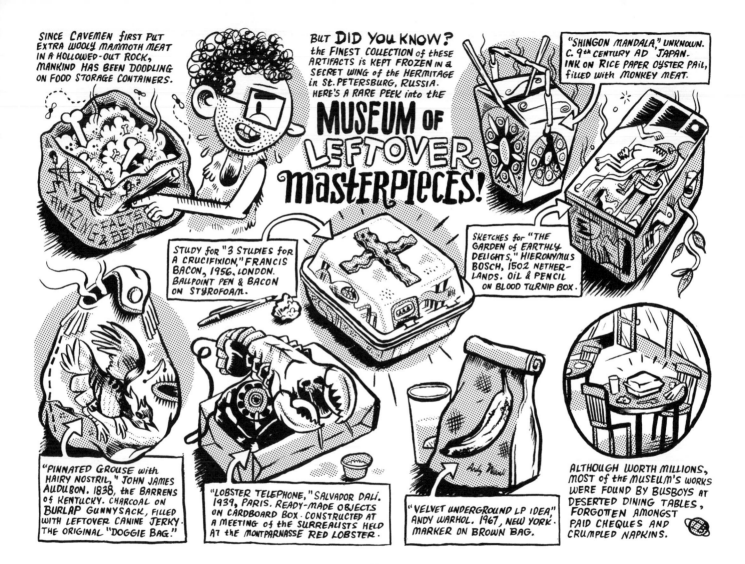

SINCE CAVEMEN FIRST PUT EXTRA WOOLY MAMMOTH MEAT IN A HOLLOWED-OUT ROCK, MANKIND HAS BEEN DOODLING ON FOOD STORAGE CONTAINERS.

BUT DID YOU KNOW? THE FINEST COLLECTION OF THESE ARTIFACTS IS KEPT FROZEN IN A SECRET WING OF THE HERMITAGE IN ST. PETERSBURG, RUSSIA. HERE'S A RARE PEEK INTO THE

MUSEUM OF LEFTOVER masterpieces!

"SHINGON MANDALA," UNKNOWN. C. 9th CENTURY AD JAPAN. INK ON RICE PAPER OYSTER PAIL, FILLED WITH MONKEY MEAT.

STUDY FOR "3 STUDIES FOR A CRUCIFIXION," FRANCIS BACON, 1956, LONDON. BALLPOINT PEN & BACON ON STYROFOAM.

SKETCHES FOR "THE GARDEN OF EARTHLY DELIGHTS," HIERONYMUS BOSCH, 1502 NETHERLANDS. OIL & PENCIL ON BLOOD TURNIP BOX.

"PINNATED GROUSE with HAIRY NOSTRIL," JOHN JAMES AUDUBON, 1838, THE BARRENS OF KENTUCKY. CHARCOAL ON BURLAP GUNNYSACK, FILLED WITH LEFTOVER CANINE JERKY. THE ORIGINAL "DOGGIE BAG."

"LOBSTER TELEPHONE," SALVADOR DALÍ, 1939, PARIS. READY-MADE OBJECTS ON CARDBOARD BOX. CONSTRUCTED AT A MEETING OF THE SURREALISTS HELD AT THE MONTPARNASSE RED LOBSTER.

"VELVET UNDERGROUND LP IDEA," ANDY WARHOL, 1967, NEW YORK. MARKER ON BROWN BAG.

ALTHOUGH WORTH MILLIONS, MOST OF THE MUSEUM'S WORKS WERE FOUND BY BUSBOYS AT DESERTED DINING TABLES, FORGOTTEN AMONGST PAID CHEQUES AND CRUMPLED NAPKINS.

76

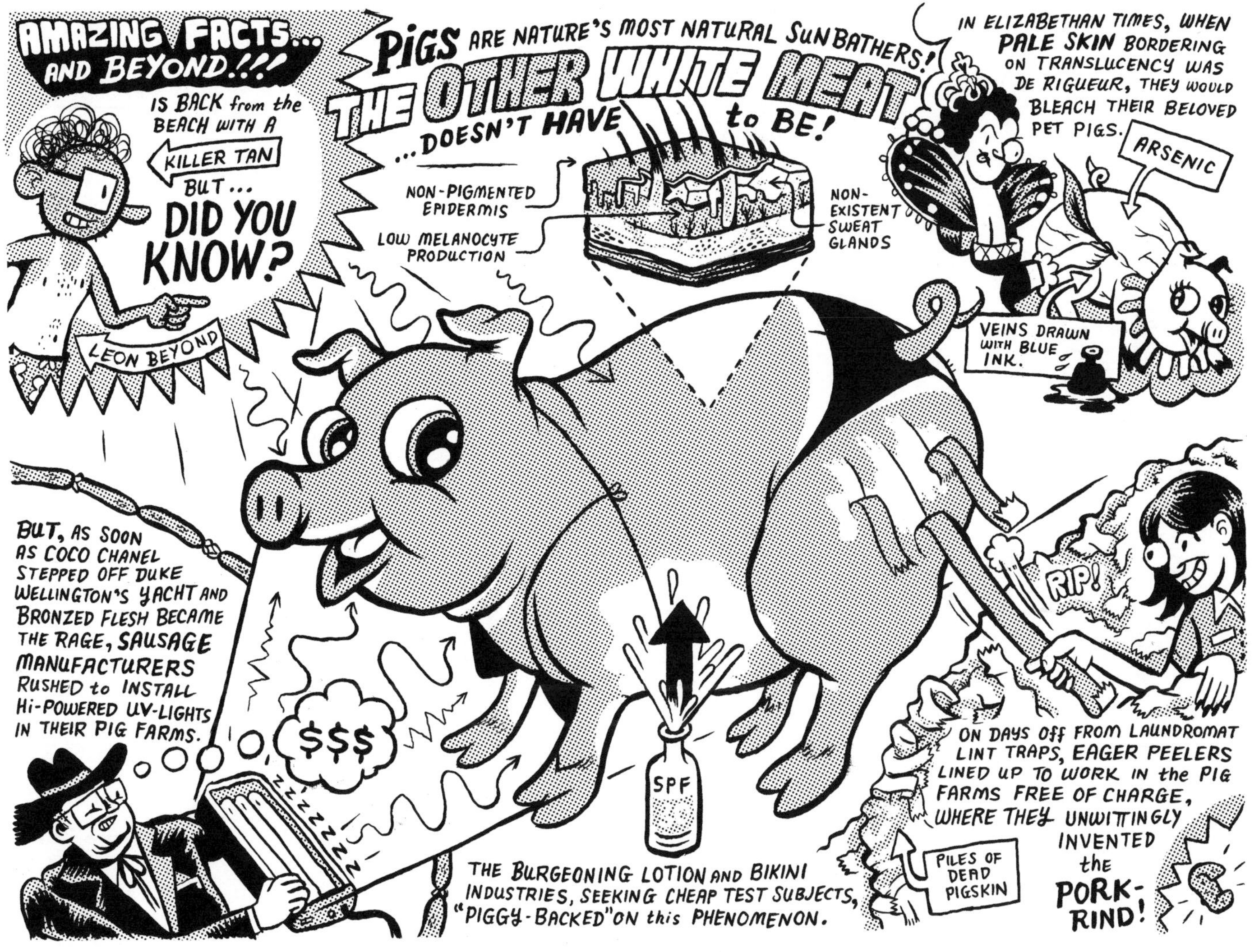
AMAZING FACTS... AND BEYOND!!!
IS BACK from the BEACH WITH A
KILLER TAN
BUT... DID YOU KNOW?
LEON BEYOND
PIGS ARE NATURE'S MOST NATURAL SUNBATHERS!
THE OTHER WHITE MEAT ...DOESN'T HAVE to BE!
NON-PIGMENTED EPIDERMIS
LOW MELANOCYTE PRODUCTION
NON-EXISTENT SWEAT GLANDS
IN ELIZABETHAN TIMES, WHEN PALE SKIN BORDERING ON TRANSLUCENCY WAS DE RIGUEUR, THEY WOULD BLEACH THEIR BELOVED PET PIGS.
ARSENIC
VEINS DRAWN WITH BLUE INK.
BUT, AS SOON AS COCO CHANEL STEPPED OFF DUKE WELLINGTON'S YACHT AND BRONZED FLESH BECAME THE RAGE, SAUSAGE MANUFACTURERS RUSHED to INSTALL Hi-POWERED UV-LIGHTS IN THEIR PIG FARMS.
$$$
SPF
RIP!
THE BURGEONING LOTION AND BIKINI INDUSTRIES, SEEKING CHEAP TEST SUBJECTS, "PIGGY-BACKED" ON this PHENOMENON.
ON DAYS OFF FROM LAUNDROMAT LINT TRAPS, EAGER PEELERS LINED UP TO WORK IN the PIG FARMS FREE OF CHARGE, WHERE THEY UNWITTINGLY INVENTED the PORK-RIND!
PILES OF DEAD PIGSKIN

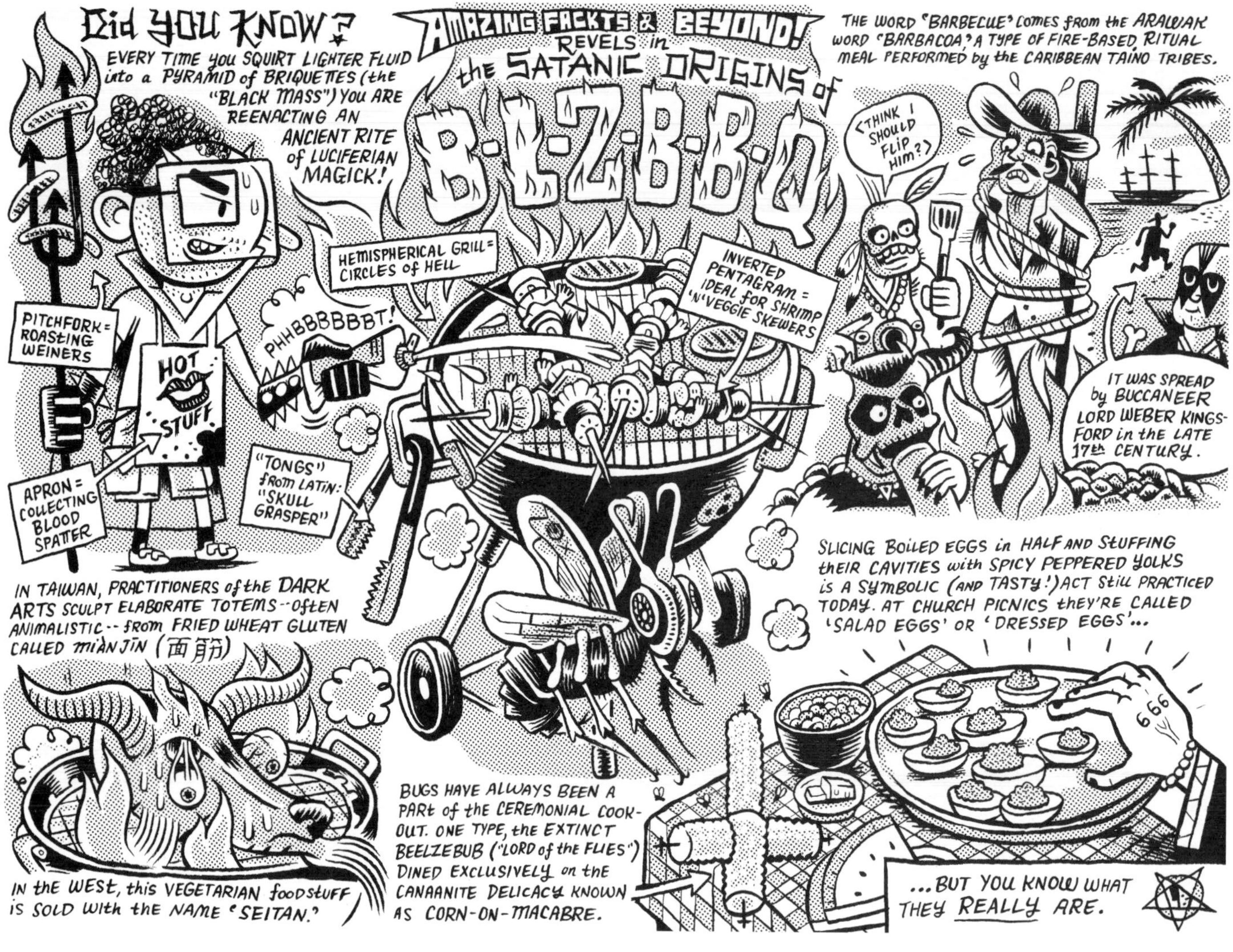
AMAZING FACKTS & BEYOND! REVELS in the SATANIC ORIGINS of
B-L-Z-B-B-Q
Did YOU KNOW?
EVERY TIME you SQUIRT LIGHTER FLUID into a PYRAMID of BRIQUETTES (the "BLACK MASS") YOU ARE REENACTING AN ANCIENT RITE of LUCIFERIAN MAGICK!
PITCHFORK = ROASTING WEINERS
HOT STUFF
APRON = COLLECTING BLOOD SPATTER
PHHBBBBBBT!
HEMISPHERICAL GRILL = CIRCLES of HELL
"TONGS" from LATIN: "SKULL GRASPER"
INVERTED PENTAGRAM = IDEAL FOR SHRIMP 'N' VEGGIE SKEWERS
THE WORD 'BARBECUE' COMES from the ARAWAK WORD 'BARBACOA,' A TYPE OF FIRE-BASED RITUAL MEAL PERFORMED by the CARIBBEAN TAINO TRIBES.
<THINK I SHOULD FLIP HIM?>
IT WAS SPREAD by BUCCANEER LORD WEBER KINGSFORD in the LATE 17th CENTURY.
IN TAIWAN, PRACTITIONERS of the DARK ARTS SCULPT ELABORATE TOTEMS--often ANIMALISTIC--from FRIED WHEAT GLUTEN CALLED MIÀNJĪN (面筋)
IN the WEST, this VEGETARIAN foodstuff is SOLD with the NAME 'SEITAN.'
BUGS HAVE ALWAYS BEEN A PART of the CEREMONIAL COOK-OUT. ONE TYPE, the EXTINCT BEELZEBUB ("LORD of the FLIES") DINED EXCLUSIVELY on the CANAANITE DELICACY KNOWN AS CORN-ON-MACABRE.
SLICING BOILED EGGS in HALF AND STUFFING their CAVITIES with SPICY PEPPERED YOLKS is A SYMBOLIC (AND TASTY!) ACT Still PRACTICED TODAY. AT CHURCH PICNICS they're CALLED 'SALAD EGGS' OR 'DRESSED EGGS'...
666
...BUT YOU KNOW WHAT THEY REALLY ARE.

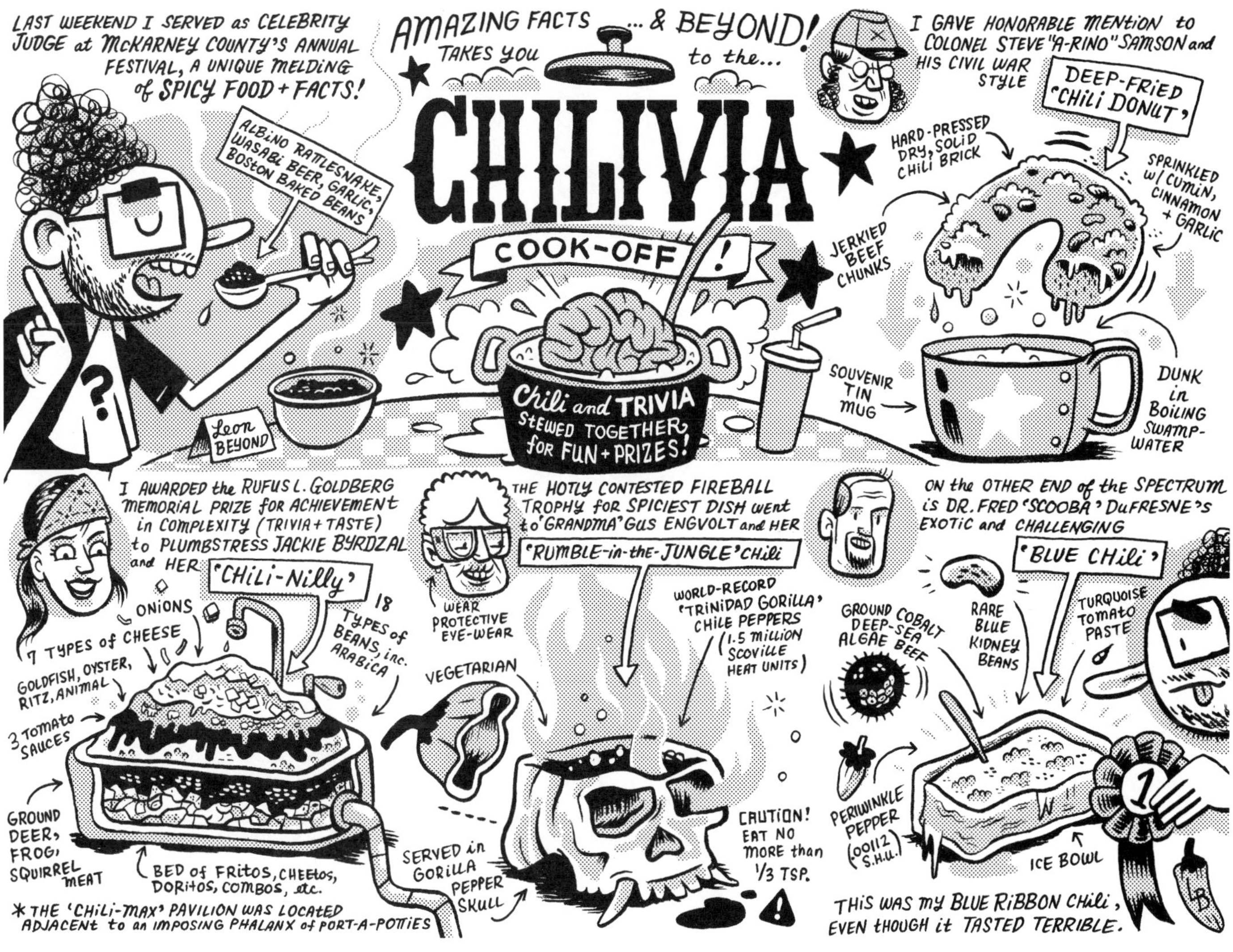
LAST WEEKEND I SERVED as CELEBRITY JUDGE at McKARNEY COUNTY'S ANNUAL FESTIVAL, A UNIQUE MELDING of SPICY FOOD + FACTS!
AMAZING FACTS ... & BEYOND! TAKES you to the...
CHILIVIA
COOK-OFF!
Chili and TRIVIA STEWED TOGETHER for FUN + PRIZES!
ALBINO RATTLESNAKE, WASABI BEER, GARLIC, BOSTON BAKED BEANS
Leon BEYOND
I GAVE HONORABLE MENTION to COLONEL STEVE "A-RINO" SAMSON and HIS CIVIL WAR STYLE
DEEP-FRIED 'CHILI DONUT'
HARD-PRESSED DRY, SOLID CHILI BRICK
SPRINKLED w/ CUMIN, CINNAMON + GARLIC
JERKIED BEEF CHUNKS
SOUVENIR TIN MUG
DUNK in BOILING SWAMP-WATER
I AWARDED the RUFUS L. GOLDBERG MEMORIAL PRIZE for ACHIEVEMENT in COMPLEXITY (TRIVIA + TASTE) to PLUMBSTRESS JACKIE BYRDZAL and HER
'CHILI-NILLY'
ONIONS
7 TYPES of CHEESE
18 TYPES of BEANS, inc. ARABICA
GOLDFISH, OYSTER, RITZ, ANIMAL
3 TOMATO SAUCES
GROUND DEER, FROG, SQUIRREL MEAT
BED of FRITOS, CHEETOS, DORITOS, COMBOS, etc.
* THE 'CHILI-MAX' PAVILION WAS LOCATED ADJACENT to an IMPOSING PHALANX of PORT-A-POTTIES
THE HOTLY CONTESTED FIREBALL TROPHY for SPICIEST DISH went to 'GRANDMA' GUS ENGVOLT and HER
'RUMBLE-in-the-JUNGLE' CHILI
WEAR PROTECTIVE EYE-WEAR
WORLD-RECORD 'TRINIDAD GORILLA' CHILE PEPPERS (1.5 MILLION SCOVILLE HEAT UNITS)
VEGETARIAN
SERVED in GORILLA PEPPER SKULL
CAUTION! EAT NO MORE than 1/3 TSP.
ON the OTHER END of the SPECTRUM is DR. FRED 'SCOOBA' DuFRESNE'S EXOTIC and CHALLENGING
'BLUE CHILI'
GROUND COBALT DEEP-SEA ALGAE BEEF
RARE BLUE KIDNEY BEANS
TURQUOISE TOMATO PASTE
PERIWINKLE PEPPER (00112 S.H.U.)
ICE BOWL
1
THIS WAS my BLUE RIBBON CHILI, EVEN THOUGH it TASTED TERRIBLE.
LB

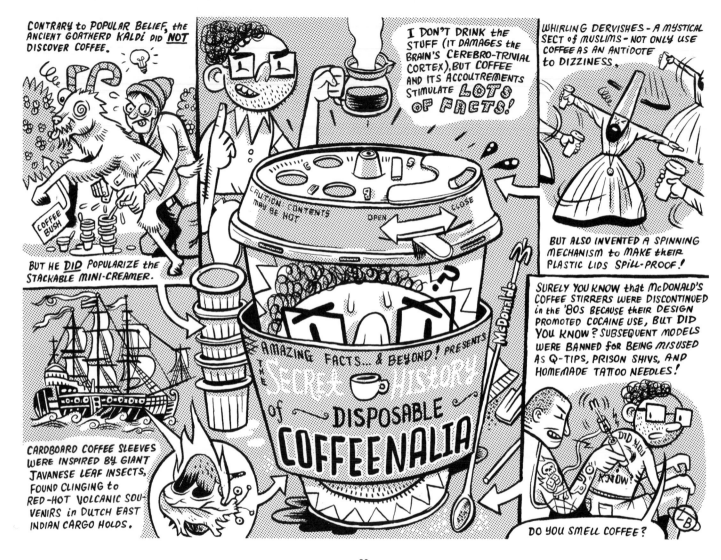

CONTRARY to POPULAR BELIEF, the ANCIENT GOATHERD KALDI DID **NOT** DISCOVER COFFEE.

BUT HE **DID** POPULARIZE the STACKABLE MINI-CREAMER.

I DON'T DRINK the STUFF (IT DAMAGES the BRAIN'S CEREBRO-TRIVIAL CORTEX), BUT COFFEE AND ITS ACCOUTREMENTS STIMULATE *LOTS of FACTS!*

WHIRLING DERVISHES - A MYSTICAL SECT of MUSLIMS - NOT ONLY USE COFFEE AS AN ANTIDOTE to DIZZINESS.

BUT ALSO INVENTED A SPINNING MECHANISM to MAKE their PLASTIC LIDS SPILL-PROOF!

CAUTION CONTENTS MAY BE HOT   OPEN   CLOSE

AMAZING FACTS... & BEYOND! PRESENTS

THE SECRET HISTORY of DISPOSABLE COFFEENALIA

SURELY YOU KNOW that McDONALD'S COFFEE STIRRERS WERE DISCONTINUED in the '80S BECAUSE their DESIGN PROMOTED COCAINE USE, BUT DID YOU KNOW? SUBSEQUENT MODELS WERE BANNED FOR BEING MISUSED AS Q-TIPS, PRISON SHIVS, AND HOMEMADE TATTOO NEEDLES!

CARDBOARD COFFEE SLEEVES WERE INSPIRED BY GIANT JAVANESE LEAF INSECTS, FOUND CLINGING to RED-HOT VOLCANIC SOUVENIRS in DUTCH EAST INDIAN CARGO HOLDS.

DID YOU KNOW!

DO YOU SMELL COFFEE?

COFFEE BUSH

McDonald's

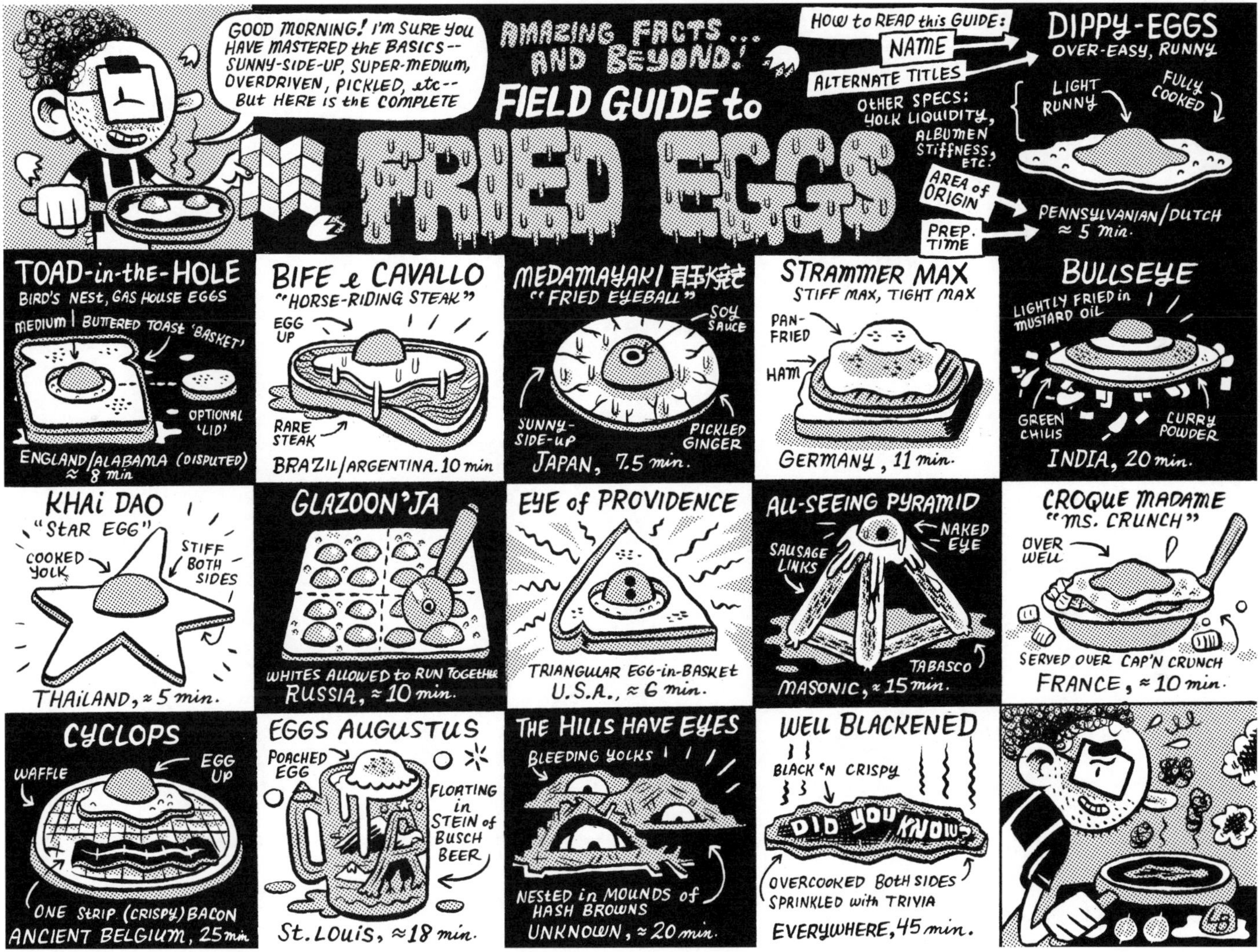
GOOD MORNING! I'M SURE YOU HAVE MASTERED the BASICS -- SUNNY-SIDE-UP, SUPER-MEDIUM, OVERDRIVEN, PICKLED, etc -- But HERE IS the COMPLETE
AMAZING FACTS... AND BEYOND!
FIELD GUIDE to
FRIED EGGS
HOW to READ this GUIDE:
NAME
ALTERNATE TITLES
OTHER SPECS: YOLK LIQUIDITY, ALBUMEN STIFFNESS, ETC.
AREA of ORIGIN
PREP. TIME
DIPPY-EGGS
OVER-EASY, RUNNY
LIGHT RUNNY
FULLY COOKED
PENNSYLVANIAN/DUTCH
≈ 5 min.
TOAD-in-the-HOLE
BIRD'S NEST, GAS HOUSE EGGS
MEDIUM
BUTTERED TOAST 'BASKET'
OPTIONAL 'LID'
ENGLAND/ALABAMA (DISPUTED) ≈ 8 min
BIFE e CAVALLO
"HORSE-RIDING STEAK"
EGG UP
RARE STEAK
BRAZIL/ARGENTINA. 10 min
MEDAMAYAKI 目玉焼き
"FRIED EYEBALL"
SOY SAUCE
SUNNY-SIDE-UP
PICKLED GINGER
JAPAN, 7.5 min.
STRAMMER MAX
STIFF MAX, TIGHT MAX
PAN-FRIED
HAM
GERMANY, 11 min.
BULLSEYE
LIGHTLY FRIED in MUSTARD OIL
GREEN CHILIS
CURRY POWDER
INDIA, 20 min.
KHAI DAO
"STAR EGG"
COOKED YOLK
STIFF BOTH SIDES
THAILAND, ≈ 5 min.
GLAZOON'JA
WHITES ALLOWED to RUN TOGETHER
RUSSIA, ≈ 10 min.
EYE of PROVIDENCE
TRIANGULAR EGG-in-BASKET
U.S.A., ≈ 6 min.
ALL-SEEING PYRAMID
NAKED EYE
SAUSAGE LINKS
TABASCO
MASONIC, ≈ 15 min.
CROQUE MADAME
"MS. CRUNCH"
OVER WELL
SERVED OVER CAP'N CRUNCH
FRANCE, ≈ 10 min.
CYCLOPS
WAFFLE
EGG UP
ONE STRIP (CRISPY) BACON
ANCIENT BELGIUM, 25 min
EGGS AUGUSTUS
POACHED EGG
FLOATING in STEIN of BUSCH BEER
St. LOUIS, ≈ 18 min.
THE HILLS HAVE EYES
BLEEDING YOLKS
NESTED in MOUNDS of HASH BROWNS
UNKNOWN, ≈ 20 min.
WELL BLACKENED
BLACK 'N CRISPY
DID YOU KNOW?
OVERCOOKED BOTH SIDES SPRINKLED with TRIVIA
EVERYWHERE, 45 min.

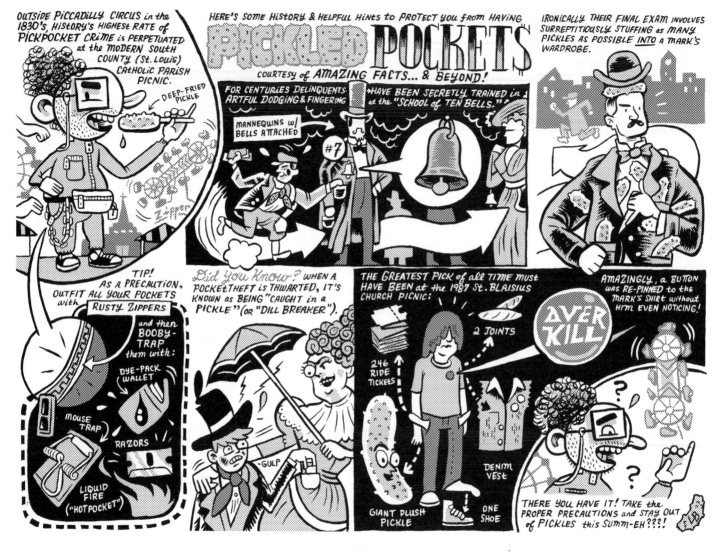

OUTSIDE PICCADILLY CIRCUS in the 1830's, HISTORY'S HIGHEST RATE OF PICKPOCKET CRIME is PERPETUATED at the MODERN SOUTH COUNTY (St. Louis) CATHOLIC PARISH PICNIC.

DEEP-FRIED PICKLE

HERE'S SOME HiSTORY & HELPFUL HiNTS TO PROTECT YOU FROM HAVING PICKLED POCKETS
COURTESY of AMAZING FACTS... & BEYOND!

FOR CENTURIES DELINQUENTS ARTFUL DODGING & FINGERING MANNEQUINS w/ BELLS ATTACHED #7 →HAVE BEEN SECRETLY TRAINED in at the "SCHOOL of TEN BELLS."

IRONICALLY THEIR FINAL EXAM INVOLVES SURREPTITIOUSLY STUFFING as MANY PICKLES AS POSSIBLE INTO a MARK'S WARDROBE.

TIP! AS A PRECAUTION, OUTFIT ALL YOUR POCKETS with RUSTY ZIPPERS and then BOOBY-TRAP them with:
DYE-PACK WALLET
MOUSE TRAP
RAZORS
LIQUID FIRE ("HOT POCKET")

Did you know? WHEN A POCKET THEFT is THWARTED, IT'S KNOWN as BEING "CAUGHT in a PICKLE" (OR "DILL BREAKER").

GULP

THE GREATEST PICK of ALL TIME MUST HAVE BEEN at the 1987 St. BLAISIUS CHURCH PICNIC:
246 RIDE TICKETS
2 JOINTS
OVER KILL
GIANT PLUSH PICKLE
DENIM VEST
ONE SHOE

AMAZINGLY, a BUTTON was RE-PINNED to the MARK'S SHIRT WITHOUT HIM EVEN NOTICING!

THERE YOU HAVE IT! TAKE the PROPER PRECAUTIONS and STAY OUT of PICKLES this SUMM-EH???!

GAMES
and ACTIVITIES

ART L. NOVAK of CARBONDALE, IL
STILL CAN'T SEE the YOUNG LADY
in the ILLUSION, ONLY the OLD HAG

AMAZING FACTS AND BEYOND!

WITH LEON BEYOND | leonbeyond@gmail.com | THE SPIRAL MEMORY GAME | ON LOCATION: WIKME, SWITZERLAND

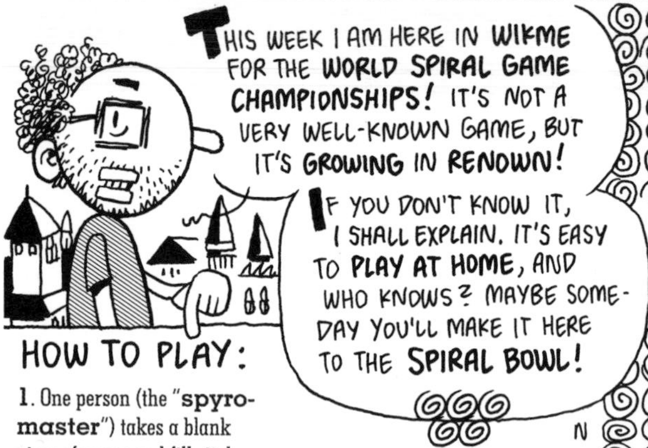
THIS WEEK I AM HERE IN WIKME FOR THE WORLD SPIRAL GAME CHAMPIONSHIPS! IT'S NOT A VERY WELL-KNOWN GAME, BUT IT'S GROWING IN RENOWN!
IF YOU DON'T KNOW IT, I SHALL EXPLAIN. IT'S EASY TO PLAY AT HOME, AND WHO KNOWS? MAYBE SOMEDAY YOU'LL MAKE IT HERE TO THE SPIRAL BOWL!

HOW TO PLAY:

1. One person (the "**spyro-master**") takes a blank piece of paper and fills it, by hand, with 676 spirals (these are called "**spyros**").

2. Each row and column of spirals is labelled with a letter, giving each individual spiral a coordinate (i.e **GF, WK, LB,** etc.)

3. Then, using a photocopier and scissors, 5 spirals are selected (called "**gyros**").

4. Now the game starts! A player (the "**gyrofinder**") is given the spyros to study for 1 minute, and then the spyros are taken away.

5. The 5 gyros are given to the gyrofinder, and if he can give their coordinates using his/her photographic memory, he/she gets 10 points each, but receives minus 1 for each wrong guess.

6. Then the gyros are returned, and gyrofinder has 30 seconds to find them—2 points for each one found.

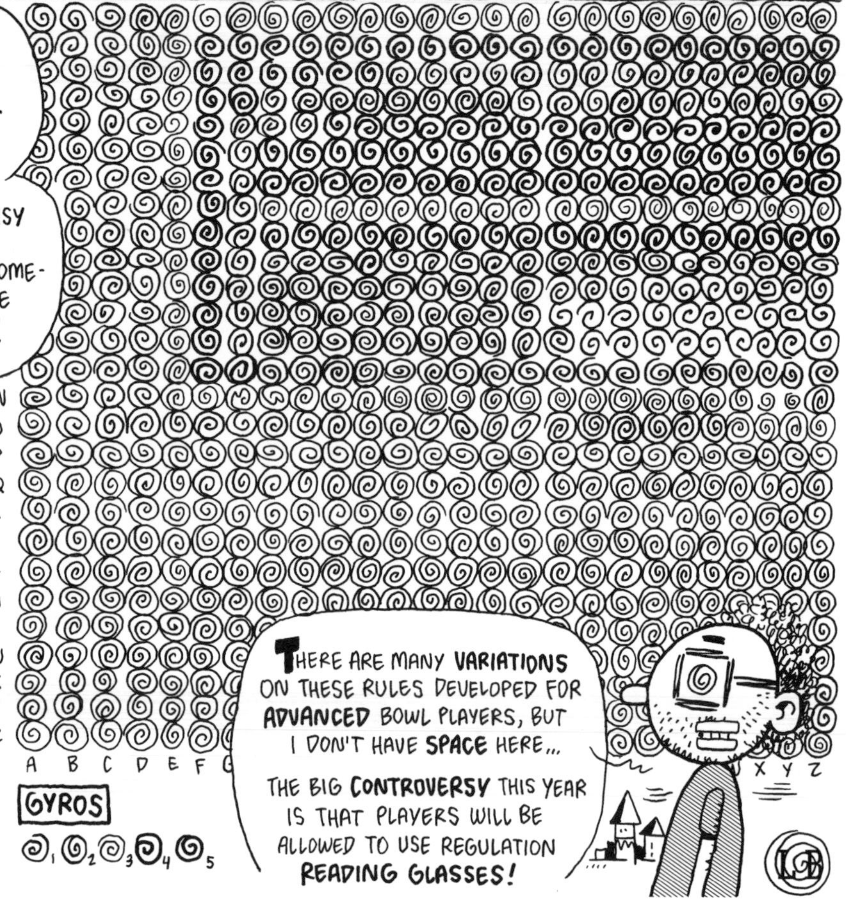
GYROS
THERE ARE MANY VARIATIONS ON THESE RULES DEVELOPED FOR ADVANCED BOWL PLAYERS, BUT I DON'T HAVE SPACE HERE...
THE BIG CONTROVERSY THIS YEAR IS THAT PLAYERS WILL BE ALLOWED TO USE REGULATION READING GLASSES!

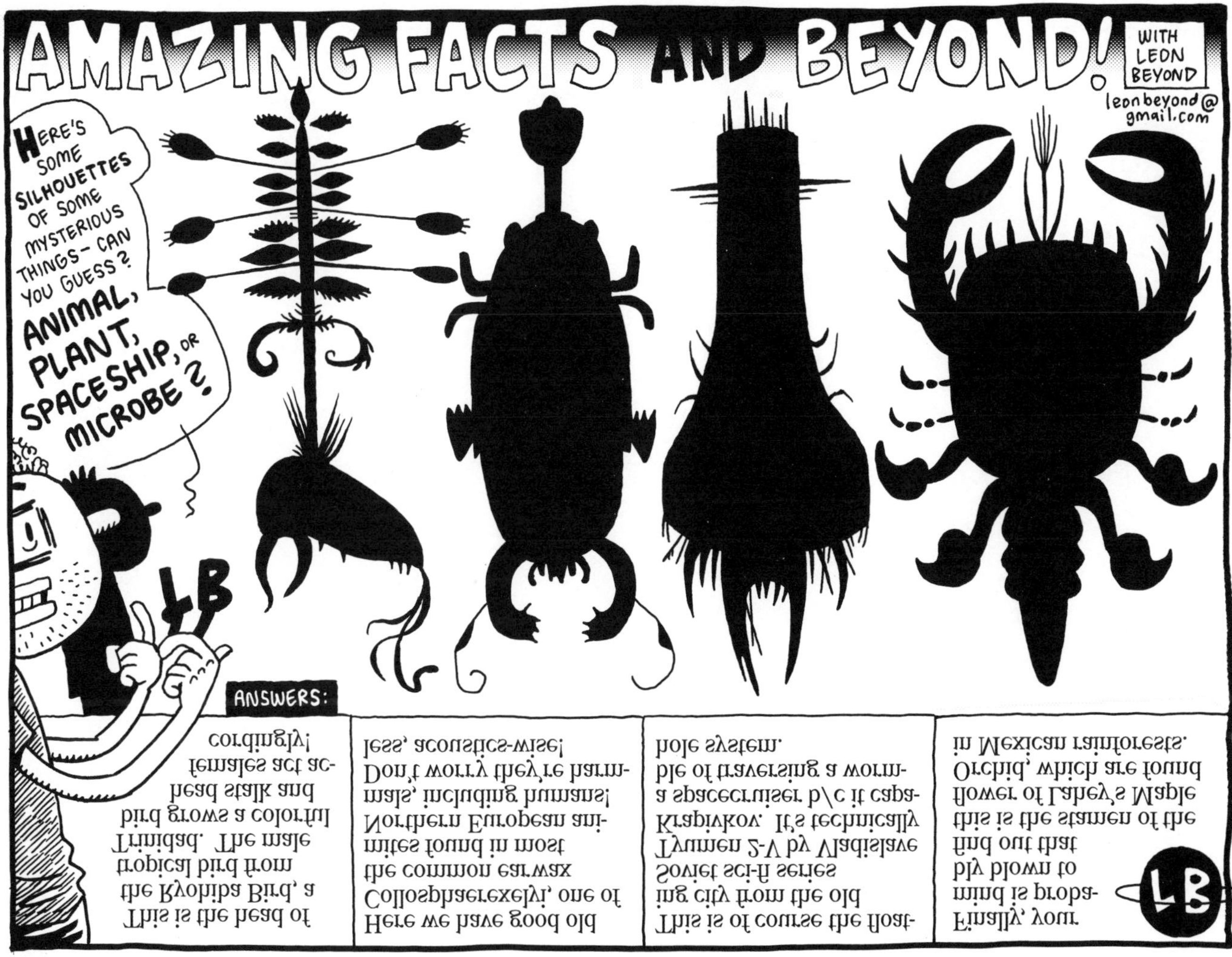
AMAZING FACTS AND BEYOND!
WITH LEON BEYOND
leonbeyond@gmail.com
HERE'S SOME SILHOUETTES OF SOME MYSTERIOUS THINGS- CAN YOU GUESS? ANIMAL, PLANT, SPACESHIP, OR MICROBE?
LB
ANSWERS:
This is the head of the Ryohida Bird, a tropical bird from Trinidad. The male bird grows a colorful head stalk and females act accordingly!
Here we have good old Collosphaerexelyi, one of the common earwax mites found in most Northern European animals, including humans! Don't worry they're harmless, acoustics-wise!
This is of course the floating city from the old Soviet sci-fi series Tyumen 2-V by Vladislave Krapivkov. It's technically a spacecruiser b/c it capable of traversing a wormhole system.
Finally, your mind is probably blown to find out that this is the stamen of the flower of Lahey's Maple Orchid, which are found in Mexican rainforests.
LB

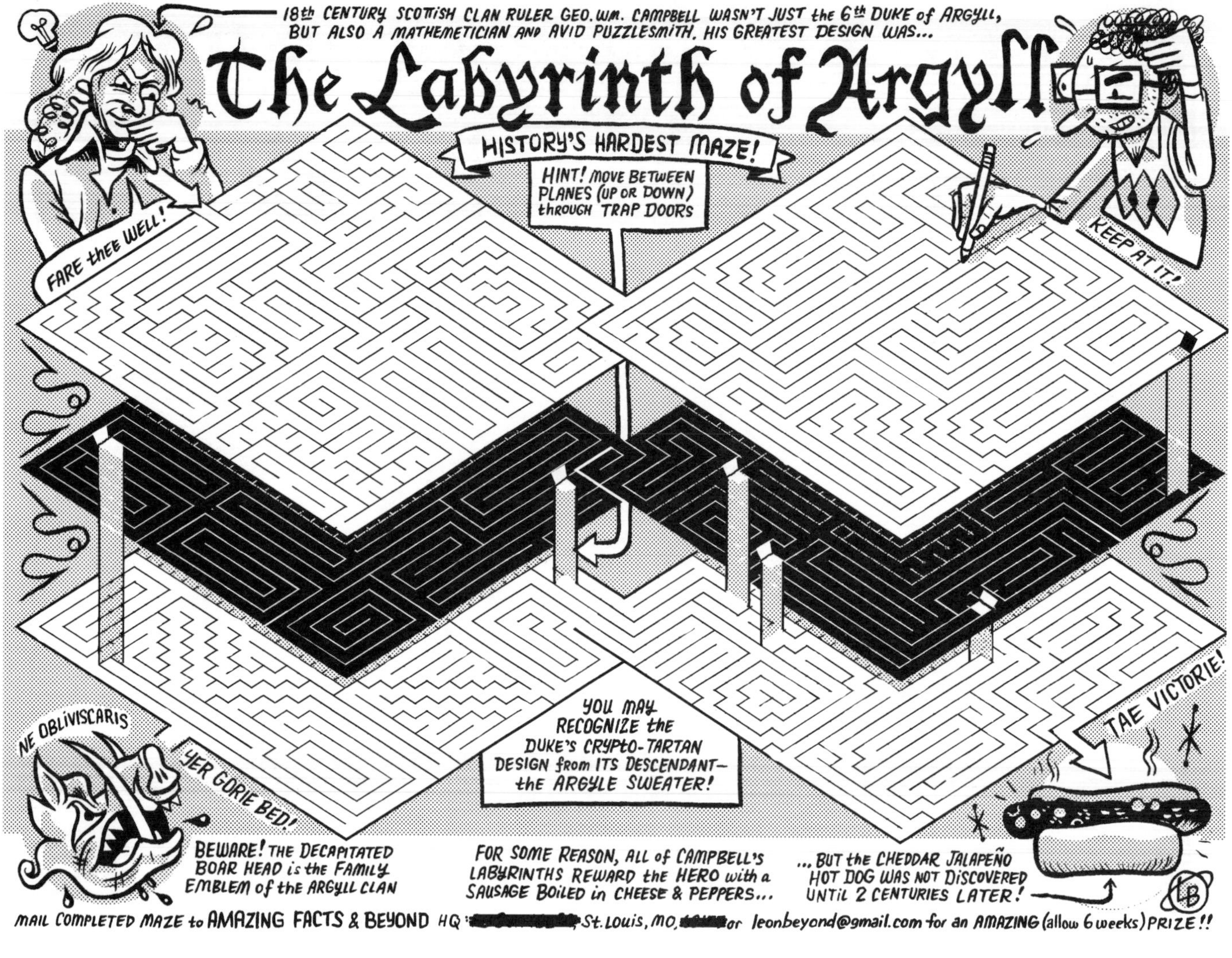
18th CENTURY SCOTTISH CLAN RULER GEO. WM. CAMPBELL WASN'T JUST the 6th DUKE of ARGYLL, BUT ALSO A MATHEMETICIAN AND AVID PUZZLESMITH. HIS GREATEST DESIGN WAS...
The Labyrinth of Argyll
HISTORY'S HARDEST MAZE!
HINT! MOVE BETWEEN PLANES (UP OR DOWN) through TRAP DOORS
FARE thee WELL!
KEEP AT IT!
NE OBLIVISCARIS
YER GORIE BED!
YOU MAY RECOGNIZE the DUKE'S CRYPTO-TARTAN DESIGN from ITS DESCENDANT– the ARGYLE SWEATER!
TAE VICTORIE!
BEWARE! THE DECAPITATED BOAR HEAD is the FAMILY EMBLEM of the ARGYLL CLAN
FOR SOME REASON, ALL of CAMPBELL'S LABYRINTHS REWARD the HERO with a SAUSAGE BOILED in CHEESE & PEPPERS...
...BUT the CHEDDAR JALAPEÑO HOT DOG WAS NOT DISCOVERED UNTIL 2 CENTURIES LATER!
LB
MAIL COMPLETED MAZE to AMAZING FACTS & BEYOND HQ: [redacted], St. Louis, MO, [redacted] or leonbeyond@gmail.com for an AMAZING (allow 6 weeks) PRIZE!!

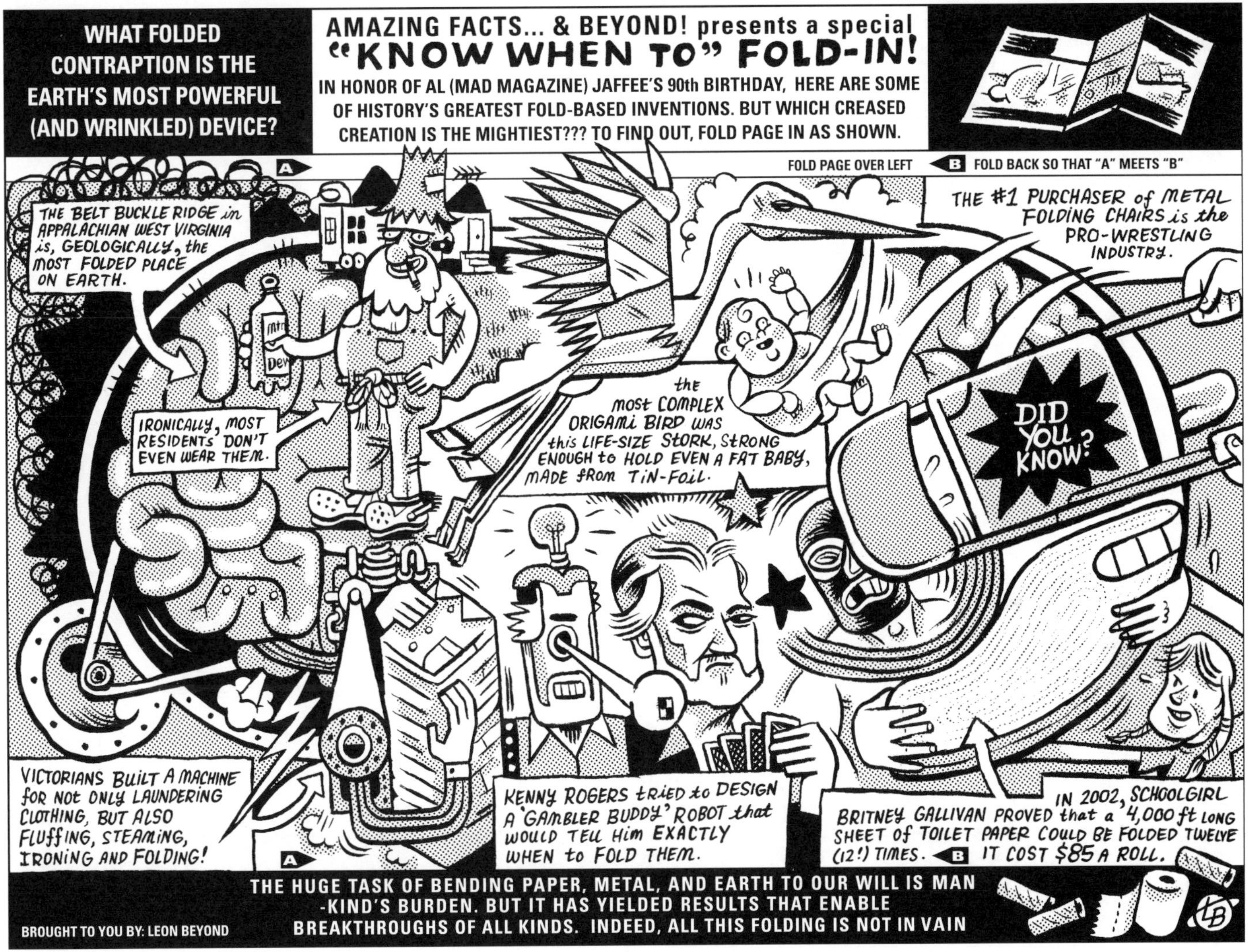

WHAT FOLDED CONTRAPTION IS THE EARTH'S MOST POWERFUL (AND WRINKLED) DEVICE?
AMAZING FACTS... & BEYOND! presents a special
"KNOW WHEN TO" FOLD-IN!
IN HONOR OF AL (MAD MAGAZINE) JAFFEE'S 90th BIRTHDAY, HERE ARE SOME OF HISTORY'S GREATEST FOLD-BASED INVENTIONS. BUT WHICH CREASED CREATION IS THE MIGHTIEST??? TO FIND OUT, FOLD PAGE IN AS SHOWN.
A
FOLD PAGE OVER LEFT
B
FOLD BACK SO THAT "A" MEETS "B"
THE BELT BUCKLE RIDGE in APPALACHIAN WEST VIRGINIA is, GEOLOGICALLY, the MOST FOLDED PLACE ON EARTH.
IRONICALLY, MOST RESIDENTS DON'T EVEN WEAR THEM.
the most COMPLEX ORIGAMi BIRD WAS this LIFE-SIZE StORK, StRONG ENOUGH to HOLD EVEN A FAT BABY, MADE from TiN-FOiL.
THE #1 PURCHASER of METAL FOLDING CHAIRS is the PRO-WRESTLING INDUSTRY.
DID YOU KNOW?
VICTORIANS BUILT A MACHINE for NOT ONLY LAUNDERING CLOTHING, BUT ALSO FLUFFING, STEAMING, IRONING AND FOLDING!
A
KENNY ROGERS tRiED to DESIGN A 'GAMBLER BUDDY' ROBOT that WOULD TELL HiM EXACTLY WHEN to FOLD THEM.
IN 2002, SCHOOLGIRL BRITNEY GALLIVAN PROVED that a 4,000 ft LONG SHEET of TOILET PAPER COULD BE FOLDED TWELVE (12!) TIMES.
B
IT COST $85 A ROLL.
THE HUGE TASK OF BENDING PAPER, METAL, AND EARTH TO OUR WILL IS MAN-KIND'S BURDEN. BUT IT HAS YIELDED RESULTS THAT ENABLE BREAKTHROUGHS OF ALL KINDS. INDEED, ALL THIS FOLDING IS NOT IN VAIN
BROUGHT TO YOU BY: LEON BEYOND
LB

AS PART of TRIVIA AWARENESS MONTH, EVERY SIX YEARS I AM ASKED to THROW OUT the FIRST PITCH AT A St. LOUIS CARDINALS' BALLGAME.

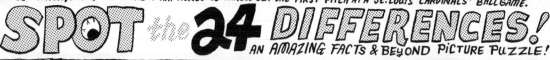

LOOK at the COMMEMORATIVE 8x10" GLOSSY from 2004, then THIS YEAR'S, AND SEE IF YOU CAN...

SPOT the 24 DIFFERENCES!

AN AMAZING FACTS & BEYOND PICTURE PUZZLE!

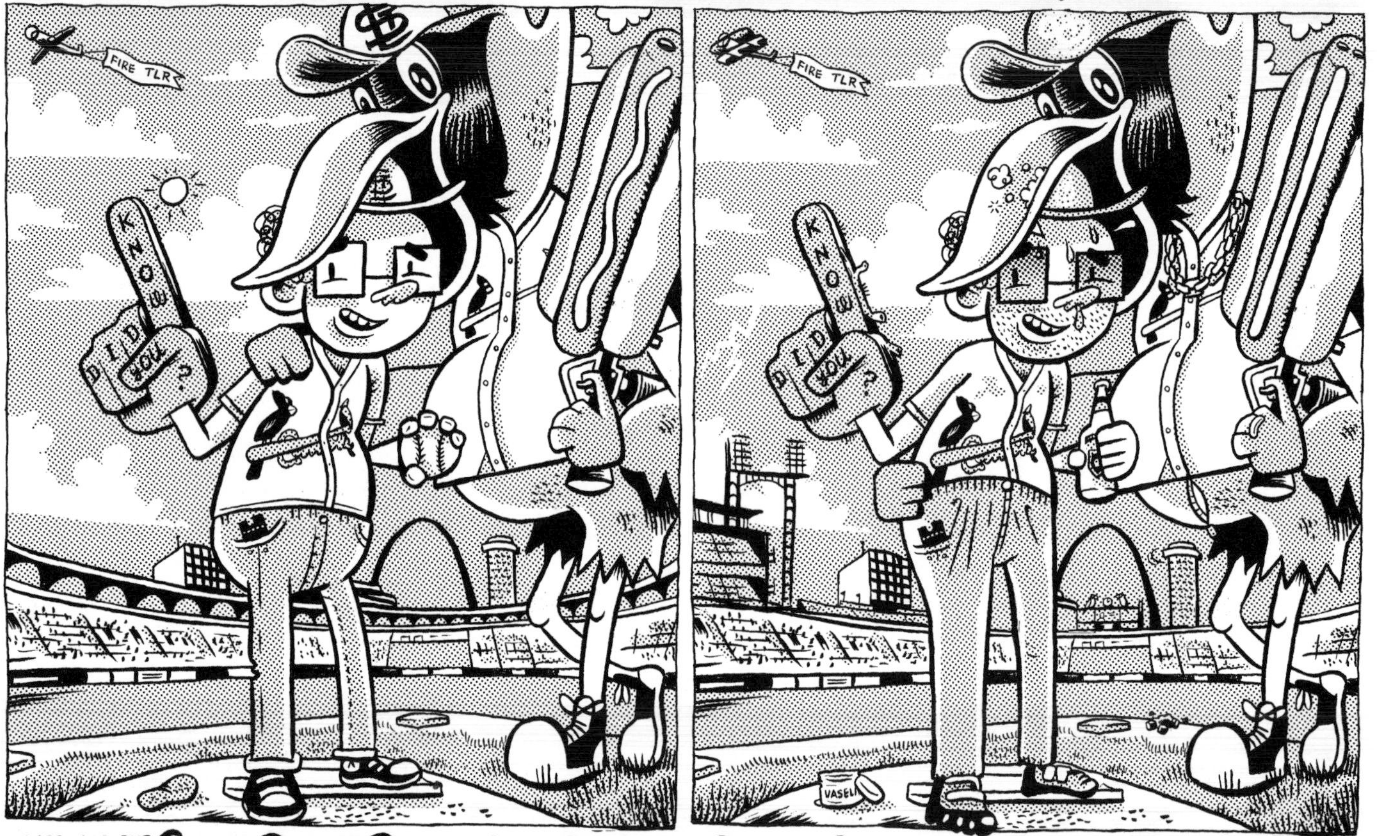
FIRE TLR
DID YOU KNOW?
FIRE TLR
DID YOU KNOW?
VASELI

1 GRAY HATS (for TRIVIA AWARENESS) 2 SUN 3 BI-PLANE 4 FOAM FINGER NOW 94% HAND TISSUE 5 THUNDERSTORM 6 FREDBIRD HANDSY 7 FREDBIRD RABID BITE
8 NACHO STAIN 9 SWEAT 10 PUJOLS-STYLE TITANIUM NECKLACE 11 MUSTARD UNSQUIGGLED 12 HOT DOG GUN DOUBLE-BARRELED 13 FREDBIRD MARRIED 14 XYZ, FREDBIRD!
15 MILLENNIUM SPINNING 16 MOM JEANS 17 TRANSITION LENSES 18 NEW BUSCH 19 CLYDESDALE POOP 20 ROSIN 21 TOE-SHOES 22 UNSHAVEN 23 BOOGER 24 BRO GOT ICED!

ANIMALS

DEEP-SEA "SATURN"
FISH — MOTHER WITH YOUNG
PICTURED HERE

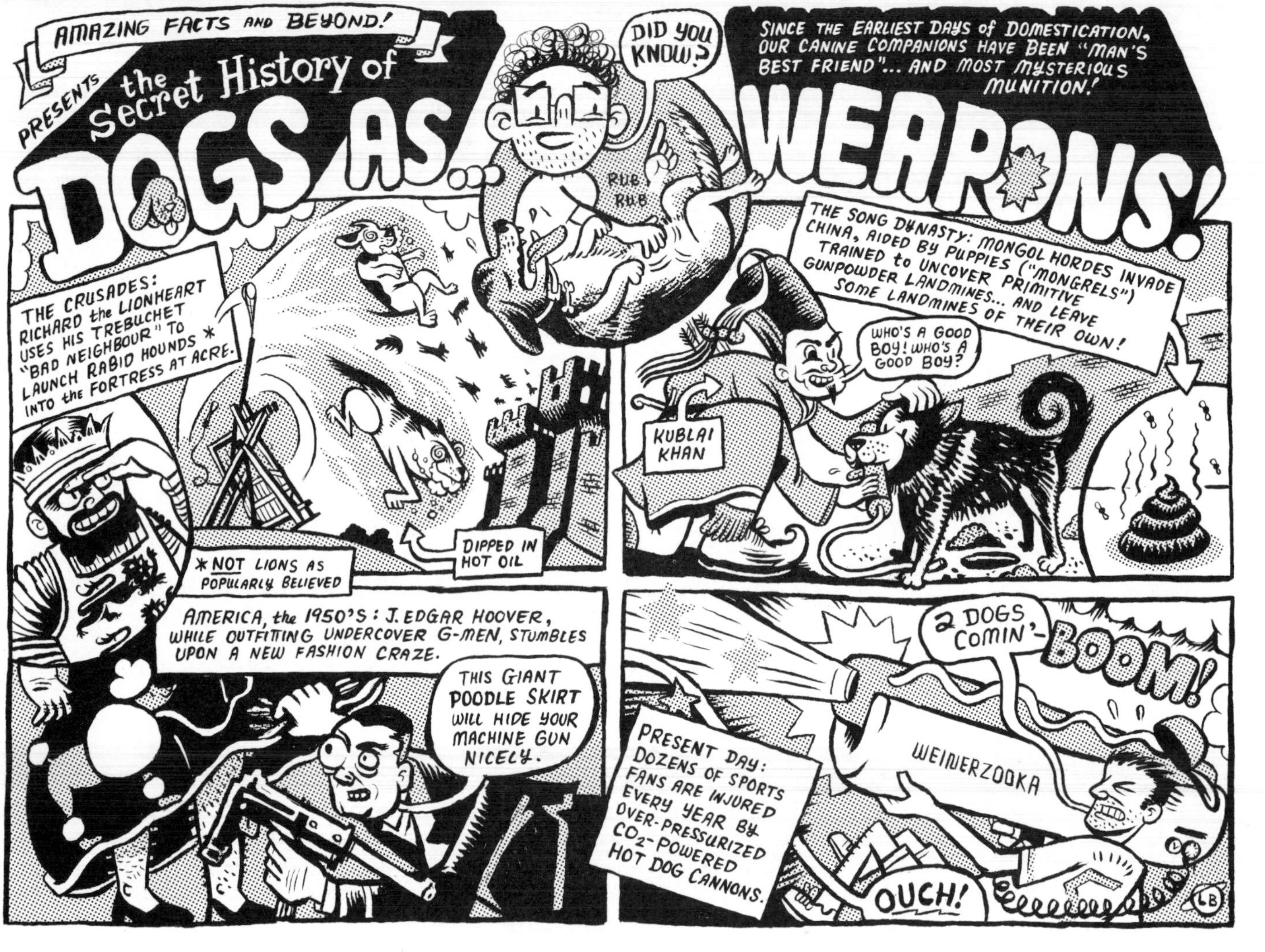

AMAZING FACTS AND BEYOND!
PRESENTS the Secret History of DOGS AS... WEAPONS!
DID YOU KNOW?
SINCE THE EARLIEST DAYS of DOMESTICATION, OUR CANINE COMPANIONS HAVE BEEN "MAN'S BEST FRIEND"... AND MOST MYSTERIOUS MUNITION!
RUB RUB
THE CRUSADES: RICHARD the LIONHEART USES HIS TREBUCHET "BAD NEIGHBOUR" TO LAUNCH RABID HOUNDS * INTO the FORTRESS AT ACRE.
DIPPED IN HOT OIL
* NOT LIONS AS POPULARLY BELIEVED
THE SONG DYNASTY: MONGOL HORDES INVADE CHINA, AIDED BY PUPPIES ("MONGRELS") TRAINED to UNCOVER PRIMITIVE GUNPOWDER LANDMINES... AND LEAVE SOME LANDMINES OF THEIR OWN!
WHO'S A GOOD BOY! WHO'S A GOOD BOY?
KUBLAI KHAN
AMERICA, the 1950'S: J. EDGAR HOOVER, WHILE OUTFITTING UNDERCOVER G-MEN, STUMBLES UPON A NEW FASHION CRAZE.
THIS GIANT POODLE SKIRT WILL HIDE YOUR MACHINE GUN NICELY.
2 DOGS COMIN'- BOOM!
WEINERZOOKA
PRESENT DAY: DOZENS OF SPORTS FANS ARE INJURED EVERY YEAR BY OVER-PRESSURIZED CO2-POWERED HOT DOG CANNONS.
OUCH!
LB

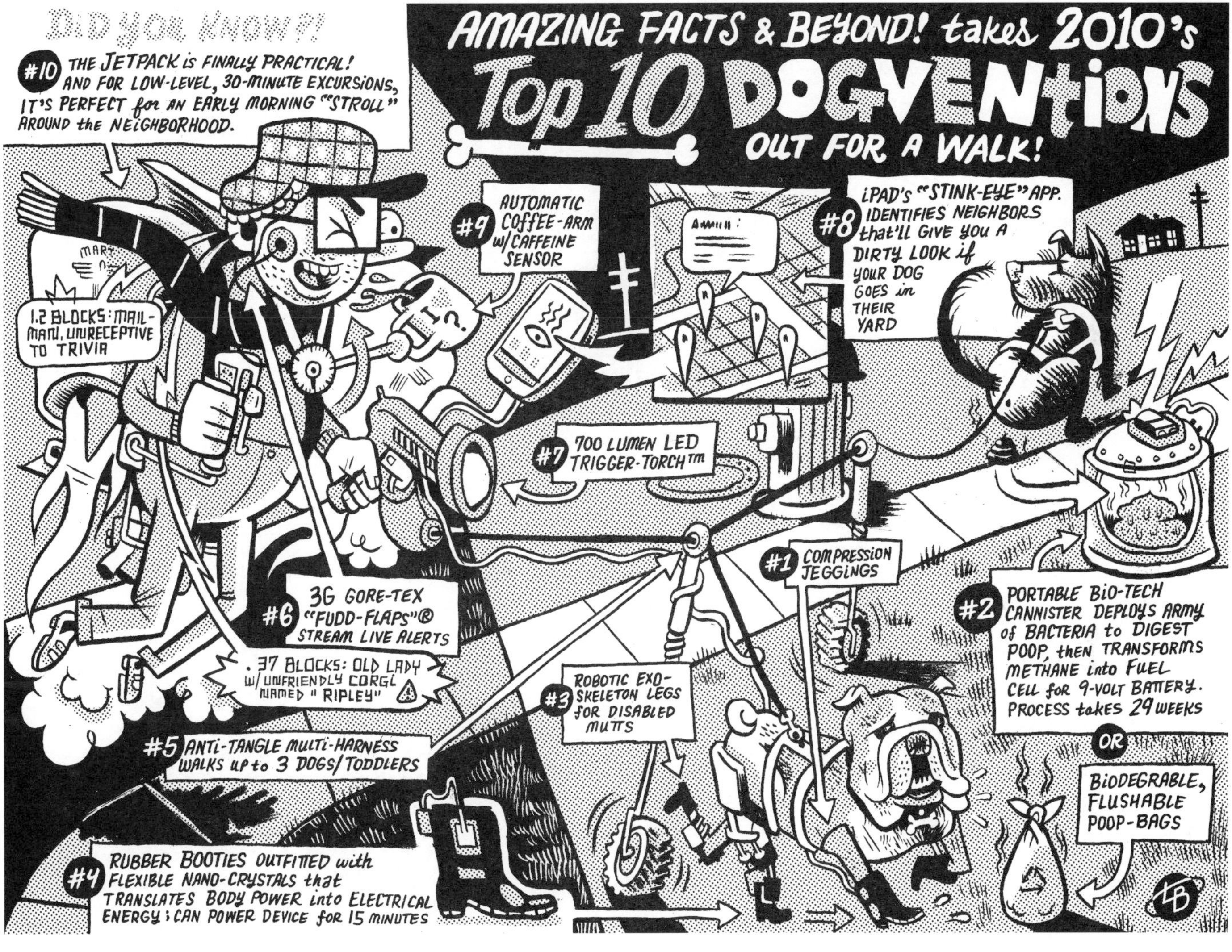
DID YOU KNOW?!
AMAZING FACTS & BEYOND! takes 2010's
Top 10 DOGVENTIONS
OUT FOR A WALK!
#10 THE JETPACK is FINALLY PRACTICAL! AND FOR LOW-LEVEL, 30-MINUTE EXCURSIONS, IT'S PERFECT for AN EARLY MORNING "STROLL" AROUND the NEIGHBORHOOD.
1.2 BLOCKS: MAILMAN, UNRECEPTIVE TO TRIVIA
#9 AUTOMATIC COFFEE-ARM w/CAFFEINE SENSOR
#8 iPAD'S "STINK-EYE" APP. IDENTIFIES NEIGHBORS that'll GIVE you A DIRTY LOOK if your DOG GOES in THEIR YARD
#7 700 LUMEN LED TRIGGER-TORCH™
#6 3G GORE-TEX "FUDD-FLAPS"® STREAM LIVE ALERTS
.37 BLOCKS: OLD LADY w/UNFRIENDLY CORGI NAMED "RIPLEY"
#1 COMPRESSION JEGGINGS
#2 PORTABLE BIO-TECH CANNISTER DEPLOYS ARMY of BACTERIA to DIGEST POOP, then TRANSFORMS METHANE into FUEL CELL for 9-VOLT BATTERY. PROCESS takes 29 WEEKS
OR
BIODEGRABLE, FLUSHABLE POOP-BAGS
#3 ROBOTIC EXO-SKELETON LEGS for DISABLED MUTTS
#5 ANTI-TANGLE MULTI-HARNESS WALKS UP to 3 DOGS/TODDLERS
#4 RUBBER BOOTIES OUTFITTED with FLEXIBLE NANO-CRYSTALS that TRANSLATES BODY POWER into ELECTRICAL ENERGY; CAN POWER DEVICE for 15 MINUTES

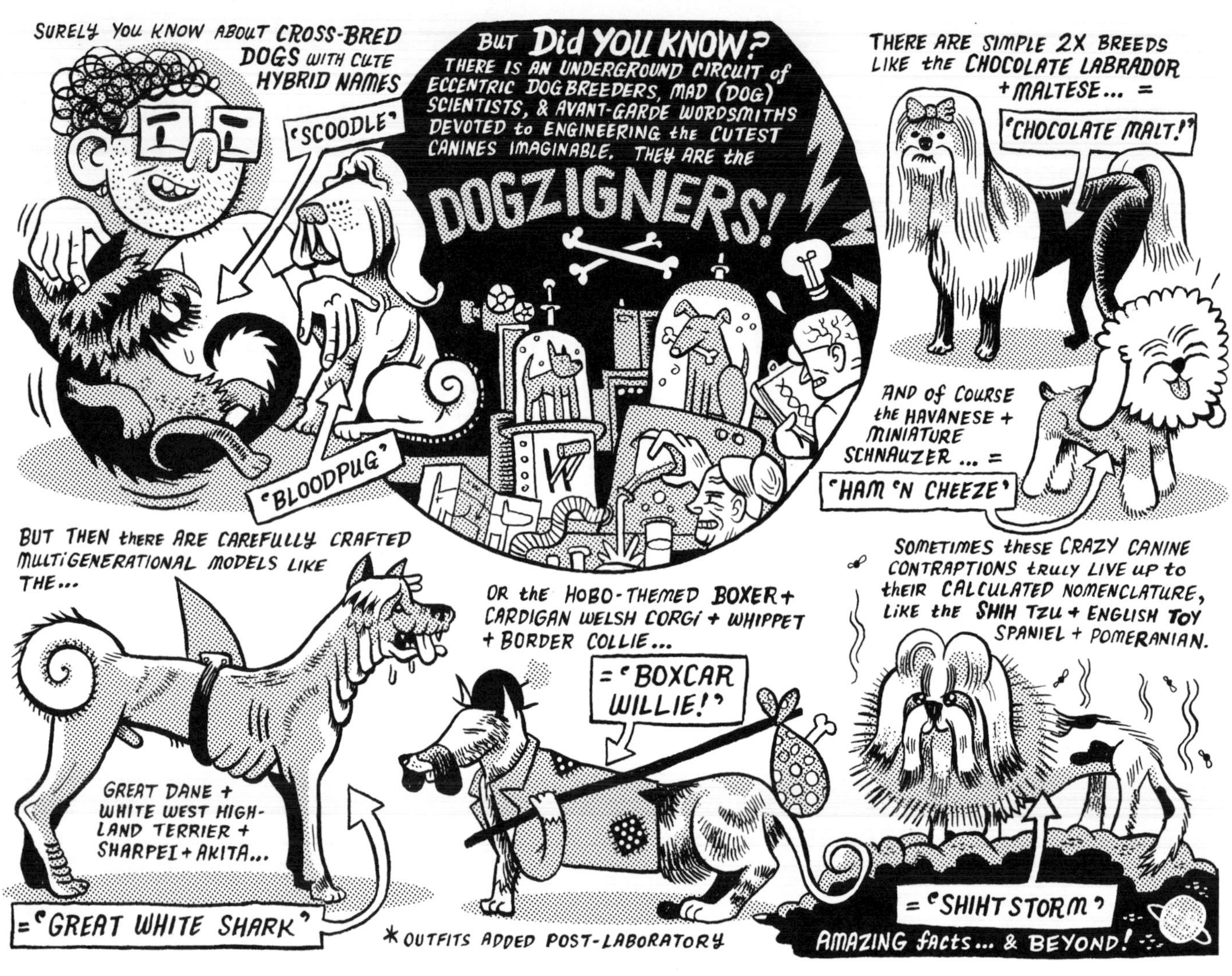
SURELY YOU KNOW ABOUT CROSS-BRED DOGS WITH CUTE HYBRID NAMES
'SCOODLE'
'BLOODPUG'
BUT Did YOU KNOW? THERE IS AN UNDERGROUND CIRCUIT of ECCENTRIC DOG BREEDERS, MAD (DOG) SCIENTISTS, & AVANT-GARDE WORDSMITHS DEVOTED to ENGINEERING the CUTEST CANINES IMAGINABLE. THEY ARE the
DOGZIGNERS!
THERE ARE SIMPLE 2X BREEDS LIKE the CHOCOLATE LABRADOR + MALTESE... =
'CHOCOLATE MALT!'
AND of COURSE the HAVANESE + MINIATURE SCHNAUZER ... =
'HAM 'N CHEEZE'
BUT THEN there ARE CAREFULLY CRAFTED MULTIGENERATIONAL MODELS LIKE THE...
GREAT DANE + WHITE WEST HIGH-LAND TERRIER + SHARPEI + AKITA...
='GREAT WHITE SHARK'
OR the HOBO-THEMED BOXER + CARDIGAN WELSH CORGI + WHIPPET + BORDER COLLIE...
='BOXCAR WILLIE!'
*OUTFITS ADDED POST-LABORATORY
SOMETIMES these CRAZY CANINE CONTRAPTIONS truly LIVE up to their CALCULATED NOMENCLATURE, LIKE the SHIH TZU + ENGLISH TOY SPANIEL + POMERANIAN.
='SHIHT STORM'
AMAZING facts... & BEYOND!

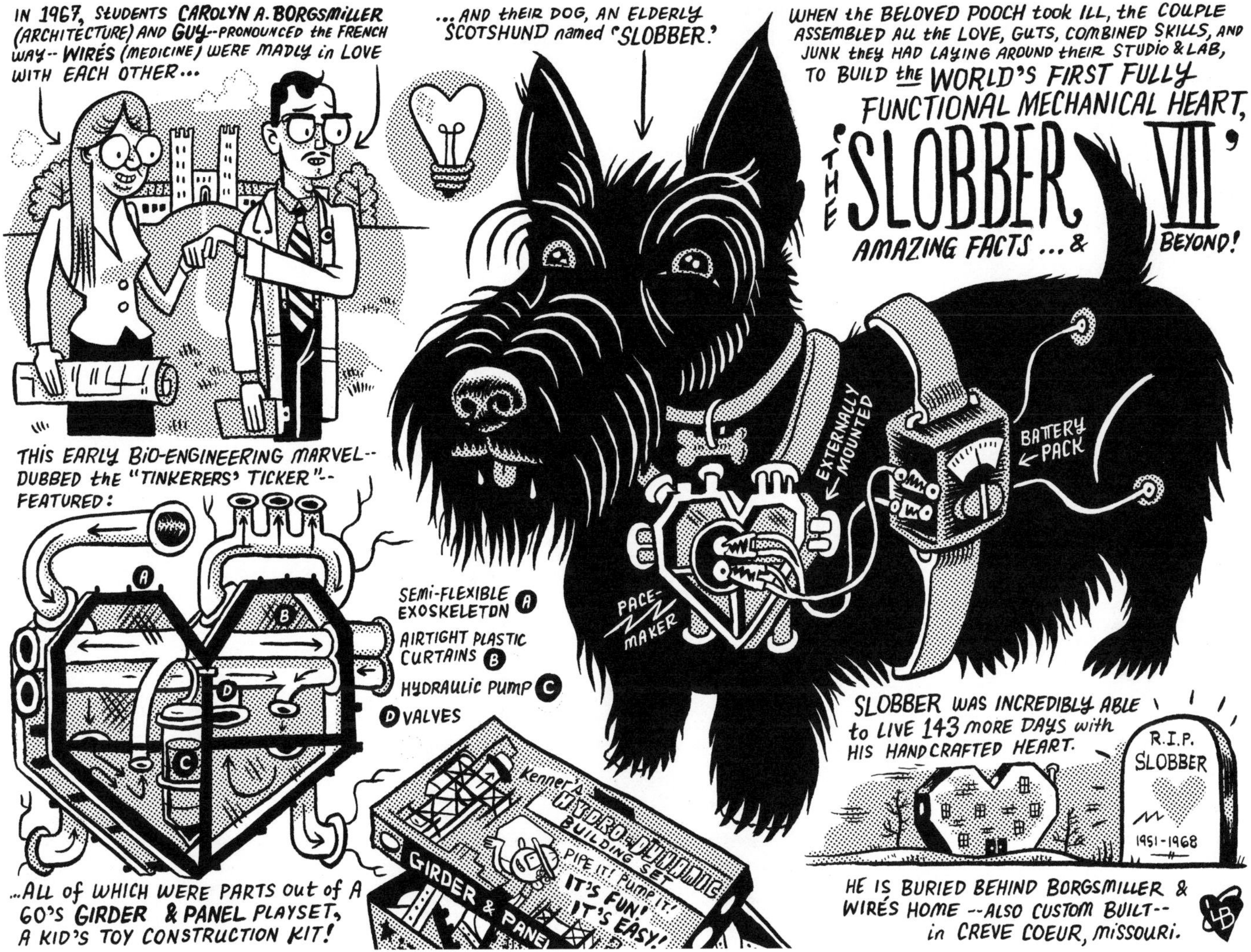
IN 1967, STUDENTS CAROLYN A. BORGSMILLER (ARCHITECTURE) AND GUY--PRONOUNCED THE FRENCH WAY-- WIRÉS (MEDICINE) WERE MADLY IN LOVE WITH EACH OTHER...
...AND THEIR DOG, AN ELDERLY SCOTSHUND NAMED 'SLOBBER.'
WHEN THE BELOVED POOCH TOOK ILL, THE COUPLE ASSEMBLED ALL THE LOVE, GUTS, COMBINED SKILLS, AND JUNK THEY HAD LAYING AROUND THEIR STUDIO & LAB, TO BUILD THE WORLD'S FIRST FULLY FUNCTIONAL MECHANICAL HEART,
THE 'SLOBBER VII'
AMAZING FACTS ... & BEYOND!
EXTERNALLY MOUNTED
BATTERY PACK
PACE-MAKER
THIS EARLY BIO-ENGINEERING MARVEL-- DUBBED THE "TINKERERS' TICKER"-- FEATURED:
SEMI-FLEXIBLE EXOSKELETON A
AIRTIGHT PLASTIC CURTAINS B
HYDRAULIC PUMP C
D VALVES
KENNER'S HYDRO-DYNAMIC BUILDING SET
PIPE IT! PUMP IT!
IT'S FUN! IT'S EASY!
GIRDER & PANEL
...ALL OF WHICH WERE PARTS OUT OF A 60'S GIRDER & PANEL PLAYSET, A KID'S TOY CONSTRUCTION KIT!
SLOBBER WAS INCREDIBLY ABLE TO LIVE 143 MORE DAYS WITH HIS HANDCRAFTED HEART.
R.I.P. SLOBBER
1951-1968
HE IS BURIED BEHIND BORGSMILLER & WIRÉS HOME --ALSO CUSTOM BUILT-- IN CREVE COEUR, MISSOURI.
LB

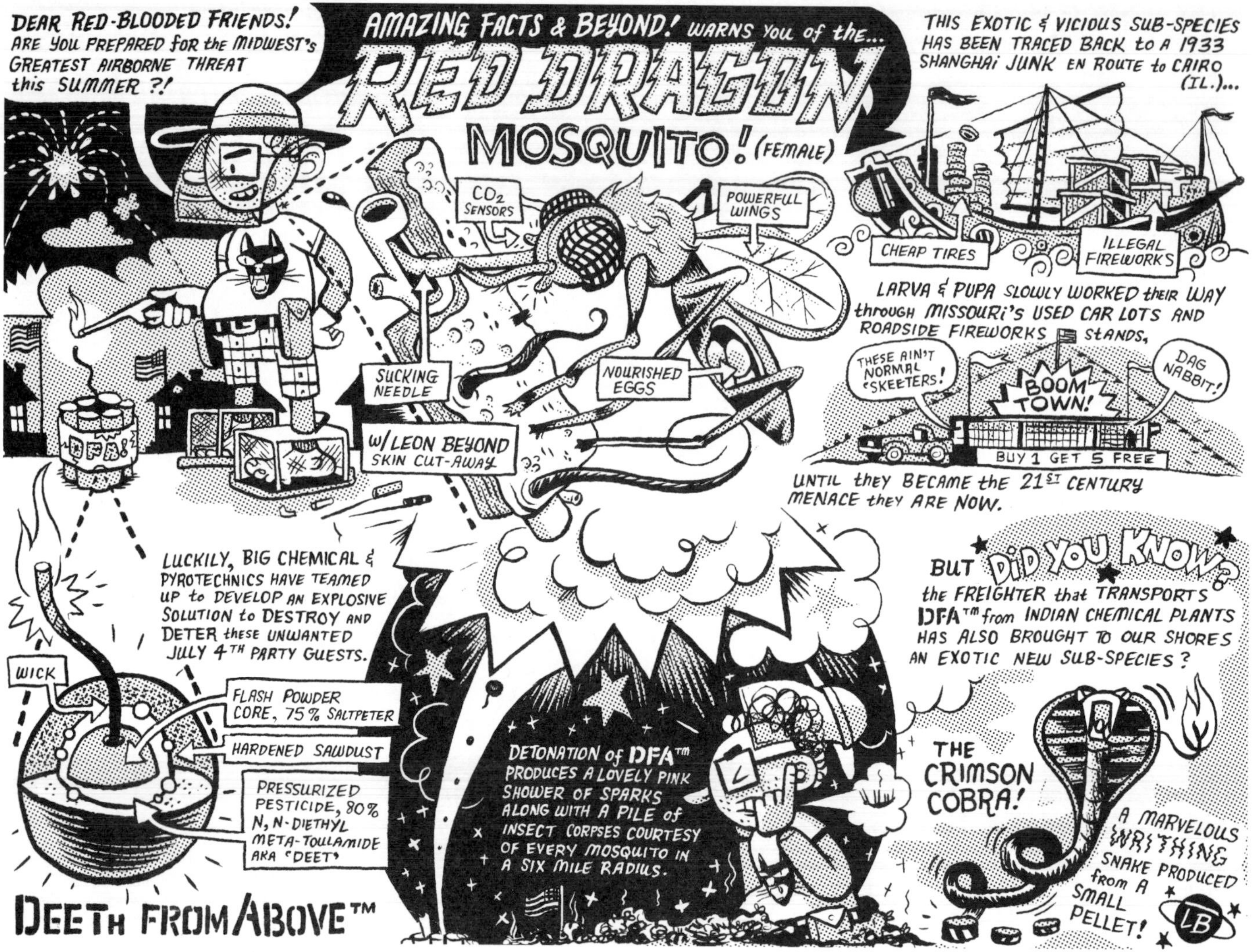
DEAR RED-BLOODED FRIENDS! ARE YOU PREPARED FOR THE MIDWEST'S GREATEST AIRBORNE THREAT THIS SUMMER ?!
AMAZING FACTS & BEYOND! WARNS YOU OF THE...
RED DRAGON MOSQUITO! (FEMALE)
THIS EXOTIC & VICIOUS SUB-SPECIES HAS BEEN TRACED BACK TO A 1933 SHANGHAI JUNK EN ROUTE TO CAIRO (IL.)...
CO2 SENSORS
POWERFUL WINGS
CHEAP TIRES
ILLEGAL FIREWORKS
LARVA & PUPA SLOWLY WORKED THEIR WAY THROUGH MISSOURI'S USED CAR LOTS AND ROADSIDE FIREWORKS STANDS,
THESE AIN'T NORMAL 'SKEETERS!
DAG NABBIT!
BOOM TOWN!
BUY 1 GET 5 FREE
SUCKING NEEDLE
NOURISHED EGGS
W/ LEON BEYOND SKIN CUT-AWAY
DFA!
UNTIL THEY BECAME THE 21ST CENTURY MENACE THEY ARE NOW.
LUCKILY, BIG CHEMICAL & PYROTECHNICS HAVE TEAMED UP TO DEVELOP AN EXPLOSIVE SOLUTION TO DESTROY AND DETER THESE UNWANTED JULY 4TH PARTY GUESTS.
WICK
FLASH POWDER CORE, 75% SALTPETER
HARDENED SAWDUST
PRESSURIZED PESTICIDE, 80% N, N-DIETHYL META-TOLUAMIDE AKA "DEET"
DEETH FROM ABOVE™
DETONATION OF DFA™ PRODUCES A LOVELY PINK SHOWER OF SPARKS ALONG WITH A PILE OF INSECT CORPSES COURTESY OF EVERY MOSQUITO IN A SIX MILE RADIUS.
BUT DID YOU KNOW? THE FREIGHTER THAT TRANSPORTS DFA™ FROM INDIAN CHEMICAL PLANTS HAS ALSO BROUGHT TO OUR SHORES AN EXOTIC NEW SUB-SPECIES?
THE CRIMSON COBRA!
A MARVELOUS WRITHING SNAKE PRODUCED FROM A SMALL PELLET!
LB

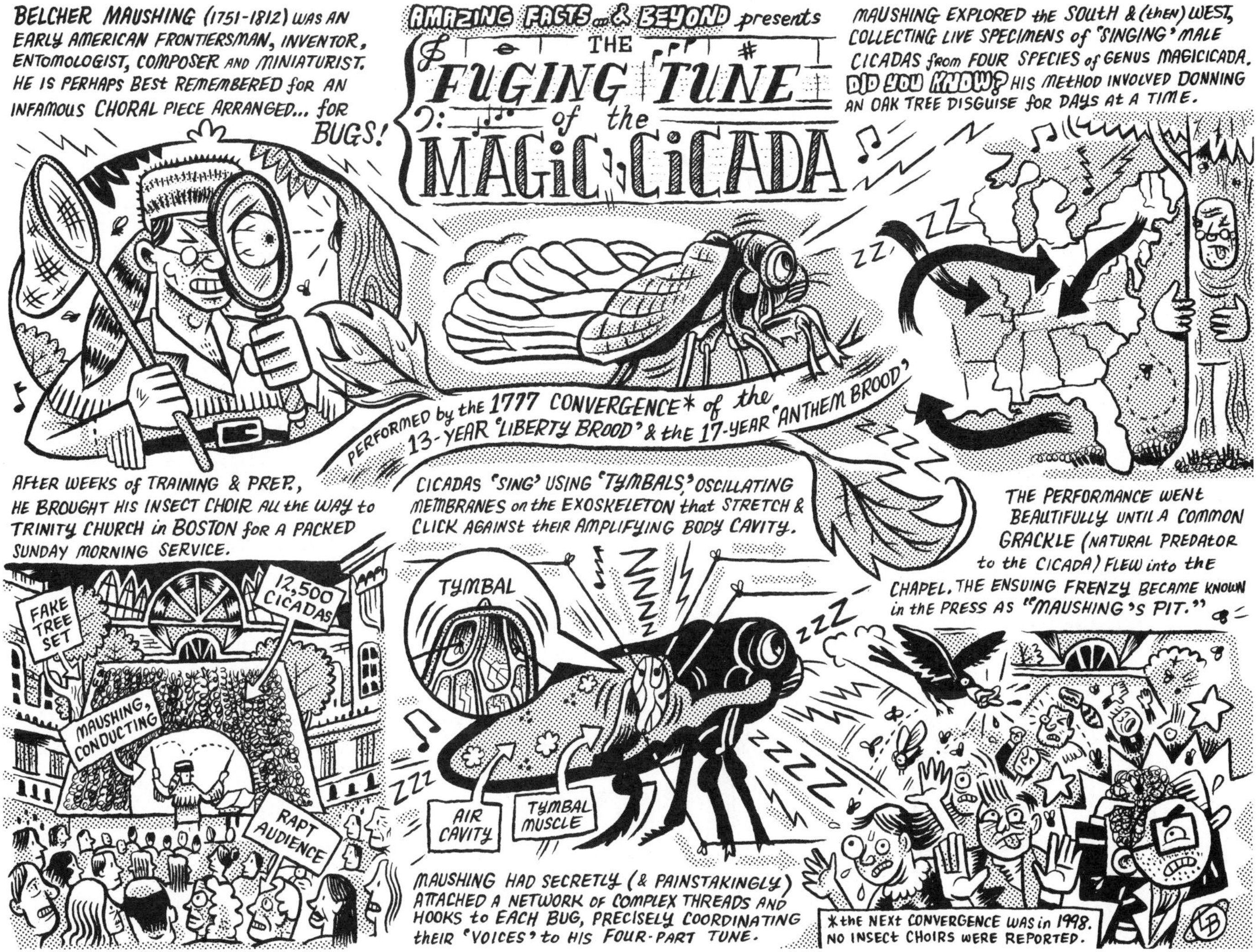
AMAZING FACTS AND BEYOND presents
THE FUGING TUNE of the MAGIC CICADA
BELCHER MAUSHING (1751-1812) WAS AN EARLY AMERICAN FRONTIERSMAN, INVENTOR, ENTOMOLOGIST, COMPOSER AND MINIATURIST. HE IS PERHAPS BEST REMEMBERED FOR AN INFAMOUS CHORAL PIECE ARRANGED... FOR BUGS!
MAUSHING EXPLORED THE SOUTH & (THEN) WEST, COLLECTING LIVE SPECIMENS OF 'SINGING' MALE CICADAS FROM FOUR SPECIES OF GENUS MAGICICADA. DID YOU KNOW? HIS METHOD INVOLVED DONNING AN OAK TREE DISGUISE FOR DAYS AT A TIME.
PERFORMED BY THE 1777 CONVERGENCE* OF THE 13-YEAR 'LIBERTY BROOD' & THE 17-YEAR 'ANTHEM BROOD'
AFTER WEEKS OF TRAINING & PREP., HE BROUGHT HIS INSECT CHOIR ALL THE WAY TO TRINITY CHURCH IN BOSTON FOR A PACKED SUNDAY MORNING SERVICE.
FAKE TREE SET
12,500 CICADAS
MAUSHING, CONDUCTING
RAPT AUDIENCE
CICADAS 'SING' USING 'TYMBALS,' OSCILLATING MEMBRANES ON THE EXOSKELETON THAT STRETCH & CLICK AGAINST THEIR AMPLIFYING BODY CAVITY.
TYMBAL
AIR CAVITY
TYMBAL MUSCLE
MAUSHING HAD SECRETLY (& PAINSTAKINGLY) ATTACHED A NETWORK OF COMPLEX THREADS AND HOOKS TO EACH BUG, PRECISELY COORDINATING THEIR 'VOICES' TO HIS FOUR-PART TUNE.
THE PERFORMANCE WENT BEAUTIFULLY UNTIL A COMMON GRACKLE (NATURAL PREDATOR TO THE CICADA) FLEW INTO THE CHAPEL. THE ENSUING FRENZY BECAME KNOWN IN THE PRESS AS "MAUSHING'S PIT."
*THE NEXT CONVERGENCE WAS IN 1998. NO INSECT CHOIRS WERE REPORTED.

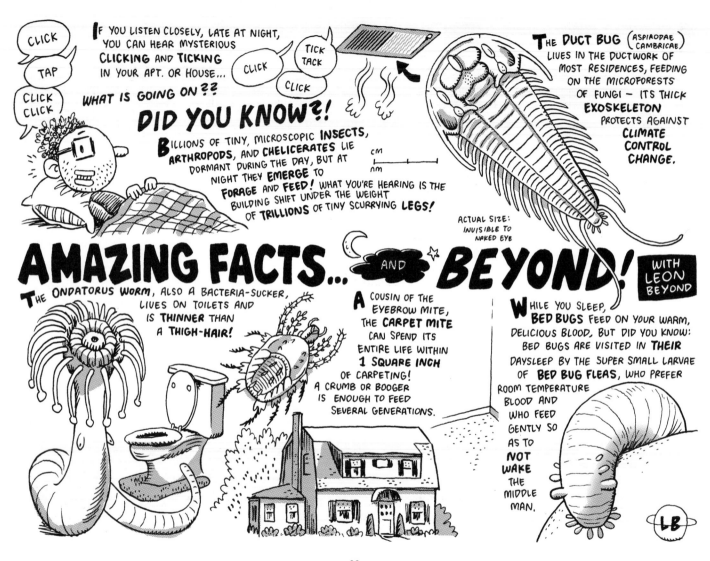

CLICK
TAP
CLICK CLICK

IF YOU LISTEN CLOSELY, LATE AT NIGHT, YOU CAN HEAR MYSTERIOUS **CLICKING** AND **TICKING** IN YOUR APT. OR HOUSE...

CLICK
TICK TACK
CLICK
CLICK

WHAT IS GOING ON ??

DID YOU KNOW?!

BILLIONS OF TINY, MICROSCOPIC **INSECTS**, **ARTHROPODS**, AND **CHELICERATES** LIE DORMANT DURING THE DAY, BUT AT NIGHT THEY **EMERGE** TO **FORAGE** AND **FEED!** WHAT YOU'RE HEARING IS THE BUILDING SHIFT UNDER THE WEIGHT OF **TRILLIONS** OF TINY SCURRYING **LEGS!**

CM
NM

THE DUCT BUG (ASPIRODAE CAMBRICAE) LIVES IN THE DUCTWORK OF MOST RESIDENCES, FEEDING ON THE MICROFORESTS OF FUNGI — ITS THICK **EXOSKELETON** PROTECTS AGAINST **CLIMATE CONTROL CHANGE.**

ACTUAL SIZE: INVISIBLE TO NAKED EYE

AMAZING FACTS... AND BEYOND!

WITH LEON BEYOND

THE **ONDATORUS WORM**, ALSO A BACTERIA-SUCKER, LIVES ON TOILETS AND IS **THINNER** THAN A **THIGH-HAIR!**

A COUSIN OF THE **EYEBROW MITE**, THE **CARPET MITE** CAN SPEND ITS ENTIRE LIFE WITHIN **1 SQUARE INCH** OF CARPETING! A CRUMB OR BOOGER IS ENOUGH TO FEED SEVERAL GENERATIONS.

WHILE YOU SLEEP, **BED BUGS** FEED ON YOUR WARM, DELICIOUS BLOOD, BUT DID YOU KNOW: BED BUGS ARE VISITED IN **THEIR** DAYSLEEP BY THE SUPER SMALL LARVAE OF **BED BUG FLEAS**, WHO PREFER ROOM TEMPERATURE BLOOD AND WHO FEED GENTLY SO AS TO **NOT WAKE** THE **MIDDLE MAN.**

LB

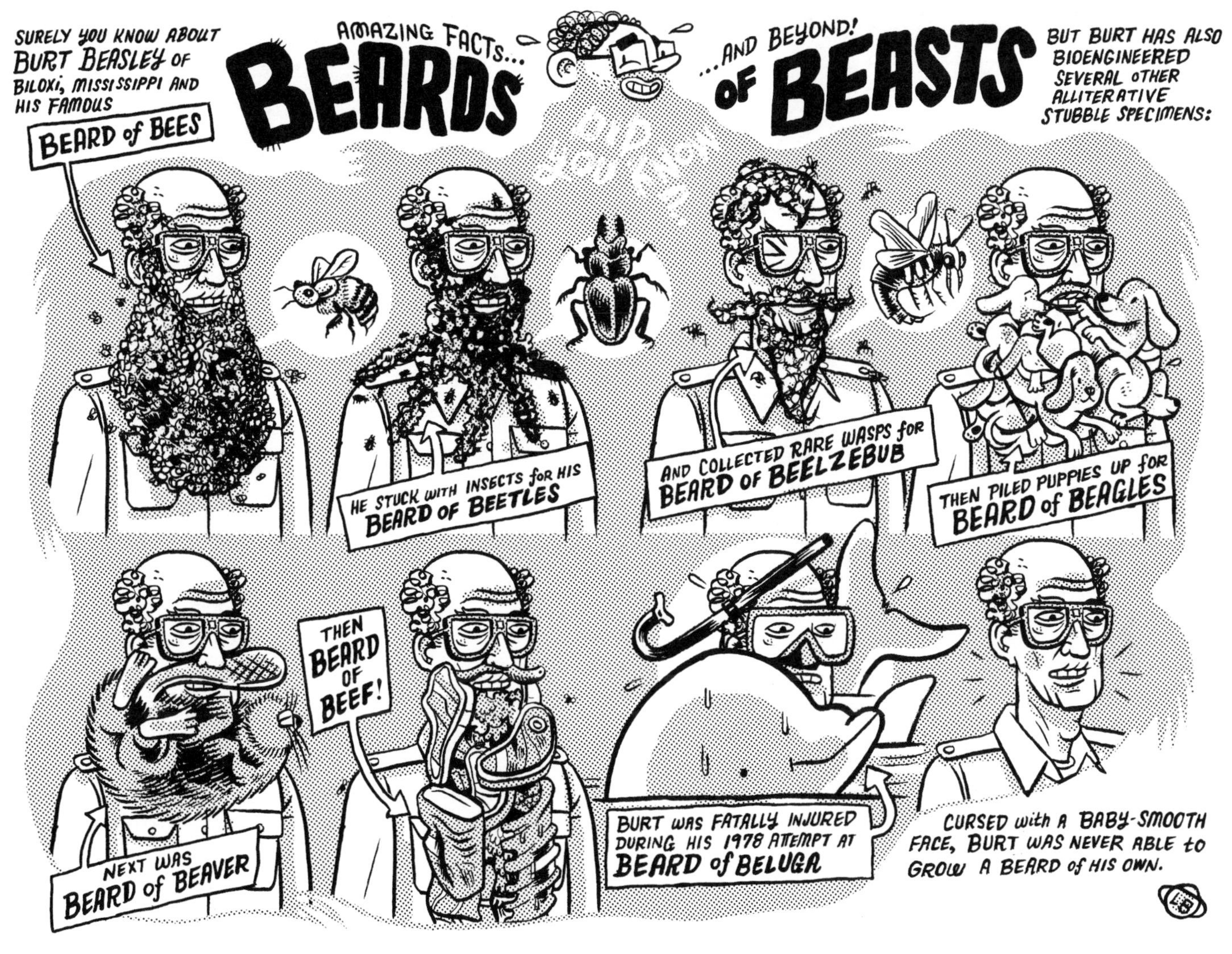
AMAZING FACTS... BEARDS ...AND BEYOND! OF BEASTS
SURELY YOU KNOW ABOUT BURT BEASLEY OF BILOXI, MISSISSIPPI AND HIS FAMOUS
BEARD of BEES
BUT BURT HAS ALSO BIOENGINEERED SEVERAL OTHER ALLITERATIVE STUBBLE SPECIMENS:
HE STUCK WITH INSECTS FOR HIS BEARD OF BEETLES
AND COLLECTED RARE WASPS FOR BEARD OF BEELZEBUB
THEN PILED PUPPIES UP FOR BEARD of BEAGLES
NEXT WAS BEARD of BEAVER
THEN BEARD OF BEEF!
BURT WAS FATALLY INJURED DURING HIS 1978 ATTEMPT AT BEARD of BELUGA
CURSED with A BABY-SMOOTH FACE, BURT WAS NEVER ABLE to GROW A BEARD of HIS OWN.

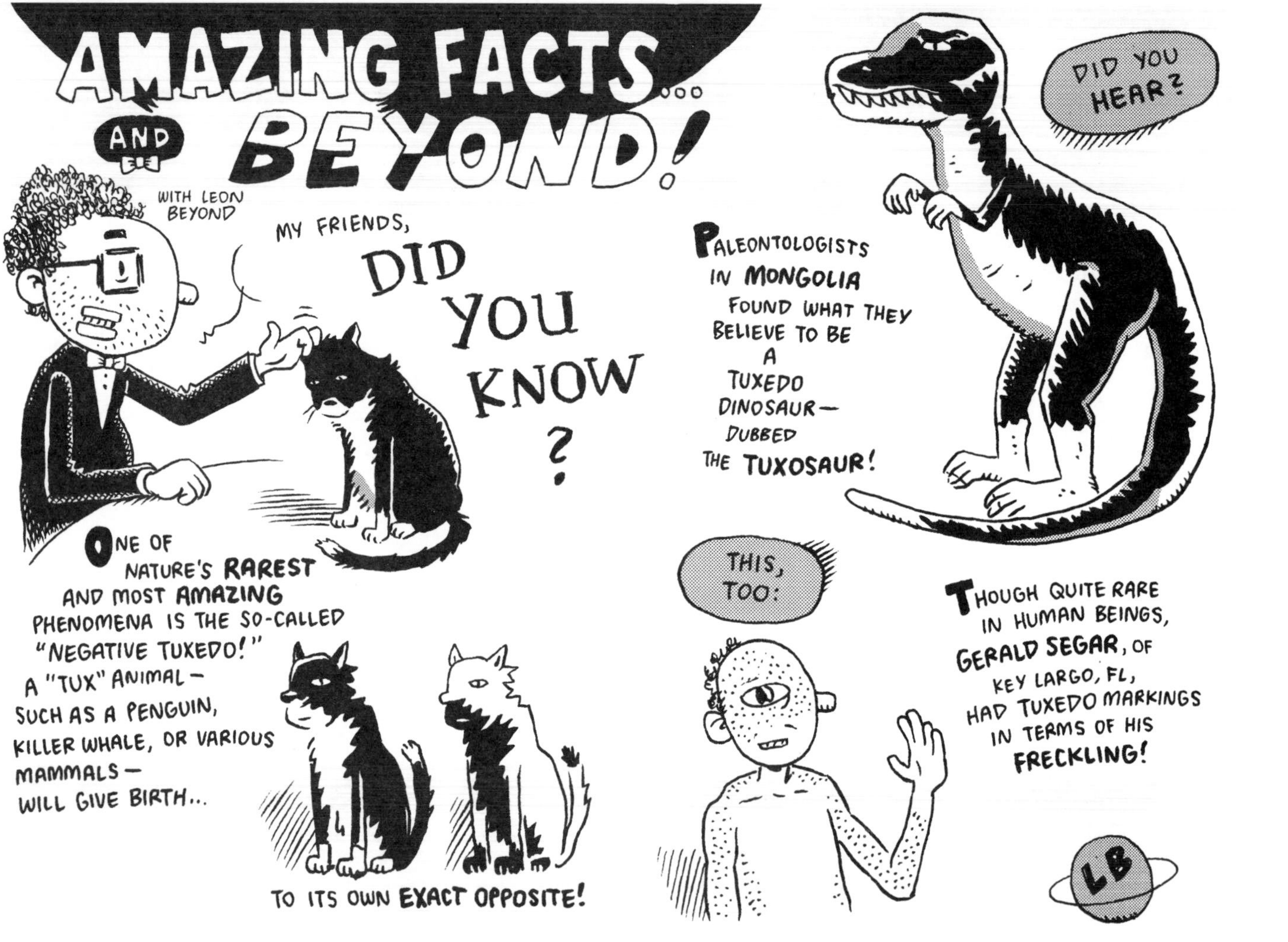
AMAZING FACTS...
AND BEYOND!
WITH LEON BEYOND
MY FRIENDS, DID YOU KNOW?
ONE OF NATURE'S RAREST AND MOST AMAZING PHENOMENA IS THE SO-CALLED "NEGATIVE TUXEDO!" A "TUX" ANIMAL — SUCH AS A PENGUIN, KILLER WHALE, OR VARIOUS MAMMALS — WILL GIVE BIRTH...
TO ITS OWN EXACT OPPOSITE!
DID YOU HEAR?
PALEONTOLOGISTS IN MONGOLIA FOUND WHAT THEY BELIEVE TO BE A TUXEDO DINOSAUR — DUBBED THE TUXOSAUR!
THIS, TOO:
THOUGH QUITE RARE IN HUMAN BEINGS, GERALD SEGAR, OF KEY LARGO, FL, HAD TUXEDO MARKINGS IN TERMS OF HIS FRECKLING!
LB

As FELLOW LOVERS of the FINE ART of TRIVIA, YOU CERTAINLY KNOW (and COULD NEVER FORGET) ABOUT the RUSSIAN ARTISTS...

...KOMAR and MELAMID WHO TAUGHT ELEPHANTS to PAINT IN 1998. But **Did You Know** THAT AT THE TIME, THAT WAS JUST ANOTHER EXAMPLE in HISTORY of FINE ARTISTS USING ANIMALS FOR THEIR OWN GAIN ?!?

PARIS, 1921:

WHILE TAKING AN EVENING STROLL, PIET MONDRIAN is STARTLED by A SPIDER...

WHICH HE KILLS — JUST BEFORE NOTICING THAT ITS WEB is BUILT USING **NO DIAGONAL LINES.**

AMAZING FACTS AND with LEON Beyond ▶ Animals and the (MOD-ERN) Art World

NYC, 1958

IN PREPARATION FOR THE **KARTOFFELSTARKE** EXPOSITION **GEORGE BRECHT** BEGINS A SERIES of EXPERIMENTAL SOUND RECORDINGS IN COLLABORATION WITH A COMMON RIVER CARP.

INCIDENTALLY, THAT RECORDING IS ALL BUT FORGOTTEN, SAVE FOR THE INFLUENCE OF ITS **IMPROVISATIONAL TECHNIQUES** ON A POPULAR 1990s FESTIVAL ROCK BAND.

By the 1980s, SEVERAL GROUPS OF ANIMAL ARTISTS DECIDED TO FOREGO HUMAN ASSOCIATION AND FORM **ALL-ANIMAL COLLECTIVES**

MOST NOTABLE AMONG THESE ARE:

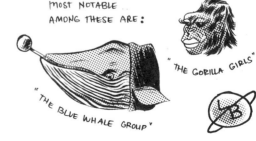

"THE GORILLA GIRLS"

"THE BLUE WHALE GROUP"

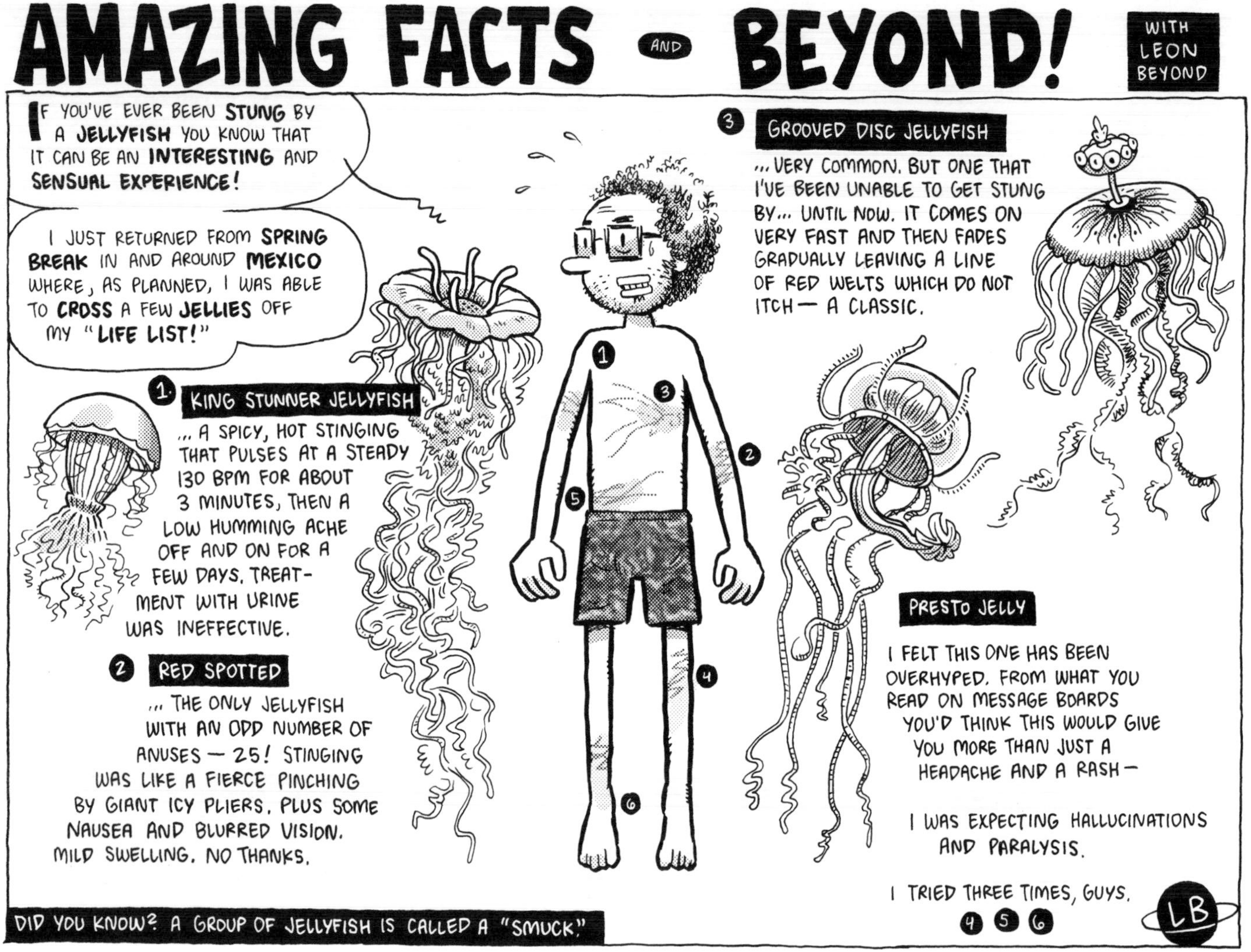
AMAZING FACTS AND BEYOND! WITH LEON BEYOND
IF YOU'VE EVER BEEN STUNG BY A JELLYFISH YOU KNOW THAT IT CAN BE AN INTERESTING AND SENSUAL EXPERIENCE!
I JUST RETURNED FROM SPRING BREAK IN AND AROUND MEXICO WHERE, AS PLANNED, I WAS ABLE TO CROSS A FEW JELLIES OFF MY "LIFE LIST!"
1. KING STUNNER JELLYFISH
... A SPICY, HOT STINGING THAT PULSES AT A STEADY 130 BPM FOR ABOUT 3 MINUTES, THEN A LOW HUMMING ACHE OFF AND ON FOR A FEW DAYS. TREAT- MENT WITH URINE WAS INEFFECTIVE.
2 RED SPOTTED
... THE ONLY JELLYFISH WITH AN ODD NUMBER OF ANUSES — 25! STINGING WAS LIKE A FIERCE PINCHING BY GIANT ICY PLIERS. PLUS SOME NAUSEA AND BLURRED VISION. MILD SWELLING. NO THANKS.
3 GROOVED DISC JELLYFISH
... VERY COMMON. BUT ONE THAT I'VE BEEN UNABLE TO GET STUNG BY... UNTIL NOW. IT COMES ON VERY FAST AND THEN FADES GRADUALLY LEAVING A LINE OF RED WELTS WHICH DO NOT ITCH — A CLASSIC.
PRESTO JELLY
I FELT THIS ONE HAS BEEN OVERHYPED. FROM WHAT YOU READ ON MESSAGE BOARDS YOU'D THINK THIS WOULD GIVE YOU MORE THAN JUST A HEADACHE AND A RASH —
I WAS EXPECTING HALLUCINATIONS AND PARALYSIS.
I TRIED THREE TIMES, GUYS. 4 5 6
DID YOU KNOW? A GROUP OF JELLYFISH IS CALLED A "SMUCK."
LB

ADVENTURES
of the MIND

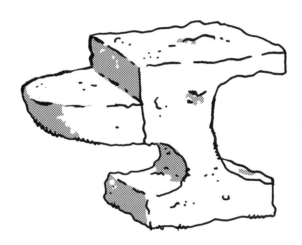

ANVIL-SHAPED CHEETO,™ 2004,
COLLECTION OF LEON BEYOND

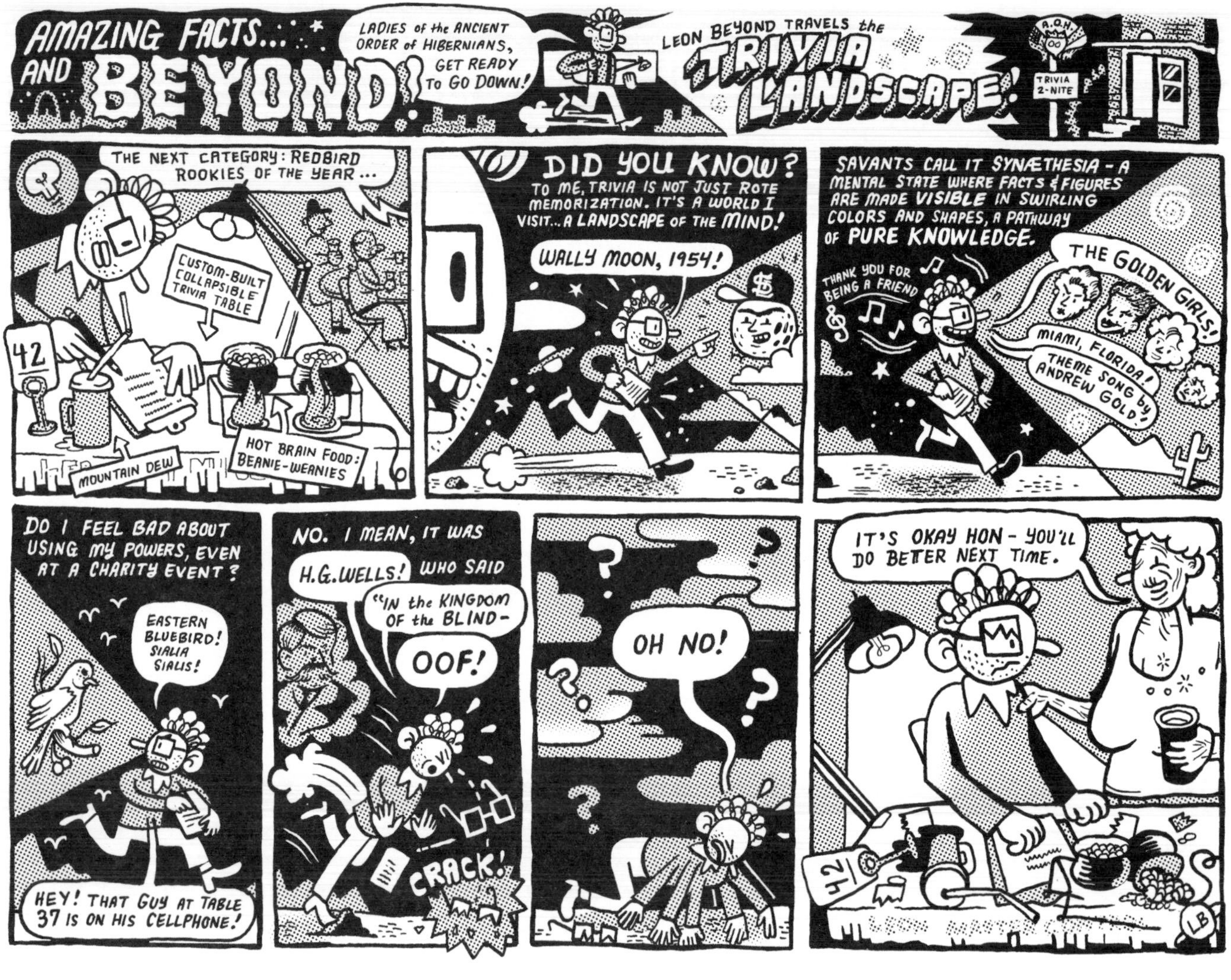
AMAZING FACTS... AND BEYOND!
LADIES of the ANCIENT ORDER of HIBERNIANS, GET READY TO GO DOWN!
LEON BEYOND TRAVELS the TRIVIA LANDSCAPE!
A.O.H.
TRIVIA 2-NITE
THE NEXT CATEGORY: REDBIRD ROOKIES OF THE YEAR...
CUSTOM-BUILT COLLAPSIBLE TRIVIA TABLE
42
HOT BRAIN FOOD: BEANIE-WEANIES
MOUNTAIN DEW
DID YOU KNOW?
TO ME, TRIVIA IS NOT JUST ROTE MEMORIZATION. IT'S A WORLD I VISIT... A LANDSCAPE OF THE MIND!
WALLY MOON, 1954!
SAVANTS CALL IT SYNÆTHESIA - A MENTAL STATE WHERE FACTS & FIGURES ARE MADE VISIBLE IN SWIRLING COLORS AND SHAPES, A PATHWAY OF PURE KNOWLEDGE.
THANK YOU FOR BEING A FRIEND
THE GOLDEN GIRLS!
MIAMI, FLORIDA!
THEME SONG by ANDREW GOLD!
DO I FEEL BAD ABOUT USING MY POWERS, EVEN AT A CHARITY EVENT?
EASTERN BLUEBIRD! SIALIA SIALIS!
HEY! THAT GUY AT TABLE 37 IS ON HIS CELLPHONE!
NO. I MEAN, IT WAS
H.G. WELLS!
WHO SAID
"IN the KINGDOM OF the BLIND-
OOF!
CRACK!
OH NO!
IT'S OKAY HON - YOU'LL DO BETTER NEXT TIME.
42
LB

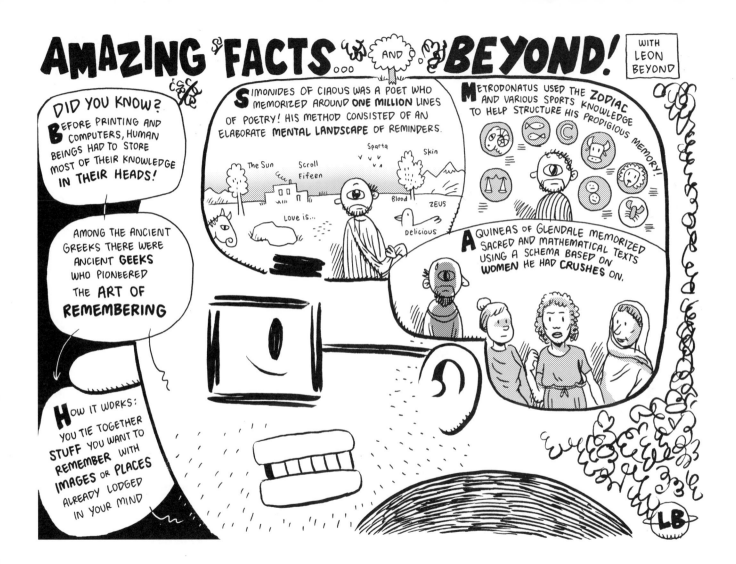

AMAZING FACTS... AND BEYOND!

WITH LEON BEYOND

DID YOU KNOW?
BEFORE PRINTING AND COMPUTERS, HUMAN BEINGS HAD TO STORE MOST OF THEIR KNOWLEDGE **IN THEIR HEADS!**

AMONG THE ANCIENT GREEKS THERE WERE ANCIENT **GEEKS** WHO PIONEERED THE **ART OF REMEMBERING**

HOW IT WORKS: YOU TIE TOGETHER **STUFF** YOU WANT TO **REMEMBER** WITH **IMAGES** OR **PLACES** ALREADY LODGED IN YOUR MIND

SIMONIDES OF CIAOUS WAS A POET WHO MEMORIZED AROUND **ONE MILLION** LINES OF POETRY! HIS METHOD CONSISTED OF AN ELABORATE **MENTAL LANDSCAPE** OF REMINDERS.

The Sun
Scroll Fifeen
Sparta
Skin
Blood
ZEUS
Love is...
Delicious

METRODONATUS USED THE **ZODIAC** AND VARIOUS SPORTS KNOWLEDGE TO HELP STRUCTURE HIS PRODIGIOUS MEMORY!

AQUINEAS OF GLENDALE MEMORIZED SACRED AND MATHEMATICAL TEXTS USING A SCHEMA BASED ON **WOMEN** HE HAD **CRUSHES** ON.

LB

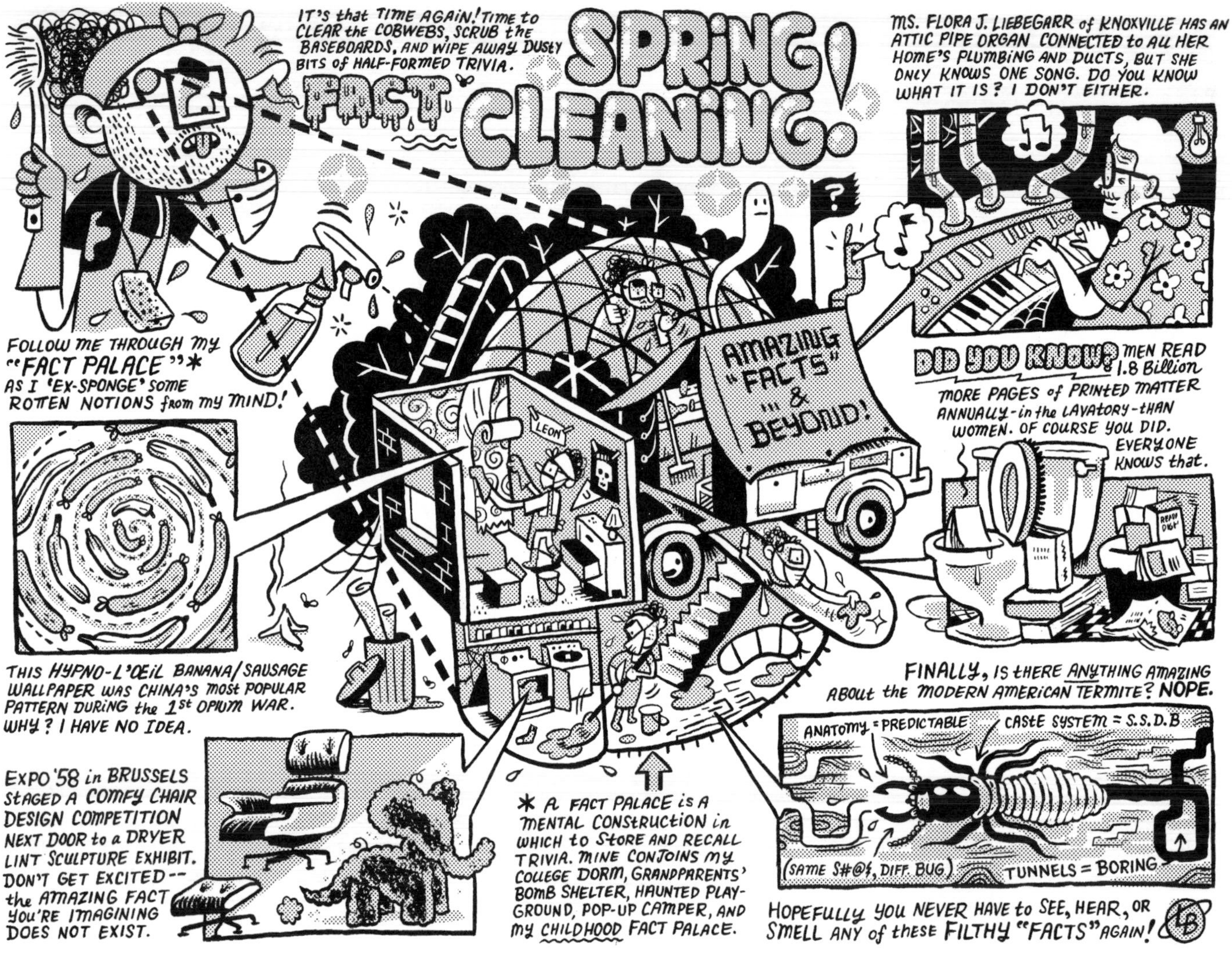

SPRING FACT CLEANING!
IT'S that TIME AGAIN! Time to CLEAR the COBWEBS, SCRUB the BASEBOARDS, AND WIPE AWAY DUSTY BITS of HALF-FORMED TRIVIA.
MS. FLORA J. LIEBEGARR of KNOXVILLE HAS AN ATTIC PIPE ORGAN CONNECTED to ALL HER HOME'S PLUMBING AND DUCTS, BUT SHE ONLY KNOWS ONE SONG. DO YOU KNOW WHAT IT IS? I DON'T EITHER.
FOLLOW ME THROUGH MY "FACT PALACE"* AS I 'EX-SPONGE' SOME ROTTEN NOTIONS from MY MIND!
LEON
AMAZING "FACTS" & BEYOND!
DID YOU KNOW? MEN READ 1.8 Billion MORE PAGES of PRINTED MATTER ANNUALLY - in the LAVATORY - than WOMEN. OF COURSE YOU DID. EVERYONE KNOWS that.
THIS HYPNO-L'OEIL BANANA/SAUSAGE WALLPAPER WAS CHINA'S MOST POPULAR PATTERN DURING the 1st OPIUM WAR. WHY? I HAVE NO IDEA.
FINALLY, IS THERE ANYTHING AMAZING ABOUT the MODERN AMERICAN TERMITE? NOPE.
ANATOMY = PREDICTABLE
CASTE SYSTEM = S.S.D.B
(SAME S#@$, DIFF. BUG.)
TUNNELS = BORING
EXPO '58 in BRUSSELS STAGED A COMFY CHAIR DESIGN COMPETITION NEXT DOOR to a DRYER LINT SCULPTURE EXHIBIT. DON'T GET EXCITED -- the AMAZING FACT YOU'RE IMAGINING DOES NOT EXIST.
* A FACT PALACE is A MENTAL CONSTRUCTION in WHICH to STORE AND RECALL TRIVIA. MINE CONJOINS MY COLLEGE DORM, GRANDPARENTS' BOMB SHELTER, HAUNTED PLAYGROUND, POP-UP CAMPER, AND MY CHILDHOOD FACT PALACE.
HOPEFULLY YOU NEVER HAVE to SEE, HEAR, OR SMELL ANY of these FILTHY "FACTS" AGAIN!
LB

AMAZING FACTS... AND BEYOND!

HEY KEVIN, IT'S LEON... WELL, ACTUALLY, I CAN'T DECIDE WHAT THE STRIP SHOULD BE ABOUT THIS WEEK... I HAVE A MENTAL **TRAFFIC JAM** OF FACTOIDS! NO, A **LOG JAM**! A **FUGUE**! A **BLOCKAGE**...

WELL, LIKE, I COULD TELL THEM ALL ABOUT THE **SMILING MARMASAN TREE** FROM AUSTRALIA, AND HOW, WHEN CUT DOWN, THE **STUMP** OF THIS SPECIES **SMILES**! YEAH, BECAUSE OF THE WAY THE WOOD GROWS, I GUESS.

(BUT THEN WHAT? A STRIP ABOUT TREES? SMILES?)

OR IT COULD BE ABOUT HOW BEAUTY AND THE BEAST STAR RON PERLMAN IS A **BIRTHMARK PSYCHIC**? HE CAN DO BOTH LOCATION **AND** DESCRIPTION!

LOWER BACK

ILLINOIS

(MOST BMPS ONLY DO LOCATION.)

OR I COULD TELL THEM ABOUT **VINCENT GIARD** — DO YOU KNOW ABOUT HIM? WHEN HE DIED HE WAS BURIED WITH HIS HEAD ENCASED IN STONE, CARVED, OF COURSE, IN HIS OWN LIKENESS — WHAT?

BECAUSE HE WAS **BURIED** WITH THE STONE HEAD AS THE **TOMBSTONE**. HE THOUGHT THAT THIS METHOD OF INTERNMENT WOULD BECOME POPULAR, BUT IT DID NOT.

SAND

OR I WAS THINKING THIS WEEK COULD BE ABOUT WHICH HOOFED ANIMALS LIKE TO BE **PETTED**, AND WHICH DO **NOT**.

GEMSBOK

YES

KLIPSPRINGER

NO

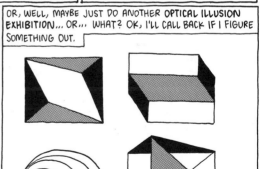

OR, WELL, MAYBE JUST DO ANOTHER **OPTICAL ILLUSION EXHIBITION**... OR... WHAT? OK, I'LL CALL BACK IF I FIGURE SOMETHING OUT.

LB

105

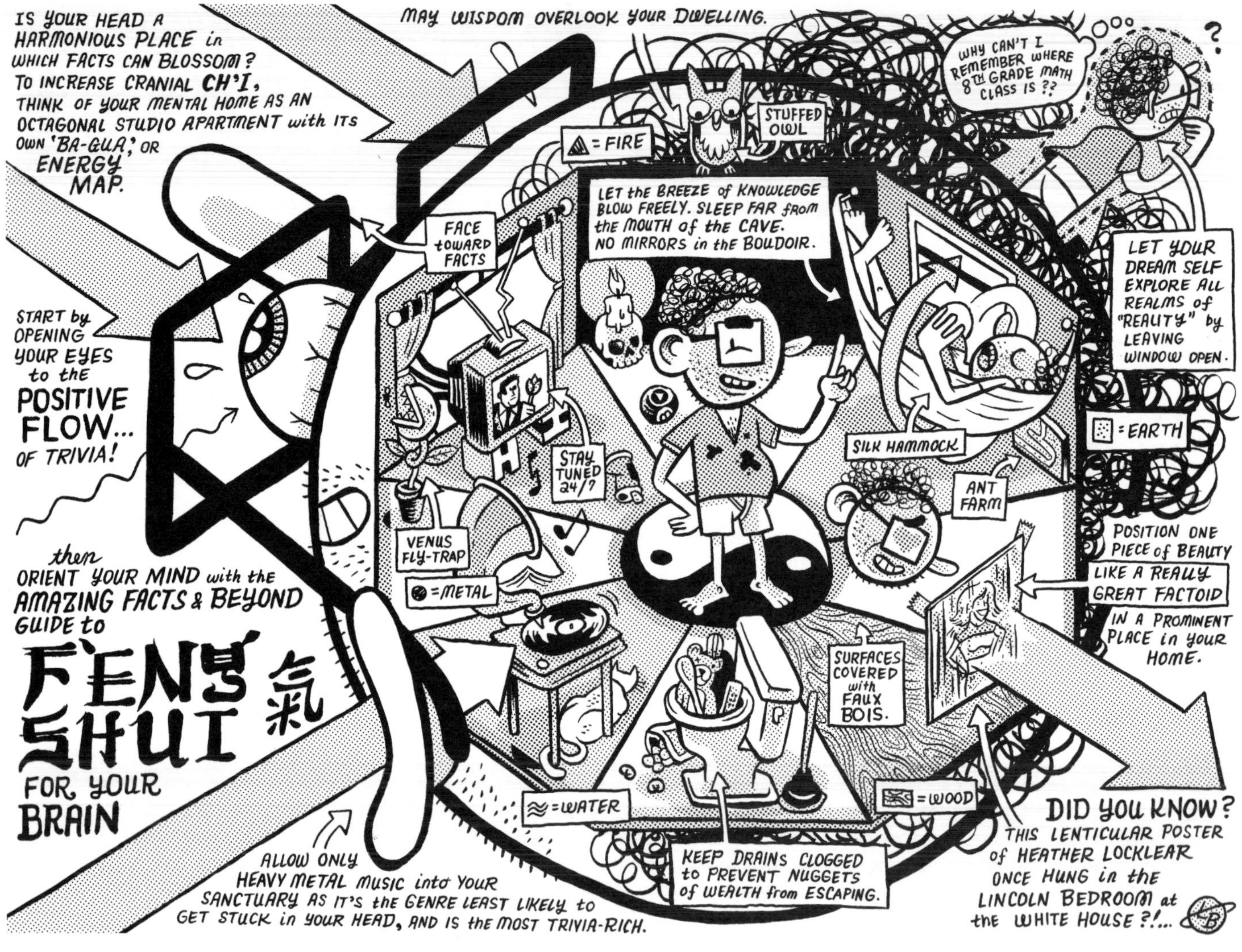
IS YOUR HEAD A HARMONIOUS PLACE in WHICH FACTS CAN BLOSSOM? TO INCREASE CRANIAL CH'I, THINK OF YOUR MENTAL HOME AS AN OCTAGONAL STUDIO APARTMENT with ITS OWN 'BA-GUA,' OR ENERGY MAP.
MAY WISDOM OVERLOOK YOUR DWELLING.
WHY CAN'T I REMEMBER WHERE 8TH GRADE MATH CLASS IS ??
STUFFED OWL
= FIRE
LET the BREEZE of KNOWLEDGE BLOW FREELY. SLEEP FAR from the MOUTH of the CAVE. NO MIRRORS in the BOUDOIR.
FACE toward FACTS
LET YOUR DREAM SELF EXPLORE ALL REALMS of "REALITY" by LEAVING WINDOW OPEN.
START by OPENING YOUR EYES to the POSITIVE FLOW... OF TRIVIA!
= EARTH
SILK HAMMOCK
STAY TUNED 24/7
ANT FARM
VENUS FLY-TRAP
= METAL
POSITION ONE PIECE of BEAUTY LIKE A REALLY GREAT FACTOID IN A PROMINENT PLACE in YOUR HOME.
then ORIENT YOUR MIND with the AMAZING FACTS & BEYOND GUIDE to FENG SHUI 氣 FOR YOUR BRAIN
SURFACES COVERED with FAUX BOIS.
= WATER
= WOOD
DID YOU KNOW? THIS LENTICULAR POSTER of HEATHER LOCKLEAR ONCE HUNG in the LINCOLN BEDROOM at the WHITE HOUSE ?!...
ALLOW ONLY HEAVY METAL MUSIC into YOUR SANCTUARY AS IT'S the GENRE LEAST LIKELY to GET STUCK in YOUR HEAD, AND IS the MOST TRIVIA-RICH.
KEEP DRAINS CLOGGED to PREVENT NUGGETS of WEALTH from ESCAPING.
LB

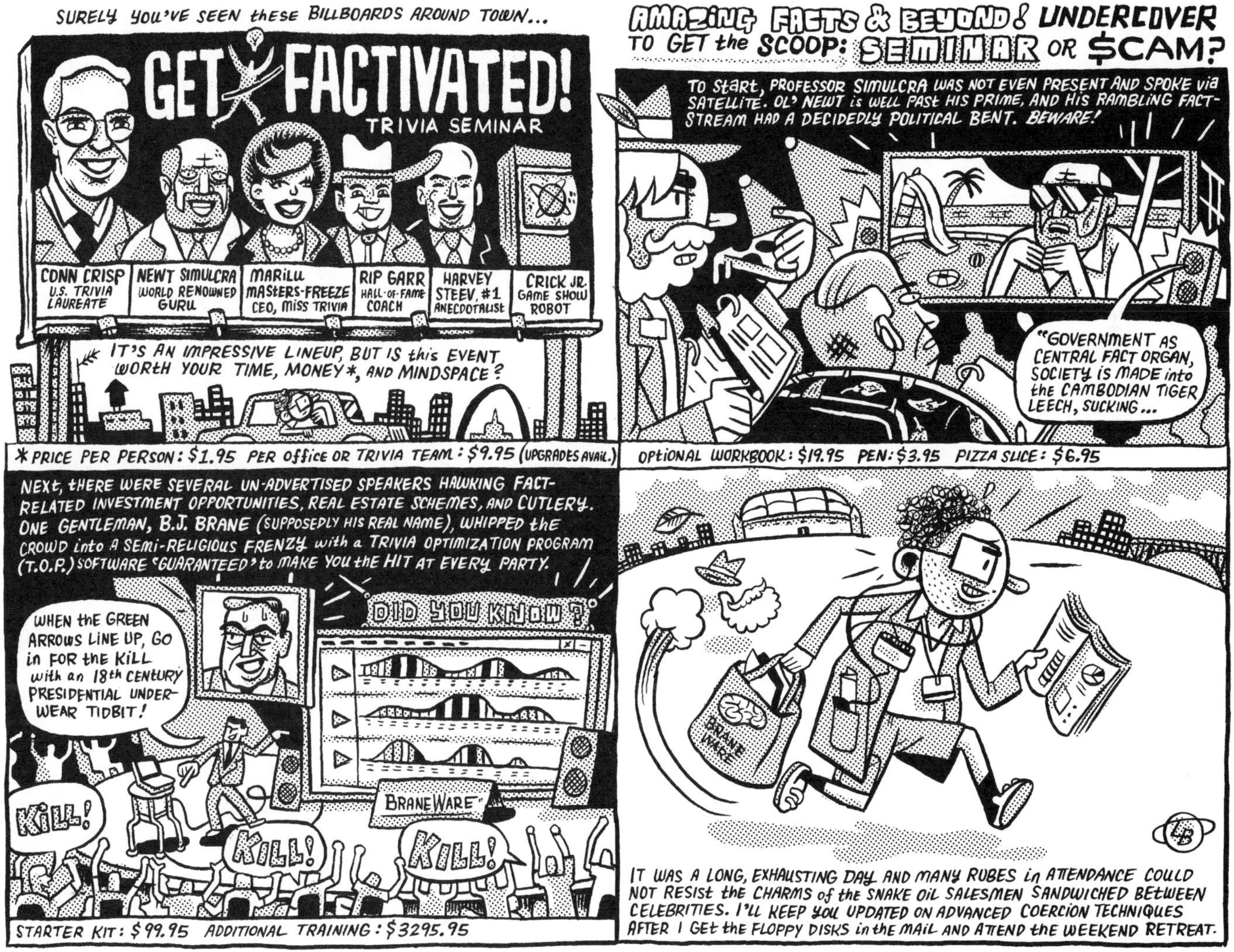
SURELY YOU'VE SEEN THESE BILLBOARDS AROUND TOWN...
GET FACTIVATED!
TRIVIA SEMINAR
CONN CRISP U.S. TRIVIA LAUREATE
NEWT SIMULCRA WORLD RENOWNED GURU
MARILU MASTERS-FREEZE CEO, MISS TRIVIA
RIP GARR HALL-OF-FAME COACH
HARVEY STEEV, #1 ANECDOTALIST
CRICK JR. GAME SHOW ROBOT
IT'S AN IMPRESSIVE LINEUP, BUT IS THIS EVENT WORTH YOUR TIME, MONEY*, AND MINDSPACE?
*PRICE PER PERSON: $1.95 PER OFFICE OR TRIVIA TEAM: $9.95 (UPGRADES AVAIL.)
AMAZING FACTS & BEYOND! UNDERCOVER TO GET THE SCOOP: SEMINAR OR $CAM?
TO START, PROFESSOR SIMULCRA WAS NOT EVEN PRESENT AND SPOKE VIA SATELLITE. OL' NEWT IS WELL PAST HIS PRIME, AND HIS RAMBLING FACT-STREAM HAD A DECIDEDLY POLITICAL BENT. BEWARE!
"GOVERNMENT AS CENTRAL FACT ORGAN, SOCIETY IS MADE INTO THE CAMBODIAN TIGER LEECH, SUCKING...
OPTIONAL WORKBOOK: $19.95 PEN: $3.95 PIZZA SLICE: $6.95
NEXT, THERE WERE SEVERAL UN-ADVERTISED SPEAKERS HAWKING FACT-RELATED INVESTMENT OPPORTUNITIES, REAL ESTATE SCHEMES, AND CUTLERY. ONE GENTLEMAN, B.J. BRANE (SUPPOSEDLY HIS REAL NAME), WHIPPED THE CROWD INTO A SEMI-RELIGIOUS FRENZY WITH A TRIVIA OPTIMIZATION PROGRAM (T.O.P.) SOFTWARE "GUARANTEED" TO MAKE YOU THE HIT AT EVERY PARTY.
DID YOU KNOW?
WHEN THE GREEN ARROWS LINE UP, GO IN FOR THE KILL WITH AN 18TH CENTURY PRESIDENTIAL UNDER-WEAR TIDBIT!
BRANEWARE
KILL!
KILL!
KILL!
STARTER KIT: $99.95 ADDITIONAL TRAINING: $3295.95
BRANE WARE
LB
IT WAS A LONG, EXHAUSTING DAY AND MANY RUBES IN ATTENDANCE COULD NOT RESIST THE CHARMS OF THE SNAKE OIL SALESMEN SANDWICHED BETWEEN CELEBRITIES. I'LL KEEP YOU UPDATED ON ADVANCED COERCION TECHNIQUES AFTER I GET THE FLOPPY DISKS IN THE MAIL AND ATTEND THE WEEKEND RETREAT.

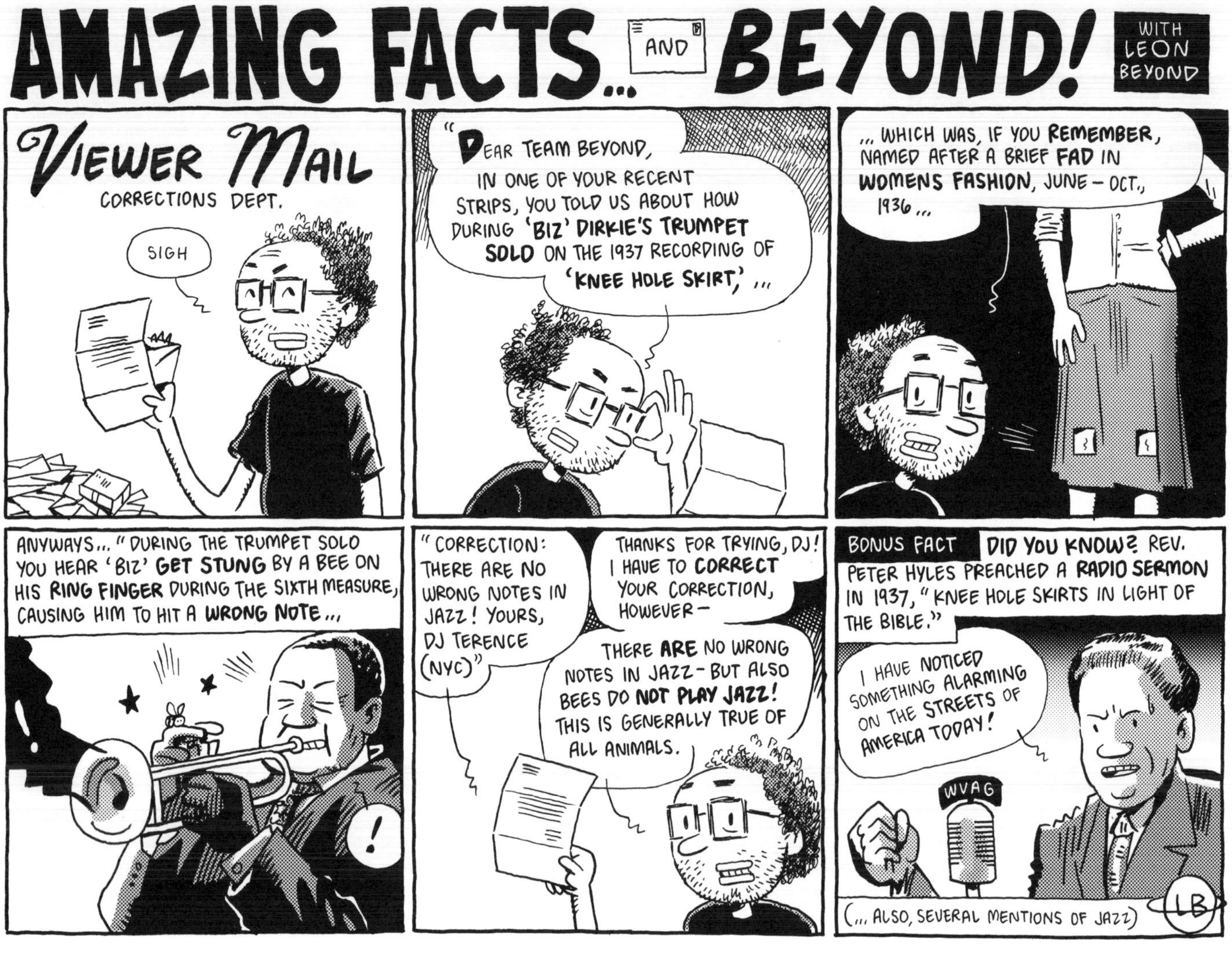
AMAZING FACTS... AND BEYOND!
WITH LEON BEYOND
VIEWER MAIL
CORRECTIONS DEPT.
SIGH
"DEAR TEAM BEYOND, IN ONE OF YOUR RECENT STRIPS, YOU TOLD US ABOUT HOW DURING 'BIZ' DIRKIE'S TRUMPET SOLO ON THE 1937 RECORDING OF 'KNEE HOLE SKIRT,' ...
... WHICH WAS, IF YOU REMEMBER, NAMED AFTER A BRIEF FAD IN WOMENS FASHION, JUNE – OCT., 1936 ...
ANYWAYS... "DURING THE TRUMPET SOLO YOU HEAR 'BIZ' GET STUNG BY A BEE ON HIS RING FINGER DURING THE SIXTH MEASURE, CAUSING HIM TO HIT A WRONG NOTE...
!
"CORRECTION: THERE ARE NO WRONG NOTES IN JAZZ! YOURS, DJ TERENCE (NYC)"
THANKS FOR TRYING, DJ! I HAVE TO CORRECT YOUR CORRECTION, HOWEVER –
THERE ARE NO WRONG NOTES IN JAZZ – BUT ALSO BEES DO NOT PLAY JAZZ! THIS IS GENERALLY TRUE OF ALL ANIMALS.
BONUS FACT
DID YOU KNOW? REV. PETER HYLES PREACHED A RADIO SERMON IN 1937, "KNEE HOLE SKIRTS IN LIGHT OF THE BIBLE."
I HAVE NOTICED SOMETHING ALARMING ON THE STREETS OF AMERICA TODAY!
WVAG
(... ALSO, SEVERAL MENTIONS OF JAZZ)
LB

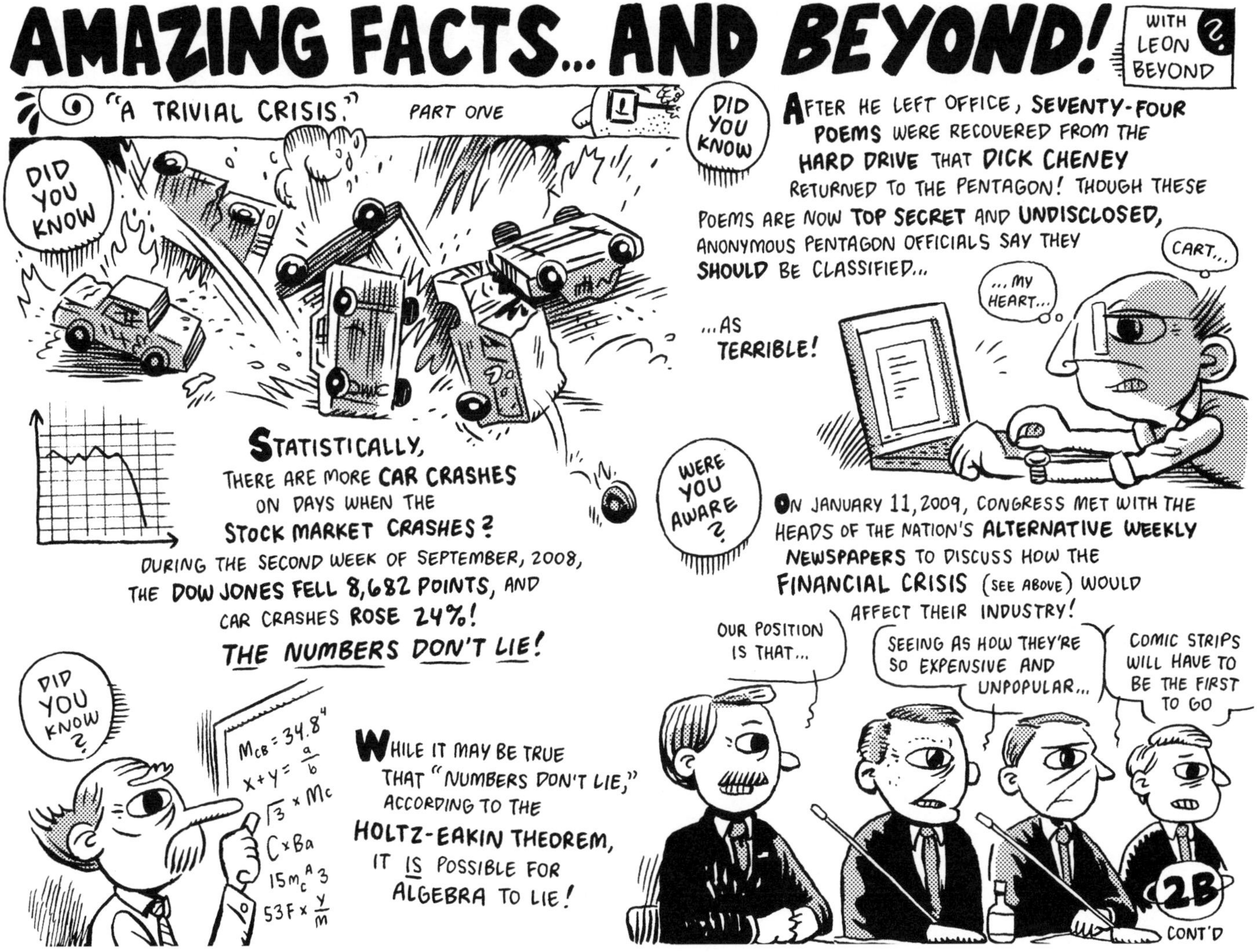
AMAZING FACTS... AND BEYOND!
WITH LEON BEYOND
"A TRIVIAL CRISIS." PART ONE
DID YOU KNOW
STATISTICALLY, THERE ARE MORE CAR CRASHES ON DAYS WHEN THE STOCK MARKET CRASHES?
DURING THE SECOND WEEK OF SEPTEMBER, 2008, THE DOW JONES FELL 8,682 POINTS, AND CAR CRASHES ROSE 24%!
THE NUMBERS DON'T LIE!
DID YOU KNOW
AFTER HE LEFT OFFICE, SEVENTY-FOUR POEMS WERE RECOVERED FROM THE HARD DRIVE THAT DICK CHENEY RETURNED TO THE PENTAGON! THOUGH THESE POEMS ARE NOW TOP SECRET AND UNDISCLOSED, ANONYMOUS PENTAGON OFFICIALS SAY THEY SHOULD BE CLASSIFIED...
...AS TERRIBLE!
...MY HEART...
CART...
DID YOU KNOW?
$M_{CB} = 34.8^4$
$x+y = \frac{a}{b}$
$\sqrt{3} \times M_C$
$C \times Ba$
$15 m_C^A 3$
$53F \times \frac{y}{m}$
WHILE IT MAY BE TRUE THAT "NUMBERS DON'T LIE," ACCORDING TO THE HOLTZ-EAKIN THEOREM, IT IS POSSIBLE FOR ALGEBRA TO LIE!
WERE YOU AWARE?
ON JANUARY 11, 2009, CONGRESS MET WITH THE HEADS OF THE NATION'S ALTERNATIVE WEEKLY NEWSPAPERS TO DISCUSS HOW THE FINANCIAL CRISIS (SEE ABOVE) WOULD AFFECT THEIR INDUSTRY!
OUR POSITION IS THAT...
SEEING AS HOW THEY'RE SO EXPENSIVE AND UNPOPULAR...
COMIC STRIPS WILL HAVE TO BE THE FIRST TO GO
2B
CONT'D

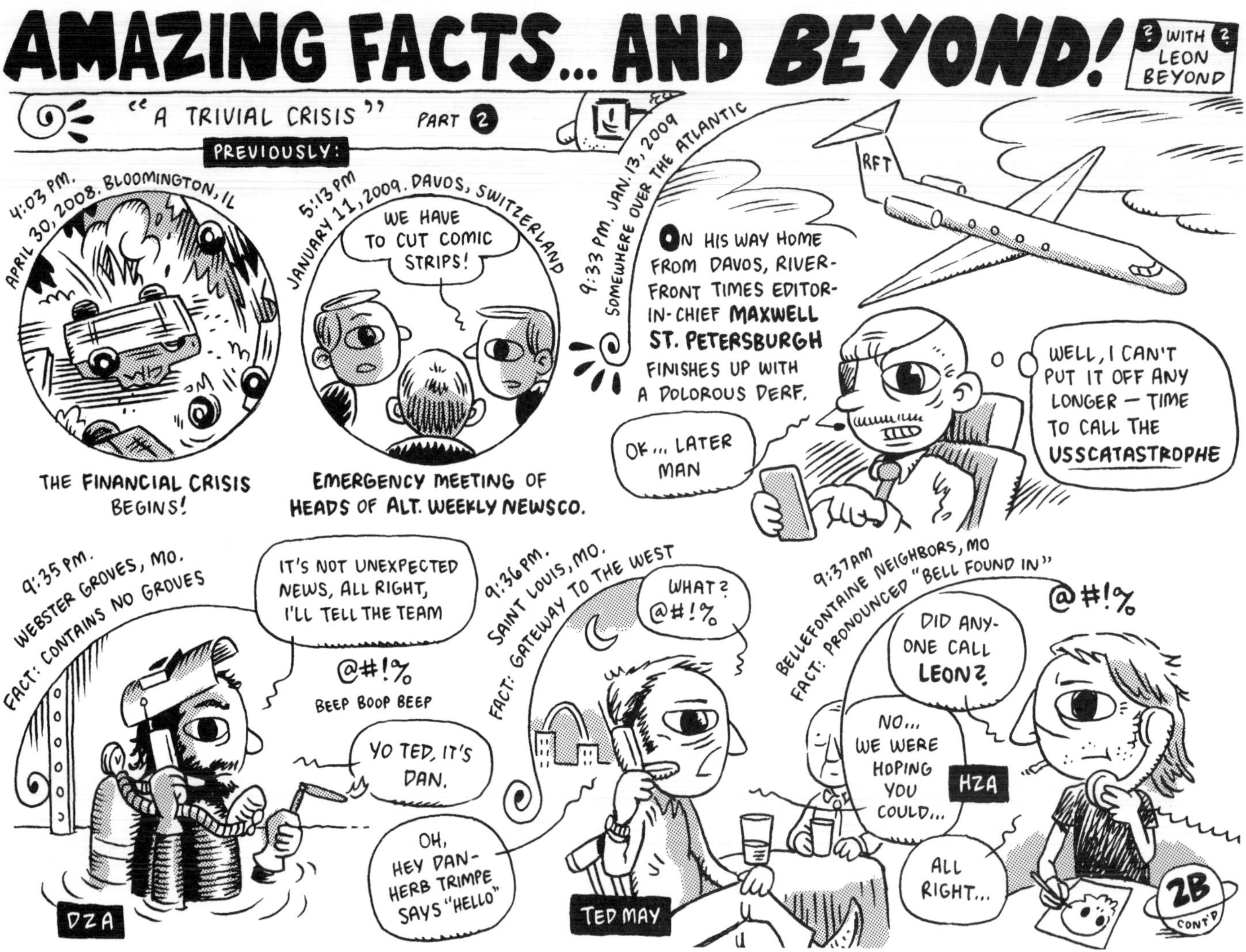
AMAZING FACTS... AND BEYOND!
WITH LEON BEYOND
"A TRIVIAL CRISIS" PART 2
PREVIOUSLY:
4:03 PM. APRIL 30, 2008. BLOOMINGTON, IL
THE FINANCIAL CRISIS BEGINS!
5:13 PM JANUARY 11, 2009. DAVOS, SWITZERLAND
WE HAVE TO CUT COMIC STRIPS!
EMERGENCY MEETING OF HEADS OF ALT. WEEKLY NEWSCO.
9:33 PM. JAN. 13, 2009 SOMEWHERE OVER THE ATLANTIC
RFT
ON HIS WAY HOME FROM DAVOS, RIVER-FRONT TIMES EDITOR-IN-CHIEF MAXWELL ST. PETERSBURGH FINISHES UP WITH A DOLOROUS DERF.
OK... LATER MAN
WELL, I CAN'T PUT IT OFF ANY LONGER — TIME TO CALL THE USSCATASTROPHE
9:35 PM. WEBSTER GROVES, MO. FACT: CONTAINS NO GROVES
IT'S NOT UNEXPECTED NEWS, ALL RIGHT, I'LL TELL THE TEAM
@#!%
BEEP BOOP BEEP
YO TED, IT'S DAN.
DZA
9:36 PM. SAINT LOUIS, MO. FACT: GATEWAY TO THE WEST
WHAT? @#!%
OH, HEY DAN-HERB TRIMPE SAYS "HELLO"
TED MAY
9:37 AM BELLEFONTAINE NEIGHBORS, MO FACT: PRONOUNCED "BELL FOUND IN"
@#!%
DID ANY-ONE CALL LEON?
NO... WE WERE HOPING YOU COULD...
HZA
ALL RIGHT...
2B CONT'D

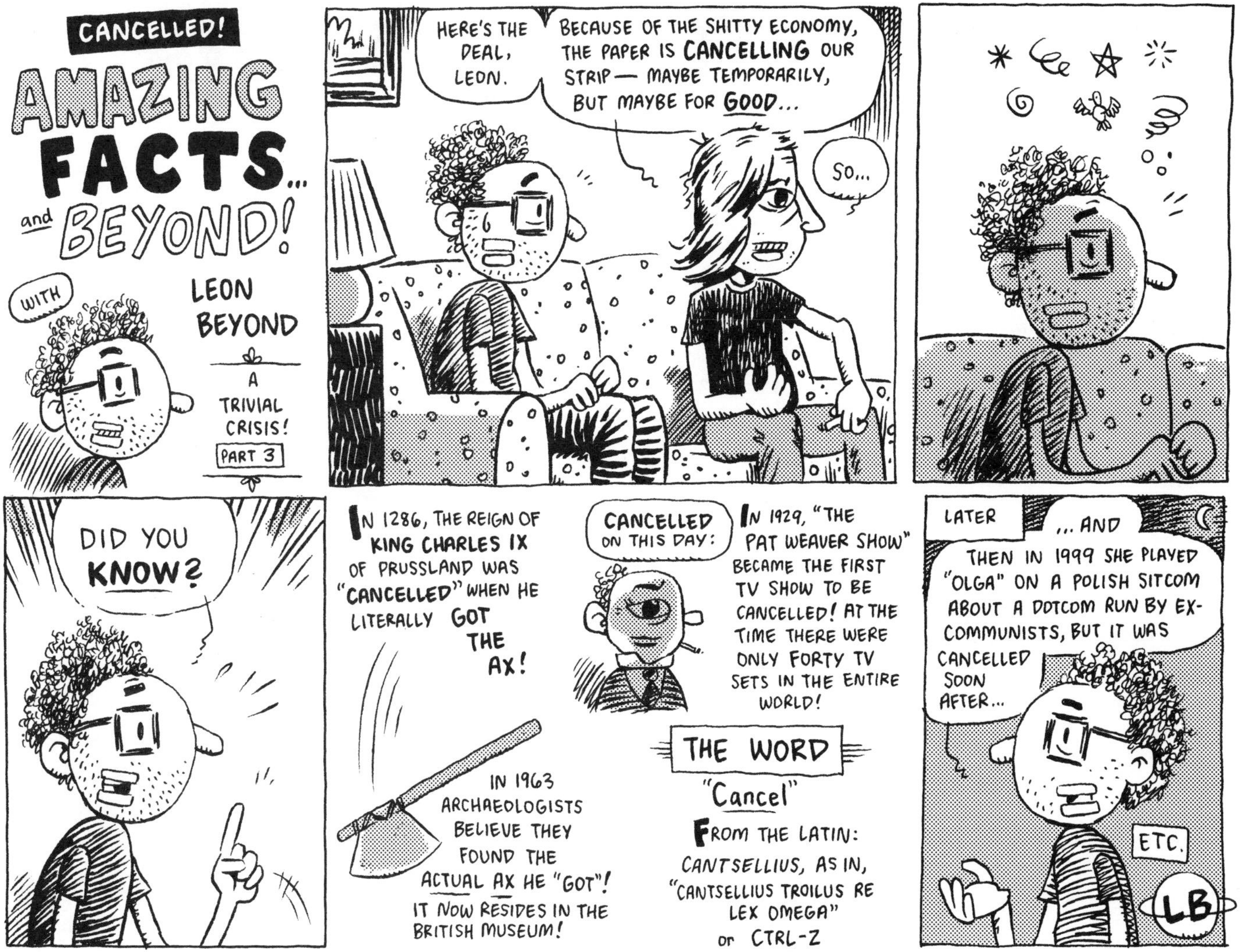
CANCELLED!
AMAZING FACTS... and BEYOND!
WITH
LEON BEYOND
A TRIVIAL CRISIS!
PART 3
HERE'S THE DEAL, LEON.
BECAUSE OF THE SHITTY ECONOMY, THE PAPER IS CANCELLING OUR STRIP— MAYBE TEMPORARILY, BUT MAYBE FOR GOOD...
SO...
DID YOU KNOW?
IN 1286, THE REIGN OF KING CHARLES IX OF PRUSSLAND WAS "CANCELLED" WHEN HE LITERALLY GOT THE AX!
IN 1963 ARCHAEOLOGISTS BELIEVE THEY FOUND THE ACTUAL AX HE "GOT"! IT NOW RESIDES IN THE BRITISH MUSEUM!
CANCELLED ON THIS DAY:
IN 1929, "THE PAT WEAVER SHOW" BECAME THE FIRST TV SHOW TO BE CANCELLED! AT THE TIME THERE WERE ONLY FORTY TV SETS IN THE ENTIRE WORLD!
THE WORD
"Cancel"
FROM THE LATIN: CANTSELLIUS, AS IN, "CANTSELLIUS TROILUS RE LEX OMEGA" or CTRL-Z
LATER
...AND THEN IN 1999 SHE PLAYED "OLGA" ON A POLISH SITCOM ABOUT A DOTCOM RUN BY EX-COMMUNISTS, BUT IT WAS CANCELLED SOON AFTER...
ETC.
LB

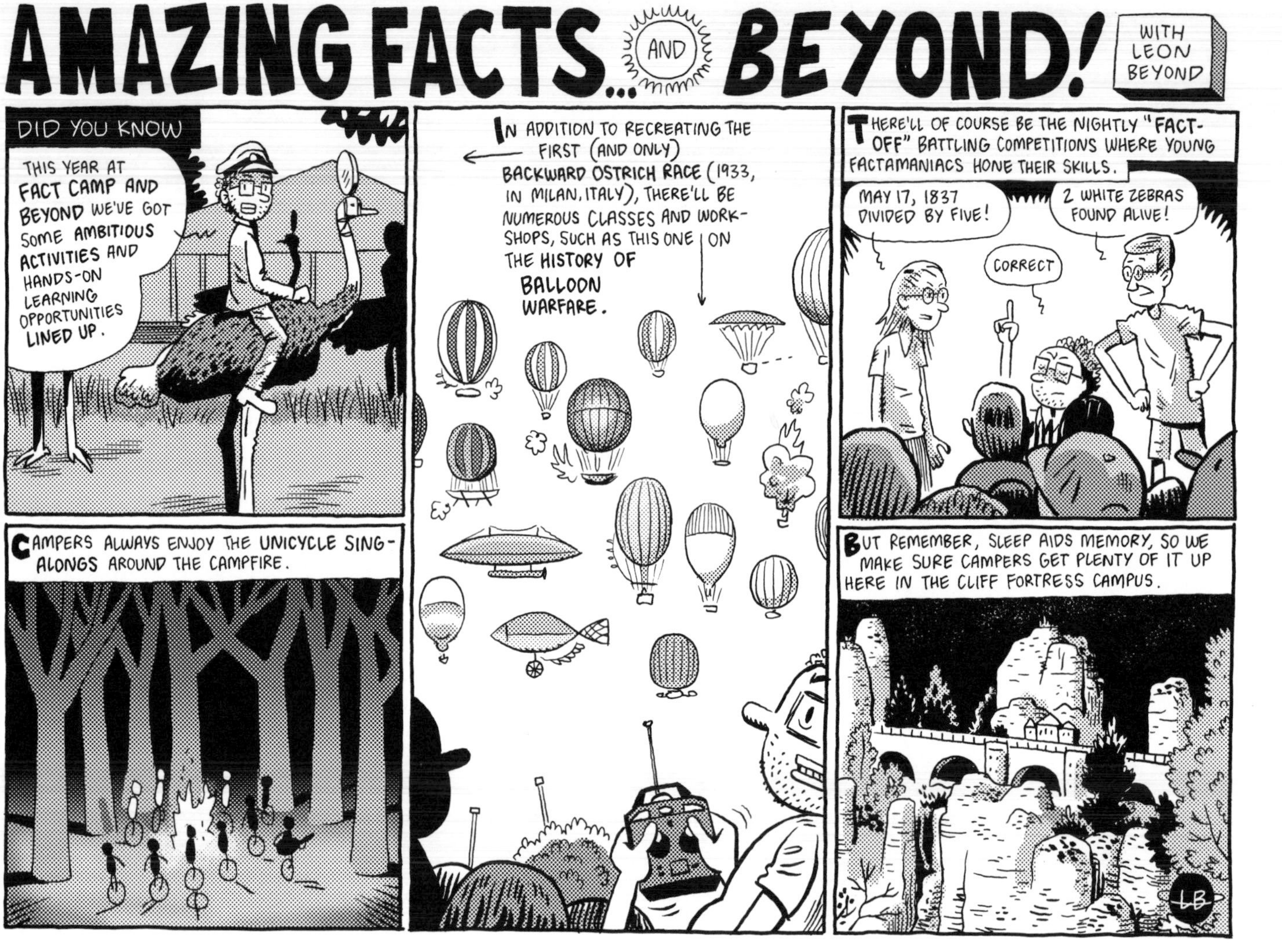
AMAZING FACTS... AND BEYOND! WITH LEON BEYOND
DID YOU KNOW
THIS YEAR AT FACT CAMP AND BEYOND WE'VE GOT SOME AMBITIOUS ACTIVITIES AND HANDS-ON LEARNING OPPORTUNITIES LINED UP.
IN ADDITION TO RECREATING THE FIRST (AND ONLY) BACKWARD OSTRICH RACE (1933, IN MILAN, ITALY), THERE'LL BE NUMEROUS CLASSES AND WORKSHOPS, SUCH AS THIS ONE ON THE HISTORY OF BALLOON WARFARE.
THERE'LL OF COURSE BE THE NIGHTLY "FACT-OFF" BATTLING COMPETITIONS WHERE YOUNG FACTAMANIACS HONE THEIR SKILLS.
MAY 17, 1837 DIVIDED BY FIVE!
2 WHITE ZEBRAS FOUND ALIVE!
CORRECT
CAMPERS ALWAYS ENJOY THE UNICYCLE SING-ALONGS AROUND THE CAMPFIRE.
BUT REMEMBER, SLEEP AIDS MEMORY, SO WE MAKE SURE CAMPERS GET PLENTY OF IT UP HERE IN THE CLIFF FORTRESS CAMPUS.
LB

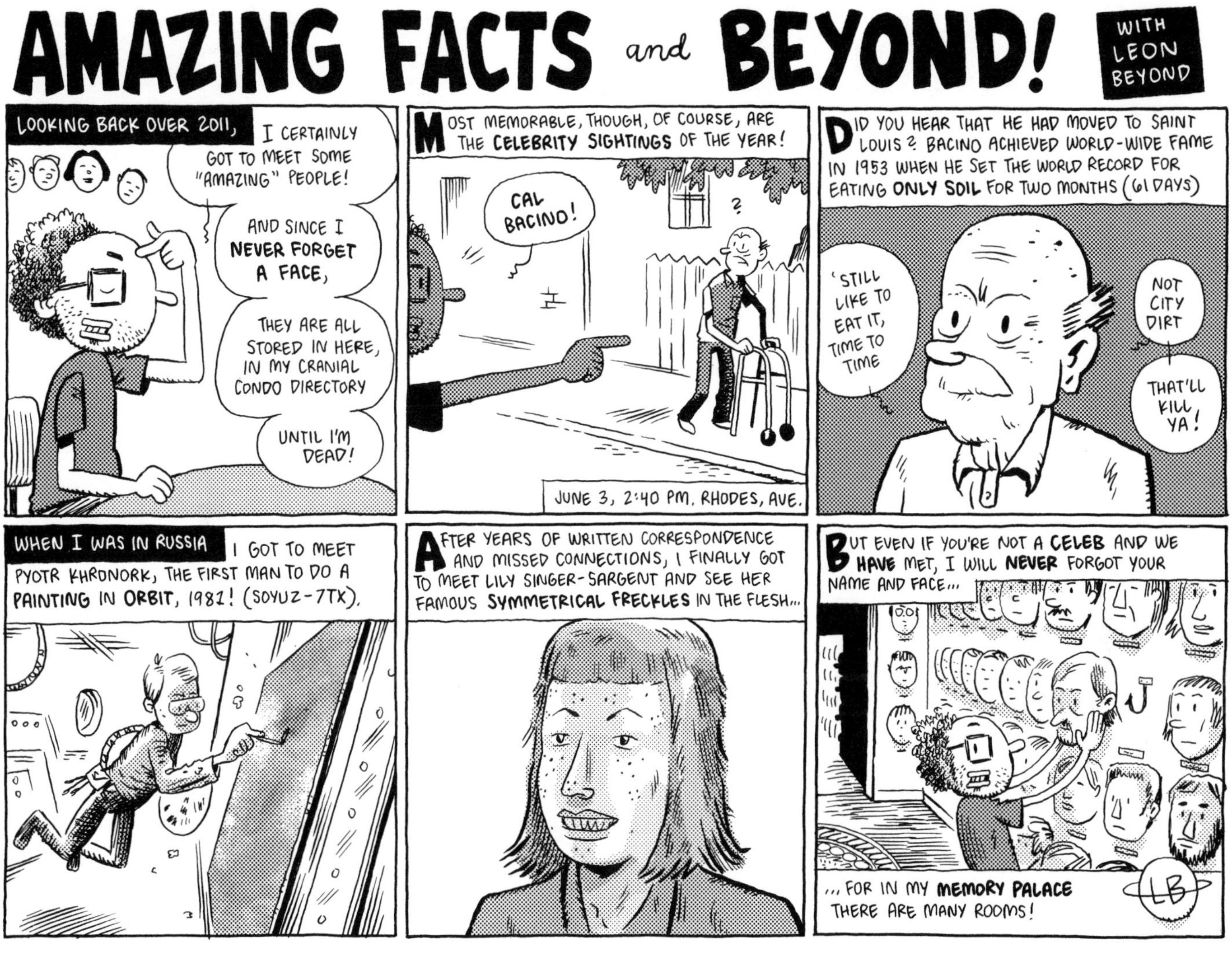
AMAZING FACTS and BEYOND!
WITH LEON BEYOND
LOOKING BACK OVER 2011,
I CERTAINLY GOT TO MEET SOME "AMAZING" PEOPLE!
AND SINCE I NEVER FORGET A FACE,
THEY ARE ALL STORED IN HERE, IN MY CRANIAL CONDO DIRECTORY
UNTIL I'M DEAD!
MOST MEMORABLE, THOUGH, OF COURSE, ARE THE CELEBRITY SIGHTINGS OF THE YEAR!
CAL BACINO!
?
JUNE 3, 2:40 PM, RHODES, AVE.
DID YOU HEAR THAT HE HAD MOVED TO SAINT LOUIS? BACINO ACHIEVED WORLD-WIDE FAME IN 1953 WHEN HE SET THE WORLD RECORD FOR EATING ONLY SOIL FOR TWO MONTHS (61 DAYS)
'STILL LIKE TO EAT IT, TIME TO TIME
NOT CITY DIRT
THAT'LL KILL YA!
WHEN I WAS IN RUSSIA
I GOT TO MEET PYOTR KHRONORK, THE FIRST MAN TO DO A PAINTING IN ORBIT, 1981! (SOYUZ-7TX).
AFTER YEARS OF WRITTEN CORRESPONDENCE AND MISSED CONNECTIONS, I FINALLY GOT TO MEET LILY SINGER-SARGENT AND SEE HER FAMOUS SYMMETRICAL FRECKLES IN THE FLESH...
BUT EVEN IF YOU'RE NOT A CELEB AND WE HAVE MET, I WILL NEVER FORGOT YOUR NAME AND FACE...
...FOR IN MY MEMORY PALACE THERE ARE MANY ROOMS!
LB

AMAZING FACTS... AND BEYOND!

WITH YOUR HOST, LEON BEYOND:

YOU KNOW WHAT?

I HAVE DEDICATED MY **LIFE** TO THE FACT THAT TRUTH IS **ODDER** THAN FICTION...

BUT!

MY LOVE FOR FACTOIDS KNOWS **SOME** BOUNDS, ACTUALLY! THERE ARE SOME 'AMAZING FACTS' I **HATE**!

THESE "MINDBLOWERS" ARE REALLY **EYEROLLERS**!

LIKE, DID YOU (GROAN) KNOW?

PRESIDENT HARRY TRUMAN SECRETLY COLLECTED TURTLES!

WHY I HATE THIS FACTOID: YOU SEE THIS ONE TROTTED OUT ALL THE TIME, BUT IT IS SO OVER-BLOWN! OK, HE HAD, LIKE, TWENTY TURTLES! GET OVER IT, LAMEBRAINS! BESIDES, A TURTLE BIT ME WHEN I WAS 2 AND I GUESS I HAVE A THING AGAINST TURTLES...

OR DID YOU (UGH) KNOW?

THE MODERN **FLYSWATTER** WAS INVENTED BY DR. FRANK CRUMBINE, WHO WAS INSPIRED BY A BASEBALL FAN YELLING "SWAT THE BALL!"

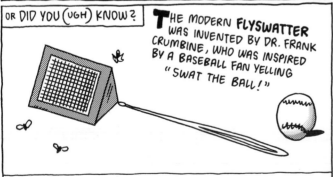

WHY I HATE THIS ONE: I SEE THIS ONE IN ALL THE MEDIOCRE COMPENDIUMS AND "BATHROOM READERS," IT EPITOMIZES THE MIDDLE-BROW FACTOID! IT'S SO PREDICTABLE.

I HATE IT WHEN PEOPLE ARE LIKE,"DID YOU KNOW, YOU CAN'T LICK YOUR ELBOW," OR "YOU CAN'T FOLD A PIECE OF PAPER MORE THAN SIX TIMES!"

I'M LIKE, UM...

THEN BAM, I DO BOTH AT THE SAME TIME!*

*FOIL + BERNOUCCI PRINCIPLE + TRIPLE JOINT DISLOCATION

LB

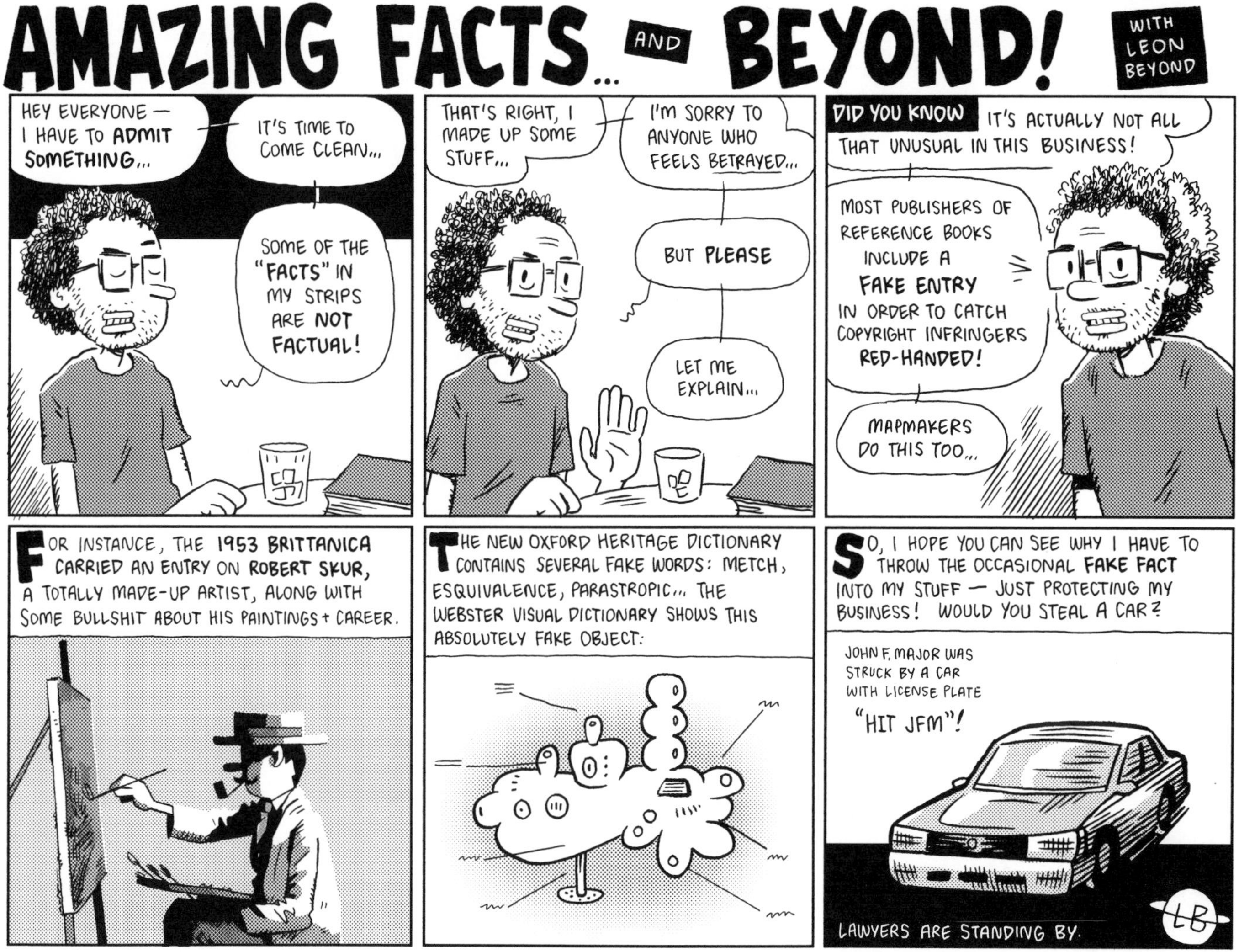
AMAZING FACTS... AND BEYOND!
WITH LEON BEYOND
HEY EVERYONE — I HAVE TO ADMIT SOMETHING...
IT'S TIME TO COME CLEAN...
SOME OF THE "FACTS" IN MY STRIPS ARE NOT FACTUAL!
THAT'S RIGHT, I MADE UP SOME STUFF...
I'M SORRY TO ANYONE WHO FEELS BETRAYED...
BUT PLEASE
LET ME EXPLAIN...
DID YOU KNOW
IT'S ACTUALLY NOT ALL THAT UNUSUAL IN THIS BUSINESS!
MOST PUBLISHERS OF REFERENCE BOOKS INCLUDE A FAKE ENTRY IN ORDER TO CATCH COPYRIGHT INFRINGERS RED-HANDED!
MAPMAKERS DO THIS TOO...
FOR INSTANCE, THE 1953 BRITTANICA CARRIED AN ENTRY ON ROBERT SKUR, A TOTALLY MADE-UP ARTIST, ALONG WITH SOME BULLSHIT ABOUT HIS PAINTINGS + CAREER.
THE NEW OXFORD HERITAGE DICTIONARY CONTAINS SEVERAL FAKE WORDS: METCH, ESQUIVALENCE, PARASTROPIC... THE WEBSTER VISUAL DICTIONARY SHOWS THIS ABSOLUTELY FAKE OBJECT:
SO, I HOPE YOU CAN SEE WHY I HAVE TO THROW THE OCCASIONAL FAKE FACT INTO MY STUFF — JUST PROTECTING MY BUSINESS! WOULD YOU STEAL A CAR?
JOHN F. MAJOR WAS STRUCK BY A CAR WITH LICENSE PLATE "HIT JFM"!
LAWYERS ARE STANDING BY.
LB

FASCINATING
ESOTERICA

ORNDORFF'S AMOEBA
AND ITS UNIQUELY-
SHAPED MITOCHONDRION

YOU PROBABLY HEARD ABOUT PIZZA MAGNATE "PAPA" JOHN SCHNATTER RE-UNITING WITH HIS BELOVED '71 Z28 CAMARO, TO THE TUNE OF 250 G's...

... SOLD TO FINANCE HIS FIRST OVEN

BUT DID YOU KNOW?! THERE ARE LOTS OF STORIES LIKE THIS AMONG THE ELITE "RAGS-to-GREASE-to-RICHES" RESTAURANTEUR SET.

IN 1985, COLONEL HARLAND SANDERS WON BACK HIS WWI-ERA INDIAN SCOUT CYCLE AT A MILITARY AUCTION AT HIS FORMER BASE...

BUCKET SEAT

... GUANTANAMO BAY IN CUBA! HE HAD TRADED THE BIKE AT WAR'S END FOR A SACK OF HERBS & SPICES.

AMAZING FACTS & BEYOND PRESENTS THE LOST LOVES of TEEN-AGED FAST-FOOD TYCOONS!

IN 1946, ORVILLE REDENBACHER BOUGHT BACK HIS BOYHOOD PET "POPPY" WHICH HE HAD SOLD TO ATTEND THE AGRI-CULTURAL SCHOOL AT PURDUE UNIVERSITY. IT COST HIM 100 TIMES WHAT HE SOLD IT FOR...

... BECAUSE THE HORSE HAD BEEN RE-NAMED "BURGOO KING" AND WON 2 OF THE 3 LEGS OF THOROUGHBRED RACING'S TRIPLE CROWN.

(NOT THE BELMONT)

Tudor's BISCUIT WORLD

THE DUKE 2.99

BOUGHT BY GRANDSON ON ebay FOR $13.50

RIGHT BEFORE HER DEATH IN 2002, MAE TUDOR CLAYTON WAS ABLE TO BUY THE EXACT PAIR OF KEDS SHE HAD AS A YOUNG RURAL WEST-VIRGINIAN WOMAN IN NEED OF SOME DOUGH.

MAE

SHE AUTHENTI-CATED THEIR IDENTITY BASED ON A BUTTER-MILK STAIN ON THE LEFT TOE!

LB

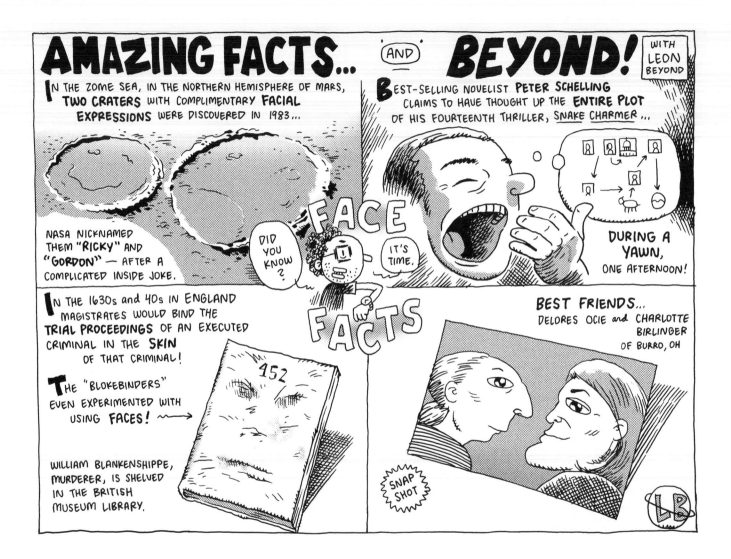

AMAZING FACTS... (AND) BEYOND!

WITH LEON BEYOND

IN THE ZOME SEA, IN THE NORTHERN HEMISPHERE OF MARS, **TWO CRATERS** WITH COMPLIMENTARY **FACIAL EXPRESSIONS** WERE DISCOVERED IN 1983...

NASA NICKNAMED THEM "RICKY" AND "GORDON" — AFTER A COMPLICATED INSIDE JOKE.

DID YOU KNOW ?

IT'S TIME.

FACE FACTS

BEST-SELLING NOVELIST PETER SCHELLING CLAIMS TO HAVE THOUGHT UP THE **ENTIRE PLOT** OF HIS FOURTEENTH THRILLER, <u>SNAKE CHARMER</u>...

DURING A YAWN, ONE AFTERNOON!

IN THE 1630s and 40s IN ENGLAND MAGISTRATES WOULD BIND THE **TRIAL PROCEEDINGS** OF AN EXECUTED CRIMINAL IN THE **SKIN** OF THAT CRIMINAL!

THE "BLOKEBINDERS" EVEN EXPERIMENTED WITH USING **FACES!** →

WILLIAM BLANKENSHIPPE, MURDERER, IS SHELVED IN THE BRITISH MUSEUM LIBRARY.

452

BEST FRIENDS... DELORES OCIE and CHARLOTTE BIRLINGER OF BURRO, OH

SNAP SHOT

LB

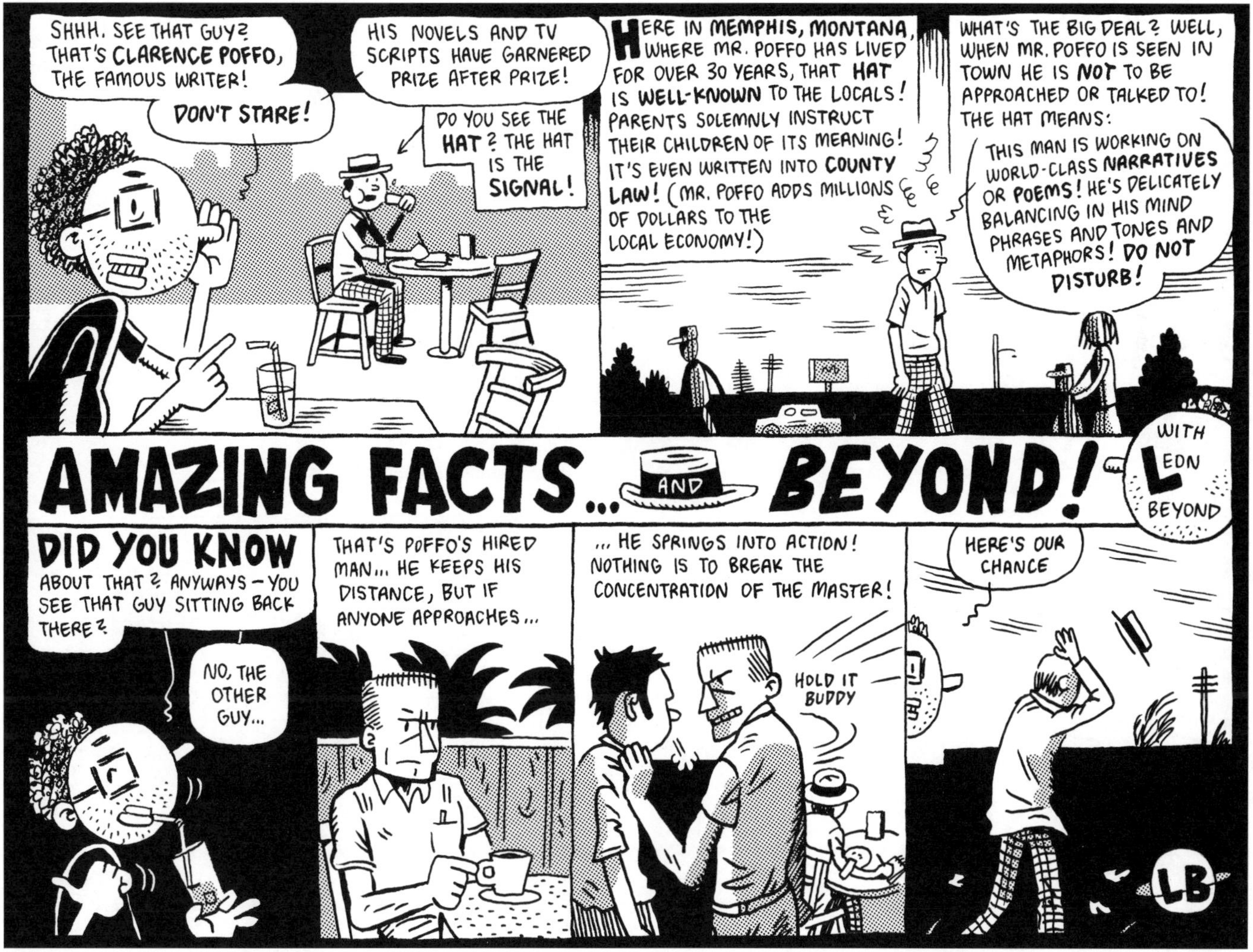
SHHH. SEE THAT GUY? THAT'S CLARENCE POFFO, THE FAMOUS WRITER!
HIS NOVELS AND TV SCRIPTS HAVE GARNERED PRIZE AFTER PRIZE!
DON'T STARE!
DO YOU SEE THE HAT? THE HAT IS THE SIGNAL!
HERE IN MEMPHIS, MONTANA, WHERE MR. POFFO HAS LIVED FOR OVER 30 YEARS, THAT HAT IS WELL-KNOWN TO THE LOCALS! PARENTS SOLEMNLY INSTRUCT THEIR CHILDREN OF ITS MEANING! IT'S EVEN WRITTEN INTO COUNTY LAW! (MR. POFFO ADDS MILLIONS OF DOLLARS TO THE LOCAL ECONOMY!)
WHAT'S THE BIG DEAL? WELL, WHEN MR. POFFO IS SEEN IN TOWN HE IS NOT TO BE APPROACHED OR TALKED TO! THE HAT MEANS:
THIS MAN IS WORKING ON WORLD-CLASS NARRATIVES OR POEMS! HE'S DELICATELY BALANCING IN HIS MIND PHRASES AND TONES AND METAPHORS! DO NOT DISTURB!
AMAZING FACTS... AND BEYOND!
WITH LEON BEYOND
DID YOU KNOW ABOUT THAT? ANYWAYS — YOU SEE THAT GUY SITTING BACK THERE?
NO, THE OTHER GUY...
THAT'S POFFO'S HIRED MAN... HE KEEPS HIS DISTANCE, BUT IF ANYONE APPROACHES...
... HE SPRINGS INTO ACTION! NOTHING IS TO BREAK THE CONCENTRATION OF THE MASTER!
HOLD IT BUDDY
HERE'S OUR CHANCE
LB

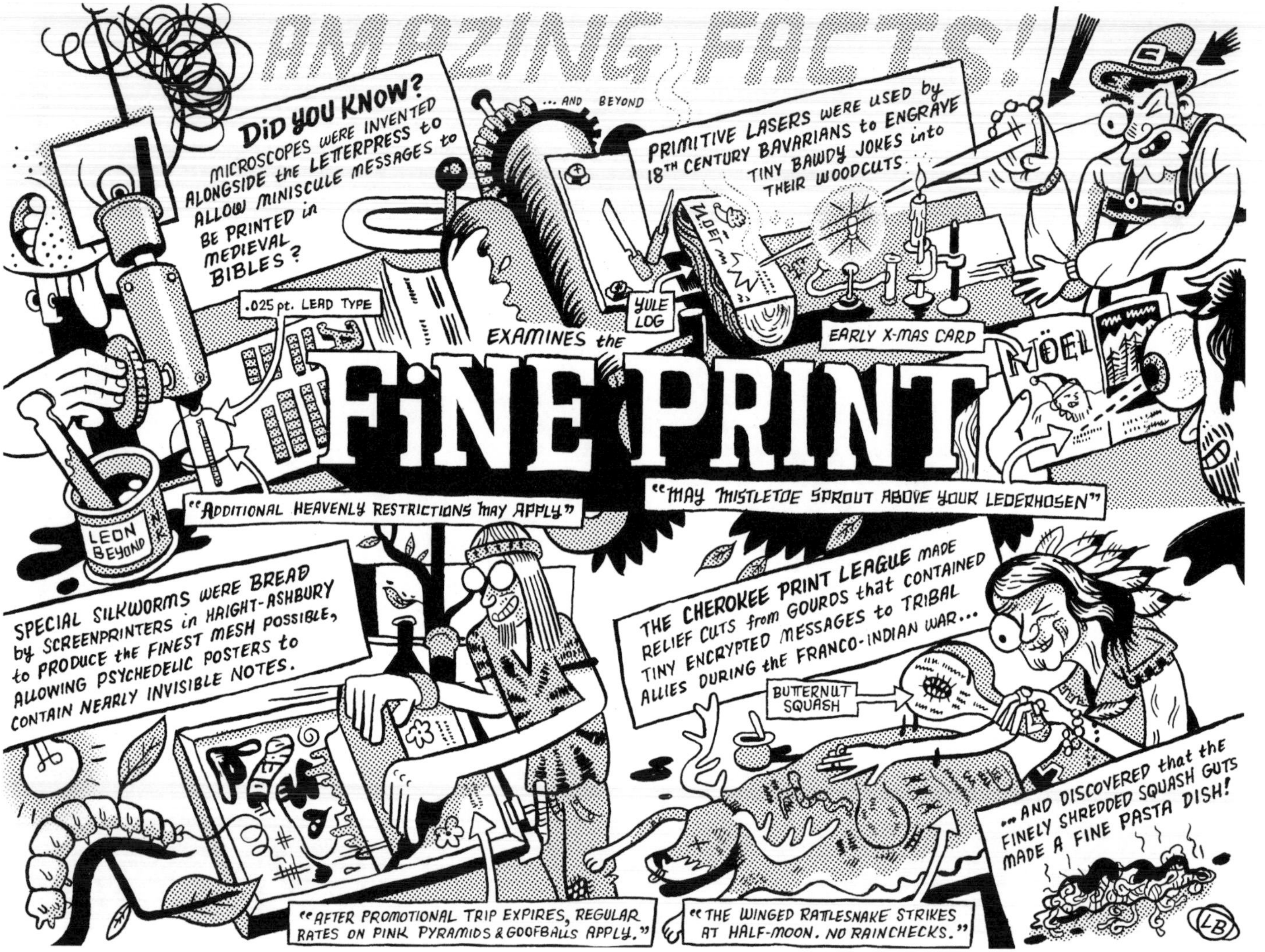
AMAZING FACTS!
... AND BEYOND
EXAMINES the
FINE PRINT
DID YOU KNOW? MICROSCOPES WERE INVENTED ALONGSIDE the LETTERPRESS to ALLOW MINISCULE MESSAGES to BE PRINTED in MEDIEVAL BIBLES?
.025 pt. LEAD TYPE
"ADDITIONAL HEAVENLY RESTRICTIONS MAY APPLY."
LEON BEYOND
PRIMITIVE LASERS WERE USED by 18TH CENTURY BAVARIANS to ENGRAVE TINY BAWDY JOKES into THEIR WOODCUTS.
YULE LOG
EARLY X-MAS CARD
NOËL
"MAY MISTLETOE SPROUT ABOVE YOUR LEDERHOSEN"
SPECIAL SILKWORMS WERE BREAD by SCREENPRINTERS in HAIGHT-ASHBURY to PRODUCE the FINEST MESH POSSIBLE, ALLOWING PSYCHEDELIC POSTERS to CONTAIN NEARLY INVISIBLE NOTES.
"AFTER PROMOTIONAL TRIP EXPIRES, REGULAR RATES ON PINK PYRAMIDS & GOOFBALLS APPLY."
THE CHEROKEE PRINT LEAGUE MADE RELIEF CUTS from GOURDS that CONTAINED TINY ENCRYPTED MESSAGES to TRIBAL ALLIES DURING the FRANCO-INDIAN WAR...
BUTTERNUT SQUASH
"THE WINGED RATTLESNAKE STRIKES AT HALF-MOON. NO RAINCHECKS."
...AND DISCOVERED that the FINELY SHREDDED SQUASH GUTS MADE A FINE PASTA DISH!
LB

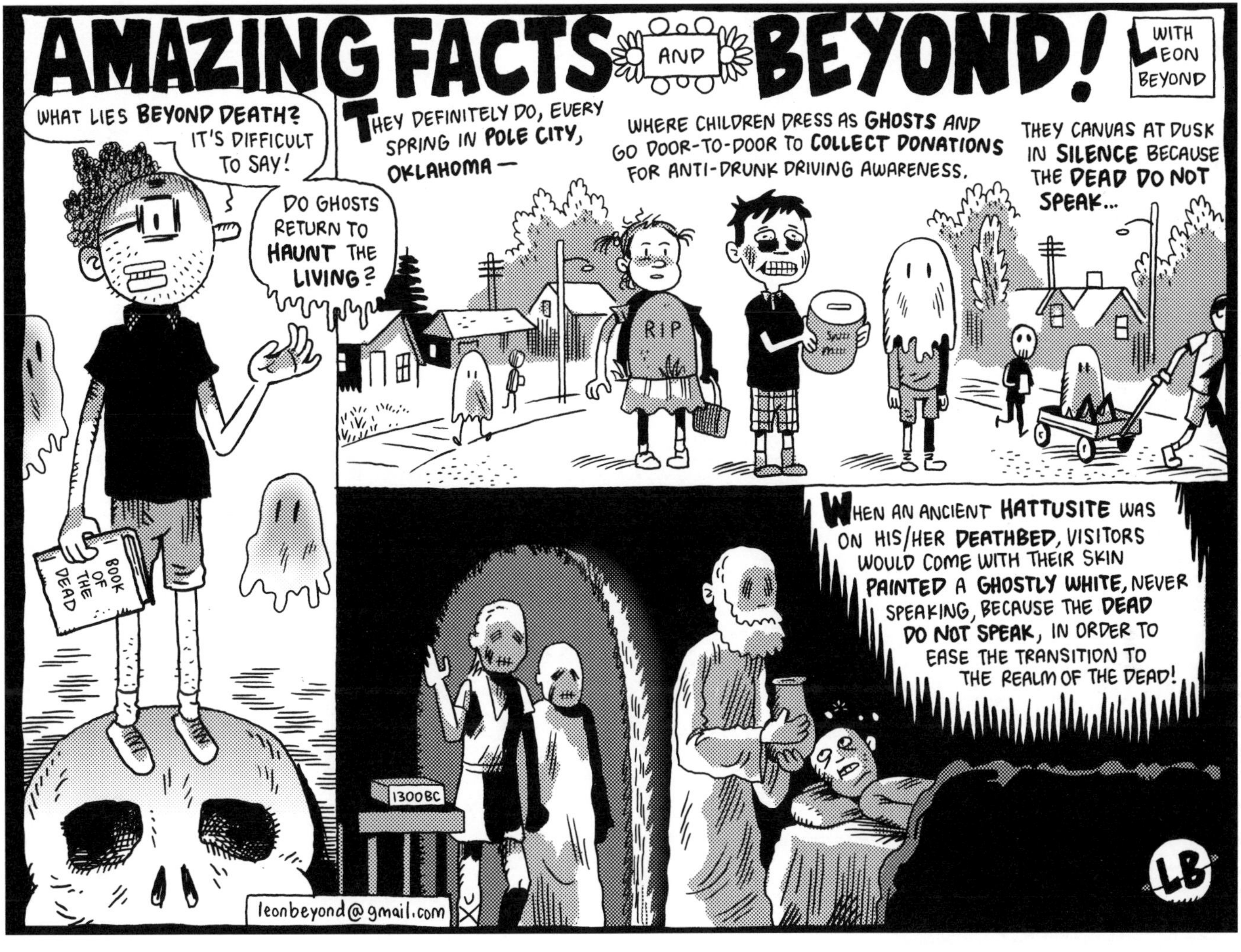
AMAZING FACTS AND BEYOND!
WITH LEON BEYOND
WHAT LIES BEYOND DEATH?
IT'S DIFFICULT TO SAY!
DO GHOSTS RETURN TO HAUNT THE LIVING?
BOOK OF THE DEAD
THEY DEFINITELY DO, EVERY SPRING IN POLE CITY, OKLAHOMA —
WHERE CHILDREN DRESS AS GHOSTS AND GO DOOR-TO-DOOR TO COLLECT DONATIONS FOR ANTI-DRUNK DRIVING AWARENESS.
THEY CANVAS AT DUSK IN SILENCE BECAUSE THE DEAD DO NOT SPEAK...
RIP
WHEN AN ANCIENT HATTUSITE WAS ON HIS/HER DEATHBED, VISITORS WOULD COME WITH THEIR SKIN PAINTED A GHOSTLY WHITE, NEVER SPEAKING, BECAUSE THE DEAD DO NOT SPEAK, IN ORDER TO EASE THE TRANSITION TO THE REALM OF THE DEAD!
1300BC
leonbeyond@gmail.com
LB

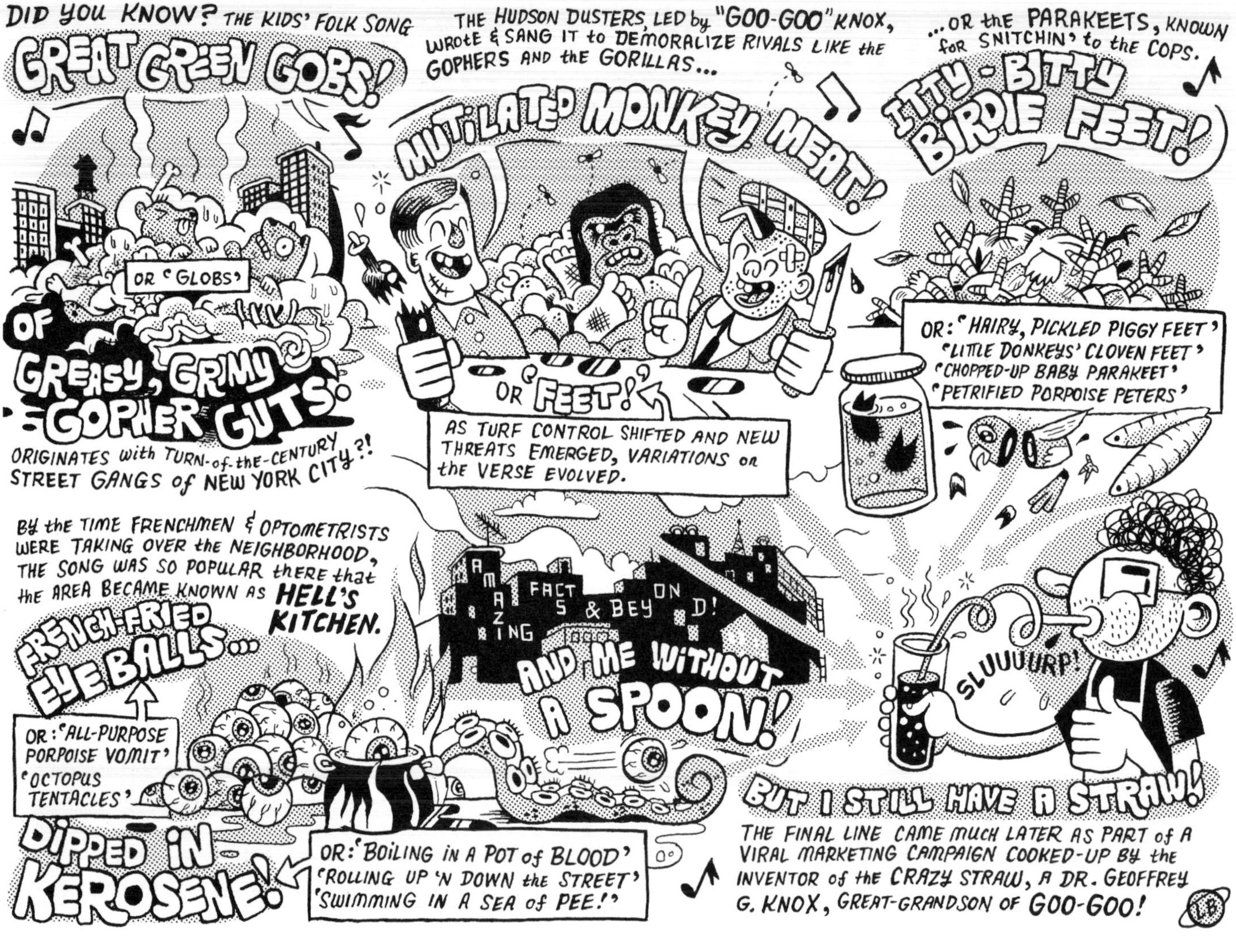

DID YOU KNOW? THE KIDS' FOLK SONG
GREAT GREEN GOBS!
OR 'GLOBS'
OF GREASY, GRIMY GOPHER GUTS!
ORIGINATES with TURN-of-the-CENTURY STREET GANGS of NEW YORK CITY?!
THE HUDSON DUSTERS, LED by "GOO-GOO" KNOX, WROTE & SANG IT to DEMORALIZE RIVALS LIKE the GOPHERS AND the GORILLAS...
MUTILATED MONKEY MEAT!
OR 'FEET!'
AS TURF CONTROL SHIFTED AND NEW THREATS EMERGED, VARIATIONS on the VERSE EVOLVED.
...OR the PARAKEETS, KNOWN for SNITCHIN' to the COPS.
ITTY-BITTY BIRDIE FEET!
OR: 'HAIRY, PICKLED PIGGY FEET'
'LITTLE DONKEYS' CLOVEN FEET'
'CHOPPED-UP BABY PARAKEET'
'PETRIFIED PORPOISE PETERS'
BY the TIME FRENCHMEN & OPTOMETRISTS WERE TAKING OVER the NEIGHBORHOOD, THE SONG WAS SO POPULAR there that the AREA BECAME KNOWN AS HELL'S KITCHEN.
FRENCH-FRIED EYEBALLS...
OR: 'ALL-PURPOSE PORPOISE VOMIT'
'OCTOPUS TENTACLES'
DIPPED IN KEROSENE!
OR: 'BOILING IN A POT of BLOOD'
'ROLLING UP 'N DOWN the STREET'
'SWIMMING IN A SEA of PEE!'
AMAZING FACTS & BEYOND!
AND ME WITHOUT A SPOON!
SLUUUURP!
BUT I STILL HAVE A STRAW!
THE FINAL LINE CAME MUCH LATER AS PART of A VIRAL MARKETING CAMPAIGN COOKED-UP BY the INVENTOR of the CRAZY STRAW, A DR. GEOFFREY G. KNOX, GREAT-GRANDSON OF GOO-GOO!
L.B.

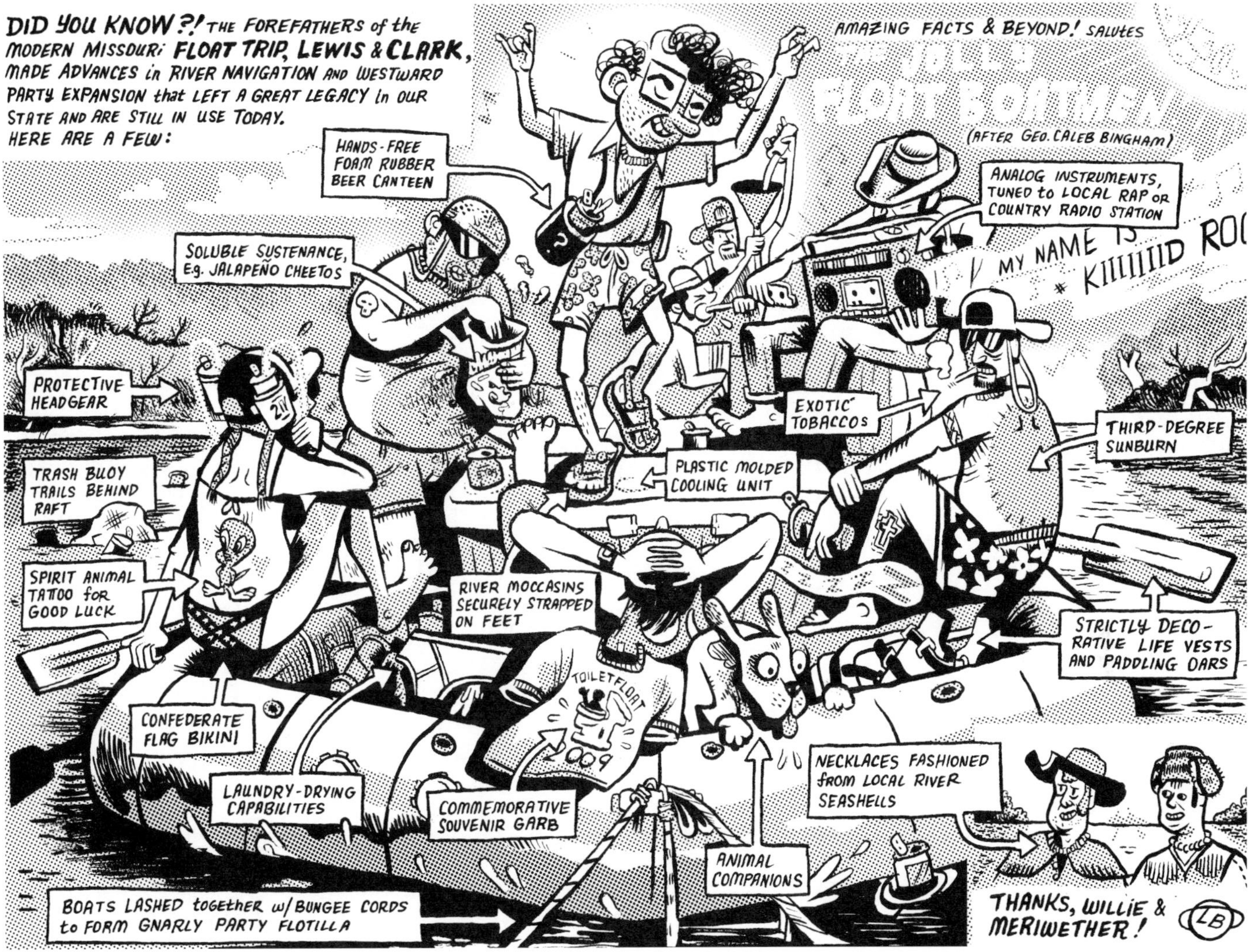
DID YOU KNOW?! THE FOREFATHERS of the MODERN MISSOURi FLOAT TRIP, LEWIS & CLARK, MADE ADVANCES in RIVER NAVIGATION AND WESTWARD PARTY EXPANSION that LEFT A GREAT LEGACY in OUR STATE AND ARE STILL IN USE TODAY. HERE ARE A FEW:
AMAZING FACTS & BEYOND! SALUtes
(AFTER GEO. CALEB BINGHAM)
HANDS-FREE FOAM RUBBER BEER CANTEEN
ANALOG INSTRUMENTS, TUNED to LOCAL RAP OR COUNTRY RADIO STATION
MY NAME IS
KIIIIIID ROC
SOLUBLE SUSTENANCE, E.g. JALAPEÑO CHEETOS
PROTECTIVE HEADGEAR
EXOTIC TOBACCOS
THIRD-DEGREE SUNBURN
TRASH BUOY TRAILS BEHIND RAFT
PLASTIC MOLDED COOLING UNIT
SPIRIT ANIMAL TATTOO for GOOD LUCK
RIVER MOCCASINS SECURELY STRAPPED ON FEET
STRICTLY DECO-RATIVE LIFE VESTS AND PADDLING OARS
TOILETFLOAT
2009
CONFEDERATE FLAG BIKINI
LAUNDRY-DRYING CAPABILITIES
COMMEMORATIVE SOUVENIR GARB
NECKLACES FASHIONED from LOCAL RIVER SEASHELLS
ANIMAL COMPANIONS
BOATS LASHED together w/ BUNGEE CORDS to FORM GNARLY PARTY FLOTILLA
THANKS, WILLIE & MERIWETHER!
LB

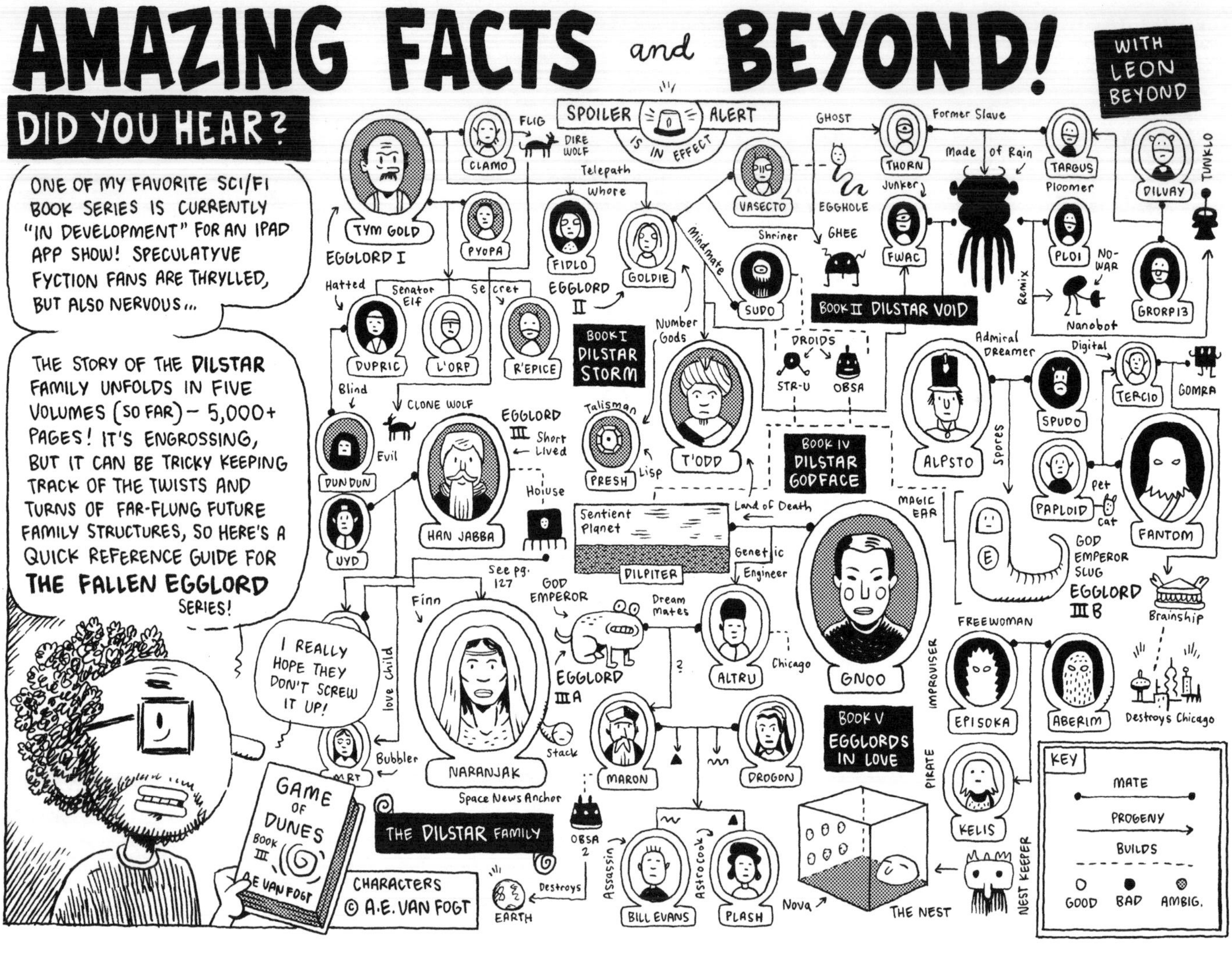
AMAZING FACTS and BEYOND!
WITH LEON BEYOND
DID YOU HEAR?
ONE OF MY FAVORITE SCI/FI BOOK SERIES IS CURRENTLY "IN DEVELOPMENT" FOR AN IPAD APP SHOW! SPECULATYVE FYCTION FANS ARE THRYLLED, BUT ALSO NERVOUS...
THE STORY OF THE DILSTAR FAMILY UNFOLDS IN FIVE VOLUMES (SO FAR) – 5,000+ PAGES! IT'S ENGROSSING, BUT IT CAN BE TRICKY KEEPING TRACK OF THE TWISTS AND TURNS OF FAR-FLUNG FUTURE FAMILY STRUCTURES, SO HERE'S A QUICK REFERENCE GUIDE FOR THE FALLEN EGGLORD SERIES!
I REALLY HOPE THEY DON'T SCREW IT UP!
GAME OF DUNES BOOK III A.E. VAN FOGT
SPOILER ALERT IS IN EFFECT
TYM GOLD
EGGLORD I
CLAMO
FLIG
DIRE WOLF
PYOPA
Telepath
Whore
FIDLO
EGGLORD II
GOLDIE
VASECTO
Mindmate
GHOST
EGGHOLE
Shriner
GHEE
SUDO
THORN
Former Slave
Made of Rain
Junker
FWAC
TARGUS
Ploomer
PLOI
NO-WAR
Remix
Nanobot
DILVAY
TUNKLO
GRORP13
BOOK II DILSTAR VOID
Hatted
DUPRIC
Senator Elf
L'ORP
Secret
R'EPICE
BOOK I DILSTAR STORM
Number Gods
DROIDS
STR-U
OBSA
T'ODD
Talisman
PRESH
Lisp
BOOK IV DILSTAR GODFACE
Admiral Dreamer
ALPSTO
Spores
Digital
SPUDO
TERCIO
GOMRA
PAPLOID
Pet
Cat
FANTOM
Blind
DUN DUN
Evil
UYD
CLONE WOLF
HAN JABBA
EGGLORD III
Short Lived
House
Sentient Planet
DILPITER
Land of Death
MAGIC EAR
GOD EMPEROR SLUG
EGGLORD III B
Brainship
Genetic Engineer
GNOO
See pg. 127
Finn
love child
NARANJAK
GOD EMPEROR
EGGLORD III A
Dream mates
ALTRU
Chicago
?
FREEWOMAN
IMPROVISER
EPISOKA
ABERIM
Destroys Chicago
MRT
Bubbler
Stack
Space News Anchor
MARON
DROGON
BOOK V EGGLORDS IN LOVE
PIRATE
KELIS
THE DILSTAR FAMILY
OBSA 2
Destroys
EARTH
Assassin
BILL EVANS
Astrocook
PLASH
Nova
THE NEST
NEST KEEPER
KEY
MATE
PROGENY
BUILDS
GOOD
BAD
AMBIG.
CHARACTERS © A.E. VAN FOGT

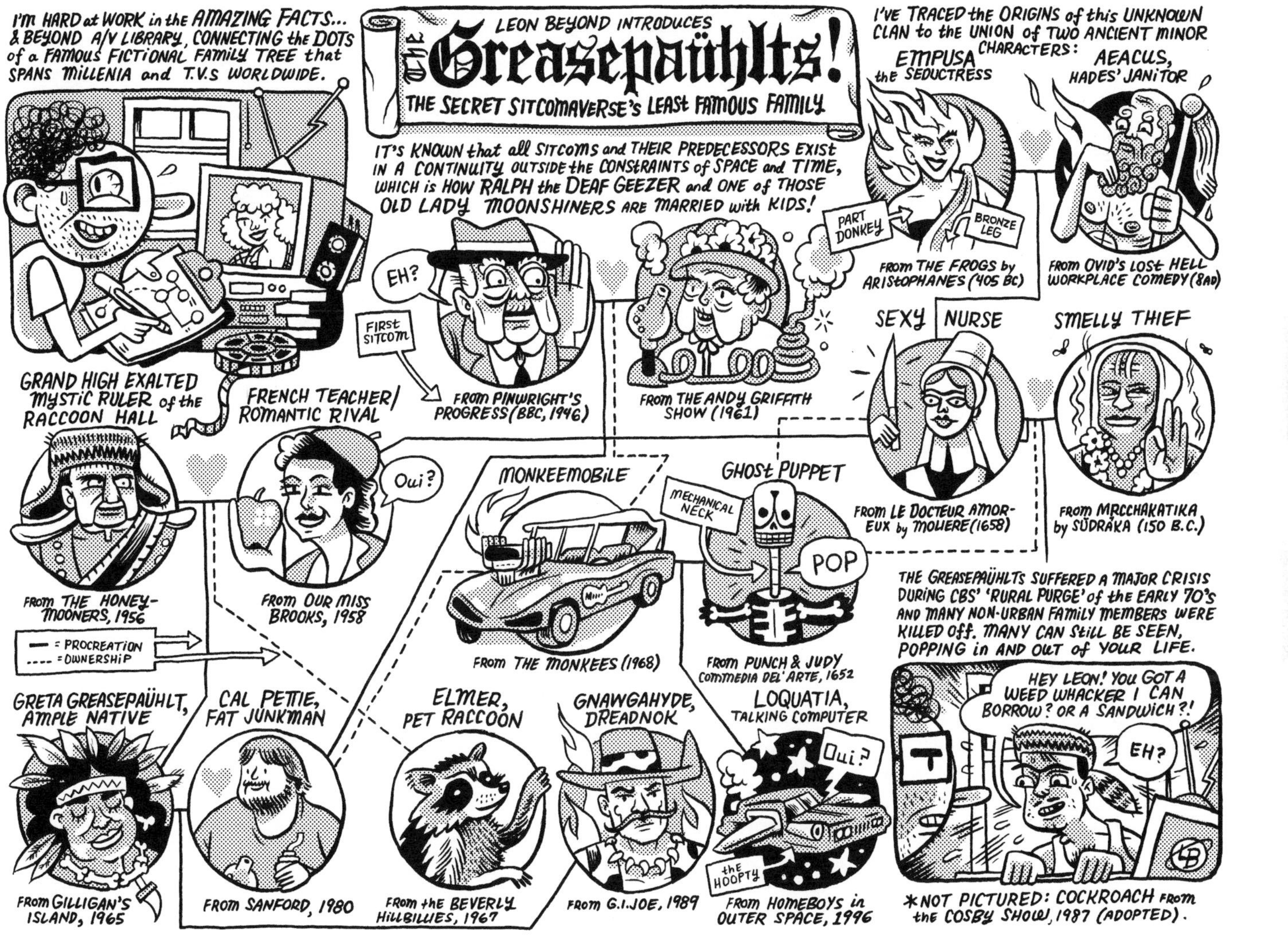
LEON BEYOND INTRODUCES
THE Greasepaühlts!
THE SECRET SITCOMAVERSE'S LEAST FAMOUS FAMILY
I'M HARD at WORK in the AMAZING FACTS... & BEYOND A/V LIBRARY, CONNECTING the DOTS of a FAMOUS FICTIONAL FAMILY TREE that SPANS MILLENIA and T.V.S WORLDWIDE.
IT'S KNOWN that all SITCOMS and THEIR PREDECESSORS EXIST IN A CONTINUITY OUTSIDE the CONSTRAINTS of SPACE and TIME, WHICH is HOW RALPH the DEAF GEEZER and ONE of THOSE OLD LADY MOONSHINERS ARE MARRIED with KIDS!
I'VE TRACED the ORIGINS of this UNKNOWN CLAN to the UNION of TWO ANCIENT MINOR CHARACTERS:
EMPUSA the SEDUCTRESS
AEACUS, HADES' JANITOR
PART DONKEY
BRONZE LEG
FROM THE FROGS by ARISTOPHANES (405 BC)
FROM OVID'S LOST HELL WORKPLACE COMEDY (8AD)
EH?
FIRST SITCOM
FROM PINWRIGHT'S PROGRESS (BBC, 1946)
FROM THE ANDY GRIFFITH SHOW (1961)
SEXY NURSE
SMELLY THIEF
FROM LE DOCTEUR AMOREUX by MOLIERE (1658)
FROM MRCCHAKATIKA by SÜDRAKA (150 B.C.)
GRAND HIGH EXALTED MYSTIC RULER of the RACCOON HALL
FRENCH TEACHER/ ROMANTIC RIVAL
Oui?
FROM THE HONEYMOONERS, 1956
FROM OUR MISS BROOKS, 1958
MONKEEMOBILE
FROM THE MONKEES (1968)
GHOST PUPPET
MECHANICAL NECK
POP
FROM PUNCH & JUDY COMMEDIA DEL' ARTE, 1652
THE GREASEPAÜHLTS SUFFERED A MAJOR CRISIS DURING CBS' 'RURAL PURGE' of the EARLY 70'S AND MANY NON-URBAN FAMILY MEMBERS WERE KILLED OFF. MANY CAN STILL BE SEEN, POPPING in AND OUT of YOUR LIFE.
= PROCREATION
= OWNERSHIP
GRETA GREASEPAÜHLT, AMPLE NATIVE
CAL PETTIE, FAT JUNKMAN
ELMER, PET RACCOON
GNAWGAHYDE, DREADNOK
LOQUATIA, TALKING COMPUTER
Oui?
the HOOPTY
HEY LEON! YOU GOT A WEED WHACKER I CAN BORROW? OR A SANDWICH?!
EH?
FROM GILLIGAN'S ISLAND, 1965
FROM SANFORD, 1980
FROM the BEVERLY HILLBILLIES, 1967
FROM G.I.JOE, 1989
FROM HOMEBOYS in OUTER SPACE, 1996
*NOT PICTURED: COCKROACH FROM the COSBY SHOW, 1987 (ADOPTED).
KB

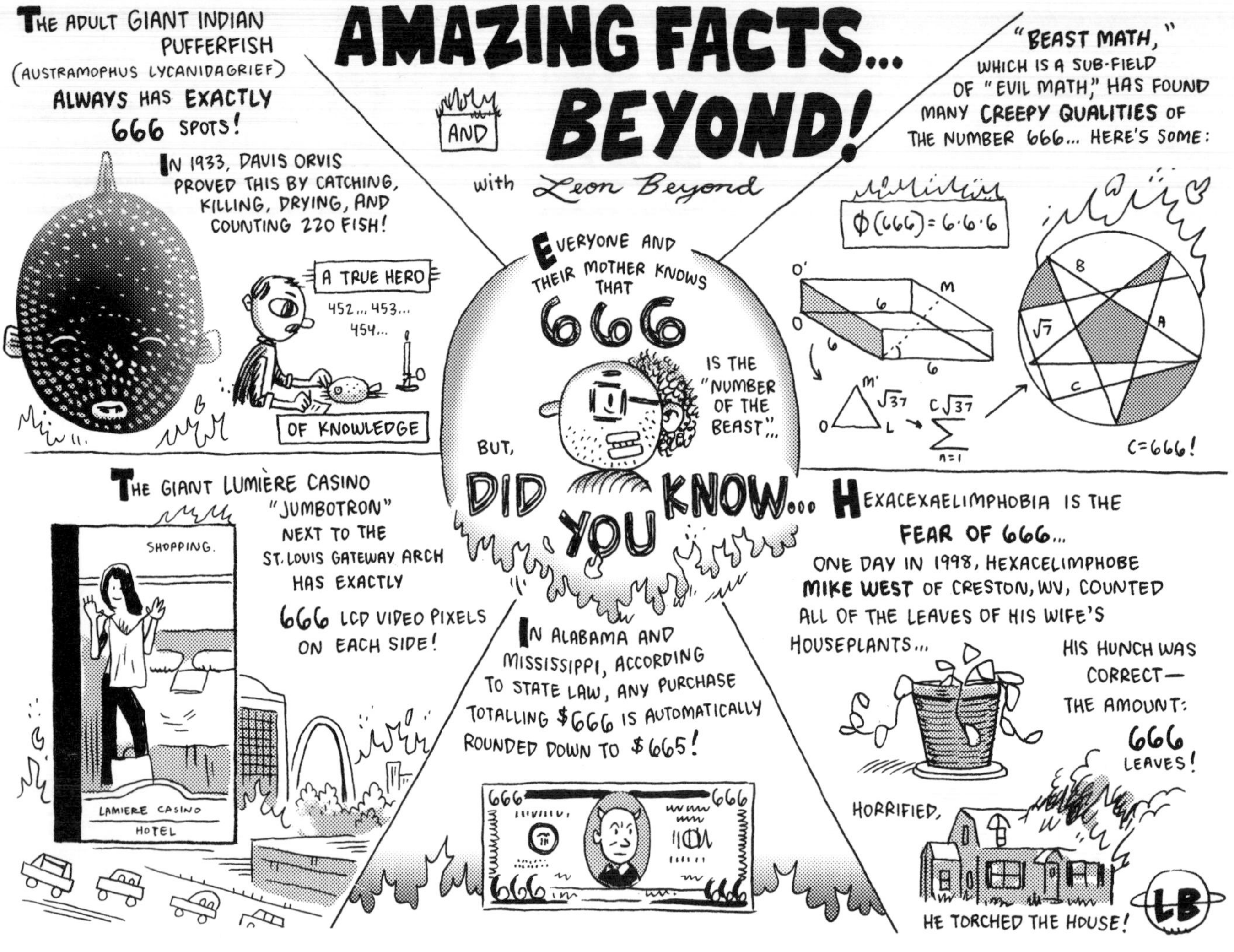

AMAZING FACTS... AND BEYOND!
with Leon Beyond
THE ADULT GIANT INDIAN PUFFERFISH (AUSTRAMOPHUS LYCANIDAGRIEF) ALWAYS HAS EXACTLY 666 SPOTS!
IN 1933, DAVIS ORVIS PROVED THIS BY CATCHING, KILLING, DRYING, AND COUNTING 220 FISH!
A TRUE HERO
452... 453... 454...
OF KNOWLEDGE
EVERYONE AND THEIR MOTHER KNOWS THAT 666 IS THE "NUMBER OF THE BEAST"...
BUT, DID YOU KNOW...
"BEAST MATH," WHICH IS A SUB-FIELD OF "EVIL MATH," HAS FOUND MANY CREEPY QUALITIES OF THE NUMBER 666... HERE'S SOME:
ϕ(666) = 6·6·6
O'
M
O
6
6
6
6
M'
√37
O
L
C √37
n=1
B
√7
A
C
C=666!
THE GIANT LUMIÈRE CASINO "JUMBOTRON" NEXT TO THE ST. LOUIS GATEWAY ARCH HAS EXACTLY 666 LCD VIDEO PIXELS ON EACH SIDE!
SHOPPING.
LAMIERE CASINO
HOTEL
IN ALABAMA AND MISSISSIPPI, ACCORDING TO STATE LAW, ANY PURCHASE TOTALLING $666 IS AUTOMATICALLY ROUNDED DOWN TO $665!
666
666
666
666
HEXACEXAELIMPHOBIA IS THE FEAR OF 666...
ONE DAY IN 1998, HEXACELIMPHOBE MIKE WEST OF CRESTON, WV, COUNTED ALL OF THE LEAVES OF HIS WIFE'S HOUSEPLANTS...
HIS HUNCH WAS CORRECT— THE AMOUNT: 666 LEAVES!
HORRIFIED,
HE TORCHED THE HOUSE!
LB

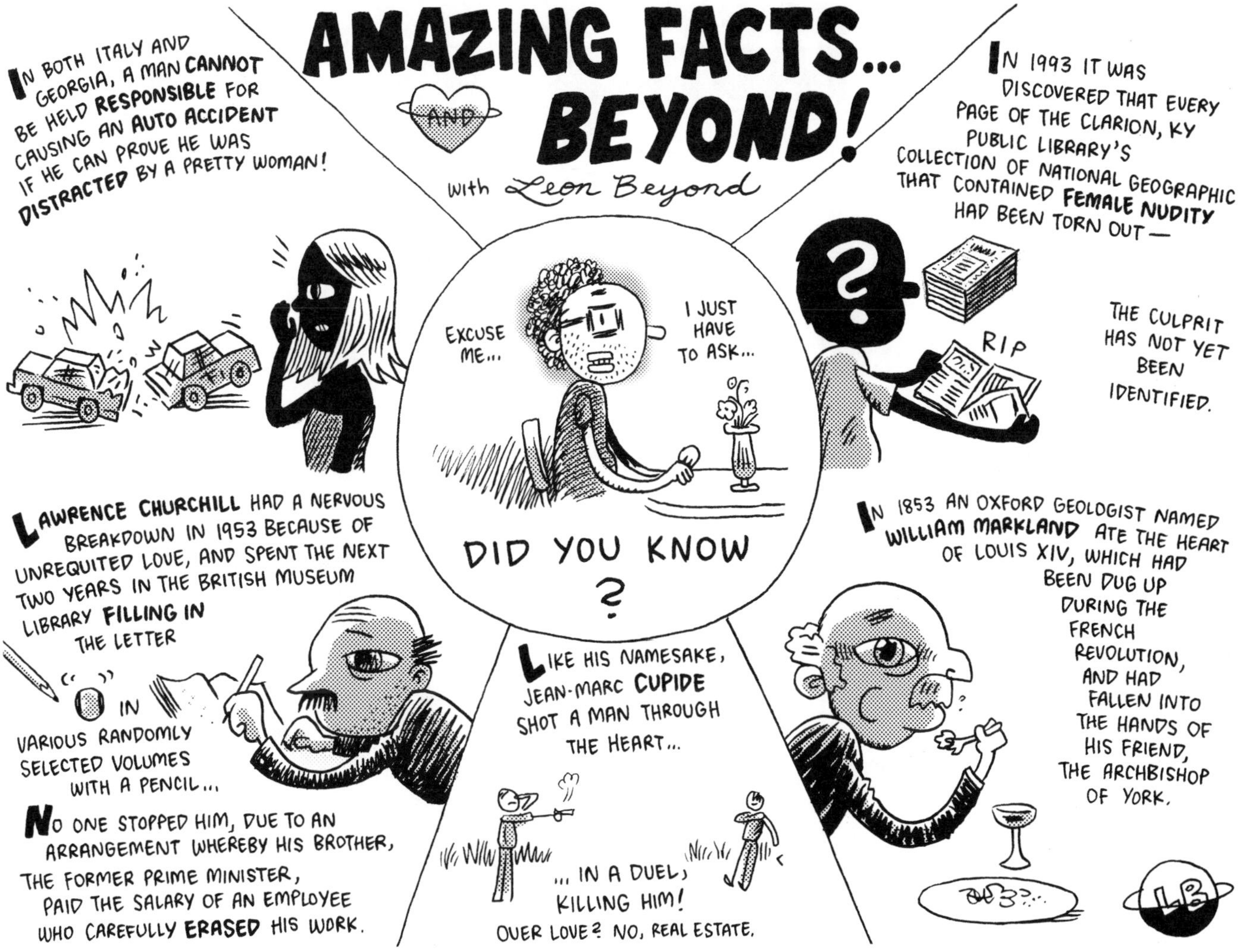
AMAZING FACTS... AND BEYOND!
with Leon Beyond
IN BOTH ITALY AND GEORGIA, A MAN CANNOT BE HELD RESPONSIBLE FOR CAUSING AN AUTO ACCIDENT IF HE CAN PROVE HE WAS DISTRACTED BY A PRETTY WOMAN!
EXCUSE ME...
I JUST HAVE TO ASK...
DID YOU KNOW ?
IN 1993 IT WAS DISCOVERED THAT EVERY PAGE OF THE CLARION, KY PUBLIC LIBRARY'S COLLECTION OF NATIONAL GEOGRAPHIC THAT CONTAINED FEMALE NUDITY HAD BEEN TORN OUT—
RIP
THE CULPRIT HAS NOT YET BEEN IDENTIFIED.
LAWRENCE CHURCHILL HAD A NERVOUS BREAKDOWN IN 1953 BECAUSE OF UNREQUITED LOVE, AND SPENT THE NEXT TWO YEARS IN THE BRITISH MUSEUM LIBRARY FILLING IN THE LETTER "O" IN VARIOUS RANDOMLY SELECTED VOLUMES WITH A PENCIL...
NO ONE STOPPED HIM, DUE TO AN ARRANGEMENT WHEREBY HIS BROTHER, THE FORMER PRIME MINISTER, PAID THE SALARY OF AN EMPLOYEE WHO CAREFULLY ERASED HIS WORK.
LIKE HIS NAMESAKE, JEAN-MARC CUPIDE SHOT A MAN THROUGH THE HEART...
... IN A DUEL, KILLING HIM!
OVER LOVE? NO, REAL ESTATE.
IN 1853 AN OXFORD GEOLOGIST NAMED WILLIAM MARKLAND ATE THE HEART OF LOUIS XIV, WHICH HAD BEEN DUG UP DURING THE FRENCH REVOLUTION, AND HAD FALLEN INTO THE HANDS OF HIS FRIEND, THE ARCHBISHOP OF YORK.
LB

AMAZING FACTS... AND BEYOND!

WITH LEON BEYOND

DID YOU KNOW?

MORRIS HAGER ROLLERSKATED FROM LA TO NYC WITH HIS TWO PET SCORPIONS ON HIS FACE TO RAISE AWARENESS OF SOMETHING HAVING TO DO WITH A DISEASE!

SOMETIMES ALL IT TAKES TO RAISE SOME **AWARENESS** IS A **STUNT** OF SOME SORT...

OR A FEAT!

OK... ON THREE...

GIOVANI SOBRIO BALANCED HIMSELF ON ONE ARM, AIMED A PISTOL AND SHOT THE WORDS "BUY WAR BONDS" INTO A BEDSHEET.

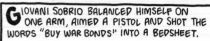

BANG

HE REPRISED THIS FEAT TWENTY YEARS LATER, WHILE BLINDFOLDED AND WITH A DEAF CAT LYING ON HIS BACK! THE MESSAGE THIS TIME: "U.S. OUT OF U.N."

SIMILARLY, IN 2004, G.T. ROSHAL "WALKED" THREE STORIES UP THE WALLS BETWEEN TWO BUILDINGS ON ACNA ST. IN AKRON, PA, TO RAISE AWARENESS OF SOMETHING HAVING TO DO WITH PLASTIC BOT-   TLES IN THE PACIFIC OCEAN!

LAST WEEK JACK AGNEW HARNASSED HIM-SELF TO A GIANT BALLOON AND LEAPT AROUND LONDON AS IF WEIGHTLESS TO RAISE AWARENESS OF SOMETHING ABOUT COAL COMPANIES DESTROYING THE EARTH.

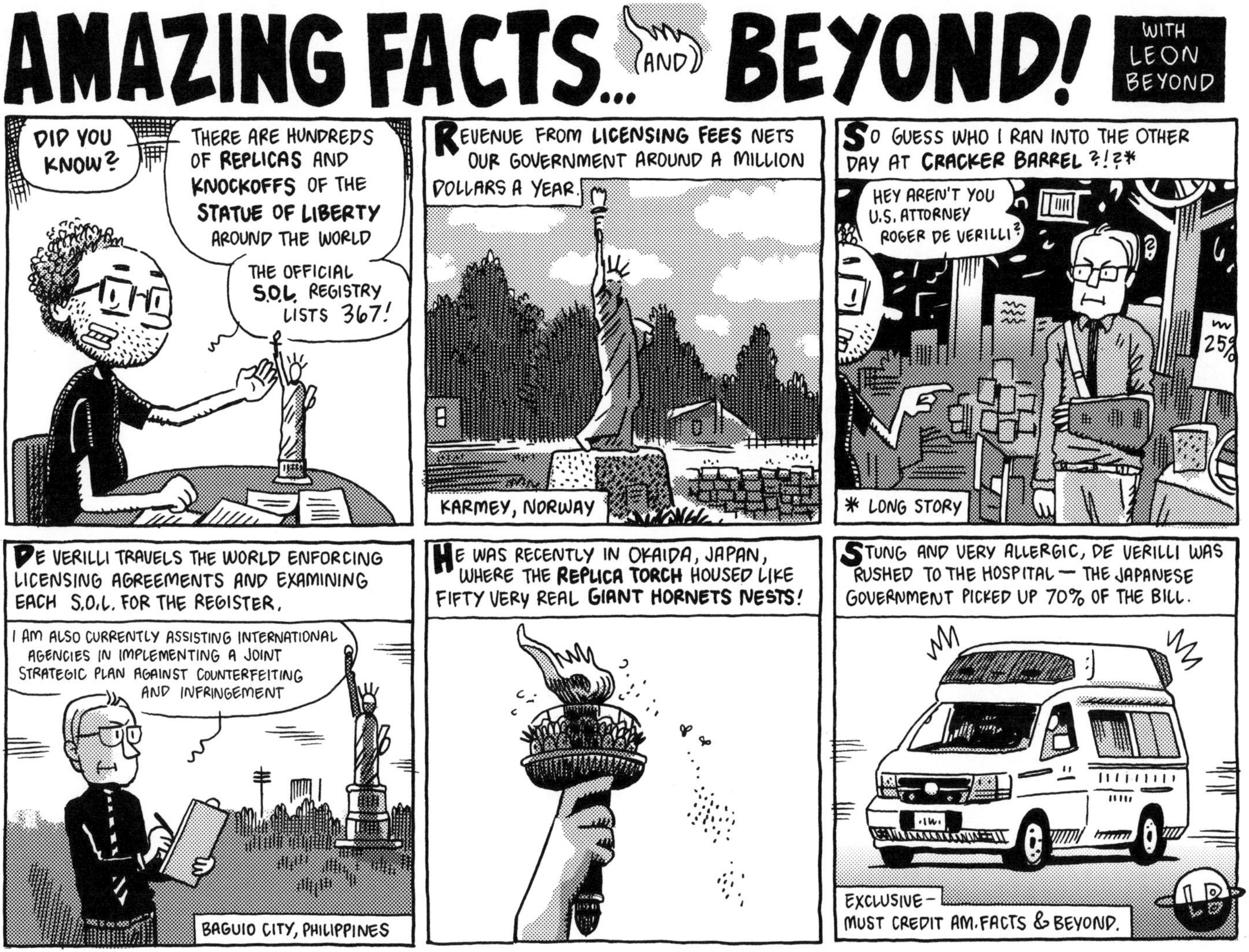
AMAZING FACTS... (AND) BEYOND!
WITH LEON BEYOND
DID YOU KNOW?
THERE ARE HUNDREDS OF REPLICAS AND KNOCKOFFS OF THE STATUE OF LIBERTY AROUND THE WORLD
THE OFFICIAL S.O.L. REGISTRY LISTS 367!
REVENUE FROM LICENSING FEES NETS OUR GOVERNMENT AROUND A MILLION DOLLARS A YEAR.
KARMEY, NORWAY
SO GUESS WHO I RAN INTO THE OTHER DAY AT CRACKER BARREL ?!?*
HEY AREN'T YOU U.S. ATTORNEY ROGER DE VERILLI?
25%
* LONG STORY
DE VERILLI TRAVELS THE WORLD ENFORCING LICENSING AGREEMENTS AND EXAMINING EACH S.O.L. FOR THE REGISTER.
I AM ALSO CURRENTLY ASSISTING INTERNATIONAL AGENCIES IN IMPLEMENTING A JOINT STRATEGIC PLAN AGAINST COUNTERFEITING AND INFRINGEMENT
BAGUIO CITY, PHILIPPINES
HE WAS RECENTLY IN OKAIDA, JAPAN, WHERE THE REPLICA TORCH HOUSED LIKE FIFTY VERY REAL GIANT HORNETS NESTS!
STUNG AND VERY ALLERGIC, DE VERILLI WAS RUSHED TO THE HOSPITAL — THE JAPANESE GOVERNMENT PICKED UP 70% OF THE BILL.
EXCLUSIVE - MUST CREDIT AM. FACTS & BEYOND.
LB

AMAZING FACTS AND BEYOND!

DID YOU KNOW? UNLIKE MUSIC, NO STANDARD FORM OF NOTATION EXISTS FOR **DANCING!** AROUND **42 SYSTEMS** OF **DANCE NOTATION** HAVE BEEN INVENTED, FROM ANCIENT TIMES UNTIL NOW!

THE MOST FAMOUS, OF COURSE, BEING THE **SHOE/DOTTED LINE (SDL)** SYSTEM, WHICH HAS BEEN IN USE SINCE SHOES WERE INVENTED. OUR MODERN SDL USAGE WAS STANDARDIZED BY A TEAM AT THE **RAND CORPORATION** UNDER HERMAN KAHN.

The [MR. DUSTY]

SOME OTHER MODERN SYSTEMS ARE THE **LABAN** AND THE **STIFFY.**

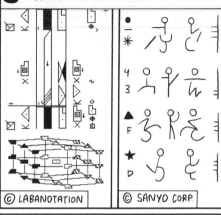

© LABANOTATION   © SANYO CORP.

ANOTHER IS THE **WINKATON,** WHICH WAS DEVELOPED PRIMARILY FOR NORWEGIAN SWORD DANCING, BUT WHICH HAS PROVED SURPRISINGLY PRACTICABLE ON **BROADWAY.**

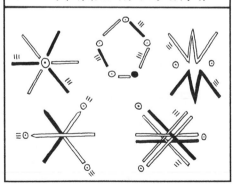

A COMPREHENSIVE NOTATION SYSTEM IS DIFFICULT TO DESIGN! THERE IS SO MUCH TO DESCRIBE, SO MUCH MOVEMENT. ICE SKATING AND SEX THERAPY ARE TWO EXAMPLES OF THE MANY FIELDS THAT WOULD BENEFIT.

THE FAMOUS DANCEWRITER H.F. BEAUX SET OUT TO RECORD HIS DAILY MOVEMENTS IN DANCE NOTATION....

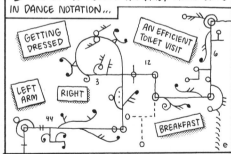

GETTING DRESSED

AN EFFICIENT TOILET VISIT

LEFT ARM   RIGHT

BREAKFAST

IT GOT TRICKY WHEN HE TRIED RECORDING THE MOVEMENTS HE MADE WHEN RECORDING HIS MOVEMENTS.... A.K.A. "GÖDEL'S PAS DE DOX."

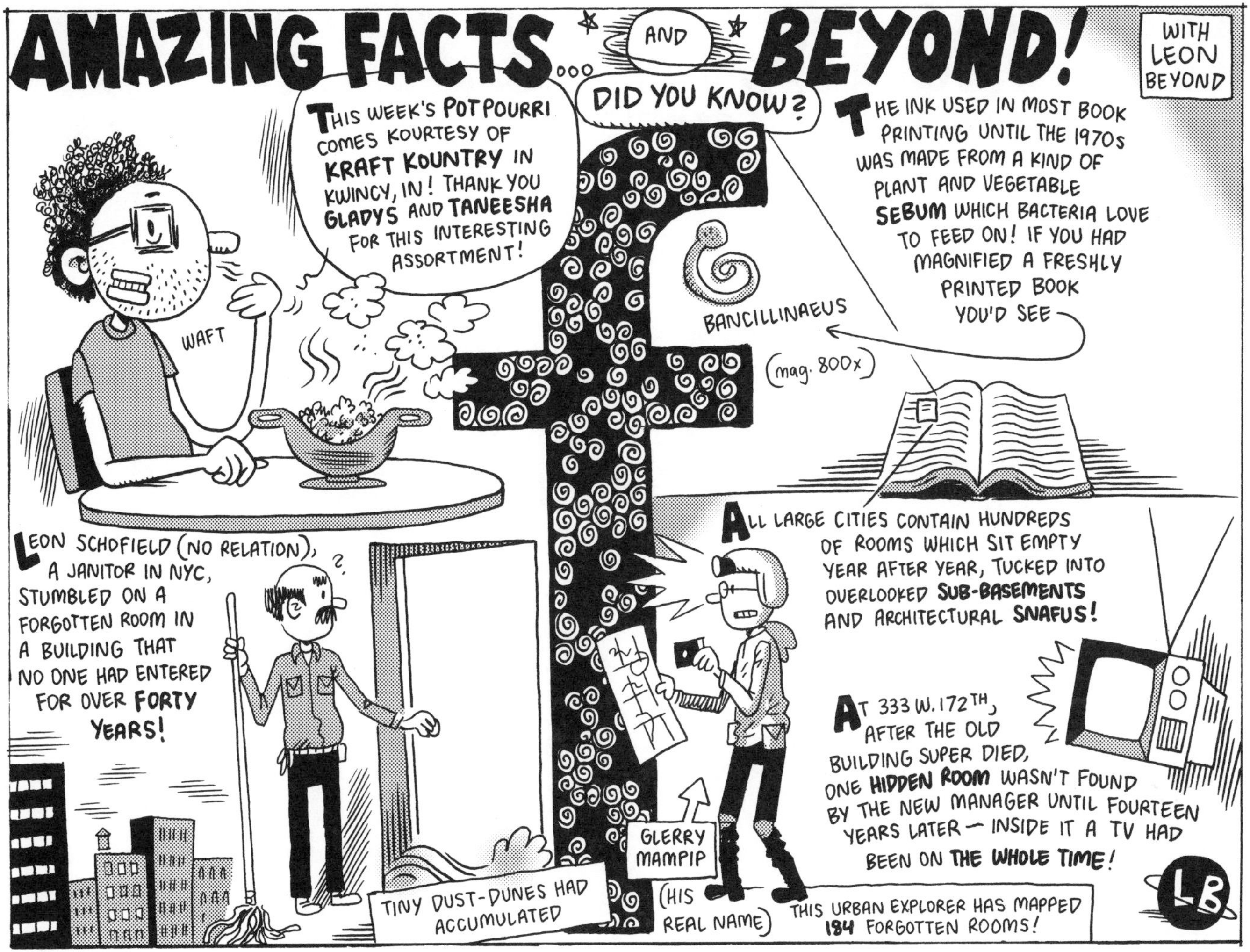
AMAZING FACTS... AND BEYOND!
WITH LEON BEYOND
THIS WEEK'S POTPOURRI COMES KOURTESY OF KRAFT KOUNTRY IN KWINCY, IN! THANK YOU GLADYS AND TANEESHA FOR THIS INTERESTING ASSORTMENT!
WAFT
DID YOU KNOW?
THE INK USED IN MOST BOOK PRINTING UNTIL THE 1970s WAS MADE FROM A KIND OF PLANT AND VEGETABLE SEBUM WHICH BACTERIA LOVE TO FEED ON! IF YOU HAD MAGNIFIED A FRESHLY PRINTED BOOK YOU'D SEE
BANCILLINAEUS
(mag. 800x)
LEON SCHOFIELD (NO RELATION), A JANITOR IN NYC, STUMBLED ON A FORGOTTEN ROOM IN A BUILDING THAT NO ONE HAD ENTERED FOR OVER FORTY YEARS!
?
TINY DUST-DUNES HAD ACCUMULATED
ALL LARGE CITIES CONTAIN HUNDREDS OF ROOMS WHICH SIT EMPTY YEAR AFTER YEAR, TUCKED INTO OVERLOOKED SUB-BASEMENTS AND ARCHITECTURAL SNAFUS!
GLERRY MAMPIP
(HIS REAL NAME)
THIS URBAN EXPLORER HAS MAPPED 184 FORGOTTEN ROOMS!
AT 333 W. 172TH, AFTER THE OLD BUILDING SUPER DIED, ONE HIDDEN ROOM WASN'T FOUND BY THE NEW MANAGER UNTIL FOURTEEN YEARS LATER — INSIDE IT A TV HAD BEEN ON THE WHOLE TIME!
LB

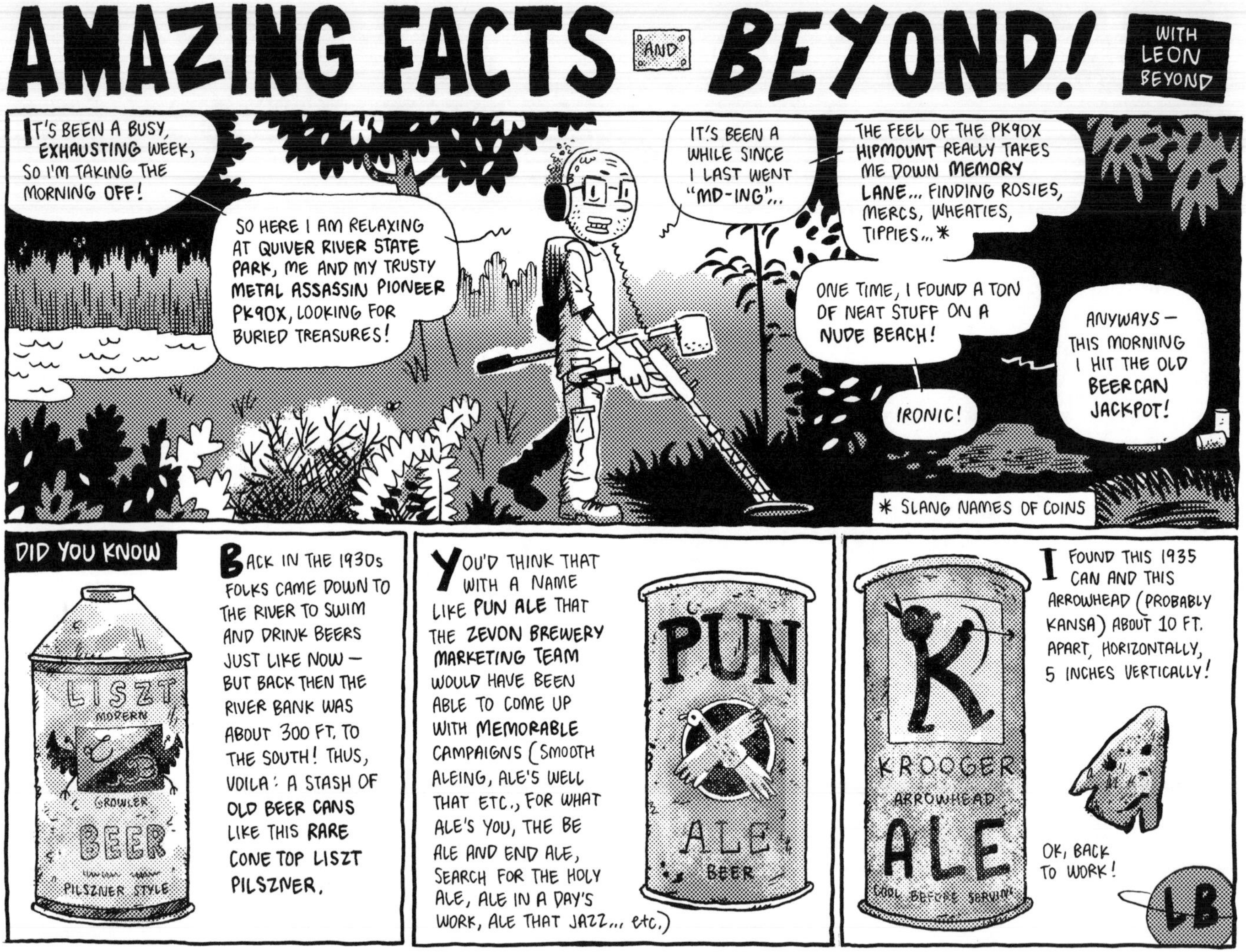
AMAZING FACTS AND BEYOND!
WITH LEON BEYOND
IT'S BEEN A BUSY, EXHAUSTING WEEK, SO I'M TAKING THE MORNING OFF!
SO HERE I AM RELAXING AT QUIVER RIVER STATE PARK, ME AND MY TRUSTY METAL ASSASSIN PIONEER PK90X, LOOKING FOR BURIED TREASURES!
IT'S BEEN A WHILE SINCE I LAST WENT "MD-ING"...
THE FEEL OF THE PK90X HIPMOUNT REALLY TAKES ME DOWN MEMORY LANE... FINDING ROSIES, MERCS, WHEATIES, TIPPIES... *
ONE TIME, I FOUND A TON OF NEAT STUFF ON A NUDE BEACH!
IRONIC!
ANYWAYS — THIS MORNING I HIT THE OLD BEERCAN JACKPOT!
* SLANG NAMES OF COINS
DID YOU KNOW
LISZT
MODERN
GROWLER
BEER
PILSZNER STYLE
BACK IN THE 1930s FOLKS CAME DOWN TO THE RIVER TO SWIM AND DRINK BEERS JUST LIKE NOW — BUT BACK THEN THE RIVER BANK WAS ABOUT 300 FT. TO THE SOUTH! THUS, VOILA: A STASH OF OLD BEER CANS LIKE THIS RARE CONE TOP LISZT PILSZNER.
YOU'D THINK THAT WITH A NAME LIKE PUN ALE THAT THE ZEVON BREWERY MARKETING TEAM WOULD HAVE BEEN ABLE TO COME UP WITH MEMORABLE CAMPAIGNS (SMOOTH ALEING, ALE'S WELL THAT ETC., FOR WHAT ALE'S YOU, THE BE ALE AND END ALE, SEARCH FOR THE HOLY ALE, ALE IN A DAY'S WORK, ALE THAT JAZZ... etc.)
PUN
ALE
BEER
K
KROOGER
ARROWHEAD
ALE
I FOUND THIS 1935 CAN AND THIS ARROWHEAD (PROBABLY KANSA) ABOUT 10 FT. APART, HORIZONTALLY, 5 INCHES VERTICALLY!
OK, BACK TO WORK!
LB

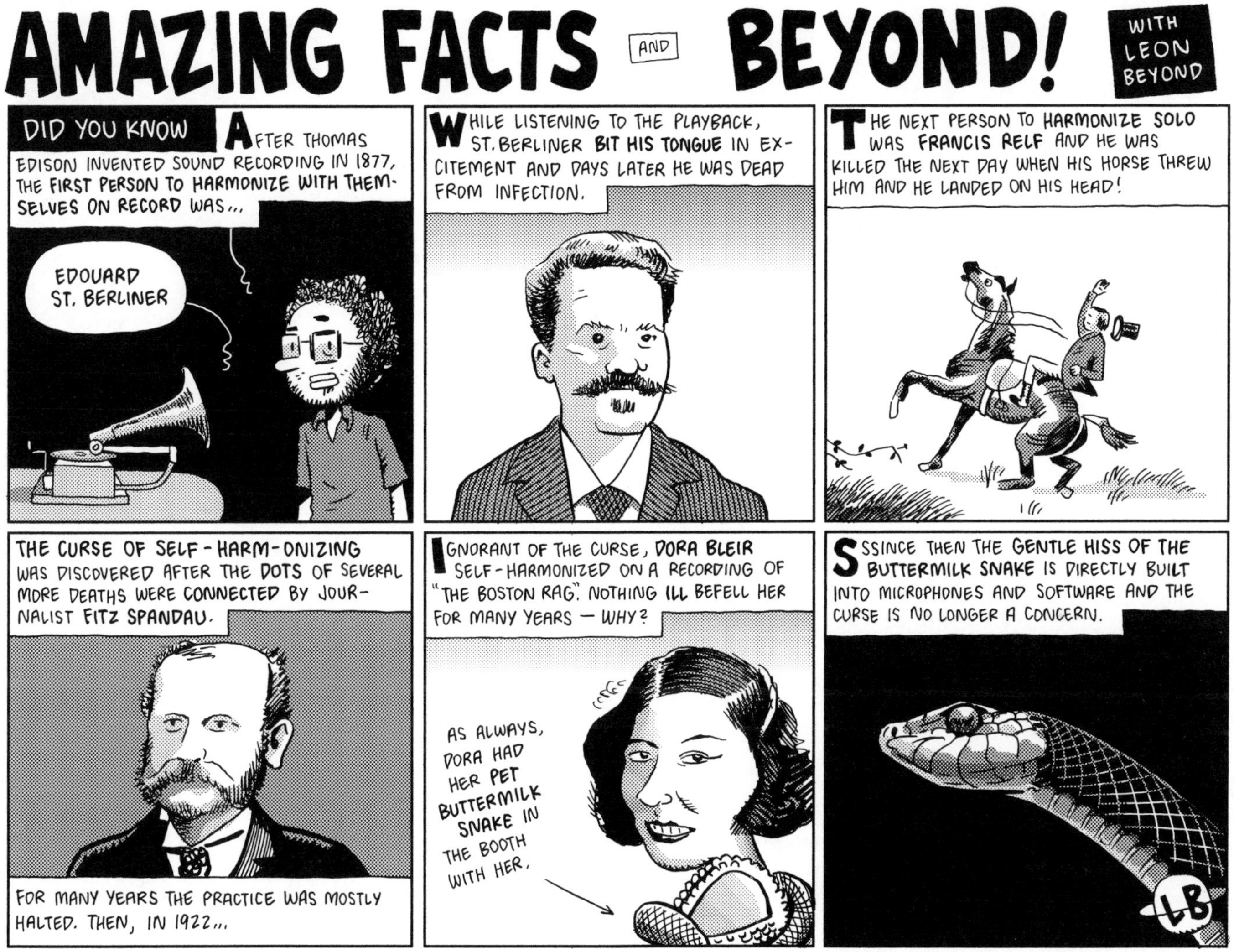
AMAZING FACTS AND BEYOND!
WITH LEON BEYOND
DID YOU KNOW
AFTER THOMAS EDISON INVENTED SOUND RECORDING IN 1877, THE FIRST PERSON TO HARMONIZE WITH THEMSELVES ON RECORD WAS...
EDOUARD ST. BERLINER
WHILE LISTENING TO THE PLAYBACK, ST. BERLINER BIT HIS TONGUE IN EXCITEMENT AND DAYS LATER HE WAS DEAD FROM INFECTION.
THE NEXT PERSON TO HARMONIZE SOLO WAS FRANCIS RELF AND HE WAS KILLED THE NEXT DAY WHEN HIS HORSE THREW HIM AND HE LANDED ON HIS HEAD!
THE CURSE OF SELF-HARM-ONIZING WAS DISCOVERED AFTER THE DOTS OF SEVERAL MORE DEATHS WERE CONNECTED BY JOURNALIST FITZ SPANDAU.
FOR MANY YEARS THE PRACTICE WAS MOSTLY HALTED. THEN, IN 1922...
IGNORANT OF THE CURSE, DORA BLEIR SELF-HARMONIZED ON A RECORDING OF "THE BOSTON RAG". NOTHING ILL BEFELL HER FOR MANY YEARS — WHY?
AS ALWAYS, DORA HAD HER PET BUTTERMILK SNAKE IN THE BOOTH WITH HER.
SSSINCE THEN THE GENTLE HISS OF THE BUTTERMILK SNAKE IS DIRECTLY BUILT INTO MICROPHONES AND SOFTWARE AND THE CURSE IS NO LONGER A CONCERN.
LB

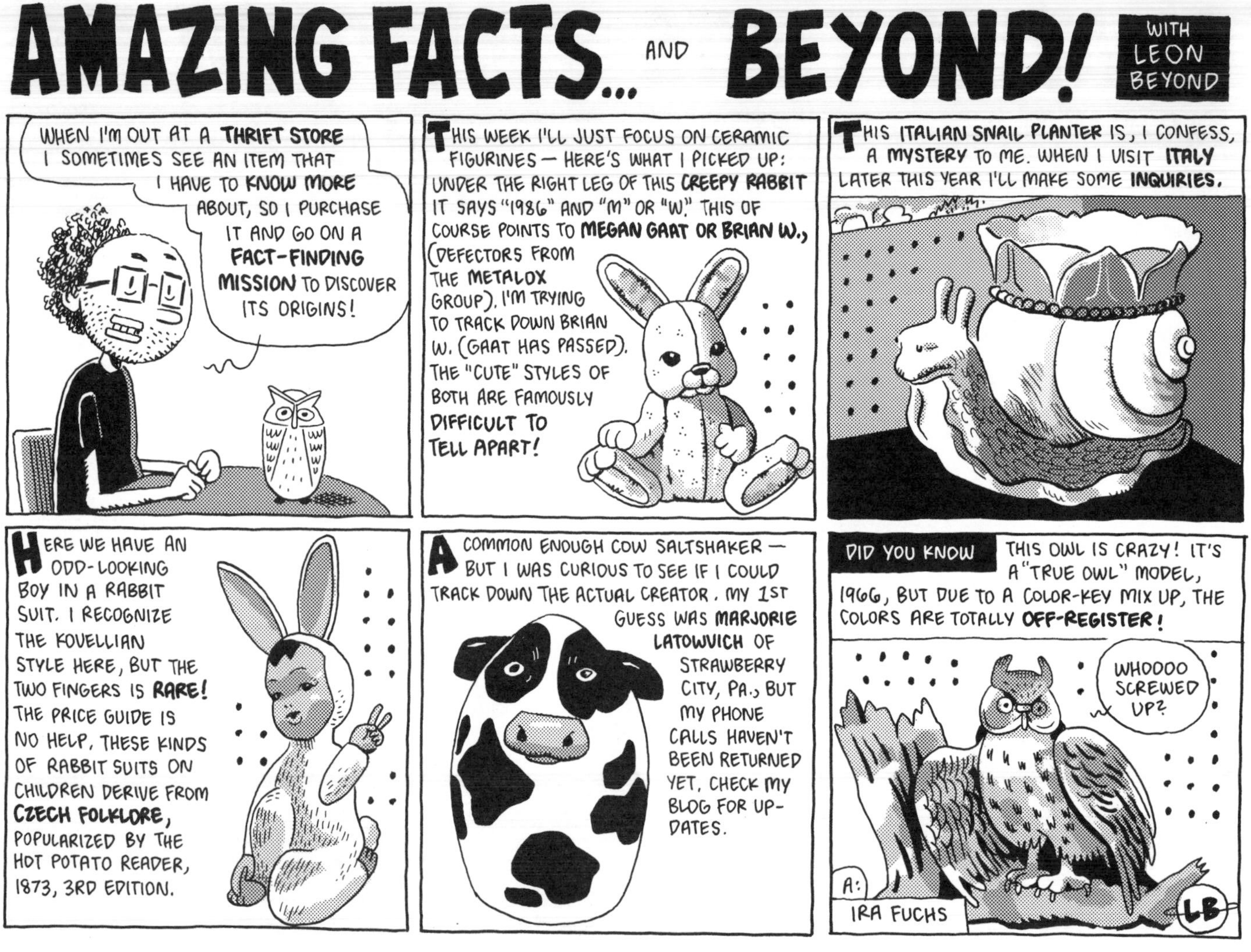
AMAZING FACTS... AND BEYOND! WITH LEON BEYOND
WHEN I'M OUT AT A THRIFT STORE I SOMETIMES SEE AN ITEM THAT I HAVE TO KNOW MORE ABOUT, SO I PURCHASE IT AND GO ON A FACT-FINDING MISSION TO DISCOVER ITS ORIGINS!
THIS WEEK I'LL JUST FOCUS ON CERAMIC FIGURINES — HERE'S WHAT I PICKED UP: UNDER THE RIGHT LEG OF THIS CREEPY RABBIT IT SAYS "1986" AND "M" OR "W." THIS OF COURSE POINTS TO MEGAN GAAT OR BRIAN W., (DEFECTORS FROM THE METALOX GROUP). I'M TRYING TO TRACK DOWN BRIAN W. (GAAT HAS PASSED). THE "CUTE" STYLES OF BOTH ARE FAMOUSLY DIFFICULT TO TELL APART!
THIS ITALIAN SNAIL PLANTER IS, I CONFESS, A MYSTERY TO ME. WHEN I VISIT ITALY LATER THIS YEAR I'LL MAKE SOME INQUIRIES.
HERE WE HAVE AN ODD-LOOKING BOY IN A RABBIT SUIT. I RECOGNIZE THE KOVELLIAN STYLE HERE, BUT THE TWO FINGERS IS RARE! THE PRICE GUIDE IS NO HELP. THESE KINDS OF RABBIT SUITS ON CHILDREN DERIVE FROM CZECH FOLKLORE, POPULARIZED BY THE HOT POTATO READER, 1873, 3RD EDITION.
A COMMON ENOUGH COW SALTSHAKER — BUT I WAS CURIOUS TO SEE IF I COULD TRACK DOWN THE ACTUAL CREATOR. MY 1ST GUESS WAS MARJORIE LATOWVICH OF STRAWBERRY CITY, PA., BUT MY PHONE CALLS HAVEN'T BEEN RETURNED YET. CHECK MY BLOG FOR UPDATES.
DID YOU KNOW
THIS OWL IS CRAZY! IT'S A "TRUE OWL" MODEL, 1966, BUT DUE TO A COLOR-KEY MIX UP, THE COLORS ARE TOTALLY OFF-REGISTER!
WHOOOO SCREWED UP?
A: IRA FUCHS
LB

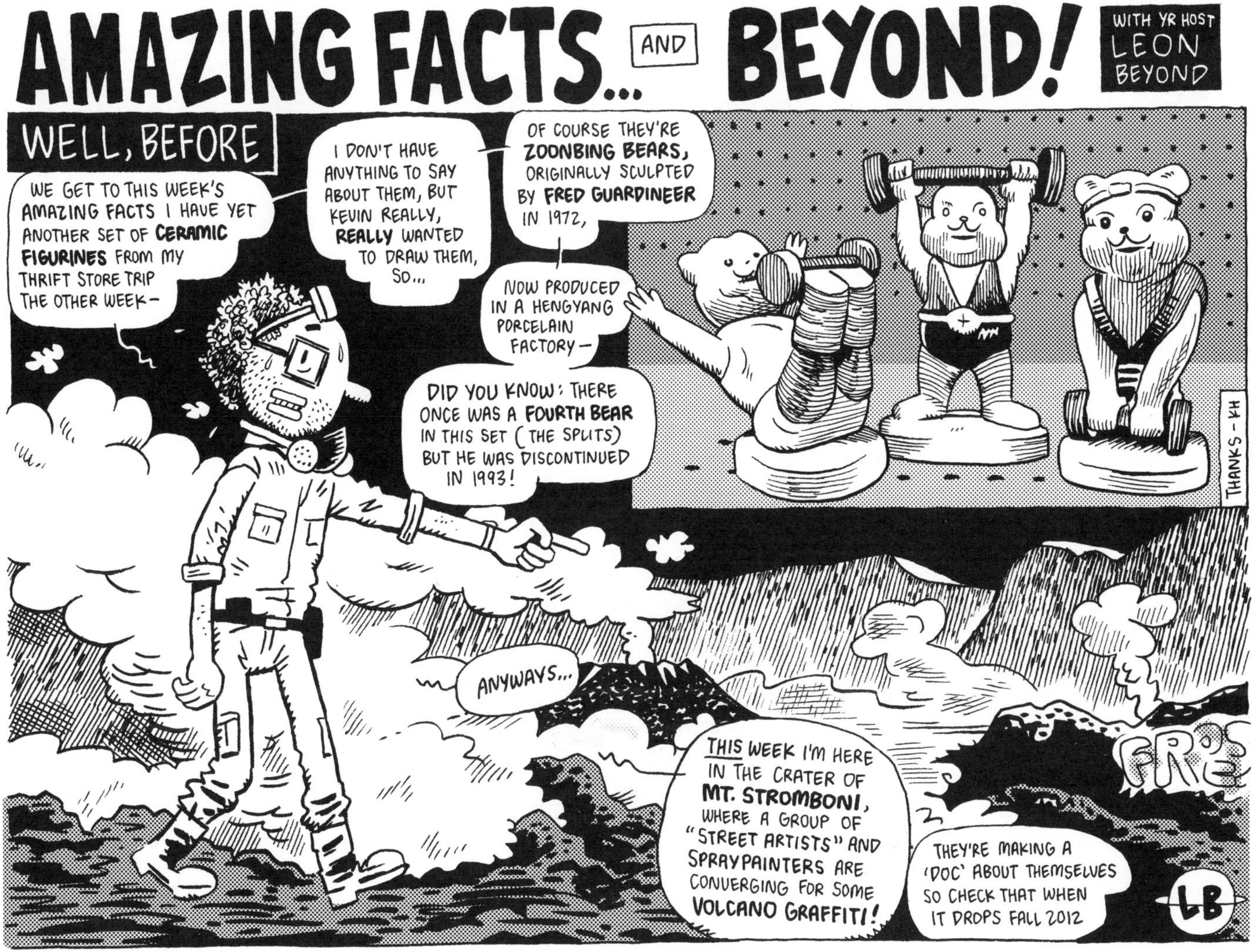
AMAZING FACTS... AND BEYOND!
WITH YR HOST LEON BEYOND
WELL, BEFORE
WE GET TO THIS WEEK'S AMAZING FACTS I HAVE YET ANOTHER SET OF CERAMIC FIGURINES FROM MY THRIFT STORE TRIP THE OTHER WEEK-
I DON'T HAVE ANYTHING TO SAY ABOUT THEM, BUT KEVIN REALLY, REALLY WANTED TO DRAW THEM, SO...
OF COURSE THEY'RE ZOONBING BEARS, ORIGINALLY SCULPTED BY FRED GUARDINEER IN 1972,
NOW PRODUCED IN A HENGYANG PORCELAIN FACTORY-
DID YOU KNOW: THERE ONCE WAS A FOURTH BEAR IN THIS SET (THE SPLITS) BUT HE WAS DISCONTINUED IN 1993!
THANKS-KH
ANYWAYS...
THIS WEEK I'M HERE IN THE CRATER OF MT. STROMBONI, WHERE A GROUP OF "STREET ARTISTS" AND SPRAYPAINTERS ARE CONVERGING FOR SOME VOLCANO GRAFFITI!
THEY'RE MAKING A 'DOC' ABOUT THEMSELVES SO CHECK THAT WHEN IT DROPS FALL 2012
LB

SPORTS

PROFESSIONAL
ABRAHAM LINCOLN
IMPERSONATOR
GRAHAM HAFEEF
WON A BRONZE
MEDAL IN THE
750 METERS
IN 1972

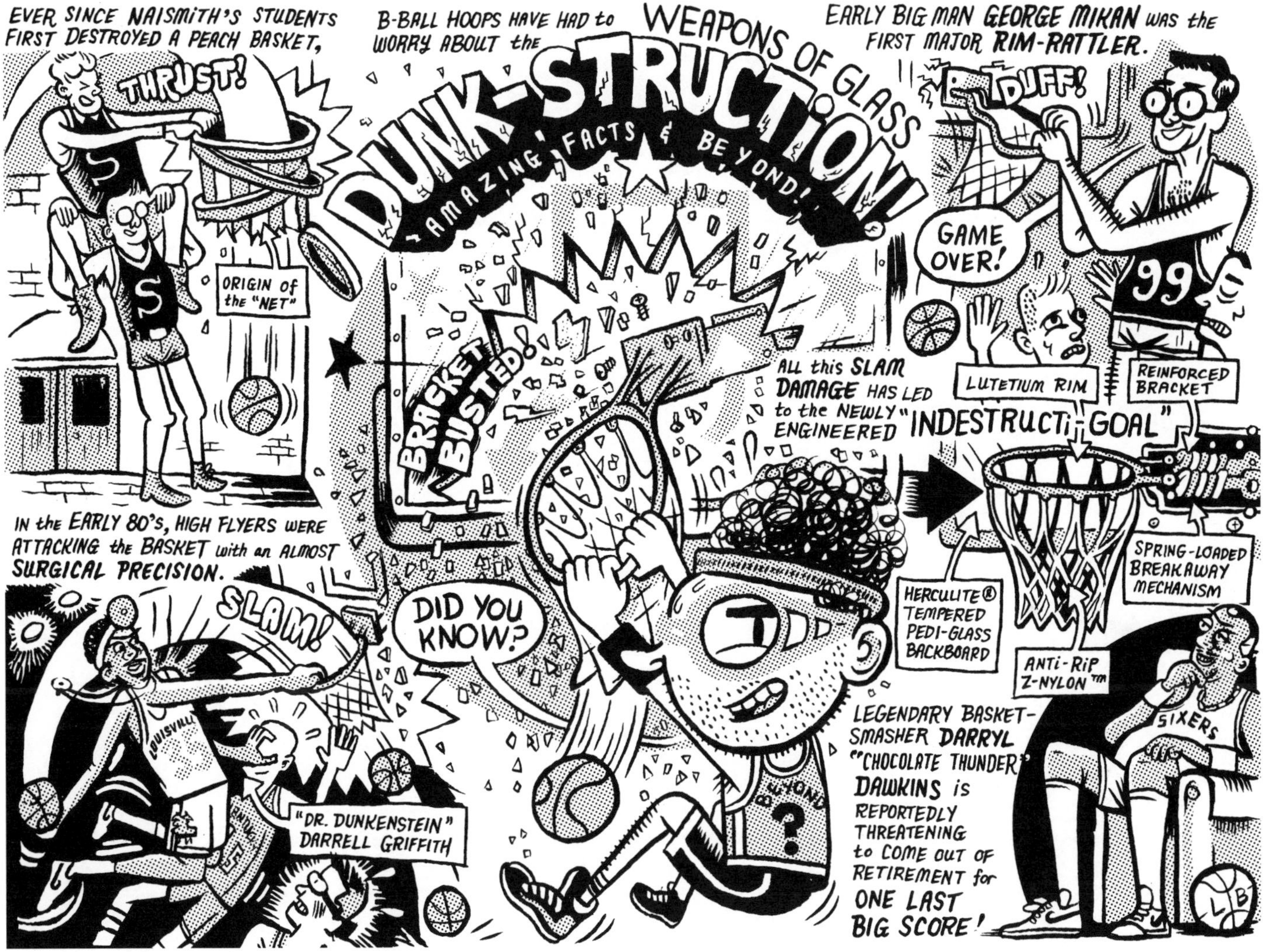
WEAPONS OF GLASS
DUNK-STRUCTION!
AMAZING FACTS & BEYOND!
EVER SINCE NAISMITH'S STUDENTS FIRST DESTROYED A PEACH BASKET,
THRUST!
ORIGIN of the "NET"
B-BALL HOOPS HAVE HAD to WORRY ABOUT the
BRACKET BUSTED!
EARLY BIG MAN GEORGE MIKAN WAS the FIRST MAJOR RIM-RATTLER.
DUFF!
GAME OVER!
99
IN the EARLY 80'S, HIGH FLYERS WERE ATTACKING the BASKET with an ALMOST SURGICAL PRECISION.
SLAM!
"DR. DUNKENSTEIN" DARRELL GRIFFITH
DID YOU KNOW?
ALL this SLAM DAMAGE HAS LED to the NEWLY ENGINEERED "INDESTRUCTI-GOAL"
LUTETIUM RIM
REINFORCED BRACKET
HERCULITE® TEMPERED PEDI-GLASS BACKBOARD
ANTI-RIP Z-NYLON™
SPRING-LOADED BREAKAWAY MECHANISM
LEGENDARY BASKET-SMASHER DARRYL "CHOCOLATE THUNDER" DAWKINS is REPORTEDLY THREATENING to COME OUT OF RETIREMENT for ONE LAST BIG SCORE!
SIXERS

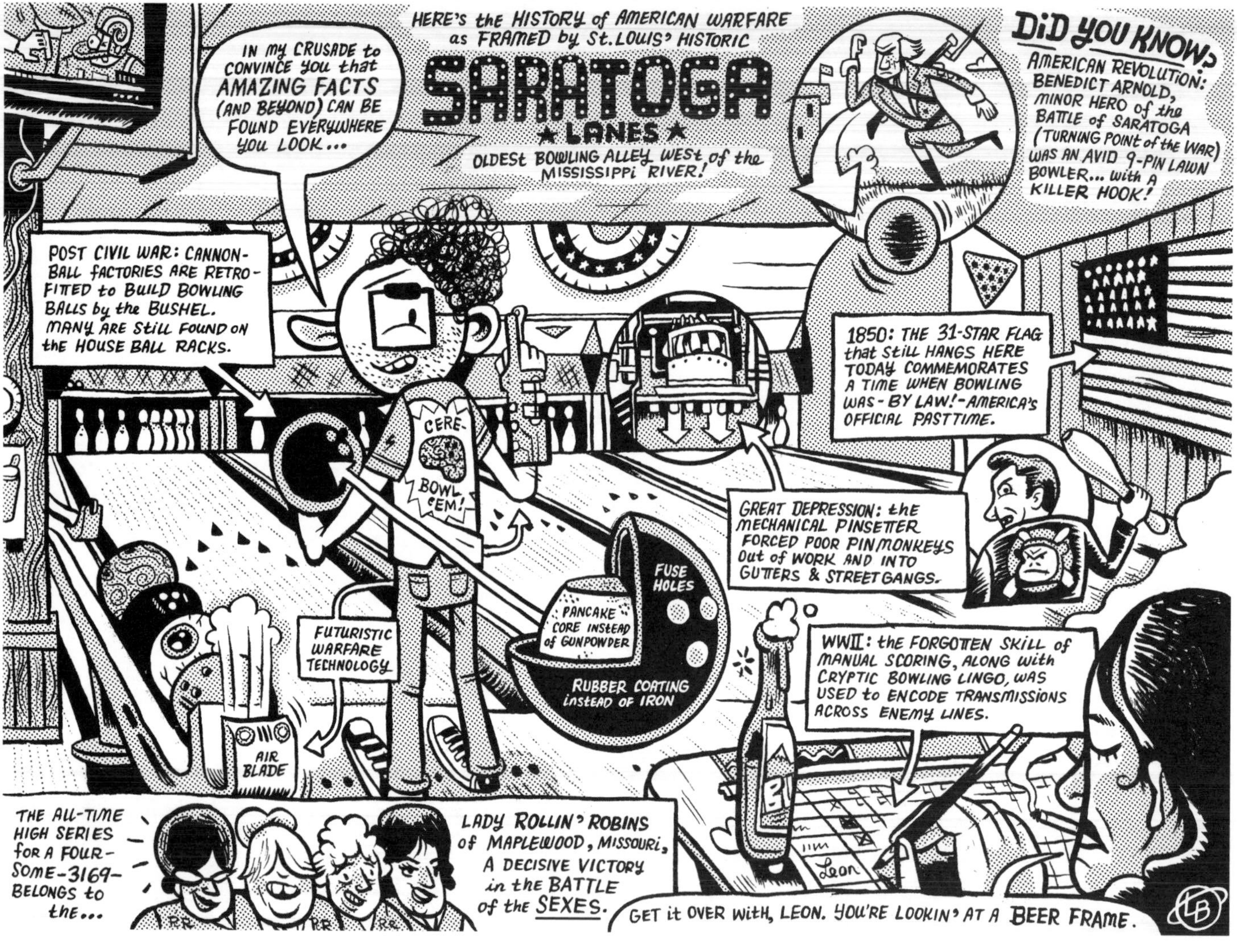
IN MY CRUSADE to CONVINCE you that AMAZING FACTS (AND BEYOND) CAN BE FOUND EVERYWHERE YOU LOOK...
HERE'S the HISTORY of AMERICAN WARFARE as FRAMED by St. LOUIS' HISTORIC
SARATOGA LANES
OLDEST BOWLING ALLEY WEST of the MISSISSIPPI RIVER!
DID YOU KNOW?
AMERICAN REVOLUTION: BENEDICT ARNOLD, MINOR HERO of the BATTLE of SARATOGA (TURNING POINT of the WAR) WAS AN AVID 9-PIN LAWN BOWLER... with A KILLER HOOK!
POST CIVIL WAR: CANNON-BALL FACTORIES ARE RETRO-FITTED to BUILD BOWLING BALLS by the BUSHEL. MANY ARE STILL FOUND ON the HOUSE BALL RACKS.
CERE-BOWL-CEM!
1850: THE 31-STAR FLAG that STILL HANGS HERE TODAY COMMEMORATES A TIME WHEN BOWLING WAS-BY LAW!-AMERICA'S OFFICIAL PASTTIME.
GREAT DEPRESSION: the MECHANICAL PINSETTER FORCED POOR PINMONKEYS Out of WORK AND INTO GUTTERS & STREET GANGS.
FUSE HOLES
PANCAKE CORE INSTEAD of GUNPOWDER
RUBBER COATING instead OF IRON
FUTURISTIC WARFARE TECHNOLOGY
AIR BLADE
WWII: the FORGOTTEN SKILL of MANUAL SCORING, ALONG with CRYPTIC BOWLING LINGO, WAS USED to ENCODE TRANSMISSIONS ACROSS ENEMY LINES.
THE ALL-TIME HIGH SERIES FOR A FOUR-SOME-3169-BELONGS to the...
LADY ROLLIN' ROBINS of MAPLEWOOD, MISSOURI, A DECISIVE VICTORY in the BATTLE of the SEXES.
Leon
GET it OVER with, LEON. YOU'RE LOOKIN' AT A BEER FRAME.

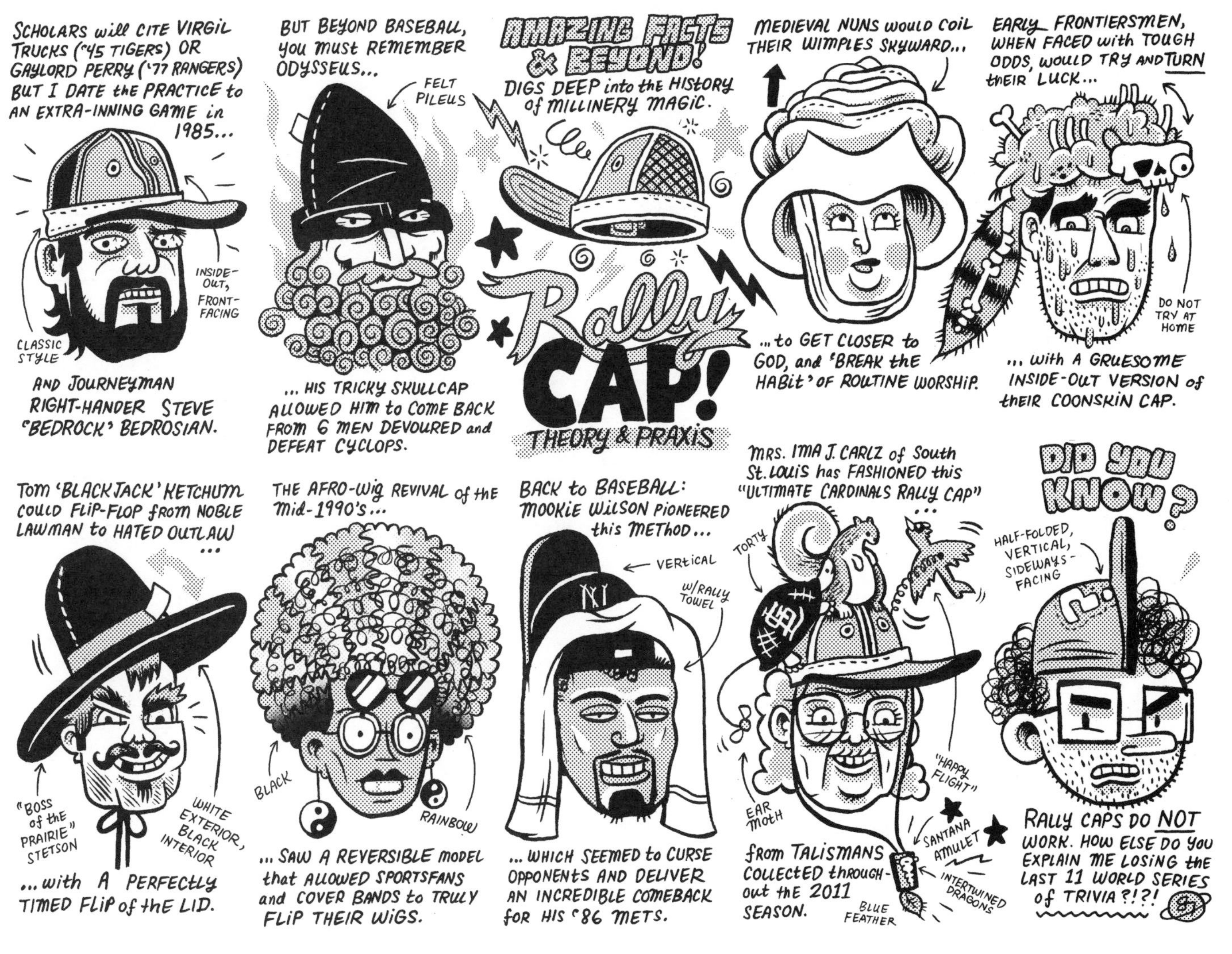
SCHOLARS will CITE VIRGIL TRUCKS ('45 TIGERS) OR GAYLORD PERRY ('77 RANGERS) BUT I DATE the PRACTICE to AN EXTRA-INNING GAME in 1985...
INSIDE-OUT, FRONT-FACING
CLASSIC STYLE
AND JOURNEYMAN RIGHT-HANDER STEVE "BEDROCK" BEDROSIAN.
BUT BEYOND BASEBALL, you must REMEMBER ODYSSEUS...
FELT PILEUS
... HIS TRICKY SKULLCAP ALLOWED HIM to COME BACK FROM 6 MEN DEVOURED and DEFEAT CYCLOPS.
AMAZING FACTS & BEYOND!
DIGS DEEP into the HISTORY of MILLINERY MAGIC.
Rally CAP!
THEORY & PRAXIS
MEDIEVAL NUNS would COIL THEIR WIMPLES SKYWARD...
... to GET CLOSER to GOD, and 'BREAK the HABIT' OF ROUTINE WORSHIP.
EARLY FRONTIERSMEN, WHEN FACED with TOUGH ODDS, would TRY AND TURN their LUCK...
DO NOT TRY AT HOME
... with A GRUESOME INSIDE-OUT VERSION of their COONSKIN CAP.
TOM 'BLACKJACK' KETCHUM COULD FLIP-FLOP from NOBLE LAWMAN to HATED OUTLAW ...
"BOSS of the PRAIRIE" STETSON
WHITE EXTERIOR, BLACK INTERIOR
... with A PERFECTLY TIMED FLIP of the LID.
THE AFRO-WIG REVIVAL of the Mid-1990's...
BLACK
RAINBOW
... SAW A REVERSIBLE model that ALLOWED SPORTSFANS and COVER BANDS to TRULY FLIP THEIR WIGS.
BACK to BASEBALL: MOOKIE WILSON PIONEERED this METHOD...
VERTICAL
W/RALLY TOWEL
NY
... WHICH SEEMED to CURSE OPPONENTS AND DELIVER AN INCREDIBLE COMEBACK for HIS '86 METS.
MRS. IMA J. CARLZ of South St. Louis has FASHIONED this "ULTIMATE CARDINALS RALLY CAP" ...
TORTY
"HAPPY FLIGHT"
EAR MOTH
SANTANA AMULET
INTERTWINED DRAGONS
BLUE FEATHER
from TALISMANS COLLECTED through-out the 2011 SEASON.
DID YOU KNOW?
HALF-FOLDED, VERTICAL, SIDEWAYS-FACING
RALLY CAPS DO NOT WORK. HOW ELSE DO YOU EXPLAIN ME LOSING the LAST 11 WORLD SERIES of TRIVIA?!?!

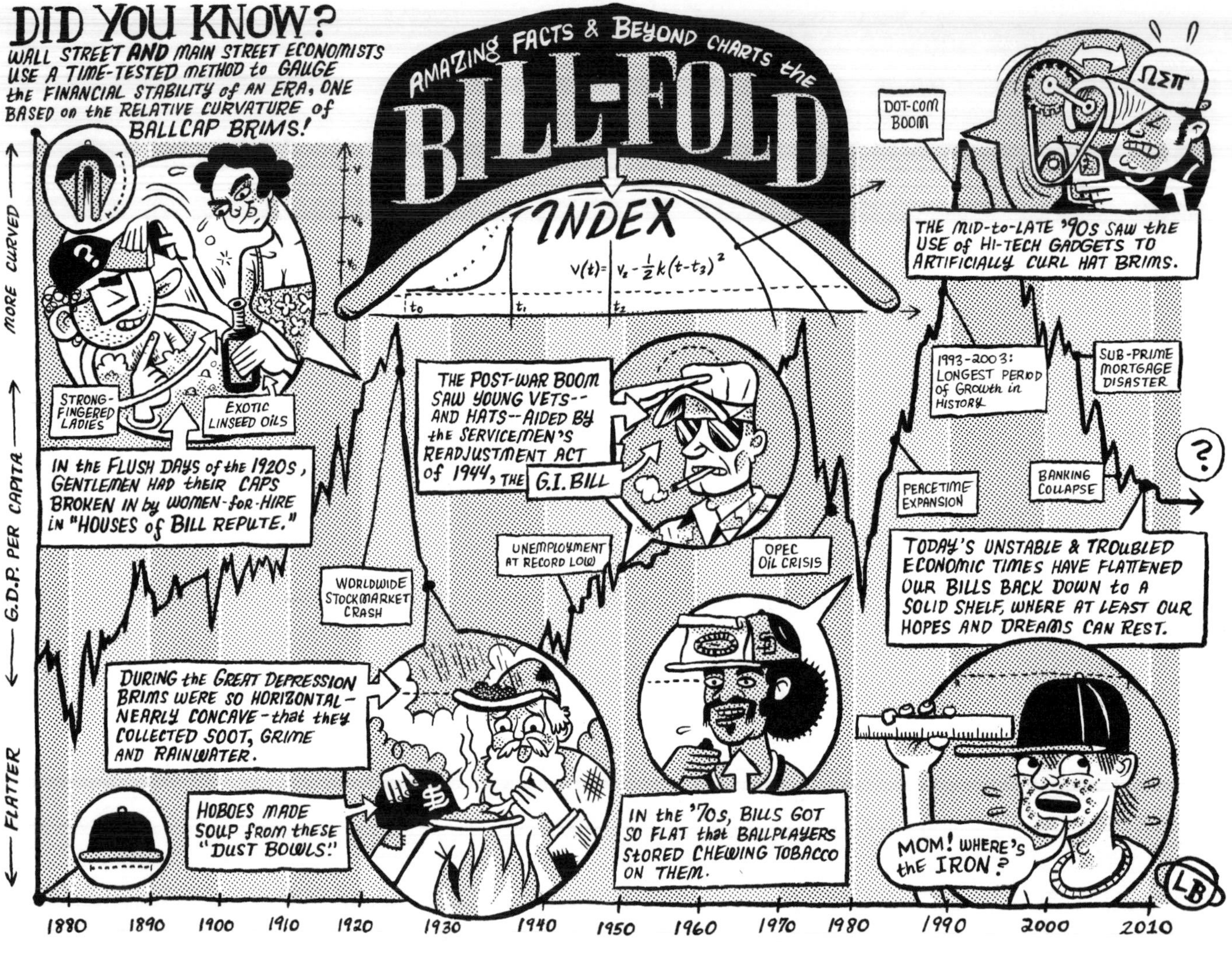

DID YOU KNOW?
WALL STREET AND MAIN STREET ECONOMISTS USE A TIME-TESTED METHOD to GAUGE the FINANCIAL STABILITY of AN ERA, ONE BASED on the RELATIVE CURVATURE of BALLCAP BRIMS!
AMAZING FACTS & BEYOND CHARTS the
BILL-FOLD
INDEX
$v(t) = v_2 - \frac{1}{2}k(t-t_3)^2$
t_0 t_1 t_2
MORE CURVED
G.D.P. PER CAPITA
FLATTER
STRONG-FINGERED LADIES
EXOTIC LINSEED OILS
IN the FLUSH DAYS of the 1920s, GENTLEMEN HAD their CAPS BROKEN IN by WOMEN-for-HIRE in "HOUSES of BILL REPUTE."
WORLDWIDE STOCKMARKET CRASH
DURING the GREAT DEPRESSION BRIMS WERE SO HORIZONTAL—NEARLY CONCAVE—that they COLLECTED SOOT, GRIME AND RAINWATER.
HOBOES MADE SOUP from these "DUST BOWLS!"
THE POST-WAR BOOM SAW YOUNG VETS—AND HATS—AIDED BY the SERVICEMEN'S READJUSTMENT ACT of 1944, THE G.I. BILL
UNEMPLOYMENT AT RECORD LOW
OPEC OIL CRISIS
IN the '70s, BILLS GOT SO FLAT that BALLPLAYERS STORED CHEWING TOBACCO ON THEM.
DOT-COM BOOM
ΩΣΠ
THE MID-to-LATE '90s SAW the USE of HI-TECH GADGETS TO ARTIFICIALLY CURL HAT BRIMS.
1993-2003: LONGEST PERIOD of GROWTH in HISTORY
SUB-PRIME MORTGAGE DISASTER
PEACETIME EXPANSION
BANKING COLLAPSE
?
TODAY'S UNSTABLE & TROUBLED ECONOMIC TIMES HAVE FLATTENED OUR BILLS BACK DOWN to A SOLID SHELF, WHERE AT LEAST OUR HOPES AND DREAMS CAN REST.
MOM! WHERE'S the IRON?
LB
1880 1890 1900 1910 1920 1930 1940 1950 1960 1970 1980 1990 2000 2010

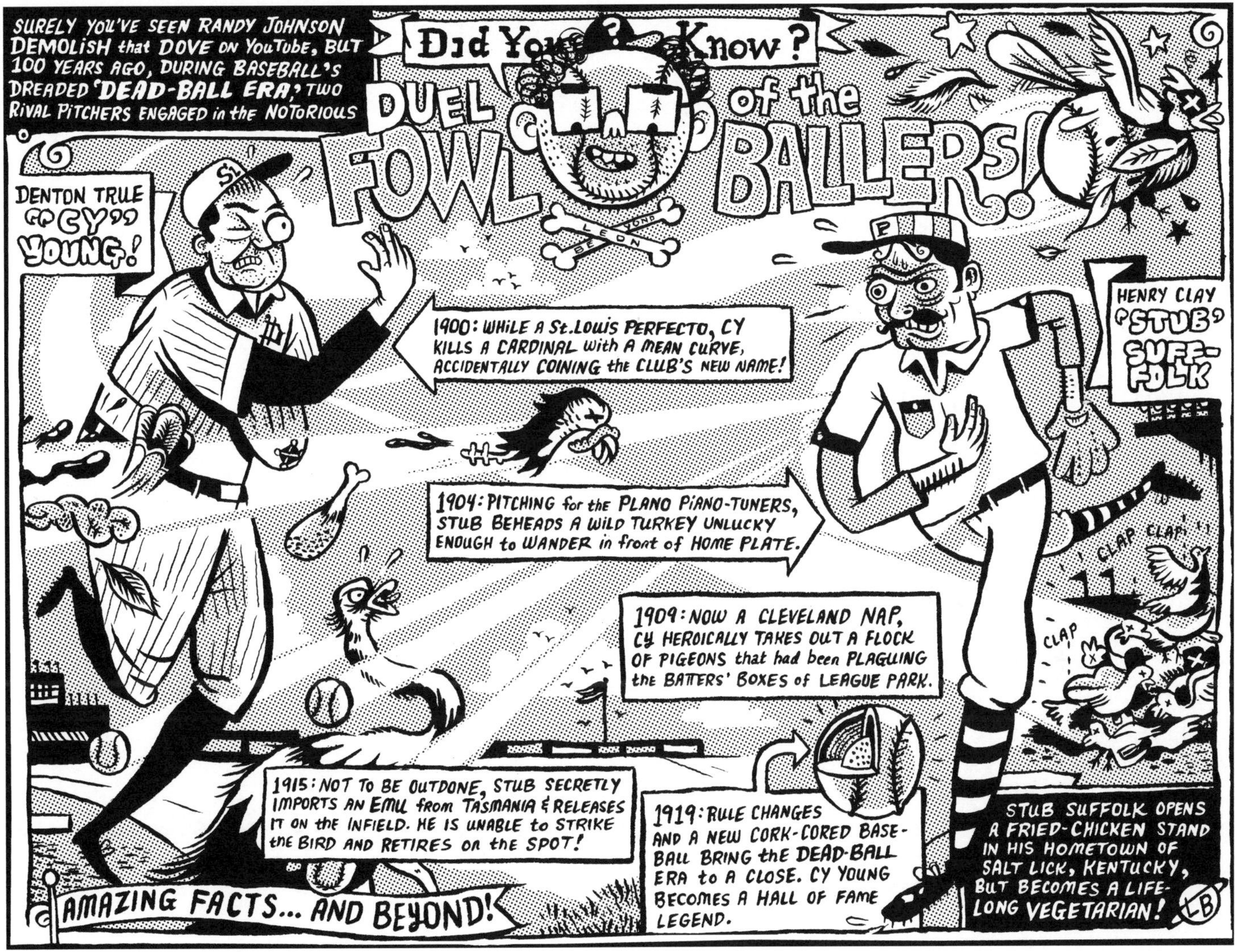
SURELY YOU'VE SEEN RANDY JOHNSON DEMOLISH that DOVE on YouTube, BUT 100 YEARS AGO, DURING BASEBALL'S DREADED 'DEAD-BALL ERA,' TWO RIVAL PITCHERS ENGAGED in the NOTORIOUS
Did You ? Know?
DUEL of the FOWL BALLERS!
LEON BEYOND
DENTON TRUE "CY" YOUNG!
HENRY CLAY "STUB" SUFF-FOLK
1900: WHILE A St. Louis PERFECTO, CY KILLS A CARDINAL with A MEAN CURVE, ACCIDENTALLY COINING the CLUB'S NEW NAME!
1904: PITCHING for the PLANO PIANO-TUNERS, STUB BEHEADS A WILD TURKEY UNLUCKY ENOUGH to WANDER in front of HOME PLATE.
CLAP CLAP
1909: NOW A CLEVELAND NAP, CY HEROICALLY TAKES OUT A FLOCK OF PIGEONS that had been PLAGUING the BATTERS' BOXES of LEAGUE PARK.
CLAP
1915: NOT TO BE OUTDONE, STUB SECRETLY IMPORTS AN EMU from TASMANIA & RELEASES IT ON the INFIELD. HE IS UNABLE to STRIKE the BIRD AND RETIRES on the SPOT!
1919: RULE CHANGES AND A NEW CORK-CORED BASE-BALL BRING the DEAD-BALL ERA to A CLOSE. CY YOUNG BECOMES A HALL OF FAME LEGEND.
STUB SUFFOLK OPENS A FRIED-CHICKEN STAND IN HIS HOMETOWN OF SALT LICK, KENTUCKY, BUT BECOMES A LIFE-LONG VEGETARIAN!
AMAZING FACTS... AND BEYOND!
LB

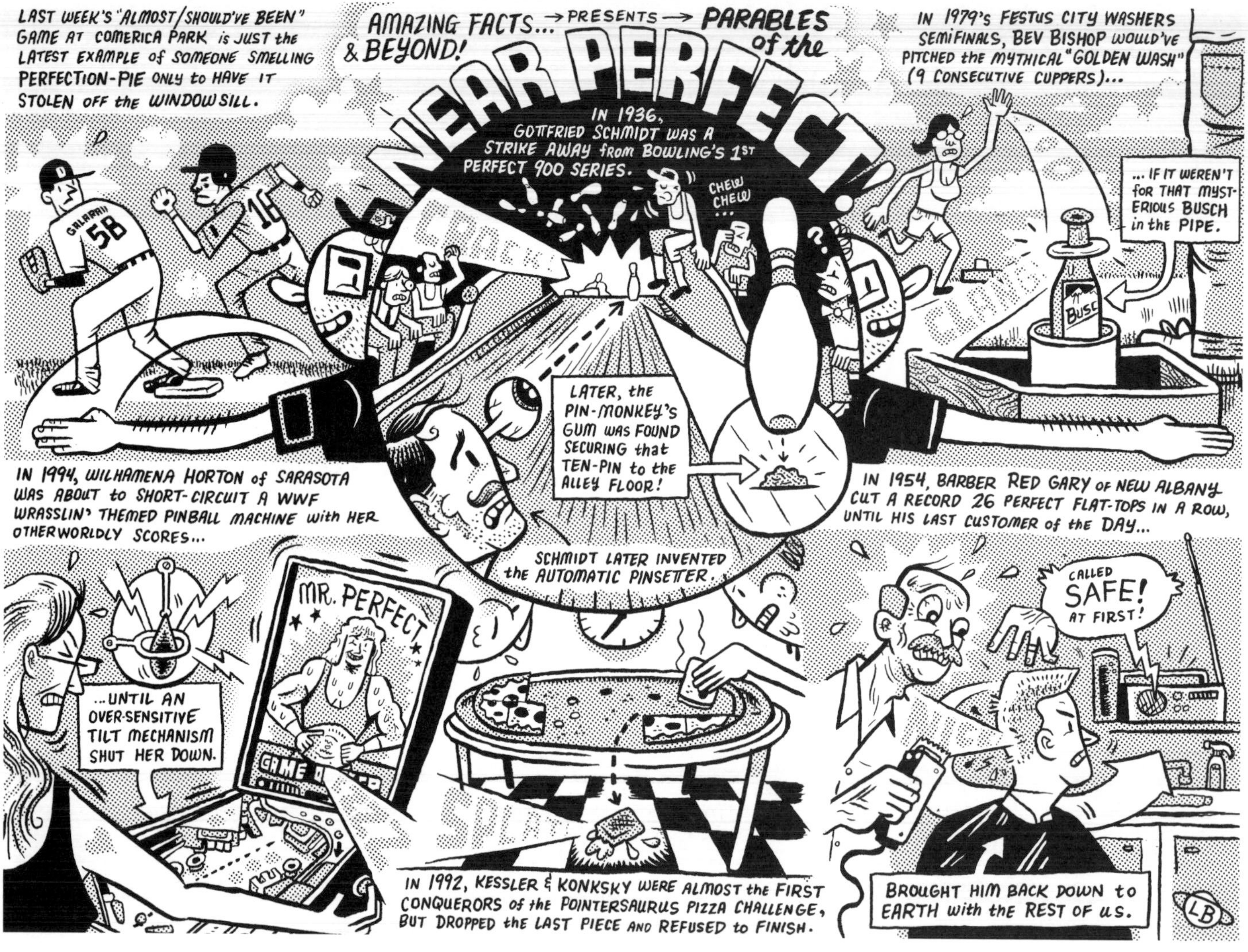
AMAZING FACTS... → PRESENTS → PARABLES & BEYOND!
of the NEAR PERFECT!
LAST WEEK'S "ALMOST/SHOULD'VE BEEN" GAME AT COMERICA PARK is JUST the LATEST EXAMPLE of SOMEONE SMELLING PERFECTION-PIE ONLY to HAVE IT STOLEN OFF the WINDOW SILL.
GALARRAGA 58
IN 1936, GOTTFRIED SCHMIDT WAS A STRIKE AWAY from BOWLING'S 1ST PERFECT 900 SERIES.
CHEW CHEW ...
LATER, the PIN-MONKEY'S GUM WAS FOUND SECURING that TEN-PIN to the ALLEY FLOOR!
SCHMIDT LATER INVENTED the AUTOMATIC PINSETTER.
IN 1979'S FESTUS CITY WASHERS SEMIFINALS, BEV BISHOP WOULD'VE PITCHED the MYTHICAL "GOLDEN WASH" (9 CONSECUTIVE CUPPERS)...
... IF IT WEREN'T FOR THAT MYSTERIOUS BUSCH in the PIPE.
IN 1994, WILHAMENA HORTON of SARASOTA WAS ABOUT to SHORT-CIRCUIT A WWF WRASSLIN' THEMED PINBALL MACHINE with HER OTHERWORLDLY SCORES...
MR. PERFECT
...UNTIL AN OVER-SENSITIVE TILT MECHANISM SHUT HER DOWN.
GAME OVER
SPLAT
IN 1992, KESSLER & KONKSKY WERE ALMOST the FIRST CONQUERORS of the POINTERSAURUS PIZZA CHALLENGE, BUT DROPPED the LAST PIECE AND REFUSED to FINISH.
IN 1954, BARBER RED GARY OF NEW ALBANY CUT A RECORD 26 PERFECT FLAT-TOPS IN A ROW, UNTIL HIS LAST CUSTOMER of the DAY...
CALLED SAFE! AT FIRST!
BROUGHT HIM BACK DOWN to EARTH with the REST OF US.
LB

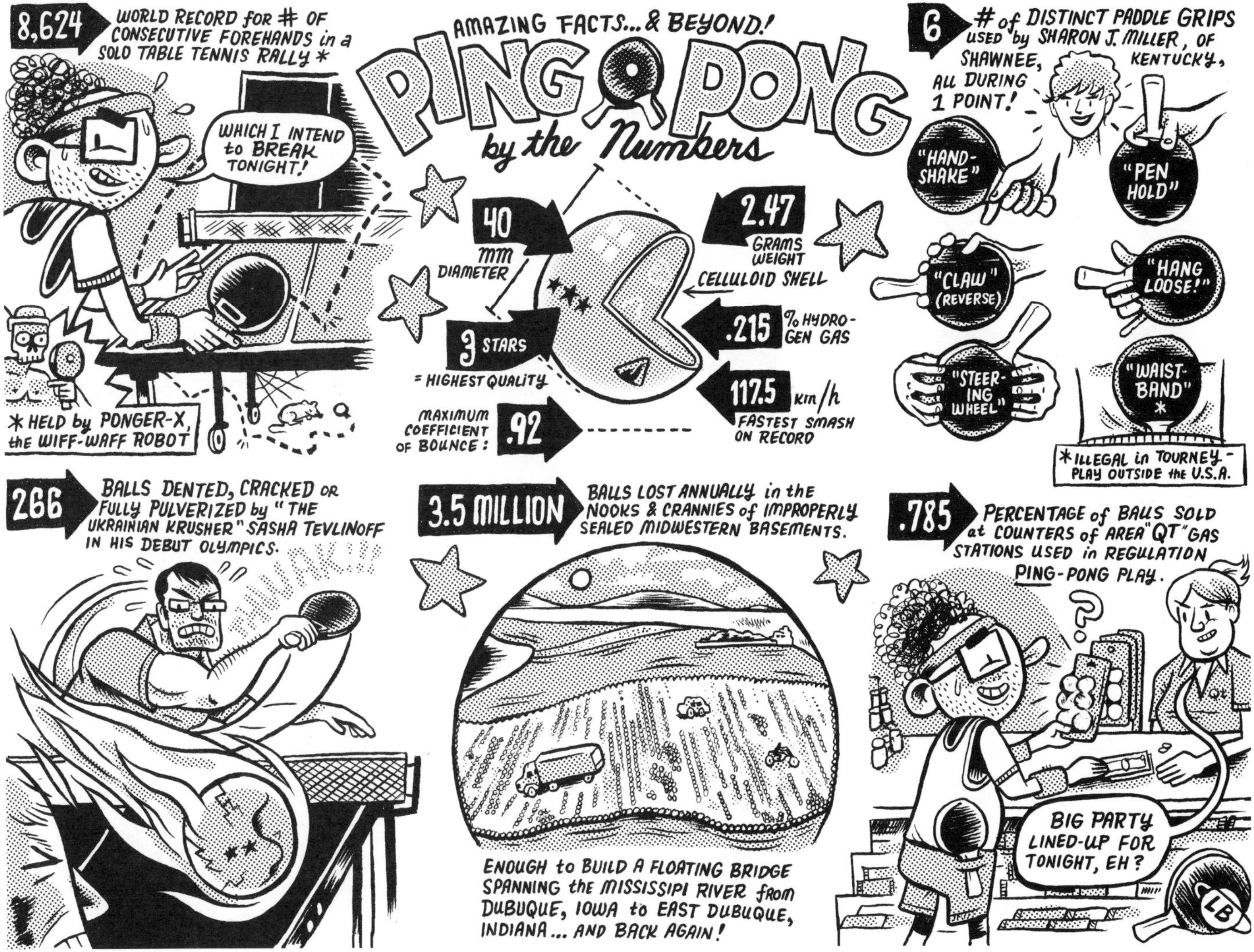
AMAZING FACTS... & BEYOND!
PING PONG
by the Numbers
8,624
WORLD RECORD for # OF CONSECUTIVE FOREHANDS in a SOLO TABLE TENNIS RALLY *
WHICH I INTEND to BREAK TONIGHT!
* HELD by PONGER-X, the WIFF-WAFF ROBOT
40
mm
DIAMETER
3 STARS
= HIGHEST QUALITY
MAXIMUM COEFFICIENT OF BOUNCE :
.92
2.47
GRAMS WEIGHT
CELLULOID SHELL
.215
% HYDRO-GEN GAS
117.5
km/h
FASTEST SMASH ON RECORD
6
# of DISTINCT PADDLE GRIPS USED by SHARON J. MILLER, OF SHAWNEE, KENTUCKY, ALL DURING 1 POINT!
"HAND-SHAKE"
"PEN HOLD"
"CLAW" (REVERSE)
"HANG LOOSE!"
"STEER-ING WHEEL"
"WAIST-BAND" *
* ILLEGAL in TOURNEY-PLAY OUTSIDE the U.S.A.
266
BALLS DENTED, CRACKED OR FULLY PULVERIZED by "THE UKRAINIAN KRUSHER" SASHA TEVLINOFF IN HIS DEBUT OLYMPICS.
3.5 MILLION
BALLS LOST ANNUALLY in the NOOKS & CRANNIES of IMPROPERLY SEALED MIDWESTERN BASEMENTS.
ENOUGH to BUILD A FLOATING BRIDGE SPANNING the MISSISSIPI RIVER from DUBUQUE, IOWA to EAST DUBUQUE, INDIANA ... AND BACK AGAIN!
.785
PERCENTAGE of BALLS SOLD at COUNTERS of AREA "QT" GAS STATIONS USED in REGULATION PING-PONG PLAY.
?
BIG PARTY LINED-UP FOR TONIGHT, EH?
LB

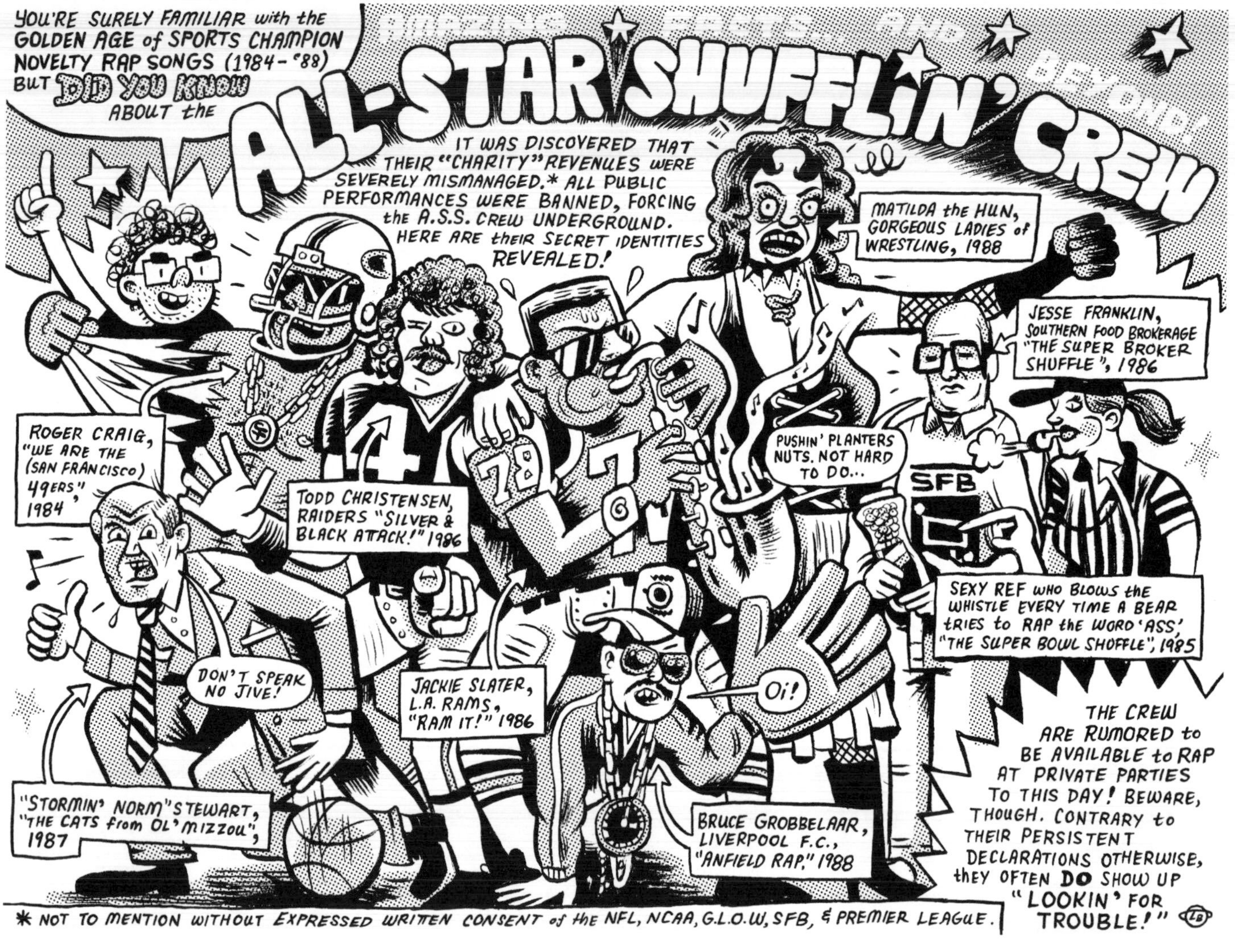

YOU'RE SURELY FAMILIAR with the GOLDEN AGE of SPORTS CHAMPION NOVELTY RAP SONGS (1984-'88) BUT DID YOU KNOW ABOUT the
AMAZING FACTS... AND BEYOND!
ALL-STAR SHUFFLIN' CREW
IT WAS DISCOVERED THAT THEIR "CHARITY" REVENUES WERE SEVERELY MISMANAGED.* ALL PUBLIC PERFORMANCES WERE BANNED, FORCING the A.S.S. CREW UNDERGROUND. HERE ARE their SECRET IDENTITIES REVEALED!
MATILDA the HUN, GORGEOUS LADIES of WRESTLING, 1988
JESSE FRANKLIN, SOUTHERN FOOD BROKERAGE "THE SUPER BROKER SHUFFLE", 1986
ROGER CRAIG, "WE ARE THE (SAN FRANCISCO) 49ERS," 1984
TODD CHRISTENSEN, RAIDERS "SILVER & BLACK ATTACK!" 1986
PUSHIN' PLANTERS NUTS. NOT HARD TO DO...
SFB
SEXY REF WHO BLOWS the WHISTLE EVERY TIME A BEAR tRIES to RAP the WORD 'ASS' "THE SUPER BOWL SHUFFLE", 1985
DON'T SPEAK NO JIVE!
JACKIE SLATER, L.A. RAMS, "RAM IT!" 1986
Oi!
THE CREW ARE RUMORED to BE AVAILABLE to RAP AT PRIVATE PARTIES TO THIS DAY! BEWARE, THOUGH. CONTRARY to THEIR PERSISTENT DECLARATIONS OTHERWISE, they OFTEN DO SHOW UP "LOOKIN' FOR TROUBLE!"
"STORMIN' NORM" STEWART, "THE CATS from OL' MIZZOU", 1987
BRUCE GROBBELAAR, LIVERPOOL F.C., "ANFIELD RAP," 1988
* NOT TO MENTION WITHOUT EXPRESSED WRITTEN CONSENT of the NFL, NCAA, G.L.O.W, SFB, & PREMIER LEAGUE.

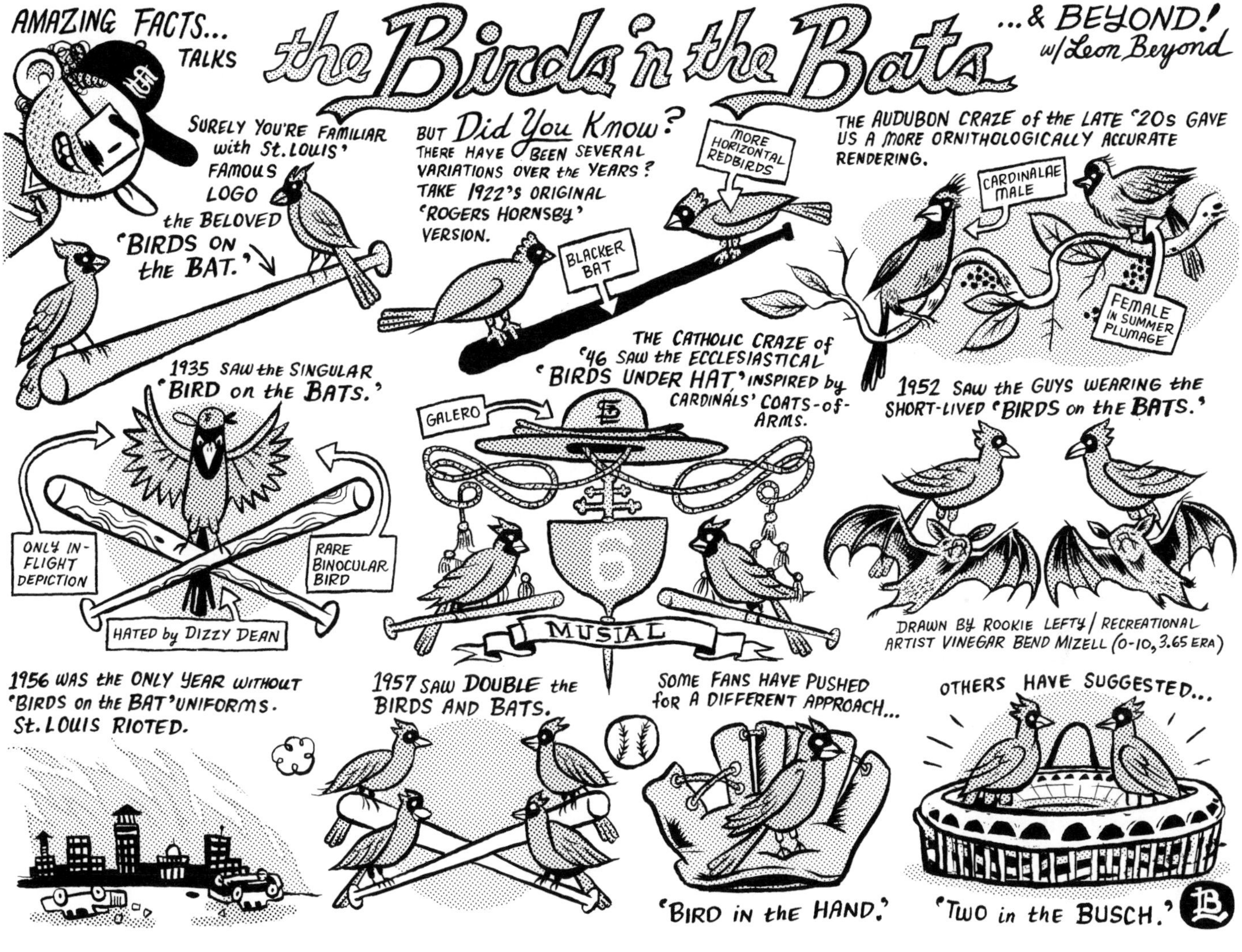
AMAZING FACTS... TALKS
the Birds 'n the Bats
...& BEYOND! w/Leon Beyond
SURELY YOU'RE FAMILIAR with St. LOUIS' FAMOUS LOGO the BELOVED 'BIRDS ON the BAT.'
BUT Did You Know? THERE HAVE BEEN SEVERAL VARIATIONS OVER the YEARS? TAKE 1922'S ORIGINAL 'ROGERS HORNSBY' VERSION.
MORE HORIZONTAL REDBIRDS
BLACKER BAT
THE AUDUBON CRAZE of the LATE '20s GAVE US A MORE ORNITHOLOGICALLY ACCURATE RENDERING.
CARDINALAE MALE
FEMALE IN SUMMER PLUMAGE
1935 SAW the SINGULAR 'BIRD on the BATS.'
ONLY IN-FLIGHT DEPICTION
RARE BINOCULAR BIRD
HATED by DIZZY DEAN
THE CATHOLIC CRAZE of '46 SAW the ECCLESIASTICAL 'BIRDS UNDER HAT' INSPIRED by CARDINALS' COATS-of-ARMS.
GALERO
6
MUSIAL
1952 SAW the GUYS WEARING the SHORT-LIVED 'BIRDS on the BATS.'
DRAWN BY ROOKIE LEFTY / RECREATIONAL ARTIST VINEGAR BEND MIZELL (0-10, 3.65 ERA)
1956 WAS the ONLY YEAR WITHOUT 'BIRDS on the BAT' UNIFORMS. St. LOUIS RIOTED.
1957 SAW DOUBLE the BIRDS AND BATS.
SOME FANS HAVE PUSHED for A DIFFERENT APPROACH...
'BIRD IN the HAND.'
OTHERS HAVE SUGGESTED...
'TWO in the BUSCH.'

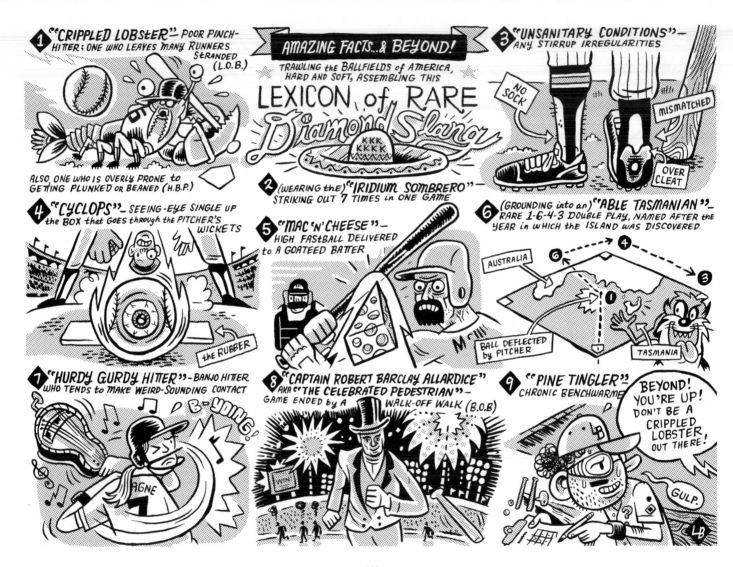

1. "CRIPPLED LOBSTER" — POOR PINCH-HITTER; ONE WHO LEAVES MANY RUNNERS STRANDED (L.O.B.) ALSO ONE WHO IS OVERLY PRONE TO GETTING PLUNKED OR BEANED (H.B.P.)

AMAZING FACTS...& BEYOND!
TRAWLING the BALLFIELDS of AMERICA, HARD AND SOFT, ASSEMBLING THIS
LEXICON of RARE
Diamond Slang
KKK
KKKK

2. (WEARING the) "IRIDIUM SOMBRERO" — STRIKING OUT 7 TIMES IN ONE GAME

3. "UNSANITARY CONDITIONS" — ANY STIRRUP IRREGULARITIES
NO SOCK
MISMATCHED
OVER CLEAT

4. "CYCLOPS" — SEEING-EYE SINGLE UP the BOX that GOES THROUGH the PITCHER'S WICKETS
the RUBBER

5. "MAC 'N' CHEESE" — HIGH FASTBALL DELIVERED to a GOATEED BATTER

6. (GROUNDING into an) "ABLE TASMANIAN" — RARE 1-6-4-3 DOUBLE PLAY, NAMED AFTER THE YEAR IN WHICH the ISLAND WAS DISCOVERED
AUSTRALIA
BALL DEFLECTED BY PITCHER
TASMANIA

7. "HURDY GURDY HITTER" — BANJO HITTER WHO TENDS TO MAKE WEIRD-SOUNDING CONTACT
B-YOING!
AGNE

8. "CAPTAIN ROBERT BARCLAY ALLARDICE" AKA "THE CELEBRATED PEDESTRIAN" — GAME ENDED BY A WALK-OFF WALK (B.O.B)

9. "PINE TINGLER" — CHRONIC BENCHWARMER
BEYOND! YOU'RE UP! DON'T BE A CRIPPLED LOBSTER OUT THERE!
GULP.

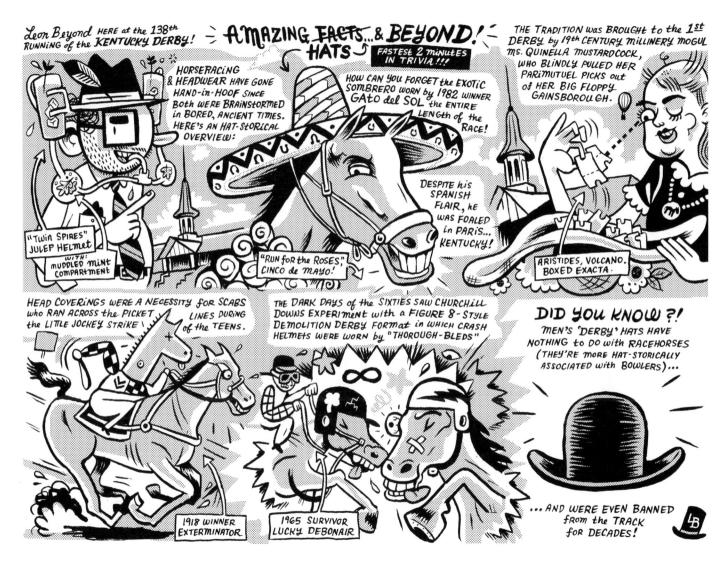

Leon Beyond HERE at the 138th RUNNING of the KENTUCKY DERBY!

AMAZING FACTS... & BEYOND! HATS

FASTEST 2 minutes IN TRIVIA!!!

HORSERACING & HEADWEAR HAVE GONE HAND-in-HOOF SINCE BOTH WERE BRAINSTORMED in BORED, ANCIENT TIMES. HERE'S AN HAT-STORICAL OVERVIEW:

HOW CAN YOU FORGET the EXOTIC SOMBRERO WORN by 1982 WINNER GATO del SOL the ENTIRE LENGTH of the RACE!

THE TRADITION was BROUGHT to the 1st DERBY by 19th CENTURY MILLINERY MOGUL MS. QUINELLA MUSTARDCOCK, WHO BLINDLY PULLED HER PARIMUTUEL PICKS OUT of HER BIG FLOPPY GAINSBOROUGH.

DESPITE his SPANISH FLAIR, he WAS FOALED in PARIS... KENTUCKY!

"Twin Spires" JULEP HELMET WITH: MUDDLED MINT COMPARTMENT

"RUN for the ROSES", CINCO de MAYO!

ARISTIDES, VOLCANO. BOXED EXACTA.

HEAD COVERINGS WERE A NECESSITY for SCABS WHO RAN ACROSS the PICKET LINES DURING the LITTLE JOCKEY STRIKE of the TEENS.

THE DARK DAYS of the SIXTIES SAW CHURCHILL DOWNS EXPERIMENT with a FIGURE 8-STYLE DEMOLITION DERBY FORMAT in WHICH CRASH HELMETS WERE WORN by "THOROUGH-BLEDS"

DID YOU KNOW?! MEN'S 'DERBY' HATS HAVE NOTHING to DO with RACEHORSES (THEY'RE MORE HAT-STORICALLY ASSOCIATED with BOWLERS)...

1918 WINNER EXTERMINATOR

1965 SURVIVOR LUCKY DEBONAIR

...AND WERE EVEN BANNED from the TRACK for DECADES!

LB

147

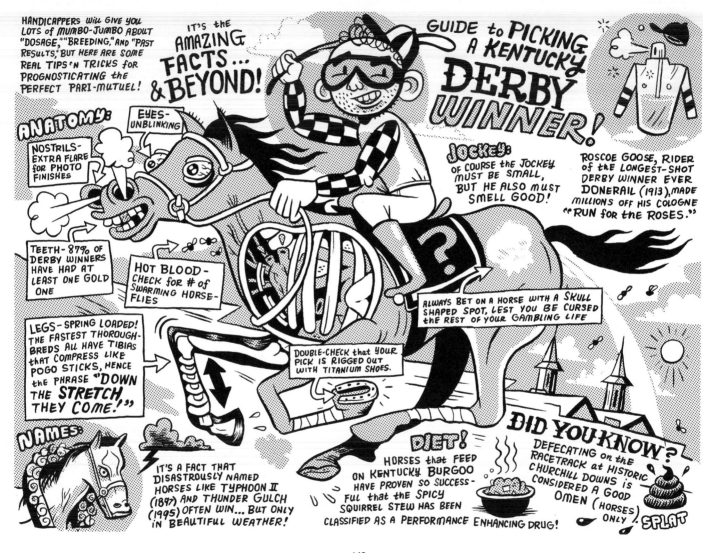

HANDICAPPERS WILL GIVE YOU LOTS OF MUMBO-JUMBO ABOUT "DOSAGE," "BREEDING," AND "PAST RESULTS," BUT HERE ARE SOME REAL TIPS 'N TRICKS FOR PROGNOSTICATING THE PERFECT PARI-MUTUEL!

IT'S THE AMAZING FACTS... & BEYOND!

GUIDE to PICKING A KENTUCKY DERBY WINNER!

ANATOMY:

EYES- UNBLINKING

NOSTRILS- EXTRA FLARE FOR PHOTO FINISHES

JOCKEY: OF COURSE THE JOCKEY MUST BE SMALL, BUT HE ALSO MUST SMELL GOOD!

ROSCOE GOOSE, RIDER OF THE LONGEST-SHOT DERBY WINNER EVER DONERAIL (1913), MADE MILLIONS OFF HIS COLOGNE "RUN FOR THE ROSES."

TEETH- 87% OF DERBY WINNERS HAVE HAD AT LEAST ONE GOLD ONE

HOT BLOOD- CHECK FOR # OF SWARMING HORSE- FLIES

ALWAYS BET ON A HORSE WITH A SKULL SHAPED SPOT, LEST YOU BE CURSED THE REST OF YOUR GAMBLING LIFE

LEGS- SPRING LOADED! THE FASTEST THOROUGH- BREDS ALL HAVE TIBIAS THAT COMPRESS LIKE POGO STICKS, HENCE THE PHRASE "DOWN THE STRETCH THEY COME!"

DOUBLE-CHECK that YOUR PICK IS RIGGED OUT WITH TITANIUM SHOES.

NAMES:

IT'S A FACT THAT DISASTROUSLY NAMED HORSES LIKE TYPHOON II (1897) AND THUNDER GULCH (1995) OFTEN WIN... BUT ONLY IN BEAUTIFUL WEATHER!

DIET! HORSES that FEED ON KENTUCKY BURGOO HAVE PROVEN SO SUCCESS- FUL that the SPICY SQUIRREL STEW HAS BEEN CLASSIFIED AS A PERFORMANCE ENHANCING DRUG!

DID YOU KNOW? DEFECATING ON the RACETRACK AT HISTORIC CHURCHILL DOWNS IS CONSIDERED A GOOD OMEN (HORSES ONLY) SPLAT

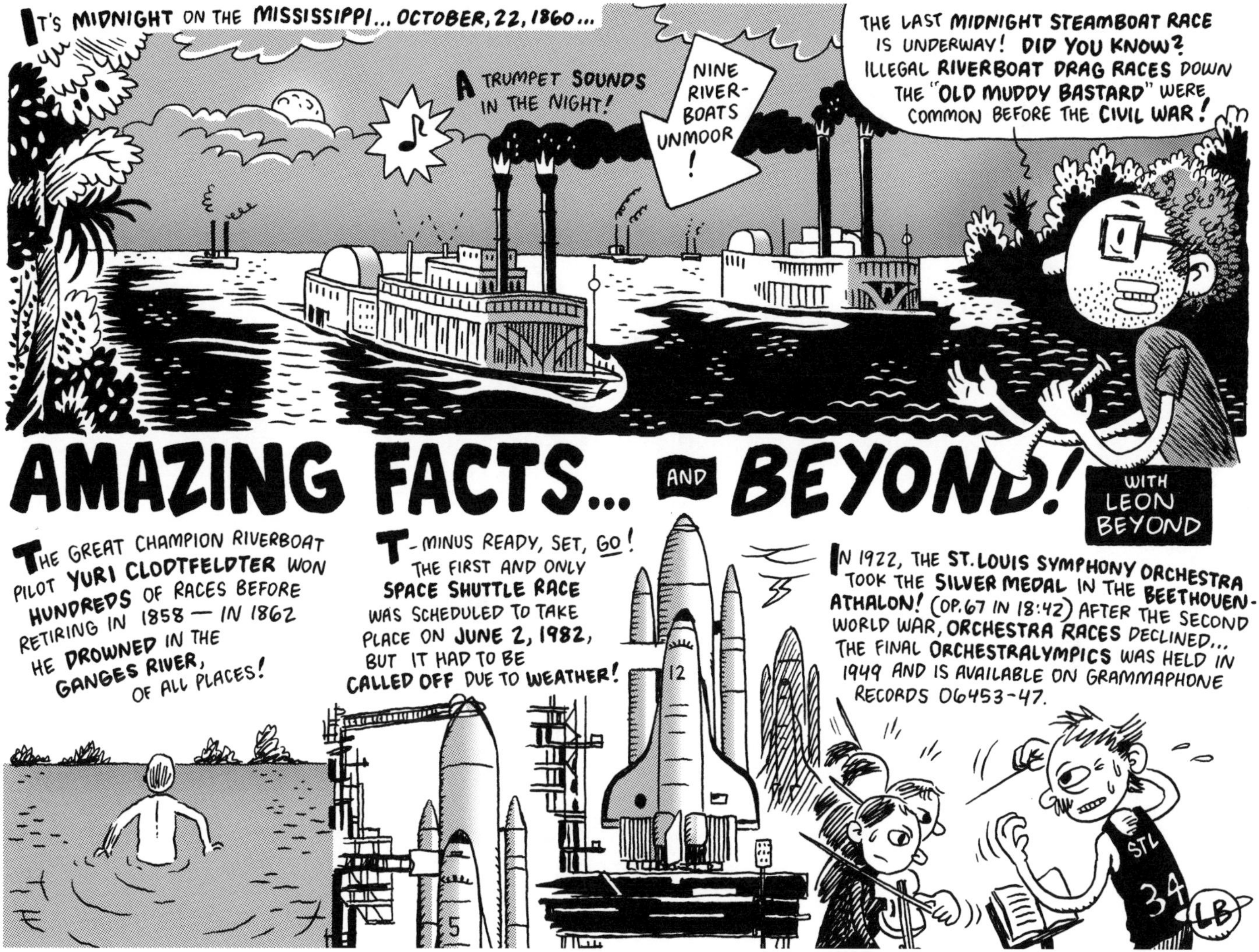
IT'S MIDNIGHT ON THE MISSISSIPPI... OCTOBER, 22, 1860...
A TRUMPET SOUNDS IN THE NIGHT!
NINE RIVERBOATS UNMOOR!
THE LAST MIDNIGHT STEAMBOAT RACE IS UNDERWAY! DID YOU KNOW? ILLEGAL RIVERBOAT DRAG RACES DOWN THE "OLD MUDDY BASTARD" WERE COMMON BEFORE THE CIVIL WAR!
AMAZING FACTS... AND BEYOND!
WITH LEON BEYOND
THE GREAT CHAMPION RIVERBOAT PILOT YURI CLODTFELDTER WON HUNDREDS OF RACES BEFORE RETIRING IN 1858 — IN 1862 HE DROWNED IN THE GANGES RIVER, OF ALL PLACES!
T-MINUS READY, SET, GO! THE FIRST AND ONLY SPACE SHUTTLE RACE WAS SCHEDULED TO TAKE PLACE ON JUNE 2, 1982, BUT IT HAD TO BE CALLED OFF DUE TO WEATHER!
IN 1922, THE ST. LOUIS SYMPHONY ORCHESTRA TOOK THE SILVER MEDAL IN THE BEETHOVEN-ATHALON! (OP.67 IN 18:42) AFTER THE SECOND WORLD WAR, ORCHESTRA RACES DECLINED... THE FINAL ORCHESTRALYMPICS WAS HELD IN 1949 AND IS AVAILABLE ON GRAMMAPHONE RECORDS 06453-47.
12
5
STL
34
LB

FURTHERMORE,
DID YOU *ALSO* KNOW:

THIS *HAIRY* EYEBALL FOUND
IN A *MOSCOW MEDICAL MUSEUM*
HAS GOTTEN A TRIM EVERY
SIX MONTHS SINCE 1872

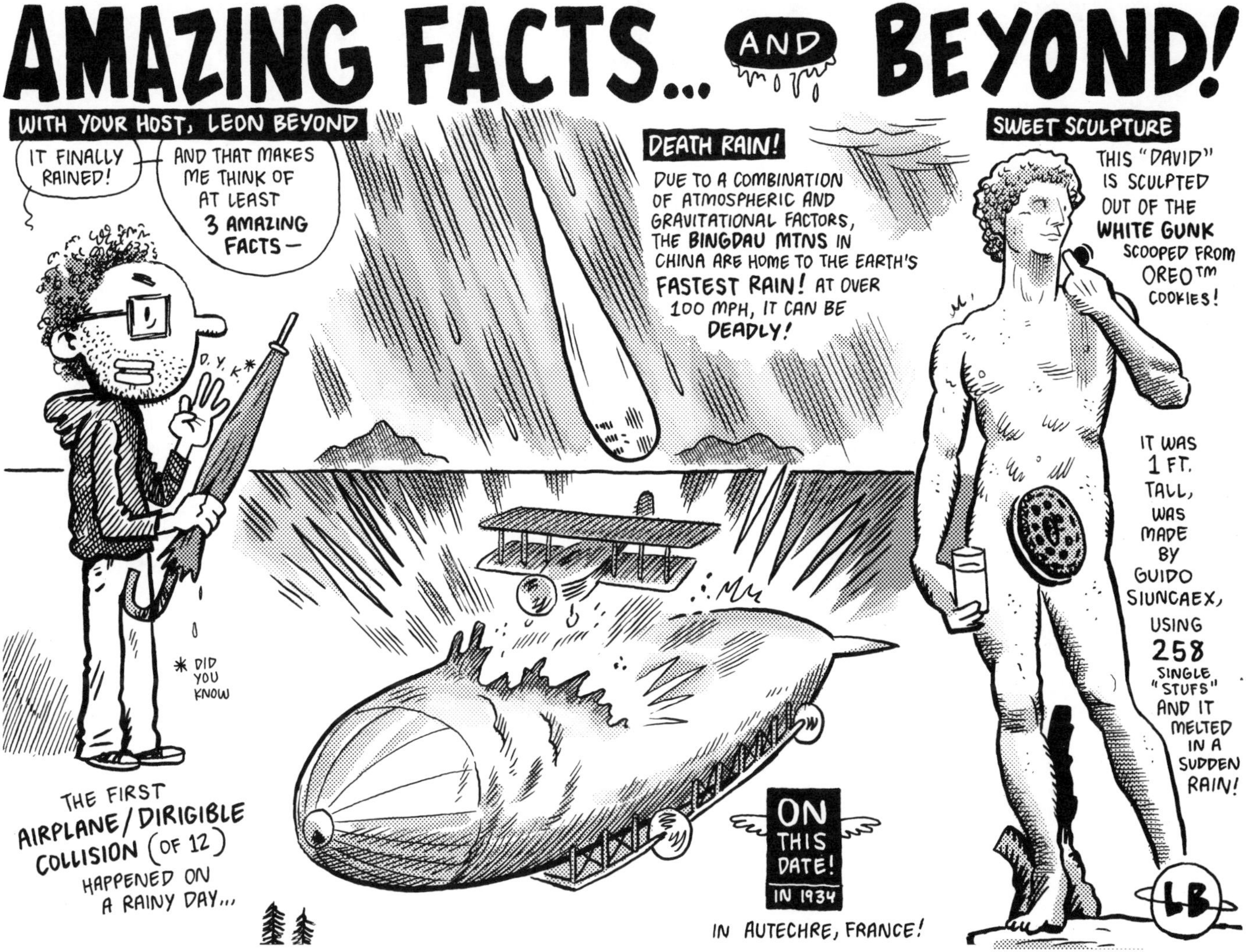
AMAZING FACTS... AND BEYOND!
WITH YOUR HOST, LEON BEYOND
IT FINALLY RAINED!
AND THAT MAKES ME THINK OF AT LEAST 3 AMAZING FACTS—
D.Y.K.*
* DID YOU KNOW
THE FIRST AIRPLANE/DIRIGIBLE COLLISION (OF 12) HAPPENED ON A RAINY DAY...
ON THIS DATE! IN 1934
IN AUTECHRE, FRANCE!
DEATH RAIN!
DUE TO A COMBINATION OF ATMOSPHERIC AND GRAVITATIONAL FACTORS, THE BINGDAU MTNS IN CHINA ARE HOME TO THE EARTH'S FASTEST RAIN! AT OVER 100 MPH, IT CAN BE DEADLY!
SWEET SCULPTURE
THIS "DAVID" IS SCULPTED OUT OF THE WHITE GUNK SCOOPED FROM OREO™ COOKIES!
IT WAS 1 FT. TALL, WAS MADE BY GUIDO SIUNCAEX, USING 258 SINGLE "STUFS" AND IT MELTED IN A SUDDEN RAIN!
LB

AMAZING FACTS... AND BEYOND!

WITH LEON BEYOND

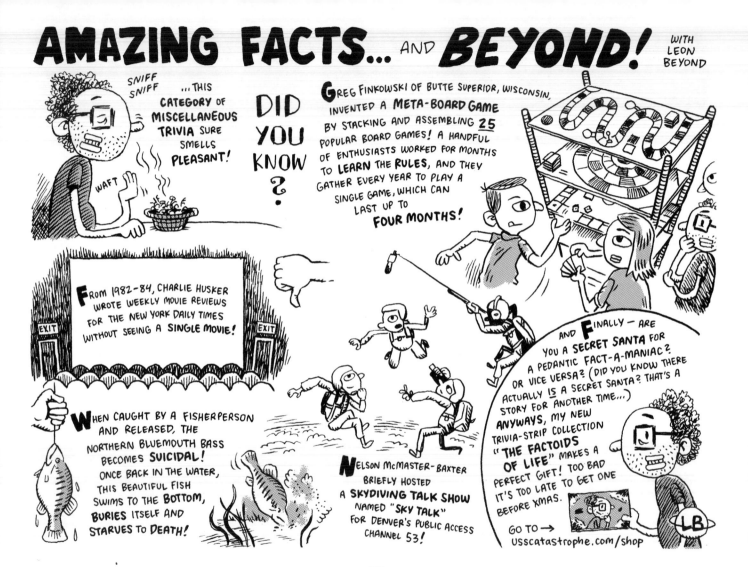

SNIFF SNIFF ...THIS CATEGORY OF **MISCELLANEOUS TRIVIA** SURE SMELLS **PLEASANT!**

WAFT

DID YOU KNOW ?

GREG FINKOWSKI OF BUTTE SUPERIOR, WISCONSIN, INVENTED A **META-BOARD GAME** BY STACKING AND ASSEMBLING **25** POPULAR BOARD GAMES! A HANDFUL OF ENTHUSIASTS WORKED FOR MONTHS TO **LEARN THE RULES**, AND THEY GATHER EVERY YEAR TO PLAY A SINGLE GAME, WHICH CAN LAST UP TO **FOUR MONTHS!**

FROM 1982-84, CHARLIE HUSKER WROTE WEEKLY MOVIE REVIEWS FOR THE NEW YORK DAILY TIMES WITHOUT SEEING A SINGLE MOVIE!

EXIT   EXIT

WHEN CAUGHT BY A FISHERPERSON AND RELEASED, THE NORTHERN BLUEMOUTH BASS BECOMES SUICIDAL! ONCE BACK IN THE WATER, THIS BEAUTIFUL FISH SWIMS TO THE **BOTTOM**, **BURIES** ITSELF AND STARVES TO **DEATH!**

NELSON MCMASTER-BAXTER BRIEFLY HOSTED A **SKYDIVING TALK SHOW** NAMED "**SKY TALK**" FOR DENVER'S PUBLIC ACCESS CHANNEL 53!

AND **FINALLY** — ARE YOU A **SECRET SANTA** FOR A PEDANTIC **FACT-A-MANIAC?** OR VICE VERSA? (DID YOU KNOW THERE ACTUALLY **IS** A SECRET SANTA? THAT'S A STORY FOR ANOTHER TIME....) **ANYWAYS,** MY NEW TRIVIA-STRIP COLLECTION "**THE FACTOIDS OF LIFE**" MAKES A PERFECT GIFT! TOO BAD IT'S TOO LATE TO GET ONE BEFORE XMAS.

GO TO → USSCATASTROPHE.COM/SHOP

LB

AMAZING FACTS... AND BEYOND!

WITH LEON BEYOND

THESE AMAZING FACTS ARE NO **LAUGHING** MATTER!

CLARA WESTON OF DES BOINES HAS A **LAUGH** SO CONTAGIOUS IT GOT HER FIRED FROM **3 JOBS!**

STEPHEN KITE OF CLEARINBURGH, SCOTLAND WAS BORN WITH A **RARE NEUROLOGICAL CONDITION** NAMED **ST. GERALD'S FIRE** ✱ WHERE ONCE THE SUFFERER BEGINS ≡ LAUGHING ≡ IT IS ALMOST **IMPOSSIBLE TO STOP!** RELIEF IS FOUND AFTER PAINFUL EXHAUSTION!

DID YOU KNOW ?

PINK SLIP #3

IN SCIENCE NEWS AND REPORTS, SPRING 1978, WE FIND THE **STRANGE CASE OF PHIL JABLONEY** OF HOUSTON, TX, WHO WAS PUZZLED WHEN HE BEGAN **WEEPING** IN RESPONSE TO **JOKES** AND **GIGGLING** WHEN **DEPRESSED!**

✱ NAMED AFTER THE LEGENDARY TALE OF **ST. GERALD,** ✱✱ WHO SUFFERED EPONYMOUSLY— AFTER DEAFENING HIMSELF AND GOUGING OUT HIS OWN EYES, HE BECAME A MONK... YET STILL HE SUFFERED FROM THE "DEVIL'S JOKE",.. UNTIL FINALLY HE WAS HACKED APART BY SOLDIERS!
✱✱ HE'S NOT OFFICIALLY A SAINT YET.

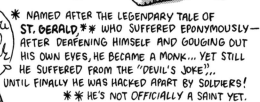

JOKE

AFTER FALLING DEAD ON ONE EVENING, A **BRAIN TUMOR** WAS FOUND, WHICH DOCTORS THEORIZE CAUSED THE MIX UPS! THE SIDEWALK

A COURT OFFICIAL NAMED **THOMAS MUNDT** MADE KING THEODOR OF **PRUSSIA** ≡ LAUGH ≡ SO LONG AND HARD THAT IN HIS EMBARRASSMENT HE HAD MUNDT **BOILED ALIVE!**

HUH! HUH! HUH!

"SPARKY" WAS TAUGHT BY HIS MASTER, **KEN DENNIS,** OF ST. GERALD, MO, TO MAKE A **LAUGH-LIKE SOUND** WHEN PEOPLE RAISE ONE EYEBROW! BUT AFTER SPARKY **BIT** THE PREGNANT **MRS DENNIS,** THEY DECIDED TO GET RID OF HIM.

LB

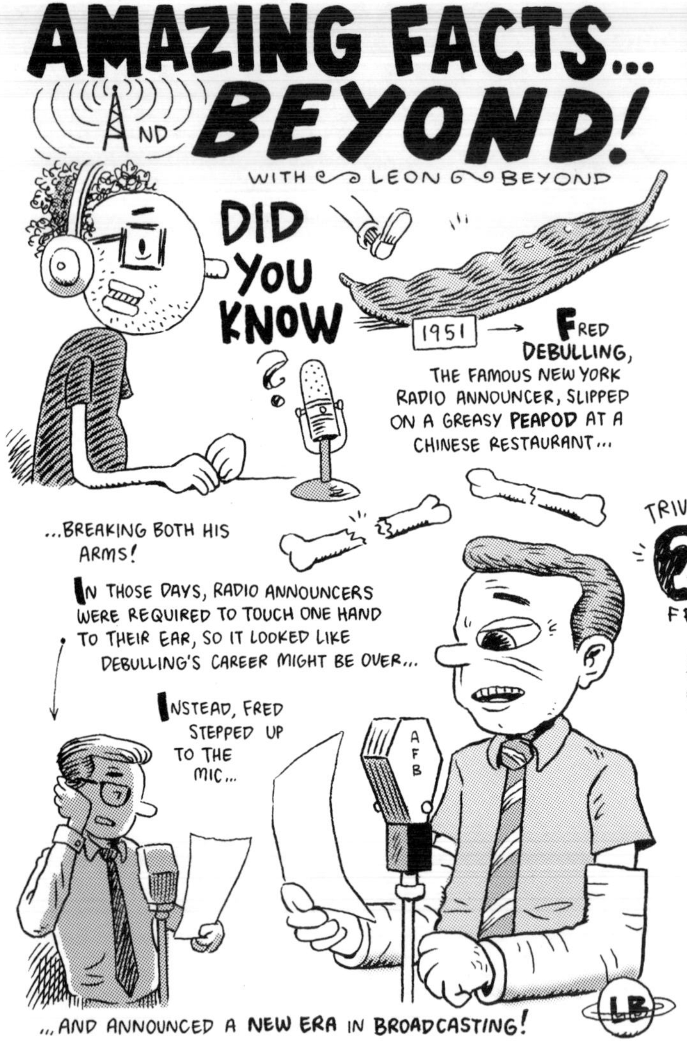
AMAZING FACTS... AND BEYOND!
WITH LEON BEYOND
DID YOU KNOW
1951 → FRED DEBULLING, THE FAMOUS NEW YORK RADIO ANNOUNCER, SLIPPED ON A GREASY PEAPOD AT A CHINESE RESTAURANT...
...BREAKING BOTH HIS ARMS!
IN THOSE DAYS, RADIO ANNOUNCERS WERE REQUIRED TO TOUCH ONE HAND TO THEIR EAR, SO IT LOOKED LIKE DEBULLING'S CAREER MIGHT BE OVER...
INSTEAD, FRED STEPPED UP TO THE MIC...
AFB
...AND ANNOUNCED A NEW ERA IN BROADCASTING!
LB

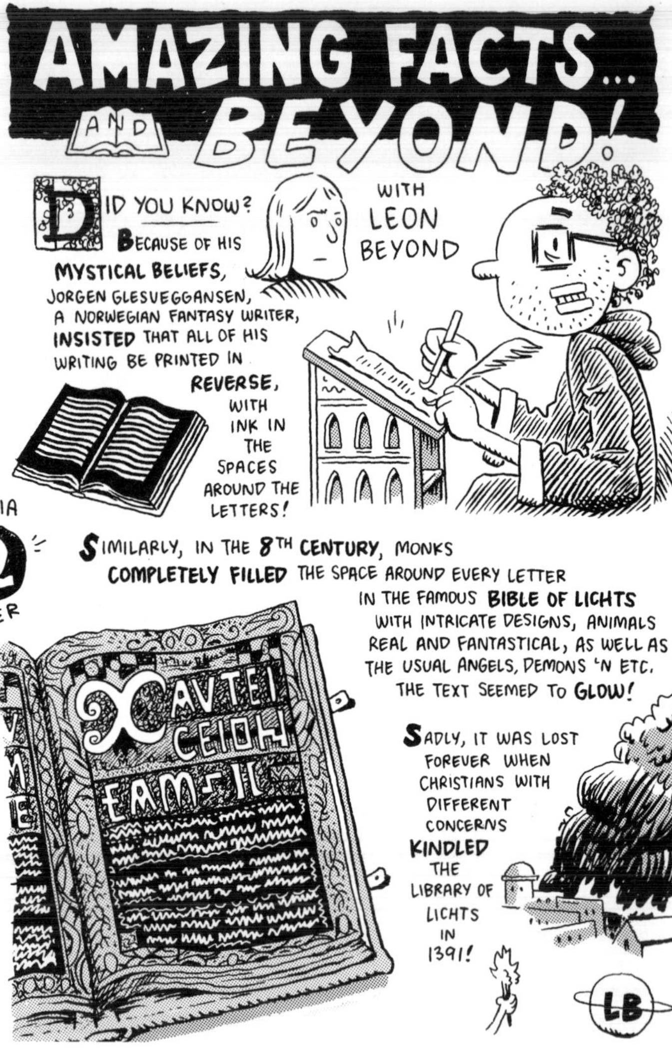
AMAZING FACTS... AND BEYOND!
DID YOU KNOW?
BECAUSE OF HIS MYSTICAL BELIEFS, JORGEN GLESVEGGANSEN, A NORWEGIAN FANTASY WRITER, INSISTED THAT ALL OF HIS WRITING BE PRINTED IN REVERSE, WITH INK IN THE SPACES AROUND THE LETTERS!
WITH LEON BEYOND
TRIVIA 2 FER
SIMILARLY, IN THE 8TH CENTURY, MONKS COMPLETELY FILLED THE SPACE AROUND EVERY LETTER IN THE FAMOUS BIBLE OF LICHTS WITH INTRICATE DESIGNS, ANIMALS REAL AND FANTASTICAL, AS WELL AS THE USUAL ANGELS, DEMONS 'N ETC. THE TEXT SEEMED TO GLOW!
SADLY, IT WAS LOST FOREVER WHEN CHRISTIANS WITH DIFFERENT CONCERNS KINDLED THE LIBRARY OF LICHTS IN 1391!
LB

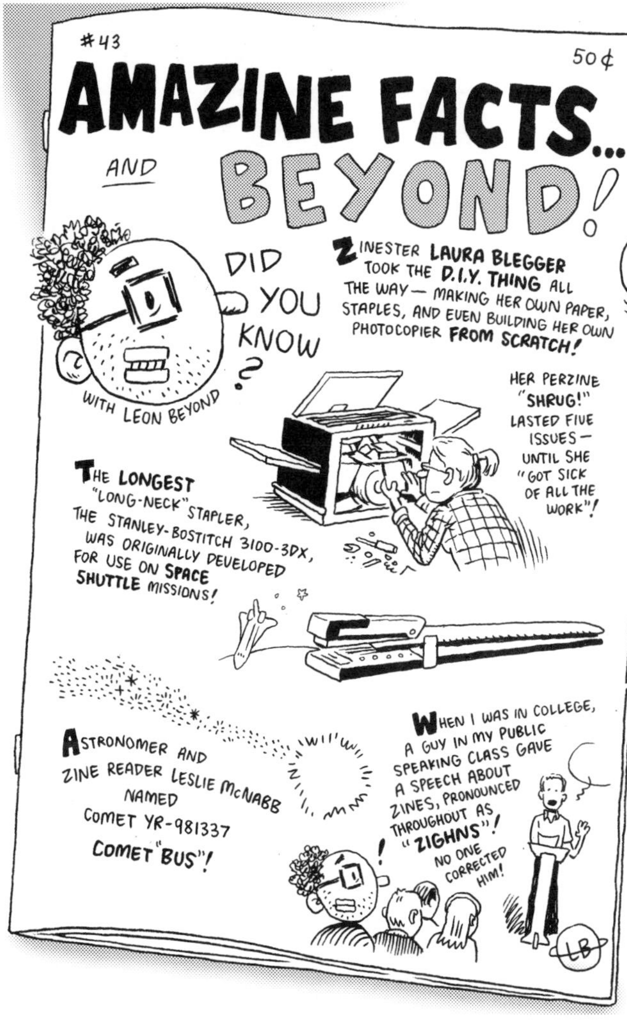

#43
50¢
AMAZINE FACTS... AND BEYOND!
DID YOU KNOW?
WITH LEON BEYOND
ZINESTER LAURA BLEGGER TOOK THE D.I.Y. THING ALL THE WAY— MAKING HER OWN PAPER, STAPLES, AND EVEN BUILDING HER OWN PHOTOCOPIER FROM SCRATCH!
HER PERZINE "SHRUG!" LASTED FIVE ISSUES— UNTIL SHE "GOT SICK OF ALL THE WORK"!
THE LONGEST "LONG-NECK" STAPLER, THE STANLEY-BOSTITCH 3100-3DX, WAS ORIGINALLY DEVELOPED FOR USE ON SPACE SHUTTLE MISSIONS!
ASTRONOMER AND ZINE READER LESLIE McNABB NAMED COMET YR-981337 COMET "BUS"!
WHEN I WAS IN COLLEGE, A GUY IN MY PUBLIC SPEAKING CLASS GAVE A SPEECH ABOUT ZINES, PRONOUNCED THROUGHOUT AS "ZIGHNS"! NO ONE CORRECTED HIM!
LB

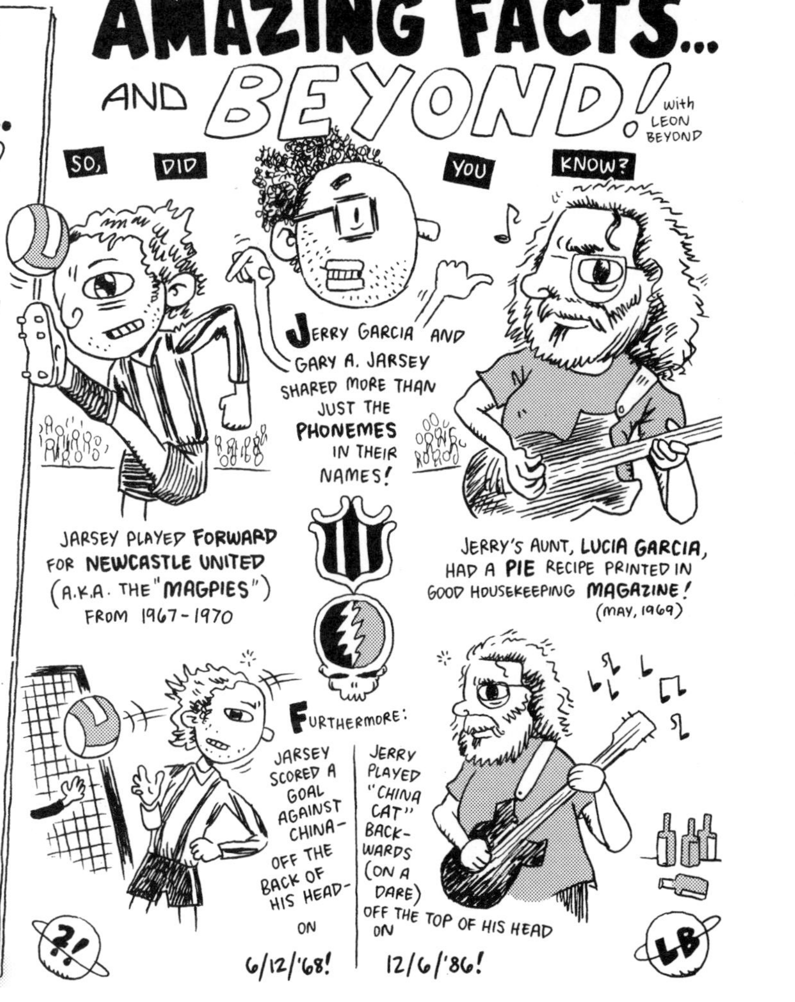

AMAZING FACTS... AND BEYOND! with LEON BEYOND
SO, DID YOU KNOW?
JERRY GARCIA AND GARY A. JARSEY SHARED MORE THAN JUST THE PHONEMES IN THEIR NAMES!
JARSEY PLAYED FORWARD FOR NEWCASTLE UNITED (A.K.A. THE "MAGPIES") FROM 1967-1970
JERRY'S AUNT, LUCIA GARCIA, HAD A PIE RECIPE PRINTED IN GOOD HOUSEKEEPING MAGAZINE! (MAY, 1969)
FURTHERMORE:
JARSEY SCORED A GOAL AGAINST CHINA— OFF THE BACK OF HIS HEAD— ON 6/12/'68!
JERRY PLAYED "CHINA CAT" BACKWARDS (ON A DARE) OFF THE TOP OF HIS HEAD ON 12/6/'86!
?!
LB

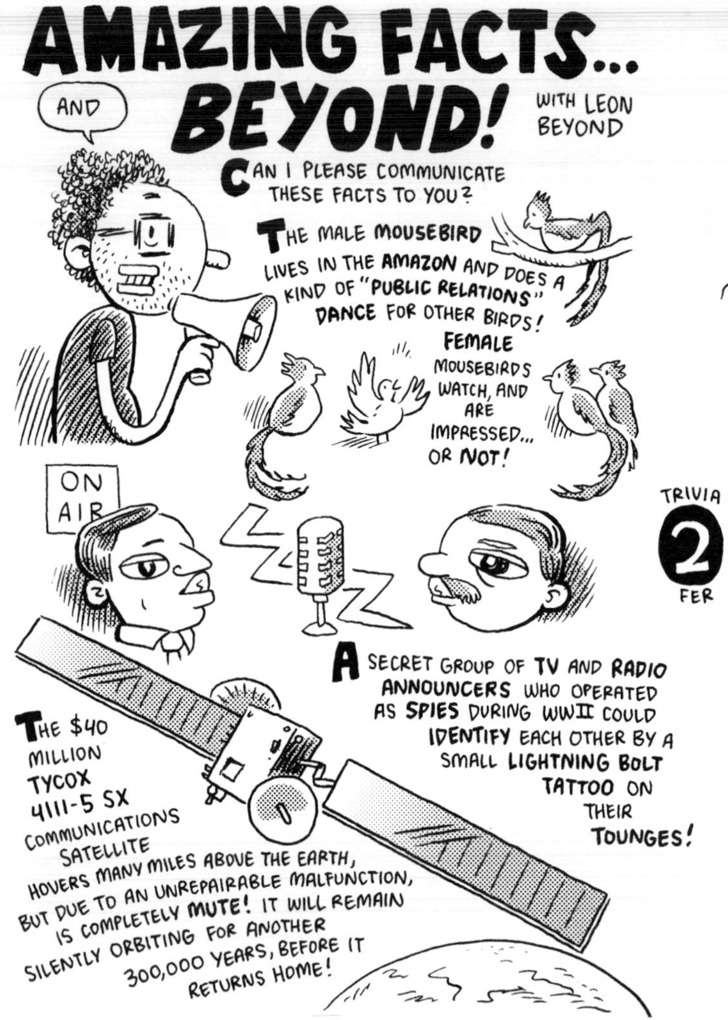
AMAZING FACTS...
AND
BEYOND!
WITH LEON BEYOND
CAN I PLEASE COMMUNICATE THESE FACTS TO YOU?
THE MALE MOUSEBIRD LIVES IN THE AMAZON AND DOES A KIND OF "PUBLIC RELATIONS" DANCE FOR OTHER BIRDS!
FEMALE MOUSEBIRDS WATCH, AND ARE IMPRESSED... OR NOT!
ON AIR
A SECRET GROUP OF TV AND RADIO ANNOUNCERS WHO OPERATED AS SPIES DURING WWII COULD IDENTIFY EACH OTHER BY A SMALL LIGHTNING BOLT TATTOO ON THEIR TOUNGES!
THE $40 MILLION TYCOX 4111-5 SX COMMUNICATIONS SATELLITE HOVERS MANY MILES ABOVE THE EARTH, BUT DUE TO AN UNREPAIRABLE MALFUNCTION, IS COMPLETELY MUTE! IT WILL REMAIN SILENTLY ORBITING FOR ANOTHER 300,000 YEARS, BEFORE IT RETURNS HOME!
TRIVIA
2
FER
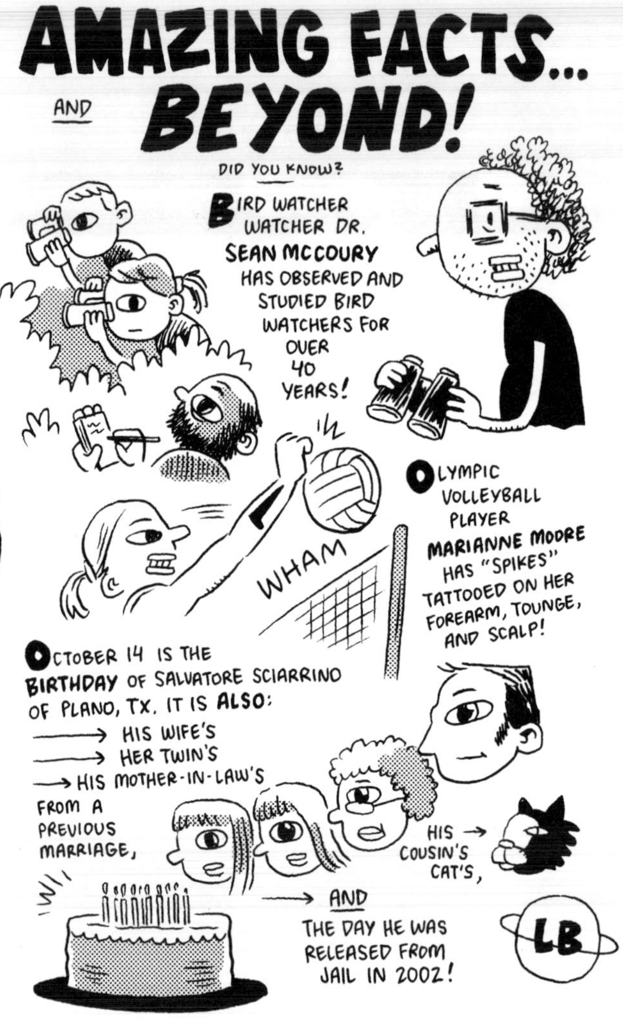
AMAZING FACTS...
AND
BEYOND!
DID YOU KNOW?
BIRD WATCHER WATCHER DR. SEAN MCCOURY HAS OBSERVED AND STUDIED BIRD WATCHERS FOR OVER 40 YEARS!
OLYMPIC VOLLEYBALL PLAYER MARIANNE MOORE HAS "SPIKES" TATTOOED ON HER FOREARM, TOUNGE, AND SCALP!
WHAM
OCTOBER 14 IS THE BIRTHDAY OF SALVATORE SCIARRINO OF PLANO, TX. IT IS ALSO:
→ HIS WIFE'S
→ HER TWIN'S
→ HIS MOTHER-IN-LAW'S FROM A PREVIOUS MARRIAGE,
HIS → COUSIN'S CAT'S,
→ AND THE DAY HE WAS RELEASED FROM JAIL IN 2002!
LB

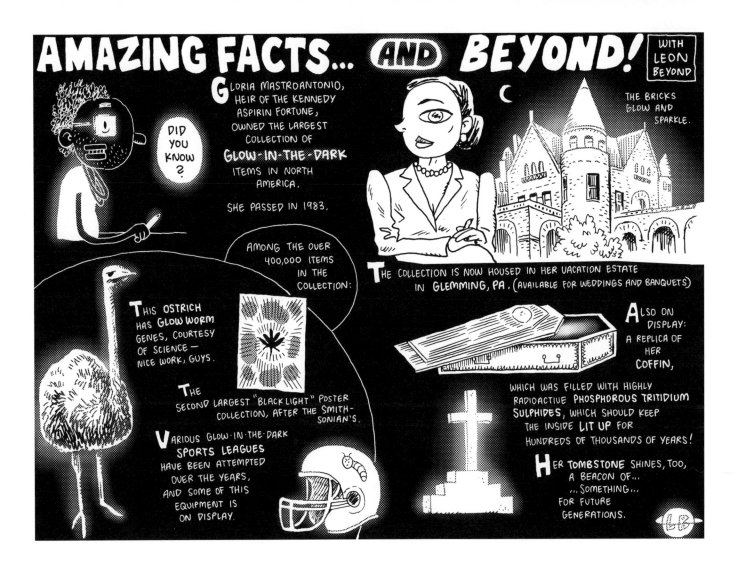

AMAZING FACTS... AND BEYOND!

WITH LEON BEYOND

DID YOU KNOW ?

GLORIA MASTROANTONIO, HEIR OF THE KENNEDY ASPIRIN FORTUNE, OWNED THE LARGEST COLLECTION OF **GLOW-IN-THE-DARK** ITEMS IN NORTH AMERICA.

SHE PASSED IN 1983.

THE BRICKS GLOW AND SPARKLE.

THE COLLECTION IS NOW HOUSED IN HER VACATION ESTATE IN GLEMMING, PA. (AVAILABLE FOR WEDDINGS AND BANQUETS)

AMONG THE OVER 400,000 ITEMS IN THE COLLECTION:

THIS OSTRICH HAS GLOW WORM GENES, COURTESY OF SCIENCE — NICE WORK, GUYS.

THE SECOND LARGEST "BLACK LIGHT" POSTER COLLECTION, AFTER THE SMITHSONIAN'S.

VARIOUS GLOW-IN-THE-DARK SPORTS LEAGUES HAVE BEEN ATTEMPTED OVER THE YEARS, AND SOME OF THIS EQUIPMENT IS ON DISPLAY.

ALSO ON DISPLAY: A REPLICA OF HER **COFFIN**, WHICH WAS FILLED WITH HIGHLY RADIOACTIVE PHOSPHOROUS TRITIDIUM SULPHIDES, WHICH SHOULD KEEP THE INSIDE LIT UP FOR HUNDREDS OF THOUSANDS OF YEARS!

HER TOMBSTONE SHINES, TOO, A BEACON OF... ...SOMETHING... FOR FUTURE GENERATIONS.

LB

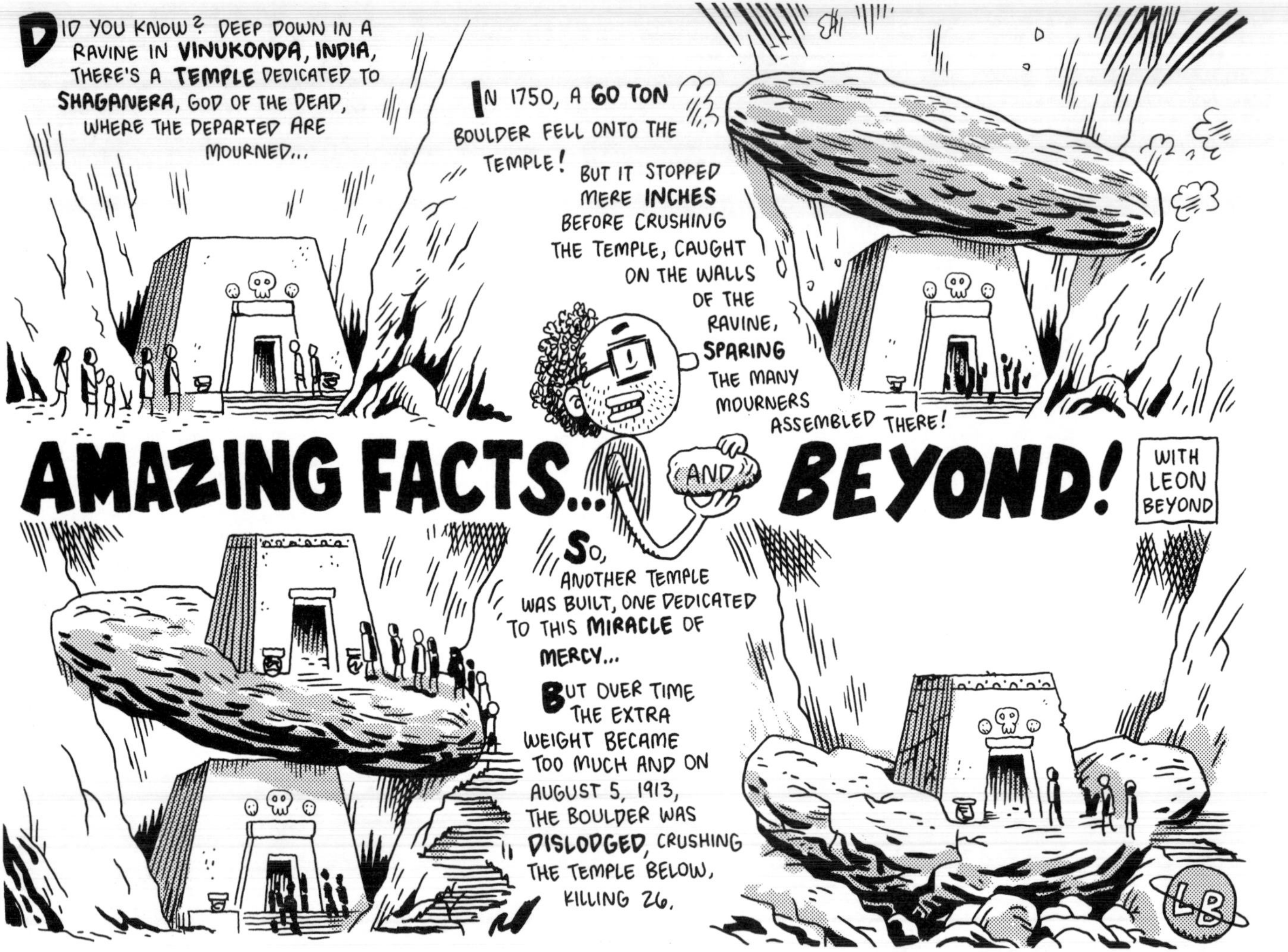
DID YOU KNOW? DEEP DOWN IN A RAVINE IN VINUKONDA, INDIA, THERE'S A TEMPLE DEDICATED TO SHAGANERA, GOD OF THE DEAD, WHERE THE DEPARTED ARE MOURNED...
IN 1750, A 60 TON BOULDER FELL ONTO THE TEMPLE!
BUT IT STOPPED MERE INCHES BEFORE CRUSHING THE TEMPLE, CAUGHT ON THE WALLS OF THE RAVINE, SPARING THE MANY MOURNERS ASSEMBLED THERE!
AMAZING FACTS... AND BEYOND!
WITH LEON BEYOND
SO, ANOTHER TEMPLE WAS BUILT, ONE DEDICATED TO THIS MIRACLE OF MERCY...
BUT OVER TIME THE EXTRA WEIGHT BECAME TOO MUCH AND ON AUGUST 5, 1913, THE BOULDER WAS DISLODGED, CRUSHING THE TEMPLE BELOW, KILLING 26.
LB

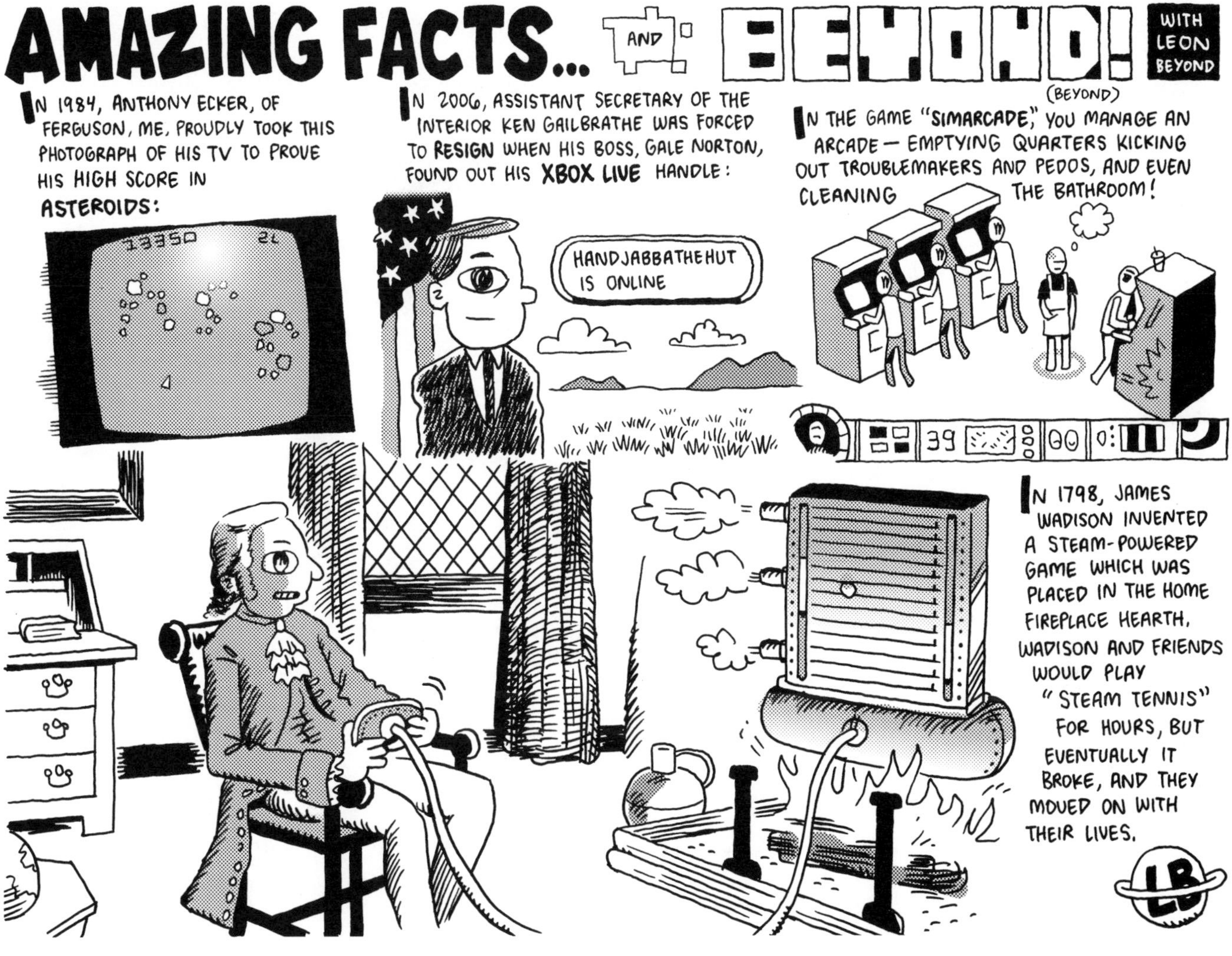

AMAZING FACTS... AND BEYOND!
WITH LEON BEYOND
IN 1984, ANTHONY ECKER, OF FERGUSON, ME, PROUDLY TOOK THIS PHOTOGRAPH OF HIS TV TO PROVE HIS HIGH SCORE IN ASTEROIDS:
13350
2L
IN 2006, ASSISTANT SECRETARY OF THE INTERIOR KEN GAILBRATHE WAS FORCED TO RESIGN WHEN HIS BOSS, GALE NORTON, FOUND OUT HIS XBOX LIVE HANDLE:
HANDJABBATHEHUT IS ONLINE
(BEYOND)
IN THE GAME "SIMARCADE," YOU MANAGE AN ARCADE — EMPTYING QUARTERS KICKING OUT TROUBLEMAKERS AND PEDOS, AND EVEN CLEANING THE BATHROOM!
39
IN 1798, JAMES WADISON INVENTED A STEAM-POWERED GAME WHICH WAS PLACED IN THE HOME FIREPLACE HEARTH. WADISON AND FRIENDS WOULD PLAY "STEAM TENNIS" FOR HOURS, BUT EVENTUALLY IT BROKE, AND THEY MOVED ON WITH THEIR LIVES.
LB

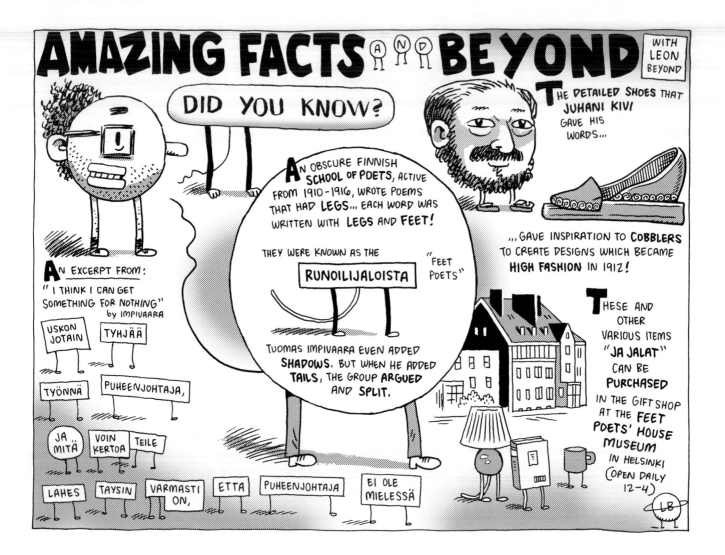

AMAZING FACTS AND BEYOND

WITH LEON BEYOND

DID YOU KNOW?

An obscure Finnish **SCHOOL OF POETS**, ACTIVE FROM 1910-1916, WROTE POEMS THAT HAD **LEGS**... EACH WORD WAS WRITTEN WITH **LEGS AND FEET!**

THEY WERE KNOWN AS THE

RUNOILIJALOISTA

"FEET POETS"

TUOMAS IMPIVAARA EVEN ADDED **SHADOWS**, BUT WHEN HE ADDED **TAILS**, THE GROUP **ARGUED** AND **SPLIT**.

An EXCERPT FROM:
"I THINK I CAN GET SOMETHING FOR NOTHING"
by IMPIVAARA

USKON JOTAIN

TYHJÄÄ

TYÖNNÄ

PUHEENJOHTAJA,

JA MITÄ

VOIN KERTOA

TEILE

LAHES

TAYSIN

VARMASTI ON,

ETTA

PUHEENJOHTAJA

EI OLE MIELESSÄ

The detailed shoes that **JUHANI KIVI** GAVE HIS WORDS...

...GAVE INSPIRATION TO **COBBLERS** TO CREATE DESIGNS WHICH BECAME **HIGH FASHION** IN 1912!

These AND OTHER VARIOUS ITEMS "**JA JALAT**" CAN BE **PURCHASED** IN THE GIFT SHOP AT THE **FEET POETS' HOUSE MUSEUM** IN HELSINKI (OPEN DAILY 12-4)

LB

160

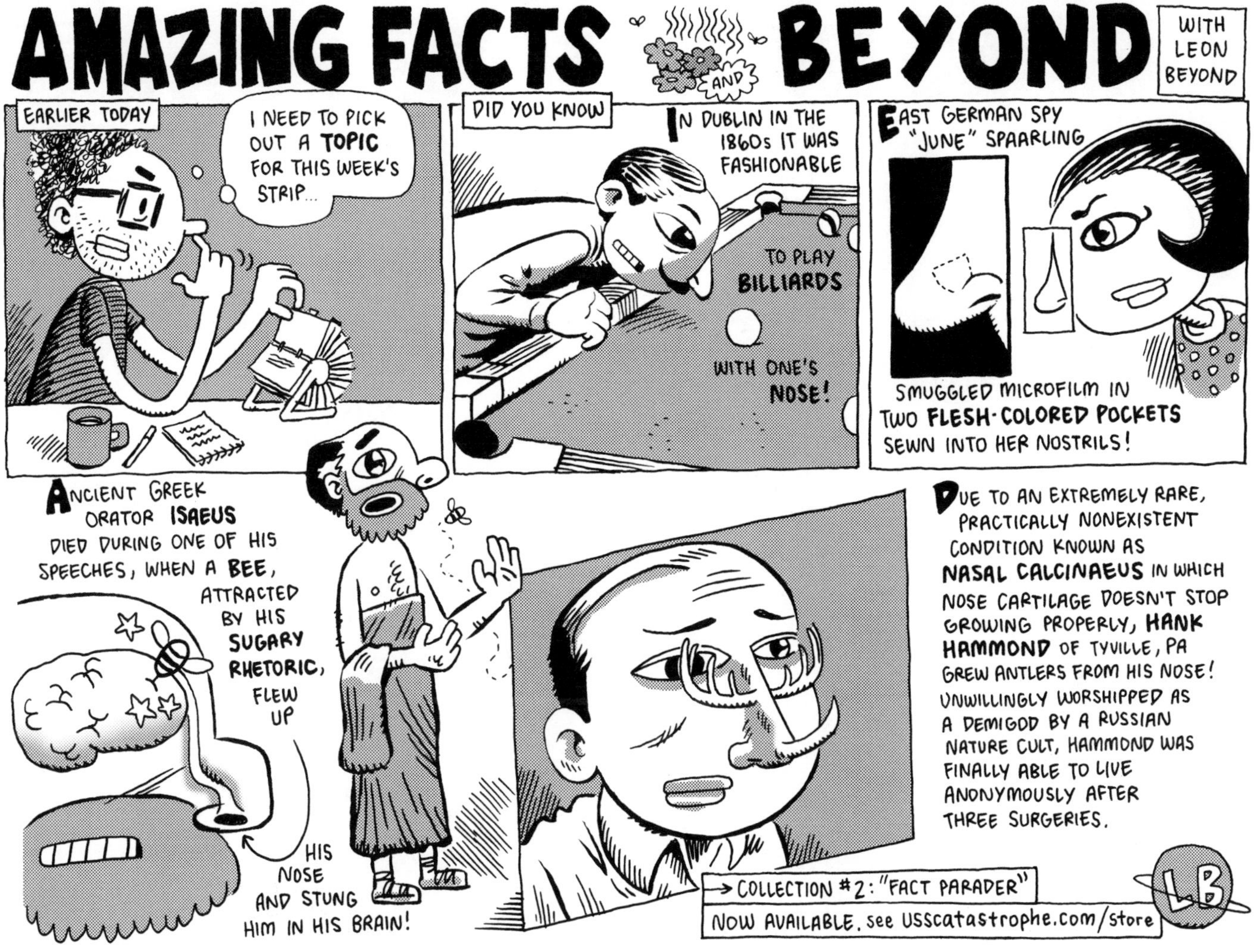
AMAZING FACTS AND BEYOND
WITH LEON BEYOND
EARLIER TODAY
I NEED TO PICK OUT A TOPIC FOR THIS WEEK'S STRIP...
DID YOU KNOW
IN DUBLIN IN THE 1860s IT WAS FASHIONABLE
TO PLAY BILLIARDS
WITH ONE'S NOSE!
EAST GERMAN SPY "JUNE" SPAARLING
SMUGGLED MICROFILM IN TWO FLESH-COLORED POCKETS SEWN INTO HER NOSTRILS!
ANCIENT GREEK ORATOR ISAEUS DIED DURING ONE OF HIS SPEECHES, WHEN A BEE,
ATTRACTED BY HIS SUGARY RHETORIC, FLEW UP
HIS NOSE AND STUNG HIM IN HIS BRAIN!
DUE TO AN EXTREMELY RARE, PRACTICALLY NONEXISTENT CONDITION KNOWN AS NASAL CALCINAEUS IN WHICH NOSE CARTILAGE DOESN'T STOP GROWING PROPERLY, HANK HAMMOND OF TYVILLE, PA GREW ANTLERS FROM HIS NOSE! UNWILLINGLY WORSHIPPED AS A DEMIGOD BY A RUSSIAN NATURE CULT, HAMMOND WAS FINALLY ABLE TO LIVE ANONYMOUSLY AFTER THREE SURGERIES.
→ COLLECTION #2: "FACT PARADER"
NOW AVAILABLE. see USScatastrophe.com/store
LB

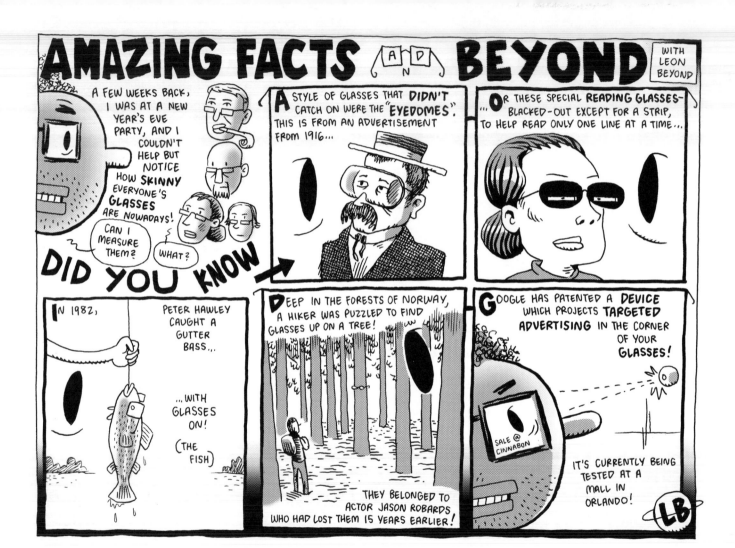

AMAGING FACTS AND BEYOND

WITH LEON BEYOND

A FEW WEEKS BACK, I WAS AT A NEW YEAR'S EVE PARTY, AND I COULDN'T HELP BUT NOTICE HOW **SKINNY** EVERYONE'S **GLASSES** ARE NOWADAYS!

CAN I MEASURE THEM?

WHAT?

DID YOU KNOW

A STYLE OF GLASSES THAT **DIDN'T** CATCH ON WERE THE "**EYEDOMES**". THIS IS FROM AN ADVERTISEMENT FROM 1916...

OR THESE SPECIAL **READING GLASSES**—BLACKED-OUT EXCEPT FOR A STRIP, TO HELP READ ONLY ONE LINE AT A TIME...

IN 1982, PETER HAWLEY CAUGHT A GUTTER BASS...

...WITH GLASSES ON!

(THE FISH)

DEEP IN THE FORESTS OF NORWAY, A HIKER WAS PUZZLED TO FIND GLASSES UP ON A TREE!

THEY BELONGED TO ACTOR JASON ROBARDS WHO HAD LOST THEM 15 YEARS EARLIER!

GOOGLE HAS PATENTED A **DEVICE** WHICH PROJECTS **TARGETED ADVERTISING** IN THE CORNER OF YOUR **GLASSES**!

SALE @ CINNABON

IT'S CURRENTLY BEING TESTED AT A MALL IN ORLANDO!

LB

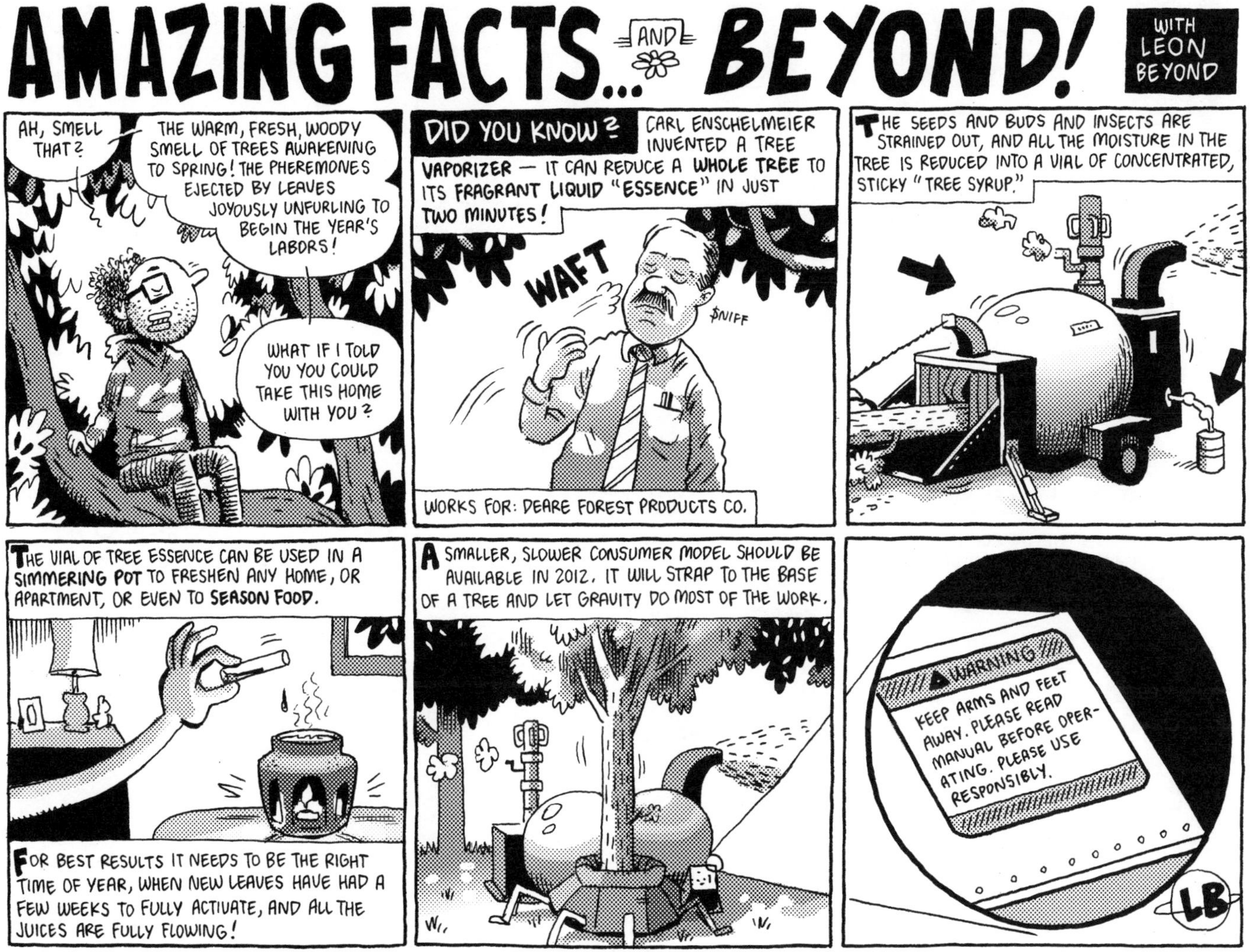
AMAZING FACTS... AND BEYOND! WITH LEON BEYOND
AH, SMELL THAT?
THE WARM, FRESH, WOODY SMELL OF TREES AWAKENING TO SPRING! THE PHEREMONES EJECTED BY LEAVES JOYOUSLY UNFURLING TO BEGIN THE YEAR'S LABORS!
WHAT IF I TOLD YOU YOU COULD TAKE THIS HOME WITH YOU?
DID YOU KNOW? CARL ENSCHELMEIER INVENTED A TREE VAPORIZER — IT CAN REDUCE A WHOLE TREE TO ITS FRAGRANT LIQUID "ESSENCE" IN JUST TWO MINUTES!
WAFT
SNIFF
WORKS FOR: DEARE FOREST PRODUCTS CO.
THE SEEDS AND BUDS AND INSECTS ARE STRAINED OUT, AND ALL THE MOISTURE IN THE TREE IS REDUCED INTO A VIAL OF CONCENTRATED, STICKY "TREE SYRUP."
THE VIAL OF TREE ESSENCE CAN BE USED IN A SIMMERING POT TO FRESHEN ANY HOME, OR APARTMENT, OR EVEN TO SEASON FOOD.
FOR BEST RESULTS IT NEEDS TO BE THE RIGHT TIME OF YEAR, WHEN NEW LEAVES HAVE HAD A FEW WEEKS TO FULLY ACTIVATE, AND ALL THE JUICES ARE FULLY FLOWING!
A SMALLER, SLOWER CONSUMER MODEL SHOULD BE AVAILABLE IN 2012. IT WILL STRAP TO THE BASE OF A TREE AND LET GRAVITY DO MOST OF THE WORK.
WARNING
KEEP ARMS AND FEET AWAY. PLEASE READ MANUAL BEFORE OPERATING. PLEASE USE RESPONSIBLY.
LB

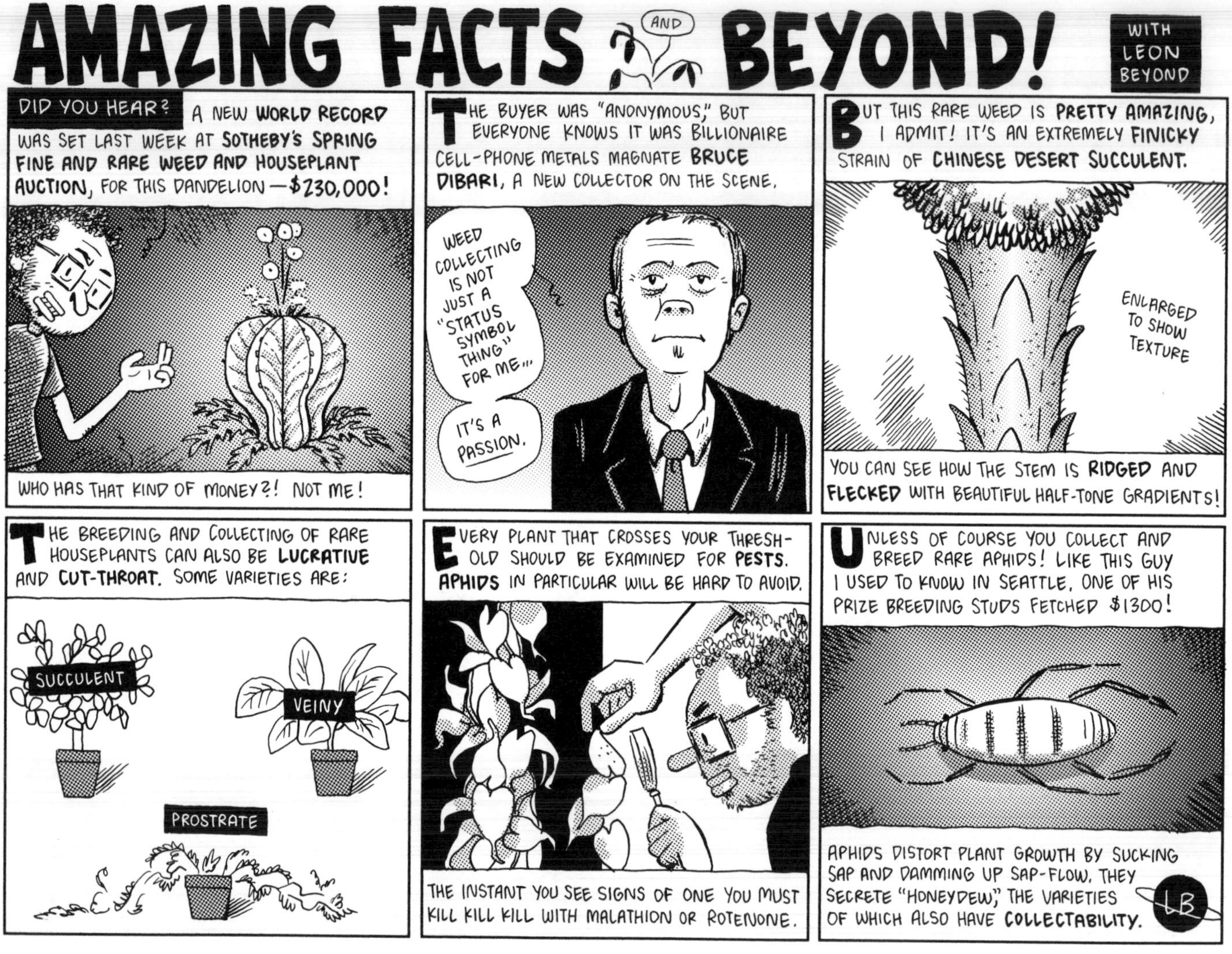

AMAZING FACTS BEYOND!

WITH LEON BEYOND

DID YOU HEAR? A NEW **WORLD RECORD** WAS SET LAST WEEK AT **SOTHEBY'S** SPRING FINE AND RARE WEED AND HOUSEPLANT AUCTION, FOR THIS DANDELION — $230,000!

WHO HAS THAT KIND OF MONEY?! NOT ME!

THE BUYER WAS "ANONYMOUS," BUT EVERYONE KNOWS IT WAS BILLIONAIRE CELL-PHONE METALS MAGNATE **BRUCE DIBARI**, A NEW COLLECTOR ON THE SCENE.

WEED COLLECTING IS NOT JUST A "STATUS SYMBOL THING" FOR ME...

IT'S A PASSION.

BUT THIS RARE WEED IS **PRETTY AMAZING**, I ADMIT! IT'S AN EXTREMELY **FINICKY** STRAIN OF **CHINESE DESERT SUCCULENT**.

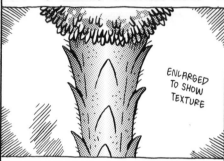

ENLARGED TO SHOW TEXTURE

YOU CAN SEE HOW THE STEM IS **RIDGED** AND **FLECKED** WITH BEAUTIFUL HALF-TONE GRADIENTS!

THE BREEDING AND COLLECTING OF RARE HOUSEPLANTS CAN ALSO BE **LUCRATIVE** AND **CUT-THROAT**. SOME VARIETIES ARE:

SUCCULENT

VEINY

PROSTRATE

EVERY PLANT THAT CROSSES YOUR THRESH-OLD SHOULD BE EXAMINED FOR **PESTS**. **APHIDS** IN PARTICULAR WILL BE HARD TO AVOID.

THE INSTANT YOU SEE SIGNS OF ONE YOU MUST KILL KILL KILL WITH MALATHION OR ROTENONE.

UNLESS OF COURSE YOU COLLECT AND BREED RARE APHIDS! LIKE THIS GUY I USED TO KNOW IN SEATTLE, ONE OF HIS PRIZE BREEDING STUDS FETCHED $1300!

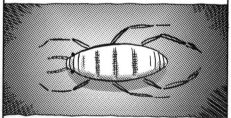

APHIDS DISTORT PLANT GROWTH BY SUCKING SAP AND DAMMING UP SAP-FLOW, THEY SECRETE "HONEYDEW," THE VARIETIES OF WHICH ALSO HAVE **COLLECTABILITY**.

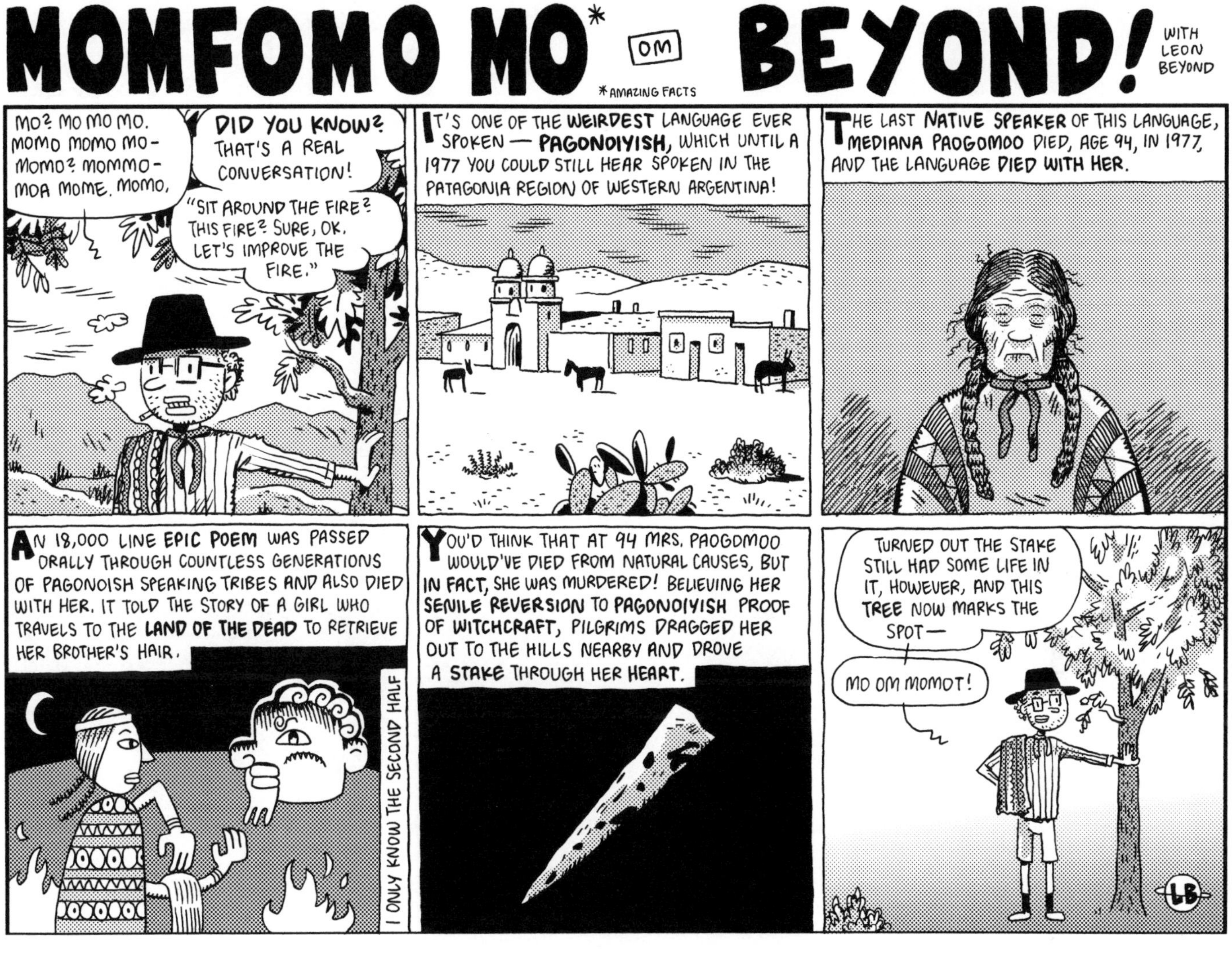
MOMFOMO MO* OM BEYOND!
WITH LEON BEYOND
*AMAZING FACTS
MO? MO MO MO. MOMO MOMO MO-MOMO? MOMMO-MOA MOME. MOMO.
DID YOU KNOW? THAT'S A REAL CONVERSATION!
"SIT AROUND THE FIRE? THIS FIRE? SURE, OK. LET'S IMPROVE THE FIRE."
IT'S ONE OF THE WEIRDEST LANGUAGE EVER SPOKEN — PAGONOIYISH, WHICH UNTIL A 1977 YOU COULD STILL HEAR SPOKEN IN THE PATAGONIA REGION OF WESTERN ARGENTINA!
THE LAST NATIVE SPEAKER OF THIS LANGUAGE, MEDIANA PAOGOMOO DIED, AGE 94, IN 1977, AND THE LANGUAGE DIED WITH HER.
AN 18,000 LINE EPIC POEM WAS PASSED ORALLY THROUGH COUNTLESS GENERATIONS OF PAGONOISH SPEAKING TRIBES AND ALSO DIED WITH HER. IT TOLD THE STORY OF A GIRL WHO TRAVELS TO THE LAND OF THE DEAD TO RETRIEVE HER BROTHER'S HAIR.
I ONLY KNOW THE SECOND HALF
YOU'D THINK THAT AT 94 MRS. PAOGOMOO WOULD'VE DIED FROM NATURAL CAUSES, BUT IN FACT, SHE WAS MURDERED! BELIEVING HER SENILE REVERSION TO PAGONOIYISH PROOF OF WITCHCRAFT, PILGRIMS DRAGGED HER OUT TO THE HILLS NEARBY AND DROVE A STAKE THROUGH HER HEART.
TURNED OUT THE STAKE STILL HAD SOME LIFE IN IT, HOWEVER, AND THIS TREE NOW MARKS THE SPOT—
MO OM MOMOT!
LB

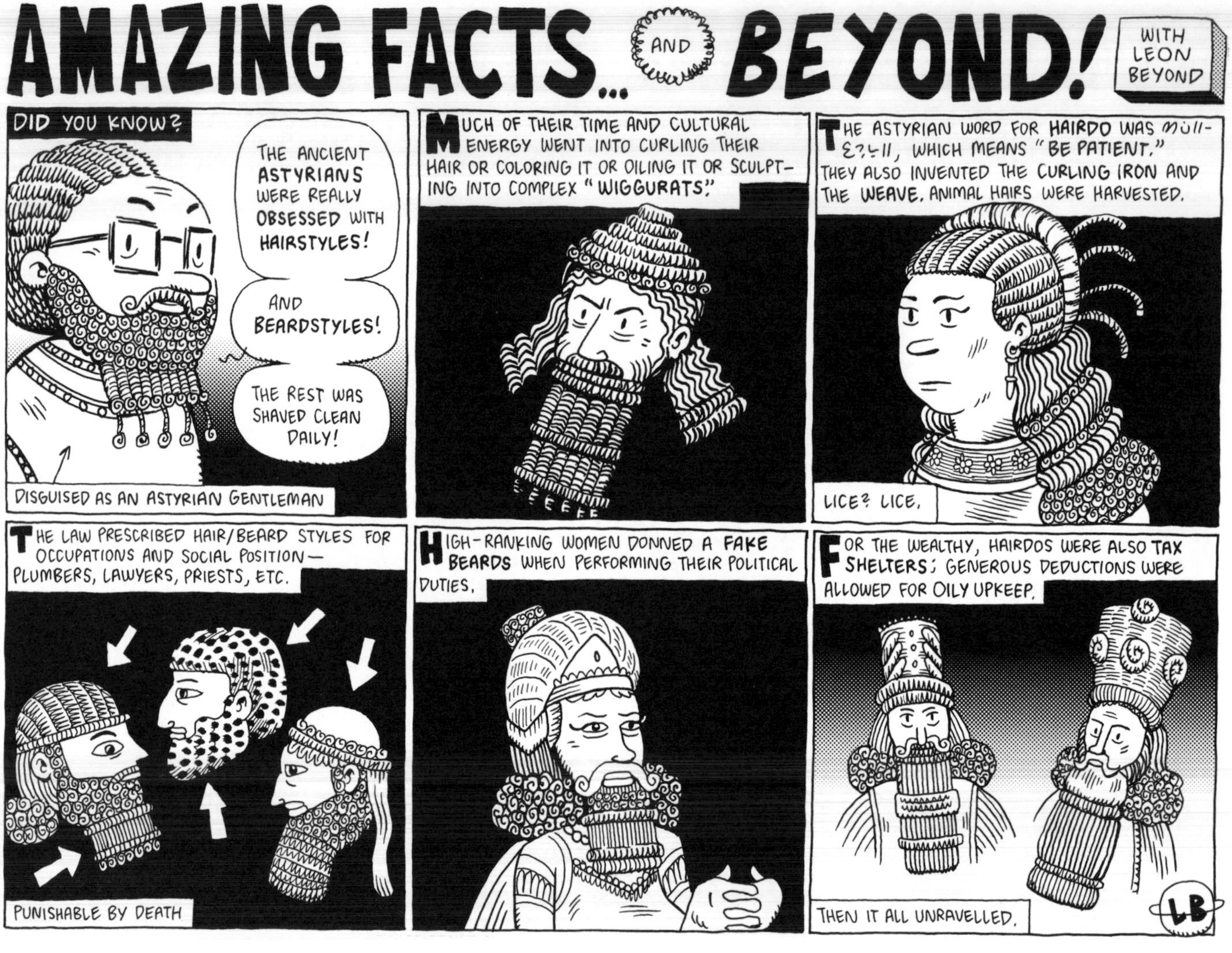
AMAZING FACTS... AND BEYOND!
WITH LEON BEYOND
DID YOU KNOW?
THE ANCIENT ASTYRIANS WERE REALLY OBSESSED WITH HAIRSTYLES!
AND BEARDSTYLES!
THE REST WAS SHAVED CLEAN DAILY!
DISGUISED AS AN ASTYRIAN GENTLEMAN
MUCH OF THEIR TIME AND CULTURAL ENERGY WENT INTO CURLING THEIR HAIR OR COLORING IT OR OILING IT OR SCULPTING INTO COMPLEX "WIGGURATS."
THE ASTYRIAN WORD FOR HAIRDO WAS , WHICH MEANS "BE PATIENT." THEY ALSO INVENTED THE CURLING IRON AND THE WEAVE. ANIMAL HAIRS WERE HARVESTED.
LICE? LICE.
THE LAW PRESCRIBED HAIR/BEARD STYLES FOR OCCUPATIONS AND SOCIAL POSITION— PLUMBERS, LAWYERS, PRIESTS, ETC.
PUNISHABLE BY DEATH
HIGH-RANKING WOMEN DONNED A FAKE BEARDS WHEN PERFORMING THEIR POLITICAL DUTIES.
FOR THE WEALTHY, HAIRDOS WERE ALSO TAX SHELTERS; GENEROUS DEDUCTIONS WERE ALLOWED FOR OILY UPKEEP.
THEN IT ALL UNRAVELLED.
LB

AMAZING FACTS AND BEYOND!

 WITH LEON BEYOND

I JUST CANNOT ENJOY THIS GOLDEN EVENING LIGHT...

...WITHOUT BEING REMINDED OF WEALTHY ECCENTRIC, BRUCE RIDGEBROOK!

DID YOU KNOW? RIDGEBROOK MARRIED INTO THE VAST DEFRACK LUMBER FORTUNE IN 1932. WHEN HIS WIFE DIED SUDDENLY IN CHILDBIRTH HE CASHED OUT AND RETREATED TO NYC TO MOURN.

HE HAD AN ARRAY OF MIRRORS — THE PRECISE NUMBER IS UNKNOWN — INSTALLED ALL OVER THE CITY, AND HIRED A TEAM OF MEN TO ADJUST THEM YEAR 'ROUND...

SO THAT EVERY EVENING, CLOUD COVER COOPERATING, THE LIGHT OF THE SETTING SUN WOULD STRIKE THE MIRRORS, MAKING ITS WAY THROUGH THE STREETS, AROUND BUILDINGS...

...TO THE WALL OF HIS PENTHOUSE APARTMENT, ILLUMINATING THE PORTRAIT OF HIS FAVORITE HUNTING DOG!

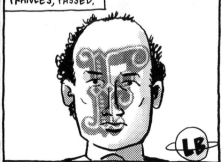

BONUS FACT WEALTHY ECCENTRIC ALCOHOLIC MOURNER DAVIS SPRINGGLEND HAD A LARGE "F" TATTOOED ON HIS FACE AFTER HIS MOTHER, FRANCES, PASSED.

LB

167

AMAZING FACTS and BEYOND!

YEAH

I KEEP BUSY, YOU KNOW... ETC.

IN ADDITION TO THIS **COMIC STRIP**, AND DOING THE **DISHES**, ETC. I'M ALSO WRITING **SEVERAL BOOKS EVERY WEEK...**

HERE'S A LOOK AT WHAT'S ON THE TO-BE-WRITTEN PILE TODAY!

CURRENTLY ON LUNCH BREAK

For CHINESE PUBLISHER TAIJIQUAN HOUSE I'M TRANSLATING RECORD OF THE GOLDEN MIRROR, THE VENERABLE **TONGUE DIAGNOSIS** MANUAL, FIRST PUBLISHED IN 1341, FOR TODAY'S AMERICAN AUDIENCE. IT'S A CHALLENGE, BUT IT'S A TOPIC CLOSE TO MY **HEART.**

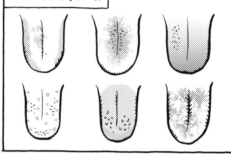

Is IT YELLOW? PINK? ARE THERE **CRACKS? LIGHT** OR **DARK** FUR? THESE ARE THE KINDS OF QUESTIONS YOU HAVE TO ASK.

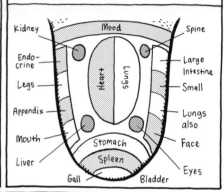

Kidney — Mood — Spine
Endo-crine — Large Intestine
Heart — Lungs
Legs — Small
Appendix — Lungs also
Mouth — Stomach — Face
Liver — Spleen — Eyes
Gall — Bladder

This NEW EDITION WILL HAVE HUNDREDS OF PAGES OF GLOSSY, FULL-COLOR PHOTOGRAPHS OF THE MANY POSSIBLE TONGUE SYMPTOMOLOGIES — SEVERAL ANGLES EACH.

ONE TIME I HAD THIS

THERE WILL BE AN APP OF COURSE.

ALSO DUE ON MONDAY ARE, LET'S SEE...

ACTUALLY, A **FAIRLY LIGHT WEEK**

- THE ART OF FAKE EXHIBITION POULTRY (TASCHEN)
- A SCRIPT FOR "BODY WARS" ON A HISTORY OF GARGLING
- SKYRIM WALKTHROUGH FOR IGN FRANCE
- GUEST BLOGGER FOR 'MIDWEST PANCAKES'

BONUS FACT

THIS PALINDROMISH ECONOLINE BELONGED TO **VAN TUT** OF AURORA, IL!

REMEMBER TO BRUSH YOUR TONGUE

LB

AMAZING FACTS and BEYOND!

EVERY YEAR

TRILLIONS OF LEAVES COME DOWN AND BECAUSE GRASS AND TREES WEREN'T MEANT TO LIVE TOGETHER IN **NATURE** THEY HAVE TO BE **GATHERED** AND **DISPOSED OF** — IF THE GRASS IS TO **LIVE!**

AND EVERY YEAR **BIZARRE** LEAVES ARE SPOTTED AND SENT IN BY YOU FOR OUR **WEIRD LEAF ROUNDUP**

SILHOUETTE CATEGORY

CARVED OUT BY A KRESTEL WORM. ACTUAL SIZE

BEFORE

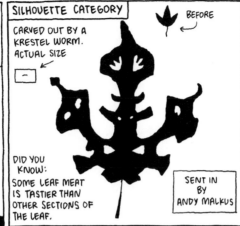

DID YOU KNOW: SOME LEAF MEAT IS TASTIER THAN OTHER SECTIONS OF THE LEAF.

SENT IN BY ANDY MALKUS

FUNGAL CATEGORY

AN AMAZING SPECIMEN OF SPIRAL STINKBALL FUNGUS — USUALLY NATIVE TO NEW ZEALAND. IT WAS FOUND BY J. ROBERTS OF FISTAL, MO. HOPE YOU WASHED YOUR HANDS, J. ROBERTS.

COLORING CATEGORY

leonbeyond@gmail.com

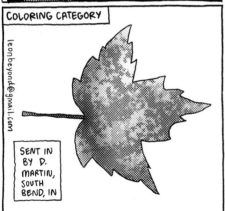

SENT IN BY D. MARTIN, SOUTH BEND, IN

MAYBE THE MOST BEAUTIFUL ONE I'VE EVER SEEN

IMAGE / TEXT CATEGORY

FOUND BY VERONICA MAY, STL

BONUS FACT | ON THIS DATE | 1897

FIRST SUCCESSFUL USE OF THE TONSILOTOME, AKA THE "TONSIL GUILLOTINE", INVENTED IN 1892 BY M. SCHAERER, OF MOOSSEEDOORFF, SWITZERLAND, ON THIS MAN, FRANCISCO GIL.

LB

CHAINSAWS

CHIHUAHUA NAMED CHAINSAW —
BELONGED TO CARL TOMSON
OF NEEDLE CITY, NEW YORK

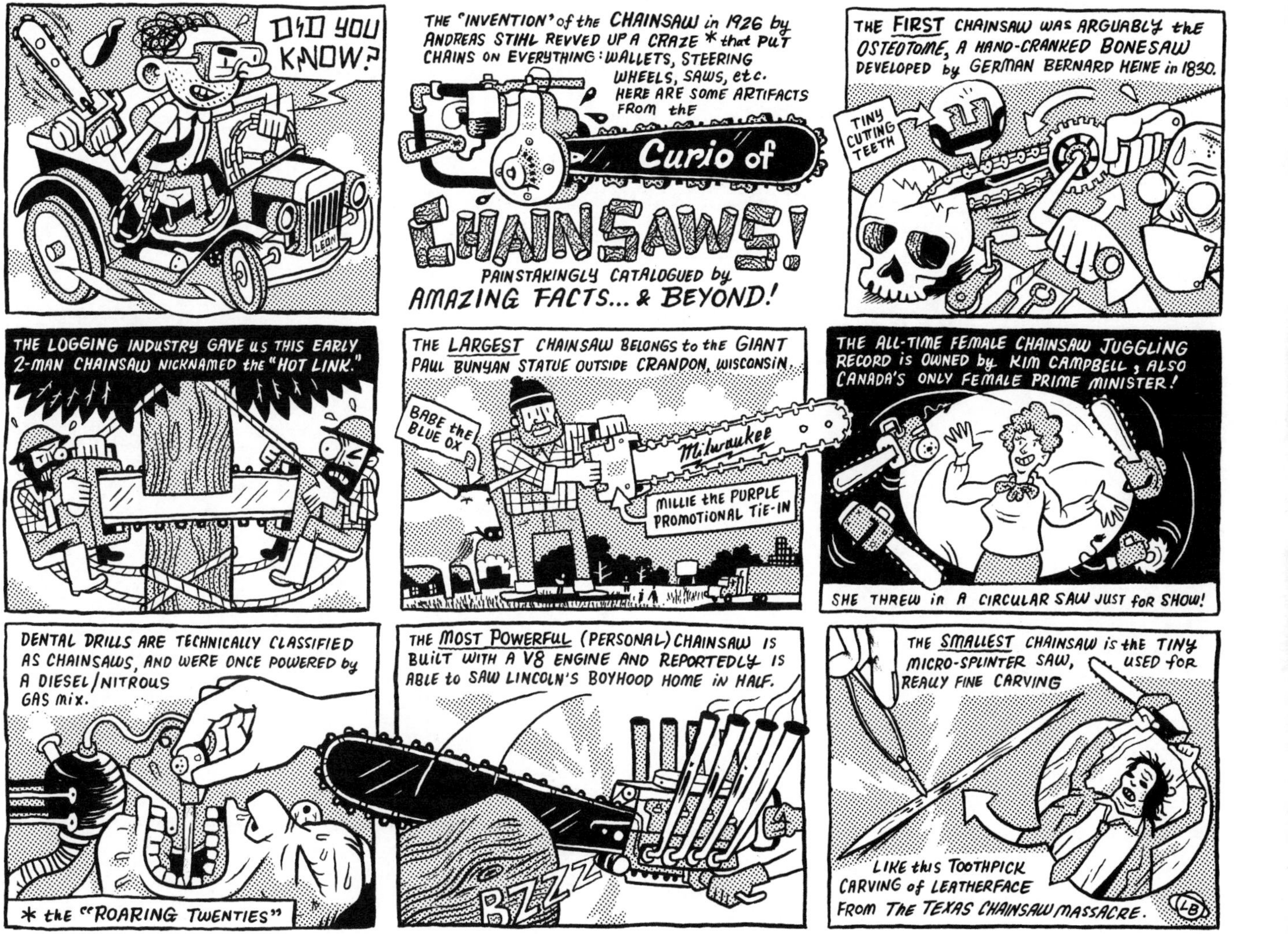
DID YOU KNOW?
LEON
THE "INVENTION" of the CHAINSAW in 1926 by ANDREAS STIHL REVVED UP A CRAZE * that PUT CHAINS ON EVERYTHING: WALLETS, STEERING WHEELS, SAWS, etc.
HERE ARE SOME ARTIFACTS FROM the
Curio of
CHAINSAWS!
PAINSTAKINGLY CATALOGUED by
AMAZING FACTS... & BEYOND!
THE FIRST CHAINSAW WAS ARGUABLY the OSTEOTOME, A HAND-CRANKED BONESAW DEVELOPED by GERMAN BERNARD HEINE in 1830.
TINY CUTTING TEETH
THE LOGGING INDUSTRY GAVE US THIS EARLY 2-MAN CHAINSAW NICKNAMED the "HOT LINK."
THE LARGEST CHAINSAW BELONGS to the GIANT PAUL BUNYAN STATUE OUTSIDE CRANDON, WISCONSIN.
BABE the BLUE OX
Milwaukee
MILLIE the PURPLE PROMOTIONAL TIE-IN
THE ALL-TIME FEMALE CHAINSAW JUGGLING RECORD is OWNED by KIM CAMPBELL, ALSO CANADA'S ONLY FEMALE PRIME MINISTER!
SHE THREW in A CIRCULAR SAW JUST for SHOW!
DENTAL DRILLS ARE TECHNICALLY CLASSIFIED AS CHAINSAWS, AND WERE ONCE POWERED by A DIESEL/NITROUS GAS mix.
* the "ROARING TWENTIES"
THE MOST POWERFUL (PERSONAL) CHAINSAW IS BUILT WITH A V8 ENGINE AND REPORTEDLY IS ABLE to SAW LINCOLN'S BOYHOOD HOME IN HALF.
BZZZZ
THE SMALLEST CHAINSAW is the TINY MICRO-SPLINTER SAW, USED for REALLY FINE CARVING
LIKE this TOOTHPICK CARVING of LEATHERFACE FROM THE TEXAS CHAINSAW MASSACRE.
LB

TIPS *and* TRICKS

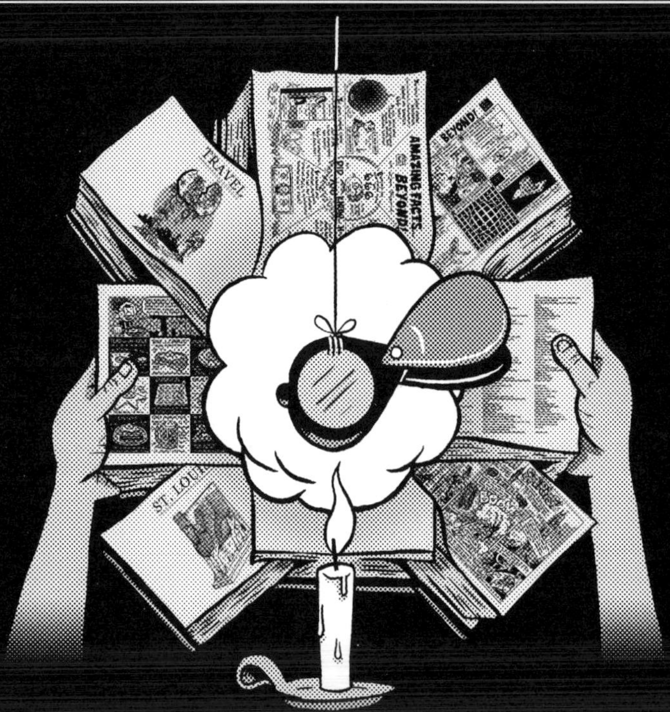
TRAVEL
AMAZING FACTS BEYOND!
BEYOND!

THE MOST AMAZING FACT, ONLY FOUND with a JEWELER'S LOUPE, BLACKLIGHT CANDLE, and FOUR (OR MORE) COPIES OF THIS BOOK

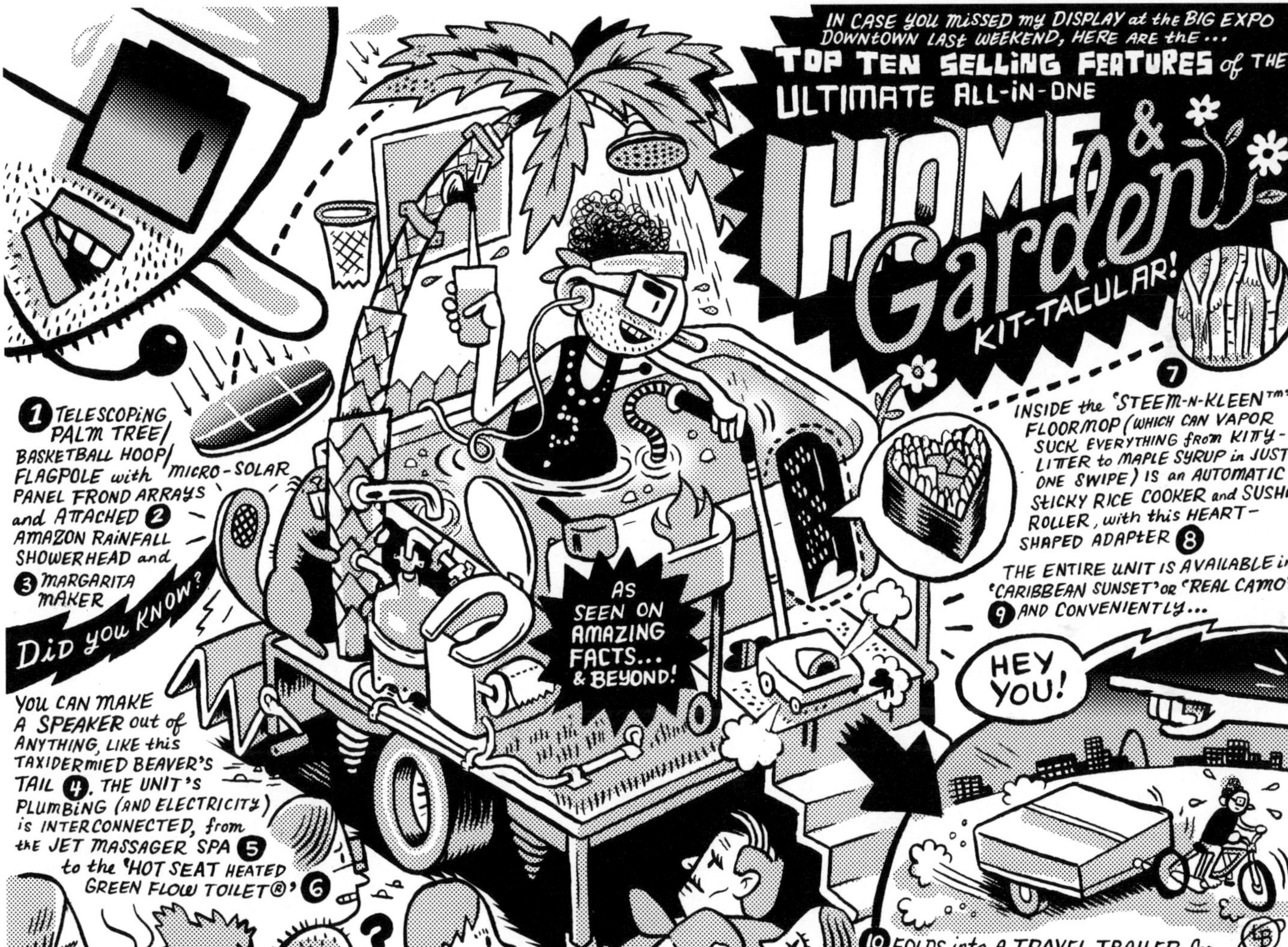
IN CASE YOU MISSED MY DISPLAY AT THE BIG EXPO DOWNTOWN LAST WEEKEND, HERE ARE THE ...
TOP TEN SELLING FEATURES OF THE ULTIMATE ALL-IN-ONE
HOME & Garden KIT-TACULAR!
1 TELESCOPING PALM TREE/ BASKETBALL HOOP/ FLAGPOLE WITH MICRO-SOLAR PANEL FROND ARRAYS and ATTACHED 2 AMAZON RAINFALL SHOWERHEAD and 3 MARGARITA MAKER
7 INSIDE the 'STEEM-N-KLEEN™' FLOORMOP (WHICH CAN VAPOR SUCK EVERYTHING from KITTY-LITTER to MAPLE SYRUP in JUST ONE SWIPE) IS an AUTOMATIC STICKY RICE COOKER and SUSHI ROLLER, with this HEART-SHAPED ADAPTER 8
THE ENTIRE UNIT IS AVAILABLE in 'CARIBBEAN SUNSET' OR 'REAL CAMO'. 9 AND CONVENIENTLY...
DID YOU KNOW?
AS SEEN ON AMAZING FACTS... & BEYOND!
HEY YOU!
YOU CAN MAKE A SPEAKER OUT OF ANYTHING, LIKE THIS TAXIDERMIED BEAVER'S TAIL 4. THE UNIT'S PLUMBING (AND ELECTRICITY) IS INTERCONNECTED, FROM THE JET MASSAGER SPA 5 to the 'HOT SEAT HEATED GREEN FLOW TOILET®' 6
10 FOLDS into A TRAVEL TRAILER for TRIVIAL TRANSPORT COSTS. LIMITED TIME OFFER!

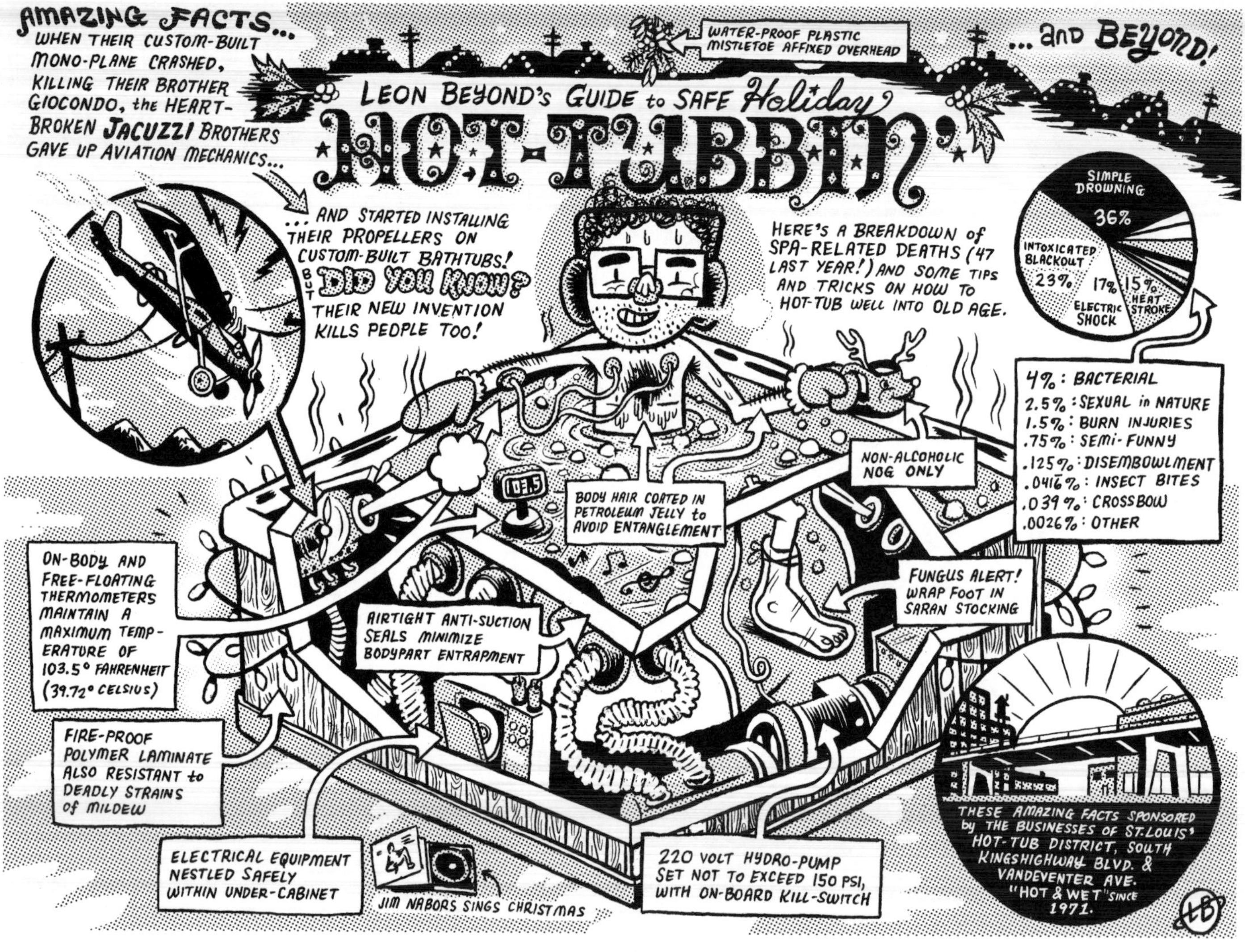
AMAZING FACTS... WHEN THEIR CUSTOM-BUILT MONO-PLANE CRASHED, KILLING THEIR BROTHER GIOCONDO, the HEART-BROKEN JACUZZI BROTHERS GAVE UP AVIATION MECHANICS...
WATER-PROOF PLASTIC MISTLETOE AFFIXED OVERHEAD
...AND BEYOND!
LEON BEYOND'S GUIDE to SAFE Holiday
HOT-TUBBIN'
...AND STARTED INSTALLING THEIR PROPELLERS ON CUSTOM-BUILT BATHTUBS! BUT DID YOU KNOW? THEIR NEW INVENTION KILLS PEOPLE TOO!
HERE'S A BREAKDOWN of SPA-RELATED DEATHS (47 LAST YEAR!) AND SOME TIPS AND TRICKS ON HOW TO HOT-TUB WELL INTO OLD AGE.
SIMPLE DROWNING 36%
INTOXICATED BLACKOUT 23%
17% ELECTRIC SHOCK
15% HEAT STROKE
4% : BACTERIAL
2.5% : SEXUAL in NATURE
1.5% : BURN INJURIES
.75% : SEMI-FUNNY
.125% : DISEMBOWLMENT
.0416% : INSECT BITES
.039% : CROSSBOW
.0026% : OTHER
NON-ALCOHOLIC NOG ONLY
103.5
BODY HAIR COATED IN PETROLEUM JELLY to AVOID ENTANGLEMENT
ON-BODY AND FREE-FLOATING THERMOMETERS MAINTAIN A MAXIMUM TEMPERATURE OF 103.5° FAHRENHEIT (39.72° CELSIUS)
AIRTIGHT ANTI-SUCTION SEALS MINIMIZE BODYPART ENTRAPMENT
FUNGUS ALERT! WRAP FOOT IN SARAN STOCKING
FIRE-PROOF POLYMER LAMINATE ALSO RESISTANT to DEADLY STRAINS of MILDEW
ELECTRICAL EQUIPMENT NESTLED SAFELY WITHIN UNDER-CABINET
JIM NABORS SINGS CHRISTMAS
220 VOLT HYDRO-PUMP SET NOT TO EXCEED 150 PSI, WITH ON-BOARD KILL-SWITCH
THESE AMAZING FACTS SPONSORED by THE BUSINESSES OF ST. LOUIS' HOT-TUB DISTRICT, SOUTH KINGSHIGHWAY BLVD. & VANDEVENTER AVE. "HOT & WET" SINCE 1971.
LB

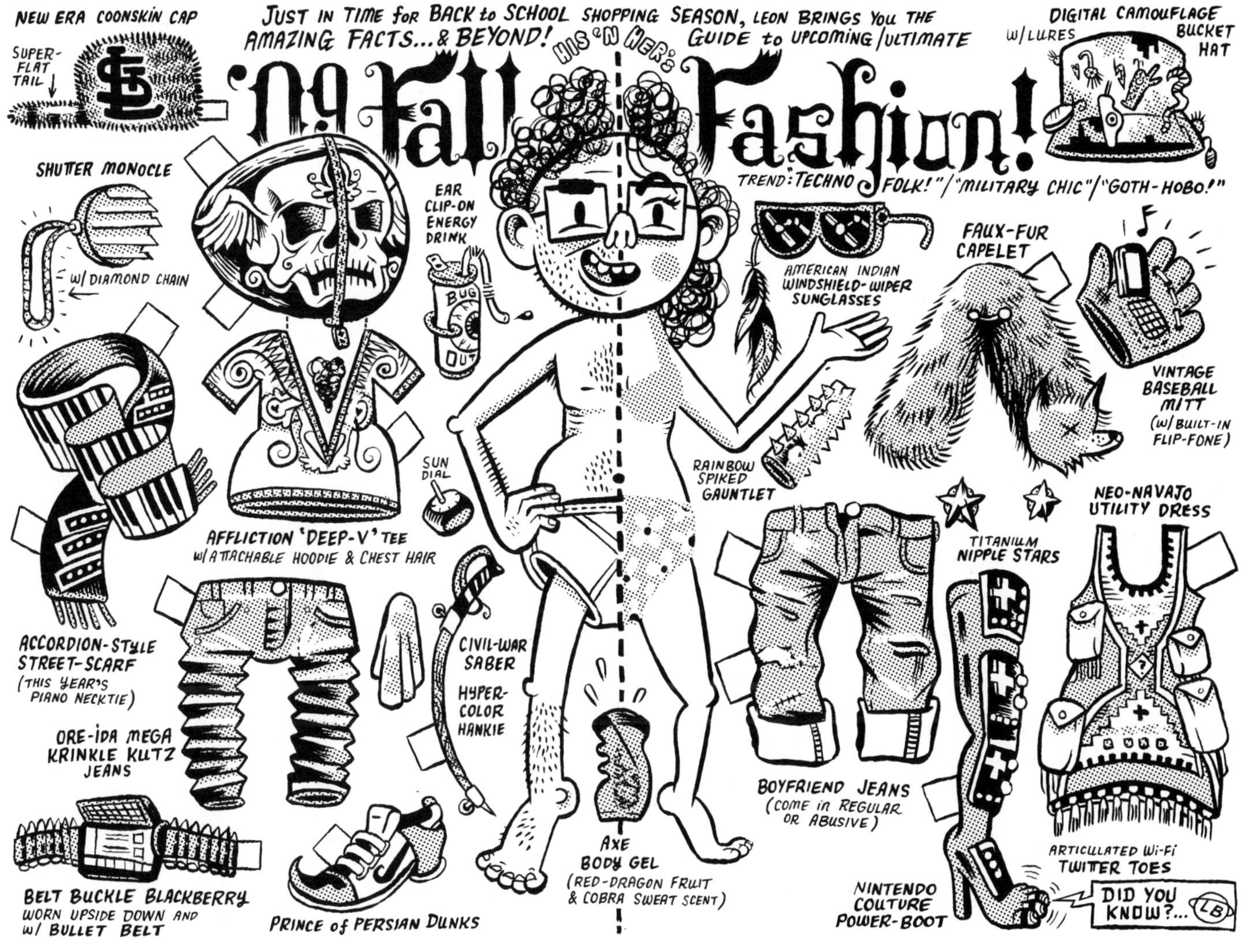

JUST IN TIME for BACK to SCHOOL SHOPPING SEASON, LEON BRINGS You THE AMAZING FACTS... & BEYOND! GUIDE to UPCOMING/ULTIMATE
HIS 'N HER'S
'09 Fall Fashion!
TREND: "TECHNO FOLK!" / "MILITARY CHIC" / "GOTH-HOBO!"
NEW ERA COONSKIN CAP
SUPER-FLAT TAIL
DIGITAL CAMOUFLAGE BUCKET HAT
W/ LURES
SHUTTER MONOCLE
W/ DIAMOND CHAIN
EAR CLIP-ON ENERGY DRINK
BUG OUT
AMERICAN INDIAN WINDSHIELD-WIPER SUNGLASSES
FAUX-FUR CAPELET
VINTAGE BASEBALL MITT (W/ BUILT-IN FLIP-FONE)
ACCORDION-STYLE STREET-SCARF (THIS YEAR'S PIANO NECKTIE)
AFFLICTION 'DEEP-V' TEE W/ ATTACHABLE HOODIE & CHEST HAIR
SUN DIAL
RAINBOW SPIKED GAUNTLET
TITANIUM NIPPLE STARS
NEO-NAVAJO UTILITY DRESS
CIVIL-WAR SABER
HYPER-COLOR HANKIE
ORE-IDA MEGA KRINKLE KUTZ JEANS
BOYFRIEND JEANS (COME IN REGULAR OR ABUSIVE)
AXE BODY GEL (RED-DRAGON FRUIT & COBRA SWEAT SCENT)
BELT BUCKLE BLACKBERRY WORN UPSIDE DOWN AND W/ BULLET BELT
PRINCE of PERSIAN DUNKS
ARTICULATED Wi-Fi TWITTER TOES
NINTENDO COUTURE POWER-BOOT
DID YOU KNOW?...
LB

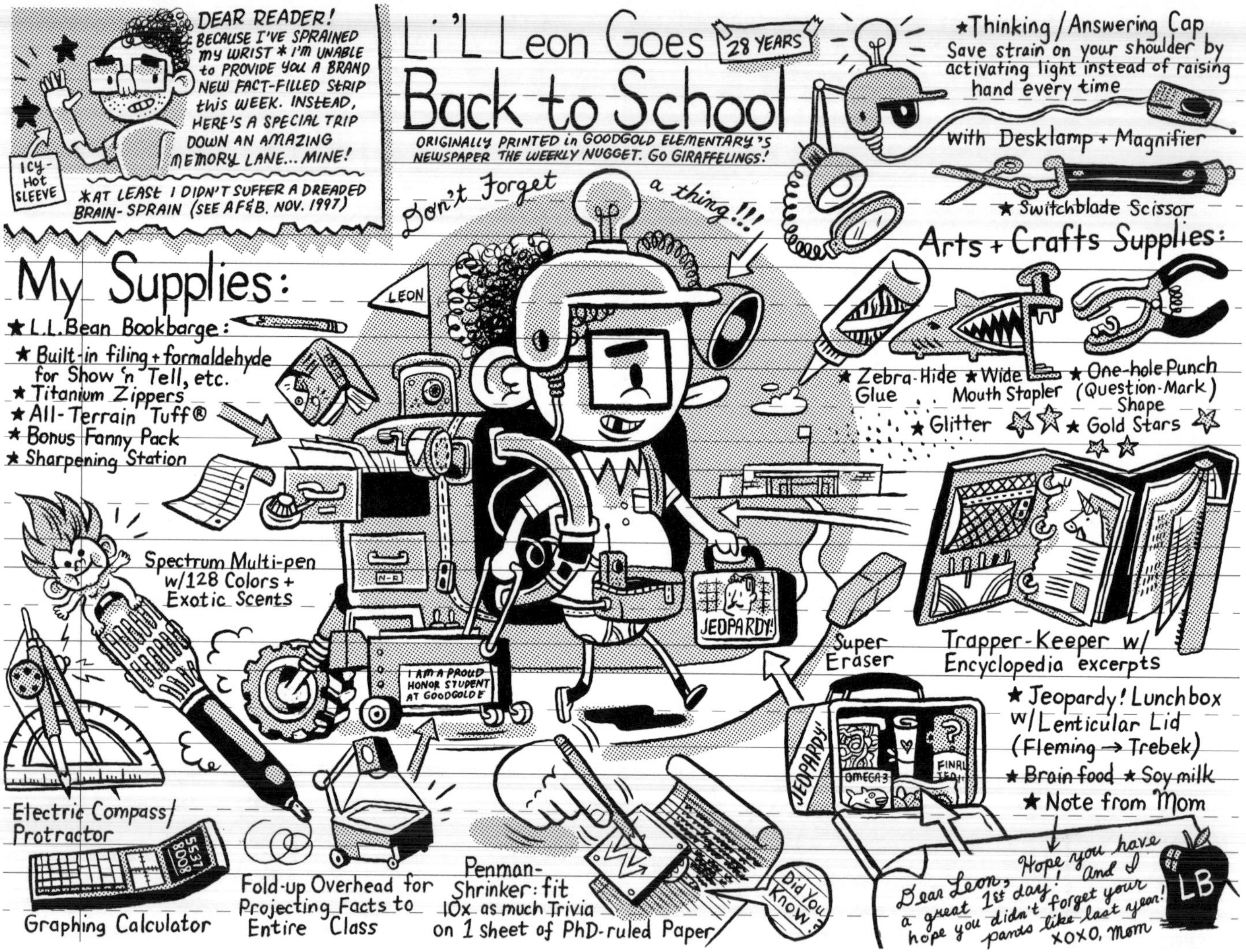
DEAR READER! BECAUSE I'VE SPRAINED MY WRIST * I'M UNABLE TO PROVIDE YOU A BRAND NEW FACT-FILLED STRIP THIS WEEK. INSTEAD, HERE'S A SPECIAL TRIP DOWN AN AMAZING MEMORY LANE... MINE!
ICY-HOT SLEEVE
*AT LEAST I DIDN'T SUFFER A DREADED BRAIN-SPRAIN (SEE AF&B. NOV. 1997)
Li'L Leon Goes 28 YEARS Back to School
ORIGINALLY PRINTED in GOODGOLD ELEMENTARY'S NEWSPAPER THE WEEKLY NUGGET. GO GIRAFFELINGS!
★Thinking / Answering Cap
Save strain on your shoulder by activating light instead of raising hand every time
with Desklamp + Magnifier
★Switchblade Scissor
Don't Forget a thing!!!
Arts + Crafts Supplies:
My Supplies:
★L.L.Bean Bookbarge:
★ Built-in filing + formaldehyde for Show 'n' Tell, etc.
★ Titanium Zippers
★ All-Terrain Tuff®
★ Bonus Fanny Pack
★ Sharpening Station
LEON
★ Zebra-Hide Glue
★ Wide Mouth Stapler
★ One-hole Punch (Question-Mark) Shape
★ Glitter
★ Gold Stars
Spectrum Multi-pen w/128 Colors + Exotic Scents
N-R
JEOPARDY!
I AM A PROUD HONOR STUDENT AT GOODGOLDE
Super Eraser
Trapper-Keeper w/ Encyclopedia excerpts
★ Jeopardy! Lunchbox w/Lenticular Lid (Fleming → Trebek)
★ Brain food ★ Soy milk
★ Note from Mom
JEOPARDY!
OMEGA 3
FINAL
Electric Compass/ Protractor
5537 8008
Graphing Calculator
Fold-up Overhead for Projecting Facts to Entire Class
Penman-Shrinker: fit 10x as much Trivia on 1 sheet of PhD-ruled Paper
Did You Know...
Dear Leon, Hope you have a great 1st day! And I hope you didn't forget your pants like last year! XOXO, Mom
LB

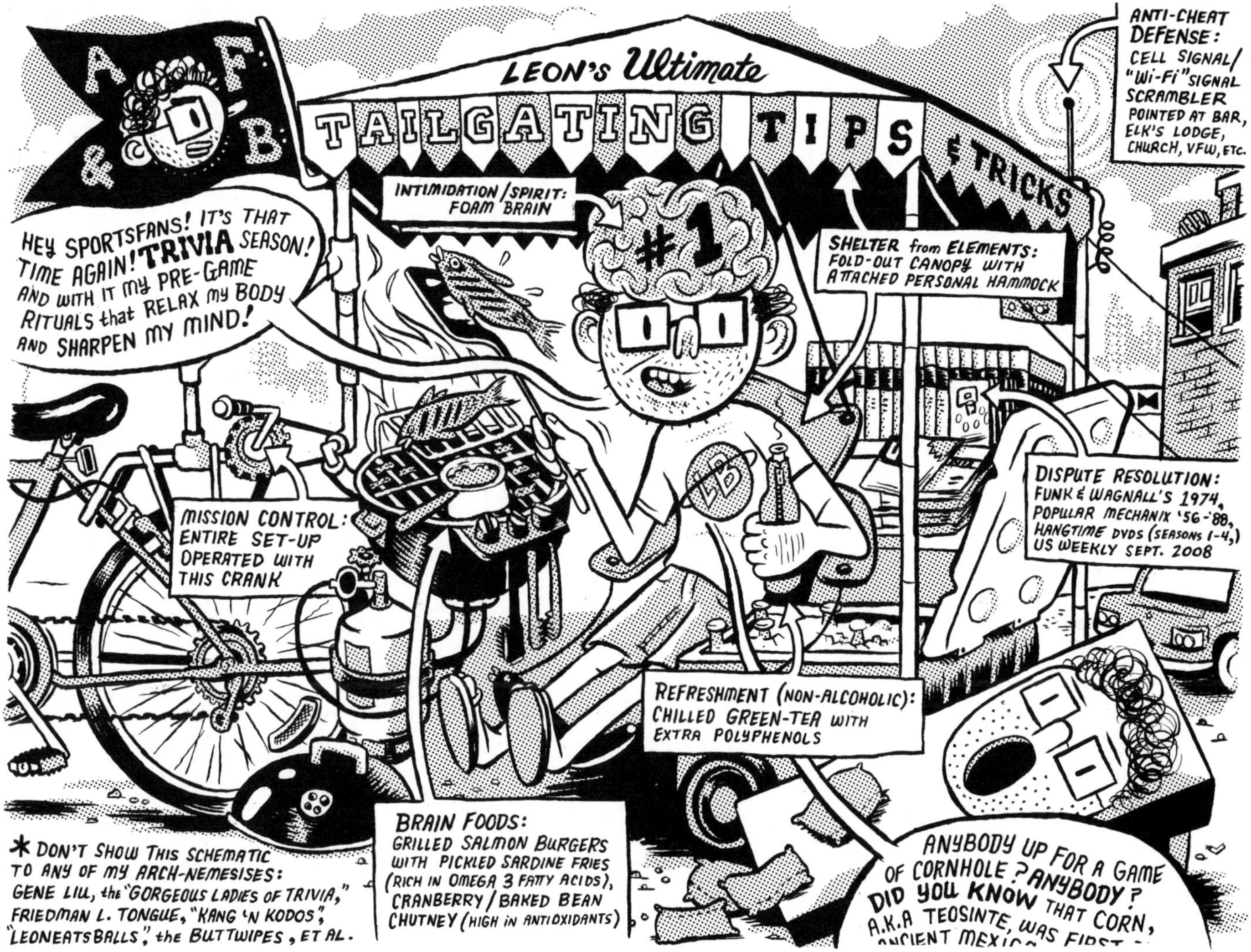
A F & B
LEON'S Ultimate TAILGATING TIPS & TRICKS
ANTI-CHEAT DEFENSE: CELL SIGNAL/ "Wi-Fi" SIGNAL SCRAMBLER POINTED AT BAR, ELK'S LODGE, CHURCH, VFW, ETC.
HEY SPORTSFANS! IT'S THAT TIME AGAIN! TRIVIA SEASON! AND WITH IT MY PRE-GAME RITUALS that RELAX MY BODY AND SHARPEN MY MIND!
INTIMIDATION/SPIRIT: FOAM BRAIN
#1
SHELTER from ELEMENTS: FOLD-OUT CANOPY WITH ATTACHED PERSONAL HAMMOCK
DISPUTE RESOLUTION: FUNK & WAGNALL'S 1974, POPULAR MECHANIX '56-'88, HANGTIME DVDS (SEASONS 1-4,) US WEEKLY SEPT. 2008
MISSION CONTROL: ENTIRE SET-UP OPERATED WITH THIS CRANK
REFRESHMENT (NON-ALCOHOLIC): CHILLED GREEN-TEA WITH EXTRA POLYPHENOLS
* DON'T SHOW THIS SCHEMATIC TO ANY OF MY ARCH-NEMESISES: GENE LIU, the "GORGEOUS LADIES OF TRIVIA," FRIEDMAN L. TONGUE, "KANG 'N KODOS", "LEONEATSBALLS", the BUTTWIPES, ET AL.
BRAIN FOODS: GRILLED SALMON BURGERS WITH PICKLED SARDINE FRIES (RICH IN OMEGA 3 FATTY ACIDS), CRANBERRY/BAKED BEAN CHUTNEY (HIGH IN ANTIOXIDANTS)
ANYBODY UP FOR A GAME OF CORNHOLE? ANYBODY? DID YOU KNOW THAT CORN, A.K.A TEOSINTE, WAS FIRST

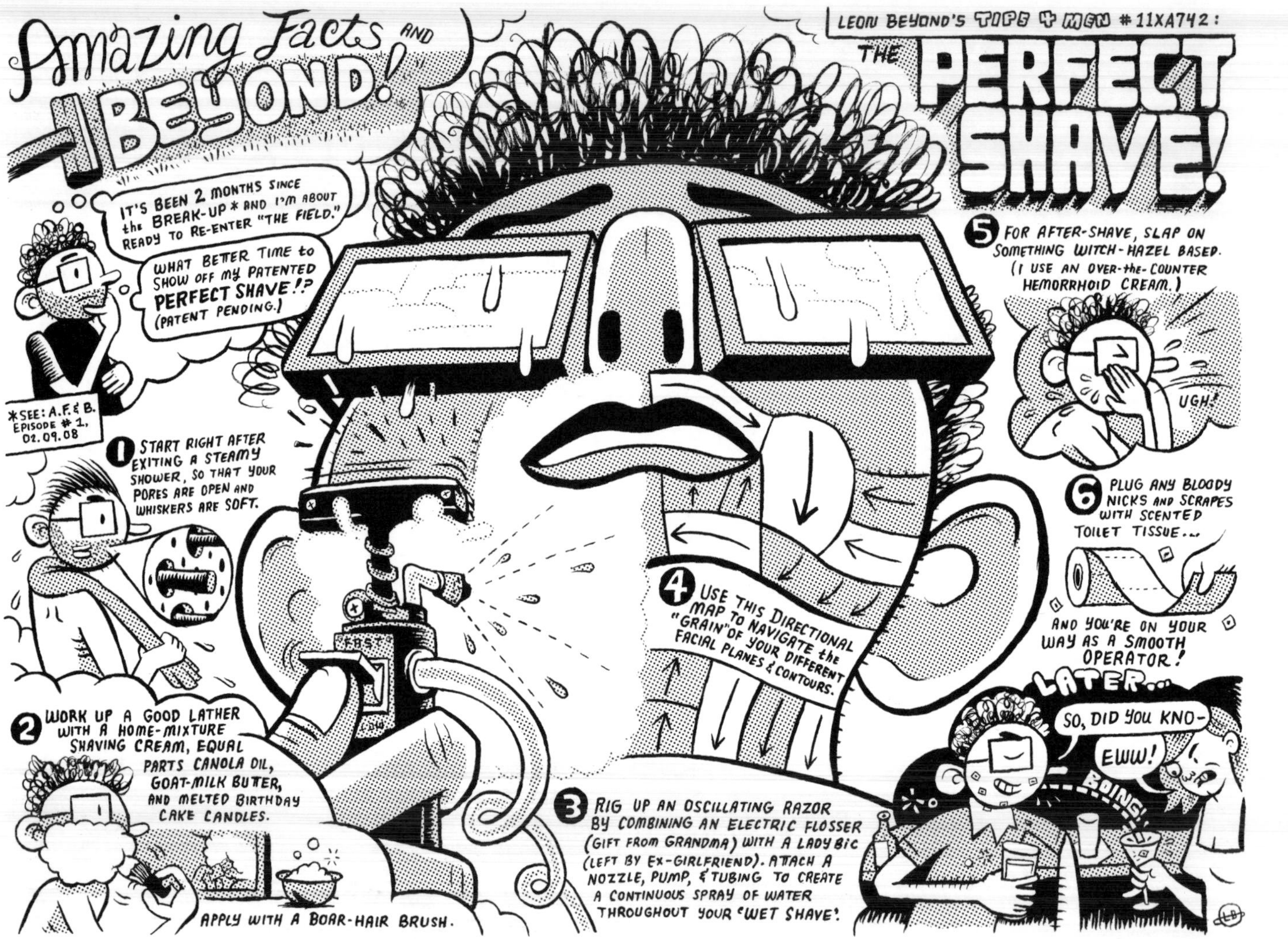

Amazing Facts AND BEYOND!
LEON BEYOND'S TIPS 4 MEN #11XA742: THE PERFECT SHAVE!
IT'S BEEN 2 MONTHS SINCE the BREAK-UP * AND I'M ABOUT READY TO RE-ENTER "THE FIELD."
WHAT BETTER TIME to SHOW OFF my PATENTED PERFECT SHAVE!? (PATENT PENDING.)
*SEE: A.F.&B. EPISODE #1, 02.09.08
1 START RIGHT AFTER EXITING A STEAMY SHOWER, SO THAT YOUR PORES ARE OPEN AND WHISKERS ARE SOFT.
2 WORK UP A GOOD LATHER WITH A HOME-MIXTURE SHAVING CREAM, EQUAL PARTS CANOLA OIL, GOAT-MILK BUTTER, AND MELTED BIRTHDAY CAKE CANDLES.
APPLY WITH A BOAR-HAIR BRUSH.
3 RIG UP AN OSCILLATING RAZOR BY COMBINING AN ELECTRIC FLOSSER (GIFT FROM GRANDMA) WITH A LADY BIC (LEFT BY EX-GIRLFRIEND). ATTACH A NOZZLE, PUMP, & TUBING TO CREATE A CONTINUOUS SPRAY OF WATER THROUGHOUT YOUR 'WET SHAVE'.
4 USE THIS DIRECTIONAL MAP TO NAVIGATE the "GRAIN" OF YOUR DIFFERENT FACIAL PLANES & CONTOURS.
5 FOR AFTER-SHAVE, SLAP ON SOMETHING WITCH-HAZEL BASED. (I USE AN OVER-the-COUNTER HEMORRHOID CREAM.)
UGH!
6 PLUG ANY BLOODY NICKS AND SCRAPES WITH SCENTED TOILET TISSUE...
AND YOU'RE ON YOUR WAY AS A SMOOTH OPERATOR!
LATER...
SO, DID YOU KNO-
EWW!
BOING!

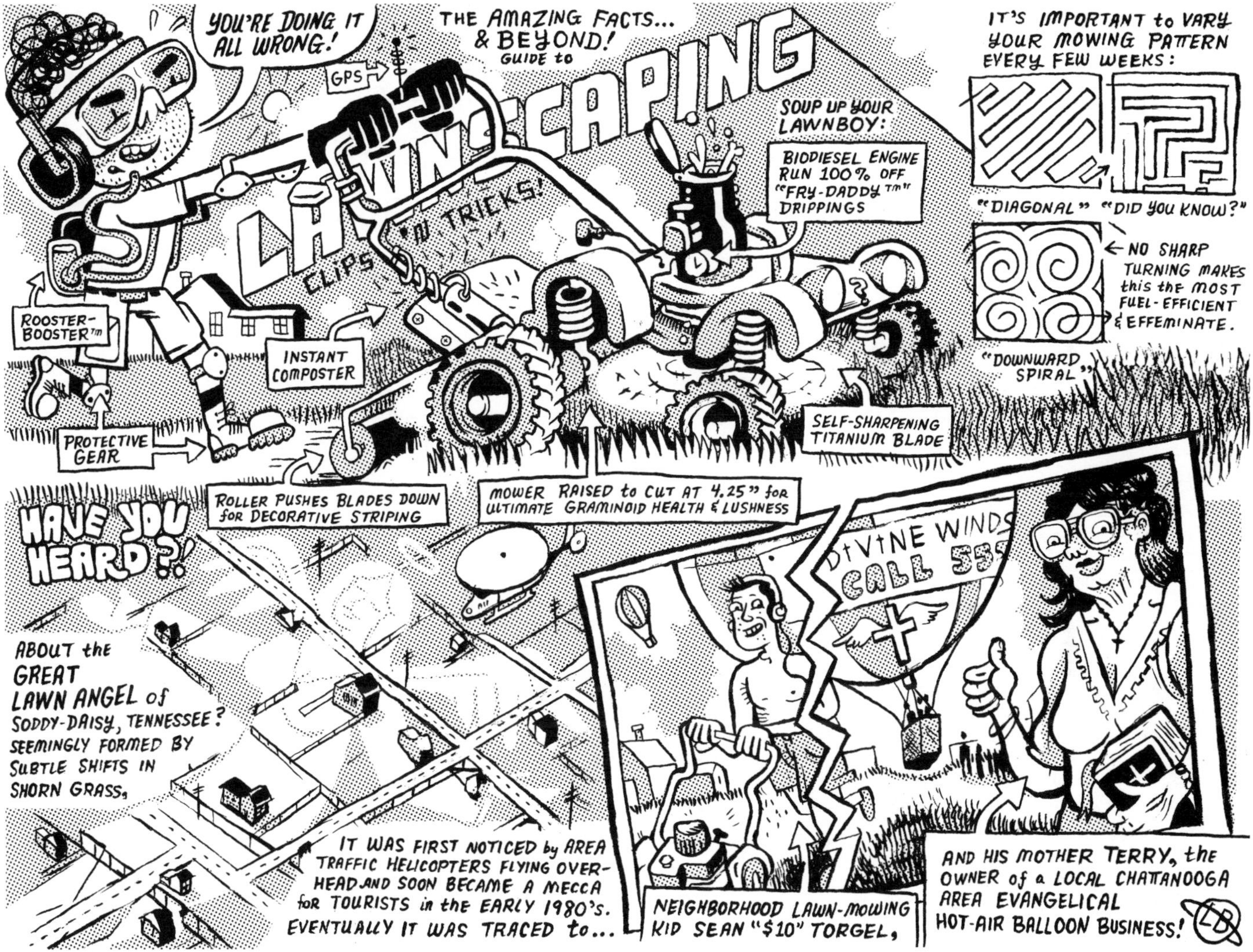

YOU'RE DOING IT ALL WRONG!
THE AMAZING FACTS... & BEYOND! GUIDE to
LAWNSCAPING
CLIPS 'N' TRICKS!
GPS
ROOSTER-BOOSTER™
INSTANT COMPOSTER
PROTECTIVE GEAR
SOUP UP YOUR LAWNBOY:
BIODIESEL ENGINE RUN 100% OFF "FRY-DADDY™" DRIPPINGS
SELF-SHARPENING TITANIUM BLADE
ROLLER PUSHES BLADES DOWN for DECORATIVE STRIPING
MOWER RAISED to CUT AT 4.25" for ULTIMATE GRAMINOID HEALTH & LUSHNESS
IT'S IMPORTANT to VARY YOUR MOWING PATTERN EVERY FEW WEEKS:
"DIAGONAL" "DID YOU KNOW?"
← NO SHARP TURNING MAKES this the MOST FUEL-EFFICIENT & EFFEMINATE.
"DOWNWARD SPIRAL"
HAVE YOU HEARD?!
ABOUT the GREAT LAWN ANGEL of SODDY-DAISY, TENNESSEE? SEEMINGLY FORMED BY SUBTLE SHIFTS IN SHORN GRASS,
IT WAS FIRST NOTICED by AREA TRAFFIC HELICOPTERS FLYING OVER-HEAD AND SOON BECAME A MECCA for TOURISTS in the EARLY 1980's. EVENTUALLY IT WAS TRACED to...
DIVINE WINDS CALL 555
NEIGHBORHOOD LAWN-MOWING KID SEAN "$10" TORGEL,
AND HIS MOTHER TERRY, the OWNER of a LOCAL CHATTANOOGA AREA EVANGELICAL HOT-AIR BALLOON BUSINESS!
LB

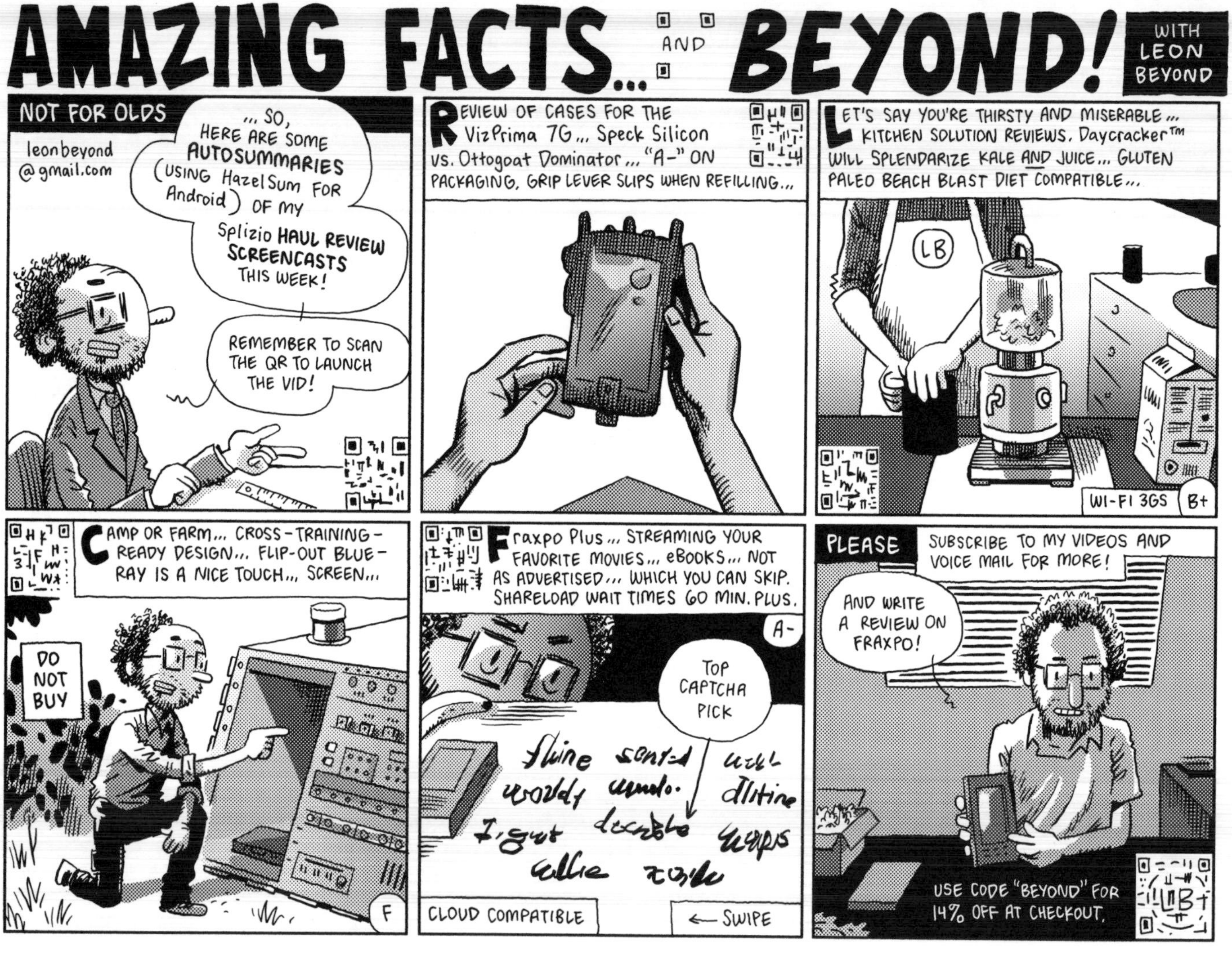
AMAZING FACTS... AND BEYOND!
WITH LEON BEYOND
NOT FOR OLDS
leonbeyond@gmail.com
... SO, HERE ARE SOME AUTOSUMMARIES (USING HazelSum FOR Android) OF MY Splizio HAUL REVIEW SCREENCASTS THIS WEEK!
REMEMBER TO SCAN THE QR TO LAUNCH THE VID!
REVIEW OF CASES FOR THE VizPrima 7G... Speck Silicon vs. Ottogoat Dominator... "A-" ON PACKAGING, GRIP LEVER SLIPS WHEN REFILLING...
LET'S SAY YOU'RE THIRSTY AND MISERABLE... KITCHEN SOLUTION REVIEWS. Daycracker™ WILL SPLENDARIZE KALE AND JUICE... GLUTEN PALEO BEACH BLAST DIET COMPATIBLE...
LB
WI-FI 3GS
B+
CAMP OR FARM... CROSS-TRAINING-READY DESIGN... FLIP-OUT BLUE-RAY IS A NICE TOUCH... SCREEN...
DO NOT BUY
F
Fraxpo Plus... STREAMING YOUR FAVORITE MOVIES... eBOOKS... NOT AS ADVERTISED... WHICH YOU CAN SKIP. SHARELOAD WAIT TIMES 60 MIN. PLUS.
A-
TOP CAPTCHA PICK
CLOUD COMPATIBLE
← SWIPE
PLEASE
SUBSCRIBE TO MY VIDEOS AND VOICE MAIL FOR MORE!
AND WRITE A REVIEW ON FRAXPO!
USE CODE "BEYOND" FOR 14% OFF AT CHECKOUT.

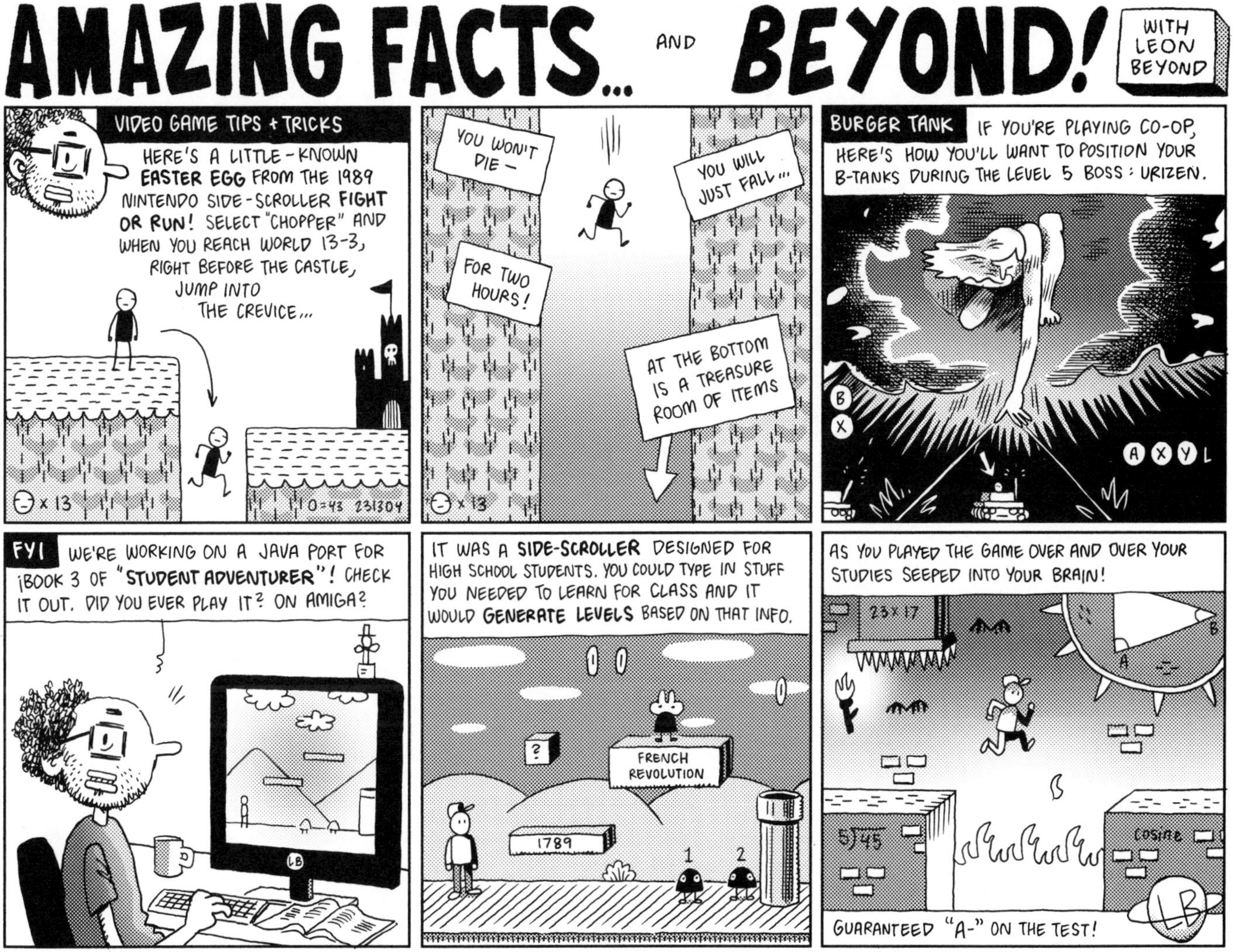
AMAZING FACTS... AND BEYOND!
WITH LEON BEYOND
VIDEO GAME TIPS + TRICKS
HERE'S A LITTLE-KNOWN EASTER EGG FROM THE 1989 NINTENDO SIDE-SCROLLER FIGHT OR RUN! SELECT "CHOPPER" AND WHEN YOU REACH WORLD 13-3, RIGHT BEFORE THE CASTLE, JUMP INTO THE CREVICE...
x 13
YOU WON'T DIE -
YOU WILL JUST FALL...
FOR TWO HOURS!
AT THE BOTTOM IS A TREASURE ROOM OF ITEMS
x 13
BURGER TANK
IF YOU'RE PLAYING CO-OP, HERE'S HOW YOU'LL WANT TO POSITION YOUR B-TANKS DURING THE LEVEL 5 BOSS: URIZEN.
B
X
A X Y L
FYI
WE'RE WORKING ON A JAVA PORT FOR iBOOK 3 OF "STUDENT ADVENTURER"! CHECK IT OUT. DID YOU EVER PLAY IT? ON AMIGA?
LB
IT WAS A SIDE-SCROLLER DESIGNED FOR HIGH SCHOOL STUDENTS. YOU COULD TYPE IN STUFF YOU NEEDED TO LEARN FOR CLASS AND IT WOULD GENERATE LEVELS BASED ON THAT INFO.
?
FRENCH REVOLUTION
1789
1
2
AS YOU PLAYED THE GAME OVER AND OVER YOUR STUDIES SEEPED INTO YOUR BRAIN!
23 x 17
A
B
5)45
COSINE
GUARANTEED "A-" ON THE TEST!
LB

MINDBLOWERS

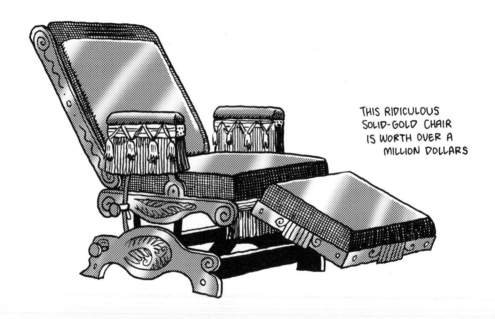

THIS RIDICULOUS
SOLID-GOLD CHAIR
IS WORTH OVER A
MILLION DOLLARS

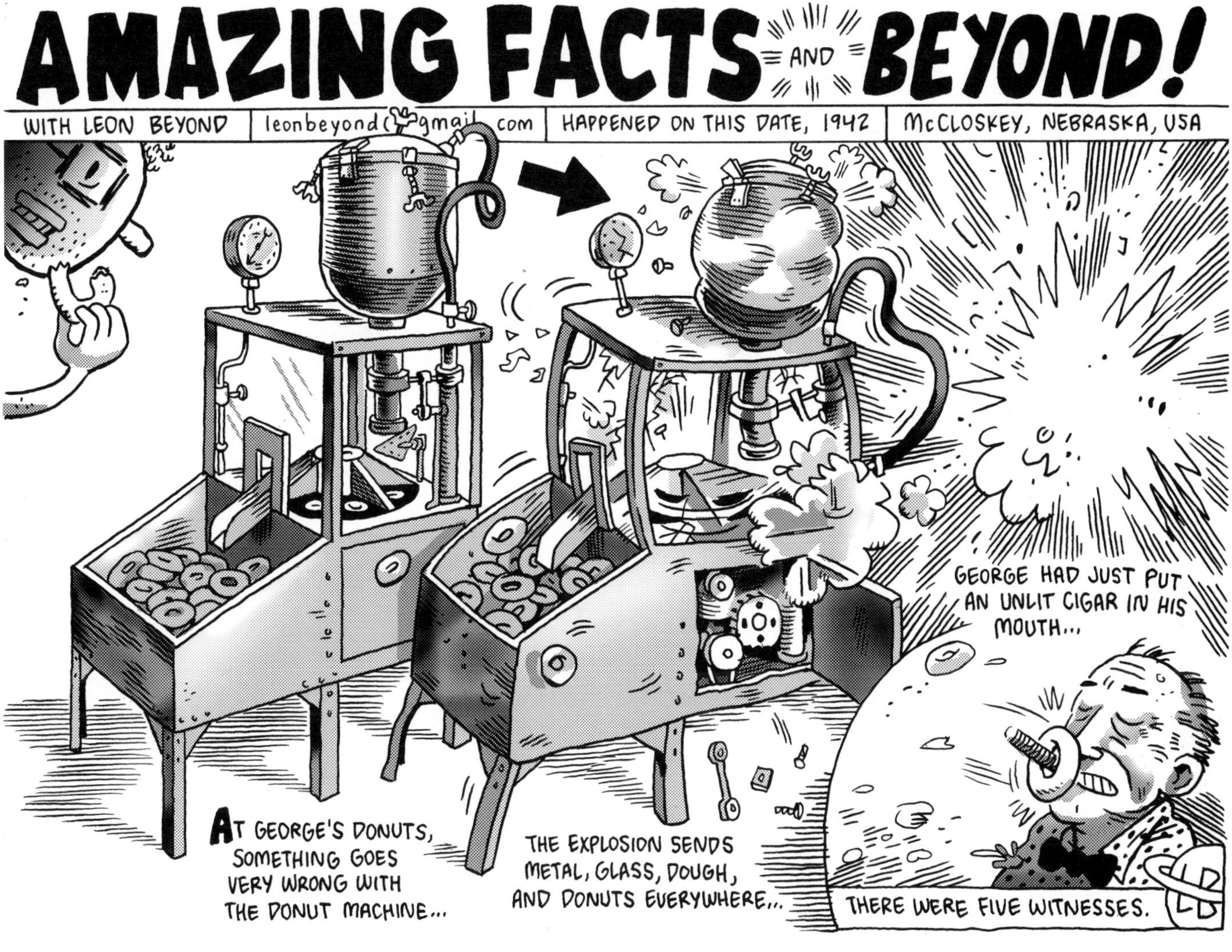
AMAZING FACTS AND BEYOND!
WITH LEON BEYOND
leonbeyond@gmail.com
HAPPENED ON THIS DATE, 1942
McCLOSKEY, NEBRASKA, USA
AT GEORGE'S DONUTS, SOMETHING GOES VERY WRONG WITH THE DONUT MACHINE...
THE EXPLOSION SENDS METAL, GLASS, DOUGH, AND DONUTS EVERYWHERE...
GEORGE HAD JUST PUT AN UNLIT CIGAR IN HIS MOUTH...
THERE WERE FIVE WITNESSES.
LB

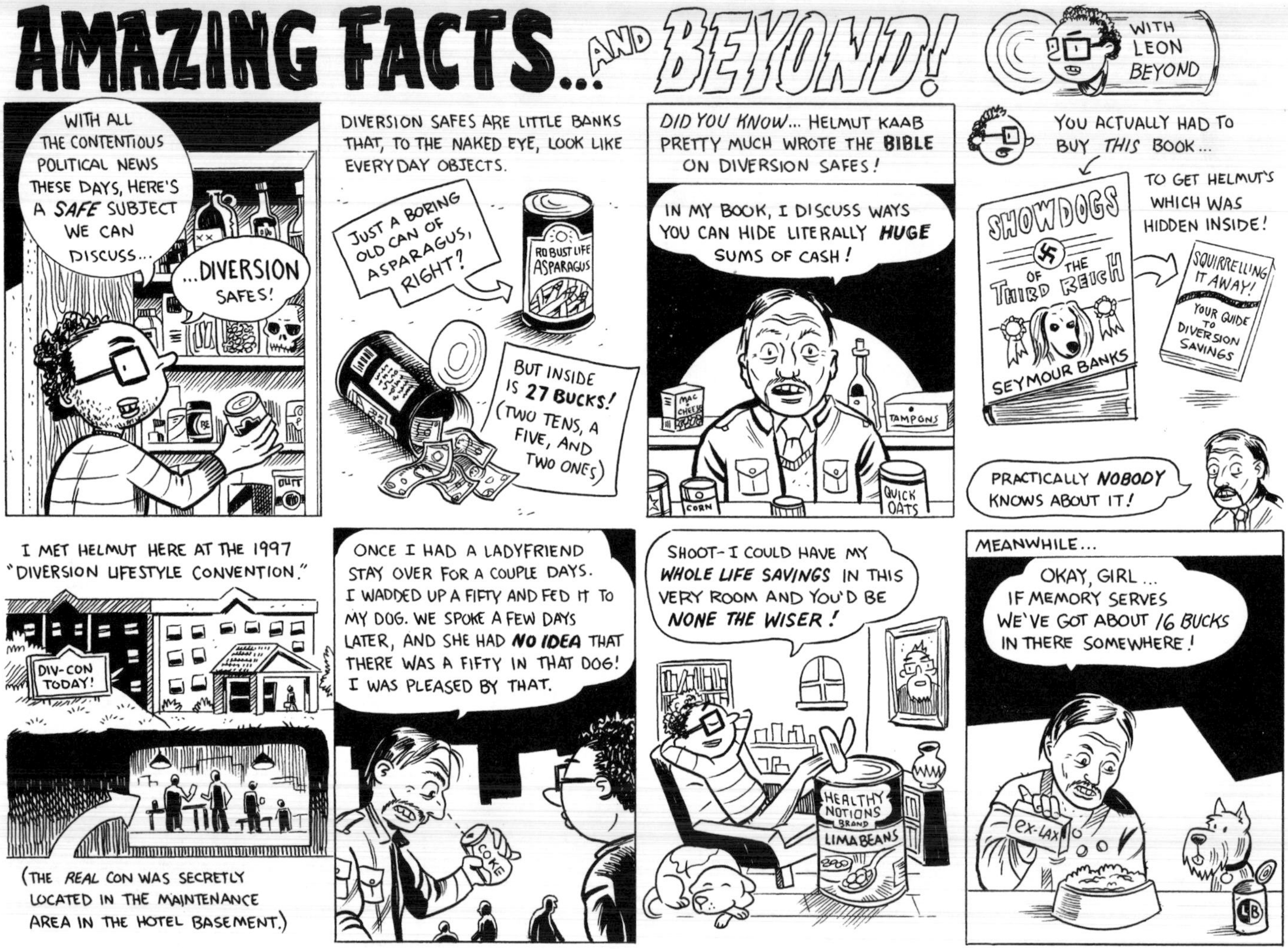
AMAZING FACTS... AND BEYOND!
WITH LEON BEYOND
WITH ALL THE CONTENTIOUS POLITICAL NEWS THESE DAYS, HERE'S A SAFE SUBJECT WE CAN DISCUSS...
...DIVERSION SAFES!
DIVERSION SAFES ARE LITTLE BANKS THAT, TO THE NAKED EYE, LOOK LIKE EVERYDAY OBJECTS.
JUST A BORING OLD CAN OF ASPARAGUS, RIGHT?
ROBUST LIFE ASPARAGUS
BUT INSIDE IS 27 BUCKS! (TWO TENS, A FIVE, AND TWO ONES)
DID YOU KNOW... HELMUT KAAB PRETTY MUCH WROTE THE BIBLE ON DIVERSION SAFES!
IN MY BOOK, I DISCUSS WAYS YOU CAN HIDE LITERALLY HUGE SUMS OF CASH!
MAC + CHEESE
TAMPONS
CORN
QUICK OATS
YOU ACTUALLY HAD TO BUY THIS BOOK...
SHOWDOGS OF THE THIRD REICH
SEYMOUR BANKS
TO GET HELMUT'S WHICH WAS HIDDEN INSIDE!
SQUIRRELLING IT AWAY! YOUR GUIDE TO DIVERSION SAVINGS
PRACTICALLY NOBODY KNOWS ABOUT IT!
I MET HELMUT HERE AT THE 1997 "DIVERSION LIFESTYLE CONVENTION."
DIV-CON TODAY!
(THE REAL CON WAS SECRETLY LOCATED IN THE MAINTENANCE AREA IN THE HOTEL BASEMENT.)
ONCE I HAD A LADYFRIEND STAY OVER FOR A COUPLE DAYS. I WADDED UP A FIFTY AND FED IT TO MY DOG. WE SPOKE A FEW DAYS LATER, AND SHE HAD NO IDEA THAT THERE WAS A FIFTY IN THAT DOG! I WAS PLEASED BY THAT.
COKE
SHOOT- I COULD HAVE MY WHOLE LIFE SAVINGS IN THIS VERY ROOM AND YOU'D BE NONE THE WISER!
HEALTHY NOTIONS BRAND LIMA BEANS
MEANWHILE...
OKAY, GIRL... IF MEMORY SERVES WE'VE GOT ABOUT 16 BUCKS IN THERE SOMEWHERE!
EX-LAX

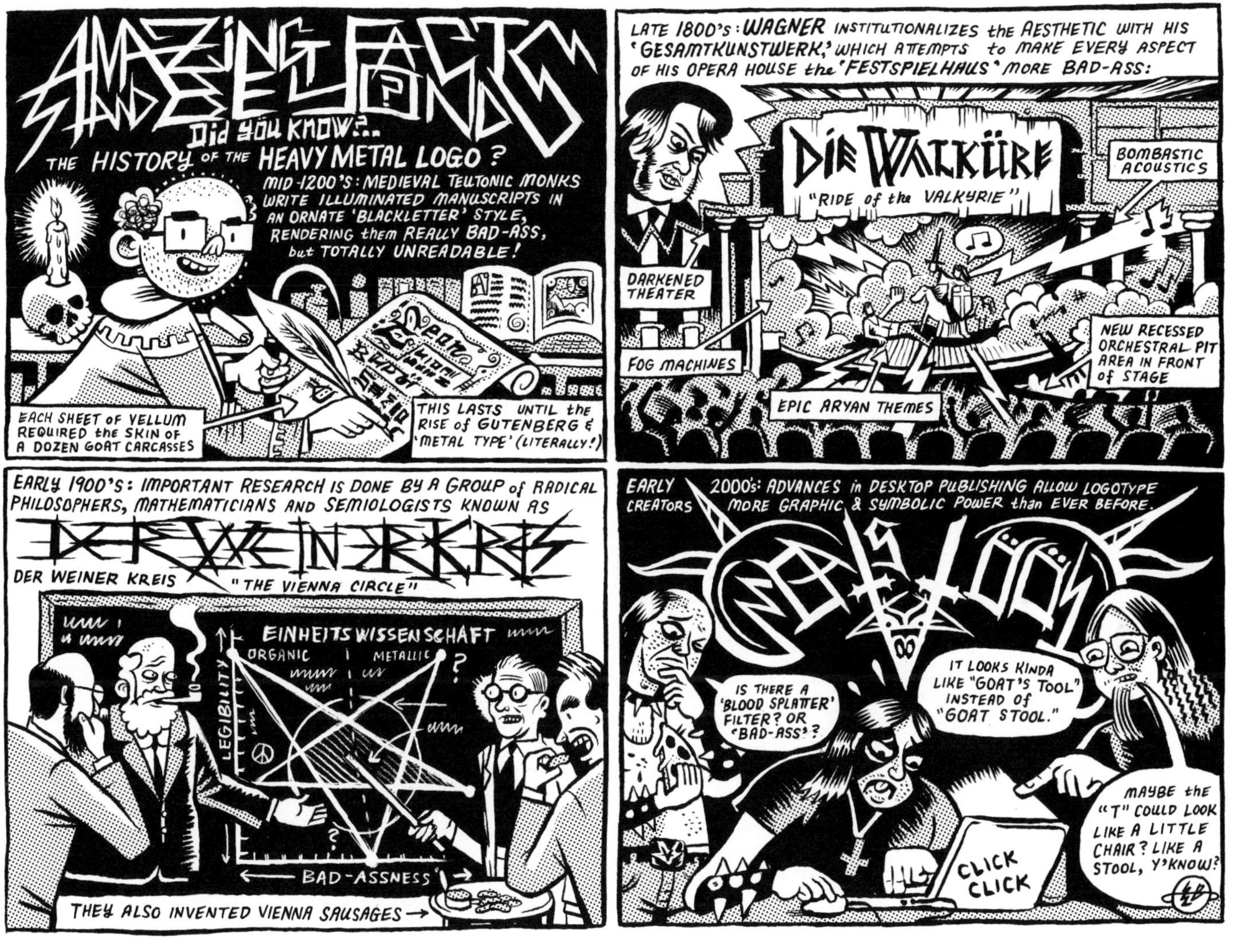
Did you know?...
THE HISTORY of the HEAVY METAL LOGO?
MID-1200'S: MEDIEVAL TEUTONIC MONKS WRITE ILLUMINATED MANUSCRIPTS IN AN ORNATE 'BLACKLETTER' STYLE, RENDERING them REALLY BAD-ASS, but TOTALLY UNREADABLE!
EACH SHEET of VELLUM REQUIRED the SKIN OF A DOZEN GOAT CARCASSES
THIS LASTS UNTIL the RISE of GUTENBERG & 'METAL TYPE' (LITERALLY!)
LATE 1800'S: WAGNER INSTITUTIONALIZES the AESTHETIC WITH HIS 'GESAMTKUNSTWERK,' WHICH ATTEMPTS to MAKE EVERY ASPECT OF HIS OPERA HOUSE the 'FESTSPIELHAUS' MORE BAD-ASS:
DIE WALKÜRE
"RIDE of the VALKYRIE"
BOMBASTIC ACOUSTICS
DARKENED THEATER
FOG MACHINES
EPIC ARYAN THEMES
NEW RECESSED ORCHESTRAL PIT AREA IN FRONT of STAGE
EARLY 1900'S: IMPORTANT RESEARCH IS DONE BY A GROUP of RADICAL PHILOSOPHERS, MATHEMATICIANS AND SEMIOLOGISTS KNOWN AS
DER WEINER KREIS
"THE VIENNA CIRCLE"
EINHEITSWISSENSCHAFT
ORGANIC
METALLIC
LEGIBILITY
BAD-ASSNESS
THEY ALSO INVENTED VIENNA SAUSAGES →
EARLY 2000's: ADVANCES in DESKTOP PUBLISHING ALLOW LOGOTYPE CREATORS MORE GRAPHIC & SYMBOLIC POWER than EVER BEFORE.
IS THERE A 'BLOOD SPLATTER' FILTER? OR 'BAD-ASS'?
IT LOOKS KINDA LIKE "GOAT'S TOOL" INSTEAD of "GOAT STOOL."
MAYBE the "T" COULD LOOK LIKE A LITTLE CHAIR? LIKE A STOOL, Y'KNOW?
CLICK CLICK

BEYOND *the* BEYOND

BEFORE

THE SAME MAPLE TREE —
BEFORE AND AFTER
HOUSING A DYSFUNCTIONAL
FAMILY OF RED SQUIRRELS

AFTER

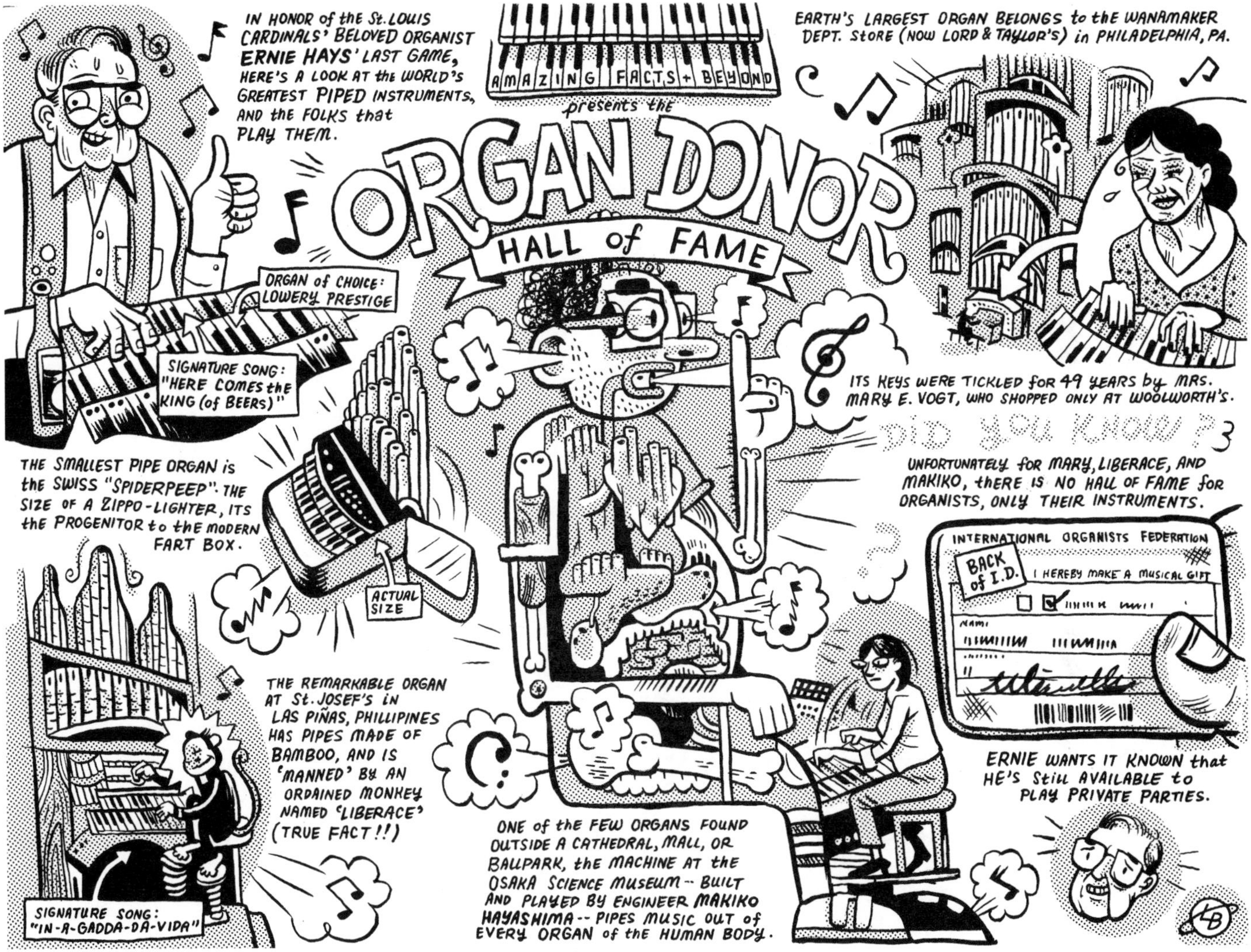
AMAZING FACTS + BEYOND
presents the
ORGAN DONOR
HALL of FAME
IN HONOR of the St. LOUIS CARDINALS' BELOVED ORGANIST ERNIE HAYS' LAST GAME, HERE'S A LOOK AT the WORLD'S GREATEST PIPED INSTRUMENTS, AND the FOLKS that PLAY THEM.
ORGAN of CHOICE: LOWERY PRESTIGE
SIGNATURE SONG: "HERE COMES the KING (of BEERS)"
EARTH'S LARGEST ORGAN BELONGS to the WANAMAKER DEPT. STORE (NOW LORD & TAYLOR'S) in PHILADELPHIA, PA.
ITS KEYS WERE TICKLED FOR 49 YEARS by MRS. MARY E. VOGT, WHO SHOPPED ONLY AT WOOLWORTH'S.
DID YOU KNOW?
UNFORTUNATELY for MARY, LIBERACE, AND MAKIKO, there IS NO HALL OF FAME for ORGANISTS, ONLY THEIR INSTRUMENTS.
THE SMALLEST PIPE ORGAN is the SWISS "SPIDERPEEP". THE SIZE OF A ZIPPO-LIGHTER, ITS the PROGENITOR to the MODERN FART BOX.
ACTUAL SIZE
INTERNATIONAL ORGANISTS FEDERATION
BACK of I.D.
I HEREBY MAKE A MUSICAL GIFT
NAME
THE REMARKABLE ORGAN AT St. JOSEF'S in LAS PIÑAS, PHILLIPINES HAS PIPES MADE OF BAMBOO, AND IS 'MANNED' BY AN ORDAINED MONKEY NAMED 'LIBERACE' (TRUE FACT!!)
SIGNATURE SONG: "IN-A-GADDA-DA-VIDA"
ONE of the FEW ORGANS FOUND OUTSIDE A CATHEDRAL, MALL, OR BALLPARK, the MACHINE AT the OSAKA SCIENCE MUSEUM -- BUILT AND PLAYED BY ENGINEER MAKIKO HAYASHIMA -- PIPES MUSIC OUT of EVERY ORGAN of the HUMAN BODY.
ERNIE WANTS IT KNOWN that HE'S Still AVAILABLE to PLAY PRIVATE PARTIES.
LB

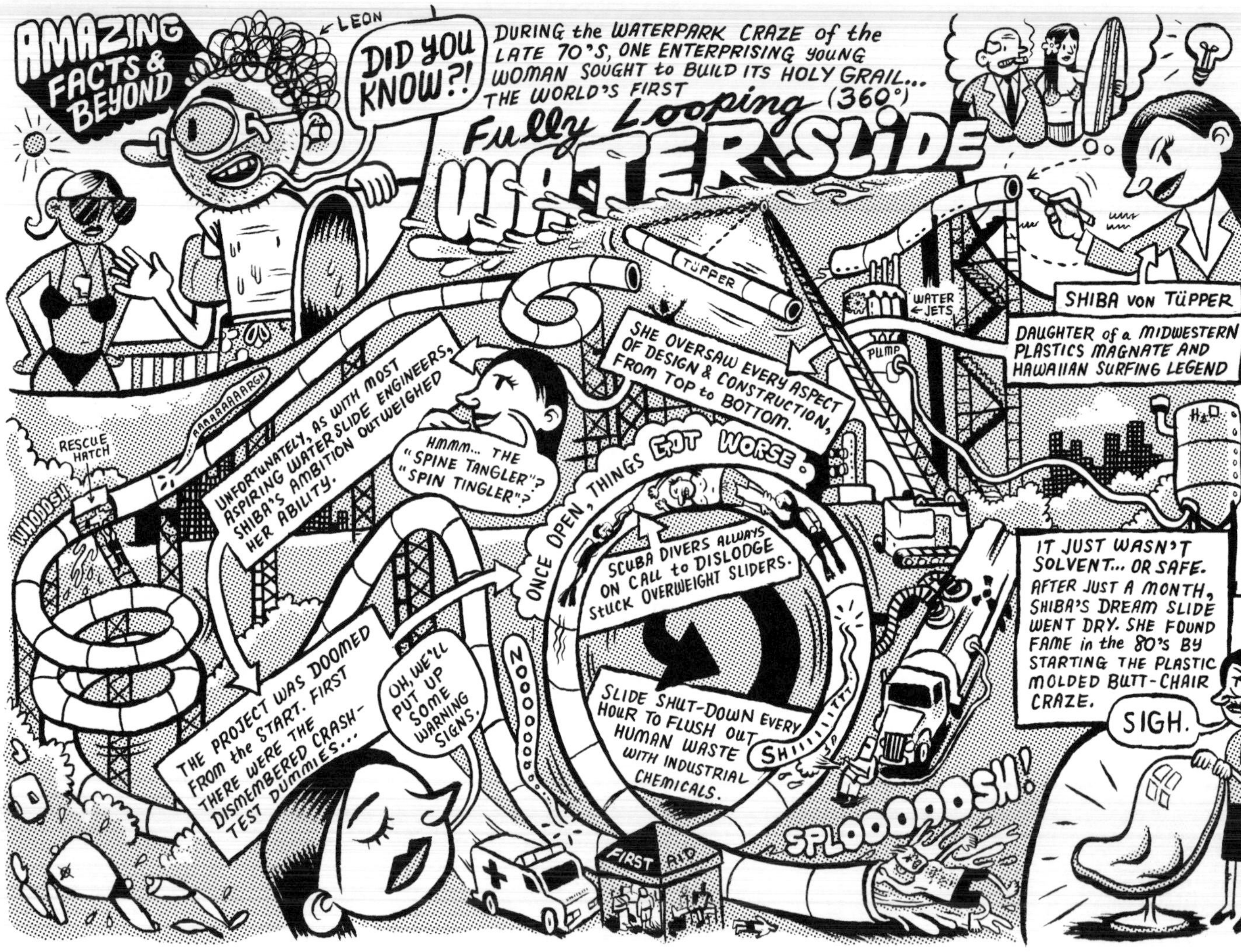
AMAZING FACTS & BEYOND
LEON
DID YOU KNOW?!
DURING the WATERPARK CRAZE of the LATE 70'S, ONE ENTERPRISING YOUNG WOMAN SOUGHT to BUILD ITS HOLY GRAIL... THE WORLD'S FIRST
Fully Looping (360°) WATER SLIDE
TÜPPER
WATER JETS
PUMP
SHIBA VON TÜPPER
DAUGHTER of a MIDWESTERN PLASTICS MAGNATE AND HAWAIIAN SURFING LEGEND
SHE OVERSAW EVERY ASPECT OF DESIGN & CONSTRUCTION, FROM TOP to BOTTOM.
UNFORTUNATELY, AS WITH MOST ASPIRING WATER SLIDE ENGINEERS, SHIBA'S AMBITION OUTWEIGHED HER ABILITY.
HMMM... THE "SPINE TANGLER"? "SPIN TINGLER"?
RESCUE HATCH
WHOOOSH!
ONCE OPEN, THINGS GOT WORSE.
SCUBA DIVERS ALWAYS ON CALL to DISLODGE STUCK OVERWEIGHT SLIDERS.
H_2O
IT JUST WASN'T SOLVENT... OR SAFE. AFTER JUST A MONTH, SHIBA'S DREAM SLIDE WENT DRY. SHE FOUND FAME in the 80'S BY STARTING THE PLASTIC MOLDED BUTT-CHAIR CRAZE.
SIGH.
THE PROJECT WAS DOOMED FROM the START. FIRST THERE WERE THE DISMEMBERED CRASH-TEST DUMMIES...
OH, WE'LL PUT UP SOME WARNING SIGNS.
NOOOOOOOOOO
SLIDE SHUT-DOWN EVERY HOUR TO FLUSH OUT HUMAN WASTE WITH INDUSTRIAL CHEMICALS.
SHIIIIIIT
FIRST AID
SPLOOOOOOSH!

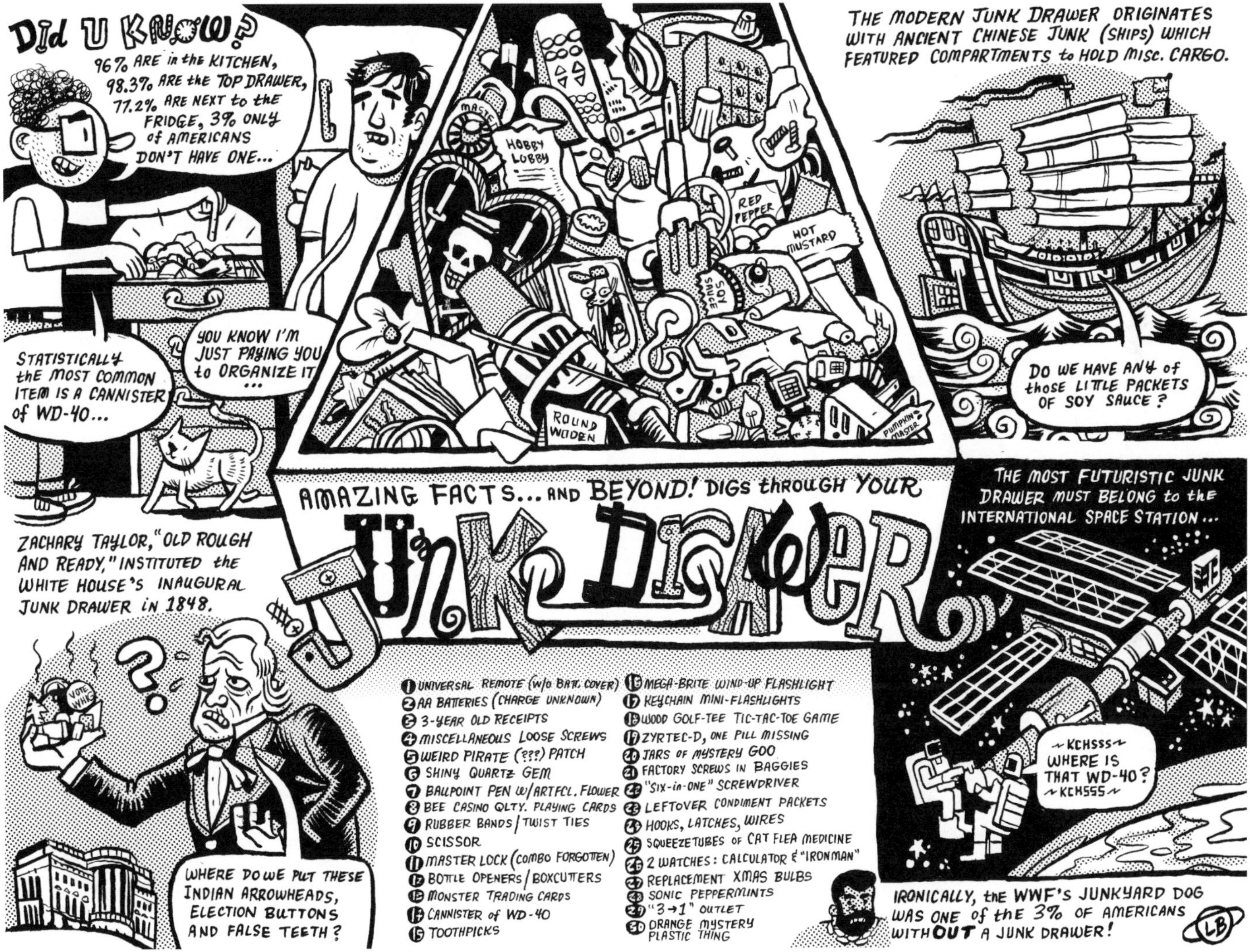
DID U KNOW?
96% ARE in the KITCHEN, 98.3% ARE the TOP DRAWER, 77.2% ARE NEXT to the FRIDGE, 3% ONLY of AMERICANS DON'T HAVE ONE...
STATISTICALLY the MOST COMMON ITEM IS A CANNISTER of WD-40...
YOU KNOW I'M JUST PAYING YOU to ORGANIZE IT...
HOBBY LOBBY
RED PEPPER
HOT MUSTARD
SOY SAUCE
ROUND WOODEN
PUMPKIN MASTER
THE MODERN JUNK DRAWER ORIGINATES WITH ANCIENT CHINESE JUNK (SHIPS) WHICH FEATURED COMPARTMENTS to HOLD MISC. CARGO.
DO WE HAVE ANY of those LITTLE PACKETS OF SOY SAUCE?
AMAZING FACTS... AND BEYOND! DIGS through YOUR
JUNK DRAWER
THE MOST FUTURISTIC JUNK DRAWER MUST BELONG to the INTERNATIONAL SPACE STATION...
~KCHSSS~ WHERE IS THAT WD-40? ~KCHSSS~
ZACHARY TAYLOR, "OLD ROUGH AND READY," INSTITUTED the WHITE HOUSE'S INAUGURAL JUNK DRAWER in 1848.
VOTE WHIG
WHERE DO WE PUT THESE INDIAN ARROWHEADS, ELECTION BUTTONS AND FALSE TEETH?
1 UNIVERSAL REMOTE (w/o BATT. COVER)
2 AA BATTERIES (CHARGE UNKNOWN)
3 3-YEAR OLD RECEIPTS
4 MISCELLANEOUS LOOSE SCREWS
5 WEIRD PIRATE (???) PATCH
6 SHINY QUARTZ GEM
7 BALLPOINT PEN w/ARTFCL. FLOWER
8 BEE CASINO QLTY. PLAYING CARDS
9 RUBBER BANDS / TWIST TIES
10 SCISSOR
11 MASTER LOCK (COMBO FORGOTTEN)
12 BOTTLE OPENERS / BOXCUTTERS
13 MONSTER TRADING CARDS
14 CANNISTER of WD-40
15 TOOTHPICKS
16 MEGA-BRITE WIND-UP FLASHLIGHT
17 KEYCHAIN MINI-FLASHLIGHTS
18 WOOD GOLF-TEE TIC-TAC-TOE GAME
19 ZYRTEC-D, ONE PILL MISSING
20 JARS OF MYSTERY GOO
21 FACTORY SCREWS IN BAGGIES
22 "SIX-in-ONE" SCREWDRIVER
23 LEFTOVER CONDIMENT PACKETS
24 HOOKS, LATCHES, WIRES
25 SQUEEZETUBES OF CAT FLEA MEDICINE
26 2 WATCHES: CALCULATOR & "IRONMAN"
27 REPLACEMENT XMAS BULBS
28 SONIC PEPPERMINTS
29 "3→1" OUTLET
30 ORANGE MYSTERY PLASTIC THING
IRONICALLY, the WWF'S JUNKYARD DOG WAS ONE of the 3% OF AMERICANS WITHOUT A JUNK DRAWER!
LB

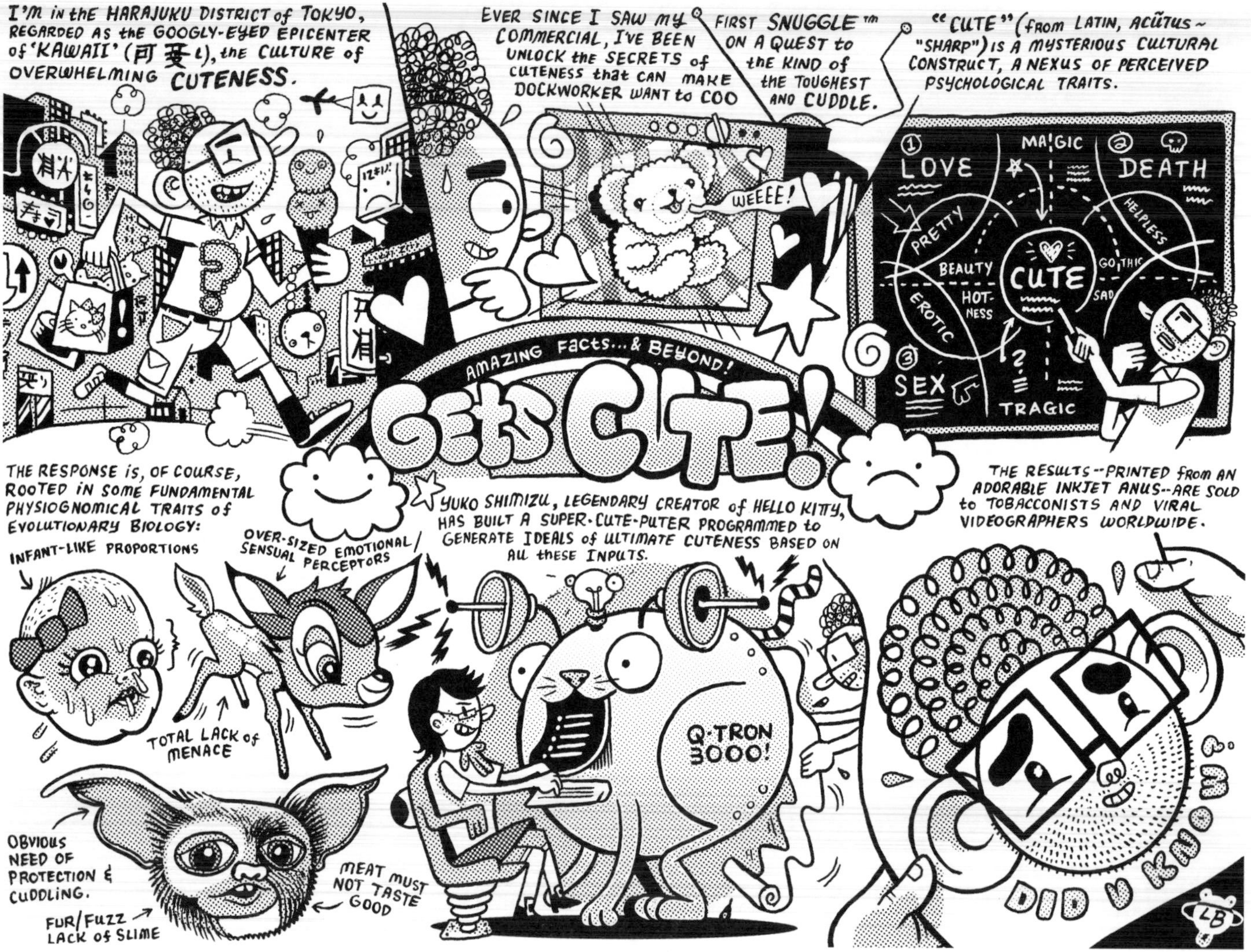
I'M IN THE HARAJUKU DISTRICT OF TOKYO, REGARDED AS THE GOOGLY-EYED EPICENTER OF 'KAWAII' (可愛い), THE CULTURE OF OVERWHELMING CUTENESS.
EVER SINCE I SAW MY FIRST SNUGGLE™ COMMERCIAL, I'VE BEEN ON A QUEST TO UNLOCK THE SECRETS OF THE KIND OF CUTENESS THAT CAN MAKE THE TOUGHEST DOCKWORKER WANT TO COO AND CUDDLE.
WEEEE!
"CUTE" (FROM LATIN, ACŪTUS ~ "SHARP") IS A MYSTERIOUS CULTURAL CONSTRUCT, A NEXUS OF PERCEIVED PSYCHOLOGICAL TRAITS.
① LOVE
MA!GIC
② DEATH
PRETTY
HELPLESS
BEAUTY
CUTE
GOTHIC
EROTIC
HOT-NESS
SAD
③ SEX
TRAGIC
AMAZING FACTS... & BEYOND!
GETS CUTE!
THE RESPONSE IS, OF COURSE, ROOTED IN SOME FUNDAMENTAL PHYSIOGNOMICAL TRAITS OF EVOLUTIONARY BIOLOGY:
INFANT-LIKE PROPORTIONS
OVER-SIZED EMOTIONAL/SENSUAL PERCEPTORS
TOTAL LACK OF MENACE
OBVIOUS NEED OF PROTECTION & CUDDLING.
MEAT MUST NOT TASTE GOOD
FUR/FUZZ LACK OF SLIME
YUKO SHIMIZU, LEGENDARY CREATOR OF HELLO KITTY, HAS BUILT A SUPER-CUTE-PUTER PROGRAMMED TO GENERATE IDEALS OF ULTIMATE CUTENESS BASED ON ALL THESE INPUTS.
Q·TRON 3000!
THE RESULTS--PRINTED FROM AN ADORABLE INKJET ANUS--ARE SOLD TO TOBACCONISTS AND VIRAL VIDEOGRAPHERS WORLDWIDE.
DID U KNOW
LB

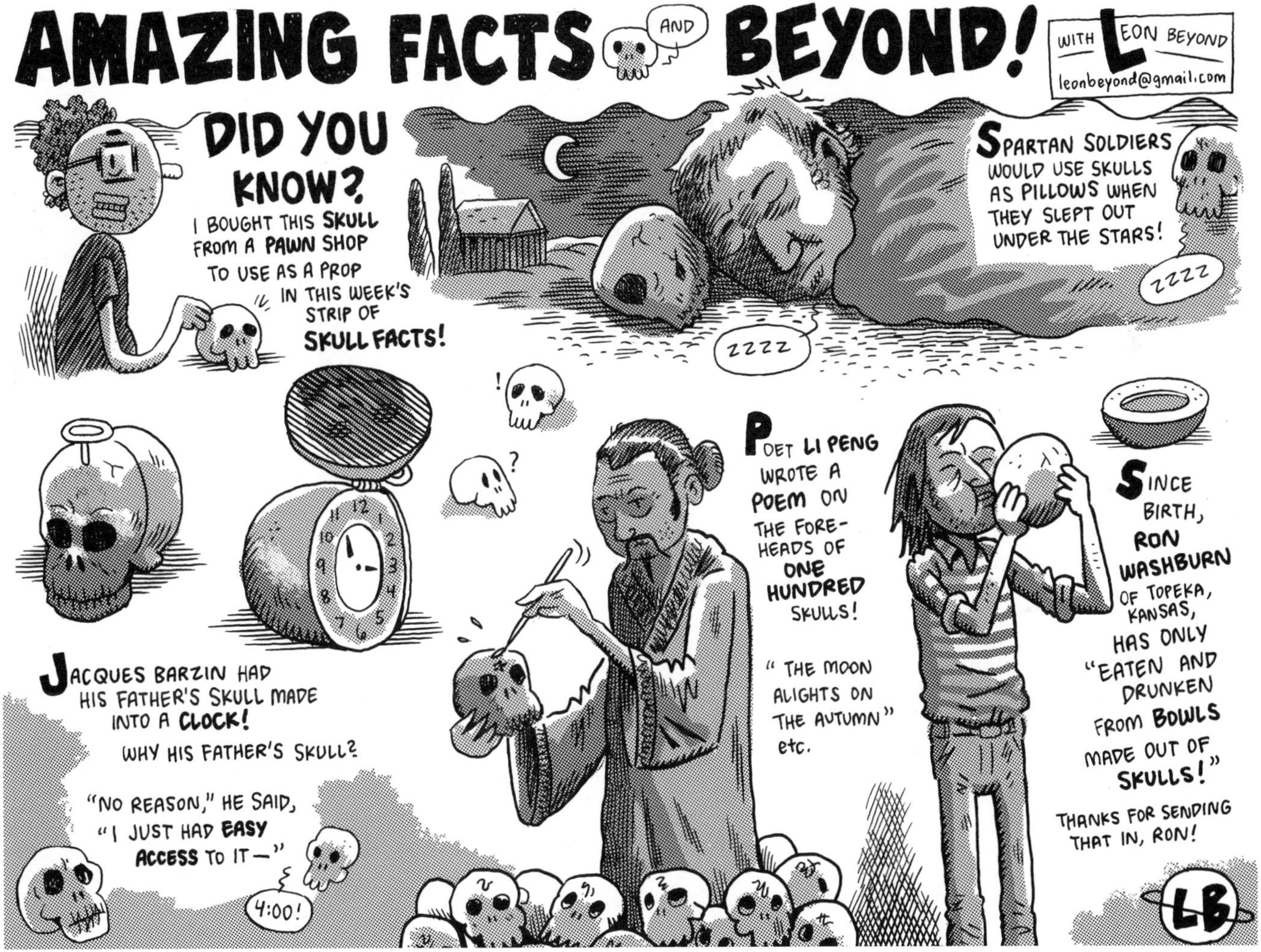
AMAZING FACTS AND BEYOND!
WITH LEON BEYOND
leonbeyond@gmail.com
DID YOU KNOW? I BOUGHT THIS SKULL FROM A PAWN SHOP TO USE AS A PROP IN THIS WEEK'S STRIP OF SKULL FACTS!
SPARTAN SOLDIERS WOULD USE SKULLS AS PILLOWS WHEN THEY SLEPT OUT UNDER THE STARS!
ZZZZ
ZZZZ
JACQUES BARZIN HAD HIS FATHER'S SKULL MADE INTO A CLOCK!
WHY HIS FATHER'S SKULL?
"NO REASON," HE SAID, "I JUST HAD EASY ACCESS TO IT—"
4:00!
POET LI PENG WROTE A POEM ON THE FOREHEADS OF ONE HUNDRED SKULLS!
"THE MOON ALIGHTS ON THE AUTUMN" etc.
SINCE BIRTH, RON WASHBURN OF TOPEKA, KANSAS, HAS ONLY "EATEN AND DRUNKEN FROM BOWLS MADE OUT OF SKULLS!"
THANKS FOR SENDING THAT IN, RON!
LB

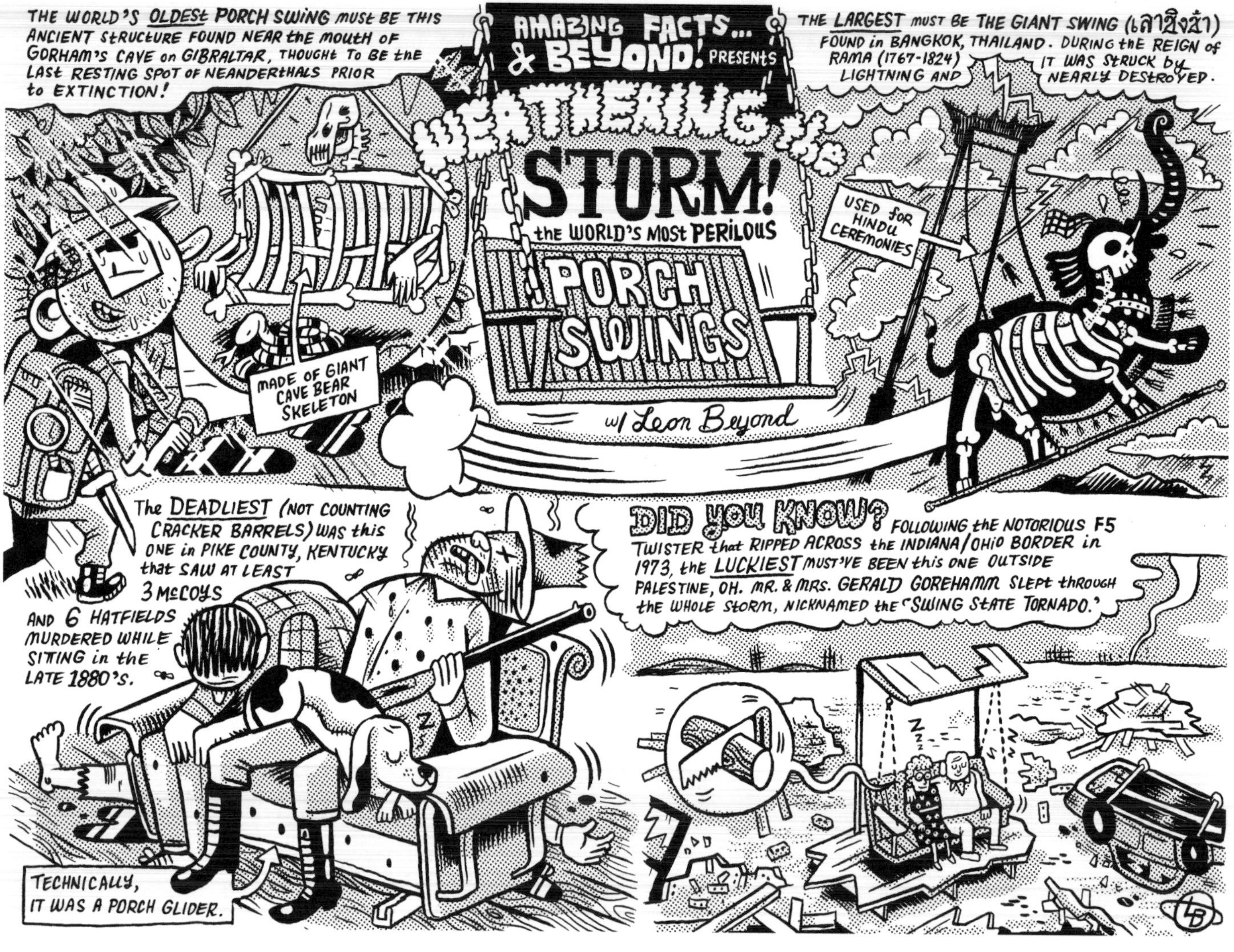

AMAZING FACTS... & BEYOND! PRESENTS
WEATHERING the STORM!
the WORLD'S MOST PERILOUS PORCH SWINGS
w/ Leon Beyond
THE WORLD'S OLDEST PORCH SWING MUST BE THIS ANCIENT STRUCTURE FOUND NEAR the MOUTH OF GORHAM'S CAVE on GIBRALTAR, THOUGHT TO BE the LAST RESTING SPOT OF NEANDERTHALS PRIOR to EXTINCTION!
MADE OF GIANT CAVE BEAR SKELETON
THE LARGEST MUST BE THE GIANT SWING (เสาชิงช้า) FOUND in BANGKOK, THAILAND. DURING the REIGN of RAMA (1767-1824) IT WAS STRUCK by LIGHTNING AND NEARLY DESTROYED.
USED for HINDU CEREMONIES
The DEADLIEST (NOT COUNTING CRACKER BARRELS) WAS this ONE in PIKE COUNTY, KENTUCKY that SAW AT LEAST 3 McCOYS AND 6 HATFIELDS MURDERED WHILE SITTING in the LATE 1880's.
TECHNICALLY, IT WAS A PORCH GLIDER.
DID you KNOW? FOLLOWING the NOTORIOUS F5 TWISTER that RIPPED ACROSS the INDIANA/OHIO BORDER in 1973, the LUCKIEST MUST'VE BEEN this ONE OUTSIDE PALESTINE, OH. MR. & MRS. GERALD GOREHAMM SLEPT through the WHOLE STORM, NICKNAMED the "SWING STATE TORNADO."
LB

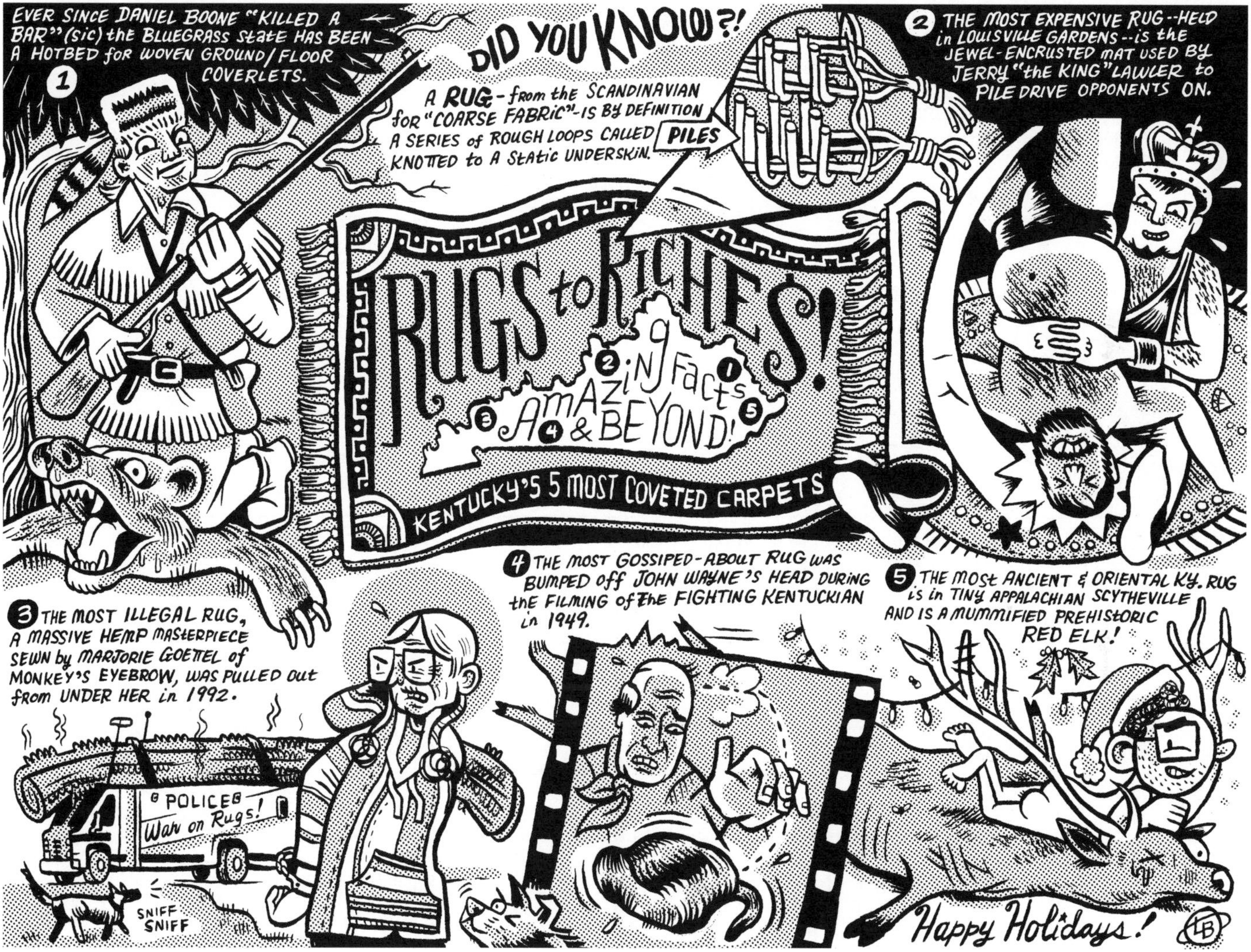
DID YOU KNOW?!
EVER SINCE DANIEL BOONE "KILLED A BAR" (sic) THE BLUEGRASS STATE HAS BEEN A HOTBED FOR WOVEN GROUND/FLOOR COVERLETS.
A RUG - from the SCANDINAVIAN for "COARSE FABRIC" - IS BY DEFINITION A SERIES of ROUGH LOOPS CALLED PILES KNOTTED to A STATIC UNDERSKIN.
PILES
2 THE MOST EXPENSIVE RUG -- HELD in LOUISVILLE GARDENS -- is the JEWEL-ENCRUSTED MAT USED BY JERRY "the KING" LAWLER to PILE DRIVE OPPONENTS ON.
RUGS to RICHES!
Amazing Facts & BEYOND!
KENTUCKY'S 5 MOST COVETED CARPETS
3 THE MOST ILLEGAL RUG, A MASSIVE HEMP MASTERPIECE SEWN by MARJORIE GOETTEL of MONKEY'S EYEBROW, WAS PULLED OUT from UNDER HER in 1992.
POLICE
War on Rugs!
SNIFF SNIFF
4 THE MOST GOSSIPED-ABOUT RUG WAS BUMPED OFF JOHN WAYNE'S HEAD DURING THE FILMING of the FIGHTING KENTUCKIAN in 1949.
5 THE MOST ANCIENT & ORIENTAL KY. RUG is in TINY APPALACHIAN SCYTHEVILLE AND IS A MUMMIFIED PREHISTORIC RED ELK!
Happy Holidays!
LB

AMAZING FACTS AND BEYOND!

WITH LEON BEYOND

1. WELL, ACCORDING TO MY CALENDAR, **2012** IS ALMOST ONE QUARTER OVER.

THIS YEAR I'M TRYING OUT A NEW KIND OF FORMAT: 1 ☐ = 3 MONTHS.

2. OF COURSE, MOST CALENDARS USE 1 ☐ = 1 DAY. DID YOU KNOW? IF 1 ☐ = 1 HOUR, YOU'D NEED **8760** BOXES, WHICH MEANS YOU'D NEED 24 CALENDARS. ($8760 \div 365 = 24$).

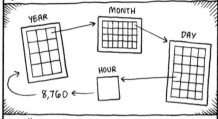

THE "LEON BEYOND FACT-AN-HOUR" CALENDAR WON "MOST INFORMATIVE" AT CALENDAR-CON 1988.

3. AROUND THE WORLD, A SMALL COMMUNITY OF EXTREME CALENDAR CREATORS HAVE CREATED SOME CALENDARS THAT ARE EXTREME. HERE ARE SOME EXAMPLES:

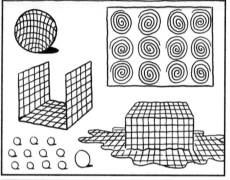

4. SOME CALENDAR SCIENTISTS ARE RECOMMENDING **BLOCK** CALENDARS, WHEREIN 1 ⬛ = 1 DAY, TO HELP WITH THE WORLD'S EXCESS PLASTIC SUPPLY.

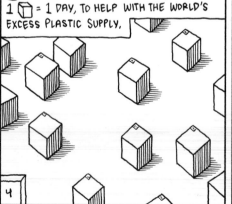

5. CALENDARS VISUALIZE AND SPATIALIZE. SOME PEOPLE IMAGINE WEEKS IN DIFFERENT WAYS:

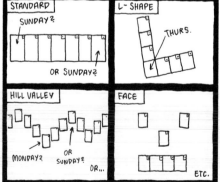

STANDARD
SUNDAY?
OR SUNDAY?

L-SHAPE
THURS.

HILL VALLEY
MONDAY? OR SUNDAY? OR...

FACE
ETC.

6. SOME PEOPLE HAVE CALENDAR-RELATED UNEASE DISORDER (CRUD), WHICH INVOLVES HATING ANYTHING TO DO WITH CALENDARS. SCIENCE HAS SHOWN THAT MANY SUFFER FROM LOW-LEVEL C.R.U.D.

ANYTIME SOMETHING GOES ON THE CALENDAR, THEY BEGIN TO VIEW THAT THING NEGATIVELY.

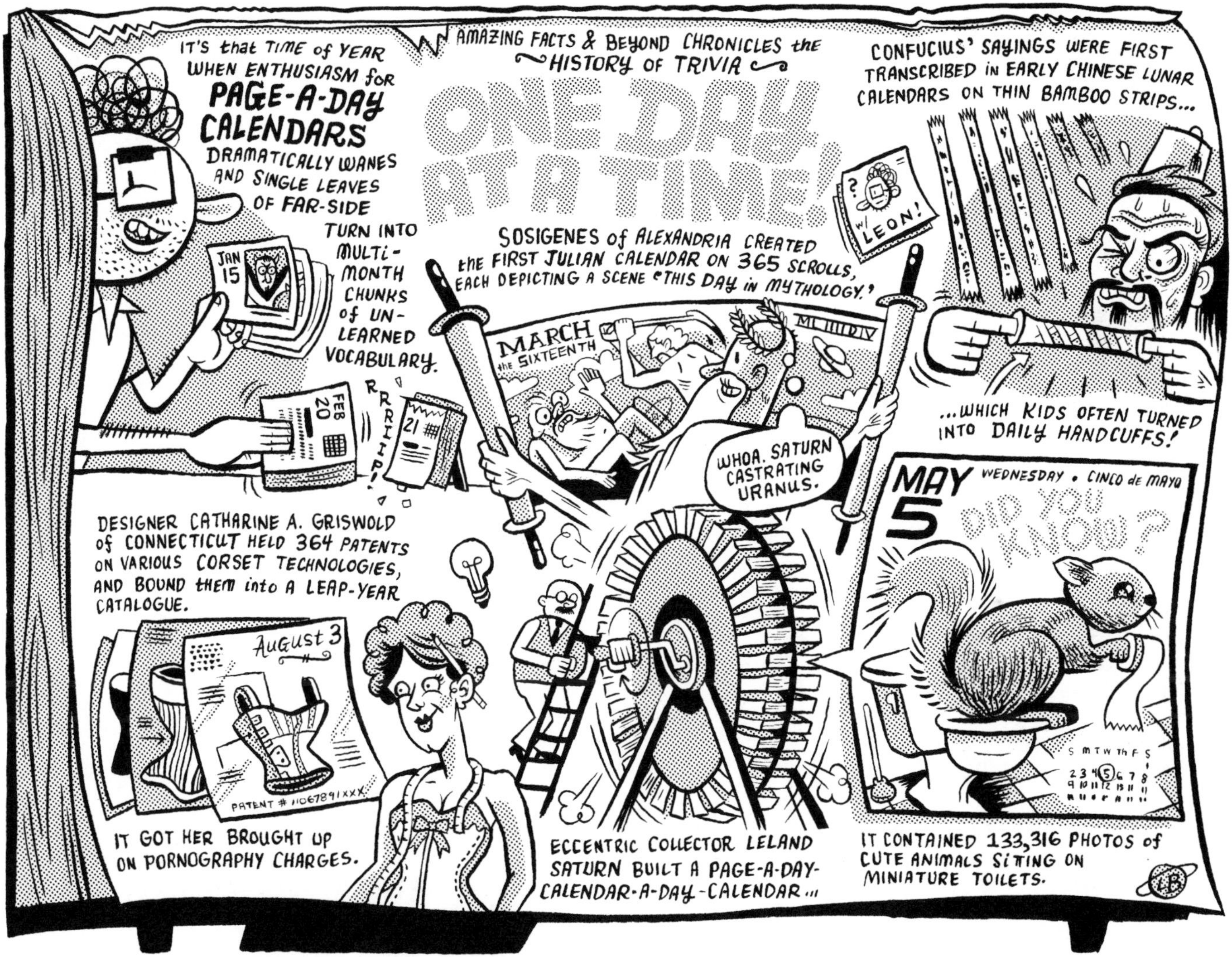
AMAZING FACTS & BEYOND CHRONICLES the HISTORY of TRIVIA
ONE DAY, AT A TIME!
IT'S that TIME of YEAR WHEN ENTHUSIASM for PAGE-A-DAY CALENDARS DRAMATICALLY WANES AND SINGLE LEAVES OF FAR-SIDE TURN INTO MULTI-MONTH CHUNKS of UN-LEARNED VOCABULARY.
JAN 15
FEB 20
21
RRRIIIP!
SOSIGENES of ALEXANDRIA CREATED the FIRST JULIAN CALENDAR ON 365 SCROLLS, EACH DEPICTING A SCENE 'THIS DAY in MYTHOLOGY.'
MARCH the SIXTEENTH
WHOA. SATURN CASTRATING URANUS.
W/ LEON!
CONFUCIUS' SAYINGS WERE FIRST TRANSCRIBED in EARLY CHINESE LUNAR CALENDARS ON THIN BAMBOO STRIPS...
...WHICH KIDS OFTEN TURNED INTO DAILY HANDCUFFS!
DESIGNER CATHARINE A. GRISWOLD of CONNECTICUT HELD 364 PATENTS ON VARIOUS CORSET TECHNOLOGIES, AND BOUND THEM into A LEAP-YEAR CATALOGUE.
August 3
PATENT # 1106789IXXX
IT GOT HER BROUGHT UP ON PORNOGRAPHY CHARGES.
ECCENTRIC COLLECTOR LELAND SATURN BUILT A PAGE-A-DAY-CALENDAR-A-DAY-CALENDAR...
MAY 5 WEDNESDAY • CINCO de MAYO
DID YOU KNOW?
IT CONTAINED 133,316 PHOTOS of CUTE ANIMALS SITTING ON MINIATURE TOILETS.
LB

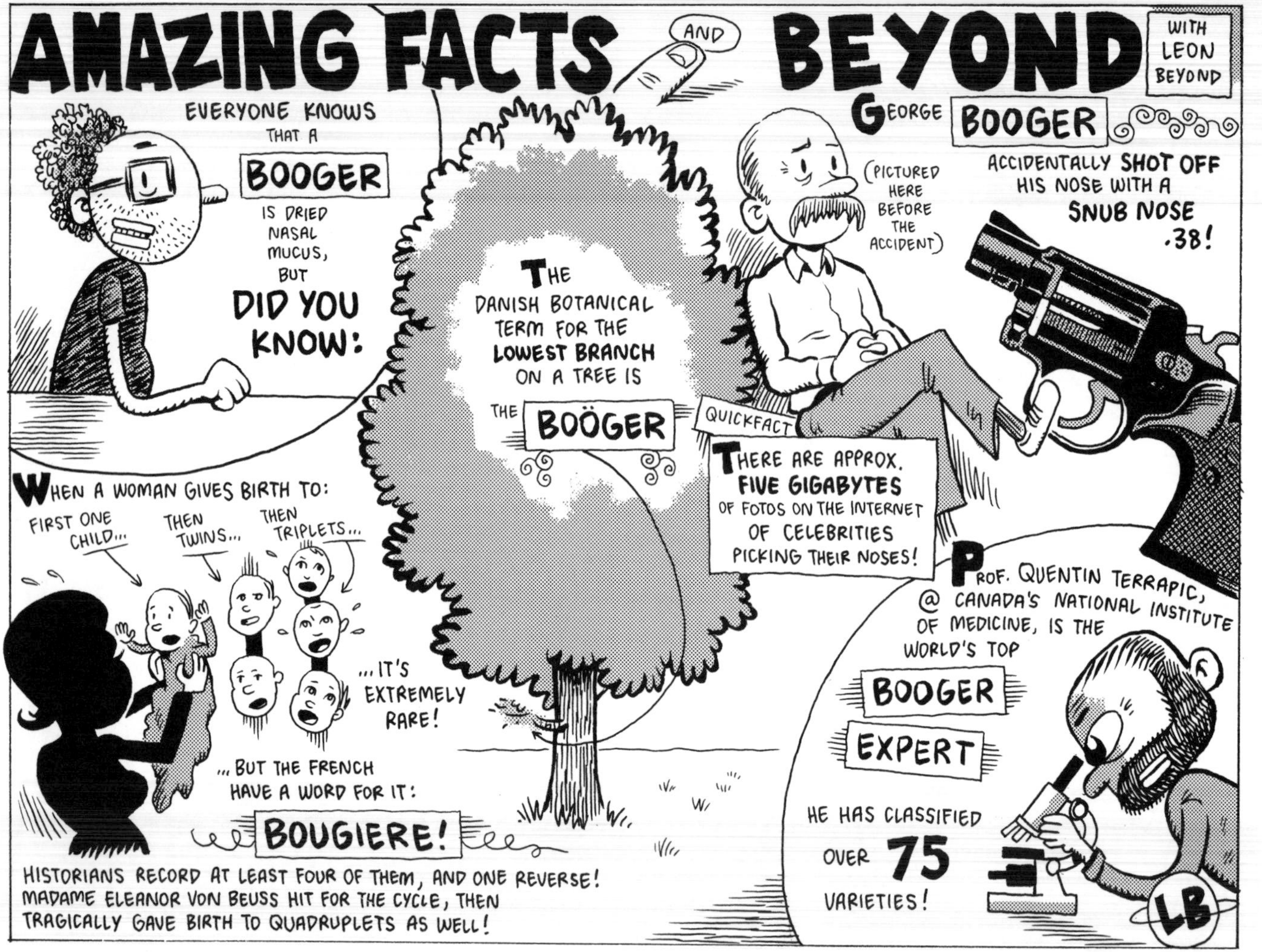
AMAZING FACTS AND BEYOND
WITH LEON BEYOND
EVERYONE KNOWS THAT A BOOGER IS DRIED NASAL MUCUS, BUT DID YOU KNOW:
THE DANISH BOTANICAL TERM FOR THE LOWEST BRANCH ON A TREE IS THE BOÖGER
GEORGE BOOGER
(PICTURED HERE BEFORE THE ACCIDENT)
ACCIDENTALLY SHOT OFF HIS NOSE WITH A SNUB NOSE .38!
QUICKFACT
THERE ARE APPROX. FIVE GIGABYTES OF FOTOS ON THE INTERNET OF CELEBRITIES PICKING THEIR NOSES!
WHEN A WOMAN GIVES BIRTH TO:
FIRST ONE CHILD...
THEN TWINS...
THEN TRIPLETS...
...IT'S EXTREMELY RARE!
...BUT THE FRENCH HAVE A WORD FOR IT:
BOUGIERE!
HISTORIANS RECORD AT LEAST FOUR OF THEM, AND ONE REVERSE! MADAME ELEANOR VON BEUSS HIT FOR THE CYCLE, THEN TRAGICALLY GAVE BIRTH TO QUADRUPLETS AS WELL!
PROF. QUENTIN TERRAPIC, @ CANADA'S NATIONAL INSTITUTE OF MEDICINE, IS THE WORLD'S TOP BOOGER EXPERT
HE HAS CLASSIFIED OVER 75 VARIETIES!
LB

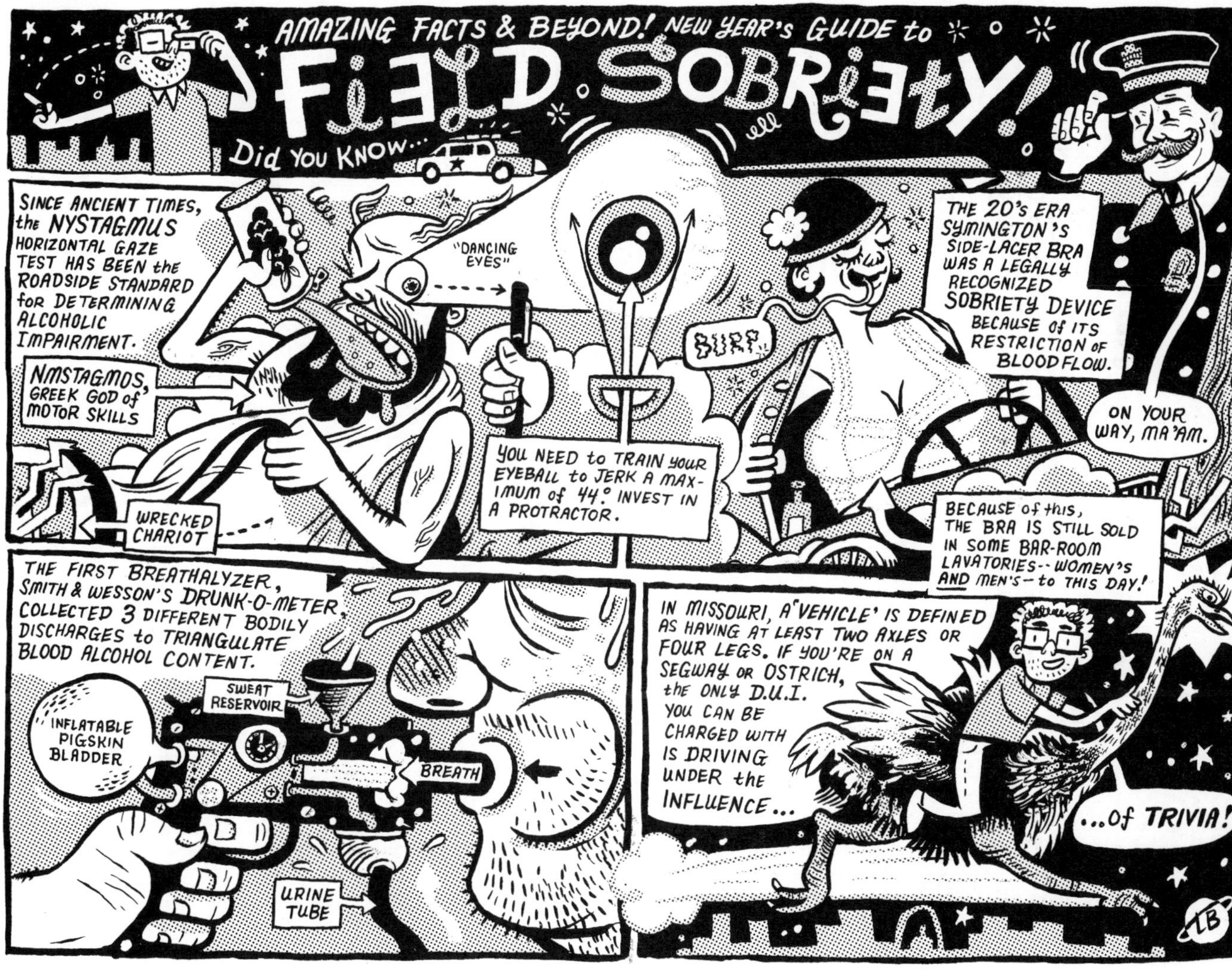
AMAZING FACTS & BEYOND! NEW YEAR'S GUIDE to
FIELD SOBRIETY!
Did YOU KNOW...
SINCE ANCIENT TIMES, the NYSTAGMUS HORIZONTAL GAZE TEST HAS BEEN the ROADSIDE STANDARD for DETERMINING ALCOHOLIC IMPAIRMENT.
"DANCING EYES"
NMSTAGMOS, GREEK GOD of MOTOR SKILLS
WRECKED CHARIOT
YOU NEED to TRAIN YOUR EYEBALL to JERK A MAXIMUM of 44°. INVEST IN A PROTRACTOR.
THE 20's ERA SYMINGTON'S SIDE-LACER BRA WAS A LEGALLY RECOGNIZED SOBRIETY DEVICE BECAUSE of ITS RESTRICTION of BLOODFLOW.
BURP
ON YOUR WAY, MA'AM.
BECAUSE of this, THE BRA IS STILL SOLD IN SOME BAR-ROOM LAVATORIES-- WOMEN'S AND MEN'S-- to THIS DAY!
THE FIRST BREATHALYZER, SMITH & WESSON'S DRUNK-O-METER, COLLECTED 3 DIFFERENT BODILY DISCHARGES to TRIANGULATE BLOOD ALCOHOL CONTENT.
SWEAT RESERVOIR
INFLATABLE PIGSKIN BLADDER
BREATH
URINE TUBE
IN MISSOURI, A 'VEHICLE' IS DEFINED AS HAVING AT LEAST TWO AXLES OR FOUR LEGS. IF YOU'RE ON A SEGWAY OR OSTRICH, the ONLY D.U.I. YOU CAN BE CHARGED WITH IS DRIVING UNDER the INFLUENCE...
...of TRIVIA!
LB

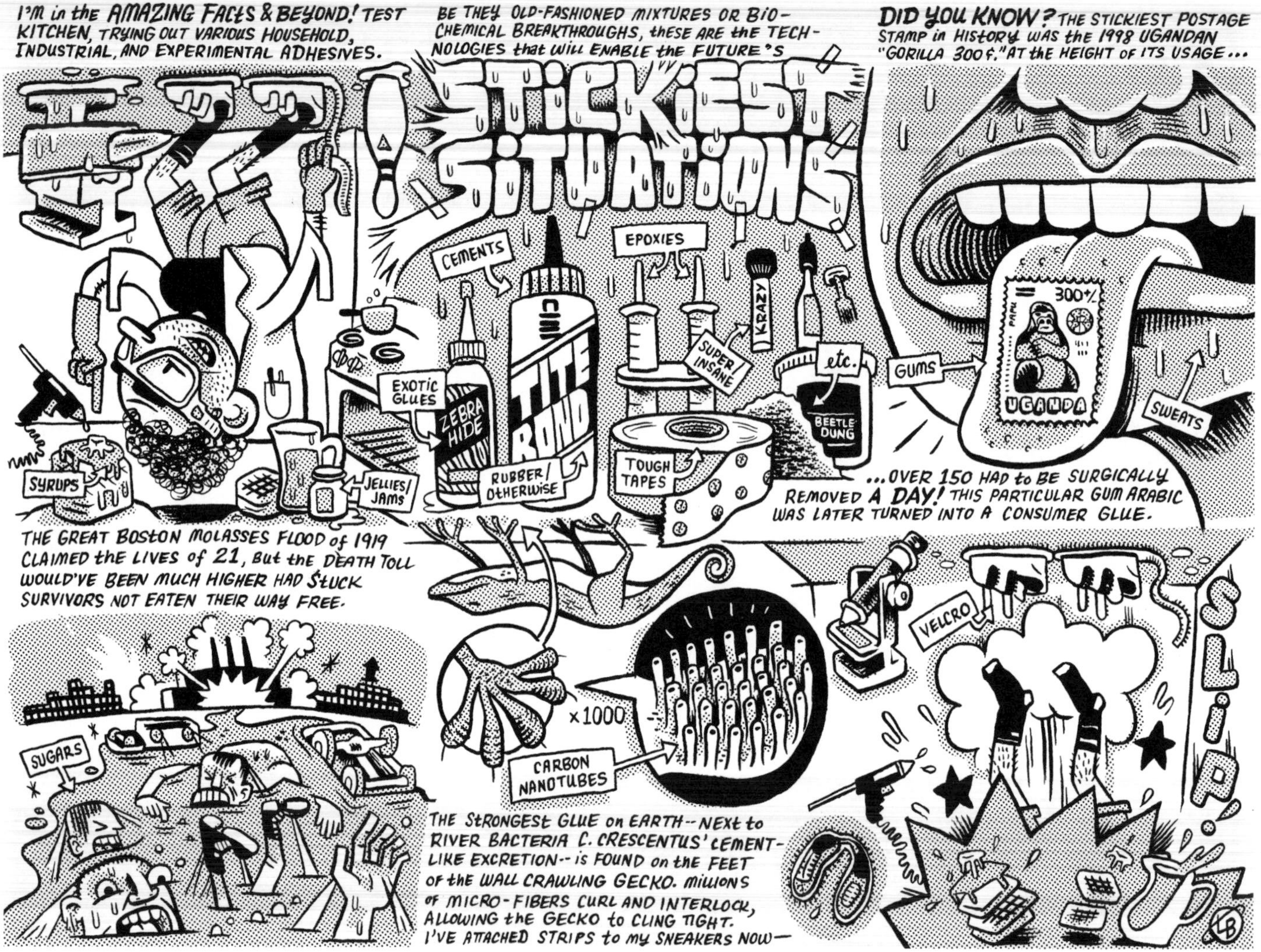
I'M in the AMAZING FACTS & BEYOND! TEST KITCHEN, TRYING OUT VARIOUS HOUSEHOLD, INDUSTRIAL, AND EXPERIMENTAL ADHESIVES.
BE THEY OLD-FASHIONED MIXTURES OR BIO-CHEMICAL BREAKTHROUGHS, THESE ARE THE TECH-NOLOGIES THAT WILL ENABLE THE FUTURE'S
STICKIEST SITUATIONS
DID YOU KNOW? THE STICKIEST POSTAGE STAMP IN HISTORY WAS THE 1998 UGANDAN "GORILLA 300¢." AT THE HEIGHT OF ITS USAGE...
CEMENTS
EPOXIES
KRAZY
SUPER/INSANE
etc.
EXOTIC GLUES
ZEBRA HIDE
TITE BOND
RUBBER/OTHERWISE
TOUGH TAPES
BEETLE DUNG
SYRUPS
JELLIES/JAMS
GUMS
300¢
UGANDA
SWEATS
...OVER 150 HAD TO BE SURGICALLY REMOVED A DAY! THIS PARTICULAR GUM ARABIC WAS LATER TURNED INTO A CONSUMER GLUE.
THE GREAT BOSTON MOLASSES FLOOD OF 1919 CLAIMED THE LIVES OF 21, BUT THE DEATH TOLL WOULD'VE BEEN MUCH HIGHER HAD $TUCK SURVIVORS NOT EATEN THEIR WAY FREE.
SUGARS
×1000
CARBON NANOTUBES
VELCRO
SLIP
THE STRONGEST GLUE ON EARTH--NEXT TO RIVER BACTERIA C. CRESCENTUS' CEMENT-LIKE EXCRETION--IS FOUND ON THE FEET OF THE WALL CRAWLING GECKO. MILLIONS OF MICRO-FIBERS CURL AND INTERLOCK, ALLOWING THE GECKO TO CLING TIGHT. I'VE ATTACHED STRIPS TO MY SNEAKERS NOW—
LB

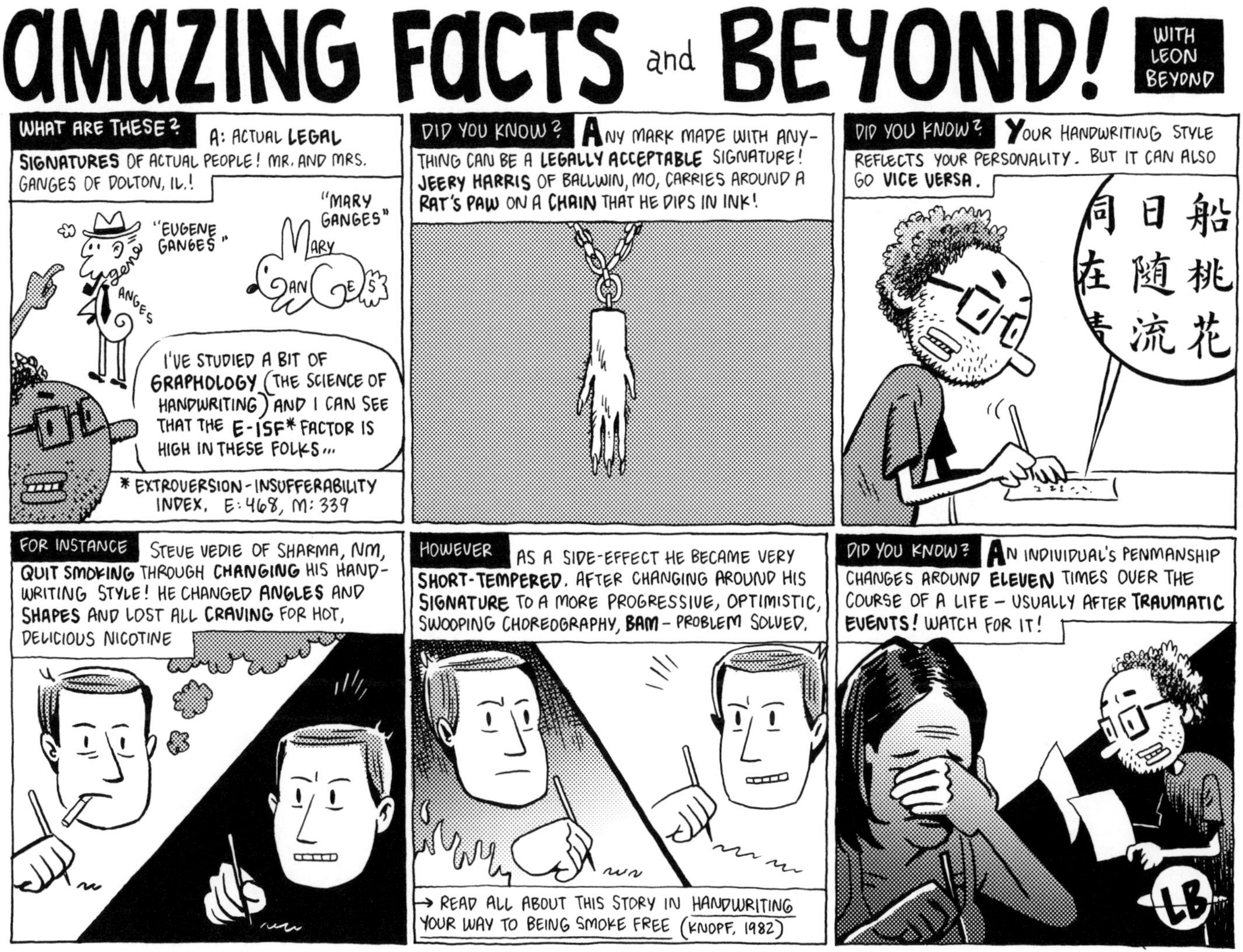
AMAZING FACTS and BEYOND!
WITH LEON BEYOND
WHAT ARE THESE?
A: ACTUAL LEGAL SIGNATURES OF ACTUAL PEOPLE! MR. AND MRS. GANGES OF DOLTON, IL.!
"EUGENE GANGES"
Eugene GANGES
"MARY GANGES"
MARY GANGES
I'VE STUDIED A BIT OF GRAPHOLOGY (THE SCIENCE OF HANDWRITING) AND I CAN SEE THAT THE E-ISF* FACTOR IS HIGH IN THESE FOLKS...
* EXTROVERSION-INSUFFERABILITY INDEX. E: 468, M: 339
DID YOU KNOW? ANY MARK MADE WITH ANYTHING CAN BE A LEGALLY ACCEPTABLE SIGNATURE! JEERY HARRIS OF BALLWIN, MO, CARRIES AROUND A RAT'S PAW ON A CHAIN THAT HE DIPS IN INK!
DID YOU KNOW? YOUR HANDWRITING STYLE REFLECTS YOUR PERSONALITY. BUT IT CAN ALSO GO VICE VERSA.
船桃花
日随流
同在青
FOR INSTANCE STEVE VEDIE OF SHARMA, NM, QUIT SMOKING THROUGH CHANGING HIS HANDWRITING STYLE! HE CHANGED ANGLES AND SHAPES AND LOST ALL CRAVING FOR HOT, DELICIOUS NICOTINE
HOWEVER AS A SIDE-EFFECT HE BECAME VERY SHORT-TEMPERED. AFTER CHANGING AROUND HIS SIGNATURE TO A MORE PROGRESSIVE, OPTIMISTIC, SWOOPING CHOREOGRAPHY, BAM – PROBLEM SOLVED.
→ READ ALL ABOUT THIS STORY IN HANDWRITING YOUR WAY TO BEING SMOKE FREE (KNOPF, 1982)
DID YOU KNOW? AN INDIVIDUAL'S PENMANSHIP CHANGES AROUND ELEVEN TIMES OVER THE COURSE OF A LIFE – USUALLY AFTER TRAUMATIC EVENTS! WATCH FOR IT!
LB

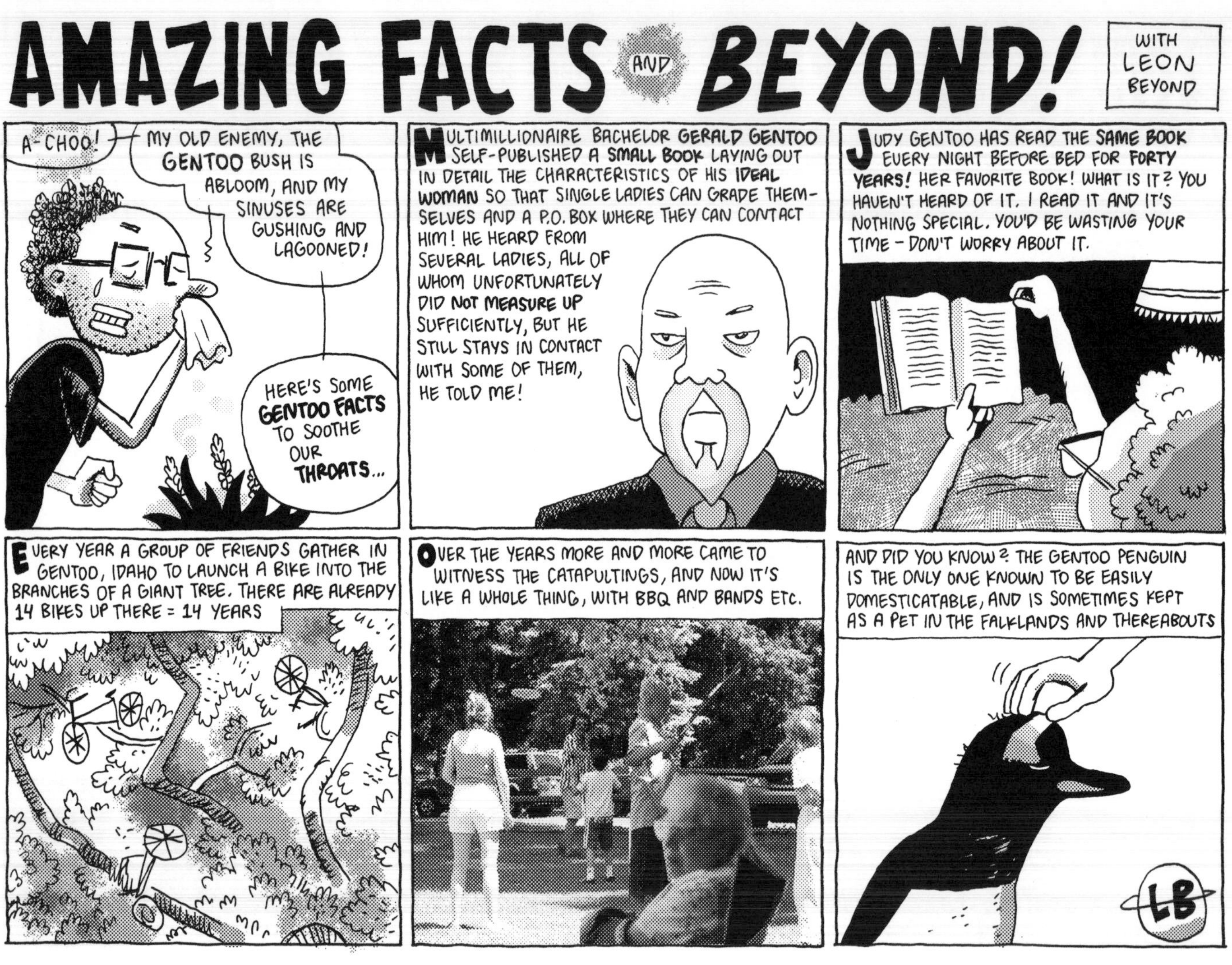
AMAZING FACTS AND BEYOND!
WITH LEON BEYOND
A-CHOO!
MY OLD ENEMY, THE GENTOO BUSH IS ABLOOM, AND MY SINUSES ARE GUSHING AND LAGOONED!
HERE'S SOME GENTOO FACTS TO SOOTHE OUR THROATS...
MULTIMILLIONAIRE BACHELOR GERALD GENTOO SELF-PUBLISHED A SMALL BOOK LAYING OUT IN DETAIL THE CHARACTERISTICS OF HIS IDEAL WOMAN SO THAT SINGLE LADIES CAN GRADE THEMSELVES AND A P.O. BOX WHERE THEY CAN CONTACT HIM! HE HEARD FROM SEVERAL LADIES, ALL OF WHOM UNFORTUNATELY DID NOT MEASURE UP SUFFICIENTLY, BUT HE STILL STAYS IN CONTACT WITH SOME OF THEM, HE TOLD ME!
JUDY GENTOO HAS READ THE SAME BOOK EVERY NIGHT BEFORE BED FOR FORTY YEARS! HER FAVORITE BOOK! WHAT IS IT? YOU HAVEN'T HEARD OF IT. I READ IT AND IT'S NOTHING SPECIAL. YOU'D BE WASTING YOUR TIME - DON'T WORRY ABOUT IT.
EVERY YEAR A GROUP OF FRIENDS GATHER IN GENTOO, IDAHO TO LAUNCH A BIKE INTO THE BRANCHES OF A GIANT TREE. THERE ARE ALREADY 14 BIKES UP THERE = 14 YEARS
OVER THE YEARS MORE AND MORE CAME TO WITNESS THE CATAPULTINGS, AND NOW IT'S LIKE A WHOLE THING, WITH BBQ AND BANDS ETC.
AND DID YOU KNOW? THE GENTOO PENGUIN IS THE ONLY ONE KNOWN TO BE EASILY DOMESTICATABLE, AND IS SOMETIMES KEPT AS A PET IN THE FALKLANDS AND THEREABOUTS
LB

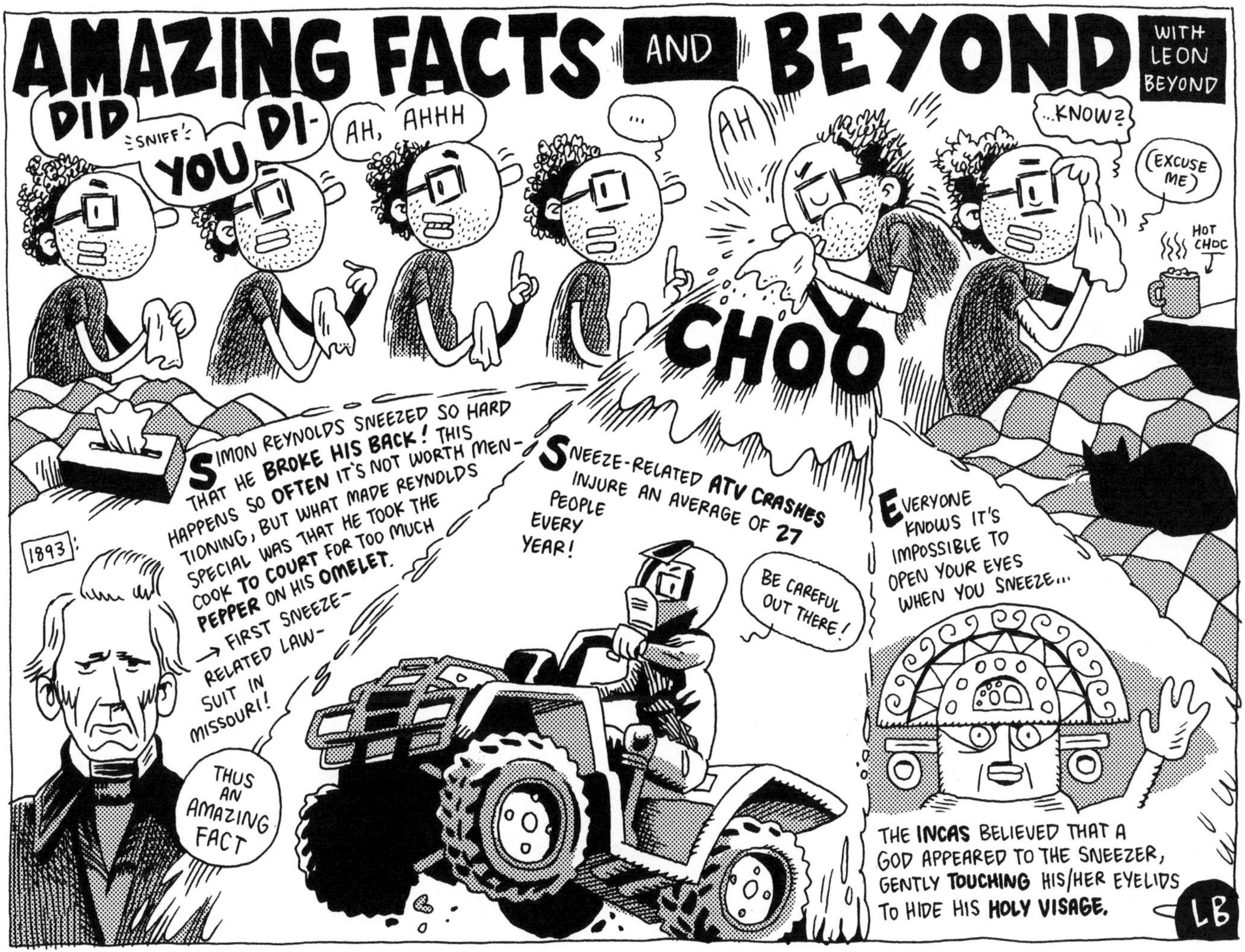
AMAZING FACTS AND BEYOND WITH LEON BEYOND
DID
SNIFF
YOU
DI-
AH, AHHH
...
AH
CHOO
...KNOW?
(EXCUSE ME)
HOT CHOC
SIMON REYNOLDS SNEEZED SO HARD THAT HE BROKE HIS BACK! THIS HAPPENS SO OFTEN IT'S NOT WORTH MENTIONING, BUT WHAT MADE REYNOLDS SPECIAL WAS THAT HE TOOK THE COOK TO COURT FOR TOO MUCH PEPPER ON HIS OMELET.
1893:
→ FIRST SNEEZE-RELATED LAWSUIT IN MISSOURI!
THUS AN AMAZING FACT
SNEEZE-RELATED ATV CRASHES INJURE AN AVERAGE OF 27 PEOPLE EVERY YEAR!
BE CAREFUL OUT THERE!
EVERYONE KNOWS IT'S IMPOSSIBLE TO OPEN YOUR EYES WHEN YOU SNEEZE...
THE INCAS BELIEVED THAT A GOD APPEARED TO THE SNEEZER, GENTLY TOUCHING HIS/HER EYELIDS TO HIDE HIS HOLY VISAGE.
LB

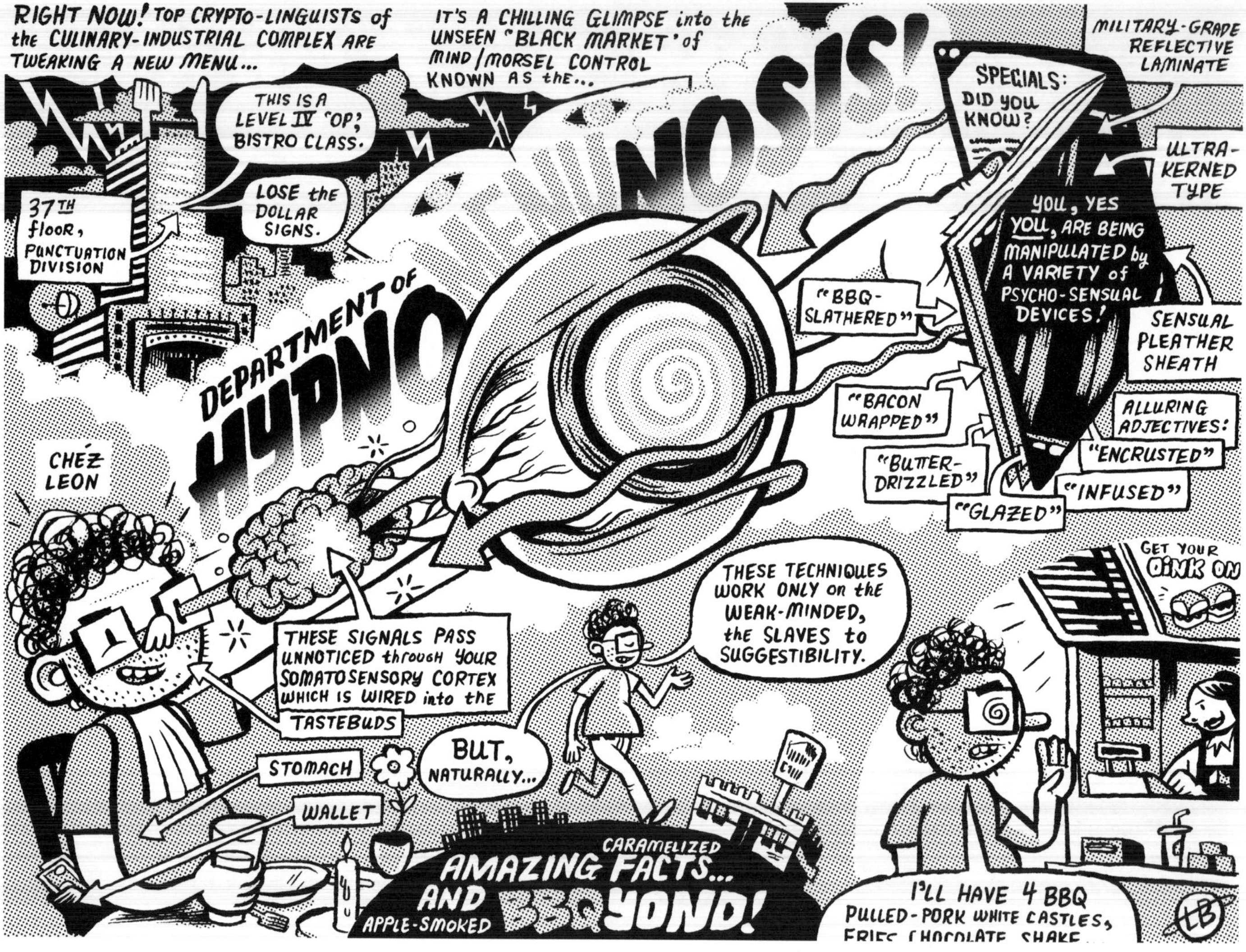
RIGHT NOW! TOP CRYPTO-LINGUISTS of the CULINARY-INDUSTRIAL COMPLEX ARE TWEAKING A NEW MENU...
IT'S A CHILLING GLIMPSE into the UNSEEN "BLACK MARKET" of MIND/MORSEL CONTROL KNOWN AS the...
DEPARTMENT OF HYPNO MENU NOSIS!
MILITARY-GRADE REFLECTIVE LAMINATE
SPECIALS: DID YOU KNOW?
THIS IS A LEVEL IV "OP," BISTRO CLASS.
LOSE the DOLLAR SIGNS.
37TH floor, PUNCTUATION DIVISION
ULTRA-KERNED TYPE
YOU, YES YOU, ARE BEING MANIPULATED by A VARIETY of PSYCHO-SENSUAL DEVICES!
"BBQ-SLATHERED"
SENSUAL PLEATHER SHEATH
"BACON WRAPPED"
ALLURING ADJECTIVES:
"ENCRUSTED"
"BUTTER-DRIZZLED"
"INFUSED"
"GLAZED"
CHEZ LEON
GET YOUR OINK ON
THESE TECHNIQUES WORK ONLY on the WEAK-MINDED, the SLAVES to SUGGESTIBILITY.
THESE SIGNALS PASS UNNOTICED through YOUR SOMATOSENSORY CORTEX WHICH IS WIRED into the
TASTEBUDS
STOMACH
WALLET
BUT, NATURALLY...
AMAZING CARAMELIZED FACTS... AND APPLE-SMOKED BBQ YOND!
I'LL HAVE 4 BBQ PULLED-PORK WHITE CASTLES, FRIES CHOCOLATE SHAKE...
LB

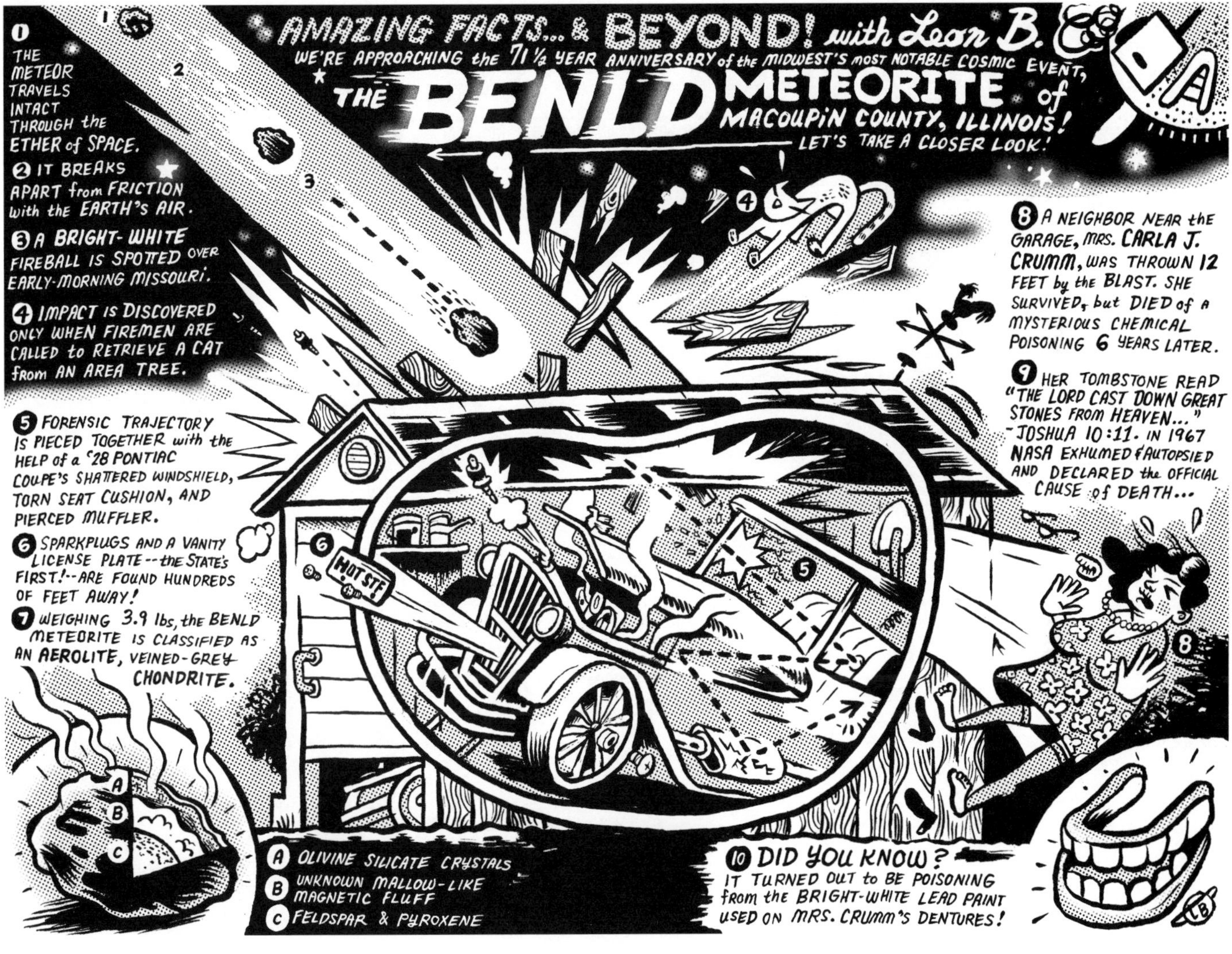
AMAZING FACTS... & BEYOND! with Leon B.
WE'RE APPROACHING the 71 ½ YEAR ANNIVERSARY of the MIDWEST'S most NOTABLE COSMIC EVENT,
THE BENLD METEORITE of MACOUPIN COUNTY, ILLINOIS!
LET'S TAKE A CLOSER LOOK!
1 THE METEOR TRAVELS INTACT THROUGH the ETHER of SPACE.
2 IT BREAKS APART from FRICTION with the EARTH'S AIR.
3 A BRIGHT-WHITE FIREBALL IS SPOTTED OVER EARLY-MORNING MISSOURI.
4 IMPACT IS DISCOVERED ONLY WHEN FIREMEN ARE CALLED to RETRIEVE A CAT from AN AREA TREE.
5 FORENSIC TRAJECTORY IS PIECED TOGETHER with the HELP of a '28 PONTIAC COUPE'S SHATTERED WINDSHIELD, TORN SEAT CUSHION, AND PIERCED MUFFLER.
6 SPARKPLUGS AND A VANITY LICENSE PLATE -- the STATE'S FIRST! -- ARE FOUND HUNDREDS OF FEET AWAY!
7 WEIGHING 3.9 lbs, the BENLD METEORITE IS CLASSIFIED AS AN AEROLITE, VEINED-GREY CHONDRITE.
8 A NEIGHBOR NEAR the GARAGE, MRS. CARLA J. CRUMM, WAS THROWN 12 FEET by the BLAST. SHE SURVIVED, but DIED of A MYSTERIOUS CHEMICAL POISONING 6 YEARS LATER.
9 HER TOMBSTONE READ "THE LORD CAST DOWN GREAT STONES FROM HEAVEN..." - JOSHUA 10:11. IN 1967 NASA EXHUMED & AUTOPSIED AND DECLARED the OFFICIAL CAUSE of DEATH...
HOT STF
A OLIVINE SILICATE CRYSTALS
B UNKNOWN MALLOW-LIKE MAGNETIC FLUFF
C FELDSPAR & PYROXENE
10 DID YOU KNOW? IT TURNED OUT to BE POISONING from the BRIGHT-WHITE LEAD PAINT USED ON MRS. CRUMM'S DENTURES!
LB

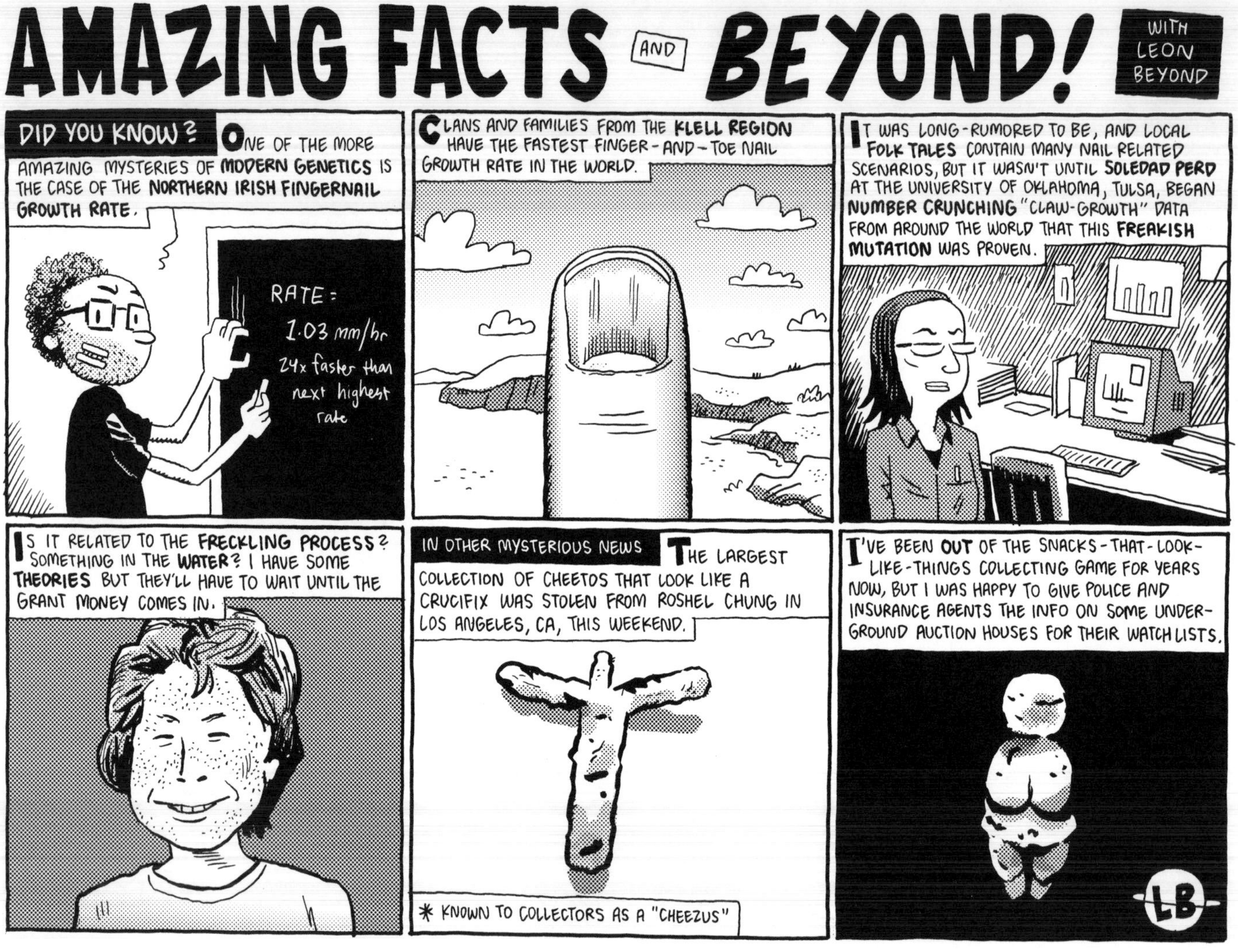
AMAZING FACTS AND BEYOND!
WITH LEON BEYOND
DID YOU KNOW?
ONE OF THE MORE AMAZING MYSTERIES OF MODERN GENETICS IS THE CASE OF THE NORTHERN IRISH FINGERNAIL GROWTH RATE.
RATE = 1.03 mm/hr 24x faster than next highest rate
CLANS AND FAMILIES FROM THE KLELL REGION HAVE THE FASTEST FINGER-AND-TOE NAIL GROWTH RATE IN THE WORLD.
IT WAS LONG-RUMORED TO BE, AND LOCAL FOLK TALES CONTAIN MANY NAIL RELATED SCENARIOS, BUT IT WASN'T UNTIL SOLEDAD PERD AT THE UNIVERSITY OF OKLAHOMA, TULSA, BEGAN NUMBER CRUNCHING "CLAW-GROWTH" DATA FROM AROUND THE WORLD THAT THIS FREAKISH MUTATION WAS PROVEN.
IS IT RELATED TO THE FRECKLING PROCESS? SOMETHING IN THE WATER? I HAVE SOME THEORIES BUT THEY'LL HAVE TO WAIT UNTIL THE GRANT MONEY COMES IN.
IN OTHER MYSTERIOUS NEWS
THE LARGEST COLLECTION OF CHEETOS THAT LOOK LIKE A CRUCIFIX WAS STOLEN FROM ROSHEL CHUNG IN LOS ANGELES, CA, THIS WEEKEND.
* KNOWN TO COLLECTORS AS A "CHEEZUS"
I'VE BEEN OUT OF THE SNACKS-THAT-LOOK-LIKE-THINGS COLLECTING GAME FOR YEARS NOW, BUT I WAS HAPPY TO GIVE POLICE AND INSURANCE AGENTS THE INFO ON SOME UNDERGROUND AUCTION HOUSES FOR THEIR WATCH LISTS.
LB

AMAGING FACTS... AND BEYOND!

I HAD TO GET MY EYES CHECKED UP THIS WEEK... WELL EVEN THOUGH THEY USED A DIFFERENT CHART THAN THE ONE I STUDIED ON, I STILL BASICALLY ACED IT.

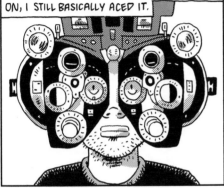

WHAT'S THE DIFFERENCE BETWEEN OPTOMETRISTS AND OPTHAMOLOGISTS? BOY OH BOY, THEY HATE IT WHEN YOU MIX THAT UP...

PLEASE HOLD STILL

HERE'S A LITTLE MNEMONIC FOR HOW TO KEEP THEM SEPARATED:

OPTOMETRISTS ARE "UP TOP OF THE LIST" AS FAR AS GETTING GLASSES.

OPTHAMALLOGISTS ARE IN STRIP MALLS.

OPTOGENARIANS ARE OLD PEOPLE.

PTO

"OPTO" MEANS "OCULAR"

AND WHILE WE'RE ON THE SUBJECT, DID YOU KNOW? A HERPETOPTOLOGIST MAKES GLASSES FOR LIZARDS, WHICH HAVE NOTORIOUSLY BAD ASTIGMATISMS.

PRESCRIPTION SUNGLASSES

AN OPTILLUSOR IS SOMEONE WHO COLLECTS AND CREATES OPTICAL ILLUSIONS.

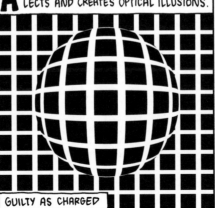

GUILTY AS CHARGED

BONUS FACT

UP UNTIL THE SUPREME COURT RULED IN IRVING VS. VIRGINIA IN 1922, IT WAS AGAINST THE LAW IN SOME STATES FOR BOOKS BY MALE AND FEMALE AUTHORS TO SHARE A SHELF...

...UNLESS THE AUTHORS WERE THEMSELVES MARRIED OR ENGAGED!

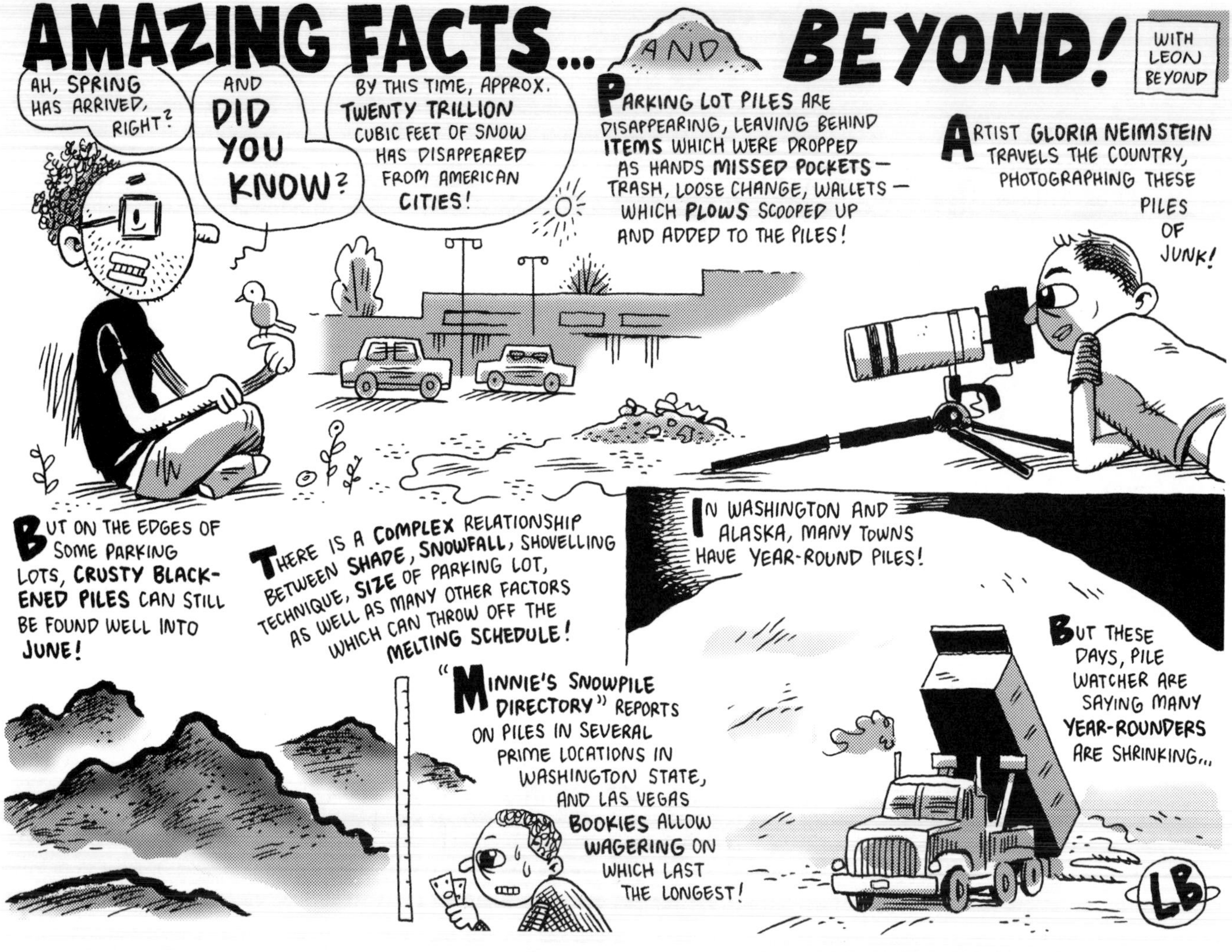
AMAZING FACTS... AND BEYOND!
WITH LEON BEYOND
AH, SPRING HAS ARRIVED, RIGHT?
AND DID YOU KNOW?
BY THIS TIME, APPROX. TWENTY TRILLION CUBIC FEET OF SNOW HAS DISAPPEARED FROM AMERICAN CITIES!
PARKING LOT PILES ARE DISAPPEARING, LEAVING BEHIND ITEMS WHICH WERE DROPPED AS HANDS MISSED POCKETS — TRASH, LOOSE CHANGE, WALLETS — WHICH PLOWS SCOOPED UP AND ADDED TO THE PILES!
ARTIST GLORIA NEIMSTEIN TRAVELS THE COUNTRY, PHOTOGRAPHING THESE PILES OF JUNK!
BUT ON THE EDGES OF SOME PARKING LOTS, CRUSTY BLACKENED PILES CAN STILL BE FOUND WELL INTO JUNE!
THERE IS A COMPLEX RELATIONSHIP BETWEEN SHADE, SNOWFALL, SHOVELLING TECHNIQUE, SIZE OF PARKING LOT, AS WELL AS MANY OTHER FACTORS WHICH CAN THROW OFF THE MELTING SCHEDULE!
IN WASHINGTON AND ALASKA, MANY TOWNS HAVE YEAR-ROUND PILES!
"MINNIE'S SNOWPILE DIRECTORY" REPORTS ON PILES IN SEVERAL PRIME LOCATIONS IN WASHINGTON STATE, AND LAS VEGAS BOOKIES ALLOW WAGERING ON WHICH LAST THE LONGEST!
BUT THESE DAYS, PILE WATCHER ARE SAYING MANY YEAR-ROUNDERS ARE SHRINKING...
LB

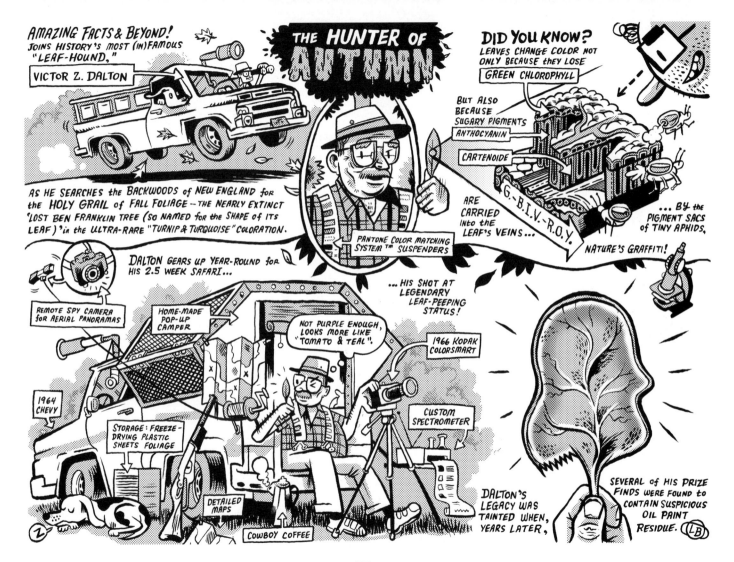

AMAZING FACTS & BEYOND! JOINS HISTORY'S MOST (IN)FAMOUS "LEAF-HOUND,"

VICTOR Z. DALTON

THE HUNTER OF AUTUMN

DID YOU KNOW? LEAVES CHANGE COLOR NOT ONLY BECAUSE THEY LOSE

GREEN CHLOROPHYLL

BUT ALSO BECAUSE SUGARY PIGMENTS

ANTHOCYANIN

CARTENOIDE

ARE CARRIED INTO THE LEAF'S VEINS...

G·B·I·V·R·O·Y·

... BY THE PIGMENT SACS OF TINY APHIDS,

NATURE'S GRAFFITI!

AS HE SEARCHES THE BACKWOODS OF NEW ENGLAND FOR THE HOLY GRAIL OF FALL FOLIAGE -- THE NEARLY EXTINCT 'LOST BEN FRANKLIN TREE (SO NAMED FOR THE SHAPE OF ITS LEAF)' IN THE ULTRA-RARE "TURNIP & TURQUOISE" COLORATION.

PANTONE COLOR MATCHING SYSTEM ™ SUSPENDERS

DALTON GEARS UP YEAR-ROUND FOR HIS 2.5 WEEK SAFARI...

REMOTE SPY CAMERA FOR AERIAL PANORAMAS

HOME-MADE POP-UP CAMPER

... HIS SHOT AT LEGENDARY LEAF-PEEPING STATUS!

NOT PURPLE ENOUGH, LOOKS MORE LIKE "TOMATO & TEAL".

1966 KODAK COLORSMART

1964 CHEVY

STORAGE: FREEZE-DRYING PLASTIC SHEETS FOLIAGE

CUSTOM SPECTROMETER

DETAILED MAPS

COWBOY COFFEE

DALTON'S LEGACY WAS TAINTED WHEN, YEARS LATER,

SEVERAL OF HIS PRIZE FINDS WERE FOUND TO CONTAIN SUSPICIOUS OIL PAINT RESIDUE.

LB

207

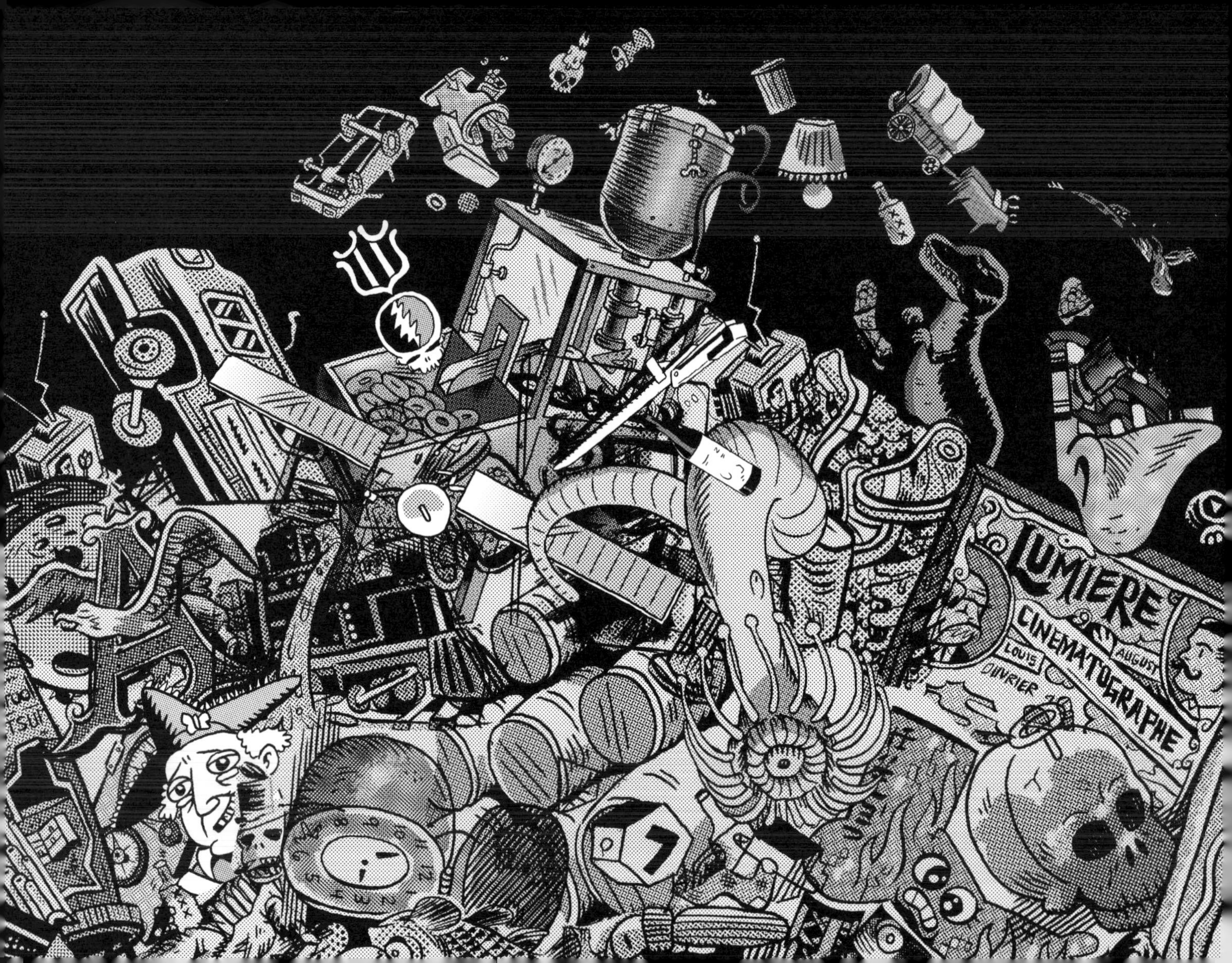
LUMIERE
CINEMATOGRAPHE
LOUIS
AUGUST
OUVRIER

3D/ SCRATCH *'n'* SNIFF

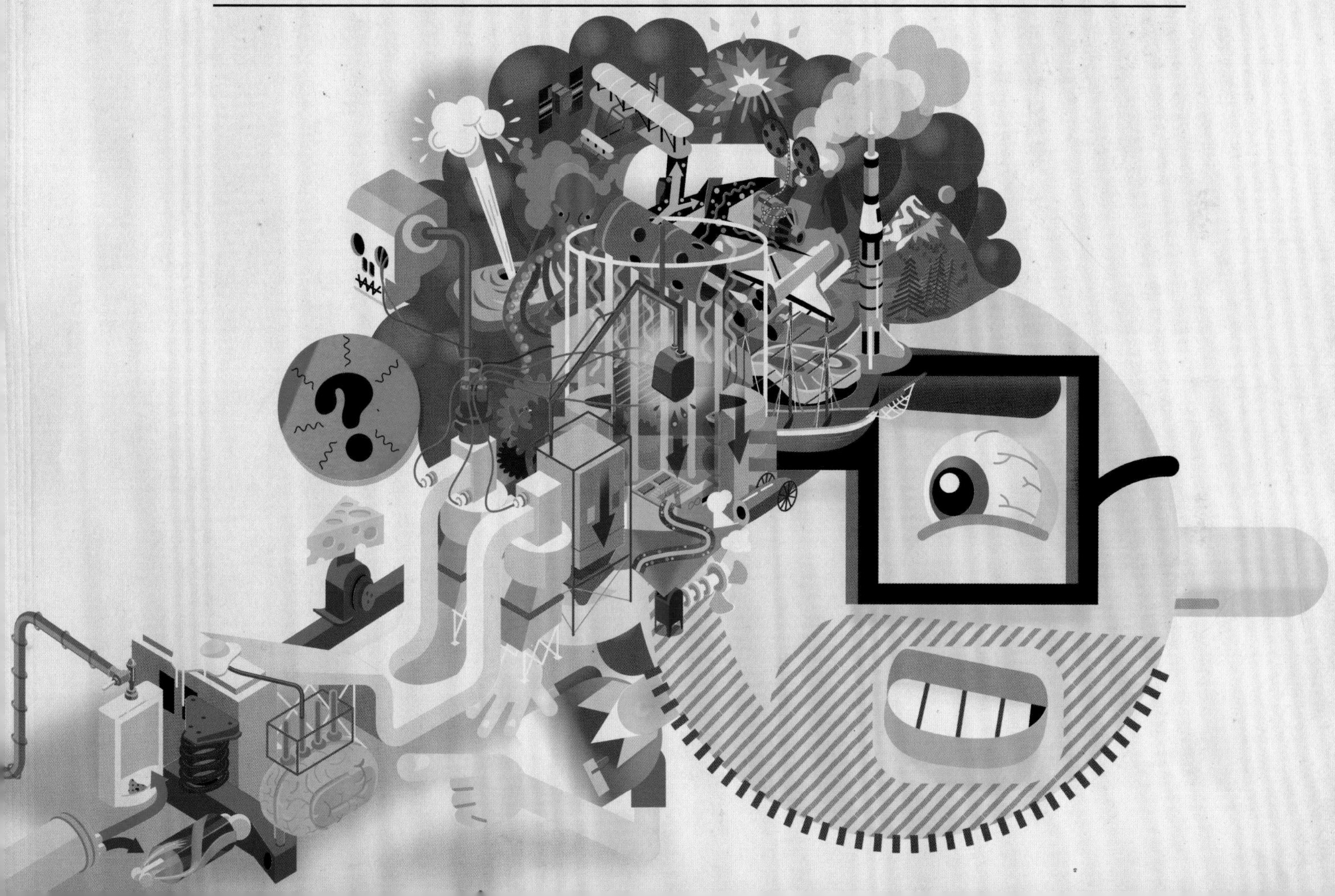

Appendix I: COVER GALLERY

Selected covers from previous collections

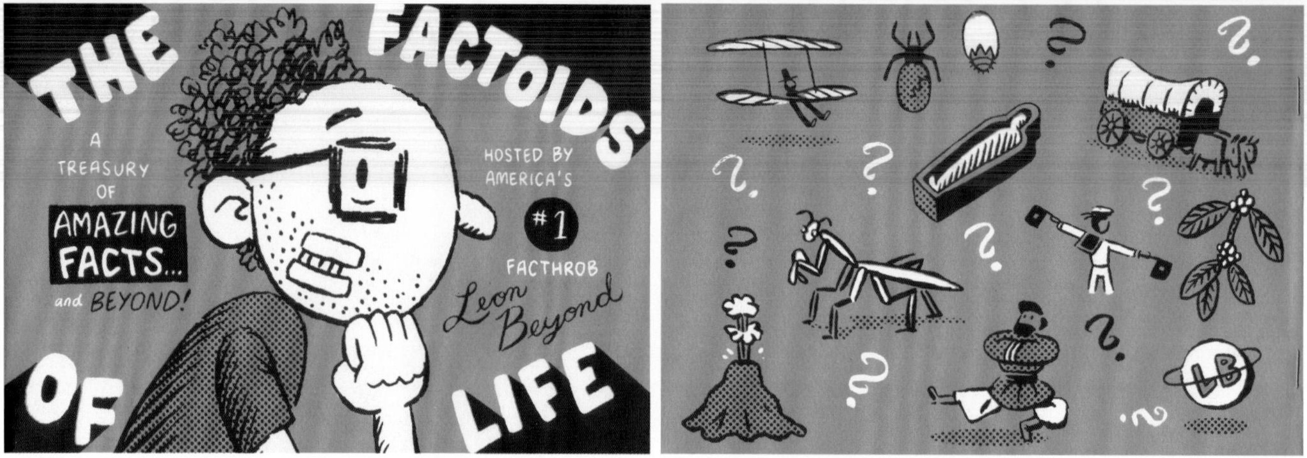
THE FACTOIDS OF LIFE
A TREASURY OF
AMAZING FACTS...
and BEYOND!
HOSTED BY AMERICA'S
#1
FACTHROB
Leon Beyond
LB

2008

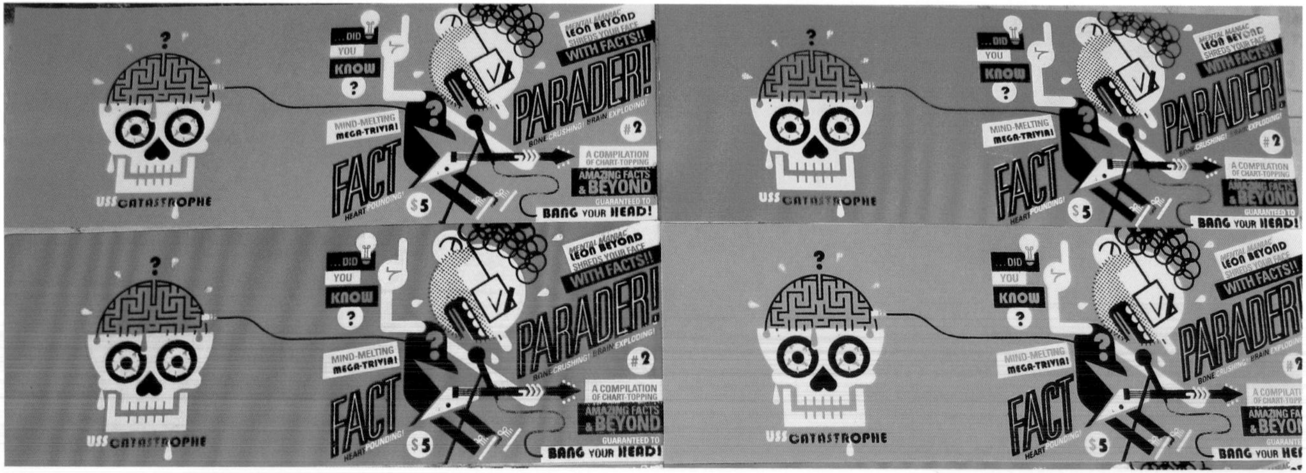
...DID YOU KNOW ?
MENTAL MANIAC LEON BEYOND SHREDS YOUR FACE WITH FACTS!!
PARADER!
BONE CRUSHING! BRAIN EXPLODING!
#2
MIND-MELTING MEGA-TRIVIA!
FACT
HEART POUNDING!
A COMPILATION OF CHART-TOPPING
AMAZING FACTS & BEYOND
GUARANTEED TO
BANG YOUR HEAD!
$5
USS CATASTROPHE

2009

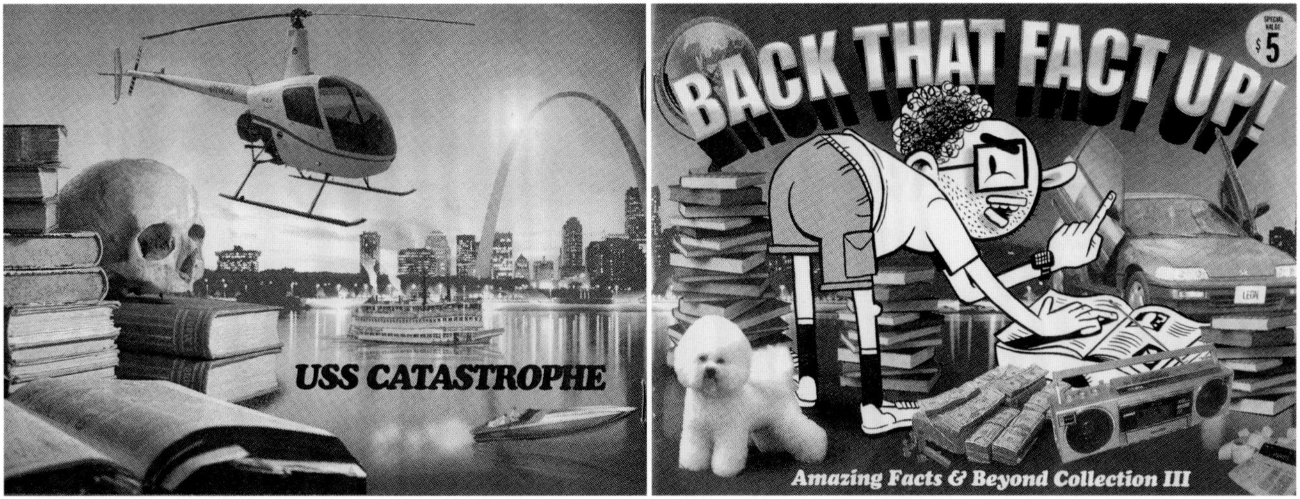
USS CATASTROPHE
BACK THAT FACT UP!
$5
LEON
Amazing Facts & Beyond Collection III

2010

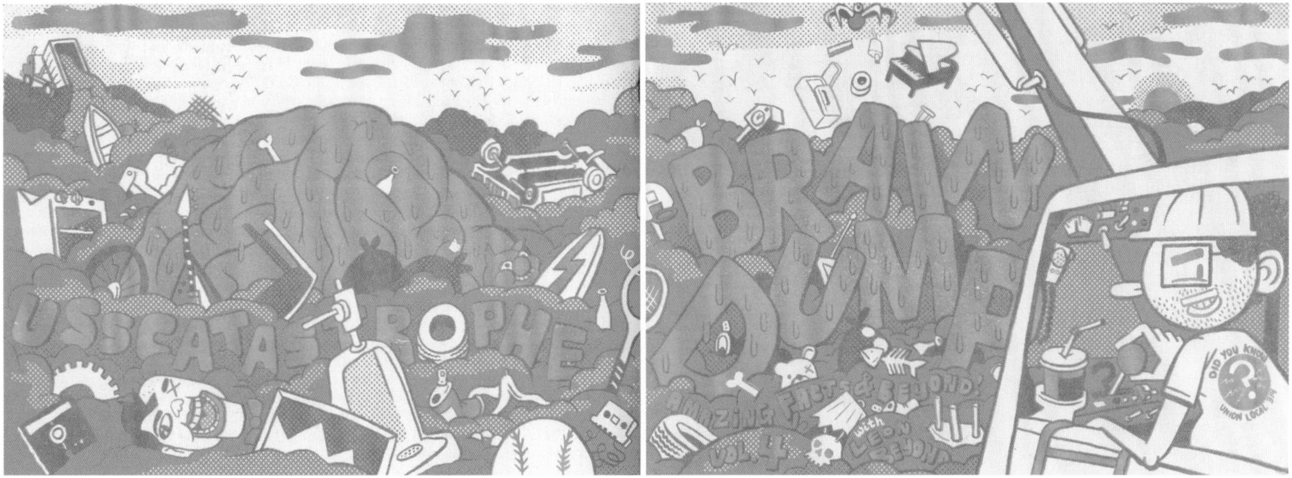
USS CATASTROPHE
BRAIN DUMP

2011

FACTUAL
HEALING
with Leon Beyond

THE LATEST
COLLECTION OF
AMAZING FACTS
&
BEYOND!
with LEON BEYOND
&
with
DAN ZETTWOCH
&
KEVIN H

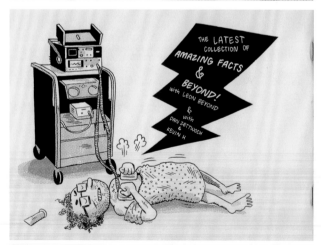

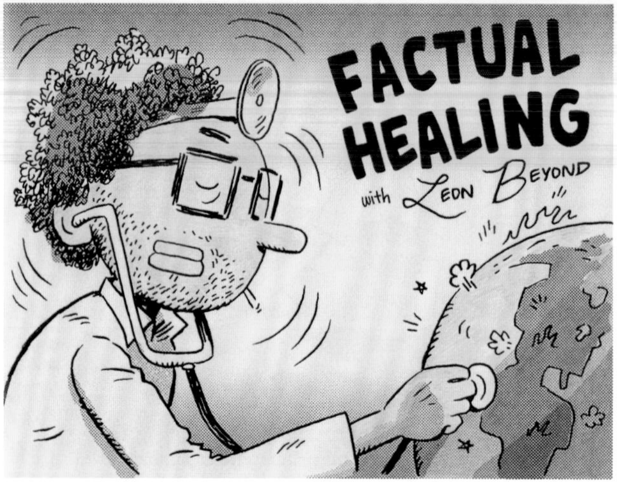

2011

Appendix II

Order of strips in which they were drawn.

Breaking Up • Car Battery Punx • Origins of H-O-R-S-E • Reflections • Leon Mnemonic • How to Beat the (Digestive) System • Writer's Block • Bible Fu • Trivia Landscape • The Perfect Shave • Cat Calendars • Cell Phones • High Spirits • Lleon • The Secret History of Dogs as Weapons • The Leon Tapes • Museum of Lightly Used Ab' Equipment • The Second Speediest Reader • Fully Looping Waterslide • On Vacation • The Other White Meat • Some Advanced Trivia • The Lying Dead • Anthropo-Romantic Polygons in Early 20th Century Newspaper Strips • Ultimate Trivia Tailgating Tips and Tricks • The Word of God • Star Clipper 20th Anniversary • Gigant-O-Lantern • Off to the Races • Cloud-Plex • Bed Bugs and Beyond • Midwestern Origins of Thanksgiving • The Tree Tomb of Hildeburg, Mississippi • Holiday Hot-Tubbin' • Pot Pourri (Smells Pleasant) • Field Sobriety • No Laughing Matter • History of the Heavy Metal Logo • Department of Hypnomenunosis • A Trivial Crisis part 1 • A Trivial Crisis part 2 • A Trivial Crisis part 3 • Vice Presidential Debate Tactics • Pods, Casts, & Kindling • All-Star Shufflin' Crew • Tux Time • Weapons of Glass Dunk-struction • The Benld Meteorite • Duel of the Fowl Ballers • DIY / Symmetry of the Universe • Red Dragon Mosquito • Pinot Beyond • Lawnscaping: Clips 'n Tricks • Partial Manifest of Traditional Pie-Habitants • Communications / Birdwatching / Volleyball • The Jolly FloatBoatMen • '09 Fall Fashion • Glow in the Dark • Lost Loves of Teenaged Fast Food Tycoons • Hearts Afire • Museum of Leftover Masterpieces • Number of the Beast • The Hunter of Autumn • The Art of Memory • All Souls' Day, 1832 • Temple Troubles • Dogzigners! • Facteroids • Great Green Gobs of Greasy Grimy Gopher Guts • Face Facts • Fine Print • The War on Xmas • Xmas $avings • Falling on New Year's • Pick Out a Good One • How I got My SWAGger Back • Glasses Menagerie • Secret History of Coffeenalia • Boogers • One Day at a Time • Leon Sneezes • Thermo-Secrets of the Sign-Twirlers • Poetry With Legs • History of Pole Dancing • National Bubble Week • The Birds 'n' the Bats • The Rise & Fall of Parking Lot Snow Piles • Digs Through your Junk Drawers • Pot Pourri (Kraft Kountry) • Picking the Kentucky Derby Winner • Curio of Chainsaws • Busy Week • Gets Cute! • Poffo's Hat • Near Perfect • The Silent Living Dead • Heat Wave • Facts About Skulls • Spot the 24 Differences • Guess the Shape • The Great Poyang Pool of Pecos County • International Doodle Week • Animals and the (Modern) Art World • The 66 Year Stink • -City Under Stench • -An Expert is Hired • -Overground Hideouts • -Can't Stop the Flow of Trivia • -How Your Brain Smells • -The Smell of Our Fathers • -Party Cave • -The Veiled Prophet • -Blowin's in the Wind • -The Game's Afoot • -The Greatest Show on Turf • -And Then Suddenly, • Ping Pong by the Numbers • On Vacation Again • Beards of Beasts • The Donut Machine Explosion Ring Toss • The Bill-Fold Index • The Spiral Memory Game • Feng Shui for the Brain • Organ Donor Hall of Fame • STL GPS Disc Golf • Saratoga Lanes • San Francisco • Cavalcade of Christmas Creeps • The Facts I Hate • Three Rain-Related Amazing Facts Off the Top of My Head • Top 10 Dogventions of 2010 • Maple Treevia • Gift Guide 2010 • Rugs to Riches! Kentucky's Most Coveted Carpets • The Nose Knows • Blowin' Smoke • In a Ken Burns Doc • The Labyrinth of Argyll • Statue of Liberty Replicas • The SLOBBER VII • Ceramic Figurine Fact-Finding Mission • Know When to Fold-In • Volcano Graffiti • The Great Blue Streak of Trail County, North Dakota • Dispatches from the Lunatic Fringe • In Search of Opening Day Jitters! • -Baseball's Most $#@% Manager • -More Prime Cards • The Tree Vaporizer • Get Factivated! • Gentoos • Weathering the Storm: The World's Most Perilous Porch Swings • Wealthy Eccentrics Mourn • Stickiest Situations • Handwriting Your Way to a Brand New You • The Ultimate Branson Show • Mysteries of Modern Genetics • The Fuging Tune of the Magic Cicada • Beercan Jackpot • Some Feats • The Satanic Origins of B-L-Z-B-B-Q • Viewer Mail • Lexicon of Rare Diamond Slang • Fact Camp • Back to School • International Doodle Week II • Field Guide to Fried Eggs • Pagonoiyish • Curl Up and Die • Can't Decide on a Topic • Rally Cap, Theory & Praxis • The Greasepaühlts • The Fallen Egglord Family Tree • Turkey Talk • Tongue Diagnosis • Seeing Red • Weird Leaf Roundup • Faces and Names • 2011 World Gift Wrapping Championships • Top Typos 20011 • Top 10 TOP TEN Lists of 2011 • Diversion Safes • Golden Arches • Video Game Tips & Tricks • Packin' Heat • Haul Review Screencast Autosummaries • Chilivia Cook-Off • Home & Garden Kit-tacular • Know Your Nebulas • Self-Harmonizing • Another Day, Another Box • World Record Weed • On the Road to MEGA-MILLION$ • Spring (Fact) Cleaning • Some Additions to My Jellyfish Life List • Amazing Hats & Beyond • Get Togethers • Move Your Feet • Pickled Pocket$ • Something to Admit • Topic: Optics

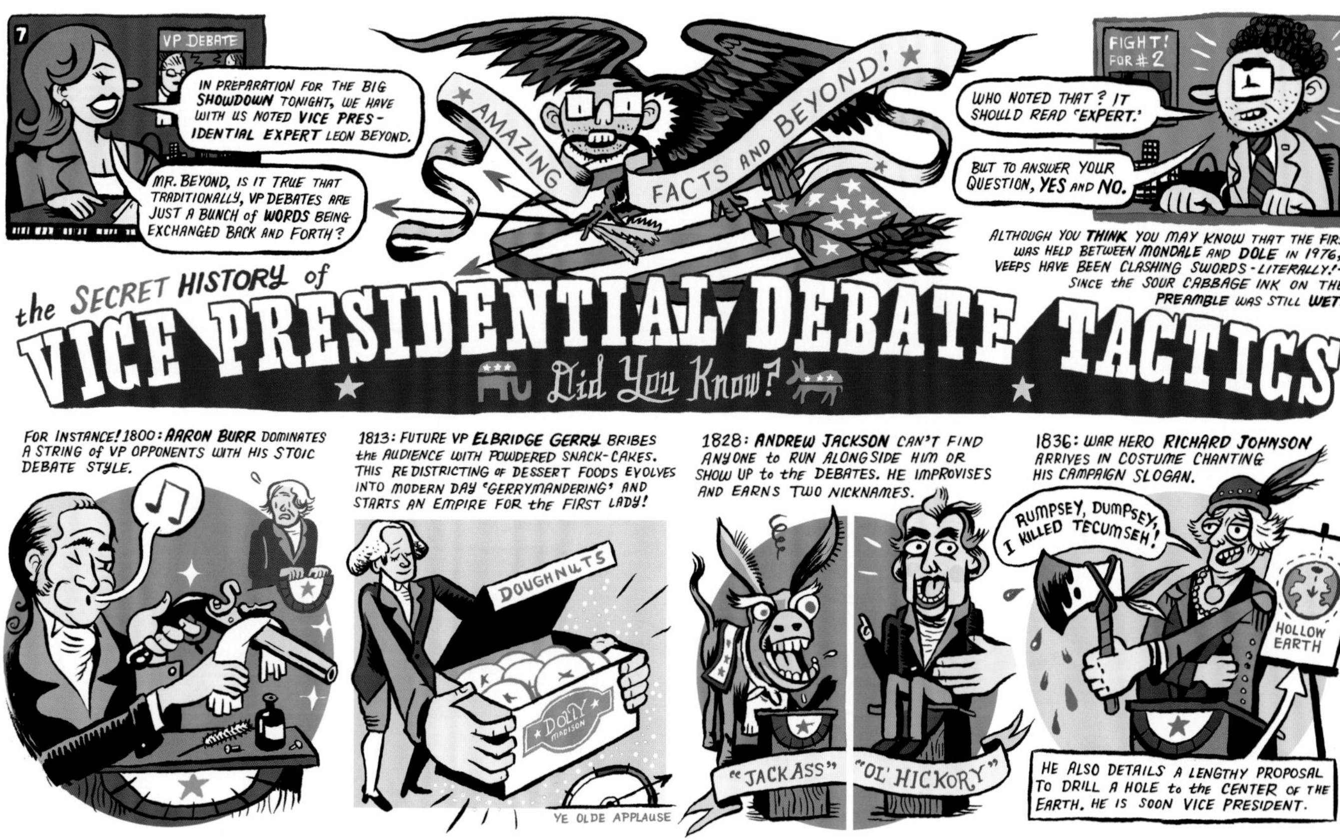
7
VP DEBATE
IN PREPARATION FOR THE BIG SHOWDOWN TONIGHT, WE HAVE WITH US NOTED VICE PRESIDENTIAL EXPERT LEON BEYOND.
MR. BEYOND, IS IT TRUE THAT TRADITIONALLY, VP DEBATES ARE JUST A BUNCH of WORDS BEING EXCHANGED BACK AND FORTH?
AMAZING FACTS AND BEYOND!
FIGHT! FOR #2
WHO NOTED THAT? IT SHOULD READ 'EXPERT.'
BUT TO ANSWER YOUR QUESTION, YES AND NO.
ALTHOUGH YOU THINK YOU MAY KNOW THAT THE FIRST WAS HELD BETWEEN MONDALE AND DOLE IN 1976, VEEPS HAVE BEEN CLASHING SWORDS - LITERALLY! - SINCE the SOUR CABBAGE INK ON THE PREAMBLE WAS STILL WET!
the SECRET HISTORY of VICE PRESIDENTIAL DEBATE TACTICS
Did You Know?
FOR INSTANCE! 1800: AARON BURR DOMINATES A STRING of VP OPPONENTS WITH HIS STOIC DEBATE STYLE.
1813: FUTURE VP ELBRIDGE GERRY BRIBES the AUDIENCE WITH POWDERED SNACK-CAKES. THIS REDISTRICTING of DESSERT FOODS EVOLVES INTO MODERN DAY 'GERRYMANDERING' AND STARTS AN EMPIRE FOR the FIRST LADY!
DOUGHNUTS
DOLLY MADISON
YE OLDE APPLAUSE
1828: ANDREW JACKSON CAN'T FIND ANYONE to RUN ALONGSIDE HIM OR SHOW UP to the DEBATES. HE IMPROVISES AND EARNS TWO NICKNAMES.
"JACKASS"
"OL' HICKORY"
1836: WAR HERO RICHARD JOHNSON ARRIVES IN COSTUME CHANTING HIS CAMPAIGN SLOGAN.
RUMPSEY, DUMPSEY, I KILLED TECUMSEH!
HOLLOW EARTH
HE ALSO DETAILS A LENGTHY PROPOSAL TO DRILL A HOLE to the CENTER of the EARTH. HE IS SOON VICE PRESIDENT.

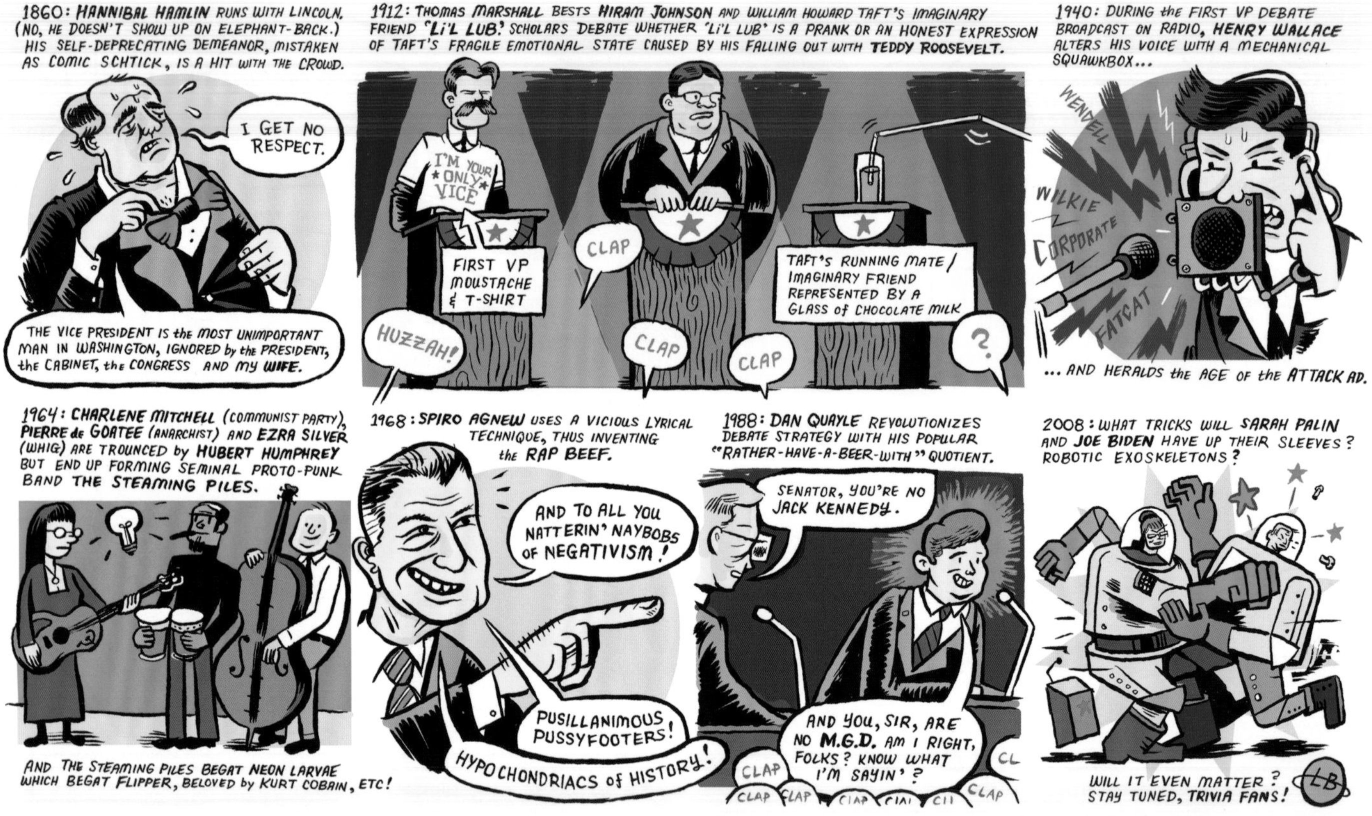
1860: HANNIBAL HAMLIN RUNS WITH LINCOLN. (NO, HE DOESN'T SHOW UP ON ELEPHANT-BACK.) HIS SELF-DEPRECATING DEMEANOR, MISTAKEN AS COMIC SCHTICK, IS A HIT WITH THE CROWD.
I GET NO RESPECT.
THE VICE PRESIDENT IS the MOST UNIMPORTANT MAN IN WASHINGTON, IGNORED by the PRESIDENT, the CABINET, the CONGRESS AND MY WIFE.
1912: THOMAS MARSHALL BESTS HIRAM JOHNSON AND WILLIAM HOWARD TAFT'S IMAGINARY FRIEND 'LI'L LUB.' SCHOLARS DEBATE WHETHER 'LI'L LUB' IS A PRANK OR AN HONEST EXPRESSION OF TAFT'S FRAGILE EMOTIONAL STATE CAUSED BY HIS FALLING OUT WITH TEDDY ROOSEVELT.
I'M YOUR ONLY VICE
FIRST VP MOUSTACHE & T-SHIRT
CLAP
TAFT'S RUNNING MATE / IMAGINARY FRIEND REPRESENTED BY A GLASS of CHOCOLATE MILK
HUZZAH!
CLAP
CLAP
?
1940: DURING the FIRST VP DEBATE BROADCAST ON RADIO, HENRY WALLACE ALTERS HIS VOICE WITH A MECHANICAL SQUAWKBOX...
WENDELL
WILKIE
CORPORATE
FATCAT
... AND HERALDS the AGE OF the ATTACK AD.
1964: CHARLENE MITCHELL (COMMUNIST PARTY), PIERRE de GOATEE (ANARCHIST) AND EZRA SILVER (WHIG) ARE TROUNCED by HUBERT HUMPHREY BUT END UP FORMING SEMINAL PROTO-PUNK BAND THE STEAMING PILES.
AND THE STEAMING PILES BEGAT NEON LARVAE WHICH BEGAT FLIPPER, BELOVED by KURT COBAIN, ETC!
1968: SPIRO AGNEW USES A VICIOUS LYRICAL TECHNIQUE, THUS INVENTING the RAP BEEF.
AND TO ALL YOU NATTERIN' NAYBOBS of NEGATIVISM!
PUSILLANIMOUS PUSSYFOOTERS!
HYPOCHONDRIACS of HISTORY!
1988: DAN QUAYLE REVOLUTIONIZES DEBATE STRATEGY WITH HIS POPULAR "RATHER-HAVE-A-BEER-WITH" QUOTIENT.
SENATOR, YOU'RE NO JACK KENNEDY.
AND YOU, SIR, ARE NO M.G.D. AM I RIGHT, FOLKS? KNOW WHAT I'M SAYIN'?
CLAP
CLAP
CLAP
CLAP
2008: WHAT TRICKS WILL SARAH PALIN AND JOE BIDEN HAVE UP THEIR SLEEVES? ROBOTIC EXOSKELETONS?
WILL IT EVEN MATTER? STAY TUNED, TRIVIA FANS!
LB

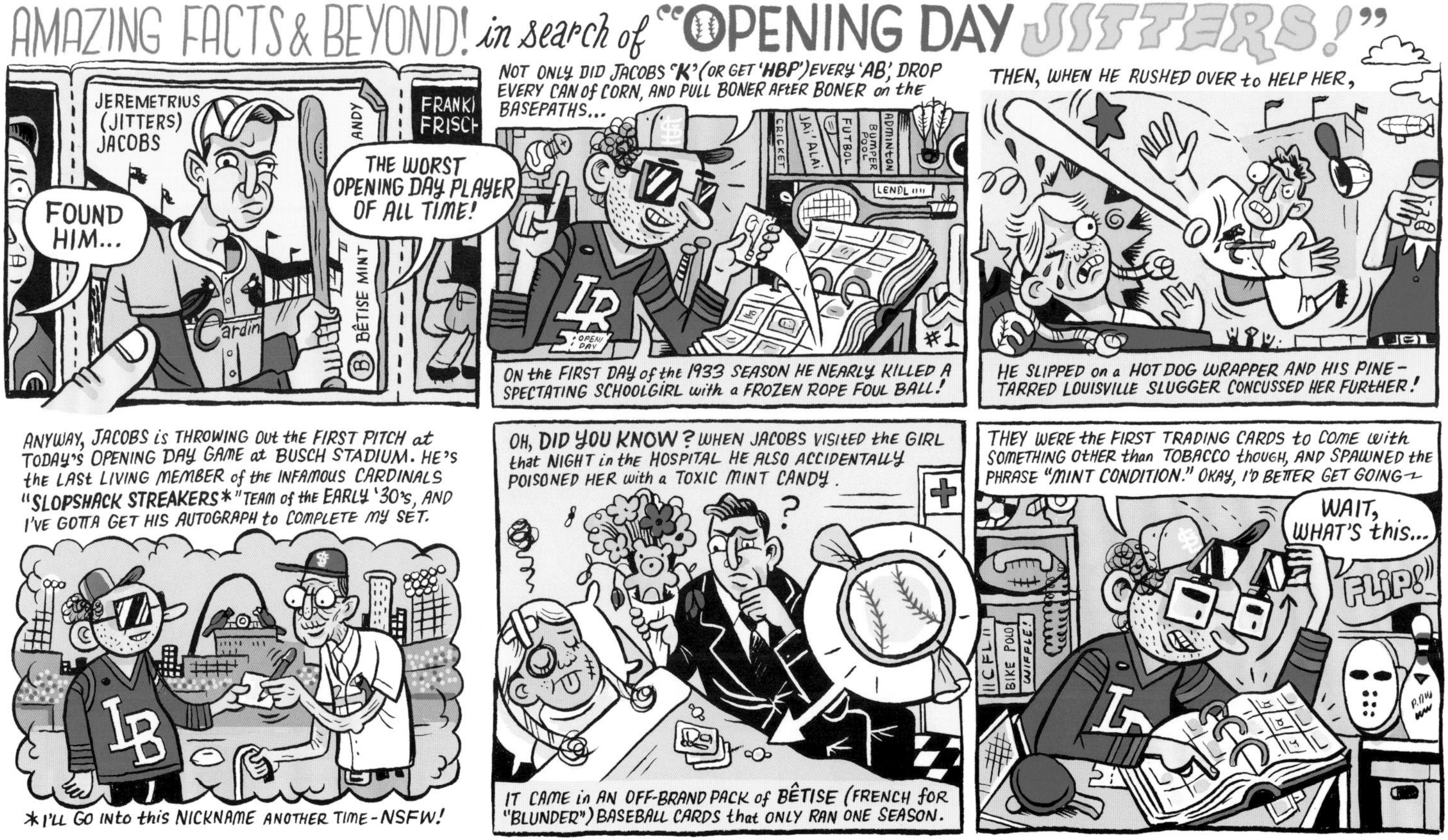
AMAZING FACTS & BEYOND! in search of "OPENING DAY JITTERS!"
JEREMETRIUS (JITTERS) JACOBS
ANDY
FRANKI FRISCH
BÊTISE MINT
FOUND HIM...
THE WORST OPENING DAY PLAYER OF ALL TIME!
NOT ONLY DID JACOBS 'K' (OR GET 'HBP') EVERY 'AB,' DROP EVERY CAN OF CORN, AND PULL BONER AFTER BONER on the BASEPATHS...
CRICKET
JAI ALAI
FUTBOL
BUMPER POOL
ADMINTON
LENDL
#1
ON the FIRST DAY of the 1933 SEASON HE NEARLY KILLED A SPECTATING SCHOOLGIRL with a FROZEN ROPE FOUL BALL!
THEN, WHEN HE RUSHED OVER to HELP HER,
HE SLIPPED on a HOT DOG WRAPPER AND HIS PINE-TARRED LOUISVILLE SLUGGER CONCUSSED HER FURTHER!
ANYWAY, JACOBS is THROWING OUT the FIRST PITCH at TODAY'S OPENING DAY GAME at BUSCH STADIUM. HE'S the LAST LIVING MEMBER of the INFAMOUS CARDINALS "SLOPSHACK STREAKERS*" TEAM of the EARLY '30's, AND I'VE GOTTA GET HIS AUTOGRAPH to COMPLETE MY SET.
*I'LL GO INTO this NICKNAME ANOTHER TIME - NSFW!
OH, DID YOU KNOW? WHEN JACOBS VISITED the GIRL that NIGHT in the HOSPITAL HE ALSO ACCIDENTALLY POISONED HER with a TOXIC MINT CANDY.
?
IT CAME in AN OFF-BRAND PACK of BÊTISE (FRENCH for "BLUNDER") BASEBALL CARDS that ONLY RAN ONE SEASON.
THEY WERE the FIRST TRADING CARDS to COME with SOMETHING OTHER than TOBACCO though, AND SPAWNED the PHRASE "MINT CONDITION." OKAY, I'D BETTER GET GOING-
WAIT, WHAT'S this...
FLIP!
CFL
BIKE POLO
WIFFLE

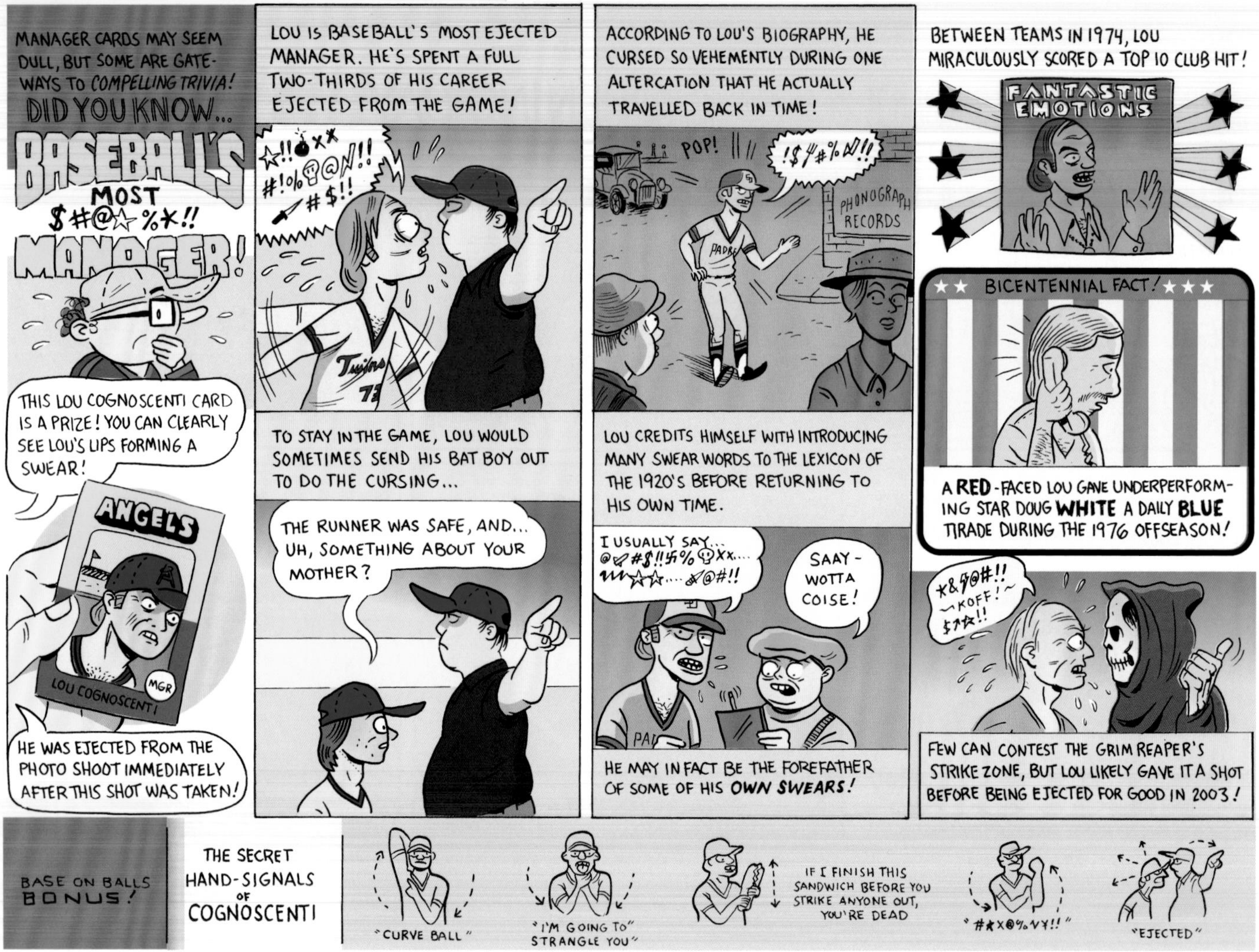
MANAGER CARDS MAY SEEM DULL, BUT SOME ARE GATE-WAYS TO COMPELLING TRIVIA! DID YOU KNOW...
BASEBALL'S MOST $#@☆%*!! MANAGER!
THIS LOU COGNOSCENTI CARD IS A PRIZE! YOU CAN CLEARLY SEE LOU'S LIPS FORMING A SWEAR!
ANGELS
LOU COGNOSCENTI
MGR
HE WAS EJECTED FROM THE PHOTO SHOOT IMMEDIATELY AFTER THIS SHOT WAS TAKEN!
LOU IS BASEBALL'S MOST EJECTED MANAGER. HE'S SPENT A FULL TWO-THIRDS OF HIS CAREER EJECTED FROM THE GAME!
Twins
TO STAY IN THE GAME, LOU WOULD SOMETIMES SEND HIS BAT BOY OUT TO DO THE CURSING...
THE RUNNER WAS SAFE, AND... UH, SOMETHING ABOUT YOUR MOTHER?
ACCORDING TO LOU'S BIOGRAPHY, HE CURSED SO VEHEMENTLY DURING ONE ALTERCATION THAT HE ACTUALLY TRAVELLED BACK IN TIME!
POP!
PHONOGRAPH RECORDS
PADRES
LOU CREDITS HIMSELF WITH INTRODUCING MANY SWEAR WORDS TO THE LEXICON OF THE 1920'S BEFORE RETURNING TO HIS OWN TIME.
I USUALLY SAY...
SAAY - WOTTA COISE!
HE MAY IN FACT BE THE FOREFATHER OF SOME OF HIS OWN SWEARS!
BETWEEN TEAMS IN 1974, LOU MIRACULOUSLY SCORED A TOP 10 CLUB HIT!
FANTASTIC EMOTIONS
BICENTENNIAL FACT!
A RED-FACED LOU GAVE UNDERPERFORMING STAR DOUG WHITE A DAILY BLUE TIRADE DURING THE 1976 OFFSEASON!
~KOFF!~
FEW CAN CONTEST THE GRIM REAPER'S STRIKE ZONE, BUT LOU LIKELY GAVE IT A SHOT BEFORE BEING EJECTED FOR GOOD IN 2003!
BASE ON BALLS BONUS!
THE SECRET HAND-SIGNALS OF COGNOSCENTI
"CURVE BALL"
"I'M GOING TO" STRANGLE YOU"
IF I FINISH THIS SANDWICH BEFORE YOU STRIKE ANYONE OUT, YOU'RE DEAD
"EJECTED"

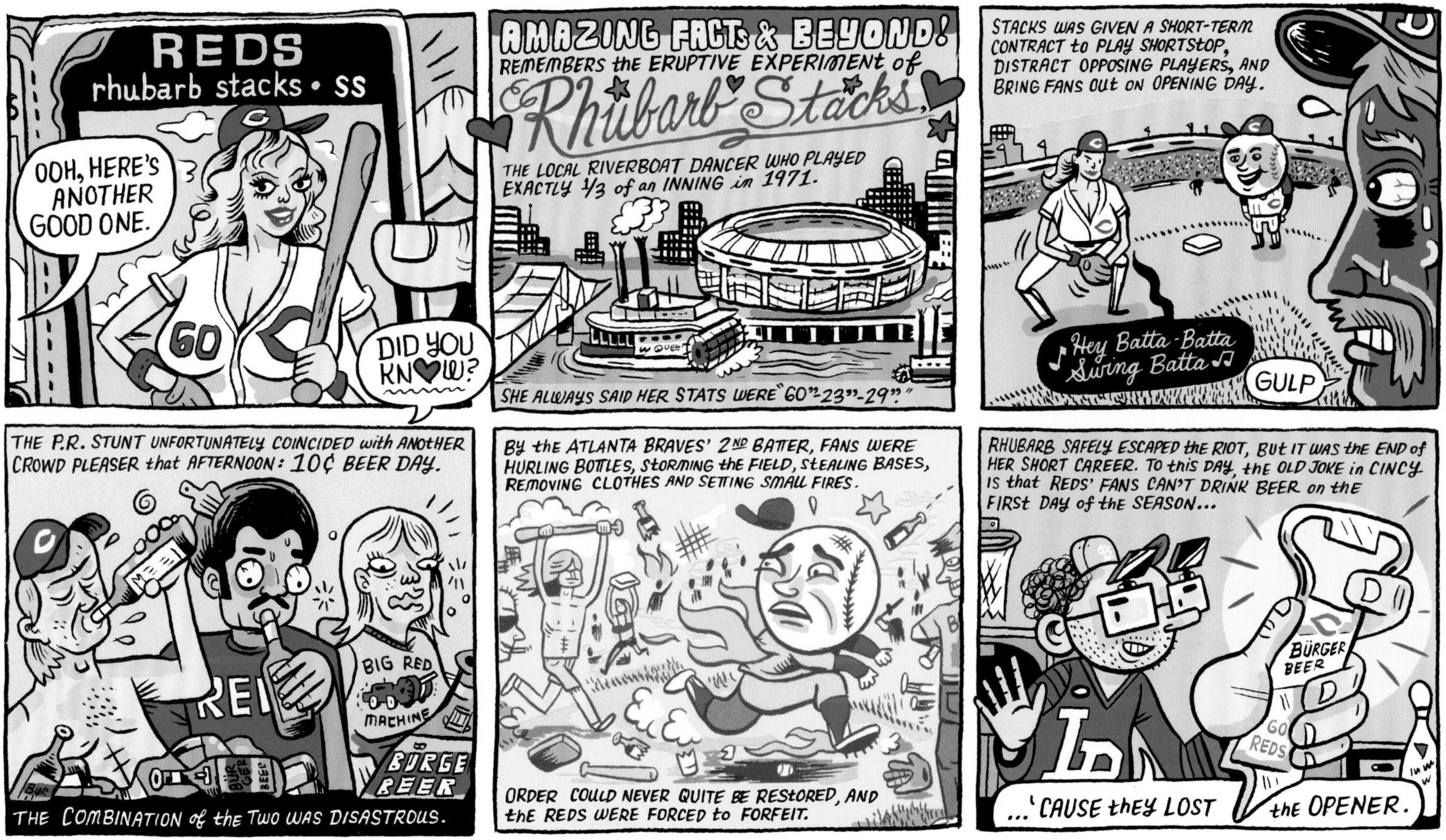
REDS
rhubarb stacks • ss
OOH, HERE'S ANOTHER GOOD ONE.
60
DID YOU KNOW?
AMAZING FACTS & BEYOND!
REMEMBERS the ERUPTIVE EXPERIMENT of
Rhubarb Stacks,
THE LOCAL RIVERBOAT DANCER WHO PLAYED EXACTLY 1/3 of an INNING in 1971.
SHE ALWAYS SAID HER STATS WERE "60"-23"-29"."
STACKS WAS GIVEN A SHORT-TERM CONTRACT to PLAY SHORTSTOP, DISTRACT OPPOSING PLAYERS, AND BRING FANS OUT ON OPENING DAY.
♪ Hey Batta-Batta Swing Batta ♫
GULP
THE P.R. STUNT UNFORTUNATELY COINCIDED with ANOTHER CROWD PLEASER that AFTERNOON: 10¢ BEER DAY.
BIG RED MACHINE
BÜRGER BEER
THE COMBINATION of the TWO WAS DISASTROUS.
By the ATLANTA BRAVES' 2ND BATTER, FANS WERE HURLING BOTTLES, STORMING the FIELD, STEALING BASES, REMOVING CLOTHES AND SETTING SMALL FIRES.
ORDER COULD NEVER QUITE BE RESTORED, AND the REDS WERE FORCED to FORFEIT.
RHUBARB SAFELY ESCAPED the RIOT, But IT WAS the END of HER SHORT CAREER. To this DAY, the OLD JOKE in CINCY IS that REDS' FANS CAN'T DRINK BEER on the FIRST DAY of the SEASON...
BÜRGER BEER
GO REDS
...'CAUSE they LOST the OPENER.

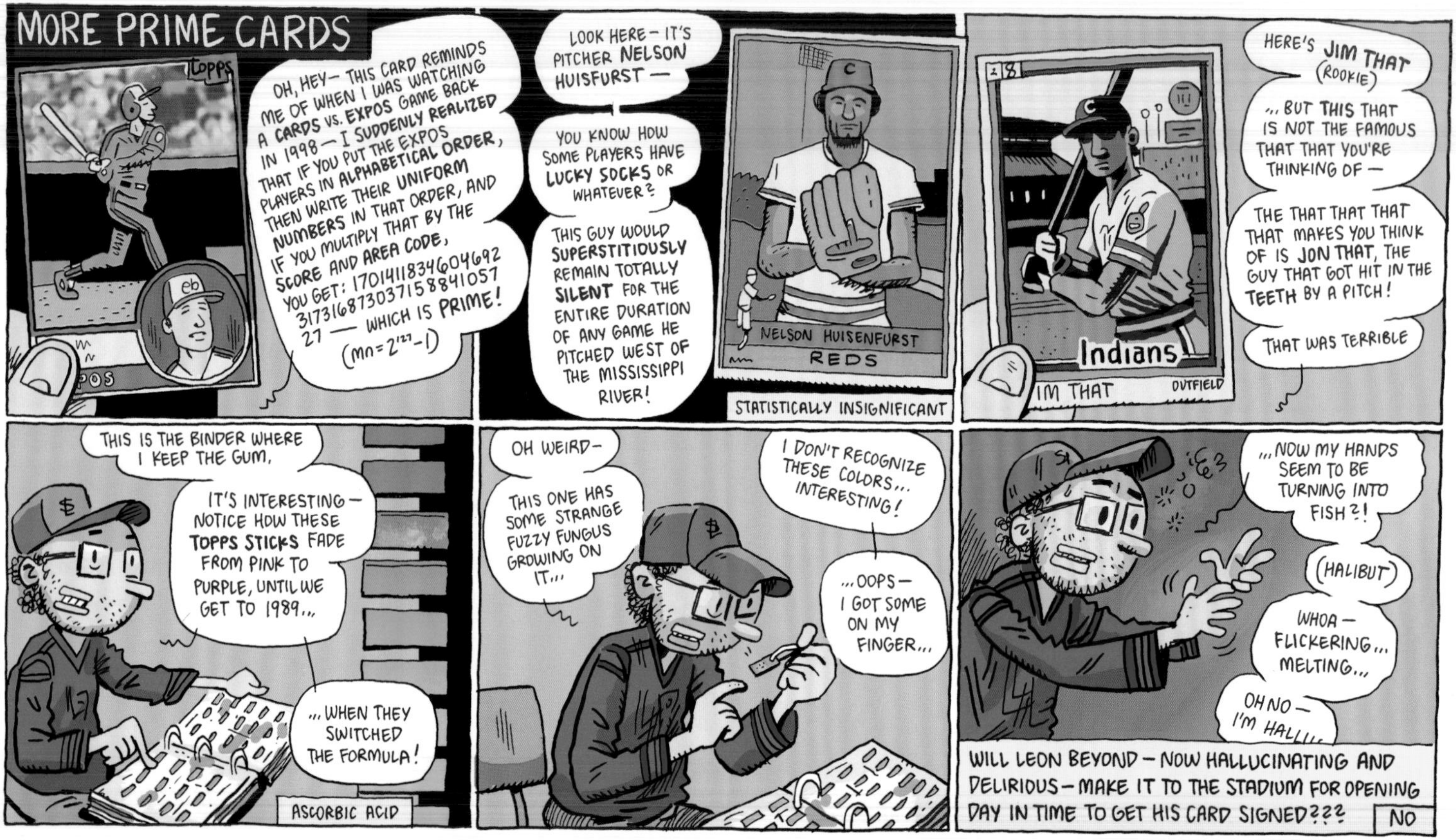
MORE PRIME CARDS
TOPPS
OH, HEY— THIS CARD REMINDS ME OF WHEN I WAS WATCHING A CARDS VS. EXPOS GAME BACK IN 1998 — I SUDDENLY REALIZED THAT IF YOU PUT THE EXPOS PLAYERS IN ALPHABETICAL ORDER, THEN WRITE THEIR UNIFORM NUMBERS IN THAT ORDER, AND IF YOU MULTIPLY THAT BY THE SCORE AND AREA CODE, YOU GET: 170141183460469231731687303715884105727 — WHICH IS PRIME!
(Mn=2^127-1)
LOOK HERE — IT'S PITCHER NELSON HUISFURST —
YOU KNOW HOW SOME PLAYERS HAVE LUCKY SOCKS OR WHATEVER?
THIS GUY WOULD SUPERSTITIOUSLY REMAIN TOTALLY SILENT FOR THE ENTIRE DURATION OF ANY GAME HE PITCHED WEST OF THE MISSISSIPPI RIVER!
NELSON HUISENFURST
REDS
STATISTICALLY INSIGNIFICANT
HERE'S JIM THAT (ROOKIE)
... BUT THIS THAT IS NOT THE FAMOUS THAT THAT YOU'RE THINKING OF —
THE THAT THAT THAT THAT MAKES YOU THINK OF IS JON THAT, THE GUY THAT GOT HIT IN THE TEETH BY A PITCH!
THAT WAS TERRIBLE
Indians
JIM THAT
OUTFIELD
THIS IS THE BINDER WHERE I KEEP THE GUM.
IT'S INTERESTING — NOTICE HOW THESE TOPPS STICKS FADE FROM PINK TO PURPLE, UNTIL WE GET TO 1989...
... WHEN THEY SWITCHED THE FORMULA!
ASCORBIC ACID
OH WEIRD —
THIS ONE HAS SOME STRANGE FUZZY FUNGUS GROWING ON IT...
I DON'T RECOGNIZE THESE COLORS... INTERESTING!
... OOPS — I GOT SOME ON MY FINGER...
... NOW MY HANDS SEEM TO BE TURNING INTO FISH?!
(HALIBUT)
WHOA — FLICKERING... MELTING...
OH NO — I'M HALL...
WILL LEON BEYOND — NOW HALLUCINATING AND DELIRIOUS — MAKE IT TO THE STADIUM FOR OPENING DAY IN TIME TO GET HIS CARD SIGNED???
NO

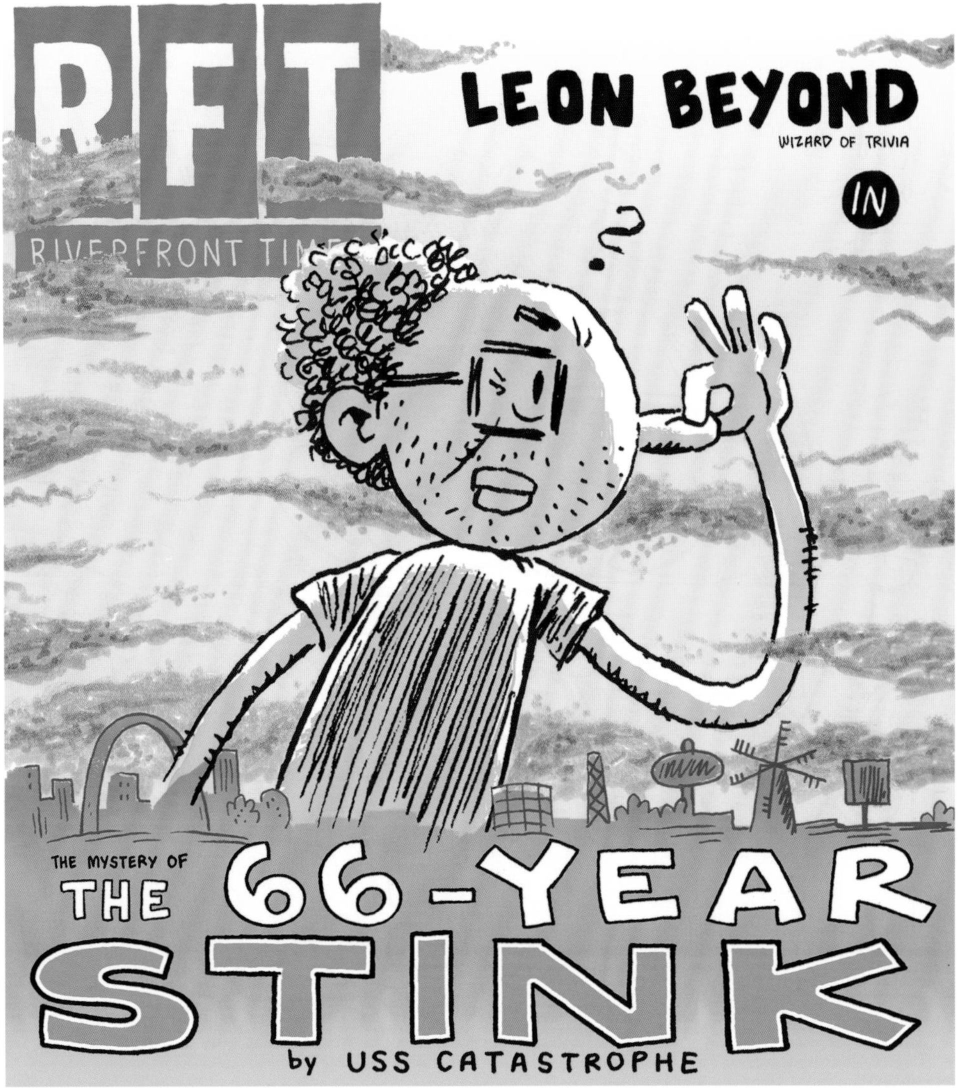
RFT
RIVERFRONT TIMES
LEON BEYOND
WIZARD OF TRIVIA
IN
THE MYSTERY OF
THE 66-YEAR
STINK
by USS CATASTROPHE

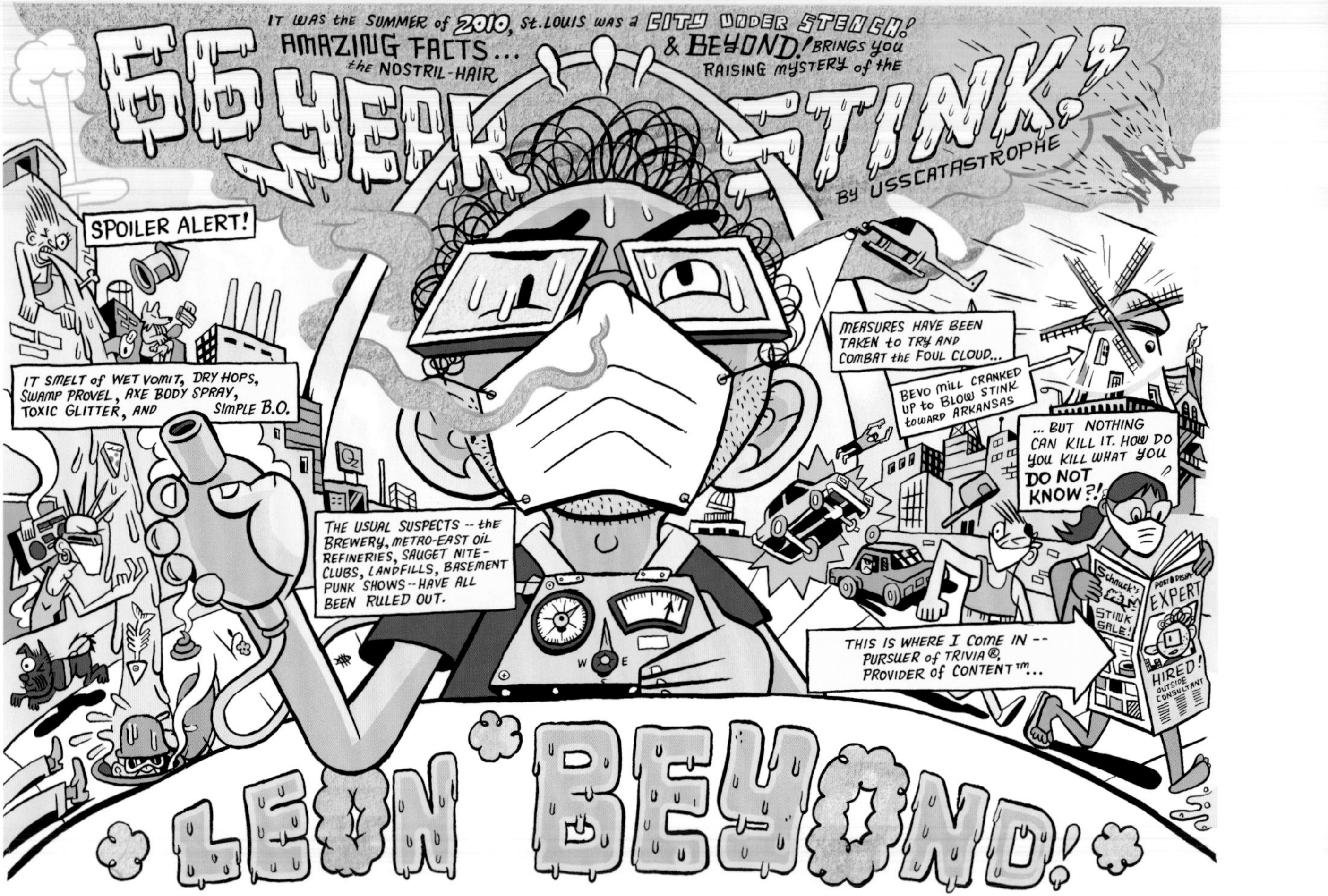
IT WAS the SUMMER of 2010, St. LOUIS WAS a CITY UNDER STENCH!
AMAZING FACTS... & BEYOND! BRINGS you the NOSTRIL-HAIR RAISING mystery of the
66 YEAR STINK!
BY USSCATASTROPHE
SPOILER ALERT!
IT SMELT of WET VOMIT, DRY HOPS, SWAMP PROVEL, AXE BODY SPRAY, TOXIC GLITTER, AND SIMPLE B.O.
THE USUAL SUSPECTS -- the BREWERY, METRO-EAST OIL REFINERIES, SAUGET NITE-CLUBS, LANDFILLS, BASEMENT PUNK SHOWS -- HAVE ALL BEEN RULED OUT.
MEASURES HAVE BEEN TAKEN to TRY AND COMBAT the FOUL CLOUD...
BEVO mill CRANKED UP to BLOW STINK toward ARKANSAS
... BUT NOTHING CAN KILL IT. HOW DO YOU KILL WHAT YOU DO NOT KNOW?!
THIS IS WHERE I COME IN -- PURSUER of TRIVIA®, PROVIDER of CONTENT™...
Schnuck's
STINK SALE!
EXPERT
HIRED! OUTSIDE CONSULTANT
W E
LEON BEYOND!

DID YOU KNOW??? *This investigative special report – inspired by real events! – ran in the Riverfront Times, Februrary 2010.*

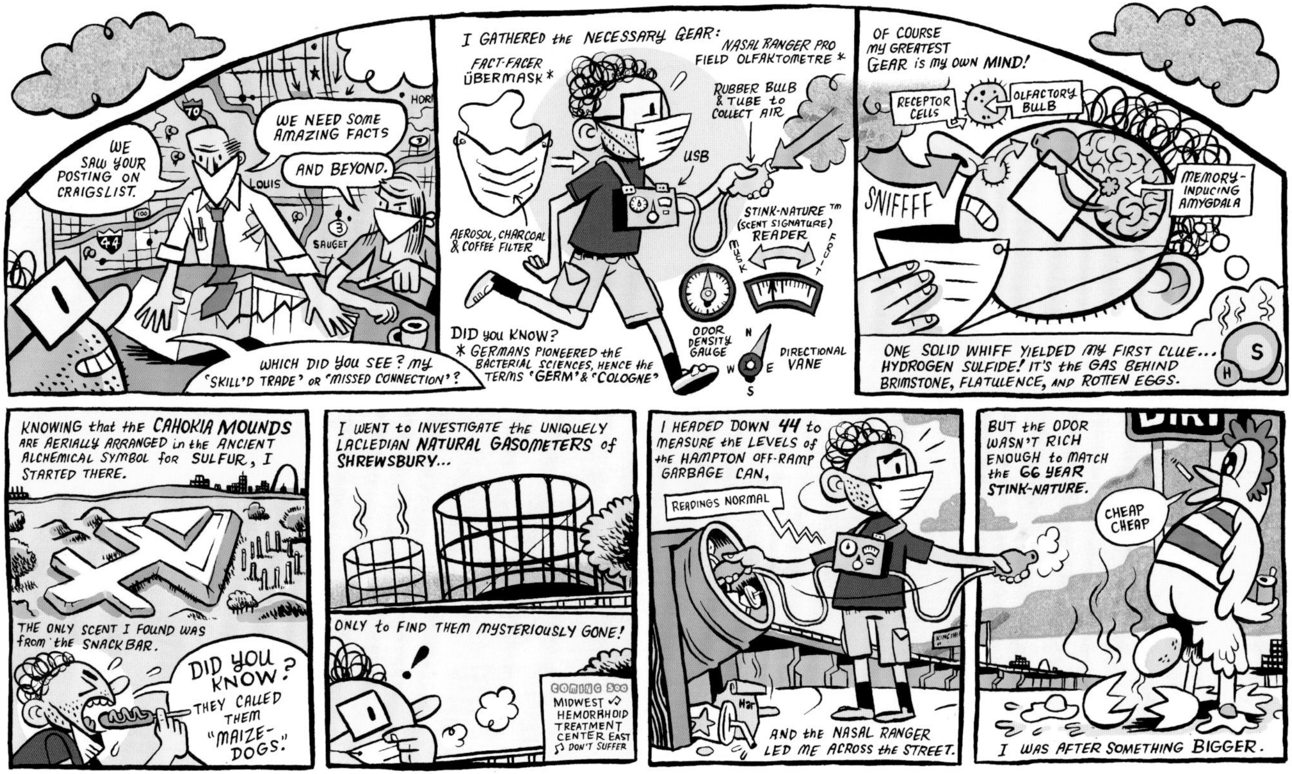
WE SAW YOUR POSTING ON CRAIGSLIST.
WE NEED SOME AMAZING FACTS
AND BEYOND.
WHICH DID YOU SEE? MY 'SKILL'D TRADE' OR 'MISSED CONNECTION'?
I GATHERED the NECESSARY GEAR:
FACT-FACER ÜBERMASK *
AEROSOL, CHARCOAL & COFFEE FILTER
NASAL RANGER PRO FIELD OLFAKTOMETRE *
RUBBER BULB & TUBE to COLLECT AIR
USB
STINK-NATURE ™ (SCENT SIGNATURE) READER
MUSK
FRUIT
ODOR DENSITY GAUGE
DIRECTIONAL VANE
DID YOU KNOW?
* GERMANS PIONEERED the BACTERIAL SCIENCES, HENCE the TERMS 'GERM' & 'COLOGNE'
OF COURSE MY GREATEST GEAR IS MY OWN MIND!
RECEPTOR CELLS
OLFACTORY BULB
MEMORY-INDUCING AMYGDALA
SNIFFFF
ONE SOLID WHIFF YIELDED MY FIRST CLUE... HYDROGEN SULFIDE! IT'S the GAS BEHIND BRIMSTONE, FLATULENCE, AND ROTTEN EGGS.
KNOWING that the CAHOKIA MOUNDS ARE AERIALLY ARRANGED in the ANCIENT ALCHEMICAL SYMBOL for SULFUR, I STARTED THERE.
THE ONLY SCENT I FOUND WAS from the SNACK BAR.
DID YOU KNOW? THEY CALLED THEM "MAIZE-DOGS."
I WENT to INVESTIGATE the UNIQUELY LACLEDIAN NATURAL GASOMETERS of SHREWSBURY...
ONLY to FIND THEM MYSTERIOUSLY GONE!
COMING SOON
MIDWEST HEMORRHOID TREATMENT CENTER EAST
DON'T SUFFER
I HEADED DOWN 44 to MEASURE the LEVELS of the HAMPTON OFF-RAMP GARBAGE CAN,
READINGS NORMAL
AND the NASAL RANGER LED ME ACROSS the STREET.
BUT the ODOR WASN'T RICH ENOUGH to MATCH the 66 YEAR STINK-NATURE.
CHEAP CHEAP
I WAS AFTER SOMETHING BIGGER.

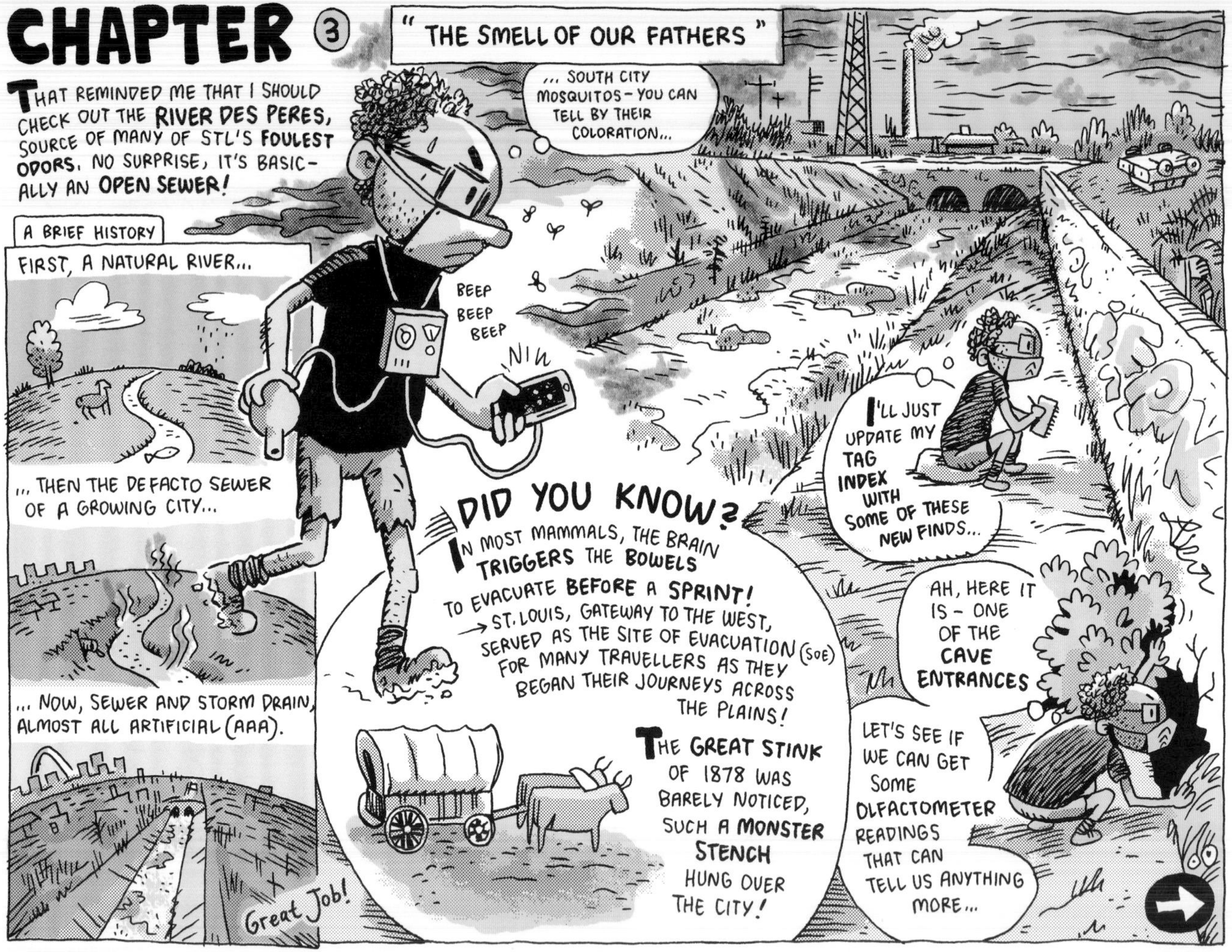
CHAPTER 3
"THE SMELL OF OUR FATHERS"
THAT REMINDED ME THAT I SHOULD CHECK OUT THE RIVER DES PERES, SOURCE OF MANY OF STL'S FOULEST ODORS. NO SURPRISE, IT'S BASICALLY AN OPEN SEWER!
... SOUTH CITY MOSQUITOS - YOU CAN TELL BY THEIR COLORATION...
A BRIEF HISTORY
FIRST, A NATURAL RIVER...
... THEN THE DEFACTO SEWER OF A GROWING CITY...
... NOW, SEWER AND STORM DRAIN, ALMOST ALL ARTIFICIAL (AAA).
Great Job!
BEEP BEEP BEEP
DID YOU KNOW?
IN MOST MAMMALS, THE BRAIN TRIGGERS THE BOWELS TO EVACUATE BEFORE A SPRINT!
→ ST. LOUIS, GATEWAY TO THE WEST, SERVED AS THE SITE OF EVACUATION (SOE) FOR MANY TRAVELLERS AS THEY BEGAN THEIR JOURNEYS ACROSS THE PLAINS!
THE GREAT STINK OF 1878 WAS BARELY NOTICED, SUCH A MONSTER STENCH HUNG OVER THE CITY!
I'LL JUST UPDATE MY TAG INDEX WITH SOME OF THESE NEW FINDS...
AH, HERE IT IS - ONE OF THE CAVE ENTRANCES
LET'S SEE IF WE CAN GET SOME OLFACTOMETER READINGS THAT CAN TELL US ANYTHING MORE...

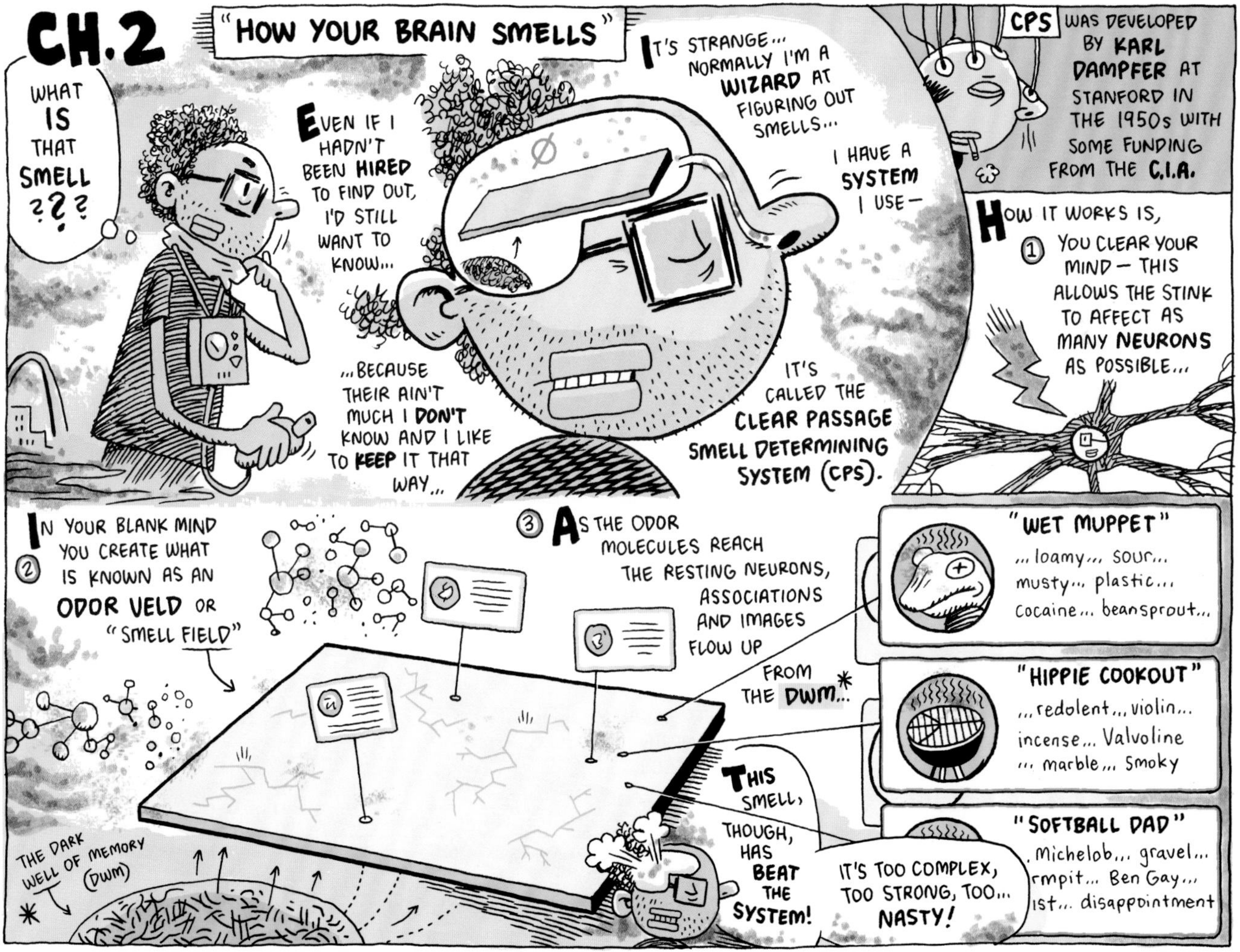
CH. 2
"HOW YOUR BRAIN SMELLS"
WHAT IS THAT SMELL ???
EVEN IF I HADN'T BEEN HIRED TO FIND OUT, I'D STILL WANT TO KNOW...
...BECAUSE THEIR AIN'T MUCH I DON'T KNOW AND I LIKE TO KEEP IT THAT WAY...
IT'S STRANGE... NORMALLY I'M A WIZARD AT FIGURING OUT SMELLS...
I HAVE A SYSTEM I USE—
IT'S CALLED THE CLEAR PASSAGE SMELL DETERMINING SYSTEM (CPS).
CPS WAS DEVELOPED BY KARL DAMPFER AT STANFORD IN THE 1950s WITH SOME FUNDING FROM THE C.I.A.
HOW IT WORKS IS,
① YOU CLEAR YOUR MIND — THIS ALLOWS THE STINK TO AFFECT AS MANY NEURONS AS POSSIBLE...
IN YOUR BLANK MIND ② YOU CREATE WHAT IS KNOWN AS AN ODOR VELD OR "SMELL FIELD"
③ AS THE ODOR MOLECULES REACH THE RESTING NEURONS, ASSOCIATIONS AND IMAGES FLOW UP FROM THE DWM*...
"WET MUPPET"
...loamy... sour... musty... plastic... cocaine... beansprout...
"HIPPIE COOKOUT"
...redolent... violin... incense... Valvoline ... marble... smoky
"SOFTBALL DAD"
...Michelob... gravel... rmpit... Ben Gay... ist... disappointment
THE DARK WELL OF MEMORY (DWM)
*
THIS SMELL, THOUGH, HAS BEAT THE SYSTEM!
IT'S TOO COMPLEX, TOO STRONG, TOO... NASTY!

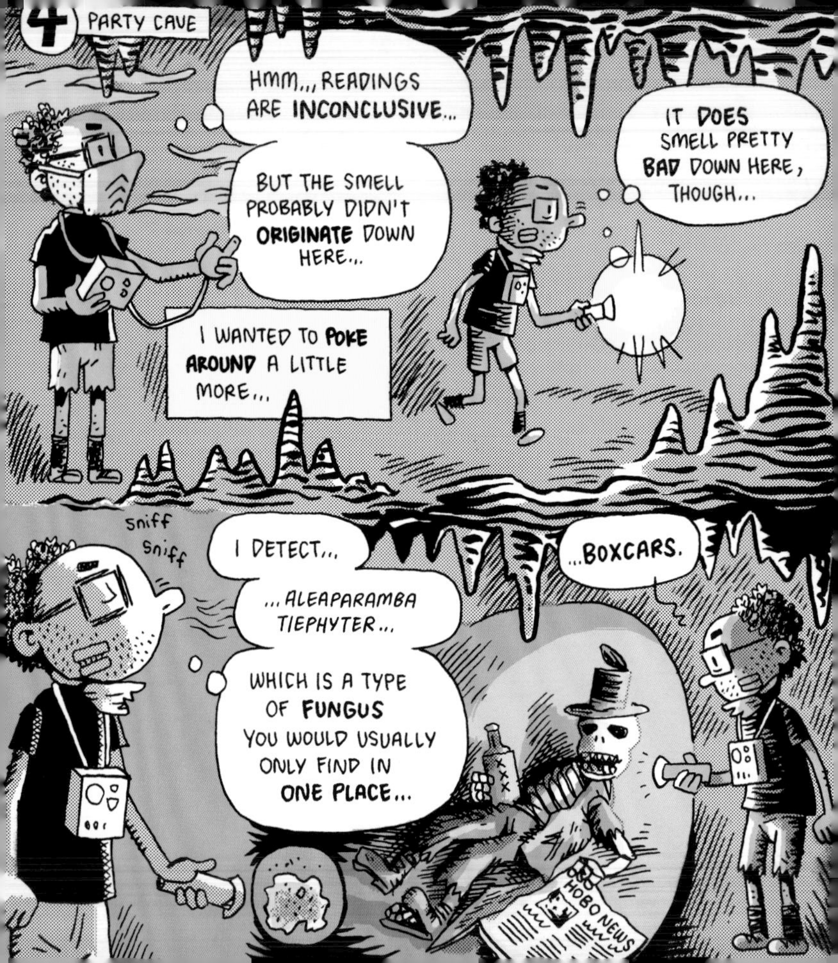
4
PARTY CAVE
HMM... READINGS ARE **INCONCLUSIVE**...
BUT THE SMELL PROBABLY DIDN'T **ORIGINATE** DOWN HERE...
I WANTED TO **POKE AROUND** A LITTLE MORE...
IT **DOES** SMELL PRETTY **BAD** DOWN HERE, THOUGH...
sniff
sniff
I DETECT...
...ALEAPARAMBA TIEPHYTER...
WHICH IS A TYPE OF **FUNGUS** YOU WOULD USUALLY ONLY FIND IN **ONE PLACE**...
...BOXCARS.
XXX
HOBO NEWS

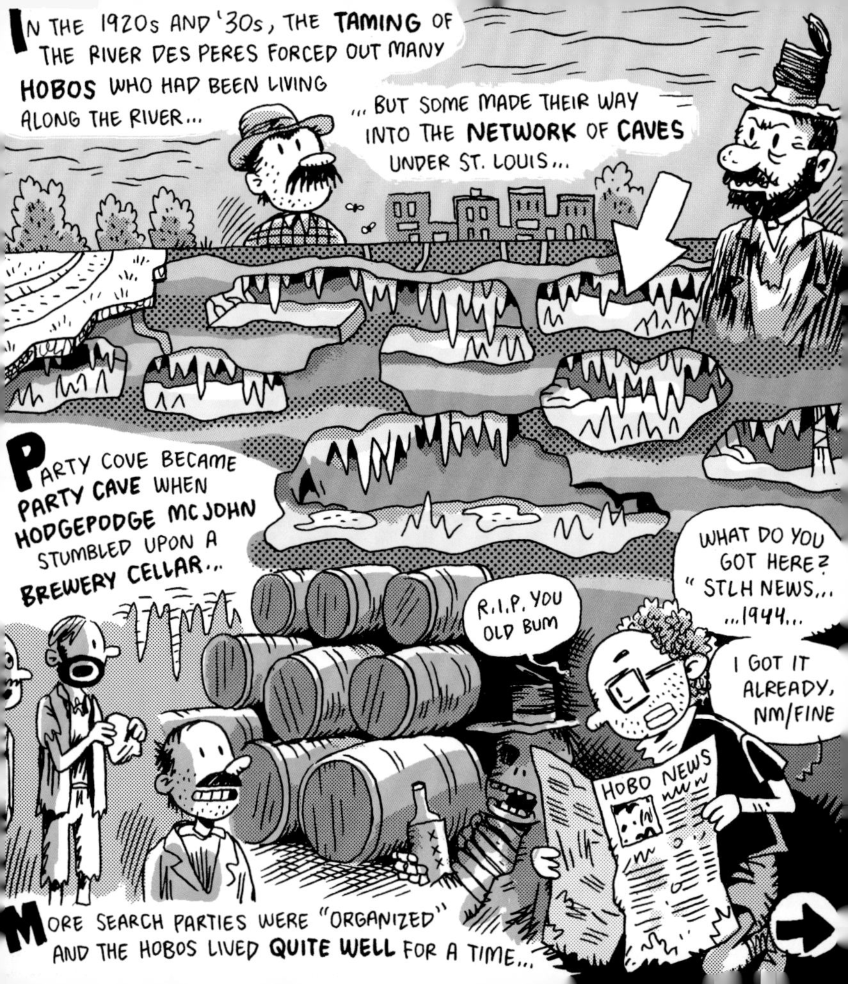
IN THE 1920s AND '30s, THE TAMING OF THE RIVER DES PERES FORCED OUT MANY HOBOS WHO HAD BEEN LIVING ALONG THE RIVER...
... BUT SOME MADE THEIR WAY INTO THE NETWORK OF CAVES UNDER ST. LOUIS...
PARTY COVE BECAME PARTY CAVE WHEN HODGEPODGE MCJOHN STUMBLED UPON A BREWERY CELLAR...
R.I.P. YOU OLD BUM
WHAT DO YOU GOT HERE? "STLH NEWS... ...1944...
I GOT IT ALREADY, NM/FINE
HOBO NEWS
XXX
MORE SEARCH PARTIES WERE "ORGANIZED" AND THE HOBOS LIVED QUITE WELL FOR A TIME...

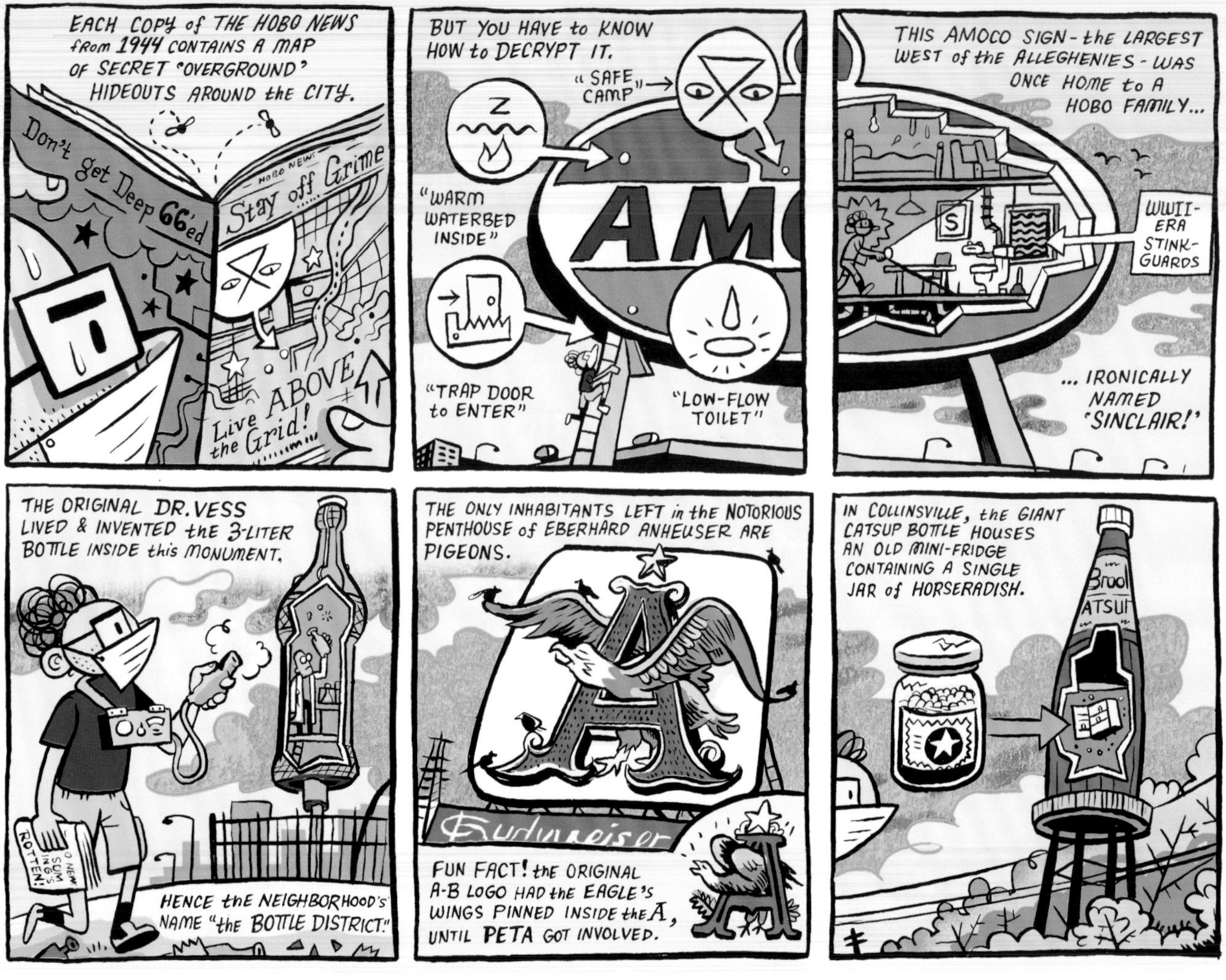
EACH COPY of THE HOBO NEWS from 1944 CONTAINS A MAP OF SECRET "OVERGROUND" HIDEOUTS AROUND the CITY.
Don't get Deep 66'ed
HOBO NEWS
Stay off Grime
Live ABOVE the Grid!
BUT YOU HAVE to KNOW HOW to DECRYPT IT.
"SAFE CAMP"
"WARM WATERBED INSIDE"
"TRAP DOOR to ENTER"
"LOW-FLOW TOILET"
AMO
THIS AMOCO SIGN - the LARGEST WEST of the ALLEGHENIES - WAS ONCE HOME to A HOBO FAMILY...
WWII-ERA STINK-GUARDS
... IRONICALLY NAMED 'SINCLAIR!'
THE ORIGINAL DR. VESS LIVED & INVENTED the 3-LITER BOTTLE INSIDE this MONUMENT.
HENCE the NEIGHBORHOOD'S NAME "the BOTTLE DISTRICT."
THE ONLY INHABITANTS LEFT in the NOTORIOUS PENTHOUSE of EBERHARD ANHEUSER ARE PIGEONS.
Budweiser
FUN FACT! the ORIGINAL A-B LOGO HAD the EAGLE'S WINGS PINNED INSIDE the A, UNTIL PETA GOT INVOLVED.
IN COLLINSVILLE, the GIANT CATSUP BOTTLE HOUSES AN OLD MINI-FRIDGE CONTAINING A SINGLE JAR of HORSERADISH.

SO FAR these LANDMARKS HAVE BEEN DEAD-ENDS on the SCENT-TRAIL BUT YOU CAN'T STOP the FLOW of TRIVIA.

DRIP

Delmar

THIS BAR & HOTEL FIXTURE IS AN EXACT REPLICA of the MOON, THE LARGEST ON EARTH,

MOONROOM

EXCEPT HAS A MANTLE of MOLTEN BUD SELECT, AND A CORE OF GOOFY MEMORA-BILIA.

BOOM

...DID YOU KNOW?

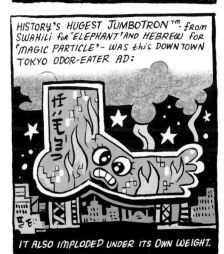

HISTORY'S HUGEST JUMBOTRON™ - from SWAHILI for 'ELEPHANT' AND HEBREW for 'MAGIC PARTICLE' - WAS this DOWNTOWN TOKYO ODOR-EATER AD:

IT ALSO IMPLODED UNDER ITS OWN WEIGHT.

NO SUCH LUCK for this St.LOUIS JUMBOTRON, WHICH IS RIGGED OUT WITH 'SCENT-SIRENS' to LURE GAMBLERS.

"SEX"

"STEAK SIZZLE"

LUMIERE PL CASINO I HO-

GASP!

LES FRÈRES LUMIÈRE DEBUTED the FIRST MOVING PICTURE in St.LOUIS in 1878.

LUMIERE CINEMATOGRAPHE
AUGUST
LOUIS
OUVRIER 4

IT WAS TITLED "OUVRIER SENTANT SA PROPRE AISSELLE" - "FACTORY WORKER SMELLING HIS OWN ARMPIT".

⑥ DID YOU KNOW? St. LOUIS' GREAT GENERAL STRIKE of 1877 WAS AMERICA'S FIRST BIG LABOR FRACAS! WORKERS OF ALL STRIPES HIT the STREETS.

RAILROADSMEN

GASSERS

NEWSIES

EXTRA! BOSSES SU-

CIGARISTS

MEAT-SCRUBBERS

ANCIENT KNIGHTS OF TOIL

AK

ST. LOUI MAN

WORKING WHISTLERS

WW

THE WAGONWASTEWOMEN UNION LOCAL 314 FOUGHT TOUGHEST... AND ARE STILL STRIKING to this DAY!

THE "REIGN of the RABBLE" CAME to A SWIFT END thanks to COPS, HIRED THUGS, & EARLY CHEMICAL WARFARE.

HORSERADISH GAS

UNION BUSTERS' RIOT GEAR PIONEERED HELMET, GAS MASK, & WHEELED JACKBOOT TECHNOLOGIES.

BY the FOLLOWING SUMMER, THINGS WERE BACK to NORMAL, EXCEPT FOR the LINGERING SMELL HANGING OVER the CITY...

THE SO-CALLED PROFOUND STENCH of SEVENTY-EIGHT!

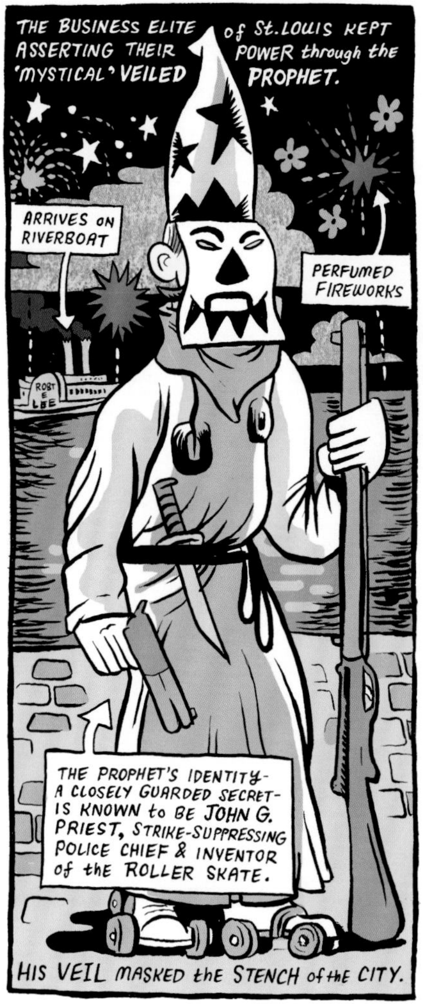
THE BUSINESS ELITE of St. LOUIS KEPT ASSERTING THEIR POWER through the 'MYSTICAL' VEILED PROPHET.
ARRIVES ON RIVERBOAT
PERFUMED FIREWORKS
ROBT E LEE
THE PROPHET'S IDENTITY - A CLOSELY GUARDED SECRET - IS KNOWN to BE JOHN G. PRIEST, STRIKE-SUPPRESSING POLICE CHIEF & INVENTOR of the ROLLER SKATE.
HIS VEIL MASKED the STENCH of the CITY.

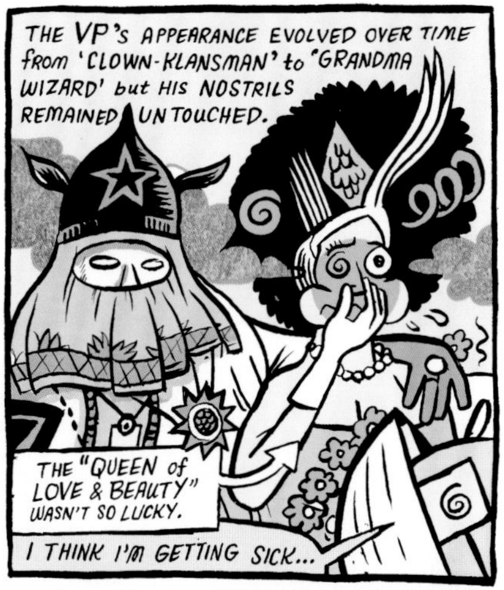
THE VP'S APPEARANCE EVOLVED OVER TIME from 'CLOWN-KLANSMAN' to 'GRANDMA WIZARD' but HIS NOSTRILS REMAINED UNTOUCHED.
THE "QUEEN of LOVE & BEAUTY" WASN'T SO LUCKY.
I THINK I'M GETTING SICK...

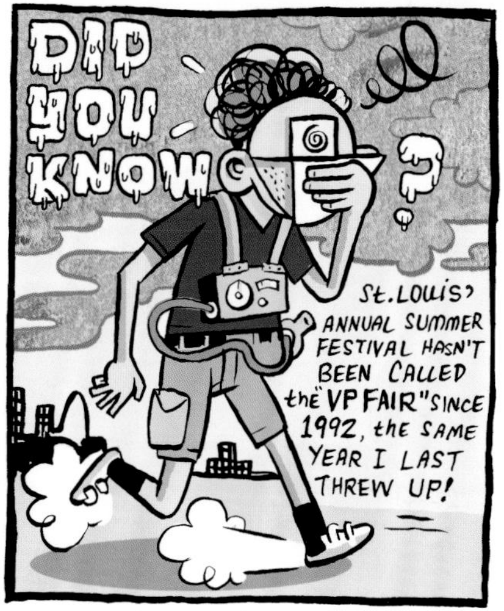
DID YOU KNOW ?
St. LOUIS' ANNUAL SUMMER FESTIVAL HASN'T BEEN CALLED the "VP FAIR" SINCE 1992, the SAME YEAR I LAST THREW UP!

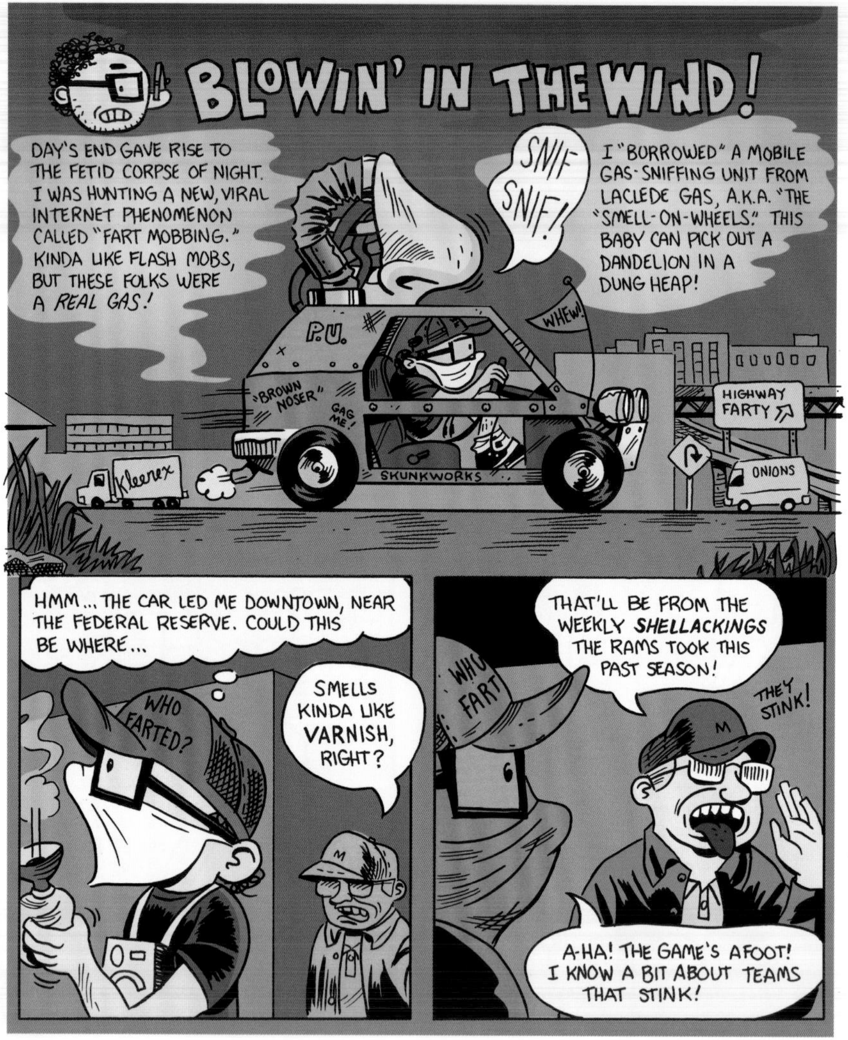
BLOWIN' IN THE WIND!
DAY'S END GAVE RISE TO THE FETID CORPSE OF NIGHT. I WAS HUNTING A NEW, VIRAL INTERNET PHENOMENON CALLED "FART MOBBING." KINDA LIKE FLASH MOBS, BUT THESE FOLKS WERE A REAL GAS!
SNIF SNIF!
I "BORROWED" A MOBILE GAS-SNIFFING UNIT FROM LACLEDE GAS, A.K.A. "THE SMELL-ON-WHEELS." THIS BABY CAN PICK OUT A DANDELION IN A DUNG HEAP!
P.U.
WHEW!
"BROWN NOSER"
GAG ME!
SKUNKWORKS
Kleenex
HIGHWAY FARTY
ONIONS
HMM... THE CAR LED ME DOWNTOWN, NEAR THE FEDERAL RESERVE. COULD THIS BE WHERE...
WHO FARTED?
SMELLS KINDA LIKE VARNISH, RIGHT?
THAT'LL BE FROM THE WEEKLY SHELLACKINGS THE RAMS TOOK THIS PAST SEASON!
THEY STINK!
A-HA! THE GAME'S AFOOT! I KNOW A BIT ABOUT TEAMS THAT STINK!

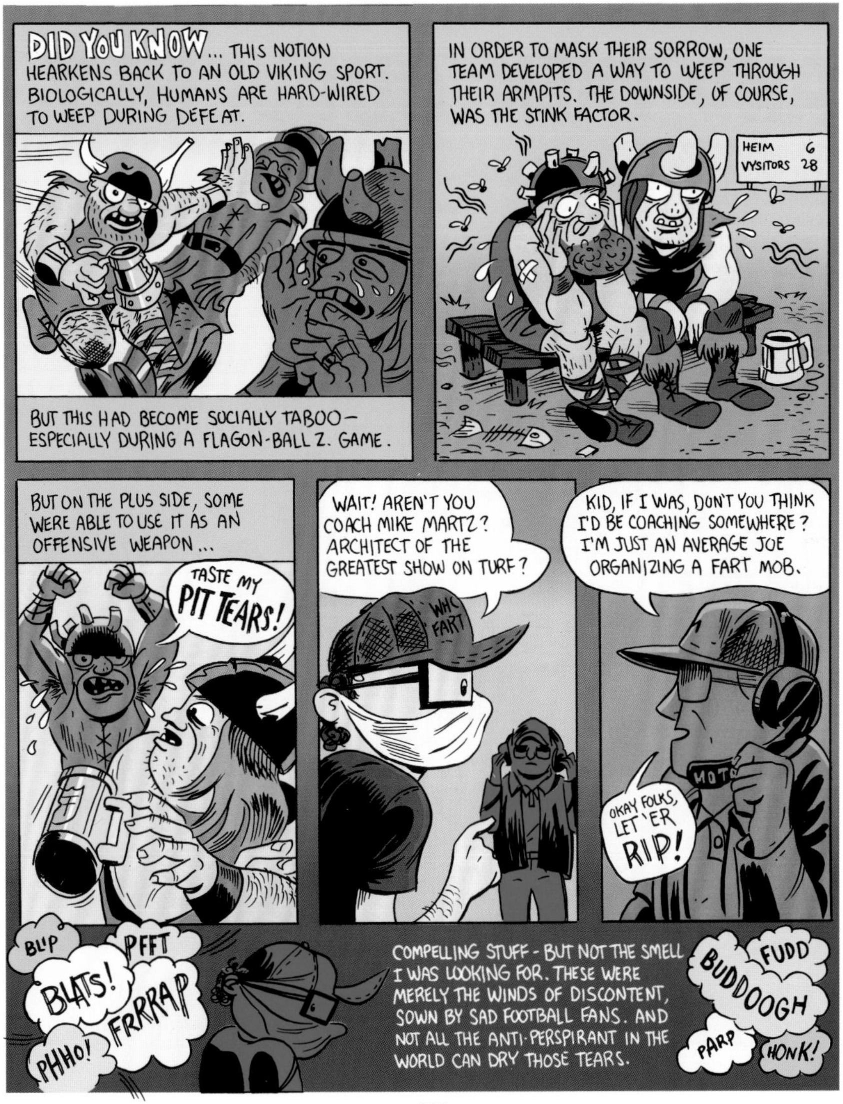
DID YOU KNOW... THIS NOTION HEARKENS BACK TO AN OLD VIKING SPORT. BIOLOGICALLY, HUMANS ARE HARD-WIRED TO WEEP DURING DEFEAT.
BUT THIS HAD BECOME SOCIALLY TABOO— ESPECIALLY DURING A FLAGON-BALL Z. GAME.
IN ORDER TO MASK THEIR SORROW, ONE TEAM DEVELOPED A WAY TO WEEP THROUGH THEIR ARMPITS. THE DOWNSIDE, OF COURSE, WAS THE STINK FACTOR.
HEIM 6
VYSITORS 28
BUT ON THE PLUS SIDE, SOME WERE ABLE TO USE IT AS AN OFFENSIVE WEAPON...
TASTE MY PIT TEARS!
WAIT! AREN'T YOU COACH MIKE MARTZ? ARCHITECT OF THE GREATEST SHOW ON TURF?
KID, IF I WAS, DON'T YOU THINK I'D BE COACHING SOMEWHERE? I'M JUST AN AVERAGE JOE ORGANIZING A FART MOB.
OKAY FOLKS, LET 'ER RIP!
BLIP
PFFT
BLATS!
FRRRAP
PHHO!
COMPELLING STUFF - BUT NOT THE SMELL I WAS LOOKING FOR. THESE WERE MERELY THE WINDS OF DISCONTENT, SOWN BY SAD FOOTBALL FANS. AND NOT ALL THE ANTI-PERSPIRANT IN THE WORLD CAN DRY THOSE TEARS.
FUDD
BUDDOOGH
PARP
HONK!

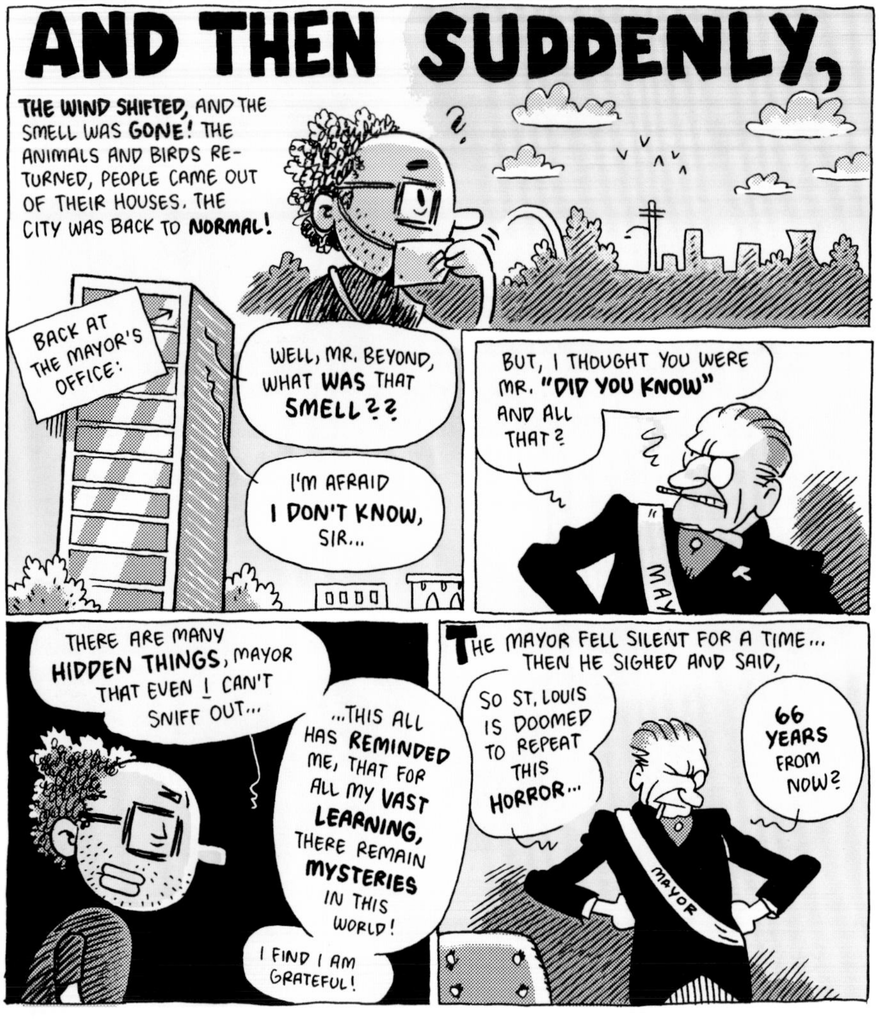

AND THEN SUDDENLY,
THE WIND SHIFTED, AND THE SMELL WAS GONE! THE ANIMALS AND BIRDS RETURNED, PEOPLE CAME OUT OF THEIR HOUSES. THE CITY WAS BACK TO NORMAL!
?
BACK AT THE MAYOR'S OFFICE:
WELL, MR. BEYOND, WHAT WAS THAT SMELL??
I'M AFRAID I DON'T KNOW, SIR...
BUT, I THOUGHT YOU WERE MR. "DID YOU KNOW" AND ALL THAT?
MAY
THERE ARE MANY HIDDEN THINGS, MAYOR THAT EVEN I CAN'T SNIFF OUT...
...THIS ALL HAS REMINDED ME, THAT FOR ALL MY VAST LEARNING, THERE REMAIN MYSTERIES IN THIS WORLD!
I FIND I AM GRATEFUL!
THE MAYOR FELL SILENT FOR A TIME... THEN HE SIGHED AND SAID,
SO ST. LOUIS IS DOOMED TO REPEAT THIS HORROR...
66 YEARS FROM NOW?
MAYOR

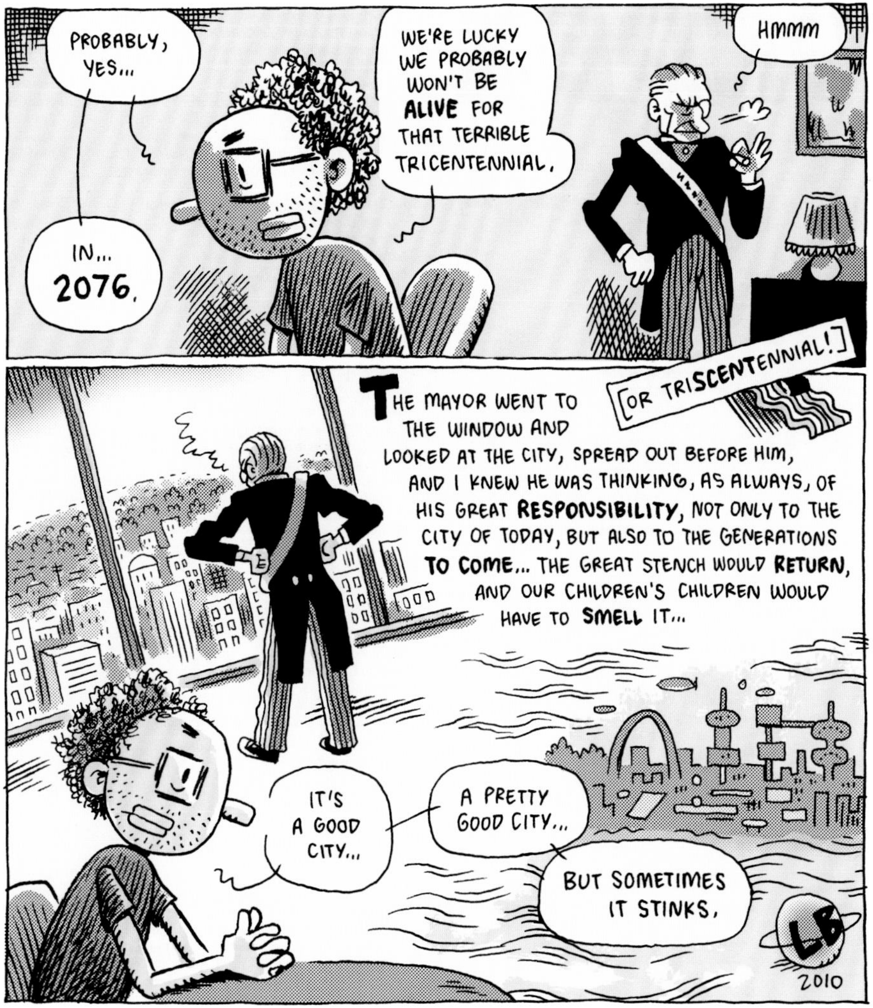
PROBABLY, YES...
IN... 2076.
WE'RE LUCKY WE PROBABLY WON'T BE ALIVE FOR THAT TERRIBLE TRICENTENNIAL.
HMMM
[OR TRISCENTENNIAL!]
THE MAYOR WENT TO THE WINDOW AND LOOKED AT THE CITY, SPREAD OUT BEFORE HIM, AND I KNEW HE WAS THINKING, AS ALWAYS, OF HIS GREAT RESPONSIBILITY, NOT ONLY TO THE CITY OF TODAY, BUT ALSO TO THE GENERATIONS TO COME... THE GREAT STENCH WOULD RETURN, AND OUR CHILDREN'S CHILDREN WOULD HAVE TO SMELL IT...
IT'S A GOOD CITY...
A PRETTY GOOD CITY...
BUT SOMETIMES IT STINKS.
LB
2010

BEYONDEX

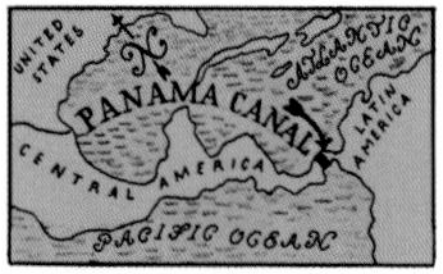
UNITED STATES
PANAMA CANAL
ATLANTIC OCEAN
LATIN AMERICA
CENTRAL AMERICA
PACIFIC OCEAN

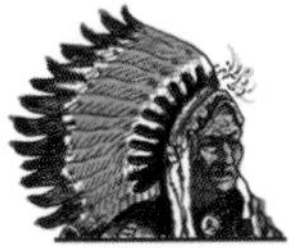
SITTING BULL

ABOUT THE AUTHORS

Leon Beyond is the author of several books, including this one. His whereabouts are currently unknown. While we were proofreading this book he stopped returning our calls. Actually, we weren't really calling him because he was calling us like six times a day. But now, who knows. If you have any information, please write PO Box 38061, Saint Louis, MO, 63138, and include a photo, or see whatthingsdo.com.

Dan Zettwoch (zedwalk) is a mystery writer and content solution implementer living in Websters Grove, Missouri. His thoughts on politics and TV shows can be seen at danzettwoch.com or his blog Zettwoch's Suitcase.

Kevin Huizenga (HIGH zing gah) is a cartoonist and fleet manager specializing in asset tracking applications. He lives with his cat, wife, and two ball pythons in Bellefondant, MO. He publishes several subscription-based newsletters. For more info write PO Box 38061, St. Louis, MO, 63138, or google.com.